**(Continued on back endsheets)**

# German Writers and Works of the Early Middle Ages: 800–1170

Dictionary of Literary Biography® • Volume One Hundred Forty-Eight

# German Writers and Works of the Early Middle Ages: 800–1170

Edited by
Will Hasty
*University of Florida*
and
James Hardin
*University of South Carolina*

 Gale Research Inc.

*An International Thomson Publishing Company*

NEW YORK • LONDON • BONN • BOSTON • DETROIT • MADRID
MELBOURNE • MEXICO CITY • PARIS • SINGAPORE • TOKYO
TORONTO • WASHINGTON • ALBANY NY • BELMONT CA • CINCINNATI OH

Printed in the United States of America

Published simultaneously in the United Kingdom
by Gale Research International Limited
(An affiliated company of Gale Research Inc.)

The paper used in this publication meets the minimum requirements
of American National Standard for Information Sciences–Permanence
Paper for Printed Library Materials, ANSI Z39.48-1984. ⊚ ™

Library of Congress Catalog Card Number 94–079402
ISBN 0–8103–5709–7

I(T)P™  Gale Research Inc., an International Thomson Publishing Company.
ITP logo is a trademark under license.

10 9 8 7 6 5 4 3 2 1

# Contents

# Contents

## Appendixes

# Plan of the Series

The advisory board, the editors, and the publisher of the *Dictionary of Literary Biography* are joined in endorsing Mark Twain's declaration. The literature of a nation provides an inexhaustible resource of permanent worth. We intend to make literature and its creators better understood and more accessible to students and the reading public, while satisfying the standards of teachers and scholars.

To meet these requirements, *literary biography* has been construed in terms of the author's achievement. The most important thing about a writer is his writing. Accordingly, the entries in *DLB* are career biographies, tracing the development of the author's canon and the evolution of his reputation.

The purpose of *DLB* is not only to provide reliable information in a convenient format but also to place the figures in the larger perspective of literary history and to offer appraisals of their accomplishments by qualified scholars.

The publication plan for *DLB* resulted from two years of preparation. The project was proposed to Bruccoli Clark by Frederick C. Ruffner, president of the Gale Research Company, in November 1975. After specimen entries were prepared and typeset, an advisory board was formed to refine the entry format and develop the series rationale. In meetings held during 1976, the publisher, series editors, and advisory board approved the scheme for a comprehensive biographical dictionary of persons who contributed to North American literature. Editorial work on the first volume began in January 1977, and it was published in 1978. In order to make *DLB* more than a reference tool and to compile volumes that individually have claim to status as literary history, it was decided to organize volumes by topic, period, or genre. Each of these free-standing volumes provides a biographical-bibliographical guide and overview for a particular area of literature. We are convinced that this organization — as opposed to a single alphabet method — constitutes a valuable innovation in the presentation of reference material. The volume plan necessarily requires many decisions for the placement and treatment of authors who might properly be included in two or three volumes. In some instances a major figure will be included in separate volumes, but with different entries emphasizing the aspect of his career appropriate to each volume. Ernest Hemingway, for example, is represented in *American Writers in Paris, 1920–1939* by an entry focusing on his expatriate apprenticeship; he is also in *American Novelists, 1910–1945* with an entry surveying his entire career. Each volume includes a cumulative index of the subject authors and articles. Comprehensive indexes to the entire series are planned.

With volume ten in 1982 it was decided to enlarge the scope of *DLB*. By the end of 1986 twenty-one volumes treating British literature had been published, and volumes for Commonwealth and Modern European literature were in progress. The series has been further augmented by the *DLB Yearbooks* (since 1981) which update published entries and add new entries to keep the *DLB* current with contemporary activity. There have also been *DLB Documentary Series* volumes which provide biographical and critical source materials for figures whose work is judged to have particular interest for students. One of these companion volumes is entirely devoted to Tennessee Williams.

We define literature as the *intellectual commerce of a nation*: not merely as belles lettres but as that ample and complex process by which ideas are generated, shaped, and transmitted. *DLB* entries are not limited to "creative writers" but extend to other figures who in their time and in their way influenced the mind of a people. Thus the series encompasses historians, journalists, publishers, and screenwriters. By this means readers of *DLB* may be aided to perceive literature not as cult scripture in the keeping of intellectual high priests but firmly positioned at the center of a nation's life.

DLB includes the major writers appropriate to each volume and those standing in the ranks immediately behind them. Scholarly and critical counsel has been sought in deciding which minor figures to include and how full their entries should be. Wherever possible, useful references are made to figures who do not warrant separate entries.

Each DLB volume has a volume editor responsible for planning the volume, selecting the figures for inclusion, and assigning the entries. Volume editors are also responsible for preparing, where appropriate, appendices surveying the major periodicals and literary and intellectual movements for their volumes, as well as lists of further readings. Work on the series as a whole is coordinated at the Bruccoli Clark Layman editorial center in Columbia, South Carolina, where the editorial staff is responsible for accuracy of the published volumes.

One feature that distinguishes DLB is the illustration policy – its concern with the iconography of literature. Just as an author is influenced by his surroundings, so is the reader's understanding of the author enhanced by a knowledge of his environment. Therefore DLB volumes include not only drawings, paintings, and photographs of authors, often depicting them at various stages in their careers, but also illustrations of their families and places where they lived. Title pages are regularly reproduced in facsimile along with dust jackets for modern authors. The dust jackets are a special feature of DLB because they often document better than anything else the way in which an author's work was perceived in its own time. Specimens of the writers' manuscripts are included when feasible.

Samuel Johnson rightly decreed that "The chief glory of every people arises from its authors." The purpose of the *Dictionary of Literary Biography* is to compile literary history in the surest way available to us – by accurate and comprehensive treatment of the lives and work of those who contributed to it.

The *DLB* Advisory Board

# Introduction

From 800 to 1170 the cultural groundwork was laid for the emergence of the German vernacular as the medium of literary expression in the great epic and lyrical works of the *Stauferzeit* (the period of the Hohenstaufen emperors) that began around 1200. This efflorescence of literature in the High Middle Ages would not have been possible without the efforts of the early-medieval German writers, who appropriated and shaped, according to their own traditions, the culture of Christian Rome, which, following the fall of the Western Roman Empire in the fifth century, had become a repository not only of the doctrines of Roman Catholicism but also of the cultural heritage of pre-Christian Greece and Rome. The Germanic tribes, at first the greatest threat to the Roman Empire, emerged after the Fall of Rome as a significant force in the safekeeping and continuation of the culture of antiquity. At the same time the Germanic tribes, absorbing the culture of the Mediterranean peoples, gained the ability to write about themselves and to record their own history.

In the early Middle Ages "Germans" in the modern sense of the word did not yet exist; individuals were identified by their tribal allegiances as Franks, Bavarians, Saxons, Langobards, and so forth. Even if the Frankish empire, under the Carolingian dynasty, served as a highway by which the Germanic peoples could later come together as a nation, the association of the term *German* with the literary developments of this period suggests a broader form of ethnic or national identity that had not yet developed. The breakup of the Frankish empire gave birth to many political entities, one of which was the Holy Roman Empire of the German Nation, founded in 800; its dissolution in 1806 preceded the formation of the modern German state. During the early Middle Ages Germans were not yet a clearly distinct people, so that some figures whose activity was of the greatest significance in the context of German culture — notably the Anglo-Saxon Alcuin — were German only in a remote sense and could also be claimed by other modern nations, just as Charlemagne is claimed by both France and Germany.

Correspondingly, during this period there was no unified German language but rather a multiplicity of West Germanic dialects (in contrast to the extinct East Germanic dialects of the Vandals, Burgundians, and Goths, and the North Germanic ancestors of the Scandinavian languages). These dialects belonged to two large linguistic groups: Old High German and Old Low German. From around 500 until around 800 the High German dialects spoken by Franks, Alemans, and Bavarians had gradually been distinguished from the Low German ones of the Anglo-Saxons, Dutch, and Flemish by the so-called second sound shift. This transformation can be illustrated by a comparison of modern German (New High German) with English, which can be view as an analogue of the Low German dialects in which the shift did not occur: *p* shifted to *pf* or *f* (as in *sleep/schlafen; pound/Pfund*), *t* to *z* (*two/zwei; time/Zeit*), and *k* to *ch* (*book/Buch; cook/Koch*).

Most of the early medieval vernacular manuscripts were written in the Old High German dialects; but there were significant exceptions, such as the *Heliand* (Savior, circa 850), which was primarily composed in Old Saxon, and the *Hildebrandslied* (Lay of Hildebrand, circa 820), in which a mixture of Low and High German features is found. The existence of these many dialects — a reflection of a tribal form of political organization — inhibited the development of a coherent German literary history. This linguistic particularism was not completely overcome even in the Middle High German period (circa 1050 to circa 1300). Middle High German was distinguished from Old High German by a flattening of the full-sounding middle and end syllables from *o* and *u* to *e*, the partial diphthongization of *î*, *û*, and *iu* to *ei*, *au*, and *eu*, respectively, and monophthongization of *ie*, *uo*, and *üe* to *î*, *û*, *û̂*, respectively, during which an increasing number of religious works in the vernacular — the so-called *Spielsmannsepen* (minstrel epics) and early courtly works such as Eilhart's *Tristrant* (circa 1160–1175) —

were written. A literary vernacular that finally overcame the linguistic barriers posed by differences of
dialect was not achieved until many centuries later,
largely as a result of the growth of a uniform chancery language in central and eastern Germany, the
Bible translation of Martin Luther in the first half of
the sixteenth century, and the efforts of the Baroque
language societies in the seventeenth century.
Hence, the relatively small amount of vernacular literature from the early Middle Ages presents itself
not in a uniform literary language but in several different dialects, the specific features of which are lost
from sight in modern German or English translations.

At least as problematic as *German* is the term
*literature* (*litterae*), which in the early Middle Ages referred to the totality of written texts. While this general understanding of *literature* still exists, today the
term is usually used more specifically to refer to creative works of fiction, poetry, and drama. In the
Middle Ages this more specific kind of literature
had not yet developed; there were no hard and fast
distinctions between literary texts in the modern
sense, on the one hand, and theological, philosophical, and historical texts, on the other. The development of an autonomous literary language seems to
coincide with the gradual emergence of the individual from the anonymous communal forms of identity that characterized the early Middle Ages: individuals first became historically visible as such
when they began to write about their own experiences. Literature did not yet provide such an instrument for early medieval writers, who were interested in the expression of communal ideals and ambitions – the most prominent of which was the glorification of God.

As one moves back to the origins of cultural
activity in German, the term *literature* needs to be
qualified in yet another way. In the Middle Ages the
term referred almost exclusively to texts written in
Latin, most of which were copies of and commentaries on the Bible and patristic writings. Many vernacular texts were translations or interpretive commentaries inserted between the lines of the Latin.
These interlinear glosses – a striking demonstration
of the dependence of the early Germans on the cultural apparatus of Christian Rome – were an exercise not merely of language but also of comprehen-
sion, in which German writers attempted to grasp
with their own rudimentary conceptual vocabulary
the complex ideas of theology and philosophy so elegantly and easily expressed in Latin. When no
suitable words or phrases were available in the vernacular, new ones had to be created, and these coin-

ages enjoyed varying degrees of success and longev-
ity. This acquisition of culture and of a literary language occurred for the most part in monastic
schools such as those at Reichenau and Saint Gall,
which were, during turbulent years of invasion and
political turmoil, the exclusive centers of literary activity. This monastic literary culture had its origins
in the activities of Irish missionaries such as Col-
umbanus and Gallus (after whom Saint Gall is
named) around 600, and in those of the Anglo-
Saxon missionary Boniface, the "apostle of the Germans," who founded the abbey of Fulda.

German vernacular texts untouched by Christian Roman culture are nonexistent. The more
purely Germanic ones, such as the *Hildebrandslied*
and the *Merseburger Zaubersprüche* (Merseburg
Charms), seem often to have been preserved by ac-
cident and are so few and isolated that some scholars have been reluctant to employ the term *Literatur*
in reference to them, preferring *Sprachdenkmäler* (language monuments). The Germanic peoples originally had no literary alphabet of their own beyond a
rudimentary angular script called runes – letters derived largely from the Greek and Etruscan alphabets that were used mainly for short texts inscribed
in wood and stone. They also had their own orally
transmitted culture. The Roman historian Publius
Cornelius Tacitus provides an often-cited report in
his *Germania* (A.D. 98) that the Germanic peoples
kept a record of their mythical past in traditional
songs that celebrated the gods from whom they believed they were descended and that they also sang
when they were about to enter battle. Although
Charlemagne's biographer Einhard says that a collection of these songs was made by the emperor,
only a single fragment, the *Hildebrandslied,* has survived (the *Elder Edda,* composed from the ninth to
the twelfth centuries in Iceland, also includes Germanic heroic-songs). Although no other written
copies of these songs have survived on the Continent, it is probable that the Germanic peoples continued their heroic-song tradition from the days of
Tacitus to the High Middle Ages and beyond.
Those who, by virtue of their literacy, were in a position to preserve these songs – the monks – were
undoubtedly familiar with this popular song tradition but do not appear to have considered it relevant to their scribal activity, although a work such
as the early-ninth-century *Waltharius* suggests that
oral traditions occasionally found their way into
writing.

It was only in their long and complex relationship to Christian Roman culture that the Germanic
ancestors of the Germans moved beyond their

orally transmitted song tradition and came to have the kind of culture that one associates with novels and philosophical systems. The earliest information on the Germanic peoples is provided by pre-Christian Roman historians such as Tacitus. Tacitus regarded the Germanic peoples as indigenous to a territory that extended east from the Rhine to Lithuania and north from the Danube to the Baltic. The physical appearance, according to Tacitus, was always the same: fierce blue eyes, reddish hair, and large frames that were suited to violent efforts but not to fatiguing labor. Later authors added colorful details: in the late fifth century Sidonius wrote that the Burgundians were seven feet tall, greased their hair with rancid butter, had enormous appetites, and spoke in stentorian tones; the Franks were gray-eyed and clean shaven, with yellow hair and close-fitting tunics. Sidonius records the striking impression made by a Frankish prince and his retinue during a visit to Lyons in 470: "The appearance of the kinglets and confederates who accompanied him inspired terror even in peacetime. Their feet were covered entirely, up to their ankles, in boots of bristly hide. Their knees, their legs, and their calves were without any covering. Besides this, they wore high, tight, and many-colored garments which hardly reached down to their bare thighs; their sleeves only covered their upper arms; their cloaks were green, embroidered with red. Their swords hung from their shoulders on baldrics, and around their waists they wore a belt of fur adorned with bosses. . . . In their right hands they held barbed lances and throwing-axes, and in their left shields, on which the light shone, white on the circuit and red on the boss, displaying both opulence and craftsmanship."

As portrayed by Tacitus, the Germanic peoples were simple, if not primitive, lacking the sophistication to refrain from blurting out their innermost thoughts. They engaged in frequent quarrels with one another, which were sometimes fatal; they loved feasting and drinking to excess; and they avoided hard work between wars, letting women, old men, and weaklings work in the fields. But if they were somewhat primitive by Roman standards, they also possessed a morality that Tacitus seems to feel Rome had lost. Tacitus portrays the Germanic peoples as largely free of avarice, taking less pleasure than most people, for example, in possessing silver and gold. Their moral code regarding marriage enjoined strict monogamy: no one in Germany, Tacitus reports, found vice amusing or called it up-to-date to seduce and be seduced; adultery, extremely rare

among the Germanic peoples, was severely punished. In his discussion of German morality Tacitus focuses on the virtues of women, leading one to suspect that the strength of the family bond depended primarily on them; as described by Tacitus, the matrimonial ceremony included provisions that suggest that the woman's relationship to her husband was that of an equal partner. During battles the women were close by, encouraging their husbands, tending to their wounds, and witnessing and comparing their acts of bravery. Tacitus reports that women were revered by the Germanic peoples, that they were believed to possess an element of holiness and a gift of prophecy, and that the surest way to put terror in the hearts of Germanic peoples was to demand their daughters as hostages.

Three institutions – the clan, the household, and the retinue – structured the social life of the Germanic tribe. The clan (Latin *stirps,* Old High German *Sibba*) was a group of families that traced its origins to a famous ancestor after whom the clan was named. The basic functions of the clan were to maintain the peace internally and to provide a common defense against outsiders. A striking manifestation of the strength of bonds within the clan was the blood feud. According to the feud mentality, transgression against a person was a crime against his or her entire clan by the entire clan of the transgressor; single crimes escalated into an enmity that could last for generations. Blood feuds arose because there was no central power to arbitrate disputes, and individuals had to depend on their own kin for security. By the time such authorities existed, the feud mentality was firmly entrenched. In spite of attempts to control them, which are visible in folk law codes such as the *Lex Salica* of the Franks, blood feuds remained an aspect of social life in Europe throughout the Middle Ages.

The household included not only blood relatives but also various dependents who stood in a relationship of obedience to the lord of the house, after whom the household was named. The primary function of the household, like that of the clan, appears to have been one of defense: members found sanctuary within the walls of their house, and outsiders crossing its threshold without the permission of its lord committed a breach of the peace that brought the severest punishment. The institution of the household provided in the figure of the lord an instance of authority that the more loosely organized structure of the clan did not possess. The powers of the lord over his dependents were referred to collectively as *munt* (Latin *mundiburdium*), which survives today in the modern German *Vormund* (guardian). Approximately one hundred households constituted a more artificial social unit, the Mark Community, which was headed by an elected chief, and the territory owned by this community was called a *Gau* (Latin *pagus*, English *shire*).

The retinue, which Tacitus calls the *comitatus* or *comites* and which was known among the Germanic peoples as *gasindi*, was based on a bond of personal loyalty that has been viewed as one of the important contributions made by the early Germanic peoples to subsequent social and political developments in medieval Europe. Each chief had a retinue of followers, called *Thegans* or *Degen* (thanes), who had sworn loyalty to their chief, ate at his table in peacetime, and fought at his side as his bodyguards in battle. Followers returning alive from a battle in which their chief had fallen harvested lifelong infamy and shame. The power and prestige of a chief was measured in large part by the quality of his retinue, and each follower, in turn, was esteemed according to the prestige of his chief. Vassalage, the basic form of political and social organization throughout the Middle Ages, has been seen by historians as an outgrowth of this bond of personal loyalty.

The highest political power originally rested in the hands of elected chiefs. Tacitus points out that these leaders were chosen on the basis of their energy and courage, and that they relied on the power of example rather than on rank. They presided over tribal gatherings of warriors, called *things* (Latin *mallus*), at which leaders were elected, treaties were decided on, and new members were adopted into the community. Sacrifices, sometimes human, were offered, and violations of assembly decisions were punished. Tacitus describes these meetings in some detail: the warriors took their seats fully armed, then hearing was given to kings or high chiefs according to their age, rank, military distinction, or eloquence. If a proposal was displeasing, the warriors shouted their dissent; if they approved, they clashed their swords and shields.

Between the sixth and the third centuries B.C. the Eastern Germanic tribes crossed from Scandinavia to the Baltic shore and made their way southeast toward the Carpathian mountains and to regions north of the Black Sea; by 200 B.C. Western Germanic peoples had reached the Rhine River and taken Bavaria away from its original Celtic inhabitants. It is in this region that, around the middle of the fourth century A.D., the Visigoth bishop Ulfila or Wulfilas composed his Gothic translation of the New Testament with specially invented letters based on the Greek alphabet.

This work, which survives in an early-sixth-century manuscript called the Codex Argenteus, written in silver ink on purple vellum, is the only significant document of the older Germanic period.

The incursions of the Huns in 376 has been viewed as a catalyst that set off a chain reaction of events that eventually led to Rome's fall. Coming from regions east of the Volga, the Huns overwhelmed the Ostrogoths and other Germanic peoples north of the Black Sea, pushing them into the Western Roman Empire. In 410 Rome was sacked by the Visigoths under Alaric. There was relatively little loss of life, and church property was spared (the Visigoths were Christians); the invasion of Italy occurred because Rome refused – or was unable – to continue paying off the hostile forces or pitting them against enemies elsewhere. Also, Germans had long since served in Roman legions (the Vandal Stilicho had been the commander of Roman forces in the West until 408). The early relationship between the Germanic peoples and the Romans was clearly not one of simple opposition, although the importance of Alaric's sacking of Rome should not be underestimated: to many it seemed that the civilized world was coming to an end, and attempts to assign blame for this cataclysm led to the composition of *De Civitate Dei* (The City of God, 413–426), in which Saint Augustine defended Christianity against the charge that the religion had so morally weakened the empire as to allow the Fall of Rome to occur. On 23 August 476 Germanic troops in Italy, who by then formed the greater part of the Roman army, elected their general Odoacer as king and deposed the last western emperor, Romulus Augustulus.

It is the great events and deeds of this time, the period of the *Völkerwanderung* (migrations of peoples), on which much of the scant surviving Germanic poetry is based. The destruction of the Burgundian kingdom on the upper Rhine in 436 provided a historical event that was to develop over centuries of storytelling into the core of the *Nibelungenlied* (Song of the Nibelungs, circa 1200). Many of Richard Wagner's music dramas are based on stories that originated during this period, which saw entire peoples struggle, emerge into the light of history, and disappear into oblivion. One of the greatest figures of this time was the Ostrogoth Theodoric the Great. Theodoric was born probably in 453 or 454, at which time the Ostrogoths were settled as *foederati* (allies of the Roman empire) on the middle Danube. In 461 he was sent to Constantinople, capital of the Eastern Roman Empire, as hostage for the good behavior of his people. Hostage-taking was a standard practice throughout the Middle Ages; hostages, often taken to guarantee that parties carried out their terms of an agreement, were often treated quite well, and such seems to have been the case with Theodoric, who may have received education in the Roman way of life and in statecraft. After being returned to his people Theodoric became dangerous to the security of Constantinople, so he was commissioned by the Byzantine emperor to invade Italy and subdue Odoacer. Theodoric took most of Italy away from Odoacer and murdered the latter at a banquet at which the two were to make peace. Claiming to rule in the name of the emperor, Theodoric gave himself the title of king. He devoted resources to the repair of the city, which had been neglected for some time, and he insisted that Romans and Goths live and work in partnership. He attempted to move the Goths toward the adoption of Roman ways of life, and he had some success in this endeavor. The obstacles, however, were great. Like most Germanic tribes, the Ostrogoths had become Arian Christians. Arianism held that Christ the Son was not equal to the Father; it thus rejected the Roman Catholic conception of the Holy Trinity. This heresy seems to have become something of a badge of distinction for the Germanic peoples, providing them with a specific identity, but it prevented the amalgamation of the Germanic peoples and the Catholic Romans. Because of such differences the Romans continued to seek a strong ally who would not only provide for their security but also share their brand of Christianity. Between 496 and 518 a West Germanic people, the Franks, were converted to Catholicism, and the possibility of an alliance of Rome and the Franks against the Arian Ostrogoths clouded the final years of Theodoric's rule. In 523 Theodoric ordered the death of the Roman statesman Boethius on the charge of treason. While awaiting execution, Boethius wrote his *De consolatione philosophiae* (The Consolation of Philosophy), which was, like Augustine's *De Civitate Dei,* to be extremely influential throughout the Middle Ages. The kingdom of the Ostrogoths outlived Theodoric but collapsed with the reconquest of Italy by the Byzantine emperor Justinian in 552–553. Thus, the fusion of Germanic and Christian Roman culture envisioned by Theodoric failed, and the Ostrogoths left little to posterity. One legacy of interest to literary scholars is Dietrich von Bern, a hero of Germanic song loosely based on Theodoric.

The major obstacle to a cultural alliance between Rome and the Germanic peoples was overcome in 496 with the conversion of the West Germanic Franks under Clovis to Roman Catholicism. This conversion provided the Franks with an official blessing for their European conquests, and the pope with a militarily strong ally that shared, at least in name, his faith. With the backing of papal Rome the Franks under Clovis defeated the Arian Burgundians and Visigoths. Eventually the realm of the Franks under Clovis and his successors, known as the Merovingian dynasty, extended over most of western Europe, from what is presently western Germany to the Pyrenees. The Merovingian kings who succeeded Clovis were murderous and fratricidal; their rule has been characterized as despotism tempered by assassination. From the early seventh century to the mid eighth century, as the Merovingian realm was fragmented by the Frankish custom of dividing the patrimony among all male offspring, power began to pass from the hands of the kings to powerful officials called *major domus* (mayor of the castle). Among these officials was Charles Martel, from whom the Carolingian dynasty would receive its name and who repulsed a Muslim incursion into Europe at Poitiers in 732. This shift of power depended on the development of vassalage: by obtaining the allegiance of powerful men the mayors of the castle became more powerful than the Merovingian kings, the last of whom was deposed in 751 by Pépin III.

On Christmas Day 800 Pépin's son Charles, who came to be known as Carolus Magnus or Charlemagne, was crowned august emperor of the Romans by Pope Leo III in Saint Peter's Cathedral in Rome. The Holy Roman Empire of the German Nation traces its origins back to this event (although the title *Sacrum Romanum Imperium Nationis Germanicae* would not be used until the fifteenth century), and all subsequent emperors would view Charlemagne as their great predecessor. Although Charlemagne chose to view himself as the inheritor of a long tradition of cultural collaboration – he had the remains of Theodoric the Great transferred from Ravenna to his palace chapel – it was under his reign that the relationship between the Germanic peoples and Christian Roman culture came to fruition. Not content with extending his realm by military conquest – a conquest that was also deemed a religious mission and pursued according to the practices of the time (heathen Saxons were reportedly butchered by the thousands at Verden in 782) – Charlemagne endeavored to establish a cultural foundation for his empire. Under his sponsorship occurred that revival of classical learning that has been called the Carolingian Renaissance. The center of this revival was the School of the Palace, headed by Alcuin, which set educational standards based on the seven liberal arts for monasteries throughout the empire. The School of the Palace attracted the most learned men of the day, and it was due to the efforts of scholars such as Alcuin, Theodulf, Angilbert, and Einhard that many of the works of classical antiquity were copied and preserved in an ornate new style of handwriting, the Carolingian minuscule, which represented a significant improvement over the often-illegible script of the Merovingian period. These men considered their activities a continuation of Roman civilization and Catholic Christianity; they made no distinction between Roman and Christian culture, viewing Virgil, Jerome, Augustine, and Gregory the Great as equally Roman. At his court Charlemagne used the pseudonym David, Alcuin the name of the Roman poet Horace, and Charlemagne's son Pépin the name Julius. The city of Aachen, or Aix-la-Chapelle, where Charlemagne principally held court, was called the second Rome. It is at least a bit ironic that Charlemagne's favorite book was reportedly Saint Augustine's *De Civitate Dei,* written some four centuries earlier in response to Rome's conquest by a Germanic people.

Although the literary activity of the Carolingian Renaissance was conducted predominantly in Latin, the German vernacular first presented itself at this time as a worthy literary medium. The *Evangelienharmonie* (Gospel Harmony), composed between 863 and 871 by the Alsatian monk Otfried von Weißenburg, is especially notable for its use of German in a monastic context, where Latin had been used almost exclusively. On the basis of their courage and wisdom, Otfried proudly asserts in his foreword, the Franks are just as worthy to hear the Gospels in their own language as the Romans were in their day; God wants to be praised in the language that he has given to his people. Similar arguments would be employed some seven centuries later by Martin Luther, who would speak on behalf not of a single Germanic tribe but of all Germans.

Charlemagne's empire disintegrated rapidly after his death in 814, and the social and political disorder that had preceded his rule returned. Uncomfortable about the pope's role in his own coronation – the pope had placed the crown on Charlemagne's head, thus symbolically claiming the right to confer the crown and scepter – Charlemagne himself had crowned his son Louis; but after his father's death Louis, known as "the Pious," journeyed to Rome and had himself crowned again by the pope. The unity of the empire was in danger even before Louis's death as each of his sons –

Lothar, Louis the German, and Charles the Bald – sought to gain advantage over the others. An alliance was formed between the two younger brothers, Louis and Charles, in the Strasbourg Oaths of 842, which were sworn by the respective kings and their armies in languages that were the ancestors of modern French and German; the political division of French-speaking from German-speaking regions of the empire that was occurring at this time had, thus, been preceded by a linguistic division. The Treaty of Verdun of 843 divided the Carolingian empire among the brothers, giving Charles the western part (corresponding roughly to modern-day France), Louis the eastern part (corresponding roughly to Germany), and Lothar the middle section, which came to be known as Lotharingia or Lorraine. When Lothar's line died out with the death of his son Louis in 875 his realm was divided up in the treaty of Mersen, and Lothar's imperial title was given to Charles the Bald. The empire was united again under Charles the Fat, a son of Louis the German; but Charles was a weak ruler, unable to deal with the invasions of the Vikings, and he was deposed in 888 by the Frankish nobility. With the end of the Carolingian empire came the end of the territorial unity that bound the ancestors of Germans together with those of other western Europeans. The subsequent history of the Holy Roman Empire is the history of the "Germans" in a more modern sense of the word. It is during this darkest period of the Middle Ages, the period of the Viking invasions, that literary activity found refuge and was preserved in monasteries scattered throughout the fragmented empire.

The gradual dissolution of the Carolingian dynasty during the ninth century was accompanied by a reorganization of political power in the territories of the major Germanic tribes, the duchies of Saxony, Bavaria, Franconia, Swabia, and Lorraine. Each of these duchies had become a powerful state within the realm, and their leaders, the *Kurfürsten* (electors), had acquired the right to select the emperor. Predictably, emperors generally emerged from the families of this select group of princes, who were interested in leaders who were strong enough to defend the realm against outside dangers but too weak or unwilling to centralize political authority. This right of the prince electors to choose the emperor was frequently a mere formality. During the Saxon dynasty from 919 to 1024 and the Salian-Frank dynasty from 1024 to 1125 stronger emperors were able to secure the monarchy for their offspring; the electoral right of the princes thus became crucial when a monarch died without a male heir.

Several powerful emperors emerged in the ninth and tenth centuries. The most significant of the Saxon emperors was Otto I, "the Great," who, like his predecessor Charlemagne, combined success on the battlefield – he won a crucial battle in 955 over the Hungarians on the Lechfeld – with an interest in fostering Christian Roman culture (during his time Byzantium was exerting its strongest cultural influences on western Europe). The Salian-Frank dynasty ruled during a turbulent period of increasing conflict between emperors and popes. Since the days of Charlemagne the emperors had generally controlled the popes and had often selected them, but this situation changed radically during the ninth century. The late Saxon and early Salian emperors had supported the reform movement begun at the monastery of Cluny in 910; the original aim of the movement was to return to the Benedictine Rule, on which monastic life had been based since Roman days, and thus to save a church that, according to many, had fallen into depravity. The separation of the church from worldly matters took a troublesome turn for the emperors when popes who also adhered to the Cluniac reform, and who were in a militarily strong position because of an alliance with the Normans in southern Italy, began to challenge the traditional right of emperors to select archbishops. Since the archbishops in Germany were the emperor's closest and strongest allies, this challenge struck at the heart of imperial power. Underlying this so-called Investiture Struggle was a broader conflict between emperors and popes for preeminence in the Christian world. An early climax in this struggle was reached in 1077 at Canossa, where the excommunicated emperor Henry IV stood barefoot in the snow for three days before being granted absolution by Pope Gregory VII. Whether a real victory for the papacy or merely political expediency on the part of Henry, this event only temporarily ended the conflict, which continued even after the Concordat of Worms in 1122 conceded to the popes the right to invest archbishops with the insignia symbolizing their religious authority. It is this struggle between emperors and popes, which gradually polarized a worldly and a spiritual authority that had previously been inextricable, that more than anything else marks the transition from the early to the High Middle Ages. This struggle, despite its traumatic political effects, was culturally productive in view of the increasing number of religious works written both in Latin and in the vernacular during the eleventh and twelfth centuries. The last emperor during the historical period covered by this volume is

Frederick I ("Barbarossa"), the first of the Hohenstaufen dynasty, who later presided over the explosion of courtly literature in the vernacular at the end of the twelfth century. This period is covered in *DLB 138: German Writers and Works of the High Middle Ages, 1170–1280.*

The present volume deals with significant German writers and anonymous works from 800 to 1170. In those cases where little is known about an author, the entries concentrate, by necessity, on his or her work. In addition to providing essential biographical and bibliographical information, each author is assessed in the light of the critical reception of his or her major works, and the works have been treated in such a way as to give the reader a sense of their atmosphere, language, and significance. Whenever possible, works are discussed individually and in chronological order (as well as this order can be determined), rather than thematically.

Each entry is headed by the full name by which the author is generally known, or the title of the anonymous work. The dates of birth and death, as well as they can be determined, appear below the author's name; in the case of an anonymous work, the approximate date of the work's composition appears below the work's title. Under the rubric MAJOR WORKS the author's works are listed in chronological order with their approximate dates of composition. If the chronology is impossible to determine, "date unknown" appears after the title of the work. Titles of works are listed as they generally appear in standard editions and are italicized. Translations by medieval authors of the works of others, and groups of songs or works with no clear title, are referred to in English. The title of a work is followed by a brief description of the age and location of significant manuscripts. The goal of this description is to provide the reader with a sense of the medieval "life" of a given work without spending too much space on disputes about the merits of different manuscripts. First publication (that is, printing); standard or critical editions of the original Middle High German text; modern German editions (if any); and English translations (if any) follow. The text of the entry assesses the author's or anonymous work's place in the literary history of the period; each entry on an author includes, to the extent possible, information on the author's life. All quotations are in the original language, and the contributor provides parenthetical idiomatic translations. The editors have attempted to keep everything in the volume comprehensible to a reader unfamiliar with German language, history, and culture. The References section at the end of the entry provides a representative selection of writings on the author or work. At the end of the volume may be found a list of books for further reading in the field of early German literature.

*— Will Hasty with the collaboration of James Hardin*

## Acknowledgments

This book was produced by Bruccoli Clark Layman, Inc. Karen L. Rood is senior editor for the *Dictionary of Literary Biography* series. Philip B. Dematteis was the in-house editor.

Production coordinator is George F. Dodge. Photography editors are Bruce Andrew Bowlin and Josephine A. Bruccoli. Photographic copy work was performed by Joseph M. Bruccoli. Layout and graphics supervisor is Penney L. Haughton. Copyediting supervisor is Bill Adams. Typesetting supervisor is Kathleen M. Flanagan. Julie E. Frick is editorial associate. The production staff includes Phyllis A. Avant, Ann M. Cheschi, Melody W. Clegg, Patricia Coate, Brigitte B. de Guzman, Denise W. Edwards, Sarah A. Estes, Joyce Fowler, Laurel M. Gladden, Mendy Gladden, Stephanie C. Hatchell, Leslie Haynsworth, Rebecca Mayo, Kathy Lawler Merlette, Jeff Miller, Pamela D. Norton, Delores I. Plastow, Patricia F. Salisbury, William L. Thomas, Jr., and Robert Trogden.

Walter W. Ross and Robert S. McConnell did library research. They were assisted by the following librarians at the Thomas Cooper Library of the University of South Carolina: Linda Holderfield and the interlibrary-loan staff; reference librarians Gwen Baxter, Daniel Boice, Faye Chadwell, Cathy Eckman, Gary Geer, Qun "Gerry" Jiao, Jean Rhyne, Carol Tobin, Carolyn Tyler, Virginia Weathers, Elizabeth Whiznant, and Connie Widney; circulation-department head Thomas Marcil; and acquisitions-searching supervisor David Haggard.

Professor Hasty would like to express his appreciation to Yale University for its support during the initial phase of his work on this project.

# German Writers and Works of the Early Middle Ages: 800–1170

# Dictionary of Literary Biography

# Alcuin

*(circa 732 – 19 May 804)*

Robert Levine
*Boston University*

and

Whitney Bolton
*Rutgers University*

MAJOR WORKS: *Poems* (780–circa 802)

**Manuscripts:** Alcuin's poems are transmitted in two manuscripts: Stuttgart, Wurtemburgische Landesmuseum, G38, dating from the ninth century; and Saint Gall, Stiftsarchiv, 565.

**First publication:** In *Opera quæ hactenus reperiri potuerunt,* edited by Andreas Quercetanus (Paris: Printed by Sebastian Cramoisy, 1617).

**Standard editions:** In *Poetae Latini Aevi Carolini,* volume 1, edited by Ernst Dümmler (Berlin: Weidmann, 1881); in *The Bishops, Kings, and Saints of York,* edited by Peter Godman (Oxford: Clarendon Press / New York: Oxford University Press, 1982).

**Editions in English:** In *The Last Poets of Imperial Rome,* translated by Harold Isbell (Baltimore: Penguin, 1971); "The Dispute between Winter and Spring," in *Poetry of the Carolingian Renaissance,* edited and translated by Peter Godman (Norman: University of Oklahoma Press, 1985), pp. 118–149.

*Letters* (circa 793–804)

**Manuscripts:** There are six English, five French, seven German, one Swiss, and three Italian manuscripts, among which are Vienna, Österreichische Nationalbibliothek, 795 (Salisburg. 140, formerly LXXI), from the eighth century, including twenty-four letters of Alcuin and Angilbert; Vienna, Nationalbibliothek, 808 (Salisbury 234, formerly XXXIV), from 802 to 804, including sixty-nine letters; and Munich, Staatsbibliothek, 4650 (Benedictus buranus 150).

**First publication:** In *Antiquae Lectionis,* volume 1, edited by Henricus Canisius (Ingolstadt: Ex officina typographica Ederiana, apud Andream Angermarium, 1601), pp. 1–123.

**Standard editions:** In *Monumenta Alcuiniana,* edited by Philipp Jaffe, Ernst Dümmler, and W. Wattenbach (Berlin: Weidmann, 1873), pp. 132–897; "Alkuini Epistolae," in *Monumenta Germaniae Historica Epistolae* IV, edited by Dümmler (Berlin, 1895), pp. 1–493; *Two Alcuin Letter-books,* edited by Colin Chase (Toronto: Pontifical Institute of Mediaeval Studies, 1975).

**Edition in modern German:** *Alcuin: Briefe an Karl den Großen,* edited by H. Schütze (Gütersloh, 1879).

**Editions in English:** Rolph Barlow Page, *The Letters of Alcuin* (New York: Forest Press, 1909); Thomas G. Sturgeon, "The Letters of Alcuin: Part One, the Aachen Period (762–796)," Ph.D. dissertation, Harvard University, 1953; translated by Stephen Allott in his *Alcuin of York: His Life and Letters* (York: Sessions, 1974).

Although Alcuin's importance as a central figure in the Carolingian Renaissance has never been seriously questioned, the quality of his literary production can be considered only part of the reason for this importance. His contemporary rival Theodulf called him "nostrorum gloria vatum" (glory of

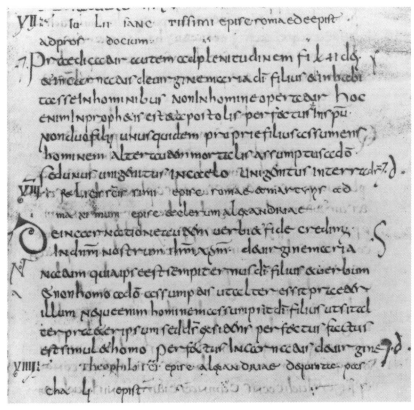

*Page from a manuscript for the Latin version of the acts of the Council of Ephesus, with marginal notations by Alcuin (Paris, Bibliothèque Nationale, Lat. 1572, fol. 79)*

our poets), but in the twentieth century even his admirers are defensive about his verse. On the other hand, modern scholars of liturgy are much interested in Alcuin. His letters, admired greatly in his own time, became models of epistolary style for later writers, both in Latin and in the vernacular. Most of the 312 letters were written between 793 and 804, the middle to the last years of his literary career. They range from short greetings, expressions of gratitude, and requests to complex compositions in a clear, unpretentious, yet demanding prose modeled on Jerome, Aldhelm, and Boniface. They deal with friendship, Christian love, humility, church politics, morality, and scientific topics; some offer advice to Charlemagne or discuss political turbulence in England. Perhaps only an aristocrat would have addressed three letters to King Aethelred upbraiding him for *rusticis moribus* (uncouth behavior) and for the sins he had committed.

When used in conjunction with the anonymous *Vita Alkuini* (Life of Alcuin, 821–829) and some of his poetry, the letters provide a picture of a late-eighth-century English aristocrat who was acquisitive, egotistical, imitative, encyclopedic, sensual, and a worldly collector of information, wealth,

and friends but who turned inward late in life. Born in Northumbria around 732, Alcuin – whose Latin name was Albinus and whose English name was Eathwine – studied at York under Archbishop Egbert and then under Archbishop Aelbert, with whom he traveled on the Continent. In 778 he took over Aelbert's office as head of the cathedral school at York. In 782 he was sent to Rome by King Aefwald to get the pallium for Eanbald, Aelbert's replacement as archbishop. On the way back he met Charlemagne in Parma, and the Frankish king offered him the chance to head the palace school that the king's father, Pépin the Short, had founded in Aachen. In 782, with the permission of his archbishop and his king, Alcuin left England to join Charlemagne.

When Alcuin arrived at Charlemagne's court, he had written a few poems in York and was, apparently, a personable, talented teacher – his English students Sigvulf, Wizo, and Fridugis followed him to Aachen, where he produced many successful scholars; nevertheless, his qualifications for a lofty intellectual position at court were not stunningly manifest. His qualifications for the benefices Charlemagne granted him were also weak since, although he had been ordained a deacon, he seems never to have been ordained to the priesthood and never took monastic vows. Some argue that the Carolingian Renaissance had started a generation before Alcuin's arrival, with Charlemagne's annexation of northern Italy in 774; the Latin of the Italians was far better than that of the Franks or Angles, and Paulinus and Peter of Pisa, who taught Charlemagne grammar, were already at Aachen. But according to Charlemagne's biographer Einhard and Alcuin's *Disputationes* and correspondence, Charlemagne listened to his Anglo-Saxon adviser in all nonpolitical matters. In addition, Alcuin would teach the aging Charlemagne rhetoric, dialectic, and astronomy.

Alcuin returned to England in 786 and again from 790 to 793, but Charlemagne denied him permission to return to York in 795, when he might have become archbishop; instead, the king granted Alcuin the abbeys of Ferrières and Saint Lupus at Troyes. In 796 Charlemagne made him abbot of Saint Martin in Tours, a monastery with two hundred members and holdings across the kingdom. Thus Alcuin remained in France from the summer of 793 until his death at Tours on 19 May 804.

Alcuin composed more than 120 Latin poems from 4 to 1,657 lines long in hexameters, distichs, adonics (with alliteration similar to that of Old English vernacular verse), sapphics, and freer liturgical forms and in a range of genres that include letters, history, hagiography, epitaphs, epigraphs, manuscript inscriptions or subscriptions, riddles, *carmina figurata* (figure poems: poems whose outlines on the page represent an object), prayers, nature poems, liturgy, poems on literary subjects, and hymns. *De Cuculo* (The Cuckoo), the "library catalogue" in the York poem, his nightingale poem, and his epitaph sometimes find their way into anthologies of medieval verse, while the rest of the poems have received scant attention.

What appears to be his earliest surviving work, dating from 780, is his verse epitaph on Aelbert; but the next is the vast poem on York, his most impressive work. A letter to Aethilhard (epistle 311) is evidence that Alcuin was still writing poetry at least as late as 802.

An occasional poem on his leaving the cathedral where he had spent most of his first half century, the York poem was written between 780 and 782 and relies heavily on material taken from the Venerable Bede's *Historia ecclesiastica gentis Anglorum* (Ecclesiastical History of the English People, 731), his lives of Saint Cuthbert, and his hymn to Ethelthryth. At line 1287, however, Alcuin records

the death of Bede; and even though he turns to Eddius for some of his material, he is constrained in the final 370 lines to be more independent. For some, these lines are the most interesting part of the poem, at least partly because in them Alcuin speaks about himself and his activities as a teacher. In lines 1525 to 1529, in the course of eulogizing Aelbert, Alcuin expresses his gratitude for the books that the archbishop gave him. The incomplete "catalogue" of the cathedral library that Alcuin offers in this poem gives some idea of the literature available to Anglo-Saxon clerics at the end of the eighth century.

In 793 a dire event elicited a more traditional kind of occasional poem from Alcuin, *De clade Lindisfarnensis monasterii* (On the Destruction of the Monastery of Lindisfarne). Vikings had raided the monastery, destroying much and killing many. In the 240-line poem Alcuin tells of the expulsion of the first parents from the unchanging joys of Paradise into the world of transience and urges the surviving monks to pray for admission to that other world where all stability and certainty abide; then he reviews the history of Lindisfarne, recalling Aidan, Eadberht, and Cuthbert (whose name he links with that of Cuthbert's biographer, Bede) and arguing that the martyrdom suffered by the monks will better serve their souls than longer life on earth. Operating within, while attempting to transcend, the genre of consolation, Alcuin draws on Roman poets and scriptural, ancient, and local history, simultaneously diminishing the disaster by setting it against the scale of human history and magnifying it by making it a new triumph in the already triumphant history of Lindisfarne.

Chief among the Roman poets to whom Alcuin constantly alludes, in the Lindisfarne poem and elsewhere, is Virgil. On the one hand, the Roman poet's name was one to conjure with since for eight hundred years he had offered the model for melodious verse; on the other hand, by his very attractiveness he symbolized all that enticed and deluded in the material world, and Alcuin praises the Song of Songs as superior to the verses of "falsi Maronis" (false Virgil) which he calls "mendacia" (lies). He certainly knew Virgil well, but other classical poets, such as Ovid, Lucan, and Horace, he seems to have known only secondhand; many of the lines he takes from their poems had become commonplace by the late eighth century. Borrowings from Christian Latin poets and prose writers – Prosper of Aquitaine, Bede, Aldhelm, Gildas, Saint Boniface, Caelius Sedulius, Arator, Juvencus, Paulinus of Nola, and

Venantius Fortunatus – however, are to be found regularly in his verse.

The subjects of Alcuin's many minor poems range from divine matters to latrines; the poems include riddles, nature poems, discussions of the art of meter, commentaries on the Bible, a description of his cell, a retelling of the fable of the cock and the wolf, and his own epitaph. Among the motifs they share are concerns with the perils of alcohol and with the imminence of death.

Alcuin wrote four didactic works in dialogue form in response to the needs of his students. In a sense, all his writing may be called educational in that it was aimed at restoring the study of the liberal arts in Europe, but these four are generally considered to be pedagogical in the strictest sense. The *Ars grammatica* consists of two parts: a conversation between Alcuin and his students and the grammar proper, in which a fourteen-year-old Frankish pupil and a fifteen-year-old Saxon pupil concern themselves mainly with morphology and etymology. (At least eight of Alcuin's letters are also concerned with grammar.) *De Orthographia* is an alphabetical list of words based mainly on Bede's work of the same name. The *Disputatio de rhetorica et de virtutibus sapientissimi regis Carli et Albini magistri* (The Debate of the Wisest King Charles and the Teacher Alcuin, about Rhetoric and the Virtues), a moralizing political treatise, is a dialogue between Charlemagne and Alcuin in which the speakers agree that the proper subjects of rhetoric are politics, law, and morals, with a final section on the four cardinal virtues. The sixteen chapters of dialogue between the questioner, Charlemagne, and the master, Alcuin, that comprise the *De Dialectica* – based on Cassiodorus, Boethius, Cicero, Marius Victorinus, Julius Victor, Quintillian, and Pseudo-Augustine – distinguish rhetoric, the art of disputation on practical matters, from dialectic, the art of disputation on theology. Derived from Secundus, Symphosius, and an anonymous *disputatio* between Hadrian and Epictetus, the *Disputatio regalis et nobilissimi juvenis Pippini cum Albino scholastico* (Dispute of the Royal and Most Noble Young Man Pépin with the Teacher Alcuin) is another pedagogical dialogue, this time with the son of Charlemagne. The first seventy-three exchanges involve figures of speech, some of which resemble kennings.

Alcuin's separate exegetical works are relatively few for a man of his station and century; trained in the rich exegetical tradition of Bede, he had the mission of transmitting that tradition to the Continent, yet he left only five derivative and relatively slight works on Genesis, some of the Psalms,

the Song of Songs, Ecclesiastes, and some of the Pauline letters, along with one far more substantial work on the Gospel of John. A work on Proverbs mentioned in the *Vita Alkuini* is lost, and several other works sometimes associated with his name are probably not his. Some further exegesis is in the letters (for example, epistle 136 to Charlemagne on Luke 22:36 and Matt. 26:52). Although his commentary on Genesis was used by Remigius of Auxerre and translated into Anglo-Saxon by Aelfric of Eynsham, the influence of his exegetical work was slight.

Alcuin's dogmatic, liturgical, and moral theological works all tend toward the same end: unity. In Charlemagne he saw a Christian monarch whose realms might come to embody the ideal of Christian unity and peace. The heresy of adoptionism claimed a large part of Alcuin's attention; he argued against the heresy at the Council of Frankfurt in 794 and in four apologetic treatises. The *Adversus Felicis haeresin libellus* (Against the Heresy of Felix), begun after the Council of Rome in 798, has seventy-two sections in which Alcuin assemblies patristic testimony against adoptionism, a position that argued that Christ as a natural human being was the adopted Son of God. It contains some of the most carefully argued theology of the Carolingian Age but is carelessly constructed. The *Contra Felicem Urgellitanum Episcopum libri VII* (Seven Books against Bishop Felix) is the written version of his oral argument against adoptionism, given at Aachen in 800, a position he also defended in the *Contra Elipandum libri IV* (Four Books against Elipandus), composed in 800, and in the *De fide sanctae et individuae Trinitatis* (On Belief in the Holy and Distinct Trinity), the last, most general, most original, most influential, and most important of his theological works, written in 802. Alcuin's most popular moral work was the *De virtutibus et vitiis liber* (Book of Virtues and Vices), written after 799; twenty-two manuscripts from the ninth century survive, and it continued to be copied long afterward. Vernacular use of it was made by writers in Old English, Middle English, and Old Norse.

Alcuin wrote lives of four saints: Martin of Tours, Vedast of Arras, Richarius, and Willibrord. The first three are prose redactions of earlier works by others; the fourth, an *opus geminatum* (work of prose and verse), is largely Alcuin's own.

Alcuin almost certainly acted as "Latin secretary" to Charlemagne, writing or editing works issued by the palace, but how large a role he played is not clear. Some works, such as one on music mentioned in the list of books in chapter 21 of the *Vita Alkuini,* as well as works mentioned by Alcuin himself in his letters and poems, seem to have disappeared.

## References:

Bernhard Bischoff, "Aus Alkuins Erdentagen," in his *Mittelalterliche Studien,* 2 (Stuttgart: Hiersemann, 1967), pp. 12–19;

Gary Baker Blumenshine, "Alkuin's Liber contra haeresim Felicis and the Frankish Kingdom," *Frühmittelalterliche Studien,* 17 (1983): 222–233;

Whitney French Bolton, *Alcuin and Beowulf: An Eighth-Century View* (New Brunswick, N. J.: Rutgers University Press, 1978);

Franz Brunhölzl, *Geschichte der lateinischen Literatur des Mittelalters* (Munich: Fink, 1975);

Donald A. Bullough, "Alkuin and the Kingdom of Heaven," in *Carolingian Essays,* edited by Uta-Renate Blumental (Washington, D.C.: Catholic University of America Press, 1983), pp. 1–69;

Pierre Courcelle, *La Consolation de Philosophie dans la tradition littéraire* (Paris: Etudes Augustiniennes, 1967), pp. 29–47;

Eleanor Shipley Duckett, *Alcuin, Friend of Charlemagne* (New York: Macmillan, 1951);

Wolfgang Edelstein, *Eruditio und Sapientia: Untersuchungen zu Alcuins Briefen* (Freiburg: Rombach, 1965);

Gerald Ellard, *Master Alkuin, Liturgist* (Chicago: Loyola University Press, 1956);

Heinrich Fichtenau, *The Carolingian Empire,* translated by Peter Munz (Oxford: Blackwell, 1968);

B. Fisher, *Die Alkuin-Bibel* (Freiburg, 1957);

A. Fiske, "Alkuin and Mystical Friendship," *Studi Medievali,* 3, no. 2 (1961): 551–575;

Peter Godman, *Poets and Emperors: Frankish Politics and Carolingian Poetry* (Oxford: Oxford University Press, 1987);

Wilhelm Heil, *Alkuinstudien* (Düsseldorf: Schwann, 1970);

Wilhelm Levison, *England and the Continent in the Eighth Century* (Oxford: Clarendon Press, 1946);

John Marenbon, *From the Circle of Alkuin to the School of Auxerre* (Cambridge: Cambridge University Press, 1981);

John I. McEnerney, "Alcuin, Carmen 58," *Mittellateinisches Jahrbuch,* 16 (1981): 35–42;

McEnerney, "Alcuin, Carmen 118," *Mittellateinisches Jahrbuch,* 19 (1984): 100–103;

Jean Meyers, "Le latin carolingien," *Moyen Age,* 96 (1990): 395–410;

Dieter Schaller, "Alkuin," in *Die deutsche Literatur des Mittelalters: Verfasserlexicon,* volume 1, edited by Kurt Ruh and others (New York & Berlin: De Gruyter, 1977), cols. 241–253;

Peter Dale Scott, "Alcuin as a Poet: Rhetoric and Belief in His Latin Verse," *University of Toronto Quarterly,* 33 (April 1964): 233–257;

Scott, "Alcuin's *Versus de Cuculo: The Vision of Pastoral Friendship,*" *Studies in Philology,* 62 (July 1965): 510–530;

R. E. Sullivan, "Carolingian Age," *Speculum,* 64 (April 1989): 267–306;

Liutpold Wallach, *Alkuin and Charlemagne* (New York: Cornell University Press, 1959).

# The Archpoet

*(circa 1130? – ?)*

Robert Levine
*Boston University*

MAJOR WORK: *Ten Poems* (circa 1159–1167)

**Manuscripts:** At least thirty-five manuscripts have survived, of which Göttingen, Universitätsbibliothek, Cod. philol. 170 provides the basis of poems I through VIII in the standard edition. Brussels, Bibliothèque Royale, 2076 is the basis for poem IX, and Pavia, Biblioteca Universitaria, Aldini 42c is the basis for poem X, the best known of the poems.

**First publication:** "Gedichte des Mittelalters auf König Friedrich I. den Staufer und aus seiner so wie der nächstfolgenden Zeit," edited by Jacob Grimm, in *Philologische und historische Abhandlungen der Königlich Preußische Akademie der Wissenschaften zu Berlin,* 28 (1843): 143–256.

**Standard edition:** *Die Gedichte des Archipoeta,* edited by Heinrich Watenphul and Heinrich Krefeld (Heidelberg: Winter, 1958).

**Edition in modern German:** *Der Archipoeta, lateinisch und deutsch,* translated by Heinrich Krefeld (Berlin: Akademie, 1992).

No one knows the name, date of birth, or date of death of the man who has become known as the Archpoet (in Latin, Archipoeta). Little about his life can be inferred from the ten poems in 714 lines his latest editor attributes to him. That he refers to Reinald von Dassel as the archbishop of Cologne indicates that he was writing between 1159, the year Reinald was elected archbishop, and 1167, the year of Reinald's death. His reference to himself as *ortus e militibus* (of knightly birth, IV 18,2) suggests that he was an aristocrat, and his mention of Salerno in poem VI may indicate a journey he undertook. In spite of the dearth of details about his life, the persona he adopted for his poetry – that of a beggar, prophet, flatterer, biblical exegete, drunkard, and lecher – has made him one of the most popular of all medieval Latin lyric poets. No poem of his twelfth-century peers – Hugh Primas, Walter of Chatillon, or the predominantly anonymous poets of the *Carmina Burana* (Songs from Benediktbeuern,

circa 1230) – has attained the popularity of stanza 12 of his tenth poem:

Mihi est propositum in taberna mori,
ut sint vina proxima morientis ori.
tunc cantabunt letius angelorum chori:
"sit deus propitius huic potatori."

(I propose to die in a tavern,
so that wine may be near my mouth as I die.
Then choruses of angels will happily sing:
"may god be kind to this drinker.")

Characteristically, the stanza combines Greco-Roman (a phrase from Ovid's *Amores*) and Judeo-Christian (a phrase from the Gospel of Luke) material to produce a comic, possibly sacrilegious series of rhyming, rhythmic trochees. The Archpoet also uses both classical and medieval prosodic patterns, demonstrating in poems V and VI competence at composing quantitative verse, while composing the others in rhythmic verse. Unlike Walter of Chatillon, he never combines quantitative and rhythmic verse in one poem.

The first poem, *Lingua balbus* (Stammering [or Stuttering] Tongue) proceeds through thirty quatrains of elegantly pious commonplaces before revealing itself to be a begging poem. Claiming to be not simply modest but inarticulate and dull-witted, the poet nevertheless has the temerity to speak in the voice of the biblical prophets. For an audience of educated clerics, the combination of arrogance and humility would establish his credentials as an authority. The usual excuse for speaking in such a voice is to deliver the vision of a prophet who is outraged at the behavior of his fellow human beings. The Archpoet, however, is motivated by his own impecunity: the wretched behavior he complains about is his own, and his complaints, consequently, become confessional.

Beginning again with the contrast of sublimity and humility, poem II offers a set of extravagant variations in trochaics on formulas of devotion and humility. It is addressed to the archbishop, to whom the Archpoet offers the role of God and Christ, while assigning himself the roles of Jonah (often considered a prefiguring of Christ) and Saint John. Poem III is another begging poem, consisting of twenty-three lines in classical hexameter with some end rhyme, with leonine rhyme throughout, and with each of the last eighteen lines ending in a monosyllable.

Poem IV begins with a disclaimer that combines the humility topos with a series of *adynata* (impossibilities) as the Archpoet proclaims that he is not the man the archchancellor thinks he is, since he does not have time for his assigned task, which Homer and Virgil would not have been able to finish in five years. He then modulates into yet another begging poem, this one in trochaic quatrains.

In poem V the poet is snatched up into heaven, where he weeps for Reinald when Augustine attacks him for reasons not revealed in the poem. Since the poem ends with a complaint against the German king Konrad III's imposition of a higher price on wine, the Archpoet may have been playfully upbraiding the archbishop for not opposing the increase. In dactylic hexameter with leonine rhyme to verse 22, followed by five stanzas of end-rhyming dactylics, poem VI portrays the poet sick at Salerno, dependent on the generosity of Reinald.

Another panegyric begging poem, with a reference to the siege of Milan, poem VII offers praise of Reinald in seven-syllable trochaic, with personification, wordplay, chiasmuses, and various other schemes and tropes. Poem VIII is a panegyric of Reinald in a six-line *Stabat Mater* strophe that would seem to bestow instant sanctity on the archbishop.

Poem IX offers straightforward praise of the territorial achievements of Emperor Friedrich I. The Archpoet again self-consciously speaks of his task as a writer, and in the penultimate stanza he pays tribute once again to the archbishop. In the one hundred lines of poem X, *Estuans intrinsecus ira vehementi* (Raging Within, with Great Anger), the poet describes himself as driven by rage, like a bird in the wind, lustful, compelled by the nature of the poetic craft to be a drunkard, but willing to turn over a new leaf and become virtuous if the archbishop will only grant him forgiveness.

In each of his poems the Archpoet pursues a narrow range of themes and genres, amplifying them with allusions to Roman and Christian biblical and liturgical texts. Thereby he produces a comic, ambiguous set of poems.

**References:**
Francis Cairns, "The Archpoet's Confession," *Mittellateinisches Jahrbuch,* 10 (1975): 100–105;

Cairns, "The Archpoet's Confession: Sources, Interpretation and Historical Context," *Mittellateinisches Jahrbuch,* 15 (1980): 87–103;

Cairns, "The Archpoet's 'Jonah-Confession' (Poem II): Literary, Exegetical, and Historical Aspects," *Mittellateinisches Jahrbuch,* 18 (1983): 168–193;

Ernst Robert Curtius, *Europäische Literatur und Lateinisches Mittelalter* (Bern: Francke, 1948); translated by Willard R. Trask as *European Literature and the Latin Middle Ages* (New York: Pantheon, 1953);

Peter Dronke, "The Archpoet and the Classics," in *Latin Poetry and the Classical Tradition,* edited by Peter Godman and Oswyn Murray (Oxford: Clarendon Press, 1990), pp. 57–72;

Dronke, "The Art of the Archpoet: A Reading of 'Lingua balbus,' " in *The Interpretation of Medieval Lyric Poetry,* edited by W. H. T. Jackson (New York: Columbia University Press, 1980), pp. 22–43;

Willibrod Heckenbach, "Zur Parodie beim Archipoeta," *Mittellateinisches Jahrbuch,* 4 (1967): 145–154;

Paul Klopsch, "Acyrus (Archipoeta vii, 11.2)," *Mittellateinisches Jahrbuch,* 4 (1967): 167–171;

Klopsch, "Zur 'Kaiser Hymnus' und 'Beichte' des Archipoeta," *Mittellateinisches Jahrbuch,* 4 (1967): 161–166;

Karl Langosch, "Zur Bittpredigt des Archipoeta," *Mittellateinisches Jahrbuch,* 4 (1967): 155–160;

Paul Lehmann, *Die Parodie im Mittelalter* (Stuttgart: Hiersemann, 1963), pp. 95–98, 135;

Marilyn B. Skinner, "The Archpoet's Use of the Jonah-Figure," *Neophilologus,* 57 (January 1973): 1–5;

G. Vinay, "Ugo Primate e l'Archipoeta," *Cultura Neolatino,* 9 (1949): 5–40;

Fritz Wagner, "Colores rhetorici in der 'Vagantbeichte' des Archipoeta," *Mittellateinisches Jahrbuch,* 10 (1975): 100–105.

# Der arme Hartmann
## (? – after 1150)

Francis G. Gentry
*Pennsylvania State University*

MAJOR WORK: *Rede vom heiligen Glouben* (between 1140 and 1160)

**Manuscript:** The work was included in the Straßburg-Molsheimer manuscript (1r–9v), which dated from around 1187 and was burned during the French siege of Strasbourg in 1870. The treatise is 3,800 lines long, with a postulated 401-line lacuna between lines 3224 and 3625. In addition to the *Rede vom heiligen Glouben,* the manuscript included Heinrich's *Litanei,* the *Straßburg Alexander,* and a *Pilatus* fragment.

**First publication and standard edition:** In *Deutsche Gedichte des zwölften Jahrhunderts und der nächstverwandten Zeit,* edited by Hans Ferdinand Massmann (Quedlinburg & Leipzig: Basse, 1837), pp. 1–42.

**Standard edition:** In *Die religiösen Dichtungen des 11. und 12. Jahrhunderts: Nach ihren Formen besprochen und herausgegeben,* volume 2, edited by Friedrich Maurer (Tübingen: Niemeyer, 1965), pp. 573–628.

Near the end of his work (line 3737) the poet of the thirty-eight-hundred-line *Rede vom heiligen Glouben* (Tract Concerning [Our] Sacred Faith, between 1140 and 1160) identifies himself as "ich arme Hartman" (I, poor Hartmann). The meaning of the fairly common epithet *arm,* a translation of the Latin *miser,* however, is not poor in the sense of destitute; rather, it is a highly stylized part of a rather traditional medieval humility formula in which the author names himself so that his audience might include him in their prayers to God (lines 3731–3742). The poet is assuming the role of a sinful, unworthy man who is trying to win the goodwill of the audience. Perhaps the best-known example of this type of humility formula is found in Hartmann von Aue's *Der arme Heinrich* (circa 1191).

To the name can be added the further biographical conjecture that Hartmann was the author of a work dealing with the Last Judgment: when that subject comes under discussion in the *Rede vom heiligen Glouben,* Hartmann declines to pursue the topic because he has already dealt with it in another work:

> wi iz dan alliz sal comen
> zo deme grozem urteile der werelt algemeine.
> daz nehabe wir niwit vermiden. iz ist alliz gescriben
> ze gehorenne unde ze gesihte in dutiscer scrifte. (lines 1630–1636)

> ([we have written] how it is all to come
> to the great judgment of the whole world.
> We did not leave out anything. It has all been written
> – to be listened to or to be read – in German.)

This work has apparently not survived.

The indication of the mode of reception of his writings — that they were listened to *or* read — leads to assumptions about his intended audience and about Hartmann's social status. At first glance it might appear that his words indicate an intended monastic or clerical audience since, around the middle of the twelfth century, these individuals would be most likely to be able to read. Works of a theological or eschatological nature designed for a monastic or clerical audience would, however, most probably have been written in Latin since the vernacular was not always welcome in monasteries and certainly not as a vehicle to express great truths. Yet Hartmann explicitly writes that his earlier treatise was in German, as is the *Rede vom heiligen Glouben.* Therefore, it seems reasonable to surmise that the individuals constituting Hartmann's intended audience were not well versed in Latin but were able to read, which leads to the conjecture that his works were intended for a noble lay audience. Although Germany lagged behind most of Europe with regard to lay literacy in the twelfth century, members of the German nobility certainly did not inhabit an intellectual wasteland, and with the emergence of a noble lay stratum sympathetic to the vernacular around the middle of the century, it is reasonable to assume that this group would be addressed by writers such as Hartmann. If this assumption is tenable, it would place Hartmann in the company of other poets of the eleventh and twelfth centuries, such as Notker von Zwiefalten and Heinrich von Melk, who admonished the nobility to be aware of their responsibilities in this world and to prepare their souls for the next. Unlike Notker von Zwiefalten, the postulated author of the *Memento mori* (circa 1080), who was a monk, Hartmann was doubtless a layperson who was proficient in Latin and theologically learned. This supposition is supported by references in the text to priests and their sacred functions of singing the Mass and consecrating the Eucharist (lines 16 and 1065–1140) in which Hartmann separates himself from the priests and their salvation-bringing activities and merges with his audience with inclusive phrases such as "uns sundigen" (we sinners). It is also assumed that Hartmann might have been a *conversus* (lay brother); *conversi* associated themselves with monasteries, often after a full life in the world, but did not take the binding vows. Thus, together with Frau Ava and Heinrich von Melk, Hartmann was probably one of the first lay poets in medieval Germany.

The *Rede vom heiligen Glouben* can best be described as a rhymed theological tract. It is not a penitential sermon like the *Memento mori* nor is it an acerbic, satirical lashing out at human society as is the case with the works of Heinrich von Melk. Rather, it is an exposition of the Nicene Creed as it appears in the Sunday liturgy, presumably for members of the laity who were not sufficiently competent in Latin. The main part of the work can be divided into four sections: on God the Father, lines 1–178; on Jesus Christ, lines 178–1640; on the Holy Spirit, lines 1641–3630; and a final section, lines 3631–3708, on topics such as baptism, confession of sins, and the resurrection of the body. An epilogue, in which the poet names himself, comprises lines 3709–3800. In each of the four main sections Hartmann quotes articles from the creed in Latin, translates them fairly exactly or paraphrases them, and then provides explications of varying lengths. Sections 2 and 3 are strikingly longer than sections 1 and 4, and section 3, in which the four-hundred-line lacuna falls, is the most extensive of all.

The *Rede vom heiligen Glouben* is not a learned theological discourse on the intricacies of the Nicene Creed and the subtleties of interpretation but a primer to aid the laity in comprehending the central mysteries of Christianity that make up the creed. It evidences a cohesive internal structure proceeding from Creation (sections 1 and 2) through Redemption and its significance (section 2), the proper conduct of life on earth (section 3), to the certainty of the final Judgment and reward for the just (section 4). In sections 1 and 2 the emphasis is on faith in the creative and redemptive actions of God. It is there that Hartmann attempts to express the ineffable – the eternity and oneness of the Trinity – trying, at the same time, to elucidate the singular tasks of the three aspects of the one God, the mystery of Creation, the Incarnation, the sacrament of the Eucharist, and the significance of the Resurrection. It is no mean undertaking, and it is one that he carries out more or less successfully. In section 3 the emphasis is on the responsibility of human beings to do good works and atone for their sins; the section is structured as a series of counsels of the Holy Spirit, all of which have to do with leading an active Christian life on earth so as to achieve salvation without disparaging earthly existence. Section 4 closes with the assurance to women and men, noble or peasant, that salvation is assured if belief in God and the articles of the creed, as well as good deeds, is present.

Although the *Rede vom heiligen Glouben* is interesting in its own right as a catechismlike document, certain parts are fascinating for the glimpse they provide into the twelfth-century mentality. In section 2, for example, a thorny problem connected with Creation is treated: did matter exist in a primal, chaotic state before the Creation? Orthodox Christian thinkers could, of course, not accept that anything existed before Creation except God: God created everything ex nihilo; he did not take preexisting matter and form it. But Plato and many thinkers after him were convinced that created matter derived from a preexistent matter (*hylē*). This concept, filtered through Christian thought, was taken up in the twelfth century by such renowned Platonists as Bernardus Silvestris and Alan of Lille. An echo of this reception is seen in *Rede vom heiligen Glouben*:

Daz di wisen hiezen yle daz nist ouch niwit me,
wen daz got von nihte machete gesihte
di vier elementa, dan abe di werlt begunde sta[n]. . . .
    (321–326)

(That which the wise men call *hylē* is [means?] nothing more
than that which God made visible from nothing
the four elements after which the world began to develop. . . .)

*Hylē*, in orthodox Christian thought, is not a substance but an action of God from which developed the four elements, which God then proceeded to order. Hartmann is describing the "instant" before

Creation, the initial act of the Creator that still existed outside of time. In addition to demonstrating the adaptation of a Platonic concept by twelfth-century Platonists and providing evidence that Hartmann had more than a passing familiarity with Platonist discourse, these lines also introduce a lengthy segment of section 2 that deals with secular wisdom (lines 321–444). In this segment Hartmann departs from his main theme and writes about the origin of earthly wisdom. As one who ostensibly was influenced by twelfth-century Platonist thought, Hartmann holds that the wisdom to which his age is heir had its origin with the ancient Greeks. The ancient wise men, he says, concerned themselves with philosophical reflection and the application of philosophy to the search for truth and the analysis of nature. They examined the heavens, determined the measurement of time, named the signs of the zodiac, and measured the distance between the earth and the heavens. Their greatest accomplishment, Hartmann writes, was to provide their spiritual heirs with the seven liberal arts. The purpose of the strivings of the ancient wise men was to engage in learning that would be useful to human beings on earth. This aim meets with Hartmann's approval; but since he is attempting to direct his listeners, as the title of his work suggests, toward a deeper understanding of the Christian faith, he must also point out that secular knowledge can extend only so far. True knowledge that transcends death can only come from Christ:

di aller besten liste di quamen von Criste,
daz ist di wisheit di da niemer nezegeit,
di niemer vertirbit in dem menscen so er stirbit. (lines 431–
    436)

(The best knowledge comes from Christ.
That is the knowledge that never diminishes,
that never ceases in the human being when he dies.)

In his view of the world and secular wisdom Hartmann strikes a reasonable chord, much as does Notker von Zwiefalten when debating the amount of alms that one should give to the poor. Secular wisdom is good and beneficial for life in this world, but this wisdom is transitory and not sufficient for salvation; on the other hand, Hartmann does not claim that secular knowledge is detrimental to one's spiritual health. The only knowledge that remains with one after death is the knowledge of truth, and that knowledge can only come from God.

Lines 2403–2488 in section 3 provide a picture of the intended addressees of Hartmann's work: the members of the nobility. Hartmann describes in de-

tail the opulent life of the nobility: the great agricultural holdings, possessions, and treasure ("michelen uop, / groz ingetume, scazzis genuge" [lines 2406–2408]); the exquisite goblets of gold and silver; the precious jewels and ivory; the expensive furs and silk;

teppit unde vorhanc vile breit unde lanc,
gevollit mit golde, als iz din herze wolde,
unde andre zirde also vile
der ich reiten nit newile. (lines 2426–2428)

([you can order made] carpets and draperies, quite
    broad and long
and completely wrought with gold, as your heart desires;
[you can order made] so many types of other glorious
    things
that I do not wish to count them all.)

Hartmann goes on to describe a nobleman in gleaming armor astride a great steed, with saddle and shield of gold; he carries a new shaft with silken pennants. He is surrounded by his squires and soldiers who will react to his every whim:

wilt du rite[n] oder ge[n], wilt du sizze[n] oder ste[n],
di beginnint din beite[n] unde tunt vil bereite,
swaz du in gebutis in dinen willen dutis. (lines 2449–
2454)

(If you wish to ride or go on foot, if you wish to sit or
    stand,
they put your [command?] into effect and readily do
whatever you order [or] whatever you indicate to them
    is your will.)

Hartmann provides descriptions of great feasts with meat and fish, wine and mead. But, he warns his listeners, in the midst of this splendor,

vil luzzil du gedinkis,
daz du bietis dicheine ere dinem sceffere,
der dirz alliz hat gegeben, da zu din selbis leben. (lines
2470–2474)

(How little you consider
that you [should] offer any sort of honor to your creator,
who has given you everything [that you have] in your life.)

Hartmann closes this description of the noble life with the nobleman enjoying his wife's favors in bed.

These lines provide a straightforward description of the emerging noble lifestyle around the middle of the twelfth century. The descriptions are detailed and cover the most important aspects of noble existence: physical comfort, followers at one's beck and call, opulent furnishings and clothes, splendid and costly food, and the pleasures provided by a beautiful woman. The moderate language that Hartmann uses in these descriptions (so unlike the invective of Heinrich von Melk) betrays a fascination with this way of life. He does not unequivocally condemn the nobility for living as they do, in spite of his use of standard descriptions of the frailty and ultimate decay of the body, which becomes a home for worms and maggots. But since the body will end up in the ground, he is more interested in the soul. It is the soul that is in danger, and to avoid that peril it would be best if the nobles abandoned their possessions, family, and friends and entered the monastery to serve God as *conversi*. But if they cannot do that, Hartmann instructs them on how to attain salvation while remaining in the world.

This program is the same one that is encountered in the works of so many of the writers from the early Middle High German period, such as Notker von Zwiefalten: the nobles should help the poor, not forget who is the author of all their wealth and joy, and control their sexual appetites but not renounce sex: "wande des fleiscis wollust daz ist der sele verlust, / swer si ubit zo unmaze unde si durch gote nit newil laze[n]" (For the pleasures of the flesh bring about the loss of the soul / [for] whoever engages [in sex] immoderately and does not intend to stop [this immoderation] for the sake of God, lines 2493–2496). Moderation in all things and a life of active Christianity will ensure the salvation of the soul regardless of one's station in life. This principle continued to fascinate German poets in the high courtly period (circa 1160 to circa 1250) in Germany. Der arme Hartmann stands in the long line of German poets, from the anonymous poet of the Old High German *Muspilli* (circa 790–circa 850) to Hartmann von Aue, Wolfram von Eschenbach, and Walther von der Vogelweide, who are concerned with "wie man zer welte solte leben" (how one ought to live in the world).

**Bibliography:**
Francis G. Gentry, *Bibliographie zur frühmittelhochdeutschen geistlichen Dichtung* (Berlin: Schmidt, 1992), pp. 75–79.

**References:**
Sister Marie P. Buttell, OSF, *Religious Ideology and Christian Humanism in German Cluniac Verse* (Washington, D.C.: Catholic University Press, 1948), pp. 47–63;

Francis G. Gentry, "'Ex oriente lux': *Translatio* Theory in Early Middle High German Literature," in *Spectrum Medii Aevi: Essays in Early German Literature in Honor of George Fenwick Jones,* edited by William C. McDonald (Göppingen: Kümmerle, 1983), pp. 119–137;

Heinz Rupp, *Deutsche Religiöse Dichtungen des 11. und 12. Jahrhunderts: Untersuchungen und Interpretationen,* second edition (Bern & Munich: Francke, 1971), pp. 134–216;

Gisela Vollmann-Profe, *Geschichte der deutschen Literatur von den Anfängen bis zum Beginn der Neuzeit,* volume 1/2: *Von den Anfängen zum Hohen Mittelalter* (Königstein: Athenäum, 1986);

Max Wehrli, *Geschichte der deutschen Literatur vom frühen Mittelalter bis zum Ende des 16. Jahrhunderts* (Stuttgart: Reclam, 1980).

# Dhuoda

*(circa 803 – after 843)*

## Linda Archibald
*Liverpool John Moores University*

MAJOR WORK: *Liber Manualis* (843)

> **Manuscripts:** Paris, Bibliothèque Nationale, 12293; Barcelona, 569, folios 57–88, Catalan copy.
>
> **Standard edition:** *Manuel pour mon fils,* edited by Pierre Riché (Paris: Éditions du Cerf, 1975).
>
> **Edition in English:** Translated by Carol Neel as *Handbook for William: A Carolingian Woman's Counsel for Her Son by Dhuoda* (Lincoln: University of Nebraska Press, 1991).

Dhuoda (also known as Dodana) is the only known female Carolingian poet and one of the few lay poets whose work has survived from the period. Her place of birth is not known, but her name suggests a northern Frankish connection. She wrote her *Liber Manualis* (Handbook, 843), a book of advice for her son William, in Latin, but her style shows the influence of Germanic half lines and stress patterns. It is likely that her first language was a Germanic one and that she wrote in Latin because most learning and literature of the time were carried on in that language.

Dhuoda's writing reveals the sort of education that could only have been afforded by a noble family. Her first documented activity is her marriage to Bernard, Duke of Septimania, at the imperial palace at Aachen on 29 June 824. Bernard was well connected through his father, Wilhelm of Gellone, who was a cousin of Charlemagne, was renowned for fighting the Saracens in northern Spain, and appears by name in many of the chansons de geste. Before their marriage Bernard had been appointed to a position at the court of his godfather, Emperor Louis the Pious; his duties included tutoring the future Charles the Bald.

When Louis the Pious's sons began to offer a potential threat to the supremacy of their father, Louis, fearful of Bernard's growing personal power and suspicious of his motives, sent him to Spain. Dhuoda went with her husband, but he sent her to live under a sort of house arrest in Uzès, in present-day southern France, soon after her son William was born on 29 November 826.

Dhuoda does not criticize Bernard in her *Liber Manualis;* indeed, she awards him nothing but the utmost respect and loyalty and encourages William to do the same. Bernard was not popular with the nobles who surrounded him, however, and was often accused of tyranny. There were persistent rumors of a relationship between Bernard and Judith, the second wife of Louis the Pious; he also stole church property during military campaigns and switched loyalties on several occasions, depending on the prevailing balance of power. Dhuoda does not directly mention these faults, but while she exhorts William to respect and honor his father she does not recommend that he emulate Bernard's behavior.

In 831 Bernard allied himself with Pépin of Aquitaine, a rival of Louis the Pious, and both were accused of treachery. Bernard built up his power base in Aquitaine, ostensibly in support of Louis the Pious; he was clearly hedging his bets, but after Louis's death, at the decisive battle of Fontenoy in 841, Bernard backed the losing side. Charles the Bald emerged as the victor, and Bernard was in danger of retribution from his former pupil. To forestall this eventuality he sent his son William to Charles's court as a hostage.

Dhuoda was still in Uzès and had just borne a second son, who had not yet been christened. Bernard had the baby brought to him, named him Bernard, and left Dhuoda with neither husband nor children. It was against this background that she wrote the *Liber Manualis* as a book of instruction for William; it was completed in 843, when he was seventeen. Forced to live apart from her children and husband, Dhuoda saw her work as a way of carrying out her duty as a wife and mother.

The *Liber Manualis* consists mostly of prose but includes four poems. There are seventy-three sections, with several introductory dedications and concluding pieces. The preface recounts the birth of William's younger brother, who is mentioned throughout the book. The first eleven sections concentrate on God; sections 12 and 13 deal with William's father. After that the book develops the theme of obedience to God and loyalty to one's earthly masters, including clergy, royalty, and statesmen. The advice echoes Christian homilies and commentaries but also covers secular matters. The large space given to practical and political considerations is distinctive in a work of the time, as is the emphasis on *astutia* (the ability to deal with people), which is not one of the celebrated Christian virtues. Dhuoda's theology is more generous than that which prevailed in her day: for example, she urges William to pray for heretics and those who have not confessed their sins – people who, according to most clerics, would merit damnation. Dhuoda recalls her family's history of violent death; fearing such a fate for her husband and sons, she is willing to believe in the power of prayer to redeem even apparently hopeless cases. This part of the work provides valuable historical information about family relationships in Frankish court circles around the time of Charlemagne.

In her varied, rather experimental approach Dhuoda follows the examples of Alcuin and Hrabanus Maurus. She demonstrates a clear grasp of poetic form, including sapphic verses and more-rhythmical sections that are reminiscent of the liturgy and of Germanic verse forms. Dhuoda's language is fluent; she quotes Scripture and lightly reflects Carolingian commentators without the scholarly tone cultivated by the monastic writers. She names three important influences: Donatus, Isidore of Seville, and Gregory the Great; others are evident though not cited by name, including Prudentius and Augustine as well as contemporary authors. There is some evidence that she read the love poems of Ovid. Her Latin is not perfect, but the Latin of most Carolingians in the mid ninth century was idiosyncratic. Many of her "errors" are colloquialisms, some are grammatical misunderstandings, and others are caused by imitation of the elaborate language of classical authors. Dhuoda did not have the benefit of a complete monastic education or of access to a large library.

What is striking, however, is the fervor and immediacy of her language as she addresses God in simple but not craven obedience and implores William to submit to the duties of son, nobleman, and Christian servant of God. She is concerned about her son and sees herself as interceding with God on his behalf. Humility formulas abound in the poem;

Dhuoda laments her physical weakness, her inability to concentrate on long prayers, and her tendency to melancholy, but the tone is one of resignation and acceptance rather than self-condemnation.

The work ends with Dhuoda's epitaph, her wishes regarding her burial, and instruction to her son on how to deal with matters of inheritance and family debts. It is not known how much longer Dhuoda lived after the writing of the *Liber Manualis,* but her husband was executed for treason a year later by Charles the Bald.

The recipient of the *Liber Manualis* followed in his father's footsteps, capturing Barcelona in 848. He threw in his lot with Pépin, the son of his father's friend Pépin of Aquitaine, and in 849 William, too, was executed for treason. In spite of his mother's efforts, William had been caught up in the same sort of intrigue and violence that had characterized his father's life. There is no reliable information on the fate of his brother Bernard.

Dhuoda has been largely ignored. She was neither statesman nor cleric, and, unlike the poetasters of the courts, she wrote for personal rather than political or religious reasons. Her concern with family honor and the proper behavior of a young nobleman of an illustrious Christian family adds to the sparse historical records of the time. Her very existence is testimony to the effectiveness of Charlemagne's educational reforms, at least for those who could afford to be tutored: the love of books and learning that is evident in her work demonstrates that her education was more than superficial. She read widely and understood complex classical works written in a Latin that was by no means straightforward.

Dhuoda had no need to dress her work up in flattering terms to impress a patron or to keep to a particular monastery or abbey "house style"; there was no bishop or schoolmaster to check the doctrinal purity of her ideas or the grammatical correctness of her language. This freedom gives her work a freshness and originality highly unusual for the period. She was aware, however, of the potential future of her little book, and on occasion she urges a general reader to take encouragement from her admonitions to her son. The inclusion of literary set pieces such as the prologue and preface, introductory and concluding chapters, and acrostics and literary allusions show a well-educated writer choosing and adapting existing literary models. Both verse and prose are within her repertoire, and theology is mixed with practical advice. Her appreciation of a wider context for her work, in terms both of antecedents and of potential audience, reveals that

Dhuoda consciously aligned herself with the literary figures of her day. In the 1990s interest in this important author was revived, and new translations, commentaries, and articles began to appear. Inclusion in major reference works and books on women writers may yet ensure that Dhuoda is brought to her rightful place in the history of early Western literature.

**References:**

P. A. Becker, "Dhuoda's Handbuch," *Zeitschrift für romanische Philologie,* 21 (1897): 73–101;

Karen Cherewatuk, "Speculum Matris: Dhuoda's Manual," *Florilegium,* 10 (1988): 49–63;

Peter Dronke, *Women Writers of the Middle Ages* (Cambridge: Cambridge University Press, 1984), pp. 36–54;

James Merchand, "The Frankish Mother: Dhuoda," in *Medieval Women Writers,* edited by Katharina M. Wilson (Athens: University of Georgia Press, 1984), pp. 1–29;

Glen W. Olsen, "One Heart and One Soul (Acts 4, 32 and 34) in Dhuoda's Manual," *Church History,* 61 (March 1992): 23–33;

Joachim Wollasch, "Eine adlige Familie des Frühen Mittelalters," *Archive für Kulturgeschichte,* 39 (1957): 150–188.

# Eilhart von Oberge

*(circa 1140 – circa 1195)*

William C. McDonald
*University of Virginia*

MAJOR WORK: *Tristrant* (circa 1160–1175)

**Manuscripts:** The work is preserved in four fragments – in Magdeburg, Regensburg, Stargard, and Sankt Paul im Lavanttal – from the late twelfth and early thirteenth centuries. These manuscripts comprise approximately 1,300 verses. The entire poem, of about 9,520 verses, is found in two manuscripts – Dresden, Sächsische Landesbibliothek, Ms. M 42, and Heidelberg, Universitätsbibliothek, Cpg 346, both from the fifteenth century. The Heidelberg manuscript is the only extant illustrated manuscript. A third fifteenth-century manuscript, Berlin, Staatsbibliothek, Preußischer Kulturbesitz, Mgf 640, preserves the conclusion of *Tristrant,* from verse 6103. It also holds the *Tristan und Isolde* (circa 1210) of Gottfried von Straßburg and a few verses from the completion of Gottfried's work by Ulrich von Türheim (circa 1230).

**First publication:** *Hienach volget die Histori von Herren Tristrant vnd der schönen Isalden von Irlannde* (Augsburg: Anton Sorg, 1484).

**Standard editions:** *Eilhart von Oberge,* edited by Franz Lichtenstein (Strasbourg: Trübner, 1877); *Tristrant: Die alten Bruchstücke,* edited by Kurt Wagner (Bonn & Leipzig: Schroeder, 1924); *Tristrant und Isalde: Prosaroman. Nach dem ältesten Druck aus Augsburg vom Jahr 1484, versehen mit den Lesarten des zweiten Druckes aus dem Jahre 1498 und eines Wormser Druckes unbekannten datums,* edited by Alois Brandstetter (Tübingen: Niemeyer, 1966); *Tristrant: Synoptischer Druck der ergänzten Fragmente mit der gesamten Parallelüberlieferung,* edited by Hadumod Bußmann (Tübingen: Niemeyer, 1969); *Tristrant: Edition diplomatique des manuscrits et traduction en Français moderne avec introduction, notes et index,* edited by Danielle Buschinger (Göppingen: Kümmerle, 1976); *Tristan und Isolde (Augsburg bei Antonius Sorg, 1484),* afterword by Helga Elsner (Hildesheim & New York: Olms, 1989);

*Tristrant und Isalde: Heidelberg, Universitätsbibliothek, Cod. Pal. Germ. 346,* edited by Norbert H. Ott (Munich: Lengenfelder, 1990).

**Edition in modern German:** *Tristrant und Isalde: Neuhochdeutsche Übersetzung,* translated by Danielle Buschinger and Wolfgang Spiewok (Göppingen: Kümmerle, 1986).

**Edition in English:** *Eilhart von Oberge's Tristrant,* translated by J. W. Thomas (Lincoln: University of Nebraska Press, 1978).

Eilhart von Oberge introduced the Tristan legend to the German cultural area with his *Tristrant,* a poem of more than ninety-five hundred verses. It is the oldest complete Tristan romance that is extant. Although Eilhart does not preserve every known Tristan episode – omitting, for example, the Gilan adventure and the equivocal oath of Isalde – he sets out to relate the full biography of the eponymous hero from birth to burial. The romance concludes with a dual miracle: King Mark, the wronged husband, forgives Tristrant and Isalde for their adulterous love; and the rosebush and grapevine over the single grave of the star-crossed lovers grow so tightly together that they are inextricably intertwined. Based on a certain *buch* (book), a French source that has not been preserved, *Tristrant* derives from the same narrative tradition as the *Tristran* of Béroul (circa 1190). Both offer the version of the Tristan story customarily designated "primitive" or "common," which focuses more on intrepid exploits than on psychology and which betrays no elevated conception of love. Although Eilhart's poem certainly arose at a secular court, court culture did not strongly influence it; chivalric manners, for instance, play only a slight role. The institution of knighthood receives short shrift: no tourneys appear, and there is only a brief reference to the knighting of Tristrant.

Eilhart's *Tristrant* was much admired in the Middle Ages; to judge by the extensive reworking of his tale, it was the most influential treatment of

stat. noch er in gegin mir niht negat. des was
ich harte ungewone. ich ne were wa uone er nu
o gesach siv das wenzin.                          S come.

vn begunde san denkin. in wirrit swaz so iz
si. ich were hi etiswer si bi. der uns habe ge hut.
bidem brunnin siv stunt. vn wart der spehere
ge ware. der mane truch den sare dare. in den
brunnin uon den mannin zuwein. der frowen
wiselit descein. daz siv ir oge dar niht ne kar
te. vn rehte also gebarre. alse si ir da niht ne
wiste. vn sprach mit grozir liste. Tristant waz
soldich her zodit. frowe daz ir helpint mir daz
mir min here sine hulde gebe. vn laze mich
wesin. als ich was in sineme hobe. uil ernist
hafte ich dir gelobe. dar zu ne helbe ich dir
niet. wane mir liebe is ge sciet. daz er dir so
gram is. des wiz zuware gewis. daz ich dir
dar zu niht ne urome. wane ich bin ze woz
te comen. non dir ane mine scult. ich was
dir durch minin heren holt. wane dv sin
nebe wertst. vn siner eren plegtst. baz den
er anderen alle. nu bin ich ze scalle. wordin

*Lines 3518–3555 in the Magdeburg fragment of Eilhart von Oberge's* Tristrant, *which dates from the end of the twelfth century, making it contemporary with Eilhart himself (Berlin, Deutsche Staatsbibliothek, Ms. germ. quart. 661)*

the Tristan legend in Germany. It served as the paradigm for the lengthy Tristan romances of Ulrich von Türheim (circa 1230) and Heinrich von Freiberg (circa 1280); the anonymous fourteenth-century Czech narrative poem *Tristram a Izalda;* the chapbook *Historie von Herrn Tristrant und der schönen Isalden von Irlande* (Story of Sir Tristrant and Isalde the Fair of Ireland), which appeared in 1484 with reprintings until 1664; and a Tristan play and poems by Hans Sachs in the sixteenth century. Of major medieval authors, Wolfram von Eschenbach was most conversant with Eilhart's poem; his *Parzival* (circa 1200–1210) includes several allusions to the story.

Despite the impressive literary reception of Eilhart's *Tristrant,* modern scholarship tends to dismiss it as a failed work of art, at best an artifact useful for the reconstruction of the archetypal Tristan story. Notwithstanding ample evidence for Eilhart's mastery of his material, manifest above all in his creation of a self-conscious narrative persona, *Tristrant* is faulted by some critics for deficient psychological motivation and excessive reliance on metaphysical determinism (in the form of chance or fate). Most believe that the poet advances a mechanistic view of the love potion and erotic passion, casting Tristrant and Isalde as cunning deceivers and fools for love.

Recent editions and translations of *Tristrant* into English and modern German are a sign of scholarly interest. A critical reappraisal has not come about, however. Because scholars are divided over the main thrust of the poem, tentative conclusions are the rule. "Tectonic" analysis, which was dominant in the 1970s, reveals the rigor of Eilhart's plot structure but is inconclusive concerning the interpretation of *Tristrant.* The poem concerns the perniciousness of lust: this force, which is capable of undermining and destroying the intrepidity of the protagonist, creates a narrative tension that can be expressed in the formula "love versus heroism." Love lays low the giant killer and dragon slayer Tristrant. Because Eilhart's ethos and style differ so markedly from the *Tristan und Isolde* (circa 1210) of Gottfried von Straßburg, which affirms the ennobling power of love, *Tristrant* research labors under comparisons – chiefly negative – with the verses of his German rival. Gottfried's work belongs to the other major branch of the Tristan tradition, the "courtly" version exemplified by the romance he adapted, the *Tristran* (circa 1175) of Thomas of Britain.

With respect to the date of composition, literary sources, sponsorship, provenance, and taxonomy, hardly any work of the twelfth century poses more questions than *Tristrant.* The manuscript stemma shows that the poem was preserved during two distinct epochs, centuries apart. Inasmuch as roughly a tenth of the early verses survive in fragments of manuscripts from the twelfth and thirteenth centuries, and, since redactions of the complete poem derive exclusively from the fifteenth century, conclusions regarding author and text are necessarily speculative. (Eilhart's name appears in fifteenth-century records alone – in verse 9446 – and even here the cognomen is not uniform.) The extent to which the main body of the poem represents a late medieval creation is simply unclear.

Of Eilhart all that is certain is his birthplace, Oberg, a village in northern Germany between Brunswick and Hildesheim. Some believe that the Eilardus de Oberge mentioned in legal documents from 1189 onward was the author; this man was a ministerial of the Guelph (Welf) family. For one official record concerning Heinrich der Löwe (Henry the Lion), the twelfth-century duke of Saxony, a youthful Eilardus was a witness. Eilhart fails to mention a literary sponsor in his work, but he could have composed it for the Saxon ducal court, which promoted vernacular literature. A consensus seems to be emerging, however, that the derivation of *Tristrant* is Rhenish rather than Saxon because the Middle and Lower Rhine would be more likely sites for the transmission of French aristocratic literature. (Indicative of the uncertainty over Eilhart's literary patronage is the assignment of the poem to regions representing the entire expanse of German geography – Limburg, Thuringia, and Regensburg.)

The dating of *Tristrant* continues to be controversial. The two principal dates proposed, circa 1170 and circa 1190, profoundly affect Eilhart's place in German literary history. If he wrote at the earlier time, he was an innovator. In fact, the Arthurian episode in *Tristrant,* according to which the hero is an illustrious member of the court of King Arthur, would make Eilhart the first German author to treat the Round Table in fiction. Arguments for a dating later than 1175 are not persuasive. The most frequently cited proof is the conformity of female love monologues in *Tristrant* and the *Eneit* (circa 1185) of Heinrich von Veldeke, which is a German version of the *Roman d'Eneas* (circa 1160). The analogous words of Isalde and Lavinia offer no proof of priority or interchange, however, because they reflect a general rhetorical tradition. Both passages do document the preoccupation of twelfth-century writers with sensual passion, the dissection of which is also a feature of Arthurian romance.

*Illustration from the fifteenth-century Heidelberg manuscript of* Tristrant *depicting Tristrant's battle with Morolt (Heidelberg, Universitätsbibliothek, Cpg 346, f17r)*

An earlier dating of *Tristrant,* between 1160 and 1175, is supported by metrical considerations as well as by archaic stylistic and linguistic features permitting the classification of the work as German *frühhöfische Epik* (early courtly epic poetry); other examples of *frühhöfische Epik* are *Trierer Floyris* (circa 1170–1180), the *Straßburger Alexander* (circa 1160–1170), and *Graf Rudolf* (circa 1170 or circa 1185). Eilhart is an epic minimalist whose poetic diction, rich in assonance, adheres to the low, or plain, style; tropes are rare. Distinguishing the early courtly ethos is a knighthood that emphasizes martial accomplishments – trials, tests, and combats. Chivalric adventures associated with the high courtly romance are only hinted at in *Tristrant* against the backdrop of the motif of the bridal quest. The Arthurian world exists, as shown by the "blades at the bed" episode – some 450 verses involving Tristrant's exploits while in the company of King Arthur, Sir Kay, and Gawain – but it inhabits the periphery. An amalgam of farce and homily, the scene exposes the negative consequences of erotic compulsion for Tristrant and Isalde. According to Eilhart, the Arthurian fellowship is normative, whereas the society of King Mark is aberrant.

The plot structure of *Tristrant* is tripartite: first, the hero's prehistory and bridal quest; second, the love potion and its effects, concluding with exile in the forest; and third, Tristrant's visits to Isalde in disguise and his adventures apart from the queen. Though Eilhart's compositional scheme mainly rests on the number three and its multiples (for example, twenty-one basic episodes and sixty-three narrative "blocks" can be discerned), the number two is also important – for instance, Tristrant's two trips to Ireland, his two poison wounds, and the two Isaldes. Some scholars, in fact, divide the poem into halves, according to the type of love depicted: inseparable love in the first half, love in separation in the second. A kind of thematic mirror of the number two is the pattern of departure/exile and return, which exposes a narration that is essentially cyclical in form. Near the center of the tale is the forest sojourn of the lovers. The woods are a wilderness, a joyless landscape entered reluctantly by Tristrant and Isalde and emblematic of their sorrow and privation.

In the prologue the narrator sets a goal of telling the full, true story of a "listig man" (clever man), Tristrant:

> ny kein man
> besserer rede ny gewan
> von werltlichin synnen,
> von manheit und von mynnen.

> (No one ever
> knew a better tale
> of worldly feats,
> of manhood, and of love.)

The order of concerns is illuminating: first are feats, next is manhood, and last is love. The tale subscribes to this hierarchy of values, patterning Tristrant as a bold hunter and warrior, a man of great physical prowess who continually strives for fame, glory, and honor. Shrewd Tristrant wears many costumes and masks — merchant, minstrel, leper, Arthurian knight, pilgrim, and fool — and inside each of these he seeks to retain his identity as bold warrior.

The story opens with King Mark of Cornwall, a ruler without wife or heir, being aided in battle by King Rivalin of Lohenois. Rivalin falls in love with Mark's sister Blankeflur and departs for home with her when the war is over. On the voyage Blankeflur perishes giving birth to Tristrant. In his father's land the boy is trained in music, manly sports, martial skills, and court etiquette. When his training is complete, Tristrant sets out for Mark's court, vowing to win honor or die in battle with the giant, Morolt of Ireland, who demands shameful tribute from the Cornish king. There is a verbal exchange between Morolt and Tristrant; the use of dialogue is characteristic of the poem. Tristrant defeats Morolt, receiving a poisoned wound in the struggle. Morolt's body is sent back to Ireland where his niece, Princess Isalde the Fair, discovers a splinter of a sword in her uncle's fatal wound.

Tristrant's own wound renders him unable to eat or drink. He is placed in a boat, with harp and sword, to die. The wind drives his skiff on the wild sea to Ireland, where Isalde, unaware of his identity, heals him with a plaster and salve. After a year's absence the hero returns to a joyous welcome in Cornwall. Mark wants to make Tristrant heir to his realm, but the jealous courtiers urge the king to marry and beget an heir instead. Not desiring a wife, Mark sets a seemingly impossible condition: two swallows have mysteriously dropped locks of a woman's hair; Mark pledges to marry her if she can be found. Tristrant, concerned that the court is faulting him for the king's marital status, resolves to search for the royal bride.

A storm again drives Tristrant's ship to Ireland, where he kills a dragon that has been terrorizing the country and cuts out its tongue. When the king's seneschal discovers the dead beast, he claims the kill; but Princess Isalde, who has been pledged in marriage to whoever might deliver the kingdom from its affliction, tells her father that the seneschal's assertions must be false. Searching the place where the dragon was slain, Isalde and her company follow the gleam of a helmet to find the injured Tristrant in a marsh. The lady revives him, and he recognizes her as the object of his bridal quest. Isalde then discovers that his sword has a notch that exactly matches the splinter in her uncle's wound and realizes that it was Tristrant who killed Morolt. Nevertheless, since she would otherwise have to marry the duplicitous seneschal, Isalde tells her father that Tristrant was the true dragon slayer. Not wanting to face Tristrant in single combat, the seneschal publicly admits his deception. The king grants Tristrant the hand of Isalde, then learns that she is intended not for Tristrant but for Mark of Cornwall.

The second narrative segment concerns the love potion that Isalde's mother prepares for the bridal pair and entrusts to Brangene, the princess's lady-in-waiting. Seeking refreshment on the journey to Cornwall, Tristrant unknowingly drinks from the potion and offers some to Isalde. Both immediately believe that they are going insane: they grow ill, then hot and cold, and almost die. (The full range of Ovidian amatory topoi is present.) When delineating the properties of the drink, the narrator stresses that Tristrant and Isalde did not wish to fall in love:

> der tranck waß so getan:
> welch wib und man
> deß truncken baiden,
> sy mochten sich nit me schaiden
> in vier jauren.
> wie gern sie eß enbaren,
> sie musten sich minnen
> mit allen iren sinnen,
> die wyl daß sie lebten.
> vier jar sie pflegten
> so grosser lieb baid,
> ja daß sie sich nit schaiden
> möchten och ainen tag.

> (The potion was of such a nature
> that any woman and man who drank it together
> could by no means leave each other
> for four years.
> However much they might want to refrain,

Jm ist licht iemant by
Der vnser hie hät ge hut
Do ward och die frow gut
Der speher do gewar
Der mon trüg och den schatten dar
Jn den brunnen von Jnen zwam
Der frowen wyßhait do schain
Vnd recht also ge bardt
Als ob su es nicht wyste
Vnd sprach mit großen listen
Tryftrand was sol ich her zü dir
Er sprach frow helffend mir
Das mir min herr sin huld gebe
Vnd mich lauße leben
Als er in sinem hof
Su sprach du mir für war geloub
Jch hilff dir dar zü nicht
Mir ist lieb das er mt pflußt
Zü dir hät vnd dir gram ist
Des bis sicher vnd gewiß
Jch will dir nicht darzü frumen
Wan ich bin an ain wort komen

*Page from the Heidelberg manuscript, with text and illustration of the scene in which*
*King Mark hides in a tree to spy on Tristrant and Isalde (Heidelberg,*
*Universitätsbibliothek, Cpg 346, lines 3526–3548)*

they had to love each other
with their whole being
as long as they lived.
But for four years
the passion was so great
that they could not part
for half a day.)

These verses describe a love from without, a fatal passion that springs from the mysterious philter. So enigmatic is the drink that some scholars speak of a two-phase love potion: its power to bind the lovers closely wanes after a time, but after the abatement of its potency Tristrant and Isalde continue to love each other with a fervor that transcends death. The dual nature of the potion is reflected in the literal and figurative functions it holds in the poem. On the one hand, it is a genuine magic drink; on the other, it is a didactic emblem. As emblem, the love potion betokens the destructiveness of sexual love. The drink initiates a chain of deceit and death that begins when, after consummation of their union, the lovers decide to substitute Brangene for Isalde on the wedding night. In persuading Brangene to sacrifice herself Isalde plays on the notion of honor, a leading motif of the episode. Fearful that Brangene will reveal her mistress's indiscretion to the king, Isalde bribes knights to put her lady-in-waiting to death. But Brangene's words save her; the would-be murderers are moved to pity, and they spare her life. Isalde regrets her actions and reconciles herself with the faithful woman.

Afterward, the omnipresent evil courtiers of Mark's realm, who hate Tristrant because of his manner of living, his striving for honor, and his favor with the king, defame the hero at court. The jealous slanderers go to Mark, seeking to win him over, but he defends his nephew. Then the king discovers Tristrant on the royal couch with the queen in his arms. Now furious, Mark speaks to Tristrant of evil love and disloyalty and orders him to leave court at once. The hero claims to be ill and, instead of leaving, meets Isalde in her orchard, where they outwit Mark's spies and are able to spend nights together. Tristrant's antagonists then conspire to test him by having Mark go off on a false hunt. Mark pretends to leave but climbs a tree to observe their rendezvous; Isalde is aware of his presence, however. Cunningly, she claims loyalty to Mark, convincing the king that she and her lover are innocent and that the wicked liegemen are telling lies about them. Tristrant and Isalde are rehabilitated.

The jealous lords strew flour between the beds of the lovers to trap them. Seeing the flour, Tristrant leaps to Isalde's bed; but his old wounds open, and he stains the bed with blood. The king discovers the blood and passes judgment on the pair: Tristrant is to be broken on the wheel and Isalde burned at the stake. They escape, however, and go into exile in the forest. They suffer great hardship for many months; their clothing falls apart, and they have no proper food. One of the king's hunters discovers the couple lying with a sword between them; he informs Mark, who comes to the hut. The king leaves behind his sword and glove but does not awaken the pair.

Tristrant meets Ugrim, a holy hermit and Mark's father confessor, in the wood. When Tristrant asks for the rite of penance, Ugrim demands that he give up the queen. Tristrant refuses and leaves without absolution. When the force of the potion wanes, the lovers believe that they must leave the forest. Ugrim seeks to mediate between them and the king. Although Tristrant returns Isalde to Mark, the sovereign, still angry, will not permit him to live on in Cornwall. Equally angry, Tristrant declares that he will ride away and do the best he can for himself.

In the third segment Tristrant returns from exile several times for furtive visits with Isalde. (The episodic structure of this portion of the tale has been frequently commented on, some scholars calling it a "string of incidents.") Tristrant arrives at the court of King Arthur in Britain, where he befriends Sir Gawain. To Gawain the hero confesses his feelings about Isalde, and by means of a stag hunt Gawain helps him return to Mark's court. Arthur's knights spend the night there; Mark, suspicious, warns all present that anyone attempting to dishonor him will be dealt with severely. The king prepares a board studded with sharp blades as a trap for Tristrant if he goes to the queen at night. In defiance of the snare Tristrant visits Isalde, cutting himself badly on the blades. To protect him from Mark, Arthur's knights inflict similar wounds on themselves. Arthur tells the irate Mark that he cannot restrain the men of the Round Table. After Arthur and his retinue leave Mark's kingdom they invite Tristrant to remain with them, but he decides to ride away in search of other lands.

Offering his services to King Havelin and his son Kehenis, Tristrant meets Kehenis's beautiful sister, Isalde of the White Hands. Tristrant fights valiantly in battle; as a reward and as a sign of attachment to Kehenis, he receives the hand of Isalde. He marries her in an attempt to get over his love for Isalde the Fair and because her name is also Isalde. He subsequently leaves his wife a chaste maiden for more than a year. Taken to task by Kehenis for his

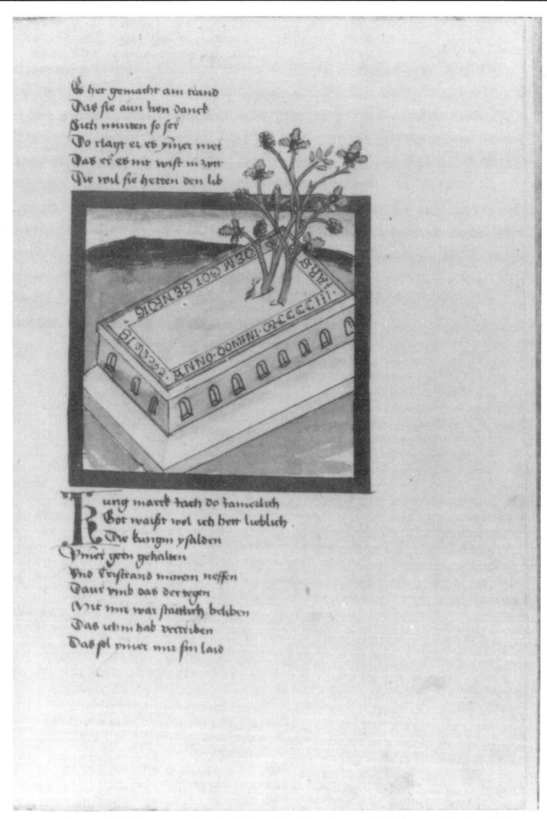

*Page from the Heidelberg manuscript, describing and depicting the grave of Tristrant and Isalde with its intertwined rosebush and grapevine (Heidelberg, Universitätsbibliothek, Cpg 346, fol. 134r)*

dishonorable actions, Tristrant claims that his wife has shown him little love, admits that he has another Isalde, and invites Kehenis to accompany him when he visits her. The two venture to Cornwall, where Tristrant resumes his relationship with Isalde the Fair.

Two intersecting motifs, disguise and deceit, dominate the narration: disguise enables Tristrant to continue his liaison with Isalde the Fair, but the pair become victims of deceit. Tristrant is wounded by the poisoned lance of Nampetenis, a nobleman and the love rival of Kehenis, and can only be healed by Isalde the Fair. Tristrant sends the queen the message that he has often suffered distress and harm for her sake and has always been faithful. Isalde comes to him on a ship with a white sail, a sign of love and healing, but Tristrant's jealous wife tells him that the sail of the arriving vessel is black. He dies believing that his beloved has abandoned him.

The two Isaldes conduct a verbal duel, after which Isalde the Fair dies of grief. The repentant Isalde of the White Hands orders that the bodies be placed in splendid caskets. King Mark learns that the lovers perished because the potion caused them to fall in love against their will; if he had only known about the drink, Mark says, he would have given Tristrant his entire kingdom. Over the grave of the lovers a rosebush and grapevine grow so tightly together that they cannot be separated without being broken.

Deeply pessimistic at its core, *Tristrant* is a poem about the effects of erotic passion. Eilhart's preoccupation is with the ignoble instincts, compulsion, and lost opportunities that such love brings forth. Contrary to common conception, the central conflict is not between love and marriage but between love and heroism. Tristrant, who fails to balance the demands of warrior and wooer, remains an exemplar of heroism until he is overcome by the frenzy of desire. The narrative unity of the poem emerges from a skeptical attitude toward *minn gezwang* (love's might). The ill-fated love of Tristrant and Isalde leads, inevitably, to permanent obsession, the erosion of status, and unrelenting misery; it also leads to the unraveling of the social fabric, making outcasts of the lovers. Love is portrayed as a force for evil – as sin – and the lovers live without grace, as these words from the Ugrim episode attest:

> durch gotz willen batt er in,
> daß er sie wider gäb,
> und so käm aber der ungehäb
> fraislichen grossen sund.

er sprach, er en kunt
vor dem tufel nicht genesen,
ob er lenger wölt weßen
an dem unrecht.

(He [the hermit] asked him [Tristrant] for God's sake to give her [the queen] up and be freed from sin, saying that he could not escape the devil if he remained longer in the wrong.)

The menacing passion that guides the actions of Tristrant and Isalde is manifestly destructive. Equally clear is that Eilhart's tale is intended as a warning to the reader. The message is that the claims of love and heroism are irreconcilable.

Even as Tristrant is torn between competing demands, so too is Eilhart's narrator pulled by conflicting impulses when assessing the hero and his milieu. The storyteller walks a fine line, creating an admiring profile of an exemplary man-of-arms and lover who is the defender of heroic ideals while condemning Tristrant's affection for Isalde as degenerate, imprudent, and threatening to the social order. The magic drink explains and excuses violations of courtly norms: seeing that the lovers act against their will, that their duplicity and lack of restraint stem from the power of the potion, the narrator and heaven itself side overtly with them, absolving them of guilt and responsibility and offering them forgiveness. Exculpation of Tristrant and Isalde also comes (in the epilogue) from King Mark, who is portrayed with more subtlety than most commentators have recognized. He is by turns a wrathful, jealous husband and a magnanimous man, and the tale ultimately exonerates him on the basis of external exigency. The ruler leaves the epic stage as a penitent who claims the reader's sympathy. He survives, whereas Tristrant and Isalde, victims of amorous passion, perish, marooned on the terrain of deceit and fatal desire.

### References:

Merritt R. Blakeslee, *Love's Masks: Identity, Intertextuality, and Meaning in the Old French Tristan Poems* (Woodbridge: Brewer, 1989);

Alois Brandstetter, "Über den Stellenwert des neugefundenen St. Pauler Fragments in der Überlieferung von Eilharts *Tristrant*," in *Festschrift für Ingo Reiffenstein*, edited by Peter K. Stein and others (Göppingen: Kümmerle, 1988), pp. 339–352;

Joachim Bumke, *Mäzene im Mittelalter: Die Gönner und Auftraggeber der höfischen Literatur in Deutschland, 1150–1300* (Munich: Beck, 1979);

Danielle Buschinger, "La composition numérique du *Tristrant* d'Eilhart von Oberg," *Cahiers de civilisation médiévale,* 16 (1973): 287–294;

Buschinger, "La structure du *Tristrant* d'Eilhart von Oberg," *Etudes germaniques,* 27 (1972): 1–26;

Buschinger, "Les structures sociales dans le *Tristrant* d'Eilhart von Oberg," *Romania,* 108, no. 1 (1987): 109–120;

Sigmund Eisner, *The Tristan Legend: A Study in Sources* (Evanston: Northwestern University Press, 1969);

Joan M. Ferrante, *The Conflict of Love and Honor: The Medieval Tristan Legend in France, Germany and Italy* (The Hague & Paris: Mouton, 1973);

W. T. H. Jackson, *The Anatomy of Love: The Tristan of Gottfried von Strassburg* (New York: Columbia University Press, 1971);

Jackson, *The Literature of the Middle Ages* (New York: Columbia University Press, 1960);

Marianne E. Kalinke, "Eilhart von Oberge," in *The New Arthurian Encyclopedia,* edited by Norris J. Lacy (New York & London: Garland, 1991), pp. 127–128;

Marion Mälzer, *Die Isolde-Gestalten in den mittelalterlichen deutschen Tristan-Dichtungen* (Heidelberg: Winter, 1991);

William C. McDonald, "Character Portrayal in Eilhart's *Tristrant,*" *Tristania,* 9 (Autumn–Spring 1983–1984): 25–39;

McDonald, "The Fool Stick: Concerning Tristan's Club in the German Eilhart Tradition," *Euphorion,* 82, no. 2 (1988): 127–149;

McDonald, "King Mark, the Holy Penitent: On a Neglected Motif in the Eilhart Literary Tradition," *Zeitschrift für deutsches Altertum und deutsche Literatur,* 120 (1991): 393–418;

McDonald, *The Tristan Story in German Literature of the Late Middle Ages and Early Renaissance* (Lewiston, N.Y.: Mellen, 1990);

Volker Mertens, "Eilhart, der Herzog und der Truchseß: Der *Tristrant* am Welfenhof," in *Tristan et Iseut, Mythe européen et mondial,* edited by Buschinger (Göppingen: Kümmerle, 1987), pp. 262–281;

Gertrude Schoepperle, *Tristan and Isolt: A Study of the Sources of the Romance,* second edition (New York: Franklin, 1960);

James A. Schultz, "Why do Tristan and Isolde Leave for the Woods?: Narrative Motivation and Narrative Coherence in Eilhart von Oberg and Gottfried von Straßburg," *Modern Language Notes,* 102, no. 3 (1987): 586–607;

Wolfgang Spiewok, "Zur Tristan-Rezeption in der mittelalterlichen deutschen Literatur," *Wissenschaftliche Zeitschrift der Ernst-Moritz-Arndt Universität Greifswald,* 12 (1963): 147–155;

Alois Wolf, *Gottfried von Straßburg und die Mythe von Tristan und Isolde* (Darmstadt: Wissenschaftliche Buchgesellschaft, 1989).

# Einhard

*(circa 770 – 840)*

Robert Levine
*Boston University*

MAJOR WORKS: *Letters* (823–836)

**Manuscripts:** Paris, Bibliothèque Nationale, fl. 11379, ninth century, f. 3–15, includes seventy-one items, of which numbers 66–71 are by Einhard (37–38 are by Einhard's wife, Imma).

**First publications:** Several in *Karoli Calviet svccessorvm aliquot Franciae regum capitvla, in diversis synodis ac placitis generalibus edita,* edited by Jacob Sirmond (Paris: Printed by S. Cramoisy, 1623); first complete edition in *Einhardi omnia quæ exstant opera,* edited by Alexandre Teulet (Paris: Renouard, 1840–1843), II: 2–174.

**Standard edition:** In *Monumenta Germaniae Historica: Epistolarum,* edited by Karl Hampe, volume 5: *Karolini Aevi III* (Berlin: Weidmann, 1899), pp. 105–145, 641.

**Edition in English:** Translated by Henry Preble as "The Letters of Einhard," annotated by Joseph Cullen Ayer, Jr., in *American Society of Church History: Papers,* second series, volume 1 (New York & London, 1913), pp. 107–158.

*Vita Karoli Magni Imperatoris* (circa 830)

**Manuscripts:** More than eighty manuscripts survive, of which five, dating from the ninth and tenth centuries and representing the three classes of extant manuscripts, form the basis for the standard edition. Vienna, Österreichische Nationalbibliothek, 510 is the oldest, having been written down not later than 850; it is also the least corrupt, although the first leaf of the *Vita Karoli Magni Imperatoris* is damaged and folio 37 is missing.

**First publication:** *Vita et gesta Karoli Magni,* edited by Hermann, Graf von Neuenar (Cologne: Printed by J. Soter, 1521).

**Standard editions:** *Einhardi Vita Karoli Magni,* edited by O. Holder-Egger, Monumenta Germaniae Historica, Scriptores rerum germanicarum in usum scholarum (Hannover: Hahn, 1911); *Eginhard, Vie de Charlemagne,* edit-

ed and translated by Louis Halphen (Paris: Champion, 1923); *Vita Karoli Magni,* edited by John F. Collins (Bryn Mawr, Pa.: Thomas Library, Bryn Mawr College, 1984).

**Editions in English:** *Einhard's Life of Charlemagne,* edited and translated by H. W. Garrod and R. B. Mowat (Oxford: Clarendon Press, 1915); *Two Lives of Charlemagne,* translated by Lewis G. Thorpe (Harmondsworth, U.K.: Penguin, 1969); *The Life of Charlemagne,* edited and translated by Evelyn Scherabon Firchow and Edwin H. Zeydel (Coral Gables, Fla.: University of Miami Press, 1972).

*Translatio et Miracula SS. Marcellini et Petri* (830)

**Manuscripts:** Metz Archives de la ville, E99, tenth century; Vatican, Vaticanus reginae Christianae 318, ninth century.

**First publication:** In *Acta Sanctorum,* edited by Joannes Bollandus and Godefridus Henschenius, volumes 19–24, 2 June (Antwerp: H. Thieullier, 1695–1715), pp. 181–206.

**Standard edition:** *Einhardi omnia quæ exstant opera,* edited by Alexandre Teulet (Paris: Renouard, 1840–1843), II: 176–377.

*Passio Martyrum Martcellini et Petri* (circa 830)

**Manuscripts:** There are three surviving manuscripts of this work: Paris, Bibliotheque Nationale, f.l. 14143, ninth century; Metz, Archives de la Ville, E99, tenth century; Vatican, Christianiae reginae 711, tenth century.

**First publication:** In *De probatis sanctorum historiis,* 7 volumes, edited by Laurentius Surius and Jacob Mossander (Cologne: G. Calenium, 1576–1581): III (1579), 555–561; VII (1581), 488–494.

**Standard edition:** "Passio Martyrum Marcellini et Petri," edited by Ernst Dümmler, in *Monumenta Germaniae Historica/Poetae Aevi Carolini,* volume 2 (Berlin: Weidmann, 1864), pp. 126–135.

**Edition in English:** Translated by Barrett Wendell as *The History of the Translation of the*

*Miniature from the manuscript for* Les Grandes Chroniques de France *(Brussels, Bibliothèque Royale; Ms. 3, fol. 76v, circa 1400) depicting Einhard and Archbishop Turpin writing their respective biographies of Charlemagne. The work then believed to be by Turpin — now known as the* Pseudo-Turpin — *was actually written in the twelfth century.*

*Blessed Martyrs of Christ, Marcellinus and Peter* (Cambridge, Mass.: Harvard University Press, 1926).

*Questio de adoranda cruce* (836)
> **Manuscript:** Vienna, Österreichische Nationalbibliothek, 956, tenth century.
> **First publication:** Ernst Dümmler, *Neues Archiv,* 11 (1896): 235–238.
> **Standard edition:** "Questio de adoranda cruce," edited by Karl Hampe, in *Monumenta Germaniae Historica: Epistolarum,* volume 5: *Karolini Aevi II* (Berlin: Weidmann, 1899), pp. 146–149.

*Collection of Psalms* (late 830s)
> **Manuscript:** Vercelli CXLIX 146–155.
> **First publication:** Excerpts edited by M. Vatasso, *Bessarione,* 31 (1915): 92–104.

Lay abbot, politician (perhaps in spite of himself), occasional theologian, hagiographer, poet, historian, perhaps an artist and an architect, Einhard certainly earned his epitaph, the seven couplets in which Hrabanus Maurus described him as wise, eloquent, and possessed of many skills. The

ninth-century historian known as the Astronomer called him "sui temporis prudentissimus virorum" (the wisest of the men of his time). His renown was such that such works were attributed to him as major parts of the *Annales regni Francorum* (Annals of the Reigns of the Franks, also called *Annales d'Einhard*), the *Annales de Fulda,* the fragmentary *Annales de Sithiu,* and the first secular Latin epic of the early Middle Ages, *Karolus Magnus et Leo Papa* (Charlemagne and Pope Leo). A treatise, *De adventu, moribus et superstitione Saxonum,* is attributed to him by Adam of Bremen, but it has not survived. In addition, he may have contributed to the continuation of the Annals of Lorsch. His letters, hagiographic texts, and poems, some of less certain attribution than others, are clearly the work of a highly competent man of letters; but his best-known accomplishment is his biography of his patron, king, and emperor, Charlemagne.

Born around 770 in Maingau (later known as Seligenstadt) into an East Frankish aristocratic family, Einhard received his education in the monastery at Fulda, a bastion of Christianity among the still unconverted Saxons that would also produce

*The church – much altered from its original appearance – built by
Einhard on his estate at Steinbach and consecrated in 827.
Einhard had planned to be buried here but was interred
at his other estate, at Seligenstadt, instead.*

Hrabanus Maurus and Walahfrid Strabo. Among his tasks at Fulda between 788 and 791 was the copying of manuscripts; each of the six surviving charters ends with the phrase *Ego Einhart scripsi*. In 794 or shortly thereafter Abbot Baugul sent him to court for further education; there, as a student of Alcuin, he rose rapidly. By 796 he belonged to the inner circle of Charlemagne's court, where his small stature earned him the nickname Nardulus (Little Nard), while his knowledge of architecture, and perhaps his ability as a craftsman and painter, earned him the name Bezaleel (after the builder of the tabernacle in Exod. 31:2–11, 35:30, and 38:22). Charlemagne put him in charge of building palatial residences in Aachen. He is also reputed to have been among the most trusted of Charlemagne's political advisers. He brought the plan for partitioning Charlemagne's kingdom to Rome in 806, and, ac-

cording to Ermoldus Nigellus, in 813, as the emperor's spokesman, he negotiated the arrangements whereby Charlemagne's son Louis the Pious, whom Einhard had tutored, was elevated to the position of coemperor.

When Louis began his reign in 814, Einhard retained his place at court and received benefices; in 817 he became adviser to Louis's son and coemperor, Lothar. In 827 he had the relics of Saints Marcellinus and Peter brought from Rome to his abbey at Michelstadt and then transferred to Maingau. These transactions and the resultant miracles are described in *Translatio et Miracula SS. Marcellini et Petri* (The Translation of the Martyrs Saints Marcellinus and Peter), of which books 1 and 2 were composed in 830, and 3 and 4 shortly afterward. This text provides some useful historical and geographical material, as well as an account of the conversation with Hilduin in the course of which Einhard discovered that he had not received all of the ashes that had been sent from Rome. The *Translatio et Miracula SS. Marcellini et Petri* became the model for justifying the theft of saints' relics. A rhythmic version of this text, the *Passio Martyrum Martcellini et Petri* (Passion of the Martyrs Marcellinus and Peter), was written at about the same time.

Einhard's literary career probably began, in the shadow of Alcuin, during his early years at court, but none of the poetry he apparently composed at that time has survived; all of his surviving literary works were produced after he had reached the age of fifty. His biography of Charlemagne is his earliest extant composition other than some letters. It draws on the *Annales royales* as well as other narrative, diplomatic, and juridical writings, although Einhard never mentions any of them – at least partly because, as he testifies in his prologue, he was an eyewitness and, therefore, in medieval terms, the most reliable kind of historian. To give effective, convincing shape to his experience, however, he used as a rhetorical (although, again, unacknowledged) model Suetonius, provoking Louis Halphen to call Einhard's book "The life of the 13th Caesar." Others have condemned the work as a piece of rhetoric rather than of history; but since history was a branch of rhetoric during the Middle Ages, Einhard might not have been unhappy with such a judgment, particularly had he known that his work would become the model for such later royal biographies as those of William the Conqueror and Frederick Barbarossa.

Reworking the *Annales royales,* other documents, and his own experiences required Einhard to suppress parts of the historical reality that modern historians sorely regret losing. In addition, fabricating a Suetonian, magisterial posture produced occasional passages that are difficult to understand. Nevertheless, Einhard's *Vita Karoli Magni Imperatoris* (Life of the Emperor Charlemagne, circa 830), the first secular biography of the Middle Ages, was praised by his contemporaries Walahfrid Strabo and Lupus of Ferrières, was copied frequently throughout the Middle Ages, and was finally reworked and incorporated into the *Grandes Chroniques,* the version of French history that was current in the fourteenth century and traditional until well into the Renaissance. In addition, Einhard's biography is the earliest text to provide evidence of a historical Roland.

The Charlemagne of the *Chanson de Roland* (Song of Roland, circa 1100), however, is a later, more hagiographic figure than the one to be found in this early-ninth-century text, although Einhard, in the preface to his life of Charlemagne, is not above adapting passages from Sulpicius Severus's *Vita S. Martini* (Life of Saint Martin). Royal biography and hagiography shared a vocabulary of panegyric in the Middle Ages, and Einhard sees to it that Charlemagne, like Augustus Caesar as described by Suetonius, observed his religious duties fastidiously; but the *Vita Karoli Magni Imperatoris* characteristically concentrates on idealizing Charlemagne for his *magnanimitas* and *constantia* rather than for his piety. The emperor's biographer does reveal that Charlemagne had a short, thick neck and three (four, according to some manuscripts) concubines.

Although Augustus is the major paradigm, Tiberius and Caligula also provide material for the portrait of Charlemagne. Using Suetonius's lives of the emperors as a model, of course, would seem to support Charlemagne's claim to being Holy Roman emperor; but Einhard always refers to Charlemagne as king, not emperor, presumably in deference to the anti-imperial position of Charlemagne's son Louis, in whose reign the *Vita Karoli Magni Imperatoris* was composed. Moreover, Einhard's borrowings from Suetonius make as often for contrasts as for similarities. In addition, he does not offer Suetonius's anecdotal detail and tells little about the administration of the kingdom – a topic to which Suetonius had paid significant attention. He does, however, strive to imitate Suetonius's Latin prose style, even when Suetonius deviates from the Ciceronian decorum for which Einhard professes admiration in his prologue. On the other hand, in his letters and in the *Translatio et Miracula SS. Marcellini et Petri* Einhard adjusts his diction and syntax to everyday Carolingian standards.

The *Vita Karoli Magni Imperatoris* begins with the well-known description of the last of the long-haired Merovingians, Childerich III, sitting ineffectually on the throne while the task of governing shifted to the mayors of the palace, Charlemagne's ancestors. A brief description of the reigns of Charles Martel and Pépin the Short follows, then an account of how the death of his brother Carloman (in 771) gave the Frankish kingdom exclusively to Charlemagne. Einhard passes over Charlemagne's youth as a subject with which everyone alive is excessively familiar (perhaps because Pépin III and Bertha were not married at the time of the birth of the future first emperor of the Holy Roman Empire) and proceeds to his acts and character. Chapters 5 to 17 list his military accomplishments at home and abroad; chapters 18 to 20 deal with his family, chapter 21 with his hospitality to foreigners, chapter 22 with his physical characteristics and habits, chapter 23 with his preference for traditional Frankish dress, and chapter 24 with his moderation in eating and drinking and his reading of the works of Saint Augustine, especially *The City of God* (412–425), at meals. Chapter 25 tells of his support for the liberal arts and of his respect for his teachers Peter of Pisa and Alcuin; chapter 26 of his religious devotion, his concern for constructing a new church at Aachen, and his reforming the singing of the Psalms; and chapter 27 of his charity toward the poor and of his particular concern for the Church of the Apostle Peter in Rome. Chapter 28 gives an account of Charlemagne's coronation in 800 and of his support for Pope Leo III. Chapter 29 describes his attempt to reconcile two different law codes applied to the Franks and his seeing to it that laws and deeds were written down. Chapters 30 to 33 describe his death in 814 and the political results.

Politics also provides much of the material in Einhard's fifty-eight surviving letters, the earliest of which is dated 823, although they also show him dealing with everyday problems such as a request for sanctuary by a husband who has married without his master's permission or a functionary who has delivered fewer than the stipulated number of pigs (and those not of the best quality).

After 830 Einhard remained far from court, although he was still a dependent of Lothar. When Louis's wife, the empress Judith, asked him to come to Compiègne to help settle a dispute between Louis and Lothar, he made the attempt; but according to one of his surviving apologetic letters to Judith his spleen and kidney prevented him from getting further than Valenciennes. In 836 his wife Imma, whom legend would eventually convert into a daughter of Charlemagne, died. At about this time, in response to a request from Lupus of Ferrières, he composed *Questio de adoranda cruce* (On Worshiping the Cross); he died in 840 in Seligenstadt.

**References:**

Erich Auerbach, *Literary Language and Its Public in Late Latin Antiquity and in the Middle Ages* (New York: Pantheon, 1965);

Helmut Beumann, "Topos und Gedankengefüge beim Einhard," *Archiv für Kulturgeschichte,* 33 (1951): 337ff.;

Marguerite Bondois, *La translation des saints Marcellin et Pierre: Etude sur Einhard et sa vie politique de 827 à 834* (Paris: Champion, 1907);

Donald Bullough, *The Age of Charlemagne* (London: Elek, 1965);

Karl Brunner, *Oppositionelle Gruppen im Karolingerreich* (Vienna, 1979);

François Louis Ganshof, "Eginhard, biographe de Charlemagne," *Bibliothèque d'Humanisme et Renaissance,* 13 (1951): 217–230;

Patrick Geary, *Furta Sacra* (Princeton: Princeton University Press, 1978);

Louis Halphen, *Etudes critiques sur l'histoire de Charlemagne* (Paris: Alcan, 1921), pp. 73–74;

Karl Hauck, ed., *Das Einhardkreuz: Vorträge und Studien der Munsteraner Diskussion zum arcus Einhardi* (Göttingen: Vandenhoeck & Ruprecht, 1974);

Sigmund Hellman, "Einhards literarische Stellung," *Historische Vierteljahrsschrift,* 27 (1932): 40–110; reprinted in *Ausgewählte Abhandlungen zur Historiographie und Geistesgeschichte des Mittelalters,* edited by Beumann (Darmstadt Wissenschaftliche Buchgesellschaft, 1961), pp. 159–230;

Arthur Jean Kleinclausz, *Eginhard* (Paris: Société d'edition Les Belles Lettres, 1942);

H. Löwe, "Religio Christiana, Rom und das Kaisertum in Einhards Vita Karoli," in *Storiographia e storia: Studi in onore di Eugenio Dupré-Theseider* (Rome: Bulzoni, 1974), pp. 1–20;

B. de Montesquiou-Fezensac, "L'arc de triomphe d'Einhardus," *Cahiers archéologiques,* 4 (1949): 79–103;

Lawrence Nees, *A Tainted Mantle* (Philadelphia: University of Pennsylvania Press, 1991).

# Eupolemius
*(flourished circa 1095)*

## Brian Murdoch
*University of Stirling*

MAJOR WORK: *Bible Poem* (circa 1095)

**Manuscripts:** The work is preserved in Besançon, Bibliothèque Municipale, MS. 536 (later twelfth century) and in Dresden, Sächsische Landesbibliothek, MS. DC 171a (early thirteenth century), both from near Merseburg. The latter manuscript is a copy of the former, which itself is not the original, and was almost completely destroyed in the bombing of Dresden in 1945, although a transcription survives.

**First publication:** "Die Messias des sogenannten Eupolemius," edited by Max Manitius, *Romanische Forschungen,* 6 (1891): 509–556.

**Standard edition:** "Eupolemius: Das Bibelgedicht," edited by Karl Manitius, in *Monumenta Germaniae Historica: Quellen zur Geistesgeschichte,* volume 9 (Leipzig: Böhlau, 1973).

The allegorical Latin *Bible Poem* (circa 1095) of Eupolemius deserves more attention than it has been given, and it merits a place in German cultural and literary history. For the entire Carolingian and Ottonian periods in Germany, down to the first decades of the twelfth century, the dominant written and literary language was Latin, with German only gradually making its presence felt as a means of literary expression. Otfried von Weißenburg's *Evangelienbuch* (Gospel Book, between 863 and 871) is a self-conscious effort, and Notker III of Saint Gall (Notker Labeo) is defensive about his use of German when he writes to Hugo of Sion on the subject of his own work. For a long time German literary histories of the early period included every scrap of material in the vernacular, even virtually incomprehensible fragments; material in Latin was included only when it was supposed that a German original lay behind it or when it filled a gap. Thus Ratpert's poem of Saint Gall (circa 890), which exists only in a Latin translation – made, presumably, because the German was felt not to be respectable – was included in these early histories, and so was

*Waltharius* (circa 825), because of the clearly Germanic nature of the content. Writers in Latin with no direct connection with German were omitted from the early histories and are frequently omitted from modern ones. Thus, to do full justice to literature in Germany in the early Middle Ages, attention would have to be paid to the schoolmaster and poet Froumund of Tegernsee, born around 960; to the *Eclogue* of Theodulus, an influential work probably written in the tenth century but once ascribed to Gottschalk in the ninth century; to Hermann der Lahme (the Lame; also known as Hermannus Contractus and Herman von Reichenau), born in 1013, the crippled polymath from south Germany; to the mid-eleventh-century poet Warnerius of Basel; and to Sextus Amarcius, who was probably from the Rhineland and whose satiric *Sermones* also date from the middle of the eleventh century. Eupolemius may, then, stand as a representative of the neglected German writers of Latin; but his unusual *Bible Poem* is worth consideration in its own right.

Scholars have only a scant idea of who Eupolemius was and when he wrote. His Greek-based pseudonym is connected with the content of the work, which is about a *polemos* (battle, struggle, war), combined with the prefix meaning "good." The poet appears to have been a German rather than – as Frederic James Edward Raby believes – a Frenchman; the work that survives under his name, with an admittedly slight, though clearly German, manuscript tradition, contains internal support for this contention in a passage in which, although several Gallic tribes are named, places in Germany are treated in great detail; the homeland of the writer seems to be the Upper Rhine. If the pseudonym is not based on the content of the poem, it may be a Greek adaptation of a German compound with the suffix *wic* (battle) – an editor of the poem, Max Manitius, suggested *Wicpert* or *Hartwic*. Evidence from the work indicates that the poet knew the *Sermones* of Sextus Amarcius; the poem cannot have been written before the latter half of the eleventh century, then, and a date not too long before 1100 seems likely. The most recent editor of the work, Karl Manitius, notes that there is no reference to the taking of Jerusalem in 1099 and argues that such an omission from the detailed comments on Jerusalem at the conclusion of the poem would be unlikely had that event taken place. The poem contains a wealth of allusions from classical and early Christian poets, but the alleged citation of the *Pentitential Hymn* of Marbod of Rennes, which was written at the end of the eleventh century and is used by Raby as evidence of a late date for Eupolemius, may simply be a shared formula.

The poem, designated in the early parts of the surviving manuscripts only as *Liber Eupolemii* (Book of Eupolemius), comprises two books of, respectively, 684 and 780 Latin hexameters containing an allegorical depiction of the Christian battle between the forces of good and evil. The work is unusual in a variety of respects. There is hardly any evidence of rhyme – a strong contrast to works such as *Ruodlieb* (circa 1075). It is also a learned work, drawing on and citing many other writings, including not only the works of such classical writers as Ovid and Lucan but also the *Sermones* of Sextus Amarcius and Warnerus's *Synodicus,* a poem, based on Theodulus's *Eclogue,* in which Sophia (Wisdom) asks for typological parallels between the Old Testament and the New: in Eupolemius's work Sophia, instead of the Muses Clio and Calliope, is invoked. The influence of the *Eclogue,* a work that contrasts classical myth and Christianity, is also patent.

In spite of the opening announcement that the poem will sing of the battle between Cacus (Evil) and the Messiah, the work is, as Karl Manitius points out, far broader. The theme is the prolonged battle between the forces of good and evil for the human race. It is an epic allegorization, with personified Greek terms for the principal protagonists, of the divine economy of history from Adam to Christ. Agatus (Good), or God, has ejected Cacus (Lucifer); the epic is concerned with the sons of Antropus (Adam, mankind): the younger, Ethnis (the heathens), and Judas, who signifies the people to whom God first revealed himself. The Fall of Man occurs when the serpent Ophites tempts Antropus and leads him into Babylonian captivity. There he marries and has his two sons, who are "mens dispar . . . ut olim / Infelicis Ade geniti de semini fratres" (as different as unhappy Adam's children . . . / [I, lines 237–238]), Cain and Abel, whose story follows. The separation of allegory and actual biblical characters is striking. Other Old Testament stories are built into a tale of the repeated attempts

of Agatus to liberate Judas, who proves unreliable in the Golden Calf scene and eventually joins the forces of evil. The Greek-based names – such as Polipater (Father of All) for Abraham – require explanation throughout, and Old Testament events are compared (often following Theodulus) with classical tales, such as the stories of Joseph and of Hippolytus (I, lines 397–401) or of Samson and of Hercules (II, lines 275–286). The allegory, in terms of medieval Christocentric historiography, is of the Old Testament age, in which the opposition to evil was not strong enough. Battles are described, with the forces of good under the leadership of Moses. When Moses asks, "Sed tamen admiror, cur non huc ipse veniret Messias . . . " (I wonder why the Messiah has not yet come here . . . [I, lines 437–438]), he is told that thirty-eight years must elapse. This figure might refer to Deut. 2:14, as Karl Manitius suggests, but it probably has behind it the same numerical exegesis of "forty minus two" that Otfrid implies in the *Evangelienbuch* for the healing miracle of the man lame for thirty-eight years in John 5:5. Forty is the product of the old law – the Decalogue – and the four Gospels, minus the two laws of Christ (love of God and of one's neighbor). The number thirty-eight, thus, designates sinful man.

The battles continue into the second book, and a triumphal speech by the forces of evil includes references to places all over the world over which they now hold sway (II, lines 468–555). Judas joins them, but Messias (the Messiah) will now be sent, disguised, from Bethlehem. Messias – that is, Christ – appears only toward the end (II, line 581), but the whole poem leads up to this point. Messias is mocked by Judas, who denies that he is the son of Agatus, and calls him "filius . . . fabri" (son of a carpenter [II, line 715]). In the final battle, in which Ethnis comes over to the forces of good, Messias is disarmed by Cacus and allows himself to be killed outside the walls of Jerusalem with five wounds (II, line 727). His death inspires Cacus with fear, and he is driven off. There is an extended *planctus* (lamentation) by the mother of Messias, but on the third day Messias's father raises him to his rightful throne.

While Eupolemius's blend of the classical and the biblical may be compared with the works of later writers, such as Gundacker von Judenberg's *Christi Hort* (Christ the Protector, circa 1300), Giles Fletcher the Younger's *Christs Victorie, and Triumph in Heaven, and Earth, over, and after death* (1610), with John Milton's poems, or, indeed, with the best-known messianic poem of later German literature, Friedrich Gottlieb Klopstock's *Der Messias* (1751–

1773), the *Bible Poem* of Eupolemius seems to have had virtually no direct later influence; it was probably written and known only within a monastic context.

**References:**

Ernst Robert Curtius, *Europäische Literatur und lateinisches Mittelalter* (Bern: Francke, 1948); translated by Willard R. Trask as *European Poetry and the Latin Middle Ages* (London: Routledge & Kegan Paul, 1953);

Max Manitius, *Geschichte der lateinischen Literatur des Mittelalters,* 3 volumes (Munich: Beck, 1911–1931), II: 599–605;

Frederic James Edward Raby, *A History of Secular Latin Poetry in the Middle Ages,* second edition, 2 volumes (Oxford: Clarendon Press, 1957), I: 363–365.

# Ezzo

## ( ? – after 1065)

### Francis G. Gentry
*Pennsylvania State University*

MAJOR WORK: *Cantilena de miraculis Christi* (circa 1060)

**Manuscripts:** The work is preserved in two manuscripts: S, Strasbourg, Bibliothèque Nationale et Universitaire, cod. germ. 278, fol. 74v, from the first quarter of the twelfth century; and V, Vorau, Kodex 276 des Chorherrenstifts Vorau in Steiermark, fol. 128r–129v. The Vorau manuscript was assembled in the latter half of the twelfth century. While the Strasbourg version is older and no doubt more authentic, only seven strophes are preserved in it. The Vorau version includes thirty-four strophes and is clearly a revision intended for a monastic audience. Both are probably revisions of a lost original. The Strasbourg version is obviously a hymn – that is, it was meant to be sung. Strophes 1 and 2 each have eight lines, and the rest have twelve lines, indicating an attempt to adhere to a systematic structural principle. The Vorau version, bespeaking its monastic origin, was clearly meant to be read either silently or aloud, and its strophes are of varying lengths, ranging from two to eighteen lines.

**First publications:** In Joseph Diemer, "Beiträge zur älteren deutschen Sprache und Literatur. 22. Ezzo's Lied von dem Anegenge aus dem Jahr 1065" (text), "Beiträge zur älteren deutschen Sprache und Literatur. 23. Ezzo's Lied von dem Anegenge aus dem Jahr 1065" (notes), *Sitzungsberichte der philosophisch-historischen Klasse der österreichischen Akademie der Wissenschaften in Wien,* 52 (1866): 183–202, 427–469 (first completion edition of V); in K. A. Barack, "Althochdeutsche Funde," *Zeitschrift für deutsches Altertum,* 23 (1879): 210–212 (S).

**Standard editions:** *Die religiösen Dichtungen des 11. und 12. Jahrhunderts: Nach ihren Formen besprochen und herausgegeben,* edited by Friedrich Maurer, volume 1 (Tübingen: Niemeyer, 1964), pp. 284–303 (V and S); *Kleinere deutsche Gedichte des 11. und 12. Jahrhunderts: Nach der Auswahl von Albert Waag,* edited by Werner Schröder (Tübingen: Niemeyer, 1972), pp. 10–26 (V and S).

Around 1060 the German vernacular was again deemed a worthy vehicle for written literary religious expression. For the first time since the Old High German *Christus und die Samariterin* (circa 900) a German work of mature quality ap-

*Page from manuscript S of Ezzo's* Cantilena de miraculis Christi, *dating from the first quarter of the twelfth century (Strasbourg, Bibliothèque Nationale et Universitaire, folio 74v)*

peared, and it forever changed literary convention in Germany. This phenomenon was the *cantalina de miraculis Christi* (Hymn about the Miracles of Christ), more commonly known as the *Ezzolied* (Song of Ezzo).

The earliest connection between the name Ezzo and a hymn composed around the middle of the eleventh century is found in the *Vita Altmanni* (Life of Altmann), written around 1130 at the monastery of Göttweig at the behest of the abbot Chadalhoh and reporting on the life of Bishop Altmann of Passau, who died in 1091. One of the episodes is a pilgrimage to the Holy Land, under the direction of Bishop Gunther of Bamberg and Archbishop Siegfried of Mainz, in which Altmann took part in 1064–1065. Also participating in this pil-

grimage, according to the *Vita Altmanni,* was a cleric named Ezzo who wrote a *Cantilena de miraculis Christi* (Hymn about the Miracles of Christ), adding that he "patria lingua nobiliter composuit" (composed [the hymn] splendidly in his mother tongue). That the "cantilena" in the vernacular by someone named Ezzo and the *Ezzolied* are one and the same is a virtual certainty. Whether the hymn was composed to be sung on the pilgrimage, as indicated by the *Vita Altmanni,* is uncertain. The first strophe of the Vorau manuscript of the *Ezzolied,* which is unique to that version, describes one other occasion on which the hymn was allegedly sung:

Der guote biscoph Guntere vone Babenberch,
der hiez machen ein vil guot werch:

er hiez di sine phaphen
ein guot liet machen.
eines liedes si begunden,
want si di buoch chunden.
Ezzo begunde scriben,
Wille vant die wise.
duo er die wise duo gewan,
duo ilten si sich aller munechen. (V, lines 1–10)

(The worthy Bishop Gunther of Bamberg
directed that a splendid work be written:
He bade his priests
to write a lofty hymn.
They began [working on] a hymn
because they were well familiar with the books [i.e., the
    Bible].
Ezzo began to write,
and Wille composed the music.
When he had created the melody,
they all rushed to become monks.)

The composer, Wille, is assumed to be identical with the man who was abbot of the Michelsberg monastery in Bamberg from 1082 to 1085; Ezzo is not identified further, but a *presbyter* Ezzo died in Michelsberg on 15 November 1100. That Gunther ordered a "splendid work" to be written in the vernacular indicates that German was considered a worthy literary instrument, at least in the Bamberg bishop's sphere of influence. This supposition is borne out by contemporary criticisms that Gunther was overly fond of secular heroic songs, especially those about Dietrich von Bern; Ezzo's insistence that he is about to relate a "true" tale can easily be viewed as a statement of clerical distrust of secular, and thus untrue, works, especially of heroic songs. It has also been postulated that this preference for some of the good things of life prompted Gunther to embark on his pilgrimage to the Holy Land to atone for his lapses; he died in Hungary in 1065 on the way home. This strophe of the Vorau *Ezzolied,* while not mentioning a pilgrimage, does connect the names of Gunther and Ezzo and establish the relationship between them. The hymn also claims to have had a perceptible effect: "They all rushed to become monks." Some scholars have associated this comment with the program carried out by Gunther between 1057 and 1061 to reform the Bamberg cathedral chapter by instituting the Augustinian Rule; possibly the *Ezzolied* was used to inspire the canons to choose the rule. Another theory as to the occasion of the composition of the *Ezzolied* is that it was written for the dedication of Saint Gangolf's in Bamberg in 1063. Helmut de Boor is of the opinion that the hymn was composed for the dedication of Saint Gangolf's and was sung on the pilgrimage the following year. Whatever the circumstances of its performance, it is clear that Ezzo's creation had a great effect on its listeners.

As is the case with many works from the early Middle High German period, the *Ezzolied* is well structured. Like the *Rede vom heiligen Glouben* (Tract Concerning [Our] Sacred Faith, between 1140 and 1160) of the arme Hartmann, the *Ezzolied* presents the immutable lessons of Christianity, beginning with Creation (S, lines 2–4; V, lines 5–8) and proceeding to the Fall (S, lines 5–6; V, lines 9–10); the Old Testament period to the mission of John the Baptist (S, line 7; V, lines 11–13); the birth of Christ and his baptism (V, lines 14–17); the miracles done during Christ's public ministry (V, lines 18–19); the Crucifixion and its significance, including the harrowing of Hell (V, lines 20–30); and concluding with a paean to the Cross (V, lines 31–34) – not, as might be expected, with the Last Judgment.

The older, more authentic Strasbourg *Ezzolied* begins with a direct address to the listeners:

Nu wil ih iu herron
heina war reda vor tuon:
von dem anegenge,
von alem manchunne. . . . (lines 1–4)

(Now I intend to relate to you, my lords,
a true tale
about Creation
and about all mankind. . . .)

The term of address ("my lords") would be quite proper for the postulated original audience of the *Ezzolied:* members of the higher clergy, of the lay nobility, or of the about-to-be-regularized cathedral chapter. That it would also be appropriate on the type of pilgrimage described in the *Vita Altmanni* goes without saying. The corresponding line in the Vorau version leaves no doubt as to its intended audience: "ich wil iu eben allen . . ." (I intend [to relate] to you all alike . . .) indicates a monastic audience, perhaps one composed of *conversi.*

In the second strophe Ezzo praises the coming of Christ and employs metaphors from the Gospel of John to describe Christ and his significance for the world:

Lux in tenebris,
daz sament uns ist:
der uns sin lieht gibit,
neheiner untriwon er nefligit.
in principio erat verbum,

daz ist waro gotes sun;
von einimo worte er bechom
dirre werlte al ze dien gnadon. (lines 9–16)


(A light shines in the dark;
one that is with us.
He who gives us his light
has never been unfaithful [to us].
In the beginning was the word;
that is, in truth, the Son of God.
Through one word, he became
the salvation of this world.)

In the remaining five strophes of the Strasbourg manuscript Ezzo relates the familiar account of the eternity of God, the creation of the world and of Adam, the Fall, and the darkness of the time preceding the advent of Christ, which was illuminated only by a few stars – prophets and other notable personalities from the Old Testament such as Abel, Enoch, Noah, Abraham, and David. With the mention of David the Strasbourg *Ezzolied* abruptly ends, but enough survives to demonstrate that Ezzo had in mind a clear logical procession of straightforward religious issues and that he had a sophisticated consciousness of form. He was not going to waste time bringing up subtle theological matters, for he was primarily concerned with depicting and celebrating the incontrovertible facts of salvation.

The Vorau scribe, on the other hand, tends to be verbose and interpolative; thirteen Vorau strophes with 156 lines correspond to seven Strasbourg ones with 76 lines. The Vorau work is also filled with much discursive monkish learning. For example, the creation of Adam is described straightforwardly in the Strasbourg manuscript:

Got, tu gescuofe al daz ter ist;
ane dih ne ist nieht.
ze aller jungest gescuofe du den man
nach dinem bilde getan,
nah tiner getate,
taz er gewalt habete.
du blies imo dinen geist in,
taz er ewic mahti sin.... (lines 29–36)


(Lord God, you created all that exists;
without you nothing is [possible].
Last of all you created man
in your image,
in your form,
so that he would have dominion.
You blew your spirit into him
so that he might live forever....)

These lines are repeated more or less intact in the Vorau version. But where line 34 in the Strasbourg

version reads "so that he would have dominion," the corresponding line 72 in the Vorau version reads "so du gewalt hete" (so that you would have dominion). It is clear that the Vorau scribe did not understand the intent of S, line 34, that God had intended to exalt man and give him dominion over all creation; it appears that the scribe was already contemplating the dreadful consequences of the Fall that are described two strophes later (V, lines 9–10; S, lines 5–6). In addition to the common strophe, the Vorau account also contains a strophe dealing with the creation of Eve that is free of misogynist overtones and that gives a description of Eden, as well as another strophe, providing details of the composition of the human body, that occurs two strophes *before* the common creation strophe. The latter strophe is a perfect example of monkish lore:

Got mit siner gewalt, der wurchet zeichen vil
      manecvalt;
der worhte den mennischen einen
uzzen von aht teilen:
von dem leime gab er ime daz fleisch,
der tou becechenit den sweiz,
von dem steine gab er imm daz pein
(des nist zwivil nehein).
von den wurcen gab er ime di adren,
von dem grase gab er ime daz har,
von dem mere gab er ime daz pluot,
von den wolchen daz muot.
duo habet er ime begunnen
der ougen von der sunnen.... (V, lines 37–50)


(With his power, God works many kinds of signs;
he formed the man
out of eight parts:
he gave him flesh from clay;
dew symbolizes sweat;
he gave him bones from stone
[there is no doubt about that].
He gave him veins from roots;
hair from grass;
blood from the ocean;
spirit from the clouds.
He formed
his eyes from the sun....)

The *Ezzolied* stands at the beginning of the resurgence of the vernacular as a vehicle of literary discourse, but it also stands at the end of a period of relative political stability in the empire. A scant generation separates it from the *Memento mori,* but in those twenty years the young King Henry IV was kidnapped at Kaiserswerth in 1062 by Bishop Anno; Empress Agnes, Henry's mother and regent of the empire, ceded enormous portions of Salian lands, and with them power, to great nobles who would prove to be a threat to the crown; savage wars were fought with the Saxons; and, perhaps most important, Henry IV and Pope Gregory VII engaged in the so-called Investiture Contest. The results of this struggle were the complete collapse of the Salian striving for effective monarchial rule; the alienation of the king from his subjects and nobles; the interdict of the church, which prohibited followers of the King from communion with the faithful; and fifty years of civil war, from which Germany never completely recovered. Christian religious writers reacted to the chaos about them by attempting to focus the attention of the mighty on the proper exercise of power on earth, for the souls of men and the well-being of the church were seen to be gravely threatened.

Unlike the *Memento mori* (circa 1080) or twelfth-century moralists such as the arme Hartmann and Heinrich von Melk, whose focus is strictly on earthly existence and its potential for inhibiting the salvation of the soul, the *Ezzolied* is a joyous celebration of the triumph of Christ over death ("von dem tode starp der tot" [death died as a result of death, V, line 347]) and over Satan, who is portrayed as the Leviathan snapping at and getting snared on the Cross. The emphasis is not on the suffering Christ of later centuries, with their Gothic crucifixes of pain and martyrdom, but on the majestic Christ the King, triumphantly wearing a crown, on a victorious Romanesque cross.

## Bibliography:

Francis G. Gentry, *Bibliographie zur frühmittelhochdeutschen geistlichen Dichtung* (Berlin: Schmidt, 1992), pp. 184–191.

## References:

Helmut de Boor, *Geschichte der deutschen Literatur von den Anfängen bis zur Gegenwart,* volume 1: *Die deutsche Literatur von Karl dem Großen bis zum Beginn der höfischen Dichtung,* ninth edition (Munich: Beck, 1979);

Sister Marie P. Buttell OSF, *Religious Ideology and Christian Humanism in German Cluniac Verse* (Washington, D.C.: Catholic University Press, 1948), pp. 40–47;

Hartmut Freytag, "Ezzos Gesang: Text und Funktion," in *Geistliche Denkformen in der Literatur des Mittelalters* (Munich: Fink, 1984), pp. 154–170;

Emil Ploß, "Ezzo 1100," in *Fränkische Klassiker: Eine Literaturgeschichte in Einzeldarstellungen,* edited by Wolfgang Buhl (Nuremberg: Nürnberger Presse, 1971), pp. 23–33;

Heinz Rupp, *Deutsche religiöse Dichtungen des 11. und 12. Jahrhunderts. Untersuchungen und Interpretationen,* second edition (Bern & Munich: Francke, 1971), pp. 33–83;

Ruth Schmidt-Wiegand, "Die Weltalter in Ezzos Gesang," in *Zeiten und Formen in Sprache und Dichtung: Festschrift Fritz Tschirch zum 70. Geburtstag,* edited by Karl-Heinz Schirmer and Bernhard Sowinski (Cologne & Vienna: Böhlau, 1972), pp. 42–51;

Gisela Vollmann-Profe, *Geschichte der deutschen Literatur von den Anfängen bis zum Beginn der Neuzeit,* volume 1/2: *Von den Anfängen zum Hohen Mittelalter* (Königstein: Athenäum, 1986);

Max Wehrli, *Geschichte der deutschen Literatur vom frühen Mittelalter bis zum Ende des 16. Jahrhunderts* (Stuttgart: Reclam, 1980).

# Frau Ava
## (? - 1127)

Ernst Ralf Hintz
*Pennsylvania State University*

MAJOR WORKS: *Johannis* (circa 1120–1125)

**Manuscript:** This work was preserved in the missing fourteenth-century Görlitzer Handschrift (G), which was formerly in Görlitz, Bibliothek der Oberlausitzischen Gesellschaft der Wissenschaften, Pergament 4°, Bll. 1r–2r.

**First publication:** In "Die Gedichte der Ava," edited by Paul Piper, *Zeitschrift für deutsche Philologie,* 19 (1887): 129–196, 275–321.

**Standard editions:** In *Die Dichtungen der Frau Ava,* edited by Friedrich Maurer (Tübingen: Niemeyer, 1966), pp. 382–397; in *Die Dichtungen der Frau Ava,* edited by Kurt Schacks (Graz: Wiener Neudrucke 8, 1986), pp. 10–43.

*Das Leben Jesu* (circa 1120–1125)

**Manuscripts:** The major work of Frau Ava is preserved in the Vorauer Handschrift (V), from the latter half of the twelfth century, Vorau, Kodex 276 des Chorherrenstifts Vorau in der Steiermark, Nr. II Bll, 115c–125a, which lacks a leaf of the work. It was also preserved in the Görlitzer Handschrift.

**First publication:** In *Fundgruben für Geschichte deutscher Sprache und Literatur,* edited by August Heinrich Hoffmann von Fallersleben, volume 1 (Breslau: Grass, Barth, 1830), pp. 140–193. Hoffmann uses only the (G) version.

**Standard editions:** In *Die Dichtungen der Frau Ava,* edited by Friedrich Maurer (Tübingen: Niemeyer, 1966), pp. 398–491; *Die Dichtungen der Frau Ava,* edited by Kurt Schacks (Graz: Wiener Neudrucke 8, 1986), pp. 44–239.

*Der Antichrist* (circa 1120–1125)

**Manuscripts:** The Vorauer Handschrift, Nr. II. Bll. 115c–125a; the Görlitzer Handschrift, Pergament 4°, Bll. 1r–24r (missing).

**First publication:** In *Fundgruben für Geschichte deutscher Sprache und Literatur,* edited by Heinrich Hoffmann von Fallersleben, volume 1 (Breslau: Grass, Barth, 1830), pp. 193–196.

**Standard editions:** In *Die Dichtungen der Frau Ava,* edited by Friedrich Maurer (Tübingen: Niemeyer, 1966), pp. 492–497; in *Die Dichtungen der Frau Ava,* edited by Kurt Schacks (Graz: Wiener Neudrucke 8, 1986), pp. 240–249.

*Das jüngste Gericht* (circa 1120–1125)

**Manuscripts:** The Vorauer Handschrift (Nr. II. Bll. 115c–125a); the Görlitzer Handschrift, Pergament 4°, Bll. 14–24r (missing).

**First publication:** In *Fundgruben für Geschichte deutscher Sprache und Literatur,* edited by Heinrich Hoffmann von Fallersleben, volume 1 (Breslau: Grass, Barth, 1830) pp. 196–204.

**Standard editions:** In *Die Dichtungen der Frau Ava,* edited by Friedrich Maurer (Tübingen: Niemeyer, 1966), pp. 498–513; in *Die Dichtungen der Frau Ava,* edited by Kurt Schacks (Graz: Wiener Neudrucke 8, 1986), pp. 250–281.

Frau Ava's poetic rendering of the history of salvation was a significant contribution to the vernacular religious literature of the German Middle Ages. Her poems, written circa 1120 to 1125, are documents of twelfth-century spirituality as well as of traditional Christian edification. In addition, Ava's poems are the earliest extant work of an identifiable woman author written in German. Nevertheless, scholars know little about the author apart from some autobiographical disclosures in her work and records of her death. It is in the final poem of the series that comprises her work that Ava tells something about her life:

Dizze buoch dihtote  zweier chinde muoter
diu sageten ir disen sin,  michel mandunge was
   under in.
nu bitte ich iuch gemeine,  michel unde chleine,

swer dize buoch lese,  daz er siner sele gnaden
    wunskende wese.
umbe den einen, der noch lebet  unde er in den
    arbeiten strebet,
dem wunsket gnaden  und der muoter, daz ist AVA.
    ( lines 393–406)

(A mother of two children composed this book.
They helped her to understand its meaning, great
    joy was theirs.
Now I beseech you all, great and small, whoever
    reads this book,
that he may ask for mercy on [the deceased son's]
    soul.
As for the one who still lives, and struggles in
    earthly works,
wish grace to him and to his mother, AVA.)

In all likelihood Ava's sons were clerics who advised her on interpreting Scripture and other religious sources. The record of her death in the necrology of the Austrian monastery of Melk notes the year as 1127 and her vocation as religious recluse. Ava probably lived in a cell in a church, maybe at the monastery of Melk itself.

The life of a recluse could be an active one as a counselor and a model of Christian conduct. Ava is likely to have led her life by the rule developed specifically for her vocation, the Regula Solitariorum of Grimlaicus, which was influential from the ninth to the fifteenth century. According to its precepts, the daily routine of the recluse encompassed not only contemplation but an active life as well. In her poems Ava advocates the exercise of charity, the giving of instruction, and the correction of error in oneself and in fellow Christians.

Peter K. Stein views lay brothers at Benedictine monasteries as the chief audience of Ava's works. Her audience may well have included lay brothers of the monastery of Melk, who, during their meals, might have heard her poems as a source of meditation and edification and as a diversion from worldly tales. Some of her listeners were, clearly, members of the aristocracy. As instruction, especially for those who lacked sufficient knowledge of Latin to follow the daily readings and pericopes, Ava's poems are an expression of the *vita activa* (active life) and her concern for the spiritual and social welfare of humankind.

In her series of four poems Ava employs pedagogical and rhetorical methods that were influenced by the rise of twelfth-century spirituality, which brought about a heightened responsibility for one's neighbor and for charitable service in one's community. The *ascensus* (ascent) pattern at the heart of Ava's work lies within a pedagogical tradition that

can be traced to late antiquity. In Saint Augustine's program of Christian culture, the *ascensus* pattern appears in book 2 of *De doctrina christiana* (On Christian Teaching, 396–426). Each of the seven levels of the purifying ascent to wisdom is also a step upward in a spiritual pilgrimage: *timor Dei* (fear of and reverence for God), *pietas* (piety), *scientia* (knowledge), and *fortitudo* (strength) – virtues that make up the active life; *consilium misericordiae* (a sense of compassion and mercy), *intellectus* (reason, a desire to turn from temporal things to eternal spiritual truths), and *sapientia* (wisdom) – virtues that constitute the contemplative life.

*Johannis,* the first poem in the series, tells of John the Baptist's future parents, Zacharias and his barren wife, Elizabeth, and of Zacharias's reaction of disbelief to the annunciation of the approaching birth of his son. Because Zacharias lacks faith in the angelic message, he is punished with muteness. Thus the listener may learn both the fear of God and the need for piety, the initial steps in the ascent to wisdom. The listener next hears of the annunciation of Jesus to Mary, who goes to dwell with Elizabeth until the birth of Johannis. In contrast to the doubting Zacharias, Mary provides a positive model of conduct by acknowledging her absolute faith in God.

After describing  the Baptist's birth and circumcision and Zacharias's regaining of speech through the intercession of the Holy Spirit, Ava recounts the exemplary character of the Baptist. She then directs the audience to the words of the Baptist:

er sprach: "Swer mit der riwe
besuochet gotes triwe,
dem nahent wærliche
diu himeliscen riche." ( lines 237–240)

(He said: "Whoever, with repentance,
seeks God's love,
to him draws near, truly,
the kingdom of heaven.")

The theme of repentance sets the tenor of the poem. Ava seeks to dispose each member of the community to correct his or her own error and to be vigilant in preventing its reoccurrence.

Ava contrasts Johannis's struggle to control the desires of the flesh by ascetic discipline with Herod's lasciviousness and its effect on his conduct: while the king enslaves himself by subjecting reason to erotic passion, Johannis upholds the rule of reason by bridling his sexual desires. In this way, the listener may learn the importance of *fortitudo.*

*The baptism of Jesus, an illustration from the Görlitz manuscript of Frau Ava's works, now lost (from Paul Piper,* Die geistliche Dichtung des Mittelalters, *volume 1, 1888)*

The poem concludes by underscoring Johannis's role as helper to the Christian listener. The correct spiritual orientation empowers Johannis to serve God and humankind, bear the ultimate witness of martyrdom, and merit the praise of Christendom.

*Das Leben Jesu* (The Life of Jesus) begins by recapitulating the annunciation to Zacharias, the mission of John the Baptist, and the machinations of Herod. This repetition forms a narrative bridge and reinforces the positive and negative models of conduct already presented. Herod plots against the Christ child, whom he fears as a potential threat to his kingship. Unlike the Magi, whose meritorious conduct is affirmed by the appearance of an angelic messenger, Herod lacks the saving force of reason – the power to resolve to learn God's will and act in accord with it. In doing the devil's bidding, Herod is himself deceived and becomes the "sun des ewigen todes" (son of eternal death, line 208). Ava

admonishes her aristocratic listeners – "Lieben mine herren" (My dear lords) – to orient themselves toward God so that they may be led safely, as were the wise men, not astray, as was Herod.

After the account of Jesus' baptism in the Jordan the author presents the major antithetical models of Christ fasting in the desert and Satan, his tempter. In the exchange between Christ and Satan, the replies of Jesus are magisterial and offer counterinstructions to those of the devil, the ultimate model of evil conduct and spiritual disorientation. Satan's defeat as tempter is intensified by the actual subjection of the devil during Christ's triumphal harrowing of hell. Christ casts down the "helle hunt" (hellhound) so that the sinner in the grasp of its jaws may escape by way of penance.

Following the scenes of Jesus' temptations in the desert, the narration recounts Jesus' miracles of healing. The failure, however, of the healed and of the disciples to bear perfect witness alerts the listener to the need for penance. Judas Iscariot's premeditated betrayal of Jesus is complemented by Peter's triple denial of Christ; Peter's insistence on his unshakable loyalty magnifies his failure.

The capture, trial, and crucifixion of Jesus place his central commandment to his disciples – that of charity – in the context of the one who gives his life out of love for a friend. Ava further teaches the importance of charity, compassion, and mercy in the dialogue between the two thieves crucified on either side of Christ. Through simplified rhetorical arguments Ava seeks to move her listener to confession, penance, and the practice of charity.

The listener's ascent to purification and wisdom continues in the accounts of the Resurrection and of Jesus' appearance before the disciples. After a brief account of the Ascension, Ava focuses on the upper room and the arrival of the Holy Spirit. The qualities from the Holy Spirit translate directly into practice as the recipients of the divine gifts are transformed by their new saving wisdom and immediately begin teaching it to others. The main body of *Das Leben Jesu* ends with Peter winning many converts as bishop in Antioch and Rome.

The transitional verses that follow are known as "Die Sieben Gaben des Heiligen Geistes" (The Seven Gifts of the Holy Spirit). They offer a catalogue of the virtues Jesus gave to his disciples. The beginning and end of the cycle of virtues – coming from and leading back to God – is *timor Dei*. The fear of God as the beginning of all wisdom leads to regret for sins committed and eventually to the other saving virtues, whose expression is the observance of the precept of charity: "daz wir den nahisten minne" (that we love our neighbor, line 2300). It is the saving virtue of reason, as the correct orientation to God, that fosters charity as a bulwark against ungodly teachings. Unlike Augustine, who places faith at the sixth level, Ava stresses the use of reason as an instrument of meditation and a means of ascending to the seventh level.

Thus, for Ava as for Augustine, the virtues form two groups. The first comprises *timor Dei, pietas, scientia,* and *fortitudo,* the virtues of the *vita activa.* The second consists of *consilium, intellectus,* and *sapientia,* the virtues of the *vita contemplativa.*

In *Der Antichrist,* a short poem of twelve strophes, the listener hears that the Antichrist, in taking possession of the world, will overthrow the existing social order. The depiction of the disintegration of familiar administrative and judicial structures amid a universal struggle for power would have been particularly distressing for Frau Ava's aristocratic audience. The author strives to mold the audience into a vigilant community; her listeners are to form a united front against a common foe. Ava shows that the Antichrist has qualities antithetical to the seven gifts of the Holy Spirit; thus she alerts her listeners to the real nature of the Antichrist and his apparent miracles. Those who lack the correct orientation to God will fall prey to the impostor's deception. The Antichrist will reign for four and one-half years and will inflict great suffering on all Christians, but a fatal spiritual error – pride – will precipitate his fall.

*Das jüngste Gericht* (The Last Judgment) is the final poem of the series comprising "dizze buoch." At the poem's outset Ava evokes a tone of salutary terror together with the hope of salvation – those who fight well in the terrible days that precede judgment will receive the crown of life. Each successive strophe introduces a new portent and brings the listener another day closer to judgment. During the first three days, as the waters of the earth decrease and then swell into a flood, Ava seeks to foster her listener's identification with the community of the faithful.

As the narrative tension heightens during the passing days, the listener experiences the reactions of those who face imminent judgment. The cries of sorrow heard on the third day intensify as the signs of the fourth, fifth, and sixth days foretell the end of the world. The chaotic behavior of fish and fowl, the sky turning blood red, and miracles regarding the sun and the moon promote the fear of God. When the winds of the seventh day roar, the unrepentant sinner whose conscience tells him he lacks God's favor will rage in fear and sorrow. The plight of the sinner may evoke in the listener a temporary identification with the potentially damned. It is in this frame of mind that the listener learns of the eighth and ninth days, when the earth begins to quake. On the tenth day Ava restores the listener's identification with the community of the faithful; addressing an aristocratic audience, she prescribes the correct and saving response to the ruin of castles:

> An dem zehenten tage,  vil luzel sul wir daz chlagen,
> so zevallent die burge,  die durch ruom geworht
>     wurden.
> Berge und veste  das muoz allez zebresten.
> so ist got ze ware  ein rehter ebenaere. ( lines 97–104)

> (On the tenth day, we ought to complain very little,
> for the castles built by fame will fall away.
> Mountains and fortresses they all must crumble.
> For God is truly a just leveler.)

The listener who has the correct relationship with God will not be troubled by the loss of worldly acclaim and power; the former seats of power and privilege will be of no consequence on the Day of Judgment. God tests the faith of everyone, regardless of that person's former social status.

The eleventh day amplifies the importance of the correct orientation to the things of this world: the listener ought to refrain from sorrow over the destruction of gold, silver, and precious objects, including "nusken unde bouge, daz gesmide der frouwen" (clasps and brooches, the jewelry of women, lines 111–112). The material wealth of the Church, too, will pass away.

After the chaotic behavior of animals and other unnatural phenomena of the twelfth day, on the thirteenth day graves open and the dead come forth to be judged. The lament of the terrified on the fourteenth day demonstrates the consequences of impenitence: they no longer possess the ability to act in accordance with reason, that is, to perform penance and gain salvation. The fifteenth day, the day of judgment, brings the purification of the world by fire in the wink of an eye.

The second half of the *Das jüngste Gericht* describes the *Parousia,* the glorious Second Coming of Christ. Preceded by the four evangelists, he awakens the dead. The good will shine like the sun, but those who made him suffer will be punished. All people will be judged according to their spiritual orientation and deeds, not their former social status: "so rihtet er rehte  dem herren unde dem chnehte, der frouwen unde der diuwe" (For he judges justly the lord and the servant, the lady and the maid, lines 185–188). The requirements for salvation cannot be fulfilled after the coming of Christ, when repentance will no longer be possible. Ava interrupts her audience's identification with the damned by addressing it with verses that highlight the need for immediate repentance and remorse for sin. The listener thus experiences another chance for salvation in an otherwise hopeless situation. Having restored the listeners to the community of the potentially saved, Ava teaches them a series of redeeming virtues. The virtues are particularly applicable to an aristocratic audience: protecting the poor, ransoming prisoners, holding court without taking bribes, showing mercy to those of lesser power, and giving alms generously. The audience learns the consequences of ignoring the advice when the narrative shifts to the punishment of the damned. When the author eventually breaks the identification of the audience with the hopeless damned, the sudden release of narrative tension evokes a feeling of euphoria that extends through the remainder of the poem.

After the account of the Last Judgment, Ava provides a recapitulation of the lesson. She also commemorates the beginning of the liturgical year at Easter, an appropriate time for spiritual reorientation, and admonishes her audience to flee from sin: "So vernemet all da bi: da sit ir edele unde fri, da nedwinget iuch sunde noch leit, daz ist diu ganze friheit" (So take note, all of you: there you are noble and free, where neither sin nor sorrow hold sway over you; that is true freedom, lines 359–362). Ava then briefly recalls the catalog of virtues and concludes with a request to her audience for its prayers.

The individual listener to Ava's poems is not taught in isolation but as a participant in a community. Each listener experiences identification with a group that merits salvation or damnation. In this way Ava seeks to move the listener to take individual initiative in implementing the lesson.

**Bibliography:**

Francis G. Gentry, *Bibliographie zur frühmittelhochdeutschen geistlichen Dichtung* (Berlin: Schmidt, 1992).

**References:**

Caroline Walker Bynum, *Docere Verbo Et Exemplum: An Aspect of Twelfth-Century Spirituality,* Harvard Theological Studies, 31 (Missoula, Mont.: Scholars Press, 1979);

Helmut de Boor and Richard Newald, *Geschichte der deutschen Literatur,* volume 1: *Von Karl dem Großen bis zum Beginn der höfischen Dichtung (770–1170),* eighth edition (Munich: Beck, 1949);

Otmar Doerr, *Das Institut der Inclusen in Süddeutschland,* Beiträge zur Geschichte des alten Mönchtums und des Benediktinerordens, 16 (Münster: Aschendorff, 1934);

Wiebke Freytag, "Geistliches Leben und christliche Bildung: Hrotsvit und andere Autorinnen des frühen Mittelalters," *Deutsche Literatur von Frauen,* volume 1: *Vom Mittelalter bis zum Ende des 18. Jahrhunderts* (Munich: Beck, 1988), pp. 65–76;

S. Eoliba Greinemann OSB, "Die Gedichte der Frau Ava: Untersuchungen zur Quellenfrage," Ph.D. dissertation, University of Freiburg, 1968;

Friedrich Heer, *Aufgang Europas: Eine Studie zu den Zusammenhängen zwischen politischer Religiosität, Frömmigkeitsstil und dem Werden Europas im 12. Jahrhundert* (Vienna & Zurich: Europa Verlag, 1949), pp. 50–51;

Ernst Ralf Hintz, "Frau Ava," *Semper Idem et Novus: Festschrift für Frank Banta* (Göppingen: Kümmerle, 1988), pp. 209–230;

Heinz G. Jantsch, *Studien zum Symbolischen in Frühmittelhochdeutscher Literatur* (Tübingen: Niemeyer, 1959);

Richard Kienast, "Ava-Studien," *Zeitschrift für Deutsches Altertum und Deutsche Literatur,* 74 (1937): 1–36, 277–308; 77 (1940): 85–104;

Paul Piper, *Die geistliche Dichtung des Mittelalters,* volume 1 (Berlin & Stuttgart: Spemann, 1888), pp. 223–238;

Hellmut Rosenfeld, "Frau Ava und der deutsche Personenname Awe," *Festgruß Hellmut Rosenfeld zum 70. Geburtstag* (Göppingen, Kümmerle, 1977), pp. 19–27;

Heinz Rupp, *Deutsche religiöse Dichtungen des 11. und 12. Jahrhunderts, Untersuchungen und Interpretationen,* second edition (Bern & Munich: Francke, 1971);

Wilhelm Scherer, *Geistliche Poeten der deutschen Kaiserzeit,* volume 2 (Strasbourg: Trübner, 1876), pp. 64–77;

C. Soeteman, *Deutsche geistliche Dichtung des 11. und 12. Jahrhunderts* (Stuttgart: Metzler, 1971);

Peter K. Stein, "Stil, Struktur, Historischer Ort und Funktion. Literarhistorische Beobachtungen und methodologische Überlegungen zu den Dichtungen Frau Avas," in *Festschrift für Adalbert Schmidt* (Stuttgart: Akademischer Verlag Hans Dieter Heinz, 1976), pp. 5–85.

# Gottschalk

*(circa 804/808 – 866/869)*

## Brian Murdoch
*University of Stirling*

MAJOR WORKS: Theological works, grammatical works, poems, and hymns

**Manuscripts:** Most of the poems are represented in a variety of manuscripts, often anonymously or with the name disguised. A major collection is found in Bern, Bürgerbibliothek, MS 584 (ninth century).

**First publication:** In *Patrologia Latina,* 221 volumes, edited by Jacques-Paul Migne, volume 121 (Paris: Migne 1841–1879), CXXI: cols 349–366.

**Standard editions:** Theological and grammatical works in *Oeuvres theologiques et grammaticales de Godescalc d'Orbais,* edited by Dom C. Lambort (Louvain, Belgium: Spicilegium Sacrum Lovaniense, 1945); poems and hymns in *Monumenta Germaniae Historica/Poetae Latini Medii Aevi,* volume 3, edited by Ludwig Traube (Berlin, 1896), pp. 703–738; in volume 4, edited by Paul von Winterfeld and Karl Strecker (Berlin, 1923), pp. 934–936; volume 6/1, edited by Strecker and Norbert Fickermann (Munich, 1951), pp. 86–106.

**Editions in English:** In *The Penguin Book of Latin Verse,* translated and edited by Frederick Brittain (Harmondsworth, U.K.: Penguin, 1962), pp. 143–146; in *Poetry of the Carolingian Renaissance,* edited and translated by Peter Godman (Norman: University of Oklahoma Press, 1985; London: Duckworth, 1985); in *Carolingian Civilization: A Reader,* edited by Paul Edward Dutton (Peterborough, Ont.: Broadview Press, 1993), pp. 394–400.

Gottschalk of Orbais, also known as Godescalc, Godescalcus the Saxon, and Gottschalk of Fulda, is one of the saddest figures of early-medieval German culture. He wrote nothing in German, but the small amount of Latin poetry by him that survives is impressive and important.

The son of a Saxon nobleman, Graf (Count) Bern, Gottschalk was dedicated to the monastery at Fulda as a *puer oblatus* (a boy offered up) – a practice abandoned not long afterward. He seems also to have spent time at the Reichenau, and he knew Walahfrid Strabo. In Fulda he came into conflict with the powerful abbot, Hrabanus Maurus, when he objected to the fact that his monastic vows had been made without his consent and attempted to have them annulled. In 829 he appealed to the Synod of Mainz to free him from his vows and to return to him the patrimony that had been paid on his behalf to the monastery. The precise result of the appeal is unclear; but Gottschalk stayed within the monastic sphere, even though he left Fulda. The inheritance seems not to have been returned to him.

In the next two decades he seems, through reading the works of Saint Augustine, to have developed his view that all individuals are predestined from eternity to salvation or damnation, thus coming into conflict with church orthodoxy.

He appears to have been at Corbie, where he met Ratramnus, to whom he dedicated a poetic epistle, then at Hautvillers, near Rheims. At Orbais, in the diocese of Soissons, he seems to have been ordained a priest by a suffragan rather than by the bishop. He visited Rome and northern Italy and traveled even further east. When he returned to Germany in 848, he was accused of heresy at the Synod of Mainz on account of his views on predestination; he was condemned, whipped, and expelled from Germany by his onetime teacher Hrabanus Maurus, who was by then archbishop of Mainz, into the charge of Hincmar, archbishop of Rheims. Hincmar brought Gottschalk before the Synod of Quiercy in 849; he was again punished physically, was forced to burn his own manuscripts, and was imprisoned under perpetual silence – which he broke several times – at Hautvillers, where he died some twenty years later. When Gottschalk died – unshriven, since he had refused to recant – Hincmar noted acidly that he had "ended his life with a death worthy of him, and gone to his own place."

Other thinkers of the time supported Gottschalk, including his friends Walahfrid Strabo and Lupus of Ferrières, and in particular (though he was perhaps also politically motivated to attack the extremely powerful and much hated Hincmar) Prudentius, bishop of Troyes, who clashed in writing with the major theologian called upon by Hincmar in his own support, John Scotus Eriugena. Since John was himself hardly an orthodox thinker, he did not really vindicate Hincmar; he resolved the issue in a philosophical sense by holding that present and future are as one with God and that evil is not a positive entity but a negation, but his solution was rejected by later synods. Ideas similar to those of Gottschalk would be revived centuries later by the Calvinists and the Jansenists.

Gottschalk's prose writings, concerned in the main with the theological controversy or with grammar, are slight, and it is difficult to assess the influence his ideas had in his own time. Attempts have been made to link his views on predestination to the notion of fate in the Old Saxon epic *Heliand* (circa 850), but such links are at best tenuous.

Gottschalk's place in literary history is assured by his poems. It has been thought that a Latin poem known as the *Ecloga Theoduli* (Eclogue of Theodulus) might be his, on the grounds that *Theodulus* is a Greek version of *Gottschalk*. A dialogue in a pastoral setting among characters whose names mean "untruth," "truth," and "thought," in which tales from classical mythology are countered by biblical stories, the work was much used in the Middle Ages as a textbook, and commentaries were written on it. Its style does not, however, match that of Gottschalk's other poems, and it may have been written a century after his time. The ten poems or poem cycles that are known to be by Gottschalk are scattered over a variety of manuscripts, with some variations in individual texts.

Some of the poems are quantitative – that is, their meters depend on the lengths of syllables – and follow classical patterns such as the Sapphic, while others are rhythmic. Gottschalk is an early exponent of the Latin hexameter with a rhyme at the caesura. He also uses *Tiradenreim,* the repetition of the same rhyme many times, especially in brief Adonic lines (those having a dactyl plus a spondee) that have the feel of a litany. The rhymes are often on the weak (or, at best, half-stressed) end syllable, but it is in the nature of Latin that two-syllable (feminine) rhymes do arise. It has been suggested that Gottschalk was influenced by Irish poets, who used deliberate rhyme patterns in some of their me-

ters. The tone and to a large extent the themes of Gottschalk's limited corpus are hymnic, and some of them have been called paraliturgical. As Otto Herding points out, early critical responses to the poetry were frequently dismissive; more recently, the individual poems have been considered in aesthetic terms and have received due praise. The natural interest in Gottschalk's life means that the dangers of an overly biographical approach to the poems have to be borne in mind; such an approach is made more tempting by the regular use of a vivid first-person poetic voice. The order in which the poems were composed is unclear.

The most attention has been paid to his song (for which music is also preserved) *Ut quid iubes, pusiole* (Why command me, my child?). It seems to have been written at the Reichenau. In thirteen six-line rhythmic and rhyming strophes (if the three strophes noted by Bernhard Bischoff in the ninth-century manuscript Angers 477 are genuine), the speaker addresses a young friend who has asked him to compose a song. Developing the biblical question "how can we sing the Lord's song in a strange land?" (Psalm 136:4), the speaker claims that he is in exile and would rather weep than sing ("plus plorare quam cantare"); there is a repeated line, "o cur iubes canere" (why do you command me to sing?). Then comes a sudden turnabout in the work as the poet speaks to a colleague (*consodalis*) and agrees to sing a song to the Lord. Next the poet addresses God, asking first for pity because he has been an exile for some time – he uses the word *diuscule,* an untranslatable diminutive meaning something like "a little bit of a long time," to match the vocative diminutives in the previous verses such as *puerule* (little lad), *fratercule* (little brother) – and then affirming his faith and begging for divine mercy. In a triumphant final strophe the poet praises God instead of complaining and agrees to provide a song – which, paradoxically, he has just done. The repetition of *psallam* (I shall sing) brings the work to a crescendo, and the reference to the *carmen dulce* (sweet song) that was asked for gains force because it falls in the same position as the heartfelt *miserere* (have pity) in the preceding strophe:

Interim cum pusione
Psallam ore, psallam mente,
Psallam voce, psallam corde
Psallam die, psallam nocte
Carmen dulce
Tibi, rex piissime. (VI, 13, lines 1–6)

(Now shall I, with the lad by me
sing with mouth and sing with mind,

sing with voice and sing with heart
sing by day and sing by night
the sweetest hymn
King most glorious, to thee.)

Just how real the young friend is (earlier critics locate him confidently in Orbais and elsewhere) is debatable; exile is a topos in Latin and German poetry, and Gottschalk does invoke the biblical parallel of the Babylonian captivity. The knowledge that he was, in a sense, an exile gives poignancy to the poem and tempts the reader to hear in it echoes of Gottschalk's own experience. But the real value of the poem is Gottschalk's control of form: the turnaround in the middle, moving away from the address downward to the boy to the hymnic statements aimed upward toward God, as well as the linking of the strophes by repeated ideas expressed in varied words.

*Ut quid iubes* is Gottschalk's best-known poem. Another poem, a longer and apparently personal plea to God for mercy, is also effective: *O deus miseri* (God Have Mercy) consists of twenty strophes, with an end rhyme and an internal rhyme on the unstressed *-i* that is maintained throughout. The speaker confesses his rejection of God in the first part of the work and asks the saints for intercession to regain God's mercy in the second part. Here, too, there is a turning point. The opening contains in the words *Deus* (God) and *servus miser* (wretched servant), a play on the name Gottschalk, and the speaker goes on to confess:

tue me, domine, fecisti     ut servirem tibi
ego miser te dimisi     et longe abivi. (VI, 2, lines 1–2)

(O my Lord, thou madest me     that I might serve thee
I ignored thee foolishly     always I would flee.)

When he realizes that he is unable to make his own plea, the poet invokes a litany of saints.

Gottschalk's use of reiterated rhyme in Adonic lines is especially pronounced in his hymns, many of them addressed to Christ. For example:

Respice flentem
quaeso clientem,
te metuentem
atque petentem
te venerantem
quin et amantem. (II, 1, lines 1–6)

(God, for thy caring
tearful, I am begging,

forever fearing
always imploring
and thee adoring
loving and yearning.)

One of the more complex of Gottschalk's poems structurally is *O mi custos* (O, My Guardian), a rhythmic work in more than seventy strophes of three lines, each strophe with a single end and caesura rhyme. The work is full of praise of Christ the Redeemer and imagery of the triune deity. Again one finds the confessional motifs that recur in so much of Gottschalk's work, the poet imploring Christ to touch him, to have pity on the sinner, to draw him forth like Lazarus. The poem is impressive because of its internal rhymes that appear in addition to the regular rhyme of the strophes – "Eripe de portis mortis / me, pater amabile" (From the fatal door draw / me, father, loved evermore) – repetitions for intensity and, again, the rhetorical paradox of asking God, in beautifully structured verse, for the words with which to worship him.

Finally, the *Horarium* is a series of rhythmic poems on the canonical hours linked with the sufferings of Christ on Good Friday; this genre was developed more fully later in the Middle Ages. There are eight poems in the cycle, each with a doxology at the end.

Gottschalk's poetry, then, is confessional and, therefore, overtly subjective and intense. It expresses the awareness of sin and the desire for mercy, constantly asking God for the power to praise while clearly demonstrating that power both in hexameters and in rhythmic poems and with a formal range that extends from the concise complexity of *Ut quid iubes* to the cumulative hugeness of *O mi custos* and the virtuoso performance of *O deus miseri*. Gottschalk's personal life was unhappy, largely because of his obsession with the theology of predestination; the subjective stance of the Saxon poet's hymns and religious poems, however, and the skill displayed in the best of them make them a major achievement in the context of poetry by Germans in the Latin Middle Ages.

### References:

Bernhard Bischoff, "Gottschalks Lied für den Reichenauer Freund," in his *Mittelalterliche Studien,* volume 2 (Stuttgart: Hiersemann, 1967), pp. 26–34;

R. R. Bolgar, *The Classical Heritage and Its Beneficiaries* (Cambridge: Cambridge University Press, 1963);

G. G. Coulton, *Studies in Medieval Thought* (London: Nelson, 1940), pp. 62–64;

Patrick S. Diehl, *The Medieval European Religious Lyric* (Berkeley & Los Angeles: University of California Press, 1985);

Peter Dronke, *The Medieval Lyric* (London: Hutchinson, 1968);

Albrecht Hagenlocher, *Schicksal im Heliand* (Cologne & Vienna: Böhlau, 1975), pp. 184–195;

Otto Herding, "Über die Dichtungen Gottschalks von Fulda," in *Festschrift für Paul Kluckhohn und Hermann Schneider* (Tübingen: Mohr, 1948), pp. 46–72;

M. L. W. Laistner, *Thought and Letters in Western Europe AD 500–900* (London: Methuen, 1957);

Max Manitius, *Geschichte der lateinischen Literatur des Mittelalters,* volume 1 (Munich: Beck, 1911), pp. 476–478, 568–574;

Rosamond McKitterick, *The Frankish Kingdoms under the Carolingians, 751–987* (London: Longman, 1983);

P. von Moos, "*O mi custos* – eine *confessio*," *Frühmittelalterliche Studien,* 4 (1970): 201–230; 5 (1971): 317–358;

Germain Morin, "Gottschalk retrouvé," *Revue Bénédictine,* 43 (1931): 303–312;

D. Nineham, "Gottschalk of Orbais," *Journal of Ecclesiastical History,* 40 (1989): 1–18;

F. J. E. Raby, *A History of Christian-Latin Poetry,* second edition (Oxford: Clarendon Press, 1953), pp. 189–192;

Raby, *A History of Secular Latin Poetry in the Middle Ages,* second edition, volume 1 (Oxford: Clarendon Press, 1953), pp. 189–192;

Fidel Rädel, "Gottschalk der Sachse," in *Verfasserlexikon,* second edition, volume 3, edited by Kurt Ruh (Berlin: De Gruyter, 1978), pp. 189–199;

Ingeborg Schröbler, "Glossen eines Germanisten zu Gottschalk von Orbais," *Beiträge* (Tübingen), 77 (1955): 89–111;

Karl Strecker, "Studien zu karolingischen Dichtern," *Neues Archiv,* 45, no. 4 (1924): 14–31;

Klaus Vielhaber, *Gottschalk der Sachse* (Bonn: Röhrscheid, 1956);

Helen Waddell, *The Wandering Scholars,* sixth edition (Harmondsworth, U.K.: Penguin, 1952).

# Heinrich von Melk

*(flourished after 1160)*

Francis G. Gentry
*Pennsylvania State University*

MAJOR WORKS: *Vom Priesterleben*; *Von des tôdes gehugde* (both after 1160)

**Manuscript:** Both works appear in the Codex Vindobonensis 2696, originally from the Dorotheenkloster in Vienna (parchment, fourteenth century) and now in the Österreichische Nationalbibliothek in Vienna. The manuscript contains eight other pieces, all dating from the last quarter of the twelfth or first half of the thirteenth century. *Von des tôdes gehugde* is found on manuscript pages 165a to 178b and is complete, with 1,043 lines. *Vom Priesterleben,* on manuscript pages 303a to 307b, is a fragment of 746 lines. Estimates of the number of missing lines range from around 400 to 1,900; the actual number is probably closer to the lower estimate. Dating is uncertain, although both were in all likelihood completed before the end of the twelfth century. Both works are written in the Bavarian-Austrian dialect.

**First publications:** "Pfaffenleben," edited by Moriz Haupt, in *Altdeutsche Blätter,* volume 1, edited by Haupt and Heinrich Hoffmann (Leipzig: Brockhaus, 1836), pp. 217–238; in Joseph Diemer, "Heinrich's Gedicht von dem gemeinem lebene und des Todes gehugede," *Sitzungsberichte der philosophisch-historischen Klasse der österreichischen Akademie der Wissenschaften in Wien,* 18 (1856): 271–310.

**Standard editions:** *Der sogenannte Heinrich von Melk: Nach R. Heinzels Ausgabe von 1867,* edited by Richard Kienast (Heidelberg: Winter, 1946); in *Die religiösen Dichtungen des 11. und 12. Jahrhunderts: Nach ihren Formen besprochen,* edited by Friedrich Maurer, volume 3 (Tübingen: Niemeyer, 1970), pp. 258–359.

The virtual identity of lines 397–402 of *Vom Priesterleben* (Of the Life of Priests, after 1160), with lines 181–186 of *Von des todes gehugde* (On the Remembrance of Death, after 1160) as well as the closely re-

lated subject matters of the two poems, suggest that they were written by the same individual. Nonetheless, the question of common authorship continues to be the subject of lively speculation. How many years lie between the composition of *Vom Priesterleben* and *Von des todes gehugde,* and which has chronological precedence, cannot be determined. What is indisputable is that among the more than ninety works that comprise Early Middle High German literature, no other piece approaches either one in keenness of observation of the moral failings of the time, in satiric embellishment, in liveliness of presentation, or in the absolutely uncompromising censure of all members of contemporary society who do not measure up to the poet's rigorous standards. Most criticism, however, is reserved for the nobility and the clergy. The moral concerns common to the two poems are representative of the age in which they were composed. At the end of *Von des tôdes gehugde*, in the midst of a description of Paradise, appear the lines:

> dar bringe du, got here,
> durch diner muoter ere
> und durch aller diner heiligen reht
> Heinrichen, dinen armen chneht;
> unt den abt Erchenfride.... (lines 1029–1033)

> (Lord God, bring to that place [Paradise]
> for the glory of your mother
> and for the sake of all your saints
> Heinrich, your humble servant, and the abbot Erkenfried.)

From these few lines a most ingenious biography was constructed for Heinrich. He was identified as a *conversus,* a lay brother associated with a monastery; the monastery in question was postulated to be the Benedictine monastery of Melk in Austria, since an abbot Erkenfried ruled that monastery from 1122 to 1163. Because of the sharpness of his attacks on his contemporaries and the depth of his acquaintanceship with courtly life, Heinrich was deemed to be a noble who, having become progressively repelled by the world and having been re-

49

jected by ungrateful children, withdrew to a monastery, immersed himself in studies, and saw it as his duty to admonish all classes of society regarding their duties as Christians. Unworthy priests became his particular target. This is an impressive biography; unfortunately, it is not an accurate one for several reasons. Abbot Erkenfried of Melk could scarcely have been Heinrich's patron, since the two works attributed to Heinrich – *Von des tôdes gehugde* and *Vom Priesterleben* – exhibit techniques in verse and rhyme of a period later than 1163 (for example, a high percentage of pure rhymes and a minimum of overlong lines of twelve to fourteen syllables). In addition, the contents of the poems display concerns and conventions of the last third of the twelfth century – the court customs, secular love lyrics, validity of sacraments administered by unworthy priests. Peter-Erich Neuser disputes the commonality of authorship; further, he claims that *Vom Priesterleben* preceded *Von des tôdes gehugde,* although the manuscript has them in the reverse order. Gisela Vollmann-Profe disputes Neuser's rearranging of the manuscript order, referring to the greater incidence of pure rhyme in *Vom Priesterleben,* which is usually indicative of a later date of composition, and concludes that the question of authorship is, at least, still open. In the final analysis, all that can be said with reasonable certainty is that the author of each work was a layman, possibly a *conversus,* who demonstrated in his writings many of the features of the popular piety movement of the twelfth century: diatribe against unworthy priests, criticism of violations of sumptuary laws, invective against the pride of the nobility, and general hostility toward the affairs of this world insofar as they interfere with the carrying out of one's duty as a Christian. It is also possible that the designation "dinen armen chneht" refers to Heinrich's affiliation with the popular religious movement *pauperes Christi* (the poor of Christ). It must be stressed, however, that Heinrich – whether there be one or two – is firmly situated within orthodox Christianity.

*Von des tôdes gehugde* represents, in spite of the title, more than an example of the memento mori genre. It is both a *Bußpredigt* (penitential sermon) and a *Standeslehre* (admonition to all three medieval estates). The poem consists of two main parts: lines 1 to 451 comprise the section "Von dem gemeinen lebene" (Concerning the Way of Life of All Estates), in which lines 1–34 serve as an introduction both to the memento mori theme and to Heinrich's general admonition to the estates; lines 452 to 1028 include two lengthy parables about the life and death of a king's son (lines 511 to 638) and the

speech of a dead knight to his son (lines 663 to 910). The remaining lines – 452 to 510, 639 to 662, and 911 to 1028 – contain memento mori admonitions. Lines 1029 to 1042 form the closing prayer, where the poet identifies himself and his patron.

Of all the estates, the clergy is taken hardest to task. Typical transgressions of priests – sexual license, prodigal lifestyle, and, especially, simony – are highlighted; the same concerns are raised in *Vom Priesterleben,* although not quite as much emphasis is placed in *Von des tôdes gehugde* on priests' predilection for sexual congress and the "good life." The term *simony,* meaning the sale of church offices, including the sacraments, derives from Acts 8:9–24, in which a new convert from Samaria, Simon Magus, offers Saints Peter and John money if they will give him the power of "laying on of hands"; Peter sternly rebukes him, saying that money cannot buy what "God has given for nothing." Heinrich was not the first to take up this topic, but his treatment of it is among the first and the most impassioned in the vernacular, demonstrating that the doings of priests were of concern to the laity.

In the pervasive anticlericalism of the various heterodox movements in the twelfth century, especially among the Cathars, the subject of unworthy priests was hotly debated. In general, these movements rejected the Catholic church and its priesthood. But even among many of the orthodox Christians and those on the borderline between heresy and orthodoxy, the inappropriate conduct of priests was a never-ending point of discussion. Of greatest concern was the question of whether an unworthy priest could administer a valid sacrament. The position among many individuals, heretics and orthodox alike, was that he could not; yet that was not the position of the church. If the consecration of the priest was valid – that is, it had been performed with oil administered by a validly consecrated bishop – the sacraments dispensed by that priest had validity. In this regard Heinrich is completely orthodox:

swa aber daz gotes wort unt diu gewihte hant
ob dem gotes tisce wurchent ensant,
da wirt der gotes lichnamen in der misse
von einem sundaer so gewisse,
so von dem heiligstem man,
der briesterlichen namen ie gewan. (lines 181–186)

(But wherever the word of God and the consecrated
   hand
act together at the altar of God,
there will come into being the body of God during the
   Mass,

*Strophe 6, line 18, through strophe 9, line 7, of Heinrich von Melk's* Vom Priesterleben *in a fourteenth-century codex (Vienna, Österreichische Nationalbibliothek, Codex Vindobonensis 2696, fol. 305r)*

from [the hands of] a sinner as certainly
as from the most pious man
who ever attained the name of priest.)

The appearance of the virtually identical lines 397–402 in *Vom Priesterleben* bears witness not only to the orthodoxy of the poet but also to the fact that this issue was of paramount interest in the latter half of the twelfth century, and not just among the clergy.

In the remainder of the section "Von dem gemeinen lebene" Heinrich castigates the foolishness of commoner women who ape the dress of nobles and the silliness of peasant women who apply makeup and assume an affected way of walking that they consider to be elegant. The arrogance and pleasure-seeking of noble men and women is taken severely to task, as is the hedonistic and self-serving nature of knighthood, all of which conspire to prompt the noble to forget his true place in society and the real task that faces him – protection of the poor and powerless. Most striking, in this context, is an invective against unjust judges:

> werltliche rihtaere
> daz sint widervehtaere
> gotes unt aller guote,
> die tragent wulfin gemuote,
> si bebirsent swaz si mugen bejagen. (lines 267–271)

(Secular judges
are enemies
of God and all good people.
They are like wolves,
they skulk after anything that they are able to hunt [that is, they attempt to snatch whatever comes into their grasp].)

The image of the unjust judge who allows himself to be bribed and the resulting terrible consequences for society – the destruction of the state of amity that should prevail among kin and between lord and vassal – is encountered again and again in medieval literature. The theme of the judge is of paramount importance in the Old High German *Muspilli* (circa 790–circa 850), for example, and is essentially the sole concern of the author of the massive *Kaiserchronik*. It is understandable that the figure of the judge would be so important: it is the judge who should stand as the guarantor of the rights of all – high and low, rich and poor – who come before him. The judge is the linchpin of medieval society; if he fails, the poor and powerless will suffer, and great harm will be done to Christian society. Thus, the judge has an immense responsibility, especially toward the least of his fellow human beings.

Heinrich is censuring the disintegration of the divinely instituted *ordo* (order) that binds his society. According to medieval *ordo* theory, in Christian society God has determined that every individual belongs to an estate, and each estate has its responsibility toward society at large; failure to fulfill that responsibility is nothing less than violation of the Divine Plan. Thus, peasants were to feed the population and, in turn, had the right to expect protection from the nobles, who also protected the church, which ministered to the spiritual needs of all and acted as a bridge between humanity and God. In the criticism of groups within his society, Heinrich concentrates on actions that represent a transgression of the *ordo*. The simoniacal priest, the peasant aping the noble, the noble more interested in pleasure than in duty, and the corrupt judge are all violating the strictures of the divinely established *ordo* and are, thus, working against the well-being of society and against God. Heinrich holds up a mirror to his society and does not like what he sees:

> Alle, die bi disen ziten lebent,
> deheines anders listes si phlegent,
> wan wie si anenander betriegen,
> bespoten unt beliegen.
> verboeset ist die niwe jugent.
> ere, zuht unt tugent
> die nigent sam um ein rat. (lines 391–397)

(All, who live in these times,
are concerned with nothing other
than how they can deceive,
ridicule, and lie to one another.
Modern youth is corrupt.
Honor, decorum, and virtue
are bent as if around a wheel.)

Priests are avaricious, Heinrich maintains a few lines further on, farmers are envious, merchants are treacherous, and women are unchaste. Society is on the road to perdition. Having established that fact and having castigated the practices of all estates, including those of his noble audience, Heinrich is ready, he says, to take up the topic of death that he mentioned in the beginning of the section.

Two major episodes form the second part of the work. Both illustrate the fate after death of an individual whose life followed the models presented in the first part. One of the best-known passages in medieval German literature occurs in the first episode when the poet urges the widow of a king's son to go to the grave and look at her dead husband. Heinrich describes a corpse in an advanced state of decomposition, prefacing each gruesome detail with a remark to the woman such as: "nu sich, in wie getaner heite diu zunge lige in sinem munde, da mit er diu trutliet chunde behagenlichen singen!"

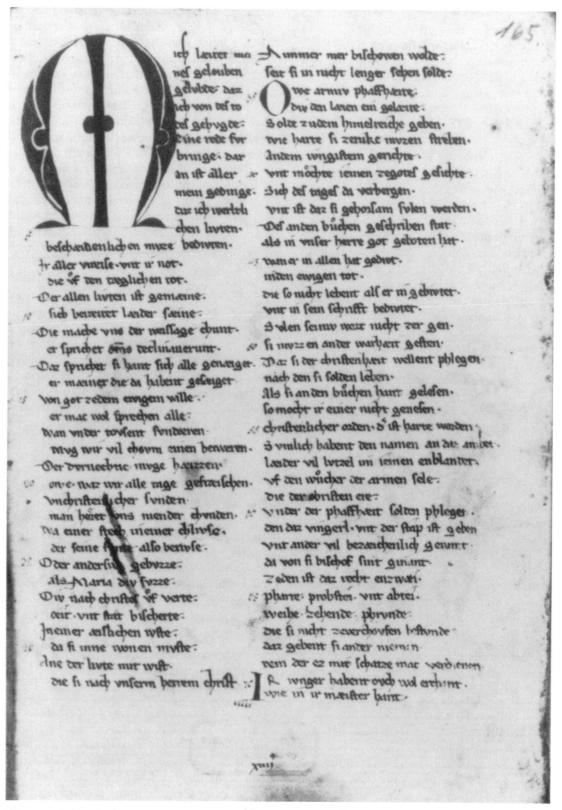

*First page of Heinrich's* Von des tôdes gehugde *in a fourteenth-century codex (Vienna, Österreichische Nationalbibliothek, Codex Vindobonensis, 2696, fol. 83r)*

("Look at the way the tongue with which he used to sing songs of love is lying in his mouth!") (lines 610–613). In his account of the king's son's life Heinrich demonstrates a close acquaintance with the customs of the court and its cultural diversions, and by means of the shocking images he is able to express what he considers the natural outcome of a too-close adherence to the attractions of earthly life.

The second episode involves a visit by a young noble to his father's grave. This episode is the more impressive of the two. It provides eloquent testimony to Heinrich's self-confidence as a writer in the vernacular as he assumes the speaking roles of both the boy and his dead father, saying to the son: "ich spriche fur in unt mit im" (I will speak for him and with him). Thus, Heinrich keeps himself present not only as a character speaking to another character but also as the poet addressing his audience, thereby demonstrating a level of stylistic sophistication not previously encountered in medieval German literature. The episode also allows him to describe at length the actions that sunder the *ordo* and the consequences that await the transgressor. Heinrich has the father go through an entire catalogue of sins that he committed, including sins of the flesh. But the most grievous sins were those that he committed by not fulfilling his obligations to the poor and powerless. The father says, "wa sint nu diu almusen, diu du begast? wa sint die durftigen, die du getroestet hast?" (Where are the alms that you distributed? Where are the needy whom you have comforted?) and "verfluochet si der tac, der mich gebaere. manige gewinnunge, di ich ane barmunge nam von witwen unt von weisen, die lazzent mich niht uz den freisen" (Cursed be the day of my birth. Many acquisitions that I took [unjustly] from widows and orphans without mercy will not let me free of the terrors [of Hell]). Since this episode of 247 lines is 120 lines longer than the first and constitutes 42 percent of the second section of the work, it is reasonable to assume that Heinrich intended to express something that would have application to the lives of his audience and that he did not want them to miss. One would have to search long to find another work of this period that is as impressive and as gripping.

*Von des tôdes gehugde* is also representative of the memento mori genre and, thus, has much in common with the earlier *Memento mori* (circa 1080) by Notker von Zwiefalten. Both writers wish to impress on their listeners that death is like a thief who can come at any time, that earthly life is over "in ictu oculi" (in the blinking of an eye), and that one

must, therefore, be constantly vigilant and prepared to die at any moment. Neither work attempts to render innocuous the inescapable fact that all must perish; indeed, just the opposite is the case. But both Heinrich and Notker move well beyond simple "scare tactics"; each emphasizes that the key to Heaven will only be secured by living a socially active Christian life while on earth. And since it is primarily the rich and powerful who are in a position to be socially active, both works are directed toward this group. Close to a century separates the two poets, however, and much has changed in the literary expectations of the lay audience as well as in the self-assuredness with which the vernacular is used as a literary vehicle. Heinrich is a masterful narrator, fully conscious of himself as a writer who is able to put vernacular expression on a stylistic par with Latin. As a result, the style of *Von des tôdes gehugde* is markedly different from that encountered in the *Memento mori*. Missing completely in Heinrich's works, for example, is the moderate tone so characteristic of Notker. Gone are the circumspection, the typically nonthreatening admonitory style, and the colorless abstraction of Hell and Heaven. Instead, Heinrich challenges his listeners, listing their faults and confronting them with the terrors of Hell; he takes obvious delight in describing the torments that await the damned as a result of their failure to carry out their responsibilities while on earth.

The Heinrich of *Von des tôdes gehugde* and *Vom Priesterleben* is a layman who speaks about theological matters on an equal level with members of the clergy. He addresses a noble, lay audience in the former work and represents the interests of this group to a clerical audience in the latter. His writing is an affirmation of the worth of the lay nobility and its view of the vital role that it plays within the Christian order of things, a role it shares with the clergy and in which it will soon be the dominant partner. This confidence and positive self-concept will find their quintessential expression in the secular tales of the courtly period, where society is shown to be improved by the actions of the nobility and not by representatives of the institutionalized church. There the path to salvation will not lead solely through the priests but also — and primarily — through the good works of each individual. The church and its priesthood will not, however, be demonized or treated contemptuously, as is the case among the heretics. On the contrary, the church will be honored but viewed as in need of guidance from laypeople following the age-old lessons of Christianity. In this respect, Heinrich stands squarely within the currents of popular piety that were aswirl in his age.

## Bibliography:

Francis G. Gentry, *Bibliographie zur frühmittelhochdeutschen geistlichen Dichtung* (Berlin: Schmidt, 1992), pp. 233–239.

## References:

Wiebke Freytag, "Das Priesterleben des sogenannten Heinrich von Melk: Redeformen, Rezeptionsmodus und Gattung," *Deutsche Vierteljahresschrift*, 52 (1978): 558–580;

Peter-Erich Neuser, *Zum sogenannten Heinrich von Melk: Überlieferung, Forschungsgeschichte und Verfasserfrage der Dichtungen "Vom Priesterleben" und "Von des tôdes gehugede"* (Cologne & Vienna: Böhlau, 1973);

Gerhild Scholz-Williams, "Against Court and School: Heinrich of Melk and Hélinant of Froidmont as Critics of Twelfth-Century Society," *Neophilologus*, 62 (October 1978): 513–526;

Scholz-Williams, *The Vision of Death: A Study of the "Memento mori" Expressions in some Latin, German and French Didactic Texts of the 11th and 12th Centuries* (Göppingen: Kümmerle, 1976);

Gisela Vollman-Profe, *Geschichte der deutschen Literatur von den Anfängen bis zum Beginn der Neuzeit*, volume 1/2: *Von den Anfängen zum Hohen Mittelalter* (Königstein: Athenäum, 1986);

Max Wehrli, *Geschichte der deutschen Literatur vom frühen Mittelalter bis zum Ende des 16. Jahrhunderts* (Stuttgart: Reclam, 1980).

# Hermann the Lame
## *(1013 – 1054)*

Linda Archibald
*Liverpool John Moores University*

MAJOR WORKS: *Compotos* (1042)

**Manuscripts:** The earliest manuscript of this work is London, British Library, Manuscript Arundel 356, 27–37. Paris, Bibliothèque Nationale, Cod. Lat. 14960 is a copy dating from about 1200 from Saint Victor in Paris.

**Standard edition:** Excerpts edited by Alfred Cordiolani, in his "Le computiste Hermann de Reichenau," *Miscellanea di Storie Ligure,* 3 (1961): 165–190.

*Martyrologia* (circa 1045)

**Manuscripts:** The earliest is a late-eleventh- or early-twelfth-century manuscript from Zwiefalten that is now at Stuttgart, Württembergische Landesbibliothek, Cod. theol. fol. 209. In Munich there are three twelfth-century texts: Bayerische Staatsbibliothek, Clm 5256, from Chiemsee; Clm 22058, from Wessobrun; and Clm 1071, from Oberaltaich. A further twelfth-century version is in Linz, Bundesstaatliche Studienbibliothek, cod. 332 (olim 258). This manuscript contains some fourteenth-century additions to Hermann's work. Another twelfth-century codex is in Engelberg, Stiftsbibliothek, Cod. 44.

**Standard edition:** In *Patrologia Latina,* 221 volumes, edited by Jacques Paul Migne (Paris: Migne, 1841–1879), CXLIII: 9–458.

*Chronicon* (circa 1048)

**Manuscripts:** Karlsruhe, Landesbibliothek, Cod. Augiensis, CLXXV, written in five different hands in the eleventh century, is the oldest and most complete version of the work, though the last part is missing. Another manuscript strand was begun in Regensburg in the eleventh century with Clm 14613.

**Standard edition:** In *Patrologia Latina,* 221 volumes, edited by Jacques Paul Migne (Paris: Migne, 1841–1879), CXLIII: 55–378.

*De astrolabio*

**Manuscripts:** There are more than forty manuscripts of these works.

**Standard edition:** In *Patrologia Latina,* 221 volumes, edited by Jacques Paul Migne (Paris: Migne, 1841–1879), pp. 389–408.

*De mensura astrolabii*

**Manuscripts:** Munich, Clm 14836, Clm 13021; Paris, Bibliothèque Nationale, 11248.

**Standard edition:** In *Patrologia Latina,* 221 volumes, edited by Jacques Paul Migne (Paris: Migne, 1841–1879), CXLIII: 481–490; in *The Astrolabes of the World 2,* edited by R. T. Gunther (Oxford, 1932), pp. 404–408.

*De octo vitiis principalibus*

**Standard edition:** Edited by Ernst Dümmler as "Opusculum Herimanni diverso metro compositum ad amiculas suas quasdam sanctimoniales feminas," *Zeitschrift für deutsches Altertum,* 13 (1867): 385–431; 432–434.

*Musica*

**Standard edition:** In *Patrologia Latina,* 221 volumes, edited by Jacques Paul Migne (Paris: Migne, 1841–1879), CXLIII: 413–442.

*Sequences*

**Manuscripts:** A complex history and disputed authorship.

**Standard edition:** In *Patrologia Latina,* 221 volumes, edited by Jacques Paul Migne (Paris: Migne, 1841–1879), CXLIII: 443–445; edited by Guido Maria Dreves, in *Analecta Hymnica medii aevi,* 55 volumes, edited by Dreves and Clemens Blume (Leipzig: Reisland, 1886–1922), XLIV (1904): 204–206; L (1907): 308–319; LII (1910): 195–196.

Hermann the Lame, also known as Hermannus Contractus and Hermann of Reichenau, was born in 1013. When he was seven, his father, Wolfrad von Altshausen, and his mother, Hiltrud, sent him to the monastery at Reichenau, where he spent the rest of his life. Unable to walk and confined to a chair that had to be carried around by his fellow monks, Hermann also had difficulty in speaking, but these disabilities did not prevent him from having a brilliant career as a teacher. Although there are legends that he visited more illustrious schools, such as the one at Augsburg, Hermann's own testimony indicates that he acquired information by borrowing works from other libraries and holding discussions with visitors. Many students came to the monastery to learn the subjects of the quadrivium from him.

Hermann's study of music went far beyond the requirements of the liturgy, and of mathematics far beyond the need to calculate the dates of Christian festivals; but the initial motivation for his study was usually related to practical matters of monastic life. One of his earliest works is the treatise that the modern world calls *Musica* and was titled by Hermann *Speculatio ad dilucidandas multiplices monochordi obscuritates*. Written soon after 1030, it reflects Hermann's analytical approach as he tries to elucidate obscure aspects of contemporary music theory. Two mnemonic verses in the work, *Ter terni sunt modi* and *ter tria iunctorum*, were in use throughout the Middle Ages.

One of his greatest influences was Notker Balbulus of Saint Gall, and Hermann was sent a copy of Notker's *Martyrologium* (896) to be brought up to date. The manuscript tradition of the martyrology genre is fraught with problems because successive authors plundered the work of previous ones, adding and omitting entries as they saw fit, usually reflecting local preferences for particular subjects. Hermann adapted and expanded Notker's martyrology using material from similar works by Bede, Ado of Vienne, and Hrabanus Maurus. The purpose of such a work was to collect the names, dates, and stories of the lives and deaths of saints to allow priests and monks to celebrate the various festivals and saints' days. Hermann worked on this task between 1039 and the mid 1040s, placing special emphasis on the locally celebrated saints Ursus, Adalbert, and Mark the Evangelist. In the course of his work Hermann came across contradictions among his sources, and even within individual texts, in regard to the dating of events. The confusion was caused by apparent errors in calculation, particularly in regard to early Christian saints, who were dated according to a mixture of Jewish, Egyptian, and early Christian calendars. To solve this problem Hermann applied mathematical and astrological techniques to the revered historical records of the Western church. This approach was rather radical for his time, since the standard practice was to copy everything, contradictions and all, and avoid the risk of appearing presumptuous or, worse, heretical.

In 1042 Hermann pursued his time measurements further, but not in the usual way – that is, by writing a reference book or teaching text summarizing existing knowledge. Instead, he wrote his *Compotos* as a theoretical exploration of the movements of the sun and moon, following the example of the pre-Christian philosophers. Hermann's work is in two parts: the first summarizes accepted opinions and was later much used as a teaching text, despite Hermann's intentions; the second part is more theoretical and dares to place arithmetically calculated dates alongside the traditional dates recorded by early Western Christians. The second part was largely forgotten, perhaps because succeeding generations could not cope with the mathematical and doctrinal difficulties of the work. It would be many centuries later, in the era of world exploration and scientific enlightenment, that Hermann's works would be understood and appreciated by readers versed in mathematics.

Hermann further applied his scientific counting methods to the writing of his *Chronicon*, which was begun not later than 1048. This work gives an account of important events from the birth of Christ onward. It is, however, not just a compendium of received information: Hermann underpins the narrative with astrological details. Events, especially astronomical ones in Hermann's source texts that do not accord with his arithmetic, are not included in the *Chronicon*. His own additions begin at the year 901, the point where the source texts cease.

Hermann wrote several practical works on mathematical instruments, especially the astrolabe. Hermann did not have access to older Greek and Arabic texts but had some knowledge of their contents through the works of authors in Spain and Lorraine, where links with the Arab world were kept faintly alive. These authors included Lupitus of Barcelona and Gerbert of Aurillac, who attempted to adapt the old knowledge to Christian uses. Hermann distilled the complicated writings of these authors into a concise set of instructions for the construction and use of the astrolabe, adapting the calculations to the longitude and latitude of Reichenau. His blueprint was used by the makers of these instruments until the mid fourteenth century. Thus, Hermann was a key figure in passing down elementary knowledge about astronomy and mathematics to the future scholars of the West.

Hermann also wrote *sequentia* (sequences), notably *Ave praeclara maris stella,* again following Notker's lead. This semisung poetic genre was fashionable as an extension of the liturgy, and the monasteries of Saint Gall and Reichenau were major centers of composition of such works. Some sequences are attributed to Hermann on the basis of clear references by other authors: for example, Gottschalk of Limburg attributes the sequence *Grates, honos, hierarchia* to Hermann. Several more are attributable to Hermann with reasonable certainty, including those dealing with the cross of Christ, the Holy Trinity, and Mary Magdalene. Other sequences, attributed to Hermann by early critics but regarded as dubious by modern scholarship, include the sequences in praise of Mary – *Alma redemptoris* and *Salve regina*. The attribution of sequences is often difficult due to a lack of manuscript evidence and the similarity of form and topic through the ages. Those definitely written by Hermann display originality in the use of Greek expressions and skillful manipulation of the Latin meters. A particularly fine example of his creative approach to the form is his sequence on the Holy Trinity, where one section is devoted to the names of God in the Latin Bible:

(6a) Pater, El Eloi
Eloe, Elion,
Ia, Sadai,
lux, Samain,
tu Eie, rex,
Sabbaoth, ineffabilis,
Adonai,
tuum nos plasma
conserva.

(6b) Proles Emmanuel,
mire mirabilis,
summe consul,
Deus fortis,
Dominus iustus,
futuri pater saeculi,
princeps pacis,
Jesu Messia,
nos salva.

Hermann also wrote a treatise addressed to a group of nuns, *De octo vitiis principalibus* (On the Eight Most Serious Sins). This piece is unlike most of Hermann's other prose works, showing none of his usual predilection for facts and figures or for theorizing. A muse, Melpomene, takes part in a dialogue with Hermann and the nuns. The work is a warning against sin and an exhortation to concentrate on the rewards of the next world rather than the distractions of this life.

Hermann's contribution to the early medieval period is hard to trace because so much of his work is a continuation of existing material or a collaboration with other monks; many attributions of texts to him are still open to question. He was undoubtedly an accomplished poet who turned his hand to various Latin meters and wore his scholarship lightly. His verse, in particular his sequences, shows a simple grace and an appreciation of tradition and style. His prose reveals knowledge of the Greek language and Greek concepts and an understanding of mathematical and scientific principles. Perhaps his greatest contribution was in the field of ideas, particularly his radical approach to the problem of conflicting sources. With a truly modern self-confidence, he applies mathematical principles to patristic and Carolingian commentaries. None of his contemporaries could match his intellect, which is why they traveled far to speak with him.

Hermann died in 1054, having charged his pupil Berthold with the transcribing of his unfinished work from wax tablets to parchment and with the continuation of his *Chronicon;* the efforts of the pupil contrast visibly with the illustrious achievements of his master. Berthold also recorded information about the life of his beloved tutor. In the ages following Hermann's death legends emerged about the man whose broken body harbored a mind that kept alive some of the insights of the ancient world through a particularly dark period in the history of science in the West.

**References:**

W. Bergmann, "Der Traktat *De mensura astrolabi* des Hermanns von Reichenau," *Francia,* 8 (1980): 65–103;

Arno Borst, "Computus: Zeit und Zahl im Mittelalter," *Deutsches Archiv für Erforschung des Mittelalters,* 44, no. 1 (1988): 1–82;

Borst, "Ein Forschungsbericht Hermanns des Lahmen," *Deutsches Archiv für Erforschung des Mittelalters,* 40, no. 2 (1984): 379–478;

R. Buchner, "Geschichtsbild und Reichsbegriff Hermanns von Reichenau," *Archiv für Kulturgeschichte,* 42 (1960): 37–60;

Buchner, "Der Verfasser der Schwäbischen Weltchronik," *Deutsches Archiv für Erforschung des Mittelalters,* 16 (1960): 389–396;

Julius Drecker, "Hermannus Contractus über das Astrolab," *Isis,* 16 (November 1931): 200–219;

Jacques Handschin, "Hermannus Contractus – Legenden – Nur Legenden?," *Zeitschrift für deutsches Altertum,* 72 (1935): 1–8;

M. Hess and P. Konzelmann, "Zur Bedeutung des Astrolabs in den Schriften Hermanns des Lahmen von Reichenau," *Archiv für Kulturgeschichte,* 62/63 (1980/1981): 49–63;

John M. McCulloch, "Herman the Lame's Martyrology through Four Centuries of Scholarship," *Analecta Bollandiana,* 104, no. 3/4 (1986): 349–370;

I. S. Robinson, "Die Chronik Hermanns von Reichenau und die Reichenauer Kaiserchronik," *Deutsches Archiv für Erforschung des Mittelalters,* 36 (1980): 84–136.

# Hildegard von Bingen
## *(1098–1179)*

Sabina Flanagan
*University of Adelaide*

MAJOR WORKS: *Scivias* (1141–1151)

**Manuscripts:** Of the ten known medieval manuscripts of *Scivias,* three are notable because they were produced in the Rupertsberg scriptorium: the illustrated manuscript Wiesbaden, Hessische Landesbibliothek, Hs 1, composed circa 1165, missing since 1945 (a handmade facsimile, produced between 1927 and 1933, is in the Bibliothek der Abtei Saint Hildegard, Eibingen); a second twelfth-century manuscript, Vatican City, Bibl. Apost. Vat., Cod. Pal. lat. 311; and the Riesenkodex, the "giant codex" prepared in the decade after Hildegard's death, containing the works for which she claimed unmediated divine inspiration (which may explain the omission of the medico-scientific works), Wiesbaden, Hessische Landesbibliothek, Hs 2. Also illustrated is a twelfth-century manuscript, Heidelberg, Universitätsbibliothek, Cod. Sal. X, 16.

**First publication:** In *Liber trium virorum et trium spiritualium virginum,* edited by Jacobus Faber (Paris, 1513); reprinted in *Sanctae Hildegardis Abbatissae Opera Omnia,* volume 197 of *Patrologia Latina,* edited by Jacques-Paul Migne (Paris: Migne, 1855), cols. 383–738.

**Standard edition:** *Hildegardis Scivias,* edited by Adelgundis Führkötter and Angela Carlevaris, volumes 43 and 43A of *Corpus Christianorum Continuatio Mediaevalis* (Turnhout: Brepols, 1978).

**Editions in English:** Excerpts translated by Bruce Hozeski as *Scivias: By Hildegard of Bingen* (Santa Fe: Bear, 1986); translated by Columba Hart and Jane Bishop as *Scivias: Hildegard of Bingen* (New York: Paulist Press, 1990).

*Epistolae* (1147–1179)

**Manuscripts:** Berlin, Staatsbibliothek Preußischer Kulturbesitz, Cod. theol. lat. fol. 699, from the second half of the twelfth century; Brussels, Bibliothèque Royale, Cod. 5387–5396 and Cod. 5527–5534; Stuttgart, Württembergische Landesbibliothek, Cod. theol. phil. 4o, 253, from the third quarter of the twelfth century; Vienna, Österreichische Nationalbibliothek, Cod. 881, from the third quarter of the twelfth century; Wiesbaden, Hessische Landesbibliothek, Hs 2 (Riesenkodex), from the 1180s; Berlin, Staatsbibliothek Preußischer Kulturbesitz, Cod. lat. 4o 674, from the beginning of the thirteenth century.

**First publication:** *Sanctae Hildegardis abbatissae in Monte S. Roberti apud Naam fluuium, prope Bingam, sanctissimae uirginis et prophetissae, Epistolarum Liber,* edited by Justus Blanckwald (Cologne: Johannis Quentel & Geruuinum Quentel, 1566).

**Standard edition:** *Hildegardis Bingensis: Epistolarium,* volumes 91 and 91A of *Corpus Christianorum Continuatio Mediaevalis,* edited by Lieven van Acker (Turnhout: Brepols, 1991, 1993).

**Edition in English:** Translated by Joseph L. Baird and Radd K. Ehrman as *The Letters of Hildegard von Bingen,* volume 1 (New York: Oxford University Press, 1994).

*Subtilitates diversarum naturarum creaturarum,* part 1: *Physica* or *Liber simplicis medicinae* (circa 1151–1158)

**Manuscripts:** The textual tradition of this work is obscure, with only one manuscript, Wolfenbüttel, Herzog-August-Bibliothek, Cod. 56, 2 Aug. 4o, dating from the thirteenth century. Two other manuscripts – Paris, Bibliothèque Nationale Cod. lat. 6952 and Brussels, Bibliothèque Royale Cod. 1494 – date from the fifteenth century.

**First publication:** *Physica S. Hildegardis Elementorum, Fluminum aliquot Germaniae, Metallorum, Leguminum, Fructuum, et Herbarum: Arborum, et Arbustorum: Piscium denique, Volatilium, et Animantium terrae naturas et operationes IV Libris mirabili experientia posteritati tradens* (Strasbourg: Joannem Schott, 1533).

**Standard edition:** In *Sanctae Hildegardis Abba*

*tissae Opera Omnia,* edited by Charles Daremberg and F. A. de Reuss, volume 197 of *Patrologia Latina,* edited by Jacques-Paul Migne (Paris: Migne, 1855), cols. 1117–1352.

*Subtilitates diversarum naturarum creaturarum,* part 2: *Causae et Curae* or *Liber compositae medicinae* (circa 1151–1158)

**Manuscript:** The unique thirteenth-century manuscript is preserved at Copenhagen, Kongelige Bibliotek, Ny. kgl. saml. 90b.

**First publication:** *Hildegardis Causae et Curae,* edited by Paul Kaiser (Leipzig: Teubner, 1903).

*Symphonia armoniae celestium revelationum* (1150s, with later additions and revisions)

**Manuscripts:** Two late-twelfth-century manuscripts contain texts and music for the cycle. Although older, dating from around 1175, the manuscript St.-Pieters-&-Paulusabdij, Dendermonde Klosterbibliothek, Codex 9 is incomplete. Eighteen additional songs are included in the cycle as found in Wiesbaden, Hessische Landesbibliothek, Hs 2 (Riesenkodex), from the 1180s.

**First publication:** In *Analecta Sanctae Hildegardis,* edited by Jean-Baptiste Pitra, volume 8 of *Analecta sacra* (Monte Cassino, 1882), pp. 441–456.

**Standard edition and edition in modern German:** *Hildegard von Bingen: Lieder,* edited by Pudentiana Barth and Joseph Schmidt-Görg (Salzburg: Müller, 1969).

**Standard edition and edition in English:** *Saint Hildegard of Bingen: Symphonia,* edited and translated by Barbara Newman (Ithaca, N.Y.: Cornell University Press, 1988).

*Ordo virtutum* (1150s?)

**Manuscript:** The work is included as part of the *Symphonia* in Wiesbaden, Hessische Landesbibliothek, Hs 2 (Riesenkodex), from the 1180s.

**First publication:** In *Analecta Sanctae Hildegardis,* edited by Jean-Baptiste Pitra, volume 8 of *Analecta Sacra* (Monte Cassino, 1882), pp. 457–465.

**Standard editions:** In Peter Dronke, *Poetic Individuality in the Middle Ages* (Oxford: Oxford University Press, 1970), pp. 180–192; *The "Ordo virtutum," of Hildegard of Bingen,* edited by Audrey Davidson (Kalamazoo, 1985).

**Edition in English:** Translated by Peter Dronke, in record liner for *Hildegard von Bingen: Ordo virtutum,* recorded by Sequentia, Harmonia Mundi 20395/96 (1982).

*Vita Sancti Ruperti* (1150s?)

**Manuscript:** Wiesbaden, Hessische Landesbibliothek, Hs 2 (Riesenkodex), from the 1180s.

**First publication:** In Hincmari Rhemensis archiepiscopi . . . epistolae, edited by Joannes Busaeus (Mainz: I. Albini, 1602), pp. 361–371.

**Standard editions:** In *Sanctae Hildegardis Abbatissae Opera Omnia,* volume 197 of *Patrologia Latina,* edited by Jacques-Paul Migne (Paris: Migne, 1855), cols. 1081–1094; in *Hildegardis Bigensis: Epistolarium,* edited by Lieven van Acker, volume 91B of *Corpus Christianorum Continuatio Mediaevalis* (Turnhout: Brepols, forthcoming 1995?).

*Lingua ignota; Litterae ignotae* (1150s?)

**Manuscript:** Wiesbaden, Hessische Landesbibliothek, Hs 2 (Riesenkodex), from the 1180s; Berlin, Staatsbibliothek Preußischer Kulturbesitz, Cod. lat. 4o 674, from the beginning of the thirteenth century.

**First publication and standard edition:** In *Analecta Sanctae Hildegardis,* edited by Jean-Baptiste Pitra, volume 8 of *Analecta Sacra* (Monte Cassino, 1882), pp. 496–502.

*Liber Vitae Meritorum* (1158–1163)

**Manuscripts:** There are four manuscripts dating from the twelfth century: Wiesbaden, Hessische Landesbibliothek, Hs 2 (Riesenkodex); St.-Pieters-&-Paulusabdij, Dendermonde Klosterbibliothek, Codex 9; Berlin, Staatsbibliothek Preußischer Kulturbesitz, Cod. theol. fol. 727, now in Tübingen, Universitätsbibliothek; and Trier, Seminarbibliothek, Cod. 68.

**First publication and standard edition:** In *Analecta Sanctae Hildegardis,* edited by Jean-Baptiste Pitra, volume 8 of *Analecta Sacra* (Monte Cassino, 1882), pp. 7–244.

*Liber Divinorum Operum* or *De Operatione Dei* (1163–1173/1174)

**Manuscripts:** Ghent, Universiteitsbibliotheek, Cod. 241, circa 1170–1171; Wiesbaden, Hessische Landesbibliothek, Hs 2 (Riesenkodex), from the 1180s; Troyes, Bibliothèque municipale, Ms 683, from the twelfth century; and the illustrated manuscript Lucca, Biblioteca Statale, Cod. lat. 1942, from the early thirteenth century.

**First publication:** In *Stephani Baluzii Tutelensis Miscellanea novo ordine digesta et non paucis ineditis monumentis opportunisque animadversionibus aucta, opera et studio,* 4 volumes, edited by Joannis Dominici Mansi (Lucca, 1761–1764), II: 377ff.

*Hildegard von Bingen (center), receiving and writing down a vision in the company of the monk Volmar of Disibodenberg and a nun; illustration from the manuscript for* Liber Divinorum Operum *(Lucca, Biblioteca Statale, Cod. lat. 1942)*

**Standard editions:** In *Sanctae Hildegardis abbatissae Opera Omnia,* volume 197 of *Patrologia Latina,* edited by Jacques-Paul Migne (Paris: Migne, 1855), cols. 739–1038; *Hildegardis Liber Divinorum Operum,* edited by Albert Derolez and Peter Dronke (Turnhout: Brepols, forthcoming 1995?).

**Edition in English:** Abridged and translated by Matthew Fox, in *Hildegard of Bingen's Book of Divine Works with Letters and Songs* (Santa Fe: Bear, 1987).

*Vita Sancti Disibodi* (1170)

**Manuscript:** Wiesbaden, Hessische Landesbibliothek, Hs 2 (Riesenkodex), from the 1180s.

**First publication:** In *Acta Sanctorum,* edited by John Bolland, Godefroid Henskens, and others (Antwerp, Brussels, Tongerloo & Paris, 1643–1894), July, volume 2, pp. 588–597.

**Standard editions:** In *Sanctae Hildegardis Abbatissae Opera Omnia,* volume 197 of *Patrologia Latina,* edited by Jacques-Paul Migne (Paris: Migne, 1855), cols. 1093–1116; in *Hildegardis Bigensis: Epistolarium,* edited by Lieven van Acker, volume 91B of *Corpus Christianorum Continuatio Mediaevalis* (Turnhout: Brepols, forthcoming 1995?).

*Solutiones triginta octo quaestionum* (1178)

**Manuscript:** Wiesbaden, Hessische Landesbibliothek, Hs 2 (Riesenkodex), from the 1180s.

**First publication:** In *Biblioteca Patrum,* volume 23 (Leyden: I. A. Huguetan, 1677), pp. 583–590.

**Standard editions:** In *Sanctae Hildegardis Abbatissae Opera Omnia,* volume 197 of *Patrologia Latina,* edited by Jacques-Paul Migne (Paris: Migne, 1855), cols. 1037–1054; in *Hildegardis Bigensis: Epistolarium,* edited by Lieven van Acker, volume 91B of *Corpus Christianorum Continuatio Mediaevalis* (Turnhout: Brepols, forthcoming 1995?).

*Expositiones Evangeliorum* (date unknown)

**Manuscript:** Wiesbaden, Hessische Landesbibliothek, Hs 2 (Riesenkodex), from the 1180s.

**First publication and standard edition:** In *Analecta Sanctae Hildegardis,* edited by Jean-Baptiste Pitra, volume 8 of *Analecta sacra* (Monte Cassino, 1882), pp. 245–327.

*Explanatio Regulae S. Benedicti* (date unknown)

**Manuscript:** Wiesbaden, Hessische Landesbibliothek, Hs 2 (Riesenkodex), from the 1180s.

**First publication:** In *Biblioteca Patrum,* volume 23 (Leyden: I. A. Huguetan, 1677), pp. 590-593.

**Standard editions:** In *Sanctae Hildegardis Abbatissae Opera Omnia,* volume 197 of *Patrologia Latina,* edited by Jacques-Paul Migne (Paris: Migne, 1855), cols. 1053-1066; in *Hildegardis Bigensis: Epistolarium,* edited by Lieven van Acker, volume 91B of *Corpus Christianorum Continuatio Mediaevalis* (Turnhout: Brepols, forthcoming 1995?).

*Explanatio Symboli S. Athanasii* (date unknown)

**Manuscript:** Wiesbaden, Hessische Landesbibliothek, Hs 2 (Riesenkodex), from the 1180s.

**First publication:** In *Biblioteca Patrum,* volume 23 (Leyden: I. A. Huguetan, 1677), pp. 594ff.

**Standard editions:** In *Sanctae Hildegardis Abbatissae Opera Omnia,* volume 197 of *Patrologia Latina,* edited by Jacques-Paul Migne (Paris: Migne, 1855), cols. 1065-1082; in *Hildegardis Bigensis: Epistolarium,* edited by Lieven van Acker, volume 91B of *Corpus Christianorum Continuatio Mediaevalis* (Turnhout: Brepols, forthcoming 1995?).

Hildegard von Bingen – visionary, poet, composer, naturalist, healer, and theologian – founded convents; corresponded with secular and ecclesiastical leaders, as well as a vast range of people of lesser rank; and ventured forth as a monastic troubleshooter, consultant exorcist, and visiting preacher. Even more remarkable for a woman of her time was the body of written work she produced. Its range – from natural history and medicine to cosmology, music, poetry, and theology – surpasses that of most of her male contemporaries; it also possesses great beauty and witnesses to Hildegard's intellectual power.

Born at Bermersheim in Rheinhesse in 1098, the tenth and last child of noble parents, Hildegard showed early signs of exceptional spiritual gifts. Looking back, she placed the onset of her visionary experiences in early childhood, although at that stage she did not understand their significance. As the monk Godfrey wrote in his and the monk Theodoric's *Vita Sanctae Hildegardis* (Life of Saint Hildegard, circa 1180s): "nomine Hildegardis, patre Hildeberdo, matre Mechtilde progenita. Qui licet mundanis impliciti curis et opulencia conspicui creatoris tamen donis non ingrati filiam prenominatam divino famulatui manciparunt. Eo quod cum ineuntis etatis eius prematura sinceritas ab omni carnalium habitudine multum dissentire

videretur" (Her parents, Hildebert and Mechtilde, although wealthy and engaged in worldly affairs, were not unmindful of the gifts of the Creator and dedicated their daughter to the service of God. For when she was yet a child she seemed far removed from worldly concerns, distanced by a precocious purity). The life they chose for her was that of a companion to Jutta, daughter of Count Stephan of Spanheim, who lived in a cell near the church of the Benedictine monks at Disibodenberg. Jutta instructed her young charge in the recitation of the Psalter, teaching her to read and (by no means an obvious corollary at the time) to write. In subsequent years Hildegard was always quick to point out how limited her formal education had been, emphasizing that she had been taught by an "indocta mulier" (unlearned woman) and, consequently, that any insight she gained into theological or secular matters was divinely inspired.

The reputation for holiness of Jutta and her pupil soon spread throughout the district, and other parents sought to have their daughters join what was developing into a small Benedictine convent on the site of the monastery of Disibodenberg. By the time Hildegard was fifteen the process seems to have been complete, for at that time she took the veil from the hands of the bishop of Bamberg.

The visionary experiences that set her apart as a child had continued, as had her recurrent illnesses. That there was a link between her visions and her state of health was recognized by Hildegard herself (some modern commentators claim that the visions were occasioned by a migraine condition). By this time, however, Hildegard had learned to conceal the visions. She confided them only to Jutta, who in turn informed the monk Volmar of Disibodenberg, who was to become Hildegard's teacher, trusted assistant, and friend until his death in 1173.

Between the time of her profession as a nun and the death of Jutta in 1136, when Hildegard was unanimously elected to head the convent, sources give only the most conventional descriptions of the kind of life she led. Within a few years, however, this situation was to change. She recalled the turning point in her life, the vision that suddenly enabled her to penetrate to the inner meaning of the texts of her religion: "Factum est in millesimo centesimo quadragesimo primo Filii Dei Iesu Christi incarnationis anno, cum quadraginta duorum annorum septemque mensium essem, maximae coruscationis igneum lumen aperto caelo veniens totum cerebrum meum transfudit et totum cor totumque pectus meum velut flamma non tamen ardens sed calens ita inflammavit.... Et repente intellectum expositionis librorum, videlicet psalterii, evangelii et aliorum catholicorum tam veteris quam novi Testamenti voluminum sapiebam ..." (And it came to pass in the eleven hundred and forty-first year of the Incarnation of Jesus Christ, Son of God, when I was forty-two years and seven months old, that the heavens were opened and a blinding light of exceptional brilliance flowed through my entire brain. And so it kindled my whole heart and breast like a flame, not burning but warming.... And suddenly I understood the meaning of the expositions of the books, that is to say of the Psalter, the evangelists and other catholic books of the Old and New Testaments ... ).

More important than this sudden access of understanding was the command that was part of the vision: Hildegard was to say and write what she learned in this way. When she hesitated to start writing, doubting that she was equal to the task and fearful of the reaction of her male contemporaries, she fell ill. She interpreted this phenomenon as a sign of God's displeasure and confided at last in Volmar. With his encouragement, and the permission of Abbot Kuno of Disibodenberg, she began recording the visions that formed the basis of *Scivias* (Know the Ways [of God], 1141–1151), a work that took her ten years to complete.

While it was still in progress a portion of *Scivias* was shown to Pope Eugenius III; reading from it to the prelates assembled at the Synod of Trier in 1147–1148, Eugenius gave papal approval both to this text and to whatever else Hildegard might produce by means of the Holy Spirit. Official recognition that Hildegard's work was divinely inspired served to disarm potential critics and allowed Hildegard a good deal of freedom to criticize the shortcomings of her secular and spiritual superiors. She saw herself as continuing the work of the prophets in proclaiming the truths that God wished humanity to know.

The longest of Hildegard's three theological works – some commentators consider *Scivias, Liber Vitae Meritorum* (Book of Life's Merits, 1158–1163), and *Liber Divinorum Operum* (Book of the Divine Works, 1163–1173/1174) a trilogy, even though Hildegard may not have envisaged them as such – *Scivias* is divided into three books of six, seven, and thirteen visions, respectively. In each case Hildegard describes the vision and then explains its meaning. The explanation, which she received via the "vox de caelo" (voice from Heaven), follows the method used by medieval exegetes to gloss written texts.

*Scivias* covers a wide range of topics in a fairly unsystematic way; Barbara Newman describes it as "a comprehensive guide to Christian doctrine ... ranged over the themes of divine majesty, the Trinity, creation, the fall of Lucifer and Adam, the stages of salvation history, the church and its sacraments, the Last Judgment and the world to come." Book 1 deals principally with the Creator and Creation. It begins with the theme of wisdom and the knowledge of God, introduces humanity, the Fall and its consequences – including prescriptions for sexual morality – and anticipates the Redemption. Book 2 expands on the theme of Redemption, considering God's remedy for the world and humankind in the fallen state depicted in the first book. Here such topics as the sacraments, the priesthood, and eucharistic theology are especially notable. Book 3 concentrates on salvation history and explores the work of the Holy Spirit in building the Kingdom of God by means of the virtues. Its apocalyptic ending includes visions of the Last Judgment and the creation of the New Heaven and Earth. The thirteenth vision incorporates an early version of Hildegard's *Ordo virtutum* (Play of the Virtues, 1150s?).

It is almost impossible to convey the powerful effect that the visions of *Scivias* produce when reviewed one after the other, but an extract from the fourth vision of book 2, dealing with the sacrament of confirmation, may give something of the flavor of the whole. Here a series of interconnected visions depicts *Ecclesia* (the Church) as a beautiful and powerful woman: "Et deinde vidi velut magnam et rotundam turrim, totamque integrum et album lapidem exsistentem, tresque fenestras in summitate sui habentem, ex quibus tantus fulgor resplenduit quod etiam tectum turris illius quod se velut in conum erexerat, in claritate eiusdem fulgoris manifestius videretur. Ipsae autem fenestrae pulcherrimis smaragdis circumornatae erant. Sed et eadem turris velut in medio dorsi praedictae muliebris imaginis posita erat, secundum quod aliqua turris in murum urbis ponitur, ita quod eadem imago prae fortitudine eius nullo modo cadere poterat ..." (And then I saw, as it were, a huge round tower entirely built of white stone, having three windows at its summit, from which such brightness shone forth that even the conical roof of the tower appeared very clearly in the brightness of this light. The windows themselves were decorated round about with most beautiful emeralds. And this tower seemed to be placed in the middle of the back

*Illustration depicting Hildegard's vision of the Trinity, from the manuscript for* Scivias. *The silver outer circle represents the Father; the human figure is the Son; and the gold inner circle is the Holy Ghost (Wiesbaden, Hessische Landesbibliothek, Hs 1 [missing since 1945]).*

of the woman mentioned above [*Ecclesia*], as a tower is placed in a city wall, so that the image might never fall, because of its strength . . . ). This section is glossed by the voice from Heaven: "Sed quod eam vides magnam et rotundam totamque integrum et album lapidem exsistentem: hoc est quod immensa est dulcedo Spiritus sancti et volubilis in gratia omnes creaturas circuiens, ita quod nulla corruptio in integritate plenitudinis iustitiae eam evacuat; quoniam ipsa torrens iter habens, omnes rivulos sanctitatis in claritate fortitudinis illius emittit, in qua nunquam maculositas ullius sordis inventa est; quia ipse Spiritus sanctus est ardens et lucens serenitas quae numquam evacuabitur et quae ardentes virtutes fortiter accendit, ac ideo omnes tenebrae ab eo fugantur" (Now the reason why you see a huge round tower entirely built of white stone is because the sweetness of the Holy Spirit is immense and comprehensively includes all creatures in its grace, so that no corruption in the integrity of the fullness of justice destroys it; since glowing, it points the way and sends forth all rivers of sanctity in the clarity of its strength, in which there is found no spot of any foulness. Wherefore the Holy Spirit is ablaze, and its burning serenity which strongly

kindles the fiery virtues will never be destroyed; so all darkness is put to flight by it). While this account is at a fairly high level of abstraction, the explanation is sometimes more concrete and specific – as where the three windows are said to represent the Trinity and the emeralds surrounding them are said to signify "viridissimis virtutibus et aerumnis apostolorum" (the most green virtues and pains of the apostles).

During the time Hildegard was writing *Scivias,* she also undertook the relocation of her convent. When she received what she took to be an order from God to move to Rupertsberg, near Bingen on the Rhine, and set up her own establishment, she met with opposition from the abbot and monks of Disibodenberg, who would suffer both spiritual and material losses from the move. But Abbot Kuno decided that the illness with which she was stricken when she found herself unable to carry out God's plan was of divine origin, and he gave his permission (if not his blessing) for the move. In 1150 Hildegard and some twenty nuns moved to her new foundation. There Hildegard faced substandard accommodations, loss of revenues, claims on the convent's inadequate resources from the surrounding populace, and internal dissension. With perseverance and, as she believed, the help of God she overcame these problems.

At this time Hildegard's writings take a somewhat more pragmatic turn. To provide for the needs of her own and surrounding communities for liturgical compositions, she continued to write the poetry and music she had first mentioned as early as 1148 in a letter to Odo of Soissons. Worked into a song cycle, these hymns and sequences were to form the mature *Symphonia armoniae celestium revelationum* (Symphony of the Harmony of Celestial Revelations, 1150s). The themes of the more than seventy hymns, sequences, antiphons, versicles, and responsaries encompass the heavenly hierarchy, with special attention to Mary and to Saint Ursula. While in modern times Hildegard's poetry had an early champion in Peter Dronke, the striking originality of her music is only now being demonstrated, both by musicological analysis and in performance.

The *Ordo virtutum,* included in some manuscripts as part of the *Symphonia,* has been called (by Bruce W. Hozeski) "the earliest morality play." In the play an errant soul wavers between the blandishments of the devil and a choir of virtues. It is possible that the play was performed by the nuns of Hildegard's convent at the dedication of the church at Rupertsberg in 1152.

Also belonging to this period are the enigmatic *Litterae ignotae* (Unknown Writing) and *Lingua ignota* (Unknown Language). The latter is a glossary of some nine hundred invented words (mostly nouns), thematically arranged. They include the names of plants and herbs and so may have been related to Hildegard's scientific interests. Although the invented alphabet is used occasionally for titles in her correspondence, her only use of the unknown language occurs in the *Symphonia.* One antiphon for the dedication of a church includes five words from the unknown language:

> O *orzchis* Ecclesia,
> armis divinis precincta
> et iacincto ornata,
> tu es *caldemia* stigmatum *loifolum*
> et urbs scientiarum.
> O, o, tu est etiam *crizanta*
> in alto sono
> et es *chortza* gemma.

Newman gives a literal translation: "O measureless Church, / girded with divine arms / and adorned with jacinth, / you are the fragrance of the wounds of nations / and the city of sciences. / O, O, and you

are anointed / amid noble sound, / and you are a sparkling gem." Whether Hildegard encouraged her nuns to speak this rather limited language with its Germanic-sounding vocabulary and Latinate syntax so as to communicate in secret, as some have suggested, has not been determined. The passing of secret messages might have been more feasible if they had used the *litterae ignotae,* Hildegard's alternative alphabet.

Hildegard's medico-scientific writings also date from these years. Such writings may reflect the fact that Benedictine monasteries at the time were often resorts of the sick and afflicted. Hildegard's *Subtilitates diversarum naturarum creaturarum* (The Subtleties of the Diverse Nature of Created Things, circa 1151–1158) has been preserved as two texts, the *Physica* (Natural History), also known as *Liber simplicis medicinae* (Book of Simple Medicine), and the *Causae et Curae* (Causes and Cures), also known as *Liber compositae medicinae* (Book of Compound Medicine).

The *Physica* consists of nine sections or books, the first and longest comprising accounts of more than two hundred plants. There follow books devoted to the elements (earth; water, including local German rivers; and air), trees, precious stones, fish, birds, mammals, reptiles, and metals. The medical uses of these objects are paramount, descriptions often being reduced to statements of their four cardinal properties – that is, whether they are hot, dry, wet, or cold. This lack of information makes some of the plants, especially those that only appear under German names, hard to identify today. For example, "Pruma valde calida est. Et qui leprosus est *Prumam* in manibus terat, et succum exprimat, et suo illo ubi leprosus est saepe liniat, et lepram mitigat. . . . Sed et flores ejus in butyro vaccarum coquat, et sic unguentem faciat, et saepe cum illo se ungat, et lepra minorabitur . . ." (Broom [?] is very hot. And let those suffering from leprosy squeeze broom in their hands and express the juice and often smear it on themselves where they are affected. . . . Or let them also cook up its flowers in butter to make an ointment and apply it frequently to themselves, and the sores will diminish).

The *Causae et Curae* consists of five sections of varying lengths. It proceeds from cosmology and cosmography to the place of humanity in the world. There follows a version of traditional humoral theory, although with some striking differences, which leads to a list of more than two hundred diseases or conditions to which humans are subject. The following two sections are concerned with cures for a selection of illnesses, using mostly herbal remedies, as foreshadowed in the *Physica*. The difference between the cures suggested in the *Physica* and those in the *Causae et Curae* is that in the latter there is some attempt to provide actual proportions for the ingredients used in the recipes. The final section includes discussions of uroscopy, cherries, and astrological prognostications (*lunaria*) according to the phase of the moon at the time of conception. Thus, "Qui in tricesima luna concipitur, si masculus est, pauper erit, et si nobilis est, semper ad inferiora descendet nec felicitatem habebit, et in corpore, viribus et carne facile deficit, sed satis diu vivet. Si vero femina est, pauper erit . . . et cum alienis hominibus libentius est quam cum notis; et non multum infirma in corpore erit et satis diu vivet" (Those conceived on the thirtieth day of the moon, if male will be poor and if noble will always descend to lower things and will not have happiness; they will easily fail in bodily strength and the flesh but will live quite a long while. Females will be poor . . . and will more willingly live among foreign folk than familiar ones; they will not be very weak in body and will live long enough).

Hildegard's production of such a variety of works in the 1150s can be seen as her response to the increased possibilities for autonomous action that she gained by the move to Rupertsberg. Ironically, her second great visionary work, *Liber Vitae Meritorum*, may owe more to the early difficulties she experienced as a result of the move to Rupertsberg than to the advantages she derived from it.

*Scivias* can be viewed, on one level, as an attempt to answer the question of how Christians should live their lives so as to reach the Heavenly City; the *Liber Vitae Meritorum* seems to be a deeper exploration of the same subject, dealing at length with the vices that beset the traveler on the way. This concentration on the negative side of human nature may have been uppermost in Hildegard's mind after the difficulties she had with some of the nuns who were dissatisfied with the move to Rupertsberg.

During this time she also suffered the defection, as she saw it, of Richardis von Stade, her friend and supporter in difficult times and her assistant in writing *Scivias*. Shortly after the move to Rupertsberg, Richardis, the sister of Archbishop Hartwig of Bremen, was appointed abbess of the convent of Bassum in Saxony. Despite Hildegard's protests (she appealed, as a last resort, to the pope), Richardis left to take up the position. Hildegard was only able to overcome her sense of betrayal when

Richardis died within a year of leaving Rupertsberg. On reflection Hildegard believed that she recognized God's hand in the affair and acquiesced in all that had happened.

In the *Liber Vitae Meritorum* the virtues are described, but more as a means of defining the corresponding vices than as a positive aid to overcoming them. The emphasis of the book is on future punishment and present penance as a way of avoiding or minimizing it. The work can be seen as an early contribution to the development of the theology of Purgatory that was to become so important a feature of the later Middle Ages.

The structure of this second visionary work is somewhat simpler than that of *Scivias*, with its series of apparently unrelated visions. The six visions of the *Liber Vitae Meritorum* are all variations on the same theme: the figure of a man superimposed on the world from the heavens to the abyss, who turns through the points of the compass and observes the various interactions between the powers of light and darkness. The methodology of this work resembles that of the later books of *Scivias* in that the boundary between the vision and its explication is not so clearly drawn as in the earliest visions. For instance, the punishments do not form part of the vision as first described but are introduced by some blanket justification such as "vidi et intellexi haec" (I saw and understood all this).

The *Liber Vitae Meritorum* covers a total of thirty-five vices and outlines the punishment and penance for each. Little prominence is given to the virtues, perhaps because they have already been described in some detail in *Scivias*. That the vices do not seem to be confined to those likely to be practiced by her nuns may reflect Hildegard's tendency, already seen in the *Physica*, for inclusiveness. Such a desire for encyclopedic completeness was common in medieval thought, as the many summae of the period attest. But some of the vices depicted, such as *tristitia saeculi* (worldly sadness), are mentioned in the *Vita Sanctae Hildegardis* as afflicting some of Hildegard's charges. The vice is described in the *Liber Vitae Meritorum*: "Quintam vero imaginem vidi, muliebrem forman habentem; ad cujus dorsum arbor stabat, quae tota arida sine foliis erat, et cujus ramis eadem imago implexa fuit. Nam ramus unus verticem capitis ejus obtexerat, et unus collum et guttur ejus circumdederat. Et unus circa dextrum brachium, unus circa sinistrum se extendit, ipsis tamen brachiis non expansis, sed ad se collectis, ac manibus ab eisdem ramis dependentibus. . . . Pedes autem illius lignei

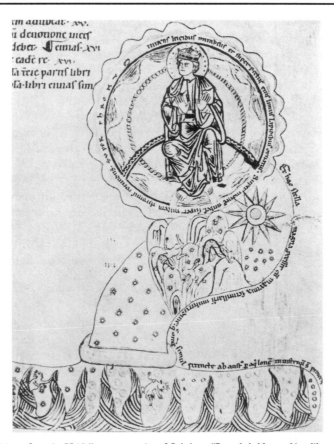

*Illustration of one of Hildegard's visions, from the Heidelberg manuscript of* Scivias: *"I . . . beheld something like an iron-colored stone of immeasurable size, above which a white cloud hovered. The cloud bore a throne of a round shape, on which a living being sat . . . on his breast coiled a black, immense band, set with pearls and priceless stones. And above the one seated on the throne . . . was stretched a golden ring that glowed with inner fire and reached from heaven down into hell. I saw glittering stars going out from the throne and countless sparks streaming together with them. Suddenly they were extinguished, and a gust of wind came that flung them widely about, finally even deep down into the abyss" (Heidelberg, Universitätsbibliothek, Cod. Sal. X, 16, fol. 111a).*

fuerunt. Alia autem indumenta non habebat, nisi quod hoc modo ramis circumdata fuit. Et maligni spiritus cum nigra nebula valde foetente venientes, ipsam invaserunt, ad quos gemendo se reclinabat" (I saw a fifth image in the form of a woman at whose back a tree was standing, wholly dried up and without leaves and by whose branches the woman was embraced. For one branch went around the top of her head, and another her neck and throat and one round her left arm and one to her right; her arms were not outstretched but held close to her body with her hands hanging down from the branches. . . . Her feet were of wood. She had no other clothes but the branches going around her. And wicked spirits coming with a very fetid black cloud swarmed over her, at which she lay down lamenting).

The explanation of the figure's attributes serves to emphasize the paralyzing effects of the vice. The sense of apathy and inability to turn either to the world or to God makes the condition sound rather like what today might be called clinical depression. The dry and lifeless tree (the symbolic opposite of all natural vitality and spiritual growth) oppresses the mind of the sufferer, preventing contrition. It constrains the neck and throat, thus preventing the assumption of the Lord's yoke or nourishment with the Food of Life. The branches hold the arms close to the body so they cannot be extended in the performance of secular or spiritual works. The blocklike feet indicate that such people do not follow the path of faith or hope. "Nullam viriditatem in viis suis habentes" (there is no greenness in their ways), as Hildegard puts it, using one of her favorite concepts. Finally, the figure is naked because "nulla gloria, nulla honestate decoratos" (it has no glory or goodness to adorn it). The evil spirits are to be taken literally, rather than symbolically; Hildegard believed in their existence and thought that they took advantage of people in such circumstances, entering into their bodies and manipulating them from within.

Around the time when she wrote the *Liber Vitae Meritorum,* Hildegard emerged even further into public life, embarking on a series of preaching tours. On the first, which took her along the river Main as far as Bamberg, she preached to monastic communities at Würzburg and Kitzingen. During her second tour in 1160 she took the highly unusual step (for a woman) of preaching in public at Trier, as well as visiting communities at Metz and Krauftal. On her third tour, undertaken sometime before 1163, she went north to Cologne and Werden; her fourth, in 1170, took her south to Zwiefalten.

In 1163 Hildegard began to write the final part of the theological trilogy, the *Liber Divinorum Operum,* considered by many to be her most impressive work. Fiona Bowie and Oliver Davies describe it as "a broad cosmological reflection on the Christian revelation from a profoundly anthropocentric point of view according to which men and women, who are themselves the 'work' of God, are called to co-operate actively with God in the perfection of his creation." Like *Scivias,* this work is divided into three parts; it comprises ten visions of varying lengths. The first book, which consists of the first four visions, deals with God's creation of the world, aided by *Charitas* (Love), and the privileged place of humanity within it. The second book, taken up by the fifth vision, develops the idea of humanity as the moral center of the world, faced with the ultimate judgment. The third book, incorporating the final five visions, is once again concerned with salvation history, especially the Incarnation and the end of time.

The central part of the work is Hildegard's meditation on the opening of Saint John's Gospel (in vision four). Although here the exegesis is virtually confined to the literal level, her subsequent commentary on the first book of Genesis in vision five interprets each verse literally; allegorically, as referring to the progress of the faith and the growth of the church; and tropologically or morally, as pertaining to the actions of the individual Christian. Her commentary on the words "And the earth was without form and void; and darkness was on the face of the deep," for example, begins with an explanation of the literal level of the text: "terra fuit inanis, scilicet forma carens, et invisibilis, lumen non habens, quia necdum splendore lucis, nec claritate solis, lunae aut stellarum illustrabatur, et inculta, quoniam nulla creatura sulcabatur, et vacua, id est incomposita, quia nondum plena erat, cum necdum viriditatem, germen, aut floriditatem herbarum, seu arborum haberet" (the earth was formless, that is to say, lacking form, and invisible, having no light because it was not yet illuminated by the splendor of light, nor the brightness of the sun, moon, or stars, and uncultivated because it had been tilled by no one, and void, that is, without order, because it was not yet full, as it did not yet have the greenness, promise, or burgeoning of plants or trees). The same passage receives an allegorical gloss: "Omnis populus, scilicet Judaicus et gentilis, qui super faciem abyssi, id est terram habitabat. . . . et caecus et surdus in agnitione Dei fuit, et vacuus a bonis operibus, quoniam ea secundum doctrinam Altissimi Filii non operabatur, donec ipse ad Patrem ascendit. Et sic super terram, quae facies abyssi est tenebrae infidelitatis erant, in qua homines Deum non cognoscentes quasi caeci vivebant" (All the people, that is, the Jews and Gentiles, who lived on the face of the deep, that is the earth . . . were blind and deaf to recognition of God, and empty of good works, since they did not live according to the teaching of the Son of the Highest, until he ascended to his Father. And thus on the earth, which is the face of the deep, was the darkness of unbelief, in which men lived, not recognizing God, as if they were blind). The tropological explanation follows: "Homo qui in moribus suis nunquam stabilis esse potest, magna inanitas est, quasi fluctuatio maris semper inundat. . . . tenebrosis factis quae ad pravos mores pertinent circumdatus est. . . . Et corpus quasi facies abyssi, anima autem velut abyssus est, quia corpus visibile et palpabile sicut facies abyssi, anima vero invisibilis et impalpabilis sicut abyssus terrae existit" (The person who can never be steadfast in behavior is quite formless and ever flooding like the sea. . . . surrounded by dark deeds which pertain to depraved actions . . . and the body is like the face of the abyss, the soul like the abyss, because the body is visible and palpable like the face of the deep, the soul invisible and impalpable).

While writing the *Liber Divinorum Operum* Hildegard also produced many letters, musical works, and other minor pieces. One was the *Vita Sancti Disibodi* (Life of Saint Disibod), written in 1170 at the request of Abbot Helenger and the monks of the parent house to supply an embarrassing lack of written evidence about their founder. She believed that by consulting her source of divine knowledge she was able to amplify whatever oral traditions had been preserved by the monastery.

Saint Disibod, despite various vicissitudes in his youth due to the rule of a tyrant in his native Ireland, maintained his devotion to religious studies and rose through the appointed grades to become a

*Illustration of Hildegard's vision of the Creation from the Lucca manuscript of her* Liber Divinorum Operum *(Lucca, Biblioteca Statale, Cod. lat. 1942, fol. 9)*

priest by the age of thirty. Later he was elected bishop, and he sought to instruct his flock in Christian ways. Schisms and apostasy were rife in Ireland, however, and after wrestling vainly for ten years with the intransigent populace he decided to take his missionary efforts elsewhere. On his travels through Germany he heard of Saint Benedict. (Since Benedict is described as having died only recently, Disibod's travels must be dated soon after 550.) After ten years he came on the wooded mountain at the junction of the Nahe and Glan that now bears his name and settled there as a hermit with three companions who had come from Ireland, Gillilaldus, Clemens, and Salustus. The fame of the hermits soon spread, and, having learned the language, Disibod began to preach the word and succor the poor and sick. He died there in the odor of sanctity thirty years later at the age of eighty. The rest of the life deals with the development of the

monastery and includes the detail that Disibod never actually became a member of the monastery he founded, preferring to maintain his eremitic way of life.

Jean Baptiste Pitra dates the *Vita Sancti Ruperti* (Life of Saint Rupert) to the years 1170 to 1173 as well, although it may have been written as early as the 1150s, as Newman suggests. On the other hand, it is not specifically mentioned in the preface to *Liber Vitae Meritorum,* which is generally taken to provide a summary of Hildegard's literary activity for the decade. In this short work Hildegard furnishes a history of the patron saint of her own convent and of his mother, who outlived him by many years. Sometime in the ninth century – her father is said to have flourished under Charlemagne – Bertha, a noblewoman and a devout Christian from the vicinity of Bingen, married a nobleman, Robold, whose faith was at best lukewarm. Widowed when their son, Rupert, was three, Bertha moved to Bingen. There she led a quasi-monastic life with a group of like-minded men, repelling many offers of marriage from the secular nobility. Bertha began to teach her son letters when he was age seven, although he wanted to be a Christian knight rather than a cleric. When he was twelve Rupert had the first of a series of prophetic dreams that resulted in his and Bertha's establishment of a hospice for the poor. There Rupert spent the next three years washing feet and making beds. Bertha and Rupert were assisted in the running of the establishment by a priest named Wigert and an unlettered man. Urged by relatives to lead a secular life, Rupert made a pilgrimage to Rome; returning, he redoubled his charitable works. At the age of twenty he fell ill with a fever and had a dream presaging his death, which occurred thirty days later. After his burial at Rupertsberg he worked many miracles. When Bertha died twenty-five years later she was buried in his tomb. Bingen was sacked by the "Normans" (that is, the Vikings) around 882, but the church where Rupert and Bertha were buried miraculously survived so that Hildegard could eventually reclaim the site for her convent.

Some of Hildegard's remaining minor works occur among her letters. Though it was common at the time for short treatises to take epistolary form, it is not clear that all were actually sent as letters. Hildegard's homilies on the Evangelists and the so-called epilogue to *Vita Sancti Ruperti,* probably delivered orally to the nuns at Rupertsberg, seem to have been subsequently written down and incorporated among the letters for want of a better place. On the other hand, the *Explanatio Symboli S. Athanasii* (Commentary on the Athanasian Creed) occurs in a letter to her own community; the *Explanatio Regulae S. Benedicti* (Commentary on the Benedictine Rule) was sent in response to a request from a German monastery; and her reply to the thirty-eight questions was directed to the monks of Villers.

Hildegard's correspondence dates from around the time of her recognition by the Synod of Trier and increases in volume and in variety of recipients until her death in 1179. More than three hundred of her letters survive, along with many letters written to her. The expectation that the letters will provide an insight into her inner thoughts and feelings is generally disappointed, however, partly because most medieval letters were intended for public consumption rather than being intimate expressions of emotion or thought. This aspect is heightened in Hildegard's case by the virtual eschewal of her own voice in preference to that of God. One of the few

exceptions is the exchange of letters relating to the move of Richardis von Stade. Another letter in which Hildegard reveals something of herself (though she declares that "Haec verba non a me . . . dico, sed ea ut in superna visione accepi profero" [The words come not from me . . . but as I received them in a vision from above]) is directed to Guibert of Gembloux, the Walloon monk who became her secretary in 1177. Some years before, he had written to Hildegard to inquire about the nature of her visionary powers. In her reply she describes how most of her knowledge comes from what she calls "umbra viventis luminis" (the shadow of the Living Light) but that sometimes, "in eodem lumine aliam lucem, que lux vivens michi nominata est, interdum et non frequenter aspicio, et quando et quomodo illam videam proferre non valeo, atque interim dum illam intueor, omnis tristicia et omnis angustia a me aufertur, ita ut tunc mores simplicis puelle, et non vetule mulieris, habeam" (in that light occasionally and infrequently I see another light, which I have been told is the Living Light, and I am unable to say when and how I see it, and while I apprehend it, all sadness and all pain is lifted from me, so that I feel like a simple girl again, and not an old woman).

In the preface to the *Liber Vitae Meritorum* Hildegard refers to her already substantial correspondence as "responsa et admonitiones" (replies and advice [or sermons]). In the manuscript known as the Riesenkodex her correspondence has been arranged in such a way as to pair requests for advice with Hildegard's responses, but other letters survive from which it seems that she sometimes gave unsolicited advice (to the emperor Frederick Barbarossa, for example) and also that she did not reply to every letter she received, as was the case with the importunate monks of Villers.

Many of the letters ask Hildegard in fairly nonspecific terms for messages of encouragement, admonition, or consolation, or simply for her prayers. Such requests came from people known to her, including her relatives, as well as from strangers. The reason such correspondents give for their faith in her help is her acknowledged gift of prophecy, in the medieval sense of being privy to God's secrets. Such, presumably, were the letters that prompted hers to Henry II of England and his queen, Eleanor of Aquitaine. Hildegard gives them general words of encouragement and admonition, indicating that the exchange took place well before the murder of Thomas Becket. She tells Henry: "Ad quemdam virum, quoddam officium habentem, Dominus dicit: Dona donationum tibi sunt, velut regendo, tegendo, protegendo, providendo, coelum habeas; sed nigerrima avis de Aquilone ad te venit, et dicit: Tu possibilitatem habes facere quodcumque volueris; fac ergo hoc et illud, et causam hanc et illam, quia tibi non est utile ut justitiam inspicias, quoniam si eam semper inspexeris, non est dominus, sed servus . . ." (To a certain man who holds a certain office, the Lord says: "Yours are the gifts of giving: it is by ruling and defending, protecting and providing, that you may reach heaven." But a bird of blackest hue comes to you from the North and says: "You are able to do whatever you want; so do this and do that; make this excuse and that excuse, for it does not profit you to have regard to Justice; for if you always consult her, you are not the master but the slave"). Sometimes, however, the narrower meaning of prophecy is assumed, as when Hildegard is asked to prognosticate on the course of an illness and the spiritual state of a husband: "O creatura Dei Luthgardis, dispone res tuas secundum necessitatem tuam, quia non video languorem viri tui ab eo recedere ante finem suum. Obsecra ergo, corripe et mone illum pro salute animae suae, quoniam multas tenebras in eo video . . ." (O Luitgard, God's creature, arrange your affairs according to your needs, because I do not see your husband's illness lifting before his end. Therefore, beg, correct and warn him for the safety of his soul, because I see much darkness in him . . . ). More-specialized concerns are to be found in an exchange of letters with the monks of Brauweiler concerning the exorcism of a young woman named Sigewize. Another group of letters addresses particular monastic concerns about the burdens of authority. There are also letters from various heads of houses who write about their desire to put aside their office for a simpler and more spiritual lifestyle.

Another series of letters charts the course of a dispute, which clouded the last year of Hildegard's life, concerning the burial of a young nobleman who had been excommunicated. Hildegard, believing that the sentence had been lifted before he died, allowed his burial at Rupertsberg. A few days later the clergy of Mainz ordered the body to be disinterred and cast out on pain of interdict. Hildegard, having consulted "the Living Light," was convinced that they were wrong but complied with the interdict, which meant refraining from singing the Divine Office and from receiving communion. In a letter to her superiors at Mainz she expounded the fundamental importance of music in the divine plan. After some further exchanges Hildegard prevailed, and the interdict was lifted. Thus, the final

months before her death in 1179 were spent peacefully at Rupertsberg, where full performance of the *Opus Dei* was restored. She has not been officially canonized by the Roman Catholic church, but her cult has local recognition.

In her letters, as in most of her other works, Hildegard's reforming mission is evident. Although she gave advice to lay and ecclesiastical figures, it can be seen that her chief concern was with reform of the clergy, since they were the ones on whom the leadership of the church and the teaching of the people depended. Indeed, she justified her prophetic role by claiming that in such disjointed times, when the world was hastening toward its end, the expected leaders and teachers had failed in their task. This was the reason that she, though a "paupercula forma" (poor weak woman), had been chosen to express God's will, whether in the extended and general form of her theological trilogy or more directly in sermons and letters.

Various events of the time gave credence to such a point of view. One such was the eighteen-year schism that began in 1159 when, on the death of Hadrian IV, two rival popes were elected. Hildegard's younger contemporary, Elisabeth of Schönau, supported (or said that God supported) Victor IV, recognized by Frederick Barbarossa; Hildegard favored Alexander III and grew increasingly disenchanted with the emperor for his support of a series of antipopes. Both visionaries linked the failure of the clergy to lead exemplary lives and to teach the people with the rise of heretical sects, notably Catharism; several of Hildegard's letters urge groups of clergy to preach against the heresy, which was gaining ground along the Rhine as well as in southern France. Some of Hildegard's more startling pronouncements on sexual matters may be seen as a response to the Catharist rejection of the body and denigration of sexuality.

Such considerations indicate the importance of viewing Hildegard's work in its historical context. Failure to do so has contributed to misreadings of Hildegard as an exponent of Creation Spirituality, environmentalism, or feminism. Hildegard's views are best understood in the context of her own times and of her entire oeuvre, rather than being selectively quarried to support currently popular positions. Such treatment ultimately diminishes, rather than enhances, her reputation. She is remarkable enough in her own right.

**Bibliographies:**

Werner Lauter, *Hildegard-Bibliographie I* (Alzey: Rheinhessischen Druckwerkstätte, 1970);

Lauter, *Hildegard-Bibliographie II* (Alzey: Rheinhessischen Druckwerkstätte, 1983).

**Biographies:**

"Vita Sanctae Hildegardis auctoribus Godefrido et
Theodorico monachis, " in *Sanctae Hildegardis
abbatissae Opera omnia,* volume 197 of *Patrologia Latina,* edited by Jacques-Paul Migne,
(Paris: Migne, 1855), cols. 91–130; translated by Anna Silvas as "Saint Hildegard of
Bingen and the *Vita Sanctae Hildegardis,*" *Tjurunga: An Australasian Benedictine Review,* 29
(1985): 22–25; 30 (1986): 63–73; 31 (1986):
32–41; 32 (1987): 46–59;

Monika zu Eltz, *Hildegard von Bingen* (Eibingen:
Abtei Sankt Hildegard, 1972);

Adelgundis Führkötter, *Hildegard von Bingen* (Salzburg: Müller, 1972);

Eduard Gronau, *Hildegard von Bingen 1098–1179:
Prophetische Lehrerin der Kirche an der Schwelle
und am Ende der Neuzeit* (Stein am Rhein:
Christiana, 1985);

Sabina Flanagan, *Hildegard of Bingen: A Visionary
Life* (London: Routledge, 1989);

Godfrey and Theodoric, *Vita Sanctae Hildegardis,*
edited by Monica Klaes, volume 126 of *Corpus Christianorum Continuatio Mediaevalis*
(Turnhout: Brepols, 1993).

**References:**

Fiona Bowie and Oliver Davies, *Hildegard of Bingen: An Anthology* (London: Society for the
Propagation of Christian Knowledge, 1990);

Anton Brück, ed., *Hildegard von Bingen, 1179–
1979: Festschrift zum 800 Todestag der Heiligen*
(Mainz: Selbstverlag der Gesellschaft für
mittelrheinische Kirchengeschichte, 1979);

Robert Cogan, "Hildegard's Fractal Antiphon,"
*Sonus,* 11 (1990): 1–19;

Peter Dronke, "The Composition of Hildegard of
Bingen's *Symphonia,*" *Sacris Erudiri,* 19 (1969–
1970): 381–393;

Dronke, "Hildegard of Bingen as Poetess and
Dramatist," in his *Poetic Individuality in the
Middle Ages* (Oxford: Clarendon Press,
1970);

Dronke, "Problemata Hildegardiana," *Mittellateinisches Jahrbuch,* 16 (1981): 97–131;

Dronke, *Women Writers of the Middle Ages: A Critical
Study of Texts from Perpetua († 203) to Margue-
rite Porete († 1310)* (Cambridge: Cambridge
University Press, 1984);

Pozzi Escot, "The Gothic Cathedral and Hidden
Geometry of St. Hildegard," *Sonus,* 5 (1984):
14–31;

Escot, "Hildegard von Bingen: Universal Propor-
tion," *Sonus,* 11 (1990): 33–40;

Sabina Flanagan, "Hildegard and the Global Possibilities of Music," *Sonus,* 11 (1990): 20–32;

Mary Ford-Grabowsky, "Angels and Archetypes:
A Jungian Approach to St. Hildegard," *American Benedictine Review,* 41 (March 1990): 1–
19;

Bruce W. Hozeski, "Hildegard of Bingen's *Ordo
Virtutum:* The Earliest Discovered Liturgical
Morality Play," *American Benedictine Review,*
26 (September 1975): 251–259;

Kathryn Kerby-Fulton, *Reformist Apocalypticism and
Piers Plowman* (Cambridge: Cambridge University Press, 1990);

Kent Kraft, "The German Visionary: Hildegard
of Bingen," in *Medieval Women Writers,* edited
by Katharina Wilson (Athens: University of
Georgia Press, 1984), pp. 109–130;

Kraft, "Hermetic Embodiment in Hildegard of
Bingen and William Blake," *Sonus,* 11
(1990): 41–52;

Hans Liebeschütz, *Das allegorische Weltbild der hl.
Hildegard von Bingen* (Leipzig & Berlin: Teubner, 1930);

Ruth Lightbourne, "The Question of Instruments
and Dance in Hildegard of Bingen's Twelfth
Century Music Drama *Ordo Virtutem,*" *Parergon,* 9 (1991): 45–67;

Janet Martin and Greta Mary Hair, "*O Ecclesia:*
The Text and Music of Hildegard of
Bingen's Sequence for St. Ursula," *Tjurunga:
An Australasian Benedictine Review,* 30 (1986):
3–62;

Constant J. Mews, "Heloise and Hildegard:
Re-visioning Religious Life in the Twelfth
Century," *Tjurunga: An Australasian Benedic-
tine Review,* 44 (1993): 20–29;

Irmgard Müller, *Die pflanzlichen Heilmittel bei Hildegard von Bingen* (Salzburg: Müller, 1982);

Barbara Newman, "Hildegard of Bingen: Visions
and Validation," *Church History,* 54 (June
1985): 163–175;

Newman, *Sister of Wisdom: St. Hildegard's Theology
of the Feminine* (Berkeley: University of California Press, 1987);

Michela Pereira, "Maternità e sessualità femmi-
nile in Ildegarda di Bingen: proposte di let-
tura," *Quaderni storici,* 44 (1980): 564–579;

Marianne Richert Pfau, "Mode and Melody Types in Hildegard von Bingen's *Symphonia*," *Sonus,* 11 (1990): 53–71;

Hildegard Ryan, "St. Hildegard and St. Bernard," *Tjurunga: An Australasian Benedictine Review,* 42 (1992): 16–28;

Oliver Sacks, *Migraine: The Understanding of a Common Disorder,* second edition (Berkeley: University of California Press, 1985), pp. 57, 106–108;

Heinrich Schipperges, *Die Welt der Engel bei Hildegard von Bingen,* second edition (Salzburg: Müller, 1979);

Miriam Schmitt, "Blessed Jutta of Disibodenberg," *American Benedictine Review,* 40 (June 1989): 170–189;

Bernhard W. Scholz, "Hildegard von Bingen on the Nature of Woman," *American Benedictine Review,* 31 (December 1980): 361–383;

Marianna Schrader and Adelgundis Führkötter, *Die Echtheit des Schrifttums der heiligen Hildegard von Bingen* (Cologne & Graz: Böhlau, 1956);

Charles Singer, "The Scientific Views and Visions of St. Hildegard (1098–1179)," in his *Studies in the History and Method of Science,* first series (Oxford: Oxford University Press, 1951), pp. 1–59;

Magna Ungrund, *Die metaphysische Anthropologie der hl. Hildegard von Bingen* (Münster: Aschendorff, 1938);

Lieven van Acker, "Der Briefwechsel der heiligen Hildegard von Bingen: Vorbemerkungen zu einer kritischen Edition," *Revue bénédictine,* 98 (1988): 141–168; 99 (1989): 118–154;

Bertha Widmer, *Heilsordnung und Zeitgeschehen in der Mystik Hildegards von Bingen* (Basel: Helbing & Lichtenhahn, 1955);

U. Wiethaus, "Cathar Influences in Hildegard of Bingen's Play *Ordo Virtutem,*" *American Benedictine Review,* 38 (June 1987): 192–203.

# Hrabanus Maurus

### (776? – 4 February 856)

### Brian Murdoch
*University of Stirling*

MAJOR WORKS: Biblical commentaries, encyclopedic works, works on church administration, theological writings, poems, hymns, letters, and sermons.

**Manuscripts:** There are many manuscripts of most of Hraban's works. Examples are Paris, Bibliothèque Nationale, Lat. 2399, 2440, 4860; Saint Gall, Cod. Sangall. 286, 878, 899; Vienna, Cod. Vindob. 1073; Amiens, Bibliothèque Municipiale, Cod. 223; Cambridge, Trinity College, B 16.3.

**First publication:** *Hrabani Opera,* 6 volumes, edited by George Colvenerius (Cologne: Hieratus, 1626–1627).

**Standard editions:** Jacques Paul Migne, ed., *Patrologia Latina,* volumes 107–112 (Paris: Migne, 1844–1864); in *Monumenta Germaniae Historica/Poetae Latini Medii Aevii/Poetae Latini Aevi Carolini,* volume 2, edited by Ernst Dümmler (Berlin: MGH, 1884), pp. 154–244; in *Monumenta Germaniae Historica/Epistola,* edited by Dümmler, volume 5 (Berlin: MGH, 1898), pp. 379–516.

**Editions in English:** Poems translated by Helen Waddell, in *Medieval Latin Lyrics* (Harmondsworth, U.K.: Penguin, 1952); translated by Peter Godman in *Poetry of the Carolingian Renaissance* (Norman: University of Oklahoma Press, 1985; London: Duckworth, 1985).

Magnentius Hrabanus Maurus (also known as Raban, Rabanus, and Rhabanus) acquired the final part of his name from his teacher, Alcuin, who gave it to him in honor of Saint Maur, the favorite pupil of Saint Benedict. He was of aristocratic birth; 776 is more likely as his date of birth than 784, which is sometimes given, and he was probably born in Mainz. He was educated first in the monastery founded by Saint Boniface at Fulda, which had become a major center of learning; he then went to Tours, where he studied under Alcuin, who had been Charlemagne's principal teacher. In Tours he came under the influence of the austere reforms of Benedict of Aniane. Early in the ninth century Hrabanus took over the school at Fulda, and he was ordained in 814. He left Fulda for a time, returned in 817, and on the death of Abbot Eigil he became abbot in 822. He retired in 842, in the troubled period of conflict after the death of Emperor Louis the Pious. Although Hrabanus supported Lothar, Louis's eldest son, after the empire was divided the new ruler of Germany, Lothar's brother Louis the German, made him archbishop of Mainz in 847. Hrabanus retained the post until his death on 4 February 856.

Hrabanus wrote an enormous amount of material, all of it in Latin. He followed in the footsteps of his celebrated teacher, Alcuin, in writing biblical commentaries and texts on church organization and education, which earned him the designation "praeceptor Germaniae" (teacher of Germany). His writings also include grammatical, theological, and encyclopedic works; homilies; letters; and poetry. Hrabanus was connected closely with most of the intellectual and literary figures in the church in his day; he was a close friend of the equally important churchman Grimald of Saint Gall, to whom he addressed an affectionate poem; more important, in his celebrated school at Fulda he taught Lupus of Ferrières, who developed an interest in classical literature in spite of some suspicions about such texts on Hrabanus's part, as well as Gottschalk of Orbais and Walahfrid Strabo, both considerable poets in Latin, and Otfried von Weißenburg, whose German *Evangelienbuch* (Gospel Book, between 863 and 871) acknowledges Hrabanus but had to be dedicated to Hrabanus's successor in the See of Mainz. Hrabanus resembles Grimald in his support and encouragement of other writers, although Grimald's literary remains are few and Hrabanus's voluminous. Hrabanus's thought is not particularly original, and in modern times the charge of plagiarism has been laid against him; in the Middle Ages, however, he was widely respected, and his works were copied time and again. He furthered the education of an important group of pupils; only his conflict with

*Hrabanus Maurus – led by his teacher, Alcuin – presenting his poem cycle* De laudibus sanctae crucis *to Saint Martin, bishop of Tours, and Hrabanus giving a copy of the work to Pope Gregory IV; miniatures in a pre-840 manuscript from the Fulda monastery (from Ewald Erb,* Geschichte der deutschen Literatur, *1965)*

Gottschalk "left one blot on [his] fair fame," according to M. L. W. Laistner, although Helen Waddell, who sees Gottschalk's heretical assertion of predestination to evil as a kind of proto-Calvinism, claims that the conflict between master and pupil was one between "two uncompromising idealists." In any case Hrabanus was, with Archbishop Hincmar of Rheims, heavily involved in the controversy over predestination and participated in the harsh treatment of Gottschalk because of the issue.

Although all of Hrabanus's own work is in Latin, he seems to have had some interest in the development of writing in the vernacular. The translation of the *Evangelienharmonie* (Gospel Harmony) of Tatian into German was probably undertaken in Fulda in his time. He also may be linked with Old High German glosses; and his pupil Otfried's *Evangelienbuch,* one of the most important works in Old High German, doubtless reflects Hrabanus's teaching. Before the appearance of Otfried's High German work and in Hrabanus's own lifetime, the Old Saxon *Heliand* (circa 850) used Hrabanus's commentary on the Gospel of Matthew.

Hrabanus's most extensive works are his biblical commentaries. He is one of the most prolific of the Carolingian exegetes, with commentaries on much of the Old Testament (including, somewhat unusually, some of the prophets) and on Matthew and the Epistles of Paul. These verse-by-verse explanations of the Bible are not original. Hrabanus, like his master, Alcuin, was a compiler, taking his interpretations from the writings of such accepted authorities as Ambrose, Augustine, Gregory the Great, Isidore of Seville, and

Bede and adding little of his own. Thus, the interpretation of the way the devil speaks through the serpent to tempt Eve in Hrabanus's *Commentaria in Genesim* is also found in Alcuin's and Bede's Genesis commentaries and derives ultimately from Augustine. Other Carolingian commentators use the same passage, and it appears regularly in later commentaries. This is not, of course, plagiarism in the modern sense, even though Hrabanus's sources regularly go unacknowledged; the technique of excerpting from the authoritative statements of the church fathers was quite usual. Hrabanus might well have been a mediator of religious ideas into German: his commentaries, like Alcuin's, enjoyed wide circulation in monastic libraries, and they have their reflection in early German religious prose and poetry not only in the *Heliand* and the *Evangelienbuch* but also in early Middle High German Old Testament poems, even if it is rarely possible to say with confidence that a poet writing in the vernacular used a specific commentary.

A similar lack of originality is clear in most of Hrabanus's other works; in the letter of dedication to an Irish monk, Macarius, attached to his *Liber de computo* (On Reckoning Time), written about 820, Hrabanus reports that he has taken much from the church fathers. His *Grammar,* similarly, comes largely from established authorities such as Priscian. So, too, his encyclopedic *De naturis rerum* (On the Nature of Things) – sometimes called *De universo* – is to a large extent a rearrangement and reworking of the much-read seventh-century encyclopedia by Isidore of Seville, the *Etymologies.* But, again, this work must not be judged by modern standards; what Hrabanus is trying to do, according to Rosamond McKitterick, is to "provide a complete dossier of learned opinion on a given subject."

Equally unoriginal, and once again indebted to Alcuin's influence, is Hrabanus's *De institutione clericorum* (On Clerical Education), which is compiled largely from Augustine's *On Christian Doctrine,* Gregory the Great's *Pastoral Rule,* and works by Isidore and Bede. It is a handbook on ecclesiastical hierarchy, on monastic education, and on preaching, and in it Hrabanus comments on the reading of Christian poets such as Arator, Juvencus, and Avitus – the same writers mentioned by Otfried in his dedicatory letter to the *Evangelienbuch.* On the other hand, Hrabanus was somewhat cautious about the reading of non-Christian classical writers. In a letter he noted that, although they might be seen as grist for the mill, anything that was not specifically Christian in such writers should be erased from the mind. Other theological writings of his include tractates on liturgy, church history, and ecclesiastic discipline; works on the soul and on the virtues and the vices; and polemics against Jewish beliefs and against magic.

Hrabanus's own poems follow at least the forms and meters of classical Latin poetry in that they are almost exclusively quantitative. Criticisms have been leveled at the prose and verse style of the Carolingians, including Hrabanus, as mannered and imitative; however justified this observation may be in general, many of Hrabanus's poems, which are often occasional or dedicatory, are stylized and even repetitious. Sometimes, however, glimpses of Hrabanus come through. In an early dedicatory poem to Abbot Eigil, for example, he declares his love for the written word, which alone can mock fate and defy death. Only one poem in rhythmic verse is certainly by him: the hundred-strophe hymn *De fide catholica* (On the Catholic Faith); the well-known hymn *Veni creator spiritus* (Come, O Creator) is incorrectly attributed, however, though often found under his name. He was, therefore, at least familiar with the rhythmic and rhyming patterns of the so-called Ambrosian hymn, used with clear rhyme and rhythm by Irish writers in particular.

Hrabanus's most complex work, *De laudibus sanctae crucis* (In Praise of the Holy Cross, circa 819), is impossible to define in modern terms. It belongs to the category of the so-called *opus geminatum* (double work) in that it contains a cycle of twenty-eight poems on the cross plus prose commentaries on the poems and a dedication. But the poems include figures and cross shapes within shapes, and the counting of individual letters is used as a structural principle. In the manuscripts the prose and verse parts are laid out side by side. The work is dedicated to Pope Gregory IV, and Hrabanus, who revised the work often, gave copies of it to various prominent men, including Louis the Pious. The number of later copies indicate its popularity. Hrabanus was influenced by Alcuin and other members of the intellectual circle around Charlemagne, who also wrote figure poems. They, in turn, were influenced by Porfyrius, who wrote at the court of Constantine the Great in the fourth century and specialized in the shape poems that would reappear in the Baroque period in Germany and in the twentieth-century *calligramme;* and Hrabanus influenced Otfried's initial and inner acrostics, his telestichs, and his play with line counts, which appear most noticeably in the dedicatory poems of the *Evangelienbuch.* Hrabanus's work is a tour de force of art and artificiality to which it is difficult to respond today. The preface, for example, has thirty-six lines, each with thirty-six letters, and includes a pattern that spells out the thirty-six-letter phrase "Magnentius Hrabanus Maurus hoc opus fecit" (Magnentius Hrabanus Maurus wrote this work).

Most critics agree that the substance of Hrabanus's poems is not profound – Max Manitius sums it up as "viel Worte und wenig Gedanken" (many words and few thoughts). Though his own works are all in Latin, Hrabanus was in support of Charlemagne's and Alcuin's view that basic prayers and sermons should be made known in German, and he notes in some of his theological writings liturgical formulas such as the *Abrenuntiatio* (baptismal vow) that are known also in German. In his brief tract *De inventione linguarum* (On the Creation of Languages) he lists various alphabets; most of these are derived from the works of Isidore and of less well known writers, but he adds the Runic alphabet. He shows an interest in etymology and in linguistic borrowing. His own activities regarding the German language are difficult to quantify and have been confused by the attachment of his name in a manuscript to a shortened version of the glossary in *Abrogans* (circa 790–800), once known as the *Hrabanisches Glossar,* even though it was written at about the time he was born. If the Old High German translation of Tatian's gospel harmony was made at Fulda it would have been under Hrabanus's abbacy, although there are no specific links between Hrabanus and that work. That the Old High German *Petruslied* (Song of Peter, circa 850) appears at the end of a manuscript of Hrabanus's Genesis commentary is, of course, entirely coincidental. Hrabanus does insert a few German words into his writings, but his real influence on German language and literature is probably indirect: as the teacher who provided Otfried with ideas on form and content; as the com-

*Ninth-century manuscript for the poem dedicating* De laudibus sanctae crucis *to the emperor Louis the Pious. The basic poem consists of fifty-one lines of thirty-seven letters each. The superimposed picture of the emperor encloses certain letters and directs the reader's eye to them in a particular order, forming a second poem that explains the allegorical meaning of the picture (Amiens, Bibliothèque Municipale, Cod. 223, fol. 3v).*

mentator who influenced the *Heliand* and other works; and, perhaps, as the promoter of the Tatian translation. His influence on Latin writers in his school – Lupus, Walahfrid Strabo, and perhaps Gottschalk – also has to be taken into account, even if Hrabanus himself was too cautious in his approach to the classics and too wooden a poet to play much of a part in the Carolingian Renaissance.

Prolific as he was, then, Hrabanus was not an original thinker, and he was not a poet of the first rank. Besides being an able administrator, however, he was a teacher who seems to have inspired a diverse group of scholars and poets. Perhaps above all else he was a compiler and gatherer. In one of his poems, a dedicatory foreword to his treatise on virtues and vices, he uses the image of picking flowers and says: "Collectoris enim nomen si noscere quaeris, Maurus dicor ego" (If you want to know the name of the collector, I am called Maurus). Hrabanus remained well known and influential for many centuries; his works were still being copied during the Renaissance and were among the earliest to be printed. Dante placed him in Paradise in one of the two circles of twelve luminaries that surround the poet and Beatrice, in the exalted company of Saint Anselm and Saint Bonaventure.

**References:**

Linda Archibald, "*Cur scriptor theotisce dictaverit*," Ph.D. dissertation, University of Stirling, 1988, pp. 191–200;

Erich Auerbach, *Literary Language and Its Public in Late Latin Antiquity and in the Middle Ages,* translated by Ralph Manheim (London: Routledge & Kegan Paul, 1965);

Georg Baesecke, "Hrabans Isidorglossierung, Walahfrid Strabus und das ahd. Schrifttum," in his *Kleinere Schriften,* edited by Werner Schröder (Bern & Munich: Francke, 1966), pp. 7–37;

Ewald Erb, *Geschichte der deutschen Literatur* (Berlin: Volk und Wissen, 1965);

Peter Godman, "Louis 'the Pious' and His Poets," *Frühmittelalterliche Studien,* 19 (1985): 240–289;

Godman, *Poets and Emperors: Frankish Politics and Carolingian Poetry* (Oxford: Clarendon Press, 1987);

J. B. Hablitzel, *Hrabanus Maurus* (Freiburg: Herder, 1906);

Paulus Ottmar Hägele, *Hrabanus Maurus als Lehrer und Seelsorger nach dem Zeugnis seiner Briefe* (Fulda: Parzeller, 1972);

Wolfgang Haubrichs, *Die Anfänge,* volume 1/i of *Geschichte der deutschen Literatur,* edited by Joachim Heinzle (Frankfurt am Main: Athenaeum, 1988);

Wolfgang Kleiber, *Otfrid von Weißenburg* (Bern & Munich: Francke, 1971);

Paul Klopsch, "Prosa und Vers in der mittellateinischen Literatur," *Mittellateinisches Jahrbuch,* 3 (1966): 9–24;

Herbert Kolb, "Isidors 'Etymologien' in deutscher Literatur des Mittelalters," *Archiv,* 205 (1968–1969): 431–453;

Raymund Kottje, "Hrabanus Maurus," in *Die deutsche Literatur des Mittelalters – Verfasserlexikon,* volume 4, second edition, edited by Kurt Ruh (Berlin: De Gruyter, 1978), pp. 166–196;

Kottje, "Hrabanus Maurus – Praeceptor Germaniae?," *Deutsches Archiv für die Erforschung des Mittelalters,* 31 (1975): 534–545;

Kottje and Harald Zimmermann, eds., *Hrabanus Maurus: Lehrer, Abt, Bischof* (Wiesbaden: Steiner, 1982);

M. L. W. Laistner, *Thought and Letters in Western Europe AD 500–900* (London: Methuen, 1957);

Max Manitius, *Geschichte der lateinischen Literatur des Mittelalters,* volume 1 (Munich: Beck, 1911), pp. 288–302;

Rosamond McKitterick, *The Frankish Kingdoms under the Carolingians, 751–987* (London: Longman, 1983);

Robert E. McNally, *The Bible in the Early Middle Ages* (Westminster, Md.: Newman, 1959);

Friedrich Neumann, "Lateinische Reimverse Hrabans," *Mittellateinisches Jahrbuch,* 2 (1965): 55–62;

F. J. E. Raby, *A History of Christian-Latin Poetry,* second edition (Oxford: Clarendon Press, 1953), pp. 179–183;

Bruno Reudenbach, "Das Verhältnis von Text und Bild in 'De laudibus sanctae crucis' des Hrabanus Maurus," in *Geistliche Denkformen in der Literatur des Mittelalters,* edited by Klaus Grubmüller, Ruth Schmidt-Wiegand, and Klaus Speckenbach (Munich: Fink, 1984), pp. 282–320;

Maria Rissel, *Rezeption antiker und patristischer Wissenschaft bei Hrabanus Maurus* (Bern & Frankfurt am Main: Lang, 1976);

Ingeborg Schröbler, "Fulda und die althochdeutsche Literatur," *Literaturwissenschaftliches Jahrbuch der Görres-Gesellschaft,* 1 (1960): 1–26;

Werner Schröder, *Grenzen und Möglichkeiten einer althochdeutschen Literaturgeschichte* (Berlin: Akademie, 1959);

Burkhard Taeger, *Zahlensymbolik bei Hraban, bei Hincmar – und im Heliand?* (Munich: Beck, 1970).

# Hrotsvit of Gandersheim

(circa 935 – circa 1000)

Katharina Wilson
*University of Georgia*

MAJOR WORKS: *Maria, Ascensio, Gongolf, Pelagius, Theophilus, Basilius, Dionysius, Agnes, Gallicanus, Dulcitius, Calimachus, Abraham, Paphnutius, Sapientia, Carmen de Gestis Oddonis Imperatoris, Primordia Coenobii Gandeshemensis* (973)

**Manuscripts:** The most complete text of Hrotsvit's works is preserved in the Emmeram-Munich Codex, Munich, Bayerische Staatsbibliothek, clm 14485 1–150. This is also the oldest extant copy of her works, dating to the early eleventh century. The manuscript is believed to have been produced at Gandersheim. The first four dramas are preserved in a manuscript of miscellaneous texts in the Cologne Stadtarchiv, cod. w 101, 1–16 and were copied toward the end of the twelfth century, probably from a prototype other than the Emmeram-Munich Codex. A late-twelfth-century copy of *Gallicanus* was incorporated into the *Alderspach Passionale,* Munich, Stadtarchiv clm 2552.

**First publication:** *Opera Hrosvite,* edited by Conrad Celtis (Nuremberg: Printed by Hieronymus Höltzel, 1501).

**Standard editions:** *Hrotsvithae Opera,* edited by Paul von Winterfeld (Berlin: Weidmann, 1902); *Hrotsvithae Opera,* edited by Helena Homeyer (Munich, Paderborn & Vienna: Schöningh, 1970).

**Edition in English:** *The Plays of Hrotsvitha von Gandersheim,* translated by Larissa Bonfante (New York: New York University Press, 1979).

Long considered to be out of the mainstream of early Germanic authors, Hrotsvit of Gandersheim (also known as Hrotsvit, Hrotswitha, and Roswitha) has now been placed firmly in the tradition of medieval Benedictine spirituality. While her hagiographic plays are without precedent in tenth-century European literature, her efforts at the didactic utilization of hagiography are not. In fact, Hrotsvit's dramatization of legendary materials bears testimony to the prominent role that hagiographic *lectiones* played in the Benedictine office.

All that is known of Hrotsvit's biography has to be gleaned from her dedicatory letters and prefaces. She was probably born in the fourth decade of the tenth century, is likely to have been of noble Saxon descent, lived as a canoness in the Imperial Abbey of Gandersheim under Gerberga II's rule, and probably died at the turn of the millennium. It is evident from her work that she considered the eremetic life – that is, total solitude in worship – and martyrdom as the two most privileged manifestations of Christian devotion. Her plays *Paphnutius* and *Abraham* reflect a particularly German brand of monastic eremetism, the custom of "Klausner" (hermits) and "Klausnerinnen" (female hermits), a practice whereby religious people did not live in a monastery but walled up alone, in a cell without doors, next to a convent or church. Martyrdom is celebrated in her dramas *Dulcitius* and *Sapientia* and in her legends *Pelagius, Dionysius,* and *Agnes;* in all but one of the five treatments of martyrdom the saint dies not only as an eloquent witness to the faith but in preserving his or her virginity from attempted seduction by male antagonists.

Hrotsvit's works consist of eight legends, six plays, two epics, and a short poem. In the principal manuscript the works are organized chronologically and generically into three books. They fall into three clearly marked creative periods, the breaks occurring after the fourth legend and the fourth play.

Book 1, comprising the legends, begins with a preface and a dedication to Hrotsvit's abbess, Gerberga II. The first legend, *Maria,* is a treatment of the Virgin's life based on an apocryphal source, the *Pseudo-Evangelium of Mattheus.* In the exordium Hrotsvit introduces her major theme: the exaltation of the virtue of virginity. *Maria* narrates Mary's childhood, her stay at the temple, her reluctance to marry, the selection by God of Joseph as her husband, the immaculate conception, and, finally, her

*Woodcut by Albrecht Dürer for the first publication of Hrotsvit of Gandersheim's works (1501). Hrotsvit is shown presenting her writings to the emperor Otto I and the archbishop of Mainz.*

motherhood. Mary's glorification is entirely Christocentric – her chastity and exemplary conduct are subordinated to her role as Jesus' mother, and the poem closes with a prayer to Christ. Hrotsvit's second legend, *Ascensio,* the shortest of her works, is drawn from a Greek source describing the ascension of Christ into Heaven. The third legend deals with the eighth-century Frankish knight Gongolf, who lived under Pépin the Short. Gongolf is a meek, courteous, wise, and chaste knight. His magnanimity and virtue are a source of envy for the devil, who uses his favorite weapon, sexuality, to plot the saintly Gongolf's destruction. Gongolf's wife, crazed with lust for a cleric, not only commits adultery but also instigates her husband's murder. She suffers for the deed and for her lack of contrition by means of a scatological miracle: an involuntary fart whenever she opens her mouth. Hrotsvit's fourth legend is based not on a written source but on an eyewitness report. It describes the martyrdom of the chaste Pelagius, a tenth-century Spanish saint who died persevering against the homosexual advances of the caliph of Cordoba, Abderrahman III. The fifth and sixth legends, *Basilius* and *Theophilus,* are the first literary treatments of the Faust legend in Germany: both concern men who make a pact with the Devil and sell their immortal souls for earthly gain. The sinners are saved at the intercession of Bishop Basilius and the Virgin Mary, respectively. Both legends present the themes of fall and conversion, sin and salvation; both show the unlimited power of prayer and contrition, which are rewarded by divine forgiveness. The seventh legend describes the martyrdom of Dionysius, the first bishop of Paris, and the last glorifies Saint Agnes, martyr for virginity, who rejects an earthly suitor in favor of the Heavenly Bridegroom and resists, with Christ's help, the ignominious attempts of her adversaries to defile her chastity when she is punished by being placed in a brothel. At the conclusion of her earthly sufferings, Christ awaits his virginal bride in the celestial bridal chamber, which Hrotsvit depicts in glowingly ecstatic passages.

The second book, Hrotsvit's most important and most original creation, comprises her plays. The book is introduced by a dedication to Gerberga, followed by a prose letter to the learned patrons of the book (sometimes identified as Gerberga's former teachers at Saint Emmeram). *Gallicanus* deals with the conversion and martyrdom of the title character, a pagan Roman general. He has been promised the hand of Constantia, Emperor Constantine's daughter, if he wages a successful war against the Scythians. Constantia, however, has taken the vow of chastity. Through divine intervention and the assistance of Saints Paul and John, Gallicanus becomes a Christian and renounces marriage. Like Constantia, he devotes the rest of his life to religion. *Dulcitius* takes place during the Diocletian persecutions of the Christians and dramatizes the martyrdom of the virgin sisters, Agapes, Chionia, and Hirena, who refuse to give up their faith and their chastity. The executioner, Dulcitius, is a philandering pagan who imprisons the girls in a room adjacent to the pantry so that he may visit them undisturbed at night. The girls spend the hours in prayer. When Dulcitius tries to seduce the virgins, a miracle happens: he is deluded so that he mistakes the pots and pans for the sisters, embraces and kisses them, and emerges so smeared and blackened with soot that his soldiers mistake him for the Devil and chase him from the palace. This instance of medieval kitchen humor is also an excellent example of the visualization of themes: external appearance is a reflection of the internal state; Dulcitius, whose soul is possessed by the Devil, appears as the *imago diaboli* in body.

*Calimachus* depicts the sin and subsequent conversion of a pagan youth. Calimachus is passionately in love with Drusiana, who has taken the vow of chastity. Learning of Calimachus's violent passion, Drusiana prays for death so as to avoid temptation, and she dies. Ablaze with lust, Calimachus bribes Fortunatus, the tomb guard, in a desperate attempt at necrophilia. Before he can profane Drusiana's body, however, he and Fortunatus both die. They are resurrected by Saint John, and Calimachus is converted to Christianity. Calimachus vividly exemplifies the Christian paradox that to live, one has to die to the world.

*Paphnutius* and *Abraham* again treat the themes of fall and conversion. In each play a harlot is con-verted by a saintly anchorite and subsequently lives an ascetic life. In *Paphnutius* the courtesan Thais is converted by a saintly hermit who aspires to this task as the result of a vision, while in *Abraham* the hermit is the courtesan's uncle and former guardian. The recognition scene between the aged Abraham, posing as a customer, and his niece Mary in the brothel has evoked special praise for Hrotsvit's talent as a dramatist. Finally, *Sapientia* deals with the martyrdom of the three allegorical virgins Fides (Faith), Spes (Hope), and Caritas (Charity), who, like the heroines of *Dulcitius,* willingly face death on earth so that they may earn eternal life in heaven. *Paphnutius* and *Sapientia* commence with dialogue lessons in music and mathematics, respectively: in *Paphnutius* the saintly hermit expounds on the mysteries of the celestial harmonies to his disciples, while in *Sapientia* the mother of the three virgins confounds the pagan emperor with her Boethian exposition of numerical values. In almost all of Hrotsvit's plays women show true heroism while men are the villains — and, what is worse, pagans. Book 2 concludes with a poem of thirty-five hexameters on the Apocalypse that is believed to have been intended for inscription under the twelve murals at Gandersheim.

Book 3 contains the two extant epics, the *Carmen de Gestis Oddonis Imperatoris* (Deeds of Emperor Otto), or *Gesta,* and the *Primordia Coenobii Gandeshemensis* (Origins of the Abbey of Gandersheim). The *Gesta* has been called one of the most successful tenth-century attempts at a Christian epic. The emperor Otto the Great is depicted as the ideal Christian ruler, a descendant of King David. He is the earthly representative of the heavenly king, deriving his just power from God; by implication, insurrection against him (and there were more than a few during Hrotsvit's lifetime) is the work of the Devil. Among the female characters of the *Gesta,* Otto's queens Edith and Adelheid stand out as paragons of feminine excellence who are described in the superlatives of the hagiographic tradition.

The *Primordia* presents the history of the Gandersheim abbey from its founding until the death of Abbess Christina in 918. The *Primordia* is replete with hagiographic topoi, legendary characters whose exemplary lives are reminiscent of the heroes and heroines of Hrotsvit's legends and dramas, miracles, and visions. The work also manifests a strong political tendency: any part that the Hildesheim bishops played in the foundation of the abbey is conspicuously ignored; rather, emphasis is placed on the role of the Liudolf family in establishing an autonomous religious house that is to be entirely in-

*The opening lines of Hrotsvit's legend* Maria *in the Emmeram-Munich Codex (Munich, Bayerische Staatsbibliothek, clm 14485, fols. 3v–4r)*

dependent of the jurisdiction and influence of the Hildesheim bishops.

The organization of the three books shows Hrotsvit to be a master of symmetry and balance. The themes and motifs of the first book are repeated in a different genre in the second; in the legends men predominate, while in the dramas women do; and the themes of the legends and dramas are transferred to a historical context in the third book.

Hrotsvit viewed the process of creating her works as an ordering, patterning, and arranging of her sources, as she says in her prefatory texts. This process is analogous to her description of God's act of creation as one of ordering according to number, measure, and weight. Evidently Hrotsvit considered the creative act, human or divine, to consist of establishing order and harmony in the organization of materials. A pronounced feature of her works is her fondness for linkage, which exists on the literal, metaphoric, and thematic levels; it occurs between lines and segments of the same work, between works of the same genre, and between works of different genres. The more pronounced correspondences exist between groups of works dealing with similar themes: the hagiographic legends and dramas, on the one hand, and the historical epics, on the other. The initial linkage between the legends and the dramas is effected by Agnes, the heroine of the final legend, at whose grave and at whose intercession Constantia, the heroine of the first drama, is healed from the double evil of leprosy and paganism. The dramas are linked by double treatments of plots: *Dulcitius* and *Sapientia* deal with the persecution and martyrdom of three allegorical sisters; *Abraham* and *Paphnutius* share the fall and conversion theme; *Gallicanus* and *Calimachus* center on the theme of conversion. The two epics, *Carmen de Gestis Oddonis Imperatoris* and *Primordia Coenobii Gandeshemensis,* concern members of the Saxon dynasty in their roles as secular rulers (*Gesta*) and religious rulers and benefactors (*Primordia*). The thirty-six-line hexameter poem on the Apocalypse of Saint John links the legends and dramas, which are hagiographic in theme and liturgical in language, on the one hand, and the epics, which are heroic and historic in theme and more secular in language, on the other, by showing Saint John as the patron saint of Gandersheim and the inspiration for the abbey's founding.

The four treatments of the fall and conversion theme in the legends *Theophilus* and *Basilius* and the plays *Abraham* and *Paphnutius* all exemplify the doctrine of heavenly grace for the repentant sinner. In the legends men sell their immortal souls to the Devil; in the dramas women sell their bodies to men. In all four treatments sinners are helped by a member of the opposite sex; this person is related to the sinner in two of the works and unrelated in the other two. In *Basilius* the servant's wife asks Bishop Basilius's help for the miserable sinner; in *Abraham* Maria's uncle sets out on the long journey to reclaim his lapsed niece. In *Theophilus* the Virgin Mary intercedes for the repentant Theophilus; in *Paphnutius* the saintly hermit of the desert seeks out and converts the famous courtesan Thais.

The four works dealing with martyrdom exemplify a reversal of the sexes of the protagonists: Pelagius and Dionysius are male martyrs; the heroines of *Dulcitius* and *Sapientia* are young girls. The sex of the persecutors, however, does not vary: all four are male pagan rulers. All four plots involve the persecution of Christians by pagans; all four contain miracles of Christ's aid to his witnesses. *Pelagius* and *Dulcitius* introduce subplots dealing with illicit love and heroically resisted seduction; in both, the protagonists' chastity is contrasted with the antagonists' promiscuity. Furthermore, in both *Dionysius* and *Sapientia* the persecution is triggered by the protagonists' missionary activity. In *Dionysius* Domitian is angered because his subjects flock to the bishop to be baptized; in *Sapientia* Antiochus is outraged because, following Sapientia's preachings on the importance of abstinence, wives no longer share their husbands' tables and beds.

*Gongolf* and *Agnes,* exemplifying the remunerative and punitive aspects of divine justice, correspond to *Gallicanus* and *Calimachus. Calimachus,* like *Gongolf,* treats of a married saint – Gongolf and Drusiana are the only married saints in Hrotsvit's legends and dramas; both of them, however, have celibate marriages. Both plots involve adulterous lust and the deaths of the protagonists because of their illicit passion. In *Calimachus,* however, Drusiana is miraculously resurrected, and Calimachus is converted at her grave, while Gongolf's adulterous wife persists in her iniquity. Again, the sexes of the protagonists in the legend are reversed in the drama: Gongolf dies because of the guiles of his adulterous wife and her lover; Drusiana is pursued by a handsome but lustful youth.

*Agnes* and *Gallicanus* both concern the preservation of the heroine's virginity and her vow to the

Heavenly Bridegroom. In both works the offer to be avoided is of honorable marriage; likewise, in both plots the would-be lovers or husbands are later converted and bear testimony for Christ the Savior. This is the only instance of a double treatment of a theme where the gender roles are not reversed: the preservation of virginity appears to be a paradigmatically female virtue. In three of the four treatments of the theme the protagonists become the catalysts of salvation for their would-be lovers or husbands. In *Gongolf,* the only version with a male protagonist, however, the catalytic role does not succeed but exacerbates the wife's iniquity.

While the linkages of the epics to the legends and dramas are less pronounced, they do exist. The historical persons of the two epics are idealized and romanticized so that they resemble the hagiographic heroes and heroines of the legends and plays. Otto I, hero of the *Gesta,* is the ideal Christian ruler. He is the pious, benevolent, and diplomatic hero, resembling Gongolf and the emperor Constantine of *Gallicanus* and marked, as they are, by his justice and mercy, and Otto's characteristics, like those of Gongolf, Pelagius, and Dionysius, link him with God and the saints. In the *Primordia* Gerberga is the living embodiment of the love of chastity and of the resolute and unchanging will that faces the temptations of the world. Like Agnes, Mary, and Constantia, Gerberga also refuses to marry her bridegroom, Bernhard, because she has taken a secret vow of chastity. Oda, ancestress of the Liudolf dynasty, is the shining example of virtuous motherhood. Like Sapientia, she survives the deaths of her daughters (except for Christina), all of whom she encourages in their religious endeavors.

Hrotsvit's protagonists in all her works are the saints of Christianity and of the Liudolf dynasty, the family of her abbess and her emperor. Her texts advocate adherence to the monastic ideal and confirm that truth is recognizable, absolute, eternal, and imitable.

## References:

Joseph von Aschbach, "Roswitha und Conrad Celtis," *Sitzungsberichte der Philosophisch-Historischen Klasse der Wissenschaften,* 56 (1867): 3–62;

Josef Bendixen, *Das Älteste Drama in Deutschland oder: Die Komödien der Nonne Hrotsvitha von Gandersheim,* 2 volumes (Altona: Hammerich & Lesser, 1850, 1853);

Barbel Bentner, "Der Traum Abrahams," *Mittellateinisches Jahrbuch,* 9 (1973): 22–30;

Sister Mary Bernardine Bergman, "Hrotsvithae Liber Tertius: A Text with Translation, Intro-

*Scene from Hrotsvit's play* Sapientia, *as performed in January 1955 by the Mercy College Players at the Lydia Mendelssohn Theatre, University of Michigan (from Sister Mary Marguerite Butler,* Hrotsvitha: The Theatricality of Her Plays, *1960)*

duction, and Commentary," Ph.D. dissertation, Saint Louis University, 1942;

Walter Berschin, "Passio und Theater: Zur dramatischen Struktur einiger Vorlagen Hrotsvits von Gandersheim," in *The Theatre in the Middle Ages,* edited by Hermann Braet, Johann Nowe, and Gilbert Tournoy (Louvain: Louvain University Press, 1985);

David Brett-Evans, *Von Hrotsvit bis Folz und Gengenbach: Eine Geschichte des mittelalterlichen deutschen Dramas* (Berlin: Schmidt, 1975);

Sister Mary Marguerite Butler, *Hrotsvitha: The Theatricality of Her Plays* (New York: Philosophical Library, 1960);

David Chamberlain, "Musical Learning and Dramatic Action in Hrotsvit's *Pafnutius,*" *Studies in Philology,* 77 (Fall 1980): 319–343;

Cornelia C. Coulter, "The 'Terentian' Comedies of a Tenth Century Nun," *Classical Journal,* 24 (April 1929): 515–529;

Rolf Denecke, "Die dichtende Nonne von Gandersheim: Zur Eröffnung des Roswitha Jahres," *Der Literat,* 15 (1973): 131;

Franz Dolger, "Die Ottonenkaiser und Byzanz," in *Karolingische und Ottonische Kunst,* edited by Hermann Aubin and others (Wiesbaden: Steiner, 1957), pp. 49–59;

Erhard Dorn, *Der sündige Heilige in der Legende des Mittelalters* (Munich: Fink, 1967);

Peter Dronke, *Women Writers of the Middle Ages: A Critical Study of Texts from Perpetua (203) to Marguerite Porete (1310)* (Cambridge: Cambridge University Press, 1984);

Reinhard Duchting, "Hrotsvitha von Gandersheim, Adam Wernher von Themar und Guarino Veronese," *Ruperto Carola,* 33 (1963): 77–89;

Eleanor S. Duckett, *Death and Life in the Tenth Century* (Ann Arbor: University of Michigan Press, 1967);

Gerhard Eis, *Die Quellen des Martenbuches* (Reichenberg: Sudetendeutscher Verlag, 1932);

Sebastian Euringer, "Drei Beiträge zur Roswitha Forschung," *Historisches Jahrbuch der Goerres-Gesellschaft zur Pflege der Wissenschaft im Katholischen Deutschland,* 54 (1934): 75–83;

Heinrich Fichtenau, "Rhetorische Elemente in der Ottonisch-salischen Herrscherurkunde," *Mitteilungen des Institutes für Österreichische Geschichtsforschung,* 69 (1960): 39–60;

A. Daniel Frankforter, "Hroswitha von Gandersheim and the Destiny of Women," *Historian,* 12 (February 1979): 295–314;

Frankforter, "Sexism and the Search for the Thematic Structure of the Plays of Hroswitha of Gandersheim," *International Journal of Women's Studies,* 2 (May–June 1979): 221–232;

Goswin Frenken, "Eine neue Hrotsvithandschrift," *Gesellschaft für ältere deutsche Geschichtskunde,* 44 (1922): 75–83;

Giulia Gatti, "Una autrice italiana alla ricerca di Rosvita," *Rassegna Mensile di Teatro,* 8–9 (Summer 1982): 10–15;

Hans Goetting, "Die Anfänge des Reichstifts Gandersheim," *Braunschweigisches Jahrbuch,* 31 (1950): 5–52;

Otto Grashof, "Das Benedictinerinnenstift Gandersheim und Hrotsvitha die 'Zierde der Benediktinerordens,' " *Studien und Mitteilungen ausdem Benedictiner und Cistercienser Orden,* 6 (1885): 303–322; 7 (1886): 87–109, 393–404;

Anne Lyon Haight, *Hrotsvitha of Gandersheim: Her Life, Times, and Works, and a Comprehensive Bibliography* (New York: Hroswitha Club, 1965);

Zoltán Haraszti, "The Works of Hrotsvitha," *More Books,* 20 (1945): 37–119, 139–173;

Mary Pia Heinrich, *The Canonesses and Education in the Early Middle Ages* (Washington, D.C.: Catholic University Press, 1924);

Helena Homeyer, *Hrotsvitha von Gandersheim* (Munich: Schoningh, 1973);

Homeyer, " 'Imitatio' und 'Aemulatio' im Werk der Hrotsvitha von Gandersheim," *Studi Medievali,* 10 (1968): 966–979;

Bruce Hozeski, "The Parallel Patterns in Hrotsvitha of Gandersheim, a Tenth-Century German Playwright, and in Hildegard of Bingen, a Twelfth-Century German Playwright," *Annuale Medievalia,* 18 (1977): 42–53;

Eril Barnett Hughes, "The Theme of Beauty in Hrotswitha's *Pafnutius* and *Sapientia,*" *Publications of the Arkansas Philological Association,* 9 (Spring 1983): 56–62;

Boris Jarcho, "Stilquellen der Hrotsvitha," *Zeitschrift für deutsches Altertum und deutsche Literatur,* 62 (1925): 236–240;

Jarcho, "Zu Hrotsvithas Wirkungskreis," *Speculum,* 2, no. 2 (1927): 343–344;

K. J. Keyser, *Rule and Conflict in an Early Medieval Society: Ottonian Saxony* (Bloomington: Indiana University Press, 1979);

Rudolf A. Köpke, *Die älteste deutsche Dichterin* (Berlin: Mittler, 1869);

Köpke, *Hrotsvit von Gandersheim* (Berlin: Mittler, 1869);

Dennis M. Kratz, "The Nun's Epic: Hroswitha on Christian Heroism," in *Wege der Worte: Festschrift für Wolfgang Fleischhauer,* edited by Donald E. Riechel (Cologne: Bohlau, 1978), pp. 132–142;

Kurt Kronenberg, *Roswitha von Gandersheim: Leben und Werk* (Bad Gandersheim: Hertel, 1962);

Hugo Kuhn, "Hrotsvits von Gandersheim dicterisches Programm," *Deutsche Vierteljahrschrift,* 24 (1950): 181–196;

Roger S. Loomis and Gustave Cohen, "Were There Theatres in the Twelfth and Thirteenth Centuries?," *Speculum,* 20 (1945): 92–98;

Kenneth de Luca, "Hrotsivit's 'Imitation' of Terence," *Classical Folia,* 28, no. 1 (1974): 89–102;

Anton Mayer, "Der Heilige und die Dirne," *Bayrische Blätter für das Gymnastische Schulwesen,* 67 (1931): 73–80;

Hermann Menhardt, "Eine unbekannte Hrotsvitha-Handschrift," *Zeitschrift für deutsches Altertum und deutsche Literatur,* 62 (1925): 233–236;

Erich Michalka, "Studien über Intention und Gestaltung in den dramatischen Werken Hrotsvits von Gandersheim," inaugural dissertation, Heidelberg University, 1968;

Bert Nagel, *Hrotsvit von Gandersheim* (Stuttgart: Metzler, 1965);

Nagel, "Roswitha von Gandersheim," *Ruperto Carola,* 33 (1963): 1–40;

Friedrich Neumann, "Der Denkstil Hrotsvits von Gandersheim," in *Festschrift für Hermann Heimpel,* volume 3 (Göttingen: Vandenhoeck & Ruprecht, 1972), pp. 37–60;

Paul Pascal, ed., *Hrotsvitha: Dulcitius and Abraham,* Bryn Mawr Commentaries (Bryn Mawr, Pa.: Thomas Library, 1985);

Mario N. Pavia, "Hrotsvitha of Gandersheim," *Folio: Studies in the Christian Perpetuation of the Classics,* 3 (1948): 41–45;

Karl Plenzat, "Die Theophiluslegende in den Dichtungen des Mittelalters," *Germanische Studien,* 43 (1926): 1–263;

Fritz Preissl, *Hrotsvith von Gandersheim und die Entstehung des mittelalterlichen Heldenbildes* (Erlangen: Palm & Enke, 1939);

Marcella Rigobon, *Il Teatro e la Latinita di Hrotsvitha* (Florence: Olschki, 1930);

Arthur J. Roberts, "Did Hrotsvitha Imitate Terence?," *Modern Language Notes,* 16 (December 1901): 239–241;

*The end of* Dulcitius *and the beginning of* Calimachus *in a late-twelfth-century manuscript for four of Hrotsvit of Gandersheim's plays (Cologne Stadtarchiv, cod. w 101, 1, fol. 8r)*

Dieter Schaller, "Hrotsvit von Gandersheim nach tausend Jahren," *Zeitschrift für deutsche Philologie,* 96 (1977): 105–114;

Margot Schmidt, "Orientalischer Einfluß auf die deutsche Literatur: Quellengeschichtliche Studie zum *Abraham* der Hrotsvit von Gandersheim," *Colloquia Germanica,* 2 (1968): 152–187;

Rolf Schulmeister, *Aedificatio und Imitatio: Studien zur intentionalen Poetik der Legende und Kunstlegende* (Hamburg: Lüdke, 1971);

Marianne Schütze-Pflugk, *Herrscher und Märtyrerauffassung bei Hrotsvit von Gandersheim* (Wiesbaden: Steiner, 1972);

L. Spitz, *Conrad Celtis the German Archhumanist* (Cambridge, Mass.: Harvard University Press, 1957);

Rosemary Sprague, "Hroswitha: Tenth Century Margaret Webster," *Theatre Annual,* 13 (1955): 16–31;

Sandro Sticca, "Drama sacro e realismo comico nel treato medioevale tedesco e francese (X–XII secoli): Da Hrotswitha di Gandersheim al Mystere d'Adam," in *L'Eredita Classica nel Medioevo: Il Linguaggio Comico* (Viterbo: Centro di Studi sul Teatro Medioevale e Rinascimentate, 1979);

Sticca, "Hrotswitha's *Dulcitius* and Christian Symbolism," *Mediaeval Studies,* 32 (1970): 108–127;

Sticca, *The Latin Passion Play: Its Origins and Development* (Albany: State University of New York Press, 1970);

Sticca, "Sacred Drama and Comic Realism in the Plays of Hrotswitha of Gandersheim," in *Acta VI: The Early Middle Ages,* edited by William Synder (Binghamton: Center for Medieval and Early Renaissance Studies, State University of New York, 1979);

Sticca, "Sacred Drama and Tragic Realism in Hrotswitha's *Pafnutius,*" in *The Theatre in the Middle Ages,* edited by Hermann Braet, Johann Nowe, and Gilbert Tournoy (Louvain: Louvain University Press, 1985);

Sticca, "Sin and Salvation: The Dramatic Context of Hrotswitha's Women," in *The Roles and Images of Women in the Middle Ages and Renaissance,* edited by R. R. Radcliff-Umstead (Pittsburgh: University of Pittsburgh Publications, 1975);

P. Ambros Sturm, "Das quadrivium in den Dichtungen Roswithas von Gandersheim," *Studien und Mitteilungen zur Geschichte den Benedictiner Ordens und seiner Zweige,* 33 (1912): 331–338;

Rudolf Vey, *Christliches Theater im Mittelalter und Neuzeit* (Aschaffenburg: Pattlock, 1960);

Hans Walther, *Hrotsvit von Gandersheim* (Bielefeld: Velhagen & Klasing, 1931);

Katharina Wilson, "Antonomasia as a Means of Character-Definition in the Works of Hrotsvit of Gandersheim," *Rhetorica,* 2 (Spring 1984): 45–53;

Wilson, *The Dramas of Hrotsvit of Gandersheim* (New York: Garland, 1987);

Wilson, "Ego Clamor Validus: Hrotsvit and Her Poetic Program," *Germanic Notes,* 14, no. 2 (1983): 17–18;

Wilson, "Hrotsvit and the Artes: Learning ad Usum Meliorem," in *Creativity, Influence, and Imagination: The World of Medieval Women,* edited by Constance Berman, Charles Connell, and Judith Rothchild (Morgantown: University of West Virginia Press, 1985), pp. 3–13;

Wilson, *Hrotsvit of Gandersheim: The Ethics of Authorial Stance* (Leiden: Brill, 1988);

Wilson, "Hrotsvit's *Abraham:* A Lesson in Etymology," *Germanic Notes,* 16, no. 1 (1985): 2–4;

Wilson, " 'Pelagius' and Calimachus," in *Medieval Women's Visionary Literature,* edited by Elizabeth Avilda Petroff (New York: Oxford University Press, 1986), pp. 114–135;

Paul von Winterfeld, *Deutsche Dichter des Lateinischen Mittelalters* (Munich: Beck, 1922);

Karl A. Zaenker, " 'Eyne hübsche Comedia Abraham genant': Hrotsvits von Gandersheims Abraham in der Übersetzung des Adam Werner von Themar," *Mittellateinisches Jahrbuch,* 17 (1982): 217–229;

Edwin Zeydel, "The Authenticity of Hrotsvitha's Works," *Modern Language Notes,* 69 (1946): 50–55;

Zeydel, "A Chronological Hrotsvitha Bibliography through 1700, with Annotations," *Journal of English and Germanic Philology,* 46 (1947): 290–294;

Zeydel, "Ekkehard's Influence upon Hrotsvitha – A Study in Literary Integrity," *Modern Language Quarterly,* 6 (September 1945): 333–339;

Zeydel, "Knowledge of Hrotsvitha's Works Prior to 1500," *Modern Language Notes,* 59 (June 1944): 382–385;

Zeydel, "On the Two Minor Poems in the Hrotsvitha Codex," *Modern Language Notes,* 60 (June 1945): 373–376.

# Lupus of Ferrières

## (circa 805 – circa 862)

### Brian Murdoch
### *University of Stirling*

MAJOR WORKS: Letters, text-critical work, works on theology and meter, *Vita Wigberti* (836), revision of the *Vita Sancti Maximini*

**Manuscript:** The letters are collected in a ninth-century manuscript from Ferrières, Paris, Bibliothèque Nationale, Lat. 2858.

**First publication:** In *Opera Stephanus Balzius,* edited by Etienne Baluze (Antwerp: F. Muquet, 1664).

**Standard editions:** *Opera Omnia,* volume 119 of *Patrologia Latina,* edited by Jacques-Paul Migne (Paris: Migne, 1852), pp. 427–700; "Vita Wigberti," edited by O. Holder-Egger, in *Monumenta Germaniae Historica/Scriptores,* volume 15/1 (Berlin: MGH, 1887), pp. 1–126; letters edited by Ernst Dümmler, in *Monumenta Germaniae Historica/Epistolae,* volume 6 (Berlin: MGH, 1925), pp. 1–126; *Loup de Ferrières: Correspondance,* 2 volumes, edited by Léon Levillain (Paris: Association Guillaume Bude, 1927, 1935; reprinted, Paris: Société d'édition "Les Belles Lettres," 1964).

**Editions in English:** *The Letters of Lupus of Ferrières,* translated by Graydon W. Regenos (The Hague: Nijhoff, 1966); excerpts translated by Peter Edward Dutton, in his *Carolingian Civilization* (Peterborough, Ont.: Broadview Press, 1993), pp. 425–433.

Servatus Lupus of Ferrières spent much of his time in France and wrote nothing in German that has survived, but his role in German literature and culture, though small, is significant. He was born in Sens around 805; his mother, Frotildis, was a West Frank and his father, Antelm, a Bavarian; the German name *Wulf* presumably lies behind *Lupus,* and the name by which he is often known, Servatus, was added later. He entered the monastery at Ferrières, but around 828 he was sent to the monastery school at Fulda to study under Hrabanus Maurus. Lupus maintained an interest in the German language and may have written in it; in one of his letters he also affirmed the value of the Frankish (French) vernacular. All of his extant works, however, are in Latin. Being at Fulda between 829 and 836 placed him in contact not only with the scholar Hrabanus, whom he much admired, but also with Walahfrid Strabo, possibly Otfried von Weißenburg, and especially Gottschalk of Orbais, who became his friend. Lupus's theological writings, the *Liber de tribus quaestionibus* (Book of Three Questions) and the subsequent *Collectaneum de tribus quaestionibus* (Supporting Extracts from the Fathers on the Three Questions), are related to the controversy that surrounded Gottschalk and his condemnation for heresy on the concept of predestination. Lupus's views on the subject support, to an extent, those of his unfortunate friend, though they are expressed with less force and are overtly closer to the thought of Saint Augustine.

Lupus made other important contacts in Fulda and at the court of Emperor Louis the Pious, most notably the historian Einhard. He copied and brought together a group of Germanic legal codes, and at the request of the abbot of Hersfeld he composed a prose life (836) of the founder of that monastery, Saint Wigbert, in which he invokes such classical historians as Livy and Sallust. Later in 836 he returned to Ferrières, where he devoted himself to literary studies — manuscript collecting, copying for purposes of text establishment, and developing his interest in classical literature. He also edited, probably about 839, the life of Saint Maximin of Trier. His work in collating and copying classical writings — perhaps his chief contribution to cultural history — has caused him to be designated the most significant Carolingian humanist.

After the death of Louis the Pious in 840, Odo, the abbot of Ferrières, supported Lothar, the nominal emperor. Odo was removed from office by Charles the Bald and replaced by Lupus, who was close both to Charles and to his mother, Empress Judith. Lupus turned Odo out of the monastery, justifying his action on grounds of self-preservation.

INCIPIT DE ORATO
RE LIBER:
PRIMUS

Cogitanti mihi saepenumero
et memoria uetera repetenti, perbea
ti fuisse quinte frater illi uideri
solent. qui in optima re publica cum
et honorib: et rerum gestarum glo
ria florerent. eum uitae cursum
tenere potuerunt. ut uel in negotio cum
dignitate esse possent, ac fuit quod
mihi quoque: initium requiescendi
atque animum ad utriusque nostrum
preclara studia referendi fore
iustum et prope ab omnib: concessum
arbitrarer. si infinitus forensi
um rerum labor et ambitionis occu
patio, cursu honorum etiam aetatis
flexu constitisset; quam spem cogi
tationum et consiliorum meorum cum
graues communium temporum tum
uarii nostri casus fefellerunt; namque qui
locus quietis et tranquillitatis
plenissimus fore uidebatur. in eo maxi

me molestiarum et turbulentissi
mae tempestates exciterunt. neque: si
nobis cupientib: atque optantib:
frui ei otio datum est. ad eas artes
quib: a pueris dediti fuimus cele
brandas in neque: colendas. nam
prima aetate incidimus in ipsam per
turbationem disciplinae ueteris et
et consulatu deuenimus in medium
rerum omnium certamen atque di
scrimen. et totum hunc locum pur omne poste con su
latum obiecimus fluctib: qui pro
nos a communi peste depulsi. in
nosmet ipsos redundarent. sed
tamen in eis asperitatib: rerum
uel angustiis temporis. obsequar
studiis nostris. et quantum mihi
fraus inimicorum, tua causa ami
corum tres publicae tribuet otii ad scri
bendum potissimum conferam, tibi
uero frater neque: hortanti deero.
neque: roganti. nam neque: auctori
tate quisquam apud me plus ualere
te potest neque: uoluntate. Ac m

*First page of Lupus's scribal copy of Cicero's* De oratore *(British Library, Harley ms. 2736)*

As abbot, Lupus attended church synods at which he played a part in the drafting of decrees. He spent time at Charles's court and was occasionally also involved (as he mentions in a letter of 844) in military campaigns, in which he suffered considerably. For his students he produced a small document on the meters used by Boethius.

The main works for which he is remembered are the more than 130 letters he wrote throughout his life to various notables and intellectuals and to others who were less well known. There are letters to the pope, to an Anglo-Saxon abbot in York, to Wanilo of Sens, to his contacts in Germany, and to friends about whom nothing further is known. They are valuable as historical documents and provide insights into Lupus's thoughts on language and literature – primarily Latin, but also German. After his death, circa 862, Lupus's letters were collected, perhaps by his pupil Heiric.

Max Manitius has referred to Lupus as "keinen bedeutenden Schriftsteller" (not a significant writer) because he did not take much part in theological controversy but was a text-critical scholar, philologist, and book collector. His theological writings and saints' lives are not of great significance, but his letters, editorial work, and copying of classical and Christian texts are of major importance. As far as his role in early German literature is concerned, it is known from one letter that he was interested in the German language and may have copied texts in it. His name has been linked with the translation from Latin into German of Tatian's *Evangelienharmonie* (Gospel Harmony, circa 830) and with the so-called *Pariser Gespräche* (Paris Conversation Book), in which phrases from that translation appear.

His literary and editorial work – copying, correcting, collating, helping to establish versions, and preserving classical texts – is extensive, and several manuscripts have been identified as his. In many of his letters he requests the loan of texts to copy; for example, he asks Pope Benedict III for a manuscript of Cicero's *De oratore* and Quintilian's *Institutiones;* he had already asked Einhard for a copy of the former work, and his reference to this text underscores his interest in classical rhetoric. He also sought copies of works by other classical writers and seems to have read the writings of Virgil, Livy, Sallust, Suetonius, Julius Caesar (whose histories did not impress him), and Boethius; other rhetorical works; and the Latin versions of the works by the Greek historian Josephus. Often he looked for second and third copies of texts to collate. In a letter he asked his friend Abbot Markward of Prüm to get him from Fulda the archetype copy of Suetonius's *Twelve Caesars;* they sent him a different copy. Books were valuable and were given to important people as gifts, and Lupus promises to take care of the books – especially when he knew them to be rare – and to return them. In one well-known passage he worries about sending a particularly valuable manuscript because it could not easily be hidden from robbers.

Some of his letters are rich in philological detail: he discusses the pronunciation, scansion, and meaning of Latin words and wonders about Greek words – he did not know that language. In a letter to Einhard (whose Latin style he much admired), written in Germany between 829 and 836, he says that a love of letters is innate in him and that the pursuit of knowledge alone was always enough to sustain him. In spite of Erich Auerbach's complaint that Lupus is never precise in the pictures he gives of his relationships, his letters do bring him and his age to life for the modern reader, especially when he discusses practical matters ranging from the activities of the Frankish royal house to the yield of wine for a given year or presents of fish. In a letter to an otherwise unknown person named Immo he responds to the question of what books he read while he was in Germany, accusing Immo of trying to make him look either vain or stupid depending on his reply; mostly he studied theology, he says, but he did get hold of a few books in German. In a letter written in July 844 Lupus tells his friend Abbot Markward of the monastery of Prüm that he is sending three young men of good birth to him "propter Germanicae linguae nanciscendam scientiam" (to learn German). Lupus clearly thought it important for the ruling class of the divided Frankish kingdoms to be bilingual.

Lupus, then, is important as an early humanist and transmitter of classical literature. He expresses occasional moral reservations about the classics, following his teacher, Hrabanus, and Hrabanus's teacher, Alcuin, but he affirms the need for aesthetic appreciation of literature. His letters are important and readable historical documents about the Carolingian period. Even in the context of German studies Lupus is of significance. Given his Franco-German background he presumably learned German early, and certainly his studies at Fulda, the major center of German learning, reinforced his knowledge of the language; and throughout his life he maintained close connections with Germany and with German scholars such as Einhard. The partition of Verdun in 843, leading eventually to the emergence of France and Germany as nation-states, came in the middle of his life, but he remains within the Latin internationalism of the intellectual – that is, largely the ecclesiastical – class of his day.

## Biography:
F. Sprotte, *Biographie des Abtes Servatus Lupus von Ferrières* (Regensburg: Manz, 1880).

## References:
Erich Auerbach, *Literary Language and Its Public in Late Latin Antiquity and in the Middle Ages,* translated by Ralph Manheim (London: Routledge & Kegan Paul, 1965);

Georg Baesecke, "Die Karlische Renaissance," in his *Kleinere Schriften,* edited by Werner Schröder (Bern & Munich: Francke, 1966), pp. 377–445;

Baesecke, *Die Überlieferung des althochdeutschen Tatians* (Halle: Niemeyer, 1948), pp. 10–12;

Charles Henry Beeson, *Lupus of Ferrières as Scribe and Text Critic: A Study of His Autograph Copy of Cicero's "De oratore"* (Cambridge, Mass.: Medieval Academy of America, 1930);

Wolfgang Haubrichs, *Die Anfänge,* volume 1/1 of *Geschichte der deutschen Literatur,* edited by Joachim Heinzle (Frankfurt am Main: Athenaeum, 1988);

Haubrichs, "Zur Herkunft der altdeutschen (Pariser) Gespräche," *Zeitschrift für deutsches Altertum,* 101 (1972): 86–103;

Haubrichs and Max Pfister, *In Francia fui* (Stuttgart: Steiner, 1989), pp. 6–11;

M. L. W. Laistner, *Thought and Letters in Western Europe AD 500–900* (London: Methuen, 1957);

Rosamond McKitterick, *The Carolingians and the Written Word* (Cambridge: Cambridge University Press, 1989);

McKitterick, *The Frankish Kingdoms under the Carolingians, 751–987* (London: Longman, 1983);

Max Manitius, *Geschichte der lateinischen Literatur des Mittelalters,* volume 1 (Munich: Beck, 1911), pp. 483–490;

Renate Schipke, "Eine von Lupus von Ferrières korrigierte Handschrift," in *Studien zur Buch- und Bibliotheksgeschichte. Hans Lülfing zum 70. Geburtstag,* edited by Ursula Altmann and Hans-Erich Teitge (Berlin: Deutsche Staatsbibliothek, 1976), pp. 33–38;

Emmanuel von Severus, *Lupus von Ferrières: Gestalt und Wert eines Vermittlers antiken Geistesgutes an das Mittelalter im IX. Jahrhundert* (Münster: Aschendorff, 1940).

# Notker Balbulus
## (circa 840 – 912)

### Linda Archibald
*Liverpool John Moores University*

MAJOR WORKS: *Gesta Caroli* (after 883)

**Standard edition:** Edited by H. F. Haefele, in *Monumenta Germaniae Historica, Scriptores rerum Germanicarum,* new series 12 (1959).

**Edition in English:** Translated by Lewis Thorpe, in *Two Lives of Charlemagne* (Harmondsworth, U.K.: Penguin, 1969).

*Vita Sancti Galli* (883–884)

**Standard edition:** Edited by Karl Strecker, in *Monumenta Germaniae Historica Poetae,* volume 4 (Berlin: Weidmann, 1923), pp. 1093ff.

*Liber Hymnorum* (884–887)

**Manuscripts:** Paris, Bibliothèque Nationale, lat. 10587 (circa 881–887); Saint Gall 484 (late tenth century).

**Standard editions:** In *Patrologia Latina,* 221 volumes, edited by Jacques-Paul Migne (Paris: Migne, 1841–1879), CXXXI: 1005–1026; *Liber Hymnorum,* edited by Wolfram von den Steinen (Bern & Munich: Francke, 1960).

*Martyrologium* (896)

**Manuscripts:** Munich 5256; Munich 22058; Saint Gall, Stiftsbibliothek, 456 and 620.

**Standard edition:** In *Patrologia Latina,* 221 volumes, edited by Jacques-Paul Migne (Paris: Migne, 1841–1879), CXXXI: 1029–1164.

*De illustribus viris* (date unknown)

**Standard editions:** In *Patrologia Latina,* 221 volumes, edited by Jacques-Paul Migne (Paris: Migne, 1841–1879), CXXXI: 993–1004; "Notkers des Stammlers *Notatio de Illustribus Viris* I: Kritische Edition," edited by Erwin Rauner, *Mittellateinisches Jahrbuch,* 21 (1986): 34–69.

Notker Balbulus (the Stammerer), known also as Notker I and Notker Poeta, is not to be confused with Notker II, also called Notker Medicus or Physicus (the Doctor), who died in 975, or the illustrious Notker III, also called Notker Labeo (of the Lip) and Notker Teutonicus (the German), who died in 1022. Notker Balbulus wrote in Latin and is remembered for his contribution to the development of the medieval *sequentia* (sequence) genre. He also wrote chronicles and hymns.

Notker was born of a noble family in Elgg, Switzerland, not far from the monastery of Saint Gall, around 840. His father died young, and Notker was brought up by Adalbert, who had fought with Charlemagne's army against the Saxons and Slavs. At the age of five or six he was placed in the Saint Gall monastery for safekeeping and education. Notker's teacher in these early days was Werinbert, one of the two Saint Gall monks to whom Otfried von Weißenburg's *Evangelienbuch* (Gospel Book, between 863 and 871) was dedicated. Other teachers were Iso and Moengal (also known by his Latin name, Marcellus), both of whom were renowned for their learning and their ability to teach a broad liberal-arts curriculum. From Moengal, Notker learned the liberal arts; he was particularly fascinated by music, and his early sequences were sung by the monks at Saint Gall.

Notker was not a healthy child, and throughout his life he avoided traveling far from the area around Saint Gall. He did visit Reichenau to exchange manuscripts and consult with monks at that monastery. His early and flattering biographer, Ekkehard IV, stresses that Notker's stammering was due to a physical defect and not to a mental one. Notker was loved by his pupils and admired for his mild manner and commitment to learning.

Many manuscripts testify to the activities of Notker Balbulus, but there are difficulties in separating his work from that of his pupils and later admirers. Notker probably began his writing career while he was still a student, and some of his hymns and sequences no doubt have their origin in this early period. His *Martyrologium* (896) is an updated version of Ado's martyrology that includes excerpts from the works of Hrabanus Maurus. Notker made sure that the saints of Ireland and Great Britain were included, as well as those of the German-speaking lands.

*Notker Balbulus at his desk; a miniature painted in 1024 (Deutsche Staatsbibliothek, Berlin)*

Notker's tasks in the library at Saint Gall included copying and updating historical texts, collating biblical materials, writing chronicles, and composing original works of prose and poetry for use within the monastery. Much of his work was directed at his pupils: he summarized and simplified complex texts and ideas for the benefit of those in his schoolroom.

Notker was asked to write down the stories and legends surrounding Charlemagne, and he did so in the *Gesta Caroli* (Deeds of Charlemagne) soon after a visit by Charles III to Saint Gall in 883. Memories of the great empire were still much discussed, particularly in the courts of Charlemagne's descendants, who were having great difficulty keeping their separate parts of the inheritance intact. None of the many surviving manuscripts of this work contain the number of chapters announced by Notker, leading to the suspicion that he never finished the work.

Notker's *Vita Sancti Galli* (Life of Saint Gall, 883–884) is preserved in an even more fragmentary

fashion: late manuscript fragments and printed editions preserve only the first book, and the second and third books survive only in fragments. The work reflects the schoolteacher's concerns even above those of the historian and scholar. It takes the form of a dialogue between Notker and his pupil Hartmann, who died in 884. Teacher and pupil alternate, speaking in both verse and prose. It appears that Notker and Hartmann actually wrote the work together, making it a dialogue in the true sense. The form of the work is unusual, and the inventiveness of the verse sections rather radical, for a saint's life. In later centuries the more traditional dialogues of Alcuin and the straightforward saints' lives of other writers appear to have been preferred, and Notker's work was not much used.

Notker's greatest achievement, apart from his lifelong teaching activities, is undoubtedly his development of the sequence genre. His *Liber Hymnorum* (Hymnbook) is a collection of these pieces, written from 884 to 887 and dedicated to Liutward, bishop

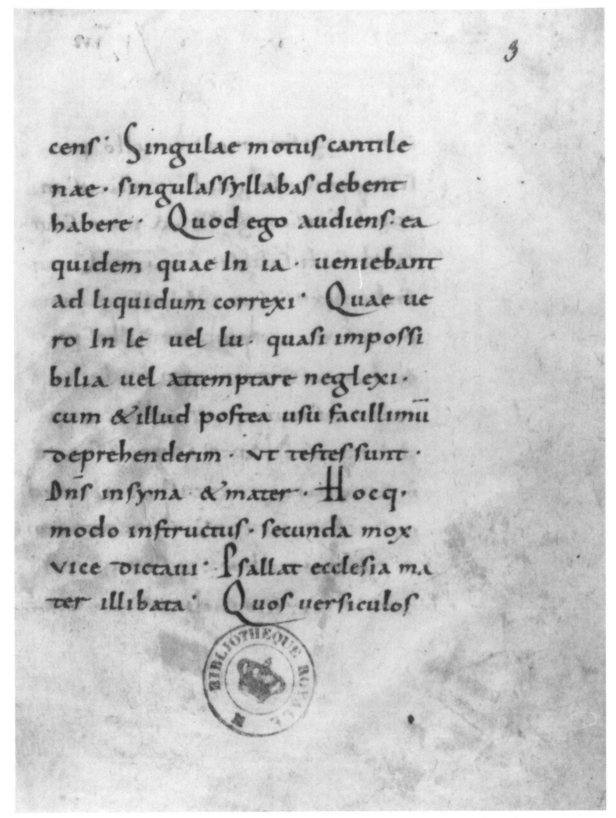

*Page from a manuscript for Notker's* Liber Hymnorum *(Paris, Bibliothèque Nationale, lat. 10587, fol. 3r)*

of Vercelli and chancellor of Charles the Fat. The many surviving manuscripts do not agree as to which sequences are Notker's. What is certain is that after his death in 912, Notker was particularly remembered in his own community as the one who wrote the sequences.

The sequence genre probably originated in Lorraine, and Notker received examples from related monasteries in that area. He improved and adapted the form, perfecting the rhythmic, as opposed to the metrical, approach to composition. Neither rhyme nor alliteration is used, and the resulting form has a quiet nobility. Notker composed both words and music and reflected on the problems of notation and stress patterns. The genre stands in stark contrast to the classical verse forms, and it has its home in the context of Christian worship. The words are simple, the style is elevated, and the topics are based on the major Christian festivals. The structure is regular, with balanced half lines, and it was a useful aid in the memorizing of ceremonial texts. Throughout Europe the sequence, including Notker's, enjoyed great popularity until well into the twelfth century.

## Biography:

Karl Langosch, *Profile des lateinischen Mittelalters* (Darmstadt: Wissenschaftliche Buchgesellschaft, 1965), pp. 137–188.

## References:

H. F. Haefele, "Studien zu Notkers *Gesta Karoli*," *Deutsch Archiv,* 15 (1959): 358–392;

P. Ladner, "Die Welt Notkers des Dichters im Spiegel seiner Urkunden," *Deutsch Archiv,* 41 (1985): 24–38;

Max Manitius, *Geschichte der lateinischen Literatur des Mittelalters,* volume 1 (Munich: Beck, 1911), pp. 363–367;

Rosamond McKitterick, "Charles the Bald (823–877) and His Library: The Patronage of Learning," *English Historical Review,* 95 (January 1980): 28–47;

F. J. E. Raby, *A History of Christian Latin Poetry* (Oxford: Clarendon Press, 1927), pp. 211–215;

Susan Rankin, "Ego itaque Notker scripsi," *Revue Bénédictine,* 101, nos. 3–4 (1991): 268–298;

Wolfram von den Steinen, *Notker der Dichter und seine geistige Welt,* 2 volumes (Bern: Francke, 1948);

Josef Szövérffy, *Die Annalen der lateinischen Hymnendichtung,* volume 1 (Berlin: Schmidt, 1964), pp. 262–312;

Hans Georg Thummel, "Fränkisches Selbstbewußtsein gegenüber Byzanz bei Notker," in *Byzanz in der europäischen Staatenwelt,* edited by Jurgen Dummer and Johannes Irmscher (Berlin: Akademie, 1983), pp. 17–25.

# Notker III of Saint Gall

*(circa 950 – 28 June 1022)*

Jerold C. Frakes
*University of Southern California*

MAJOR WORKS: Boethius's *De Consolatione philosophiae*
   **Manuscripts:** Saint Gall, Stiftsbibliothek 825, pp. 4–271 (~ 1025); Zurich, Zentralbibliothek C121 (462), foll. 49v–51v (eleventh century < Saint Gall, later than Saint Gall 825).

Martianus Capella's *De nuptiis Philologiae et Mercurii*
   **Manuscript:** Saint Gall, Stiftsbibliothek 872, pp. 2–170 (eleventh century).

Boethius's translation of Aristotle's κατηγορίαι
   **Manuscripts:** Saint Gall, Stiftsbibliothek, Codex Sangallensis 818, pp. 3–143 (eleventh century); Saint Gall, Stiftsbibliothek 825, pp. 275–338 (eleventh century).

Boethius's translation of Aristotle's περὶ ερμηνείας
   **Manuscript:** Saint Gall, Stiftsbibliothek 818, pp. 143–246 (eleventh century).

Psalms (and *Cantica,* Lord's Prayer, Apostolic Creed, Athanasian Creed)
   **Manuscripts:** (1) Saint Gall recension (before 1020): Saint Gall, Stiftsbibliothek, Codex Sangallensis 21, pp. 8–575 (mid twelfth century), formerly in and probably written in Einsiedeln, in Saint Gall by the seventeenth century; dependent on a mid-eleventh-century codex (S or Vadianus), still extant in the seventeenth century, now lost (many sixteenth- and seventeenth-century manuscripts and books cite it); seventeen fragments, most dating from the eleventh century; further fragments incorporating later revisions (see *Notkers des Deutschen Werke,* volumes 8 and 10 edited by James C. King and Petrus W. Tax [Tübingen: Niemeyer, 1972–  ], VIII: pp. xvi–xix, X: pp. 609–610); (2) Vienna recension (eleventh-century abridged Bavarian version, probably < Wessobrunn; Psalms 51–100 lacking): Vienna 2681, foll. 1–103v, 108–212r, 213–232r (twelfth century).

**Standard editions:** *Die Schriften Notkers und seiner Schule,* 3 volumes, edited by Paul Piper (Freiburg: Mohr, 1882–1883); *Notkers des Deutschen Werke,* 7 volumes, edited by E. H. Sehrt and Taylor Starck (Halle: Niemeyer, 1933–1955); *Notkers des Deutschen Werke,* 10 volumes, Altdeutsche Textbibliothek, edited by James C. King and Petrus W. Tax (Tübingen: Niemeyer, 1972–  ).

At about the same time that Gerbert d'Aurillac, the future Pope Sylvester II, was working through Boethius's *Consolatio* with the young emperor Otto III, Notker III was laboring over the same text across the Alps in Saint Gall, providing his monastic pupils with a medieval student's translation of and commentary on this seminal text from classical literature. This form of translation-commentary-exegesis for students was his life's work and makes him exemplary of a certain significant type of intellectual life in the European Middle Ages.

Notker is called "the Third" to distinguish him from his prior namesakes in the monastery of Saint Gall: Notker I *Balbulus* (the stammerer) or *poeta* (the poet), famous for his Latin sequences; Notker II *medicus* or *physicus* (the physician), also known as *piperisgranum* (peppercorn) because of his fiery temper; Notker *abbas,* abbot of Saint Gall (971–975). Notker III was called *Labeo* by his monastic brothers, probably because of his having a large lip (or lips); he has been called *Teutonicus* (the German – at the end of his translation of the Athanasian Creed is entered the epitaph: "Notker Teutonicus domini finitur amicus, / Gaudeat ille locis in paradysiacis") in acknowledgment of his accomplishments as an early and innovative translator into and proto-linguist of the German language; as master of the Saint Gall monastic school, he was also called Notker *magister.*

The few details of his life which are known are either extrapolated from his works (especially a twelfth-century copy of a letter Notker wrote a few years before his death to Bishop Hugo of Sitten [998–1017], Brussels, Royal Library 10615–10729,

*Page from a book of vows from the Saint Gall monastery. The signatures "ego Notker" on lines 4, 7, and 10 are attributed to Notker III (Stiftsarchiv Sankt Gallen).*

58 ra, edited by Paul Piper, volume 1, pp. 859–861) or are transmitted in three contemporary documents written by others: the *Casuum Sancti Galli Continuatio (MGH SS* II, 149ff.) and the *Liber benedictionum* (Saint Gall 393, especially the "Epitaphium quatuor scolarum magistris ęque tumulatis" and "De aliis sincellitis," ll. 62–83; ed. J. Egli, *Mittheilungen zur vaterländischen Geschichte* XXXI), both by Notker's pupil Ekkehard IV, and the *Annales Sancti Galli Maiores (MGH SS* I, 72–85). Notker was born into a noble family from Thurgau in northeastern Switzerland (the name Notker was rare outside this region), in the same district as Saint Gall. The district also supplied Saint Gall with several other important members, beginning with Ekkehard I and including Ekkehard IV, the historian of the early period of the monastery. Notker came to Saint Gall quite early in life, one of the four nephews whom Ekkehard I brought to the monastery to be monks, and he remained there throughout a long life, during which he became head of the monastic school and one of its greatest scholars. Ekkehard IV, one of his students and an important scholar in his own right, honored him in his *Liber benedictionum* with an intimate portrayal in twenty-two leonine hexameters. According to Ekkehard IV, Notker was of exemplary piety and humility and was a most helpful, thoughtful, and dedicated teacher. The poem itself, as well as the interlinear glosses by Ekkehard IV, treats of Notker's death in an emotional account. On his deathbed he confessed as his worst sin that as a young man he killed a wolf while wearing his habit; he had the poor assembled and fed around his deathbed, so that his last impression of earthly life would be their joy. The Saint Gall *Totenbuch* characterizes him as *doctissimus et benignissimus uir.* He died at first vespers of Saint Peter's eve (that is, on the evening of 28 June 1022), the feast of the saint to whom he was especially devoted; under 29 June 1022 the Saint Gall *Totenbuch* contains the entry: "obitus Notkeri doctissimi atque benignissimi magistri." He was a victim of the plague which Henry II's army had brought over the Alps from Italy; nine others in Saint Gall died during this outbreak of the plague, including the abbot, Purchard II, three other teachers, and four additional monks. This stunning loss to the monastic school, coupled with the antihumanistic bias of the Cluniac monastic reform movement that soon swept through the region, dealt a crippling blow to the Saint Gall school from which it never recovered. For by 1030 the reform had reached Saint Gall and by mid century secular learning had generally lost even its already re-stricted role as a pedagogical servant to ecclesiastical learning.

Notker can best be characterized as a gifted pedagogue. He was not by any means a profound or particularly original thinker, but he was a perceptive compiler and talented translator, had an impressive ability to manipulate his Alemannic dialect of Old High German to express foreign cultural ideas, and used and probably devised an orthographic and accentuation system for his native dialect. As far as is known, only his *De musica* was composed solely in Alemannic; otherwise he wrote in Latin and translated (most of) his works into Alemannic. The translations are usually also accompanied by commentary and occasionally even brief explanatory essays inserted into the texts. These commentaries, too, are not composed but rather compiled by Notker from his readings in a relatively wide but clearly circumscribed body of learned literature. For a time scholars held that much of Notker's actual translation work was carried out by assistants, but on the basis of more recent stylistic analyses a kind of stylistic unity is now taken as evidence of Notker's sole authorship.

Notker's dedication as a pedagogue was directly responsible for his writings, as he explains in his letter to Hugo of Sitten: he attempted to translate into the vernacular and to clarify the syllogistic, metaphorical, or dialectical expressions of Aristotle, Cicero, and others. He also notes in the letter that he devoted himself to such work because of the exigencies of the classroom, although he would have preferred to concentrate on scholarly studies ("artibus autem illis quibus me onustare uultis ego renunciaui neque fas mihi est aliter quam sicut instrumentis frui. sunt ecclesiastici libri, et precipue quidem in scolis legendi, quos impossibile est sine illis prelibatis ad intellectum integrum duci"). These *artes* to which he would have preferred to devote himself were the seven liberal arts (*septem artes liberales;* Notker calls them *die siben bûoh-líste* [the seven book-sciences]), the so-called trivium and quadrivium of late antique and (sporadically) medieval curricula. Notker views them, as the citation indicates, as means to a theological end: the understanding and interpretation of the Bible and other religious texts. Notker thus emphasized ecclesiastical writings as the primary focus for his students, intellectual and linguistic access to which was eased in his view by a knowledge of the liberal arts, which ultimately justifies his own translation and commentary work. Even in his work on the liberal arts, his focus is often, though not always, beyond the text at hand, for his comments quite often impose a bla-

Et quaecumq̃ · infingularib · funt · Iiu
fint oub eine halb uuar · ander halb
lugi · diu man uone ein lubhen fprichet ·
Yt focratef é albuf · nonẽ focratefalbuf ·
Lirne andifemo gemále · uuiolih uni
uerfalia · unde pafticularia · unde op
pofita · ein anderen fin ·

UNIUERSALES CONTRARIAE

Omnif
homo
albuf é

Nulluf
homo
albuf é

Uniuerfalef poffunt fimul ·
ẽẽ falfe · non autẽ fimul

OPPOSITI

CONTRAD

VERAE

LATERALES

Larralui fi uere
uere fc'particula
ticularef · ñ ideo ue
Sifalfe r unuifalef · ñ
ticulef · Et fi
fe fneceffarig

Siueru é unuif
le falfe é particu
Lare · Si an falfe
uniúfale uerú
é particulare

fino uniuerfalef
ref · Et fi uere ̃ par
re f uniuerfalefbu
neceffariofalfe fpar
falfe fparé fal
uniúfalef

LATERALES

OPPOSITI

CTRADICT

Particularef poffunt
fimul ẽẽ uere · ñ autẽ fimul ·
FALSAE

Quidam
homo
albuf é

Quidam
homo alb
huf nõ

PARTICULARIS SUBCONTRARIAE ·

QUAECUMQ̃ · AUTEM · IN UNIUERSALIB,
non uniuerfaliter · ñ femp hec uerẽ
illa falfa · Indefinita nefkeident nieht ·
uuar · unde lugi · fiu fint fament ein

tantly and not immediately relevant Christian interpretation (compare Ingeborg Schröbler on this *interpretatio christiana*). Late in life Notker turned directly to ecclesiastical translations: of the Psalms, of Gregory the Great's *Moralia in Job* (which, according to Ekkehard IV, he finished on the day of his death and which is now lost).

The works are primarily philosophical and theological but also include other literary works commonly read in the medieval schools (*Disticha Catonis*, Virgil's *Bucolica*, Terence's *Andria;* all three lost). The philosophical texts derive primarily from the part of the medieval curriculum known as the trivium: grammar (in the broad sense, including language and literary studies), dialectic (again in a broad sense, including philosophical argumentation), and rhetoric. Foremost is Boethius's *Consolatio*, a storehouse of Neoplatonic cosmology and Stoic ethics, designed by its author both as a didactic dialogue and an analysis of fortune, human fate, divine providence, the highest good, and the problem of evil. Its heuristic progression makes it an ideal classroom text to increase gradually the sophistication of the students' logical and rhetorical thinking, as well as their knowledge of an advanced Latin philosophical style and vocabulary; it also provides an introduction to Latin metrics via its virtuosic variety of poetic meters. In addition to the treatment of their own specific topics in the field of logic (in the larger sense of the use of language [*logos*] in general and the rules of discourse in particular), the Boethian translation-commentaries on Aristotle's κατηγοριαι (*Categoriae*) and περι ερμηνειας (*De interpretatione*) served this same introductory didactic purpose. The two treatises form part of the Aristotelian *Organon* (tool), as designated by later commentators, who considered logic a tool of philosophical work; Aristotle himself considered logic a preliminary to all scientific study. In the *Categoriae* Aristotle treats the distinction between simple terms and propositions, the "categories" (substance, quantity, quality, relation, place, time, position, state, action, and affection). The *De interpretatione* is, along with the *Analytica priora,* the most important of the Aristotelian logical treatises; it treats the form and interrelationship of logical statements, statements of fact versus contingent or conditional statements, the meaning of affirmation and denial. The other minor treatises, not mentioned by Notker in his letter to Hugo, but attributed to him — *De syllogismis* (edited by Piper, volume 1, pp. 596–622), *De partibus logicae* (edited by Piper, volume 1, pp. 591–595), and *De arte rhetorica* (edited by Piper, volume 1, pp. 623–684), *De definitione* (edited by

Elias von Steinmeyer, *Sprachdenkmäler,* no. xxv, pp. 118–120) – are in Latin with Alemannic examples.

In the fields of the quadrivium (arithmetic, music theory, geometry, astronomy), which complete the secular curriculum of the medieval European clerical education, Notker's *principia mathematicae* is lost, but his *Computus* (edited by G. Meier, *Die sieben freien Künste im Mittelalter,* Schulprogram Einsiedeln 1887, pp. 31–34) on the reckoning of the date of Easter (a common type of treatise and, in a religious sense, obviously an important skill) also is in some sense an introduction to mathematics. Notker also translated Martianus Capella's fifth-century *De nuptiis,* which is not so much an introduction to the liberal arts as it is a survey or compendium of the fields themselves; it is constructed as an elaborate allegory of the wedding of Philologia, an intellectually curious human, and the god of wisdom, Mercury. Martianus's excruciatingly difficult and circuitous style is typical of late Latin learned (or quasi-learned) allegories. Thus both its content and its linguistic difficulty made it perfectly suitable as a school text and a candidate for a translation-commentary. Only the first two of the nine books have been transmitted in Notker's translation; perhaps that is all that he completed, for they provide the mytho-allegorical frame story that precedes the seven books devoted to the individual liberal arts. Finally, among the texts on the quadrivium, is the brief and now fragmentary work *De musica* (edited by Piper, volume 1, pp. 851–859), which is, despite its Latin title, completely in German. It briefly treats music theory, the monochord, and the modes.

For several reasons, Boethius's *Consolatio* and Martianus's *De nuptiis* are pedagogical texts without peer for the medieval schools, and they well illustrate Notker's method of working. They are both written in the form called "Menippean satire" (*satura Menippea*), in which poetry and prose sections alternate; the *Consolatio,* whose frame fiction is a philosophical debate, includes a wealth of rhetorical figures and juridical and philosophical argumentative forms; the first two books of *De nuptiis,* on the other hand, provide the frame for Martianus's treatises on the seven liberal arts; the frame itself consists of the preparations for the wedding of Philology and Mercury, including descriptions of the deities of the Greco-Roman pantheon, their attributes and functions. A careful reading of these two works would then provide students with contextualized examples of the construction of philosophical arguments, a wide range of rhetorical devices, examples of many Roman verse forms, models of both simple and direct prose style in some Boethian passages and late Latin's florid and almost impenetrable prose in Martianus, a clear instance of the late antique Stoic-Neoplatonic melting pot of philosophical systems (with a subsumed Christianity as well), and a wealth of information concerning Greco-Roman mythology.

Notker often interrupts text and translation in order to identify the given rhetorical device in use at the moment, which in some intellectually complex passages might almost lead the modern reader to believe that Notker did not grasp the philosophical import of the matter at hand. But one must always keep in mind the purpose of Notker's translation-commentary – to help beginning students comprehend the Latin of the original, begin to understand the argumentative logic characteristic of such treatises, and to recognize standard rhetorical devices in use in this text and elsewhere. Thus he is far less interested in the content per se of the *Consolatio, De nuptiis,* or the other treatises, and he comments rarely on the point of the arguments at hand. Instead his primary interest in them is as pedagogical examples of logical and rhetorical figures; that is, he treats the whole as a pedagogical, not a scholarly, text. In this sense Notker's approach differs little from even advanced-level seminars in Classics until very recently, in which attention to form and accuracy of translation was paramount while "content" was ignored or simply assumed.

Notker's theological works included, according to his letter to Hugo, a translation of Boethius's *De trinitate* and *Job* (according to Ekkehard: the *Moralia in Job* of Gregory the Great), which was only one-third complete at the time of Notker's letter to Hugo, but which he was able to complete just before his death. Both works are lost. Of his theological works only Notker's *Psalter* survives. It is the only work of Notker's whose manuscript tradition indicates anything like a broad popularity (one complete and many fragmentary manuscripts). In 1027 Empress Gisela ordered a copy made of both the *Psalter* and *Job* (compare Ekkehard IV's gloss on his poem: "Kisila imperatrix operum eius auidissima, psalterium ipsum et Iob sibi exemplari sollicite fecit"). During the twelfth century the Codex Vindobonensis 2681 of the *Psalter* was edited and revised, probably in Wessobrunn; its Bavarian dialect forms deviate sharply from Notker's Alemannic, and his commentary has been sharply reduced to primarily theological matters; the verses of the Psalms are no longer split into sentences as in Notker's original work, and the Latin words of the commentary have also been translated into German; other words have often been substituted for Notker's terms in the translation. Perhaps these changes point to an adaptation by the monastic agents of the Cluniac reform.

The text traditions of Notker's works are generally securely based in eleventh-century Saint Gall, soon after Notker's death. Many of the manuscripts are still there. The manuscripts now in Zurich are originally also from there, as is the Latin basis of the Saint Gall recension of the *Psalter;* the connections of the Bavarian strand of the *Psalter* tradition, and the quaternio of Saint Gall tractates now in Brussels 10615–10729 (originally < Trier, with its original from Lotharingia), back to Saint Gall are now unclear. According to Ekkehard IV, two lines of Notker's own script are found in Saint Gall, Stiftsbibliothek 621, page 351 (in Orosius, *Historia aduersus paganos*).

Notker's Alemannic text was not the focus of his work but rather simply an instrument employed to allow his students easier access to the base (Latin) text, as he writes to Hugo: "cito capiuntur per patriam linguam quae uix aut non integre capienda forent in lingua non propria." Thus Notker was not at all the patriotic humanist attempting to invent German prose or develop a national literature that the Romantic period wished to see in him. He was simply a concerned teacher who did what Latin teachers with realistic appraisals of their beginning students have over the centuries recurringly done; he prepared a translation crib for them. With this focus on the Latin, not the Alemannic text, Notker's work as translator clearly had far less to do with trying to invent the "althochdeutsche Begrifflichkeit" imputed to him by modern scholars than with the propaedeutic purpose of making the Latin texts accessible to his students, even more so than the Latin paraphrase could. Thus the conceptual vocabulary must be seen as a by-product of a strictly pedagogical practice, and loan translation less an attempt to incorporate the Latin into German than simply to make clear the processes of Latin word formation (see here Evelyn S. Coleman and Georg Braungart). By the same token the untranslated Latin terms incorporated into the Alemannic text are not signs of incomplete translation, but rather indications of the direct ties back to the *primary* (in all senses) text – the Latin original, toward which the German text always points (Braungart).

The Alemannic text was not conceived as a strict equivalent for the Latin text, but rather was, coupled with the Latin comments and glosses which Notker added, more generally to provide the stu-

doter chalber uften dinen atrare dui der lichent Half fone de
ro fueigo genomenui·nube in sca eccta gezogene uingelinga
scof & innocentes· also laurentius uuas unde uincentius & ce

T E R I T A L E S
H I H E I H T E L L E C T V D A V I D· C V M V E H I R E T
D O E C H I D V M E V E T A H H V H E I A V I T S A V L
E T D I X I T· V E H I T D A V I D I H D O M V M A B I
M E L E C H· Anaxpm siehet distu sternumest dauidis·uuanda
sin fient anaxpe bier urresset uuirdet·den doech idumeus
bezeichenet·Vmbe dauidis Kenide sluoch doech sacerdotes·
umbe christus Kenide slahet
antichristus martyres·;
UI O G LORIA
RIS IH MALITIA QVI
potens es·Cheden alle mit
dauid·uuaz Kuollichost du
dih inarge·du dir mahtig pist·
He mugen oih tier unde uuir
me ubelo tuon·Iniquita
die·Vuaz Kuollichost
ununeben allen dag·
andermo
newuotrist
dir daz Kuol
lingua tua·Gn

re tota
du dih
D u tuost ico
daz tu dir
ziu duncbet
tib·Iniustitian          cogitauit
rebt ahtota din zunga·Gnrehbt uuas dir in muote unde in

*Page from the Saint Gall recension of Notker's translation of the Psalms. This page comprises the end of Psalm 50 and the beginning of Psalm 51 (Saint Gall, Stiftsbibliothek, Codex Sangallensis 21).*

dents with an understanding of the purport of the original. Certainly there is no attempt on Notker's part to provide a stylistic equivalent of the Latin in his Alemannic rendering. But he regularly takes great pains toward semantic precision, often by using multiple (partial) synonyms in addition to explanation, so as to convey shades of meaning. Since the point of the Alemannic text is to illuminate the Latin, rather than to stand on its own, Notker often imitates Latin grammatical constructions in his translation, which are nonidiomatic in German: accusative plus infinitive, ablative absolute (lacking an ablative, Notker uses dative), various participial constructions. Here, too, the pedagogical value for his students, as well as the use of the vernacular as means not end, is clear.

Notker's method in general was neither complex nor original, but its classroom efficacy is quite obvious. He divided a given Latin sentence into shorter syntactic units, often also rewriting and simplifying the syntax, translated each unit into Alemannic, and frequently appended an explanation, most often in Alemannic but using Latin technical terms or the Latin terms under discussion. He rearranged the Latin syntax by, for instance, placing substantive and attributive adjectives together, placing the verb in an independent clause after an initial subject or adverb, rather than, as in the more formal Latin of his base texts, at the end of the sentence. Such rearrangement might reflect the conversational Latin of the (northern) monasteries of the time, or it might rather have simply been of greater assistance for Notker's students, who could have found their way through a somewhat Germanized Latin syntax more easily than the stylistically difficult originals. Particularly with respect to the rearrangement of the text, the Latin tract *Quomodo vii circumstantie rerum in legendo ordinande sint* (edited by Piper, volume 1, pp. xiii–lxxxix) is relevant, and Herbert Backes has even suggested that this text from Saint Gall is to be understood as the key to the syntactic and semantic analysis and organization of the Latin and Alemannic texts, and should in fact be attributed to Notker himself. If so, much is explained about Notker's structuring of his text (called *ordo naturalis* in the treatise), as well as about his understanding of his larger project in general. It would also provide a clear example of a general tendency in his work, to build his larger translation-commentaries in part on his own earlier briefer studies, as is also clear in the excerpting of his Latin-Alemannic tract on rhetoric in book II of his *Consolatio* commentary (compare Stefan Sonderegger, 1986).

In addition to strict translation, Notker also includes word glosses, many of which seem to be neologisms. It is most often impossible to determine when he himself invented new vocabulary and when he is making use of a prior tradition: *uuîolîchî qualitas* was already in use by his time, but *bûoh-lîste artes liberales* may not have been. In any case, however, his frequent use of multiple possible glosses indicates that he is aware of the theoretical and practical problems inherent in his task. He also includes longer geographical, historical, or scientific comments and, especially in the *Psalter,* comments on theological issues. Notker's explanations and comments taken as a whole are, as was generally the case with medieval commentaries, derivative from a long and broad tradition: he made great use of the work of, among others, Remigius of Auxerre and other Carolingian commentaries on Martianus and Boethius, of Augustine's *Enarrationes in psalmos* on the Psalms, and Boethius's comments on Aristotle in his own translation-commentary. Notker's procedure in making use of various commentary traditions is interesting in itself: selecting material, editing, weighing conflicting opinions, elaborating, condensing (see especially Peter Ganz for a perceptive analysis of Notker's method here).

Notker calls his method of vernacular prose explanations "pene inusitatum" (practically unprecedented), confirming both the suspicion, based on the paucity of evidence, that there had in fact been little such work and also that Notker was either unaware of or little influenced by the prior work of others that does survive (for example, the translation of Tatian's *Diatessaron* a century and a half earlier or the earlier Alemannic Psalms translation). Certainly there was still no tradition of scholarly prose. While the romantic notions of nineteenth-century scholarship that Notker invented German scholarly prose are to be rejected (certainly other monastic teachers throughout Europe before him had explained Boethius and Aristotle via the Boethian translations to their students in the vernacular), it is still Notker's most impressive accomplishment that he produced such a large body of work and that it was written down and preserved for the use of later generations of students in Saint Gall.

A great deal has been made by scholars of Notker's use in his Alemannic translation-commentary of Latin technical terms and phrases, termed *Misch-prosa* (mixed or macaronic prose) by German scholars. This usage seems, however, only natural in context: Notker was preparing a teaching text – a translation-commentary-introduction – for his students to some of the most linguistically and intellectually challenging texts they would confront in the course of their studies. For some of the stock rhetorical, philosophical, and legal terms, there were no precise Alemannic equivalents; for others he first had to invent and introduce such a translation; for still others the Latin term had itself already become part of the vernacular of those educated in the monastery (much as a Latinate vocabulary is today unconsciously part of intellectual discourse in English).

Without question the aspect of Notker's work that has interested modern scholars most is not the philosophical or theological acumen of his commentaries nor generally his level of intellectual sophistication but, rather quite specifically, the phonetic and orthographic features of his texts. Notker's *Anlautgesetz* (law of initial consonants) is perhaps the most prominent feature of a carefully constructed orthographic system. Its primary rule is: except when preceded by a syntactic pause (that is, at the beginning of a sentence and other syntactic speech-units, inconsistently definable in the usage of the manuscripts) or a word ending in a vowel, nasal or liquid, word-initial *b, d, g* are devoiced to *p, t, k* — *unde der brûoder / tes prûoder hûs*. Further details of the application of this and related rules in Notker's usage are debated by scholars. Notker's works also make use of a system of vowel accentuation, preserved especially in his translation of Boethius's *Consolatio;* in his letter to Hugo, Notker claims that all German words except the article should have an accent mark: the acute accent marks stressed short vowels and the (first letter of the) diphthongs *ei, ou,* and the digraph *iu* (ü:); the circumflex marks long vowels and the (first letter of the) diphthongs *ie, uo, io, ia;* the circumflex is not restricted to stressed vowels.

To modern secular eyes it is sometimes surprising that despite the fact that he spent almost his entire life in the monastery, including his childhood, Notker displays in his writings a broad experience of life beyond the walls of the cell and the scriptorium. But one must remember that Saint Gall was a so-called great monastery: a huge, almost self-sufficient estate in itself, with scores of smaller and larger holdings in the immediate and extended area, hundreds of stone and wooden buildings, fruit and vegetable gardens, grain crops for bread and beer, livestock numbering in the hundreds and their attendant industries (slaughterhouses, smokehouses, candle making, hide tanning, and so forth). Thus, when Notker knows about carpentry, shipping, market fairs, flora and fauna of the mountains, astronomy, and folk sayings and rhymes, he indicates that his world was larger than could be gotten only from books.

From the nonnationalistic perspective that is beginning to make inroads into Notker scholarship, Notker's achievement is less stellar than once thought, but within the limits of his work and in concert with his own goals, his work is of great historical interest. His innovations in pedagogical method and in orthography had no immediate successors, even in Saint Gall. It was only his *Psalter* that inspired any significant imitation. Otherwise his works were soon forgotten outside of Saint Gall. There, however, he was still known and described by Konrad von Fabaria in the second quarter of the thirteenth century as "nogkerum magistrum artis theorice non pigrum" (in the *Continuatio casuum sancti Galli*). Notker's works probably had great "inhouse" significance at the time and were designed precisely for that purpose: they were textbooks for daily use and were hardly conceived as scholarly treatises for the advancement of intellectual endeavor. Rather they were designed to initiate young monastic students to the church's collection of secular "great books": Boethius, Aristotle, Martianus. Their success could only be known from the eleventh-century monastic classroom.

**Bibliographies:**

Evelyn S. Coleman, "Bibliographie zu Notker III. von St. Gallen," in *Germanic Studies in Honor of Edward Henry Sehrt,* edited by Frithjof A. Raven, Wolfram K. Legner, and James C. King (Coral Gables: University of Miami Press, 1968), pp. 61–76;

Evelyn S. Firchow, "Bibliographie zu Notker III. von St. Gallen. Zweiter Teil," in *Spectrum Medii Aevi: Essays in Early German Literature in Honor of George Fenwick Jones,* edited by W. C. McDonald, Göppinger Arbeiten, no. 362 (Göppingen: Kümmerle, 1983), pp. 91–110.

**References:**

Herbert Backes, *Die Hochzeit des Merkurs und der Philologie: Studien zu Notkers Martian-Übersetzung* (Sigmaringen: Thorbecke, 1982);

Herbert Bolender, "Notkers *Consolatio* – Rezeption als widerspruchsfreie Praktik: Eine Hypothese," *Beiträge zur Geschichte der deutsche Sprache und Literatur,* 102 (1980): 325–338;

Georg Braungart, "Notker der Deutsche als Bearbeiter eines lateinischen Schultextes: Boethius De Consolatione Philosophiae," *Zeitschrift für deutsche Philologie,* 106 (1987): 2–15;

J. M. Clark, *The Abbey of St. Gall as a Centre of Literature and Art* (Cambridge: Cambridge University Press, 1926);

Evelyn S. Coleman, "Die Lehnbildungen in Notker Labeos *Consolatio*-Übersetzung: Ein Beitrag zur Lehngutforschung," Ph.D. dissertation, Harvard University, 1963;

Alfred K. Dolch, *Notker Studien, Teil I und II: Lateinisch-althochdeutsches und althochdeutsch-lateinisches Wörterverzeichnis zu Notkers Boethius De Consolatione Philosophiae, Buch I,* New York University Ottendorfer Memorial Series, no. 16 (Leipzig: Borna, 1928);

Dolch, *Notker Studien, Teil III: Stil- und Quellenprobleme zu Notkers Boethius und Martianus Capella,* New York University Ottendorfer Memorial series, no. 16 (Leipzig: Borna, n.d.);

Jerold C. Frakes, *The Fate of Fortune in the Early Middle Ages: The Boethian Tradition* (Leiden: Brill, 1987);

Peter Ganz, "Geschichte bei Notker Labeo," in *Geschichtsbewußtsein in der deutschen Literatur des Mittelalters: Tübinger Colloquium 1983* (Tübingen: Niemeyer, 1985), pp. 1–16;

D. H. Green, "The Primary Reception of the Works of Notker the German," *Parergon: Bulletin of the Australian and New Zealand Association for Medieval and Renaissance Studies,* new series 2 (1984): 57–78;

Ernst Hellgardt, "Notker Teutonicus: Überlegungen zum Stand der Forschung," *Beiträge zur Geschichte der deutschen Sprache und Literatur,* 108 (1986): 190–205;

Paul Hoffmann, *Die Mischprosa Notkers des Deutschen,* Palaestra 58 (Berlin: Mayer & Müller, 1910; New York: Johnson, 1967);

Jürgen Jaehrling, *Die philosophische Terminologie Notkers des Deutschen in seiner Übersetzung der Aristote-lischen "Kategorien,"* Philologische Studien und Quellen, no. 47 (Berlin: Schmidt, 1969);

Gerhard Köbler, *Verzeichnis der normalisierten Übersetzungsgleichungen der Werke Notkers von St. Gallen,* Göttinger Studien zur Rechtsgeschichte, no. 9 (Göttingen: Musterschmidt, 1971);

Emil Luginbühl, *Studien zu Notkers Übersetzungskunst* (Weida in Thür: Thomas & Hubert, 1933; reprinted, Berlin: De Gruyter, 1970);

G. Meyer von Knonau, ed., *St. Gallische Geschichtsquellen, III: Ekkehart's (IV.) Casus Sancti Galli,* Mittheilungen zur vaterländischen Geschichte, nos. 15–16 (Saint Gall: Huber, 1877);

Horst D. Schlosser, "Formwille in Notkers *Consolatio*-Bearbeitung," in *Festschrift Gottfried Weber,* edited by Heinz Otto Burger and Klaus von See (Bad Homburg: Gehlen, 1967), pp. 79–107;

Ingeborg Schröbler, *Notker III. von St. Gallen als Übersetzer und Kommentator von Boethius' De Consolatione Philosophiae,* Hermaea, new series 2 (Tübingen: Niemeyer, 1953);

Edward H. Sehrt, ed., *Notker-Glossar: Ein althochdeutsches-lateinisches-neuhochdeutsches Wörterbuch zu Notkers des Deutschen Schriften* (Tübingen: Niemeyer, 1962);

Sehrt and Wolfram K. Legner, eds., *Notker-Wortschatz* (Halle: Niemeyer, 1955);

Stefan Sonderegger, *Althochdeutsch in St. Gallen: Ergebnisse und Probleme der ahd. Sprachüberlieferung in St. Gallen vom 8. bis ins 12. Jahrhundert,* Biblioteca Sangallensis, no. 6 (Saint Gall: Ostschweiz, 1970);

Benedikt Vollmann, "Simplicitas Divinae Providentiae: Zur Entwicklung des Begriffs in der antiken Philosophie und seiner Eindeutschung in Notkers 'Consolatio'-Übersetzung," *Literaturwissenschaftliches Jahrbuch,* 8 (1967): 5–29.

# Notker von Zwiefalten

*(?– 6 March 1095)*

Francis G. Gentry
*Pennsylvania State University*

MAJOR WORK: *Memento mori* (circa 1080)

**Manuscript:** The work appears only on the final pages of an eleventh-century parchment manuscript from the Monastery of Ochsenhausen in the Allgäu containing parts 3 and 4 of Gregory the Great's *Moralia in Job,* Strasbourg, Bibliothèque Nationale et Universitaire, cod. germ. 278, fol. 154v–155r. The *Memento mori* was copied by a later hand than that of the *Moralia;* the dating suggestions range from end of the eleventh or beginning of the twelfth century to around 1130. The manuscript contains the first seven strophes of the so-called *Straßburger Ezzolied.*

**First publication:** In K. A. Barack, "Althochdeutsche Funde," *Zeitschrift für deutsches Altertum,* 23 (1879): 212–216.

**Standard editions:** In Rudolf Schützeichel, *Das alemannische Memento mori: Das Gedicht und der geistig-historische Hintergrund* (Tübingen: Niemeyer, 1962), pp. 126–133 (with translation into modern German); in *Die religiösen Dichtungen des 11. und 12. Jahrhunderts: Nach ihren Formen besprochen und herausgegeben,* volume 1, edited by Friedrich Maurer (Tübingen: Niemeyer, 1964), pp. 249–259; in *Deutsche Dichtung des Mittelalters,* volume 1: *Von den Anfängen bis zum hohen Mittelalter,* edited by Michael Curschmann and Ingeborg Glier (Frankfurt am Main: Fischer, 1987), pp. 148–154 (with translation into modern German).

**Edition in English:** Translated by Francis G. Gentry as "Noker's [*sic*] 'Memento mori,'" *Allegorica,* 5 (Winter 1980): 7–18.

The final line of the *Memento mori* (circa 1080), "daz machot all ein Noker" (No[t]ker has made all this), appears to contain the name of the poet. Yet scholars are of divided opinion on this matter. According to some, *Notker* does not refer to the poet but to the scribe who produced the copy. After all,

it is argued, the line does not say that Notker *scripsit* (wrote) all this but that he *fecit* (made) it – a difference of which a monk schooled in Latin would surely be aware. Others believe that *Notker* does refer to the poet; examples, they claim, can be found in Latin and German literature in which *facere* or *machon,* respectively, are used to describe the process of writing. The difficulty then is to determine which of the several Notkers known from German intellectual history of that period is meant. Since Marlies Dittrich's essay of 1935, most scholars have identified the poet of the *Memento mori* with the abbot of the reform monastery of Zwiefalten. (Dittrich posits that this Notker was both the poet and the scribe.) Zwiefalten is relatively close to the monastery of Ochsenhausen, where the manuscript was found, and it is located in the Alemannic language area. In any case, whether Notker was poet, scribe, or both, the work with which his name is associated has not ceased to arouse the interest and, indeed, the passions of scholars.

The *Memento mori* is a penitential sermon in rhyme. Rhymed sermons were reasonably common in early Middle High German literature and were probably delivered on special days in the church calendar, such as saints' feast days. A penitential sermon calls for repentance of one's sins and preparation for the afterlife; this type of sermon would likely have been delivered during Lent, the season of penitence.

That these works were written in the vernacular leads one to postulate a lay audience; but the use of the vernacular does not necessary rule out a clerical audience, for many monks, as well as secular priests, did not possess a command of Latin beyond the minimum necessary for carrying out their tasks. In the case of the *Memento mori,* however, there is little doubt concerning the intended audience. With the simple but powerful admonition "nu denchent, wîp unde man, war ir sulint werdan" (Now reflect, o women and men, upon where you will be journeying), Notker makes clear that his work is not meant for a monkish audience; "wîp unde man" is a typical circumlocution for "everyone," but it also means exactly what it says: "women and men." In addition, some of the themes that Notker takes up in his work – for example, the correct disposition of wealth so that it does not prevent the salvation of the soul – would have more application to laypersons.

The *Memento mori* consists of 152 lines in nineteen strophes but is not complete. A lacuna occurs between lines 61 and 62 (strophes 8 and 9). This gap is not indicated in the manuscript but is revealed by a logical inconsistency: "ter eino ist wise unde vruot, / tes wirt er verdamnot" (The one is wise and good, / therefore he will be damned). Estimates of the length of the gap range from two lines to an entire strophe. The title, *Memento mori,* was given to the work by its first editor, K. A. Barack. The work can be divided into three main parts: strophes 1 to 6; strophes 7 to 11; and strophes 12 to 17. The final two strophes, 18 and 19, which may or may not be original, are supplements in which the poet laments the deceit of the world and calls on God to aid the seeker of paradise in escaping the pitfalls of the earthly life.

The first part introduces the basic themes of the work: life is a journey; the destination of the journey is paradise; this world is pleasant and, because of this pleasantness, dangerous; it is dangerous not because it actively imperils one's immortal soul but because its beauty is so attractive that one forgets that the purpose of life is to rejoin God. Again and again one is reminded that death is inevitable. After opening with a direct address to his listeners, Notker continues to personalize the introduction of these topics by using the personal pronoun *ir* (you): you love this fragile brittle world, but you will have it only for a short while; you will have to leave this life. In strophes 2 to 5, which illustrate in more detail the themes of the journey and preparedness for death, Notker does not address his audience directly but uses the general terms *sie* (they) and *er* (he): they thought that they could live here and also that they would attain eternal joy; how seldom did they consider where they, in the end, were to journey (strophe 3); he does this (that is, cleave to the world) until the end; thus he has nothing, either here or there (strophe 5). In strophe 6 Notker summarizes what he has said in the preceding strophes and returns to the personal form of address, *ir:* "ir sulent all ersterben" (you will all die). Notker does not, however, indulge in vivid, picturesque depictions of heaven and hell; he avoids

hyperbolic descriptions of the vanity of the world and the terrors of eternal punishment. Instead, he presents general theses about the meaning of existence taken from traditional Christian theology. He does not wish to frighten his listeners but to appeal to their reason. He reminds them that although the earth is beautiful, nothing there is permanent – least of all the human being. Notker places squarely before his listeners the inevitability of death and the judgment of the soul.

In the second part of the work Notker turns to the correct conduct of life on earth, borrowing heavily from Augustinian thought. In strophe 7 he addresses his listeners directly and reminds them that God created them all. Because they are all descended from Adam, they ought to live together in love and peace. Some have not done so, and this transgression is a grievous one. In strophe 9, after the lacuna and the statement "wirt er verdamnot" (he will be damned), Notker explains the nature of the offense: "tes rehten bedarf ter armo man, tes mag er leidor niewit han, / er nechouf iz also tiuro, tes varn se al ze hello" (The poor and powerless man needs fair treatment. Unfortunately he cannot have it / unless he pays dearly for it. For that reason they will all go to hell). The meaning of *reht* has been hotly debated in the scholarly literature, and it may not be amenable to precise determination. But since the theology of the work is obviously Augustinian (as can be seen especially in the theme of the journey) and since there are several direct quotations and paraphrases from Augustine, it is reasonable to propose that the meaning be sought in the works of the bishop of Hippo. There the equivalent Latin term is *justitia* ( justice). For Augustine, *justitia* is the foundation of all Christian virtues, including love. As Notker says in strophe 7, "to gebot er iu ze demo lebinne mit minnon hie ze wesinne" (in this life [God] commanded that you live together with love). Notker appears to be saying that those who do not live according to the principle of love, those who deprive the powerless of their just and fair expectations, and those who will ultimately suffer the eternal torments of hell because of this transgression are the addressees of the *Memento mori*: members of the lay nobility. When dealing with this sin, Notker abandons the circumspection that informed the first six strophes of the poem and assigns the offenders to the deepest pit of hell (strophes 9 and 10). Strophe 11, the final strophe of part 2, provides a solution:

Ube ir alle einis rehtin lebitint, so wurdint ir all geladet in

ze der ewigun mendin, da ir iemer soltint sin.
taz eina hant ir iu selben, daz ander gebent ir dien
   armen.
von diu so nemugen ir drin gen, ir muozint iemer der
   vor sten.


(If you all lived according to one principle governing
   fair treatment, you would all be invited
into the eternal joy, where you would always remain.
But one kind of fair treatment you accord to your
   selves and another you grant to the poor and powerless.
In this way you will never enter [heaven]; you will have to
   remain standing before [the gates].)


Like strophe 6 in part 1, strophe 11 offers a sum-
ming up of the lessons of the previous strophes;
and, again, the listeners are addressed directly with
the pronoun *ir*. Notker explains that if they all live
according to the original *reht* of God, that is, "mit
minnon hie ze wesinne" (to live together with love),
salvation is assured. If, however, they live according to two sets of principles – one type of *reht* for
themselves and another for the poor and powerless
– they will be lost. Thus, in strophe 11 Notker has
explained the nature of the sin that he introduced in
strophe 9: it is the failure to love all one's neighbors
equally. This is not a call for equality, as some
scholars maintain; it is a demand that Christian
society function according to the Christian principles of love and justice, giving each his or her due
within the hierarchical structure of society.

In part 3 Notker returns to the theme of the
journey through life. Strophe 14 offers a concrete
example of the *minne* (love) and *reht* (fairness, justice) introduced in part 2: the proper disposition of
wealth:

Habit er sinin richtuom so geleit, daz er vert an arbeit,
ze den sconen herbergon vindit er den suzzin lon.
des er in dirro werlte niewit gelebita, so luzil riwit iz in
   da.
in dunchit da bezzir ein tac, tenne hier tusinc, teist war.


(If he has so arranged his wealth that he departs
   without travail,
in the beautiful lodgings he will find his sweet recom
   pense.
The time which he has not lived on earth – how little
   he regrets it there!
One day there seems better to him than a thousand here.
   That is the truth.)


Notker's proposal is quite traditional and in keeping
with the Augustinian injunction that one should
give only part of one's wealth to the poor and
should retain enough for oneself; in strophe 15

Notker says, "habit er iet hina gegebin, tes muoz er
iemer furdir lebin" (if he has given anything away,
he will have everlasting life). He closes the third
part of the *Memento mori* as he did parts 1 and 2,
addressing his listeners directly. The world is indeed beautiful, he says, but it can be dangerous to
one's spiritual health if one cleaves too much to it.
For no matter how attractive life on earth may be,
leaving it is inescapable: "diu vart diu dunchit iuh
sorcsam, ir chomint dannan obinan, / tar muozint ir
bewindin, taz sund ir wol bevindin" (The journey
seems arduous to you [but] since you come from up
there [that is paradise, God], / you must return.
That you will discover well enough).

Thus the *Memento mori* progresses from the
death of the body to the possible death of the soul
and ends with the purpose of existence, reunion
with God. Nonetheless, the work deals with life, not
death. Notker's concern is to impart to his listeners
the type of behavior that they must perform to attain paradise: to follow the commandment of God
to love one's fellow human beings. The commandment demands active engagement in the affairs of
life and charity toward those in less advantaged positions in society. Notker is presenting the standard
lessons of Christianity to demonstrate that although
times may have changed, the admonitions of Christ
are still valid.

The *Memento mori* was composed during the Investiture Contest of 1076 to 1122, which resulted in
the disintegration of the Salian monarchy. It was a
time of chaos, setting pope against emperor, noble
against noble, and noble against king. It was a period of great strife and injustice in which the poor
and powerless suffered greatly. In an era when the
powerful were failing to carry out their duties as
Christian princes, it is not surprising that a churchman would concern himself with admonitions to the
rich and powerful to return to the proper path.
Notker's work is a Christian social document that
calls for adherence to the traditions of the Christian
faith that he saw to be gravely threatened by the political and social disintegration taking place in the
tumultuous final quarter of the eleventh century.

**Bibliography:**

Francis G. Gentry, *Bibliographie zur frühmittelhochdeutschen geistlichen Dichtung* (Berlin: Schmidt,
   1992), pp. 191–196.


**References:**

Marlies Dittrich, "Der Dichter des Memento mori,"
   *Zeitschrift für deutsches Altertum,* 72 (1935): 57–
   80;

Francis G. Gentry, "Notker's Memento mori and the Desire for Peace," *Amsterdamer Beiträge zur älteren Germanistik,* 16 (1981): 25–62;

Gentry, "*Vruot . . . Verdamnot?:* Memento mori vv. 61–62," *Zeitschrift für deutsches Altertum,* 108, no. 4 (1979): 299–306;

Gert Kaiser, "*Das Memento mori:* Ein Beitrag zum sozialgeschichtlichen Verständnis der Gleichheitsforderung im frühen Mittelalter," *Euphorion,* 68, no. 4 (1974): 337–370;

Hugo Kuhn, "Minne oder reht," in *Dichtung und Welt im Mittelalter,* second edition (Stuttgart: Metzler, 1969), pp. 105–111;

Heinz Rupp, *Deutsche religiöse Dichtungen des 11. und 12. Jahrhunderts. Untersuchungen und Interpretationen,* second edition (Bern & Munich: Francke, 1971), pp. 11–32;

Rudolf Schützeichel, *Das alemannische Memento mori: Das Gedicht und der geistig-historische Hintergrund* (Tübingen: Niemeyer, 1962);

Gisela Vollmann-Profe, *Geschichte der deutschen Literatur von den Anfängen bis zum Beginn der Neuzeit,* volume 1/2: *Von den Anfängen zum hohen Mittelalter* (Königstein: Athenäum, 1986);

Max Wehrli, *Geschichte der deutschen Literatur vom frühen Mittelalter bis zum Ende des 16. Jahrhunderts* (Stuttgart: Reclam, 1980);

Gerhild Scholz Williams, *The Vision of Death: A Study of the "Memento mori" Expressions in Some Latin, German and French Didactic Texts of the 11th and 12th Centuries* (Göppingen: Kümmerle, 1976).

# Otfried von Weißenburg

*(circa 800 – circa 875?)*

Albert L. Lloyd
*University of Pennsylvania*

MAJOR WORK: *Evangelienbuch* (between 863 and 871)

**Manuscripts:** The only complete manuscript is the Codex Vindobonensis 2687, Österreichische Nationalbibliothek, Vienna, designated V. Written at Weißenburg in the ninth century, it contains four illustrations (one full-page color miniature of the Crucifixion and three colored pen-and-ink drawings), marginal notations in Latin in red ink, and a carefully corrected text. Both the marginal notations and the corrections in the text are believed to be by Otfried himself. Also dating from ninth-century Weißenburg is the strangely mislabeled Codex palatinus latinus 52, in Heidelberg, designated P. With the exception of several missing pages at the beginning and in book 5, it is a good, though somewhat less elegantly executed, copy of V, possibly written by the same two principal scribes who produced V. The manuscript also includes the Old High German *Georgslied*. A third manuscript, the Freising Codex, designated F, Munich, Bayerische Staatsbibliothek, Cod. germ. mon. 14, was written about 900 at the request of Bishop Waldo of Freising by a scribe who identifies himself as Sigihard. It lacks the four dedications and book 1, chapter 2, but adds two two-line prayers at the end, usually referred to as "Sigihard's Prayers"; according to the paleographer Bernhard Bischoff, however, they were not written by the same hand as the rest of the manuscript, and, therefore, their authorship is uncertain. F appears to have been copied from V or a closely related manuscript, but with many errors and an increasing number of Bavarian forms as the work progresses. Finally, fragments of a fourth manuscript, which had been cut up to make bindings for books and has, therefore, been designated the Codex discissus (cut-up

manuscript), or D, are in Bonn and Wolfenbüttel (the Berlin fragments were lost during World War II). Formerly thought to be another ninth-century Weißenburg manuscript, it has now been established as having been written as late as the second half of the tenth century, probably at Fulda.

**First publication:** *Evangeliorum Liber: Veterum Germonorum grammaticæ, Poeseos, theologiæ, præclarum monimentum. Euangelienbuch in altfrenckischen reimen durch Otfriden von Weißenburg, Münch zu S. Gallen, vor sibenhundertjaren beschriben,* edited by Matthias Flacius Illyricus (Basel, 1571 [based on P]).

**Standard editions:** *Otfrids von Weißenburg Evangelienbuch,* 3 volumes, edited by Johann Kelle (Regensburg: Manz, 1856–1881; reprinted, Aalen: Zeller, 1963 [based on V, with listing of variants from other manuscripts]); *Otfrids Evangelienbuch, herausgegeben und erklärt,* edited by Oskar Erdmann (Halle: Waisenhaus, 1882 [based on V]); *Evangelienbuch: Textabdruck mit Quellenangaben und Wörterbuch,* edited by Erdmann (Halle: Waisenhaus, 1882; sixth edition, edited by Ludwig Wolff, Tübingen: Niemeyer, 1973 [based on V]); *Otfrids Evangelienbuch,* 2 volumes, edited by Paul Piper (Freiburg & Tübingen: Mohr, 1882, 1887 [based on P]).

**Editions in modern German:** Translated by Johann Kelle as *Christi Leben und Lehre, besungen von Otfrid* (Prague: Tempsky, 1870; reprinted, Osnabrück: Zeller, 1966); translated by Richard Fromme as *Otfrids Evangelienbuch aus dem Altdeutschen frei übersetzt* (Berlin: Furche, 1928); excerpts translated by Gisela Vollmann-Profe as *Otfried von Weißenburg: Evangelienbuch* (Stuttgart: Reclam, 1987).

Otfried (or Otfrid) von Weißenburg occupies a special position in the history of early German literature, in part because he is the first German writer whose name is known but also – and more significantly – because he produced one of the most important literary works of the first three centuries of vernacular literature in Germany. His *Evangelienbuch* (Gospel Book, between 863 and 871) is the longest work of the period, consisting of 7,104 long lines, three verse dedications totalling 312 additional long lines, and a prose letter in Latin to Liutbert, archbishop of Mainz, seeking his approval for the work. It is also the first large-scale work that is not a translation from the Latin; it is the first German work to use end rhyme; and the Vienna manuscript ( V ) is the first illustrated German book.

Although considerably more information is available about Otfried's life than about those of most other medieval German writers, much is still unknown. What is known comes mostly from Otfried's dedications to the *Evangelienbuch*, supplemented by monastery records. There is no doubt about the name of the author, which appears in its Latinized form *Otfridus* three times: in the acrostic and telestich that adorn the dedication to Bishop Salomo of Constance; with additional information linking him firmly to the Alsatian monastery Weißenburg in the dedication to his friends, the Saint Gall monks Hartmut and Werinbert; and in the letter to Liutbert, where he describes himself as "Otfridus quamvis indignus tamen devotione monachus presbyterque exiguus" (Otfried, though undeserving, yet by devotion a monk and humble priest). Also in the letter he says that he was a student of Hrabanus Maurus, who directed the well-known school at Fulda from 822–847. The dedications provide one final and important piece of information: since Liutbert, who is addressed by Otfried as archbishop of Mainz, occupied that position from 863 to 889, and since Bishop Salomo (whom Otfried also calls his teacher, though when and where they came in contact remains unclear) died in 871, it is possible to date the completion of the *Evangelienbuch* with unusual precision as between 863 and 871.

That is the extent of the biographical information that can be gleaned from the work; elsewhere Otfried's name rarely occurs. It appears twice in Weißenburg *Urkunden* (charters); once, possibly, in a fragmentary tenth-century Latin poem in which an Otfried, a teacher in the Weißenberg school, is mentioned, though apparently without great respect (or perhaps Otfried is being compared to some less admirable contemporary; the poem is unclear); and a few times in monastic lists. On the basis of the lists, Wolfgang Haubrichs has deduced some addi-

tional significant dates: Otfried took his monastic vows between 812 and 819; if he was then fifteen years old (the usual age at which such vows were taken), his birth date can be calculated as circa 800. The date of his death is uncertain, but it was probably not long after completion of the *Evangelienbuch*.

Although this work represents the crowning achievement of Otfried's life, recent paleographic investigations have revealed other facets of his activities as theologian and scholar. During the quarter century beginning about 850 the Weißenburg library experienced the greatest period of expansion in its history, acquiring many volumes from elsewhere but also producing a large quantity (at least thirty-three known manuscripts) in its own scriptorium. During this period commentaries, Latin and Old High German glosses, and other writings pertaining to nearly all the books of the Old and New Testaments were assembled in the monastery library. The natural assumption that the same person must have been responsible for both the surge in biblical scholarship and the subsequent production of the *Evangelienbuch*, with its elaborate theological interpretations, is supported by paleographic evidence: the same hand that entered the corrections in manuscript V of the *Evangelienbuch*, which have long been attributed to Otfried, has been identified by Wolfgang Kleiber in at least eight and possibly nine other manuscripts produced at that time at Weißenburg. The major portions of these manuscripts were written down by various scribes – in some cases, apparently, pupils learning the scribal art – but Otfried's distinctive hand is seen in the marginal commentaries and Latin glosses, as well as in key sections of the texts such as the beginning, the end, chapter headings, and in corrections. In addition, two manuscripts of works by Priscian and Prudentius, much used as instructional materials in the trivium in monastic schools, contain 168 Old High German glosses by Otfried.

The *Evangelienbuch* is a poetic treatment of Christ's life and mission, written in the South Rhine Franconian dialect of Old High German. It consists of five books: book 1 deals with the birth of Christ and the events leading to it, and his youth up to his baptism by John the Baptist; books 2 and 3 cover the calling together of the disciples and Jesus' teachings and miracles; book 4 treats the Passion; and book 5 tells of the Resurrection, Ascension, and Day of Judgment. Each book contains twenty-four to thirty-seven chapters with Latin titles, and the books are preceded by Latin titles and tables of contents. Book 1 begins with an important introductory chapter that tells why the author wrote the book in

DE INRISIONE SACERDOTU ET OMNIU PTEREUNTIUM

*Page from manuscript V of Otfried von Weißenburg's* Evangelienbuch. *The marginal notations in this manuscript are believed to have been written by Otfried himself (Vienna, Österreichische Nationalbibliothek, Codex Vindobonensis 2687, fol. 145v).*

German and includes an invocation; book 5 ends with a prayer and an epilogue. Outside this "inner frame" is – at least in the major manuscripts – an "outer frame" consisting of a dedication to Louis the German, King of the Franks; the Latin letter to Archbishop Liutbert; and the dedication to Bishop Salomo, all at the beginning of the work; and, at the end, the dedication to his friends Hartmut and Werinbert. The three verse dedications are ornamented with acrostics and telestichs. The letter to Liutbert contains invaluable information about Otfried's literary intentions, his poetic techniques, and his problems in dealing with the barbaric German (Franconian) language, which does not obey proper (Latin) spelling rules, and so forth.

The *Evangelienbuch* is not simply a Gospel harmony like the Old High German *Evangelienharmonie* (circa 830) of Tatian nor a straightforward narrative like the Old Saxon *Heliand* (circa 850), but a combination of narrative and interpretation. Otfried says in the letter to Liutbert that at the beginning and end of the book he has made careful selections from the four Gospels and striven to present a sequential, fairly complete account. In the middle, however (which he apparently completed last), both because of his own weariness and so as not to overburden the reader he has omitted much detail concerning Jesus' parables, miracles, and teachings and has simply related episodes as they occurred to his "poor memory." However seriously one may take this statement, there is no doubt that the theme of the *Evangelienbuch* is the central position of Jesus Christ in God's plan of redemption for humanity; details that do not contribute substantially to this theme could be sacrificed, and indeed some would have to be if the work were not to become unwieldy, for Otfried supplements the Gospel story with sometimes lengthy theological interpretations based on the various biblical commentaries current at the time. These interpretations are frequently signaled by the headings *Spiritaliter, Mystice,* or *Moraliter.* Although Otfried does not always clearly differentiate the first two, normally under *Spiritaliter* he gives the spiritual as opposed to the literal sense of the story, under *Mystice* he makes specific connections to church dogma, and under *Moraliter* he draws moral lessons from the story.

Not only is the *Evangelienbuch* the first extant German work employing end rhyme instead of traditional Germanic alliteration – the short *Petruslied* (Song of Peter), which was at one time considered to be earlier, was probably written around 900 or shortly after and seems to have been influenced by Otfried, rather than vice versa – but there is also good reason to believe that Otfried invented this new German verse form. One cannot rule out earlier, more primitive efforts; but several considerations point to Otfried as an innovator rather than as someone who was simply building on an established tradition. Among these considerations are his struggle to master the technique, evident in the clearly perceptible development of his skill as the work progresses, as well as his attempt in the letter to Liutbert to explain and defend a verse form that is not bound by a classical quantitative metrical system but is based on end rhyme – an ornamental figure especially popular in classical *Kunstprosa* (artistic prose) but not normally a basic structural element even when it began to appear in later verse. Moreover, Otfried complains in the same letter that his native Franconian is considered a barbaric language because it has neither been fixed in writing nor cultivated through grammatical-rhetorical arts.

The basic unit of Otfriedian poetic structure is the "short line," containing four beats or stresses and a relatively, though not absolutely, regular alternation of stressed and unstressed syllables (exceptionally short or exceptionally long lines are rare). To achieve this goal Otfried uses synaloepha (elision), as he says in the letter to Liutbert. In general, his system seems to have been to omit in writing those unstressed vowels whose sounds could be omitted in normal speech but to place a dot below those to be omitted solely for metrical reasons. As might be expected, he is not entirely consistent in applying this complicated system, often forgetting dots or confusing the two types of vowels. Variety in the form of the short lines is produced through different patterns of main and secondary stresses; the usual line contains two of each, though lines with three apparently equal stresses also occur. One of the four stresses must always fall on the last syllable of the line; if, as often happens, this syllable is a normally unstressed ending, it nevertheless bears a secondary stress.

Two short lines are linked by end rhyme – or, more properly, *homoeoteleuton,* a stylistic device defined by Latin grammarians and rhetoricians as the use of words with similar-sounding endings. This technique differs from the modern concept of end rhyme in two ways: only similarity, not identity of sounds is required, and only the final syllables – even if weakly stressed – need rhyme. Thus, although Otfried's rhyme frequently seems somewhat primitive to the modern reader, it represents an advance over the Latin tradition. To be sure, simple end syllable rhyme often occurs, as in *thanne: helle, redinon: giwidaron,* or more frequently with inclusion

*Miniature of the Crucifixion in manuscript V of the* Evangelienbuch
*(Vienna, Österreichische Nationalbibliothek,*
*Codex Vindobonensis 2687)*

of the preceding consonant, as in *ziti : noti, firwesti : gilusti;* there is even rhyme of a strongly stressed root syllable with a (metrically) secondarily stressed end syllable, as in *not : giredinot, sar : wuntar* (which also contain different vowel lengths). But both full rhyme of main syllables, such as *heil : deil, mag : dag,* and two-syllable rhyme, ranging from mere assonance (the vowels of the syllables rhyme, but the consonants differ), as in *eino : adeilo, bouma : gilouba,* to pure rhyme, such as *bithenkit : wenkit, reino : kleino,* are prevalent.

In form, therefore, Otfried's verse actually consists of rhyming couplets; in the manuscripts, however, these couplets are written – perhaps in part under the influence of alliterative verse – as long lines separated by a caesura, indicated by a period and a space between the short lines. Furthermore, two couplets, or two long lines, are grouped as a strophe, marked throughout by large red initials at the start of the first long line and indentation of the second, and even more clearly in the poetic dedications by the acrostics

formed from the initials of the first long lines and the telestichs formed from the last letters of the second long lines, which are separated from the rest of the line and written as red capitals. Occasionally groups of several strophes form syntactic or semantic units; Wolfgang Kleiber's attempt to find a significant pattern in these larger groupings based on different sizes of the red initials, however, is not convincing.

At four significant points the work achieves a near-lyrical tone, in part through the use of a refrain: in book 2, chapter 1, on the text "In the beginning was the word"; in book 5, chapter 1, dealing with the allegorical significance of the Cross; in book 5, chapter 19, on the Day of Judgment; and in book 5, chapter 23, the concluding chapter of the text proper, contrasting the perfection of the heavenly kingdom with the imperfection of the kingdom of earth. It is in these chapters, especially, that Otfried's poetic skill is unmistakable.

The source or sources from which Otfried derived his metrical scheme is a much disputed question, which has been unnecessarily complicated by an aberration that has stubbornly persisted in the scholarship since Paul Hörmann's dissertation on Otfried's metrics in 1939: the notion that Otfried's verse is somehow based on Latin hexameter. Although attempts to force his four-stress couplets into a six-stress pattern have been uniformly unsuccessful, this misconception has been kept alive primarily by a highly questionable reading of two lines in book 1, chapter 1, where Otfried advises his fellow Franconians: "Díhto io thaz zi nóti  theso séhs ziti, / thaz thú thih so girústes in theru síbuntun giréstes" (Write thus diligently throughout the six ages, / so that you may be prepared to rest in the seventh.) Obviously referring to the six ages of the human being followed by heavenly rest and to the six ages of the world followed by the kingdom of heaven, these lines have been interpreted on still another level as poetological instructions: "Write in hexameter, followed by a rest." Gisela Vollmann-Profe's demonstration of the impossibility of such an interpretation may finally put this theory to rest; the larger question of sources, however, must still be addressed. Otfried may have drawn inspiration from several literary genres. Certainly a basic connection with the so-called Ambrosian hymns cannot be denied: although the few indisputably genuine hymns written by Ambrosius in the fourth century are generally considered to be constructed according to classical quantitative metrical rules and lack rhyme, the later hymns, which were widely known throughout Europe, are of the new rhythmic-accentual type, frequently with end rhyme. Like Otfried's verse, the hymns are in four-line stanzas, and each line has four beats or stresses, the fourth of which always falls on the last syllable. Objections that a "lyrical" hymn form would be unsuitable for a biblical epic can be countered by the many examples of medieval Latin *ritmi* (rhythmic, as opposed to metrical, poems), ranging from hymns to lengthy biblical paraphrases, which were beginning to compete with the traditional hexameters. Indeed, the *ritmi,* which occupied a position somewhere between traditional metrical verse and *Kunstprosa* and often employed end rhyme, may well have been a further influence on Otfried. Finally, Otfried was surely well acquainted with Germanic alliterative verse and must have known the *Heliand.* To this background may be attributed his composition in apparent long lines (though similar forms can be found in late Latin poetry as well), his conversion of the four equal stresses of the Ambrosian hymns to a pattern of main and secondary stresses,

and the remnants of alliteration, particularly in the early parts of his work.

An even more vexing question is that of the structural principle underlying the *Evangelienbuch*. It is accepted that number symbolism occupied an important position in medieval thought and writing, but, especially in the 1960s and 1970s, scholars vied with each other in seeking such symbolism in every structural feature of medieval literature, including the *Evangelienbuch*. Lines were counted, added, multiplied, and divided, and the results led to widely divergent conclusions: the entire work was planned in the shape of a cross (according to Haubrichs and Gunter Gürich) or a *figura quadrata* (according to Johannes Rathofer, whose theory was modified by Heinz Klingenberg); elaborate structures were identified in individual books in the arrangement of strophe groups, and so forth. Apart from showing that numbers can be manipulated to prove virtually anything, these studies have led to a contradiction: on the one hand, Otfried is depicted as a mediocre poet struggling to subject the rude, unpolished German language to rules of rhyme and rhythm (to say nothing of spelling); yet, on the other hand, he is supposed to be a master of sophisticated number symbolism equal to the greatest writers. More recently there has developed a healthy skepticism of such nit-picking analyses of number symbolism in medieval writings. Nevertheless, care must be taken not to throw out the baby with the bathwater. Otfried himself provides a tantalizing clue to one structural principle he apparently considered basic to his work. In the letter to Liutbert a significant passage occurs: "Although the books of the Gospels are four, these (here) . . . I have divided into five because their (i.e., the Gospels')" holy, four-square (numerical) evenness adorns the (numerical) oddness of our five senses, and (through this) all things superfluous in us, not only in the way of deeds but also of thoughts, turn toward the exaltation of heavenly things" (translation by Francis P. Magoun, Jr.). That he contrasts the perfection of the even, four-square number of the Gospels with the imperfection of the odd number of the senses is apparent; the remainder of the passage, however, is less clear. How is the one to "adorn" the other? How are the "superfluous" things in us to be turned to heavenly things? Given the significance attached to numbers, one would expect to find something more specific behind these somewhat vague ideas. Though the exact meaning may continue to elude the modern reader, an interpretation advanced by Klingenberg has the advantages of simplicity and demonstrable validity for medieval thought. Medieval writers on

*Page from the Freising Codex of the* Evangelienbuch *(Munich, Bayerische Staatsbibliothek, Cod. germ. mon. 14)*

*arithmetica* were fascinated by the relationship of two figures: the *quadrangulum* (square) and the *gnomon* (right-angle figure). A square is even, a *gnomon* is odd; when a square and a *gnomon* are combined, a larger square is created:

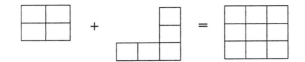

Thus, when Otfried speaks of the equal number of the Gospels "adorning" the unequal number of the senses, he may be referring to the combination of the perfect (that is, even) square represented by the four Gospels and the imperfect (odd) *gnomon* represented by the five senses, which produces a greater perfect square – the "exaltation of heavenly things" – and eliminates the "superfluous" odd number. Although Klingenberg's attempt to extend this analogy to the detailed structure of the chapters and books is highly questionable, and even the basic premise is unprovable, at least his interpretation is one that Otfried himself could hardly fault, even if it were not the one he intended.

While the Latin letter to Liutbert and the first chapter of the *Evangelienbuch*, on why the author wrote the book in German, offer a wealth of information, they also tantalize the reader with unclear and apparently contradictory statements that have fueled much controversy among scholars. This much, however, is clear: Otfried says in the letter that he was asked by certain worthy monastic brothers and a *veneranda matrona* (reverend lady) named Judith (whose further identity is unknown) to compose a selection of the Gospels in German to counter the assault of secular songs on the ears of the pious. The brothers and the lady also complained that while pagan poets such as Virgil, Lucan, and Ovid used Latin to glorify the deeds of their people and Christian poets such as Juvencus, Arator, and Prudentius used the same language to glorify the deeds of Christ, the Franks had been sluggardly in composing poetry in their language. This thought is taken up again in chapter 1 and developed into a patriotic call for the Franks, who are in all things the equal of all other peoples, not to lag behind the others in their dedication to the praise of God. But Otfried also says that he has chosen to write the work in German (Franconian) so that those who do not understand Latin or who find its difficulties too frightening may read and correctly understand the word of God; this idea also recurs in chapter 1.

Even these apparently straightforward statements raise several questions. How was the *Evangelienbuch* supposed to compete with secular songs? Was it intended to be sung also or recited as poetry, or, as J. Knight Bostock has phrased it, must one imagine the monks "in their cells reading with their fingers in their ears, rather than singing lustily in competition with the light-hearted folk outside"?

Of these alternatives, the first two, though in the past the subject of much argument, can be brought together quite simply: the work was neither strictly recited nor strictly sung in the modern sense of the words but was probably chanted, in a type of recitative known as *accentus,* which contrasted with *concentus,* the fully developed melody of a song. But there are many indications that the work was also intended to be read by an individual: for example, such adornments as the acrostics and telestichs could hardly be appreciated in any other way. Indeed, there is evidence that at least one individual did read the work; in manuscript P a later hand has scratched in the entry: "Kicila diu scona min filo las" (Beautiful Kicila read much in me). Kicila may be the empress Gisela, who in 1027 also ordered copies of the works of Notker Labeo for her own use. It is, therefore, probably best to conclude, with Dennis Green, that Otfried may well have intended his *Evangelienbuch* both for public delivery and private reading.

A second question concerns the intended audience. Unlike the *Heliand,* the *Evangelienbuch* was evidently not written for the "folk"; on the other hand, it has been argued that Otfried's repeated statement that he wrote for those who could not understand Latin would seem to rule out his fellow monks as a potential audience. Once again, it is probably most appropriate to assume several intended and actual audience types, corresponding to the different types of transmission.

One form of oral delivery was almost certainly intended as mealtime reading in the monastic refectory. It was customary to select a reader who would chant selections from the Bible, works of the Church Fathers, and so forth. Since the purpose of these readings was primarily mental relaxation and spiritual inspiration, and since the company often included lay brothers and guests who did not understand Latin, as well as some less-educated monks who might have had difficulty understanding biblical exegesis in chanted Latin, the use of the vernacular was appropriate. There is an indication that in at least one monastery the *Evangelienbuch* was used for such a purpose: the short prayers appended to the Freising manuscript (F) have been shown to be

Old High German renderings of the Latin prayer *Tu autem Domine miserere nobis* (Oh Lord, have mercy on us), with which it was customary to conclude all refectory readings. It is also possible that Otfried hoped for readings of his work at the imperial court and other gatherings of Christian nobility; in his dedication to Ludwig he expresses the hope that the king may "cause it to be read (aloud)."

As to private reading, Otfried's Latin marginal notes referring the reader to the appropriate passages in the Vulgate point to a reader who is sufficiently well versed in Latin to read the Bible but may feel more comfortable with a work in the vernacular. This description need not rule out the solitary monk reading in his cell, given the rather uneven level of education in the monasteries even after the reforms instituted by Charlemagne. The book may also have been used in monastery schools, where the use of the vernacular, the interpretations, and the Latin cross-references would have been of pedagogical value – though Otfried, unlike Notker Labeo a century later, does not say specifically that he wrote his work "out of love for his students." Of course, Otfried surely hoped for educated lay readers as well, and if Kicila is in truth Empress Gisela, he had at least one.

Otfried's theology is based on the biblical commentaries of his time, especially those of Bede, Hrabanus Maurus, and Alcuin, but the variety and richness of his exegetical sources have led some to suspect that he made use of an existing compilation. Despite many attempts, however, no such single source has been positively identified. Since Kleiber's demonstration of Otfried's role in developing a library of biblical texts and commentaries at Weißenburg, one is more inclined today to see Otfried himself as the compiler of his sources, and the Weißenburg library as his compilation.

The *Evangelienbuch* must have been well known during the last third of the ninth century and the early tenth century: since a copy was surely sent to each of the persons to whom it was dedicated, there must have been copies in Mainz, Constance, and Saint Gall in addition to Weißenburg. It is known that manuscript F was made at Freising and, if B. Bischoff is correct, manuscript D at Fulda, though the late date of the latter makes it probable that it was a copy of an earlier one, perhaps one sent to his old school at Fulda by Otfried. Otfried's inspiration can also be seen in the short burst of rhymed poems that followed his work, such as the *Petruslied, Ludwigslied* (Song of Louis III, 881 or 882), *Georgslied* (Song of Saint George, 896), *Christus und die Samariterin* (Christ and

the Samaritan Woman, circa 950), and *Psalm 138* (tenth century).

Thus, it is a mystery why Otfried and his work vanished without a trace. He must have been an important figure at Weißenburg, but his death is nowhere recorded, nor is he mentioned in later chronicles or referred to by other medieval writers; not until the end of the fifteenth century was he rediscovered by the humanist abbot of the monastery of Sponheim, Johannes Trithemius, who gives an admiring but inaccurate report of Otfried and his work. Then, during the sixteenth century, the manuscripts of the *Evangelienbuch* were discovered by German humanists – first manuscript F by Beatus Rhenanus, who published only a few brief selections, then manuscript P by an Augsburg physician, Pirminius Gassar; the first complete edition (1571) by Mathias Flacius Illyricus was based on Gassar's copy of P. Perhaps the loss of interest in the *Evangelienbuch* may be attributed to the growing opposition within the church to religious writings in the vernacular; indeed, from the end of the ninth century until the appearance of Notker III of Saint Gall (Notker Labeo) at the end of the tenth and beginning of the eleventh centuries, little of importance was written in German. The fate of Otfried himself, however, remains a mystery.

To some extent, the career of the *Evangelienbuch* in the Middle Ages was repeated in modern times. Earlier modern scholars, with few exceptions, labeled the work mediocre, comparing it unfavorably with the *Heliand*. Comments such as Rudolf Koegel's "Regarded as a poetic work of art, the *Evangelienbuch* ranks very low" and Gustav Ehrismann's "Otfried did not possess an outstanding poetic talent" were typical. Therefore, after the great editions and philological studies of the late nineteenth century, Otfried scholarship languished until the 1960s. Then, a new wave of scholarly interest in Otfried brought with it a flood of books and articles and a reevaluation of his work.

The *Heliand* may appeal more to the modern reader, but the *Evangelienbuch* was written neither for the modern reader nor for the same audience as the *Heliand*. The *Heliand* stood at the end of a long poetic tradition, and its poetic weaknesses are those of decadence; the *Evangelienbuch* represents the beginning of a new German verse form, and its weaknesses are those of a birth struggle. A comparison not with the popular *Heliand* but with more comparable late Latin biblical epics gives a truer picture of Otfried's accomplishment. In contrast to the *Heliand,* which is basically a narrative of the life of Jesus, Otfried combines the traditional features of

Latin religious poetry and achieves a balance between narration and interpretation – and does so while struggling with a rude and unpolished language "unused to being restrained by the regulating curb of the art of Grammar," as he says in the letter to Liutbert (Magoun's translation). Even if the *Evangelienbuch* did not succeed in supplanting secular songs, as Otfried had hoped, certainly to the monks hearing it in the refectory it must have seemed far more palatable than the works of Juvencus, Sedulius, or Arator. And at times, as even his critics have admitted, Otfried rises to heights of true poetic skill – as in his depiction of the Last Judgment, which is in part strongly reminiscent of the Old High German *Muspilli* (circa 790–circa 850) and in part an anticipation of the later popular sequence *Dies irae*:

In ímo man thar lésan mag    theiz ist ábulges dag,
árabeito, quísti,    joh managoro ángusti;
Thaz íst ouh dag hórnes    joh éngilliches gálmes,
    thie blásent hiar in lánte,    thaz worolt úfstante;
Theist dag ouh nîbulnísses    joh wíntesbruti, léwes!
    thiu zuei firwáhent thanne    thie súntigon alle;
Hérmido ginóto    joh wénagheiti thráto
    (waz mag ih zéllen thir hiar mér?) – thes ist ther dág
    al foller!
Lási thu io thia rédina,    wio drúhtin threwit thánana?
    that dúat er zi gihúgte,    er thanne hímil scutte.
Wér ist manno in lánte    ther thánne witharstánte,
    thanne er iz zi thíu gifíarit    thaz sih ther hímil ruarit;
Thánne er mit giwélti    ist inan fáltonti
    (queman mág uns thaz in múat!)    so man sinan lívol
    duat.

(Therein [in the prophets] one reads: that is a day of
wrath, of distress, torment,    and great anguish;
That is a day of the trumpet    and of the sound of
angels who blow their horns here    to summon the
    world to rise;
That is a day of darkness    and of storm winds, alas!
these blow away then    all sinners.
Of much pain    and great misery
[what more can I tell you here?] – of that is this day
    full!
Did you also read the account,    what the Lord threatens for us?
there he gives notice    that he will shake the heavens.
Who of the people in this land    can withstand that,
when he brings it to pass    that the heavens move;
When he with force    actually folds them up
[Let us just imagine that!]    as one does one's book.)

## Bibliography:

Johanna Belkin and Jürgen Meier, *Bibliographie zu Otfrid von Weißenburg und zur altsächsischen Bibeldichtung* (Berlin: Schmidt, 1975).

## References:

Bernhard Bischoff, "Paläographische Fragen deutscher Denkmäler der Karolingerzeit," *Frühmittelalterliche Studien*, 5 (1971): 101–134;

J. Knight Bostock, *A Handbook on Old High German Literature* (Oxford: Clarendon Press, 1955);

Helmut De Boor, *Untersuchungen zur Sprachbehandlung Otfrids: Hiatus und Synaloephe* (Breslau: Marcus, 1928);

De Boor and Richard Newald, *Geschichte der deutschen Literatur*, volume 1: *Die deutsche Literatur von Karl dem Großen bis zum Beginn der höfischen Dichtung*, ninth edition (Munich: Beck, 1979);

Gustav Ehrismann, *Geschichte der deutschen Literatur bis zum Ausgang des Mittelalters*, volume 1 (Munich: Beck, 1954);

Oskar Erdmann, *Untersuchungen über die Syntax der Sprache Otfrids* (Halle: Waisenhaus, 1874; reprinted, Hildesheim: Olms, 1973);

Ulrich Ernst, *Der Liber Evangeliorum Otfrids von Weißenburg: Literarästhetik und Verstechnik im Lichte der Tradition* (Cologne: Böhlau, 1975);

Dennis H. Green, "Zur primären Rezeption von Otfrids Evangelienbuch," in *Althochdeutsch*, volume 1, edited by R. Bergmann and others (Heidelberg: Winter, 1987), pp. 737–777;

Gunter Gürich, "Otfrids Evangelienbuch als Kreuzfigur," *Zeitschrift für deutsches Altertum und deutsche Literatur*, 95 (August 1966): 267–270;

Reinildis Hartmann, *Allegorisches Wörterbuch zu Otfrieds von Weißenburg Evangeliendichtung* (Munich: Fink, 1975);

Wolfgang Haubrichs, *Ordo als Form: Strukturstudien zur Zahlenkomposition bei Otfrid von Weissenburg und in karolingischer Literatur* (Tübingen: Niemeyer, 1969);

Haubrichs, "Otfrids St. Galler Studienfreunde," *Amsterdamer Beiträge zur älteren Germanistik*, 4 (1973): 49–112;

Ernst Hellgardt, *Die exegetischen Quellen von Otfrids Evangelienbuch* (Tübingen: Niemeyer, 1981);

Paul Hörmann, "Untersuchungen zur Verslehre Otfrids" *Literaturwissenschaftliches Jahrbuch der Görres-Gesellschaft*, 9 (1939): 1–106;

Dieter Kartschoke, *Altdeutsche Bibeldichtung* (Stuttgart: Metzler, 1975);

Kartschoke, *Bibeldichtung: Studien zur Geschichte der epischen Bibelparaphrase von Juvencus bis Otfrid von Weißenburg* (Munich: Fink, 1975);

Wolfgang Kleiber, ed., *Otfrid von Weißenburg*, Wege der Forschung, no. 419 (Darmstadt: Wissenschaftliche Buchgesellschaft, 1978);

Kleiber, *Otfrid von Weißenburg: Untersuchungen zur handschriftlichen Überlieferung und Studien zum*

*Aufbau des Evangelienbuches* (Bern & Munich: Francke, 1971);

Heinz Klingenberg, "Zum Grundriß der ahd. Evangeliendichtung Otfrids," *Zeitschrift für deutsches Altertum und deutsche Literatur,* 99 (March 1970): 35–45; 101, no. 3 (1972): 229–243;

Rudolf Koegel, *Geschichte der deutschen Literatur bis zum Ausgang des Mittelalters,* volume 1, part 2 (Strasbourg: Trübner, 1897);

D. E. Le Sage, "Aspects of the Divine Power in Otfrid's *Evangelienbuch,*" *Amsterdamer Beiträge zur älteren Germanistik,* 6 (1974): 5–48;

Albert L. Lloyd, "Vowel Shortening and Stress in Old High German. II: Otfrid," *Journal of English and Germanic Philology,* 63 (October 1964): 679–695;

Francis P. Magoun, Jr., "Otfrid's *Ad Liutbertum,*" *PMLA,* 58 (December 1943): 869–890;

Donald A. McKenzie, *Otfrid von Weißenburg: Narrator or Commentator?* (Stanford: University Press; London: Cumberlege, Oxford University Press, 1946);

Rainer Patzlaff, *Otfrid von Weißenburg und die mittelalterliche Versus-Tradition* (Tübingen: Niemeyer, 1975);

Fidel Rädle, "Otfrids Brief an Liutbert," in *Kritische Bewahrung: Beiträge zur deutschen Philologie. Festschrift für Werner Schröder zum 60. Geburtstag* (Berlin: Schmidt, 1974);

Johannes Rathofer, "Zum Bauplan von Otfrids *Evangelienbuch,*" *Zeitschrift für deutsches Altertum und deutsche Literatur,* 94 (1965): 36–38;

Heinz Rupp, "Otfrid von Weißenburg und die Zahlen," *Archiv für das Studium der neueren Sprachen,* 201 (1965): 262–265;

Werner Schröder, "Neues zu Otfrid von Weißenburg," *Beiträge zur Geschichte der deutschen Sprache und Literatur* (Tübingen), 96 (1974): 59–78;

Schröder, "Otfrid von Weißenburg," in *Die deutsche Literatur des Mittelalters: Verfasserlexikon,* second edition, volume 7 (Berlin: De Gruyter, 1989), pp. 172–193;

Rudolf Schützeichel, *Codex Pal. lat. 52: Studien zur Heidelberger Otfridhandschrift, zum Kicila-Vers und zum Georgslied,* Abh. der Akad. der Wissenschaften in Göttingen, Phil.-histor. Klasse, no. 130 (Göttingen: Vandenhoeck & Ruprecht, 1982);

Otto Springer, "Otfrid von Weißenburg: *Barbarismus et Soloecismus* – Studies in the Medieval Theory and Practice of Translation," *Symposium,* 1, no. 2 (1947): 54–81;

Petrus Tax, "Bilaterale Symmetrie bei Otfrid," *Modern Language Notes,* 80 (1965): 490–491;

Gisela Vollmann-Profe, *Kommentar zu Otfrids Evangelienbuch* (Bonn: Habelt, 1976).

# Pfaffe Konrad
*(flourished circa 1172)*

Jeffrey Ashcroft
*University of Saint Andrews*

MAJOR WORK: *Das Rolandslied* (circa 1172)

**Manuscripts:** The transmission of this work is exceptional in that the virtually complete manuscript P and the substantial fragments A and S date from before 1200, within thirty years of the composition of the poem; all appear to derive from a common manuscript. The smaller fragments T, W, E, and M are ascribed to the early thirteenth century. All these manuscripts contain closely related versions of the text tradition. Manuscript P, Heidelberg, Universitätsbibliothek, cod. pal. germ. 112, comprises 9,094 lines of rhymed couplets; it lacks one double folio (approximately 150 lines) following line 3082. It has thirty-nine pen-and-ink illustrations, whose stylistic affiliation is disputed: English influence has been proposed, though the majority of scholars relate them to Bavarian schools of manuscript illumination. Carl Wesle described the scribal dialect of manuscript P as Upper German with an admixture of Central German elements. Thomas Klein pointed to many Low German features and cast doubt on Wesle's view that it was written in Bavaria. A codicological analysis by Barbara Gutfleisch concludes that the manuscript was written in Thuringia. Paleographical features suggest a date toward the end of the twelfth century. The incomplete manuscript A, containing 4,521 lines of the text, formerly in the Städtische Bibliothek, Strasbourg, was destroyed by fire in 1870; the reliability of a transcript made by Johann Georg Scherz in 1727 is uncertain. Scherz printed engravings of two miniatures, which modern scholars have ascribed to the Regensburg-Prüfening school of book illustration, but he did not indicate how many illustrations the manuscript contained. While Wesle held it to be a Bavarian copy of a source whose scribal dialect was North Rhenish Franconian, Klein shows that this source was Eastphalian. The manuscript is tentatively dated to the last third of the twelfth century. The Schwerin fragments designated S, Schwerin, Wissenschaftliche Allgemeinbibliothek, comprise five double leaves of parchment containing lines 905 to 1843 and 8599 to 8805. Space was left for illustrations, which, however, were not carried out. Manuscript S, earlier regarded as Upper German with East Central German and Low German dialect admixture, has been localized by Klein in North Germany, perhaps in Northeastern Saxony. It dates from the twelfth century. The Arnstadt-Sondershausen fragment T, Sondershausen, Stadt- und Kreisbibliothek, Hs.-Br. 2, is a single leaf containing lines 1769 to 1869, dating from the first quarter of the thirteenth century; its scribal dialect is West Central German. The single-leaf Kauslersches Bruchstück, designated W, of similar date, preserves lines 4217 to 4311; it was at one time in Stuttgart, but its present whereabouts are unknown. The scribal dialect combines Central and Low German elements. The Erfurt fragment designated E, Erfurt, Wissenschaftliche Allgemeinbibliothek, cod. CA 4 65, retrieved from a bookbinding, has lines 3265 to 3350, though with many gaps. Its language appears to be West Central German, and it dates from around 1225. Fragment M, Marburg, Hessisches Staatsarchiv, Bestand 340 v. Dörnberg, Türkensteurregister 1603, also used as bookbinder's scrap, consists of two small pieces of parchment with lines 2221 to 2227, 2248 to 2254, 2276 to 2282, and 2305 to 2321. It dates from the second quarter of the thirteenth century; Low German dialect features suggest a northern origin.

**First publication:** *Ruolandes liet,* edited by Wilhelm Grimm (Göttingen: Dieterich, 1838).

**Standard editions:** *Das Rolandslied,* edited by Karl Bartsch (Leipzig: Brockhaus, 1874 [based on manuscript A]); *Das Rolandslied des Pfaffen Konrad*, edited by Carl Wesle (Bonn: Klopp, 1928 [diplomatic edition of manuscript P]; reprinted, Halle: Niemeyer, 1955, 1963; revised by Peter Wapnewski, Tübingen: Niemeyer, 1967).

**Standard edition and edition in modern German:** *Das Rolandslied des Pfaffen Konrad*, edited by Dieter Kartschoke (Stuttgart: Reclam, 1993).

**Edition in English:** Translated by J. W. Thomas as *Priest Konrad's Song of Roland* (Columbia, S.C.: Camden House, 1984).

Pfaffe Konrad's *Das Rolandslied* (Song of Roland, circa 1172), an adaptation of the Old French *Chanson de Roland* (circa 1100), is one of the earliest large-scale works of secular epic poetry in Middle High German and stands on the threshold of the great phase of vernacular narrative literature at the end of the twelfth and the beginning of the thirteenth centuries. It is the first major treatment in Germany of the theme of Crusade; with this theme, and with its exposition of Carolingian history — the theocratic kingship of Charlemagne and his imperial holy war to conquer and convert the heathen — it incorporates key ideological concerns of the German Empire in the age of Friedrich I (Barbarossa). As *phaffe* (cleric or ordained priest), Konrad belongs to an important category of clerical writers who had a vital role in the emergence of vernacular literature in the twelfth century and in the genesis of the cultural values and forms of *curialitas* (courtliness).

The question of Konrad's identity is connected with the question of the identity of his patrons. In the epilogue of the *Rolandslied* (lines 9017 to 9094) Konrad names them as "herzog Hainrich" (Duke Henry) and "di edele herzoginne, aines richen chüniges barn" (noble duchess, child of a mighty king). They have asked him, he says, to translate "daz buoch gescriben ze den Karlingen" (the book written in France), and he describes how he faithfully rendered it first into Latin, then into German. He praises their court, illuminated by the eternal light, as a nursery of courtly virtues and feudal loyalty. The duke is extolled as the David of his age, an all-conquering converter of the heathen who offers up body and soul in the service of his Creator; Konrad exhorts all who hear the story to pray for the salvation of the ducal couple.

In 1843 Wilhelm Grimm identified Konrad's patrons as Heinrich der Löwe (Henry the Lion), Duke of Saxony and Bavaria, and his second wife, Mathilda, daughter of Henry II of England. Their marriage in 1168 would, thus, be the earliest possible date for the commission to translate the *Chanson de Roland*, a manuscript of which Mathilda might have brought with her from England. Grimm suggests that Konrad was "eine für seine zeit gelehrter, in sprachen bewanderter mann, vielleicht capellan an dem hofe des herzogs" (a man learned by the standards of his time, versed in languages, perhaps chaplain at the ducal court). In that case, Konrad would have been at the court of Brunswick, Heinrich's main residence and power center. In his edition of 1874, however, Karl Bartsch declared the language of the *Rolandslied* too archaic for the period around 1170; believing manuscript A, whose dialect he analyzed as Rhenish Franconian with Bavarian coloring, to be a direct reflex of Konrad's original text, he assumed that Konrad came from the Franconian Rhineland but was resident in Regensburg and that his patrons were Heinrich der Löwe's parents, Herzog Heinrich der Stolze (Duke Henry the Proud) and his wife, Gertrud, daughter of the emperor Lothar III, and that they had commissioned the poem before Heinrich der Stolze's death in 1139. This thesis was elaborated in 1883 by Edward Schröder, who detailed textual and thematic links between the *Rolandslied* and *Die Kaiserchronik* (Chronicle of Emperors), written in Regensburg after 1147; Schröder claimed that Konrad was the author of both works. Carl Wesle in 1924, Martin Lintzel in 1926, and Dieter Kartschoke in 1965 refuted Schröder's attribution of the *Kaiserchronik* to Konrad, though conceding that it had a direct influence on his work, and argued cogently for Heinrich der Löwe and Mathilda as his patrons. In 1968 Karl Bertau placed the *Rolandslied* in the context of Heinrich der Löwe's cultural policy in the 1170s; Eberhard Nellmann, Karl-Ernst Geith, Marianne Ott-Meimberg, Jeffrey Ashcroft, and Maria Dobozy have shown how the poem reflects Heinrich's ideological concerns and ambitions and his prosecution of the Northern Crusade in his Saxon duchy. Attempts to promote Heinrich Jasomirgott, Duke of Bavaria from 1141 to 1156, who was married first to Gertrud and later to Theodora, niece of the Byzantine emperor Manuel I Comnenos, as Konrad's patron have proved unpersuasive. The present consensus holds firmly that the *Rolandslied* was composed circa 1172 at the behest of Heinrich der Löwe.

At the same time, it is still generally assumed that Konrad is to be sought in Regensburg. Yet the arguments in support of this assumption look increasingly tenuous. Suggested identifications (by André de Mandach and Romuald Bauerreis) of Konrad with historically documented clerics of that name in Regensburg are unconvincing in the absence of any evidence of their literary activity or of a connection with Heinrich der Löwe. The duke visited Bavaria infrequently and briefly; his court resided at Brunswick, which he vigorously promoted as the political, religious, and cultural focus of his territory. Joachim Bumke's view that Konrad might have been a cleric serving in a ducal chancery in Regensburg is untenable, given Karl Jordan's demonstration that Heinrich's administrative staff was based in Brunswick. Only the manuscript transmission offers any seemingly firm link with Bavaria: the early manuscripts display a complex and puzzling blend of linguistic features in which northern and central German dialect phonology and orthography are arbitrarily combined with Bavarian and Alemannic forms. While Wesle held that the linguistic base of manuscripts A, P, and S was Bavarian and that the more northerly elements had arisen in the manuscript transmission, Thomas Klein and Barbara Gutfleisch adduce paleographical and codicological evidence that radically challenges the older view, arguing that northern features were present in the common archetype and intermediate sources of the early manuscripts and ascribing these and the later fragments to central and northern German scribal traditions.

Jeffrey Ashcroft has adduced new evidence to support Grimm's contention that Konrad was a chaplain at Heinrich der Löwe's court in Brunswick. Witness lists of legal charters issued by Heinrich in the 1170s cite a Conradus who was in the duke's service in 1174 and 1176, and probably as early as 1171: he is specified as "capellanus ducis" (ducal chaplain) and described as "dominus Conradus Sueuus" (Sir Conrad the Swabian) and "magister Conradus presbiter" (Master Conrad the priest). Since several of Heinrich's court chaplains were also canons of the cathedral of Saint Blasius in Brunswick, it is possible that the Conradus who appears in the first extant list of the canons in 1196 may be this chaplain. There is no proof that the chaplain Conradus of the charters is the Pfaffe Konrad of the *Rolandslied,* but he is, at least, a preeminently well-qualified candidate: a man of theological learning (*magister* is a prestigious title denoting the graduate of an institution of higher clerical education, possibly in France, where many German clerics were educated in the later twelfth century); a priest, whose designation as *presbiter* in the charters suggests that liturgical and pastoral, rather than notarial, duties were his prime function at the Brunswick court; a ducal chaplain, one of a small group of highly educated clerics who served the duke as

an administrative and executive cadre and performed important religious and cultural commissions; a Swabian who may have come to Saxony from the Welf lands in south Germany – an origin that could help to explain the dialect mixture of the early manuscripts. The identification of *capellanus* Conradus as the author of the *Rolandslied* would account for the breadth of the latter's theological learning, perhaps for his ability to translate the French source, for the trust the ducal couple placed in him, for his commitment to the imperial and crusading concerns of Heinrich der Löwe, and for his lavish praise of his patrons.

In his epilogue Konrad asserts, in a conventional formula, that he translated his French source without additions or omissions (lines 9084 to 9085); and he does tell the story of Roland and Charlemagne with essential fidelity. The emperor Karl, commanded by God to conquer the pagans in Spain and to convert them to Christianity, summons his barons to war. Imbued with religious fervor, they wear the crusaders' badge of the cross and are promised eternal reward if they die in battle. A punitive campaign leaves the heathen king Marsilie beleaguered in his last stronghold, Saragossa. He sues for peace, pledging to accept the Christian faith if the Frankish army withdraws. After long deliberation Karl and his princes send Genelun, Roland's stepfather, as envoy to Marsilie's court to test the sincerity of the heathen proposal. To avenge himself on Roland, who nominated him for this perilous mission, Genelun plots the betrayal of the Christian army and accepts lavish bribes from Marsilie and his barons. Karl, at Genelun's instigation, crowns Roland as his viceroy in Spain, leaves Roland behind with a small force of warriors to enforce the pact with Marsilie, and returns with his army to Aachen. Immediately a vast heathen host attacks Roland and his men. Urged by his comrade-in-arms Olivir to summon the emperor back by sounding his war horn, Olivant, Roland refuses, greeting the battle against overwhelming odds as a God-given opportunity for martyrdom in the chivalric service of God. After brave resistance, sustained by divine help, his army is annihilated; Roland is the last to perish, having finally sounded the horn, and he surrenders his imperial commission to the angel whom God sends to conduct his soul to eternal life. Karl returns to the battlefield and finds the bodies of his men. Distraught with grief, he is admonished by the angel to rejoice at their martyrdom and to exact vengeance on the heathen. Aided by divine miracles, he defeats the pagans, reinforced and led by their emperor, Paligan, in a second cataclysmic battle. He bears the bodies of the fallen Christian saints back to France and arraigns the traitor, Genelun; a trial by combat, in which God gives victory to the emperor's champion, leads to Genelun's execution.

Despite Konrad's claim that he has merely reproduced what he found in his source, there are important differences of emphasis and theme in the *Rolandslied* as compared with the extant redactions of the *Chanson de Roland*. It may be that the version available to Konrad was different from these redactions; he may have known the Latin *Chronicle of Pseudo-Turpin,* a history of the events purporting to have been written by Bishop Turpin, a character in the epic who plays a prominent part as adviser to the emperor and as a warrior in Roland's army; there is some slight evidence of earlier German poems on Charlemagne and Roland. It seems most likely, however, that Konrad himself chose to develop and adapt his source in ways that give revealing insights into his motivation as a clerical poet and into his perception of the interests and expectations of his patrons.

Konrad is an intrusive narrator who, in the manner of the preacher or the exegetical commentator, insistently guides his audience's reception of the story by exhorting them to recognize and emulate his heroes as exemplars of Christian virtue and interjects biblical quotations and paraphrases (for example, in lines 3941 to 3960 and 5155 to 5170). The explicit theological perspective Konrad superimposes on the story is one major new thrust of his version and is especially apparent in sections where, so far as can be determined, he supplements or significantly amends his source. Thus, he adds an introduction (lines 1 to 360) in which Karl prays for and receives a divine commission to conquer and convert the pagans in Spain; here Konrad depicts the emperor as a model theocratic monarch and a figure of personal sanctity (though without expressly denoting him as a saint, as the canonization of Charlemagne by the German church at the instigation of Friedrich Barbarossa in 1165 would have allowed him to do), and he describes the mobilization of the Christian army as the summoning of a Crusade, stressing the warriors' purity of motivation and religious fervor. Konrad greatly expands the council episode (lines 891 to 1537), laying consistent emphasis on the unanimity of the princes in seeking an outcome conducive to "gotes ere" (the honor and renown of God) and isolating Genelun as the only one of Karl's counselors who puts material and secular interests before the demands of God and the Christian empire. In his handling of the crucial scene in which Roland refuses to sound his horn to recall Karl as the heathens prepare to attack, Konrad effaces the conflict in his source between Roland's pride and Olivir's caution; in his version both greet the battle as a heaven-sent opportunity for chivalric self-abnegation and martyrdom (lines 3845 to 3898). In these instances, climactic moments of tension and drama in the *Chanson de Roland* are sacrificed as Konrad suppresses all elements of fallibility in his heroes and makes them exemplary embodiments of a spiritualized commitment to religious ideals.

Konrad is not, however, simply imposing a "precourtly" or even "anticourtly" asceticism, as earlier scholars tended to claim. Konrad's conception of Christian chivalry in the *Rolandslied* is a major literary contribution to the efforts of the church, evident since the middle of the eleventh century, to evolve a theology of Christian warfare and to define knighthood as a religious vocation; the most spectacular outcome of these efforts was the Crusades, beginning in 1095 with the expedition that captured Jerusalem and established a Christian kingdom in the Holy Land. In turning the Carolingian warriors of the *Rolandslied* into high medieval crusaders, Konrad deploys his intimate awareness of the themes and idioms of twelfth-century crusading propaganda and piety. The appeals and sermonlike speeches with which Karl and Archbishop Turpin mobilize and motivate the warriors (lines 87 to 106, 243 to 272, and 3905 to 3940) show clear evidence of Konrad's acquaintance with, especially, the writings of Saint Bernard of Clairvaux. Bernard led the recruitment of the Second Crusade in France and Germany in 1146–1147 and since 1128 had been the chief advocate and spiritual patron of the military orders of the Templars and Hospitalers, whose combination of the vocations of monk and knight he hailed as a "nova militia" (new chivalry) in which the soldier of Christ "ut corpus ferri, sic animum fidei lorica induitur" (puts the breastplate of faith on his soul in the same way as he puts a breastplate of iron on his body) so that, "utrisque nimirum munitus armis, nec daemonem timet, nec hominem" (defended by both kinds of armor he fears neither demon nor man). Konrad's warriors, too,

waren uzen unt innen
beslozen mit uesten ringen.
der stal schirmtte dem ulaische,
diu heilige minne dem gaiste. (lines 4861–4864)

(were girded within and without
with sturdy chain mail.
steel protected their flesh,
divine love their spirits.)

Quotations of the gospel injunction to leave all behind and take up the cross and of the parable of the vineyard, and the exposition of the themes of reward and remission of penance, in the speeches of Karl and Turpin (lines 181–221, 245–272, 971–1010, 5399–5404) rehearse common motifs of the preaching of the Crusade. In other instances Turpin and Konrad, as the narrator, appear to paraphrase Saint Bernard's injunctions to the Templars when they prescribe how the knights should combine the virtues of monk and warrior (lines 260 to 272, 3452 to 3458, and 5755 to 5828).

Beyond the broad concern of the clerical poet to set up role models of Christian chivalry for his secular audience, and beyond the general currency of crusading ideals and enthusiasm in the twelfth century, Konrad's enlistment of the Carolingian epic heroes into the *nova militia* has a more precise motivation: he is able to praise his patron, Heinrich der Löwe, as conqueror and converter of the heathen in the epilogue of the *Rolandslied* because Heinrich's campaigns to extend his Saxon duchy into the lands beyond the river Elbe, occupied by the Slavic peoples known as the Wends, were acknowledged by the church as Crusades. As early as 1108 the church in Magdeburg had appealed for armed support from the knighthood in Saxony and in Lorraine and Flanders, which had recently provided major contingents for the First Crusade to the Holy Land, declaring that the missionary church in eastern Europe was "our Jerusalem" defended by the soldiers of Christ. In 1147 Saint Bernard and Pope Eugene III formally granted the status of Crusade to the campaign against the Wends and allowed the German nobles to fulfill their crusader's vow by fighting in Saxony as an alternative to joining the main expedition to the Holy Land. Heinrich der Löwe was one of those who "took the Cross" and fought in the war against the Slavs. Throughout the 1150s and 1160s the extension of his territories in Slav Transalbinia was a high priority for Heinrich, and the Saxon church sought to persuade the power-hungry duke to combine his territorial ambitions with the religious mission to convert the pagans. At the climax of his political career, in 1172, Heinrich led an armed pilgrimage of a thousand knights and clerics to Jerusalem, though he was thwarted in his evident hope of experiencing military action in the Holy Land itself. In Jerusalem he became a generous patron of the Templars and Hospitalers. These contacts of Konrad's patron with the military orders, as well as the presence in Saxony of monasteries of the Cistercian order (the order to which Saint Bernard belonged) and the fact that between the Second Crusade in 1147 and the Third Crusade of 1189 Saxony was the prime focus of crusading in Germany, provide a historical framework for Konrad's knowledge of and deep commitment to the ideal of crusading chivalry.

Yet the Crusade that the *Rolandslied* depicts is not summoned and directed by pope or saintly abbot. It is the emperor Karl who conceives the expedition to convert the pagans in Spain; it is to the emperor that God sends his angel to authorize the war in his name; and it is Karl who appeals to his warriors to serve in the army of God and to imitate the self-sacrifice of Christ and who promises the martyr's crown to those who die. A further major thrust of Konrad's adaptation of the epic of Charlemagne and Roland is the elaboration of the themes, central to the *Chanson de Roland,* of the theocratic nature of Karl's kingship, of his supreme authority over Christendom, and of his claim to universal dominion of the world he is charged to conquer and convert as "uoget uon Rome" (protector of the Roman Church and Empire). In Konrad's poem the sacral power of the emperor and the unquestioning allegiance he commands as God's earthly regent subsume and relegate all other secular loyalties or bonds of fealty. The patriotic pride in "dulce France" (sweet France), the concern for personal reputation, and the ties of kinship that also motivate the warriors of the *Chanson de Roland* are here overridden by the all-important sense of serving Karl, the "heiliger kaiser" (sacral emperor), and, through him, God himself. Only the traitor Genelun puts personal enmity against Roland, concern for his lands and family, and the lure of wealth before his duty to the emperor, and for doing so, Konrad condemns him as a Judas. Karl's army is drawn from many Christian lands; his counselors equate "gotes ere" (the honor of God) with "des richis ere" (the honor of the empire); in battle the warriors are "di cristen" (the Christians), "gotes chint" (the children of God), whose allegiance to Karl is coextensive with their redemptive service of God. The heathen emperor Paligan makes rival claims of universal sovereignty, threatening to seize Aachen and Rome for the heathen idols Machmet (Muhammad) and Apollo; in the final great battle scene of the poem the two emperors fight in single combat, and Karl, with miraculous aid from God, asserts the inviolability of the Christian cause.

What underlies both the *Chanson de Roland* and the *Rolandslied* – the holy war of the empire in the defence of Christendom – is a historical theme much older than the idea of Crusade. Its conception goes back to the first stage of the Christianization of the Roman Empire under Constantine; it was central to the Christian renewal of the Roman Empire

geriht unz an den tot. peſtatigen ſin ere. genelun
ſach dar ungerne. Rolant ſprach zu dem
chaiſer herre riu an ſine reiſe. harte urolichen.
haun zu francriche. den uan ſcol furen. herre
al nach dinen eren. gotes hulde haſtu hie er
worven. habe du dehaine ſorgem. dar ich uner
entrinnen dannen. der uan ne ſcol mir nichet
ſo lichte enphallen. ſo der hantſriuch geneliute.
dine furſten du niene ſume. got ſpar din ere.
der kaiſer wainte uil ſere. uil dicke er in chuſ
te. er druhte in an ſine bruſte. er beſwaif in
mit den armen. er ſprach nu mure iz got er
barmen. daz ich dich bi mir lazen. ia ne mag
ich nicht dar zu geben mure. daz ich da fure
name. het dar ich dich tagelichen ſehe.

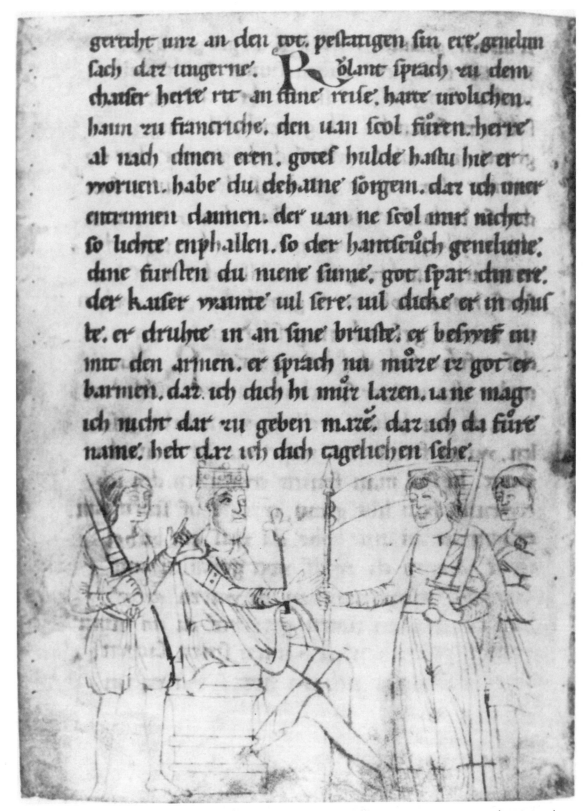

Page from manuscript P of Das Rolandslied of Pfaffe Konrad, with an illustration showing the emperor Karl (Charlemagne)
bestowing the viceroyalty of Spain on Roland (Heidelberg, Universitätsbibliothek, cod. pal. germ. 112, fol. 43v)

126

by Charlemagne; it finds expression in vernacular literature in the *Ludwigslied* (Song of Ludwig) of 881 or 882. Konrad's innovation is to synthesize the Carolingian theme of imperial holy war with the twelfth-century ideal of Crusade. In this respect he reflects the broad pattern of the German reception of the crusading idea. While in 1095 Pope Urban II appealed to the French knighthood to serve God as soldiers of Christ, and none of the Western Christian kings joined the First Crusade (though chroniclers report that in the popular imagination Charlemagne was expected to rise from the dead to lead the expedition), between 1145 and 1147 Saint Bernard recruited Louis VII of France and Konrad III of Germany. Thus, the first significant entry of Germany into the crusading movement took place under royal leadership and in some measure presupposed a merging of Crusade and holy war. Twenty years after the *Rolandslied* was written, Friedrich Barbarossa certainly envisaged the Third Crusade as an imperial war in which the emperor would lead the united forces of Christendom. In the more immediate context of the genesis of Konrad's work, Heinrich der Löwe's Saxony, the synthesis of holy war and Crusade had a particular resonance. The still-pagan Saxons had been integrated into the Christian empire and faith by Charlemagne; he and his imperial successors, notably Otto the Great, had prosecuted holy war against the Slavs on the eastern marches of Saxony. In Helmold of Bosau's *Chronicle of the Slavs,* written around the same time as the *Rolandslied,* Heinrich's wars beyond the Elbe are seen as completing and surpassing the endeavors of these great predecessors. Moreover, Heinrich laid great stress on his ancestral link with Charlemagne and, as the grandson of the emperor Lothar II, on his own royal blood. His marriage to Mathilda of England was a further assertion of this quasi-royal status. When Konrad, in the epilogue of the *Rolandslied,* celebrates Heinrich as the prince of his time who may best be compared with King David, he implies the duke's qualification to stand as an equal beside the emperor, on whose crown David was depicted, and to inherit the mantle of the "Kaiser Karl" whom his poem portrays. The fusion of imperial mission and Crusade in the Northern Crusade is endorsed and propagated in the *Rolandslied.*

Konrad's work is not, however, crude propaganda for the Welf prince Heinrich as the true heir to the imperial crown of Charlemagne. The epic characters of Karl and Roland (the latter bears on his shield the lion device of Heinrich and his dynasty) offer legitimizing images of kingship and chivalry with which the poem's patron may well

have identified himself. At the same time, however, they set up formidably idealized models for Heinrich, who was regarded by many contemporaries, and portrayed at times even by the Saxon chronicler Helmold of Bosau, as an overweeningly arrogant, ruthless, and unprincipled pursuer of power and material gain. Konrad also lays consistent emphasis throughout the epic on the exemplary unanimity and cooperation of emperor and princes. This aspect, too, must have had specific resonance for Heinrich and his court. It was the emperor Friedrich Barbarossa who had secured Heinrich's claim to the duchy of Bavaria and who granted him unparalleled latitude to build up his power in Saxony. In return, Heinrich supported Friedrich at his accession in 1152 and in his military campaigns throughout the 1150s and 1160s. Only after 1174 did Heinrich begin to withhold this support, suffering eventually for doing so by being deposed from his imperial fiefs and banished from Germany. In this respect, too, it may be asserted that Pfaffe Konrad held up before his patron not so much a flattering mirror as an ideal prescription that, in the end, Heinrich was unable to fulfill.

With this synthesis of holy war and Crusade, the grandiose portrait of theocratic kingship in the figure of Karl and the intensely spiritualized model of redemptive chivalry that Roland typifies, Konrad's adaptation of Carolingian historical legend stands at the center of politico-religious ideology in the second half of the twelfth century. The *Rolandslied* offered potent literary images for key concerns of the German empire under Friedrich Barbarossa: the reassertion of its theocratic sanction, its sacral authority, and its universal pretensions, for which Charlemagne served as a legitimizing prototype in Friedrich's propaganda and historiography. The poem had special resonance in Welf Saxony, for by celebrating the achievements of Charlemagne as conqueror and converter of the heathen it might redound to the glory of his descendant Heinrich der Löwe, validating his aggressive policies in Transalbinia and promoting the Welf dynasty's pretensions to royal status. Konrad's exposition of Christian knighthood encapsulates the church's endeavors to reform feudal warrior society on the threshold of the age in which secular poets took over from clerics the articulation of the ethical ideals of chivalry. Few works of medieval German literature present such sharply focused insights into the specific functions literature could perform for its patrons and audiences. The *Rolandslied* is preeminently a piece of political poetry; and if Konrad was the chaplain Conradus, saliently positioned at the

Brunswick court of Heinrich der Löwe, one can understand with an equally rare precision how the clerical poet was able to reinterpret the traditional story of the *Chanson de Roland* with such relevance for his contemporaries.

Although the manuscript transmission of the *Rolandslied* ceases soon after 1200, its influence on later generations was not negligible. Konrad's poem was "erniuwet" (renewed) by the poet known as Der Stricker in a free adaptation; scholars have dated this work either between 1215 and 1225 or circa 1233 and given it the title *Karl der Große* (Charlemagne). In this form it remained popular (more than forty manuscripts are recorded) until the late Middle Ages, particularly among the Deutschorden (Teutonic Knights), the warrior monks who prosecuted the Northern Crusade in the Baltic lands from the thirteenth to the fifteenth centuries. Large sections of Konrad's own text were incorporated into the *Karlmeinet* (Young Karl) compilation of Charlemagne stories sometime after 1300.

Direct influence of the *Rolandslied* on the major literature of the immediately following generation was slight. It may be that when Walther von der Vogelweide casts himself as an angelic messenger reminding Heinrich der Löwe's son, the emperor Otto IV, that he is God's "voget" (defender) on earth and should mount a Crusade, Walther intends to create associations with the opening lines of the poem Pfaffe Konrad wrote for Otto's father. But only Wolfram von Eschenbach's *Willehalm* (circa 1210–1220), which depicts warfare against Islam in the reign of Charlemagne's son, Louis the Pious, refers unmistakably and significantly to the text and themes of the *Rolandslied*. Wolfram's narrative is the only other adaptation into German of an Old French historical epic in this period. Wolfram's depiction of Carolingian holy war and crusading chivalry contrasts sharply, however, with Konrad's. Above all, Wolfram calls into question the whole ideological and theological justification of warfare in the name of God. While Konrad portrays the heathen as an evil empire and their chivalry as worldly vanity and thralldom to the devil, Wolfram argues that all humans are children of the divine father and asks, as Christian and heathen dead litter another battlefield, whether it is not a great sin to slaughter "gotes hantgetât" (God's handiwork) as if people of different faith were merely beasts. *Willehalm* breaks off uncompleted with a gesture of humane acknowledgment of religious differences. Its audience – whose literary images of chivalry, and even of Crusade, were formed by the more secularized moral optimism, emancipated from clerical

fanaticism, of Heinrich von Veldeke, Hartmann von Aue, and Wolfram himself – may already have begun to be repelled by the harsh imperative Konrad has the angel promulgate to Karl:

> daz lut wirdit bekeret;
> di dir abir widir sint,
> die heizent des tuvelis kint
> unt sint allesamt uirlorin;
> die slehet der gotes zorn
> an libe unt an sele:
> die helle puwint si imermere. (lines 58–64)

> (the people shall be converted,
> but those who oppose you
> shall be called children of the devil
> and shall perish without exception.
> God's wrath shall smite them,
> both body and soul,
> they shall dwell in hell for evermore.)

While Pfaffe Konrad was in the literal sense a courtly poet, one of the first who can be related closely to a known princely patron, the ascetic rigor of the *Rolandslied* is in some respects profoundly at odds with the cultural and ethical values of the greatest literature of the high medieval courts. Modern readers who share Wolfram's disquiet about Konrad's enthusiasm for the conversion of the heathen by fire and sword may remind themselves that men and women still kill and are killed in the name of religion and that the *Rolandslied* voices attitudes that have not yet been dispensed with.

**References:**

Jeffrey Ashcroft, "Konrad's *Rolandslied*, Henry the Lion, and the Northern Crusade," *Forum for Modern Language Studies,* 22 (April 1986): 184–208;

Ashcroft, "Magister Conradus Presbiter: Pfaffe Konrad at the Court of Henry the Lion," in *Literary Aspects of Courtly Culture,* edited by Donald Maddox and Sara Sturm-Maddox (Cambridge: Brewer, 1994), pp. 301–308;

Ashcroft, "*Miles dei – gotes ritter:* Konrad's *Rolandslied* and the Evolution of the Concept of Christian Chivalry," *Forum for Modern Language Studies,* 17 (April 1981): 146–166; reprinted in *Knighthood in Medieval Literature,* edited by W. H. Jackson (Edinburgh: Scottish Academic Press, 1982), pp. 146–166;

Ashcroft, "*Si waren aines muotes:* Unanimity in Konrad's *Rolandslied* and Otto's and Rahewin's *Gesta Frederici*," in *Medieval Knighthood IV,* edited by Christopher Harper-Bill and

and Ruth Harvey (Woodbridge: Boydell, 1992), pp. 23–50;

Herbert Backes, *Bibel und Ars Praedicandi im "Rolandslied" des Pfaffen Konrad* (Berlin: Schmidt, 1966);

Romuald Bauerreis, "Die Siegburger Klosterreform in Regensburg, die 'Kaiserchronik,' das 'Rolandslied' und der Pfaffe Konrad," *Studien und Mitteilungen zur Geschichte des Benediktinerordens*, 82 (1971): 334–343;

Karl Bertau, "Das deutsche *Rolandslied* und die Repräsentationskunst Heinrichs des Löwen," *Der Deutschunterricht*, 20, no. 2 (1968): 4–30; reprinted in *Literarisches Mäzenatentum im Mittelalter,* edited by Joachim Bumke (Darmstadt: Wissenschaftliche Buchgesellschaft, 1982), pp. 331–370;

Joachim Bumke, *Mäzene im Mittelalter: Die Gönner und Auftraggeber der höfischen Literatur in Deutschland 1150–1300* (Munich: Beck, 1979);

Maria Dobozy, *Full Circle: Kingship in the German Epic* (Göppingen: Kümmerle, 1985);

Dobozy, "The Theme of the Holy War in German Literature 1152–1190: Symptom of Controversy between Empire and Papacy?," *Euphorion*, 80, no. 4 (1986): 341–362;

Karl-Ernst Geith, *Carolus Magnus: Studien zur Darstellung Karls des Großen in der deutschen Literatur des 12. und 13. Jahrhunderts* (Bern: Francke, 1977);

Christian Gellinek, "The Epilogue of Konrad's *Rolandslied,* Commission and Dating," *Modern Language Notes,* 83 (April 1968): 390–405;

Wilhelm Grimm, "Der Epilog zum *Rolandsliede,*" *Zeitschrift für deutsches Altertum,* 3 (1843): 281–288;

Barbara Gutfleisch, "Die Überlieferung des 'Rolandsliedes' des Pfaffen Konrad: Stand und Probleme ihrer Erforschung," M.A. thesis, University of Munich, 1990;

Karl Jordan, *Heinrich der Löwe: Eine Biographie,* second edition (Munich: Beck, 1980);

Jordan, ed., *Die Urkunden Heinrichs des Löwen Herzogs von Sachsen und Bayern* (Weimar: Böhlau, 1941);

Dieter Kartschoke, *Die Datierung des deutschen "Rolandsliedes"* (Stuttgart: Metzler, 1965);

Kartschoke, "*in die latine bedwungin.* Kommunikationsprobleme im Mittelalter und die Übersetzung der 'Chanson de Roland' durch den Pfaffen Konrad," *Beiträge zur Geschichte der deutschen Sprache und Literatur,* 111 (1989): 196–209;

Thomas Klein, "Untersuchungen zu den mitteldeutschen Literatursprachen des 12. und 13.

Jahrhunderts," inaugural dissertation, University of Bonn, 1982;

Rita Lejeune and Jacques Stiennon, *The Legend of Roland in the Middle Ages* (New York: Phaidon, 1971);

Martin Lintzel, "Zur Datierung des deutschen *Rolandsliedes,*" *Zeitschrift für deutsche Philologie,* 51 (1926): 13–33;

André de Mandach, *Naissance et développement de la chanson de geste en Europe,* volume 1: *La Geste de Charlemagne et Roland* (Paris & Geneva: Droz, 1961);

Eberhard Nellmann, "Karl der Große und König David im Epilog des deutschen *Rolandsliedes,*" *Zeitschrift für deutsches Altertum,* 94 (1965): 268–279; reprinted in *Die Reichsidee in der deutschen Literatur des Mittelalters,* edited by Rüdiger Schnell (Darmstadt: Wissenschaftliche Buchgesellschaft, 1983), pp. 222–238;

Nellmann, "Pfaffe Konrad," in *Die deutsche Literatur des Mittelalters: Verfasserlexikon,* volume 5, edited by Kurt Ruh (Berlin & New York: De Gruyter, 1984), pp. 115–131;

Friedrich Neumann, "Wann entstanden *Kaiserchronik* und *Rolandslied?,*" *Zeitschrift für deutsches Altertum,* 91 (1961–1962): 263–329;

Friedrich Ohly, "Die Legende von Karl und Roland," in *Studien zur frühmittelhochdeutschen Literatur,* edited by L. Peter Johnson, Hans-Hugo Steinhoff, and Roy Albert Wisbey (Berlin: Schmidt, 1974), pp. 292–343;

Ohly, "Zum Dichtungsschluß *Tu autem, domine, miserere nobis,*" *Deutsche Vierteljahrsschrift,* 47 (February 1973): 26–68;

Ohly, "Zum Reichsgedanken des deutschen *Rolandsliedes,*" *Zeitschrift für deutsches Altertum,* 77 (1940): 189–217;

Marianne Ott-Meimberg, *Kreuzzugsepos oder Staatsroman? Strukturen adeliger Heilsversicherung im deutschen "Rolandslied"* (Zurich & Munich: Artemis, 1980);

Horst Richter, *Kommentar zum "Rolandslied" des Pfaffen Konrad* (Bern & Frankfurt am Main: Lang, 1972);

Edward Schröder, "Die Heimat des deutschen *Rolandsliedes,*" *Zeitschrift für deutsches Altertum,* 27 (1883): 70–82;

Peter Wapnewski, "Der Epilog und die Datierung des *Rolandsliedes,*" *Euphorion,* 49, no. 3 (1955): 262–282;

Carl Wesle, "*Kaiserchronik* und *Rolandslied,*" *Beiträge zur Geschichte der deutschen Sprache und Literatur,* 48 (1924): 223–258.

# Pfaffe Lamprecht

*(flourished circa 1150)*

J. Wesley Thomas
*University of Kentucky*

**MAJOR WORKS:** *Tobias* (circa 1145)

> **Manuscript:** All that remains of Lamprecht's version of the apocryphal Book of Tobit appears on two somewhat damaged parchment leaves of the late twelfth century that were used in the binding of a manuscript volume. The fragments – Berlin, Staatsbibliothek Stiftung Preußischer Kulturbesitz, Ms. germ. qu. 1418, presently in the Krakow University Library – are in the Moselle Franconian dialect and include the first 274 verses of the work.
>
> **First publication:** In "Neue Funde aus dem zwölften Jahrhundert," edited by Hermann Degering, *Beiträge zur Geschichte der deutschen Sprache und Literatur,* 41 (1916): 513–553 (*Tobias* text: 528–536);
>
> **Standard editions:** In *Die Werke des Pfaffen Lamprecht nach der ältesten Überlieferung,* edited by Hans Ernst Müller (Munich: Callwey, 1923), pp. 62–71; in *Die religiösen Dichtungen des 11. und 12. Jahrhunderts,* edited by Friedrich Maurer, volume 2 (Tübingen: Niemeyer, 1965), pp. 522–535.

*Alexander* (circa 1150)

> **Manuscripts:** The work survived in different forms in three manuscripts: two on parchment from the twelfth century and one on paper from the fifteenth century. The oldest and closest to the original is in the Bavarian-Austrian dialect, with traces of Moselle-Franconian, and is in the medieval Styrian monastery at Vorau (cod. 276). A second, in Rhenish Franconian, was destroyed with the city library of Strasbourg during the Franco-Prussian War, but its contents had been published. The fifteenth-century manuscript is in the library of the University of Basel (Hs. E. 26). It is a world chronicle in the Alemannic dialect into which a version of Lamprecht's work was inserted.

**First publications:** In *Denkmäler deutscher Sprache und Literatur aus Handschriften des 8ten bis 16ten Jahrhunderts,* edited by H. F. Massmann (Munich: Jaquet, 1827), pp. 16–75 (Strasbourg text); in *Deutsche Gedichte des elften und zwölften Jahrhunderts,* edited by Joseph Diemer (Vienna: Braumüller, 1849; reprinted, Darmstadt: Wissenschaftliche Buchgesellschaft, 1968), pp. 183–226 (Vorau text); *Die Basler Bearbeitung von Lamprechts Alexander,* edited by Richard Maria Werner (Tübingen: Literarischer Verein in Stuttgart, 1881).

**Standard editions:** *Lamprechts Alexander: Nach den drei Texten, mit dem Fragment des Alberic von Besançon und den lateinischen Quellen,* edited by Karl Kinzel (Halle: Waisenhaus, 1884); in *Das Alexanderlied des Pfaffen Lamprecht; Das Rolandslied des Pfaffen Konrad,* edited by Friedrich Maurer (Leipzig: Reclam, 1940; reprinted, Darmstadt: Wissenschaftliche Buchgesellschaft, 1964), pp. 5–46 (Vorau text).

**Edition in English:** In *The Strassburg Alexander and the Munich Oswald: Pre-courtly Adventure of the German Middle Ages,* translated by J. Wesley Thomas (Columbia, S.C.: Camden House, 1989), pp. 1–11, 21–81.

If Pfaffe (Priest) Lamprecht's *Tobias* (circa 1145) had survived in full, it would have been no more than a minor product of a long tradition of Bible translation and adaptation that reached back almost to the beginning of German literature; but his *Alexander* (circa 1150) signaled the dawn of a new era on which it, directly or indirectly, exerted a significant and manifold influence. It was the first German work to make use of French literature, which was to provide subject matter and literary conventions for the Hohenstaufen Renaissance, and it was the first of many narratives to use classical figures and settings. It was also innovative with respect to its secular hero and tone and its emphasis on the childhood education of a future monarch. Indeed, while revealing a pronounced theological tendency, Lamprecht's *Alexander* marks the beginning of a development in which German fiction escaped the domination of the church and the nobility replaced the clergy as the chief arbiter of literary tastes. Through its Strasbourg continuation the work also provided an influential model of supple narrative verse for the courtly romances that followed.

Little is known of the man who called himself Pfaffe Lamprecht. Literary influences on and from *Alexander* place the work between the anonymous *Kaiserchronik* (Chronicle of the Emperors, circa 1147) and Pfaffe Konrad's *Rolandslied* (Song of Roland, circa 1172) and thus provide an approximate date for its composition, while the superiority of its organization and expression to that of *Tobias* suggests that the latter was written earlier. The author's language and a reference in *Tobias* to Trier suggest that that city was his birthplace, but he may have moved to a more important center in the same linguistic area to find a suitable sponsor and library. He knew Latin and French and had a broad, but not fully reliable, knowledge of the Scriptures. The many digressions in both works provide no autobiographical information other than to reveal a marked pedagogical trait, but his silence on certain occasions may tell something of the author's nature. For example, one might have expected a Christian priest to condemn Alexander's hanging of three thousand citizens of Tyre because of their resistance; but Lamprecht's apparent indifference may be only a sign of the times, for, in a period when the church was vigorously supporting the Second Crusade, there may have been little sympathy in Germany for the infidels of Asia Minor.

With its mixture of piety and oriental superstition, the Apocrypha's charming story of Tobit, his son Tobias, the latter's bride, and the angel Raphael was quite popular with the clergy of the medieval and early modern periods. Martin Luther declared that, if it was fiction, it was beautiful and profitable fiction, the work of a gifted poet. During the Assyrian captivity of his tribe, Tobit lives in Ninevah and prospers for a while, but his persistence in observing the biblical law and aiding his fellow Israelites eventually causes all his property to be seized. When he also loses his sight and becomes dependent on the labor of his wife and son, Tobit despairs and prays to God to forgive his sins and let him die. At the same time Sarah, a relative of Tobit in another city, is praying for death or relief from humiliation and disgrace. She has been married seven times, and an evil demon caused each husband to die on the wedding night. God hears both prayers and sends the archangel Raphael to take care of these matters.

Remembering a large sum of money that he had entrusted to a kinsman in Medea years earlier, Tobit sends his son to reclaim it. When Tobias looks for a guide, Raphael appears in the guise of a laborer who knows the country. The two stop at Sarah's home on the way and, encouraged by his companion, Tobias asks for her hand in marriage. He is not deterred by her father's warning about the fate of her previous husbands, for Raphael has told him how to handle evil spirits. On the wedding night the bridegroom burns the heart and liver of a fish on a censer, and the fumes drive the demon away forever.

During the two weeks of festivities that follow, Raphael goes on alone to Medea and retrieves the money. When he, Tobias, and Sarah return to Ninevah, Tobias smears fish gall on his father's eyes, as Raphael had instructed him, and Tobit's sight is restored. The angel identifies himself, tells them to write in a book all that has happened, and disappears. Continuing to do good works, Tobit lives on happily for many years. On his deathbed he directs his son and daughter-in-law to leave Ninevah, whose destruction has been foretold by the prophet Nahum, and go to Medea to be with Sarah's parents. After his father and mother are buried, Tobias does as he has been bidden and lives to see the prophecy fulfilled. Lamprecht's version is an adaptation rather than a translation of the Vulgate account. The surviving portion — which breaks off at the point where Tobit loses his property — confuses minor characters, relates episodes out of chronological order, and weakens the continuity of the tale with references to events in other Old Testament sources. It is possible that Lamprecht's knowledge of the work came largely from references in homilies and patristic writings rather than from the biblical text itself. In any event, his primary goal here apparently was edification, not entertainment. Still, the composition of *Tobias* may well have inspired Lamprecht to a more ambitious and more literary undertaking.

The spectacular campaigns of Alexander the Great, his journeys into fabulous lands, and his early death by assassination took such firm hold on the popular imagination that for centuries legends had gathered around his name. At some period between 200 B.C. and A.D. 300 many of these legends were tied together with a bare thread of history by an anonymous Alexandrian to create what eventually became one of the world's most successful romances. By the end of the Middle Ages about two hundred versions in thirty-five languages had appeared from Iceland to Java. Because the Renaissance erroneously attributed it to Callisthenes, a historian and companion of Alexander, the work is commonly referred to as the *Pseudo-Callisthenes*.

The West first became acquainted with this romance in the fourth century through a Latin translation from the Greek, *Res gestae Alexandri Macedonis* (The Deeds of Alexander of Macedonia), by Julius Valerius. But the chief source of most Western versions was a tenth-century Latin translation by Archpriest Leo of Naples of a variant form, known as the *Historia de Preliis* (History of the Battles), that was transmitted in many interpolated or abbreviated editions. The fame of the Macedonian king was also spread through historical accounts, the most important of which was the *Gesta Alexandri Magni* (Deeds of Alexander the Great), by Quintus Curtius Rufus, a Roman writer of the first century A.D. Adaptations of his work and of those of Valerius and Leo were the sources of the earliest Alexander romance in a vernacular tongue, composed in a hybrid French-Provençal by Albéric of Besançon (or Pisançon) early in the twelfth century; only the first 105 verses are extant.

The historical situation at this time certainly helped to make Alexander an attractive subject for fiction. The crusades had awakened the interest of Europeans in the Orient, and Westerners could regard the Macedonian warriors, who wrested what was to be the Holy Land from the Persians and pressed into the mysterious realms beyond the Euphrates, as forerunners of their own crusaders. Alexander also had an advantage over other characters of Greek and Roman literature in that he was a biblical figure, appearing as an agent in the divine plan in the introductory verses of 1 Maccabees and, presumably, in Daniel's dream of the beasts that symbolized the four world empires. The connection with the Scriptures not only placed the king in a familiar religious setting but probably also made him a more acceptable hero to the only writers of the period, the clergy.

Albéric's work was the chief source for Lamprecht's. The latter employs the same verse form – short lines with couplet rhyme – as many religious narratives of his day, but he does not handle it smoothly: his meter is uneven, and his verses are often too long. On the other hand, his story is well organized, and its rapidly moving account of travel and conflict would certainly have held the attention of the audiences to whom it was read. After telling of Alexander's childhood, education, and remarkable feats as a youth, Lamprecht presents a concise history of the campaign against Darius as his sources had reported it.

On succeeding his father as king of Macedonia, Alexander determines to take vengeance on the king of Persia for having collected tribute from Macedonia. He raises an army and sails west to subjugate Sicily, Rome, and Carthage, then moves east along the African coast to Egypt, where he founds Alexandria. His army and coffers swollen by these conquests, he invades Asia Minor, laying waste to the land. He meets little resistance until he reaches Tyre, which is conquered and destroyed only after a fierce and bloody battle. This struggle is followed by a much greater conflict when the Macedonian warriors and their allies are confronted by the Persian host. After only 1,533 verses the Vorau manuscript, thought by most scholars to comprise all that Lamprecht wrote, ends abruptly with a brief, makeshift conclusion – probably added later by a scribe – in which Alexander slays Darius.

Continuations appear in the Strasbourg and Basel manuscripts. The one at Basel is based on a lost thirteenth-century version that probably had no significant effect on other writings and, in its present corrupted state, has little literary value. But Lamprecht's poem as it appears, revised and completed, in the Strasbourg manuscript is perhaps the most important work of the German precourtly period.

Since the new author knew Latin, he was probably a cleric, and his language places him in the middle Rhine area; but nothing more is known of him, not even his name. Nearly all of the changes he made in Lamprecht's work deal with prosody. Words and phrases are inserted to smooth over transitions, new material – often innocuous line fillers – is supplied to convert the overlong verses into two or even three trimeter or tetrameter lines, and unstressed syllables are added or dropped to form even rhythmical patterns. The resulting poetic expression is much more supple and polished.

In this version Darius is not slain by Alexander but by two of his own men. The Macedonian king thereupon takes over the Persian Empire and leads his army east toward India to intercept King Porus, who, he has learned, is coming to the aid of Darius. There is another bloody conflict, which ends with the death of Porus and the defeat of his host. Alexander moves into the land of Occidratus, whose people go naked and have neither cities nor houses; traverses a wilderness filled with monstrous beasts, scorpions, and flesh-eating bats; and, after

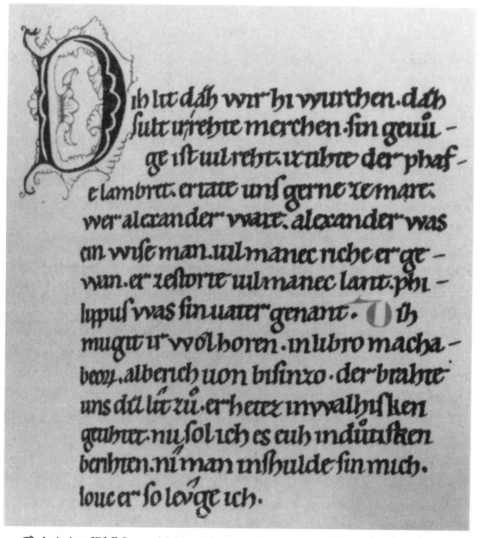

*The beginning of Pfaffe Lamprecht's* Alexander *in the Vorau manuscript (Vorau monastery, codex 276)*

further marvelous adventures, spends an idyllic summer in a beautiful forest with a throng of lovely maidens who spring full-grown from great buds in the spring and fade and die with the flowers when winter comes.

Alexander and his army pass through other strange lands and arrive at last at the end of the world, where he becomes the guest and lover of Candacis, a wise and immensely rich queen who takes him to meet an assembly of gods. Continuing his journey, the king enters the land of the Amazons, from whom he demands tribute; when they refuse and remind him that he would gain little glory in a war against women, he leaves them in peace. Alexander's fame has now spread to all parts of the earth, and many kingdoms send him tribute. Since his pride has grown with his renown, the king decides to conquer Paradise.

Plagued constantly by thunder and lightning, his warriors push on to the Euphrates, then build ships and row day after day up the swift current through fierce storms of rain, hail, and snow until they reach a high, far-reaching wall. Coming at last to a door, the king's messengers pound on it until an old man comes to ask what they want. When he is told that the mighty Alexander is there and demands tribute, he goes away and returns with a small stone for them to take to their lord with a warning that he should leave at once if he wishes to escape God's punishment.

Heeding the admonition, the king returns to Greece, where an ancient Hebrew explains the mystery of the stone. Asking for scales, he places the stone in one pan and gold bars in the other. No matter how much gold is added, the stone outweighs it; but when the gold is replaced by a feather and a little earth, the pan with the stone rises. The teaching is clear: no amount of wealth or power can satisfy human avarice, but it is easily stilled by the grave.

Most of the episodes in the continuation, which makes up nearly 80 percent of the whole, are based on a version of *Historia de Preliis* and, to a lesser extent, on a redaction of *Res gestae Alexandri Macedonis*. The flower-maiden story appears to have been inspired by an oriental tale brought back by crusaders, and the final adventure draws on a twelfth-century Latin work, *Iter ad Paradisum* (Journey to Paradise), that derives from the *Babylonian Talmud*.

The Strasbourg variant of *Pseudo-Callisthenes* differs from all the preceding ones in that the most important episodes relate to a significant theme that surfaces repeatedly from beginning to end and adds a new dimension to the adventure romance. With the familiar words of Solomon (Eccles. 1.2), "Vanitatum vanitas et omnis vanitas," the Strasbourg *Alexander* introduces a story of a man's unquenchable desire to subdue all lands, acquire all knowledge, and thus make a personal and lasting impression on a world in which all things are transitory.

The first warning of the ultimate futility of this striving comes from the dying Darius, who compares his past unparalleled greatness to his present condition and counsels Alexander not to suffer the same fate. Ignoring the admonition, Alexander continues with his plan to dominate the world. But in the land of Occidratis he learns the limits of power: since they have renounced both possessions and aspirations, he can neither take from the inhabitants nor give them anything worthwhile. On hearing that Alexander is mortal, one of the natives wishes to know why he has been performing such wonders – after all, in the end he, like all lesser men, is doomed to die.

The brevity of life, the fleeting nature of happiness, and the pitiless reality of death underscore this question in the flower-maiden episode which follows: after the Macedonians have spent a summer of inexpressible beauty and joy with them, the maidens sicken and die. That Alexander was profoundly impressed by this event is evident later when he meets the gods in an ancient vault, for he asks them not where there are more worlds to conquer but only the time of his own death.

The Candacis adventure relates to the *vanitas* theme in several ways. Alexander enters the land to learn its customs rather than to demand tribute, thus showing a temporary shift from obsession with conquest to a quest for knowledge. He is outwitted by the queen and placed at her mercy, which shakes his faith in his invincibility. The wise and loving Candacis, with her immense wealth, beautiful castles, and luxurious life, represents a temptation to give up his campaign, settle down with her, and renounce his striving for eternal fame.

But the king cannot be diverted from his goal. He journeys on through many lands, gaining both knowledge and tributaries. At last, through his failure before the walls of Paradise and the teaching of the stone, Alexander learns his limitations and becomes at least partly aware of the emptiness (*vanitas*) of worldly aspirations. And, indeed, when he died, says the narrator, he retained just seven feet of earth, no more than the poorest man who ever lived.

Although the pious narrator condemns his overweening pride, the king is presented as a Faustian, rather than an evil, figure. And there is no authorial protest when Alexander declares that men must act according to the natures they have been given and that he, Alexander, must do that which satisfies him as long as he is master of his spirit. In not challenging this statement the author shows himself to be much closer to the courtly ideals to come than to the Cluniac asceticism of the past. It is significant that Alexander's eventual acceptance of his limitations does not lead to a renunciation of all desires and aspirations.

In addition to a central theme, the work uses four motifs to achieve unity. One is the epithet *wunderlîch* (wondrous), which is frequently employed to describe Alexander and link him with the many creatures and events that evoke the reader's astonishment. Another is the luck or fortune motif, which adds suspense to the plot by constantly reminding Alexander and the reader that there is an enigmatic, unpredictable force that can bring down the mightiest and shrewdest of monarchs. The third is the love motif, important because it reveals the gentler, more human side of the hero and because it exerted a significant influence on the courtly romances that followed. The final motif is a series of symbolic gifts, the last of which is the stone that Alexander receives.

With regard to style, there is a clear dividing line between the work of Lamprecht and that of his successor. In the earlier section the narrator hurries from one episode to another, from conflict to conflict, pausing only briefly now and then to interpolate references to biblical figures and places. In the continuation the pace, even of the military campaign, is more deliberate, and there is time for descriptions of landscapes, unusual fauna, and Candice's elegant palace. There is also a fairly consistent alternation between perilous and pleasant scenes.

In one important respect, the function of the narrator, both sections are in full agreement. Although he does not have as prominent a role as his counterparts in the works of such later writers as Hartmann von Aue and Wolfram von Eschenbach, the presence of the narrator is felt throughout. He uses the first person, addresses his audience in the second person, and occasionally comments on the action and his hero. The story is clearly a tale that is told, and told by one who leaves his stamp on it.

Since about twenty years separate the composition of the Lamprecht part from that of the continuation, the development of the full story covers almost all of the precourtly period. The changes in the expectations of the audience during this time are apparent in many ways, most notably in the character of the hero. The earlier author portrays him as a rude and violent Old Testament despot who threatens to crucify all the Carthaginians, hangs the citizens of Tyre, and becomes so enraged at meeting resistance that he falls down in a fit. But at the midpoint of the reign of Friedrich Barbarossa, an era of peace and imperial splendor in Germany, monarchs were supposed to be generous and compassionate as well as shrewd and brave. And so the hero takes on new virtues in the continuation and finally, ceasing to lust after war and power, behaves and rules with the widely acclaimed *mâze* (proper moderation) of the courtly period. The result, it can be argued, is the first *Erziehungsroman* (education novel) in German literature, a forerunner of such works as Hartmann von Aue's *Erec* (circa 1180) and *Iwein* (circa 1203) and Wolfram von Eschenbach's *Parzival* (circa 1200–1210), the heroes of which learn through their errors and become wise and enlightened rulers.

The content changes markedly in the course of Alexander's travels. What begins as a realistic tale of war and conquest becomes a fantasy romance in which battles are replaced by fierce monsters as sources of suspense, and the half-familiar lands and cultures of the Bible and the Crusades make way for wondrous realms and quite alien peoples. The new scenes and exploits had a significant impact on the courtly romances that followed. A lengthy description of a marvelous castle with magnificent furnishings and of the splendid feast held there echoes through dozens of later medieval narratives that also portray the search for strange and fearful adventures as the duty of all true knights. And Alexander's relationship with a beautiful queen of the East may well have suggested to subsequent authors the possibility of the service of ladies and a love affair playing a major role in a tale of adventure.

Shortly after the completion of the Strasbourg *Alexander* three German works appeared that show significant textual similarities to it and, like it, use French models: Pfaffe Konrad's *Rolandslied* (Song of Roland, circa 1172), Eilhart von Oberge's *Tristrant* (circa 1170–1190), and the anonymous *Graf Rudolf* (Count Rudolf, circa 1185); the latter two works also appear to have been influenced by the prosody of the Strasbourg *Alexander*. Its wondrous adventures and ethnographic marvels of the Far East probably inspired similar ones in a fourth narrative of the period, the anonymous *Herzog Ernst* (Duke Ernst, circa 1190).

The strongest influence was exerted on Heinrich von Veldeke's *Eneit,* which was based on the *Roman d'Enéas* and completed about 1185. Hundreds of parallel passages show the extent of Heinrich's borrowing of rhymes, phrases, and expressions from the Strasbourg *Alexander,* but what he gained from its prosody was more important. By adding pure rhyme to its short lines, regular meter, and formulaic line and rhyme fillers, he created the poetic medium that was used by the courtly poets of the following generation.

Among the thirteenth-century German writers who made use of material from Lamprecht and his Strasbourg collaborator are Wirnt von Grafenberg, Wolfram von Eschenbach, the Albrecht who wrote *Der jüngere Titurel* (The Later Titurel, circa 1275), Konrad von Würzburg, the anonymous author of *Wolfdietrich B* (circa 1225–1250), and Ulrich von Liechtenstein. It is likely that Ulrich got his idea for composing a romance in the first person, with himself as the hero, from a long letter in which Alexander relates his adventures in the Far East to his mother and his old teacher, Aristotle.

The later Middle Ages and the early modern period produced many German accounts of Alexander – in romances, short stories, chronicles, history Bibles, chapbooks, and dramas – but all appear to have drawn from Latin sources when they did not borrow from each other. Yet they, too, are indebted to Lamprecht, for it was he who made the Macedonian conqueror a popular subject of literature in Germany. The best of the German Alexander romances is that of Rudolf von Ems, only half finished after 21,643 verses, which is thought to have been composed about 1240 for King Heinrich, the son of Emperor Friedrich II. It expresses the spirit of his time by portraying Alexander as a model of courtly virtue, an ideal knight and ruler quite unlike Lamprecht's tyrannical and quick-tempered warrior-king.

**References:**

Herwig Buntz, *Die deutsche Alexanderdichtung des Mittelalters* (Stuttgart: Metzler, 1973);

George Cary, *The Medieval Alexander* (Cambridge: Cambridge University Press, 1956);

Gilbert de Smet, "Die *Eneide* Heinrichs von Veldeken und der Strassburger *Alexander*," *Leuvense Bijdragen,* 57 (1968): 130–149;

Wolfgang Fischer, *Die Alexanderliedkonzeption des Pfaffen Lamprecht* (Munich: Eidos, 1964);

Dennis H. Green, "The *Alexanderlied* and the Emergence of the Romance," *German Life and Letters,* 28 (April 1975): 246–262;

A. T. Hatto, "The Elephants in the *Strassburg Alexander*," in *The Medieval Alexander Legend and Romance Epic: Essays in Honour of David J. A. Ross,* edited by Peter Noble and others (Millwood, N.Y.: Kraus, 1982), pp. 85–105;

Arthur Hübner, "Alexander der Große in der deutschen Dichtung des Mittelalters," *Die Antike, 9* (1933): 32–48;

Dennis M. Kratz, *The Romances of Alexander* (New York & London: Garland, 1991);

Cola Minis, "Über die ersten volkssprachigen Alexander-Dichtungen," *Zeitschrift für deutsches Altertum und deutsche Literatur,* 88 (1957): 20–39;

Friedrich Pfister, *Kleine Schriften zum Alexanderroman* (Meisenheim am Glan: Hein, 1976);

Josef Quint, "Die Bedeutung des Paradiessteins im *Alexanderlied*," in *Formenwandel: Festschrift zum 65. Geburtstag von Paul Böckmann,* edited by Walter Müller-Seidel and Wolfgang Preisendanz (Hamburg: Hoffmann & Campe, 1964), pp. 9–26;

Kurt Ruh, *Höfische Epik des deutschen Mittelalters,* volume 1: *Von den Anfängen bis zu Hartmann von Aue* (Berlin: Schmidt, 1967);

Werner Schröder, "Der Pfaffe Lamprecht," in *Die deutsche Literatur des Mittelalters: Verfasserlexikon,* volume 5, edited by Kurt Ruh (Berlin: De Gruyter, 1985), cols. 494–510;

Schröder, "Zum Vanitas-Gedanken im deutschen *Alexanderlied*," *Zeitschrift für deutsches Altertum und deutsche Literatur,* 91 (1961): 38–55;

Eberhard Sitte, *Die Datierung von Lamprechts Alexander* (Halle: Niemeyer, 1940);

Karl Stackmann, "Die Gymnosophisten-Episode in deutschen Alexander-Erzählungen des Mittelalters," *Beiträge zur Geschichte der deutschen Sprache und Literatur* (Tübingen), 105, no. 3 (1983): 331–353;

Peter Stein, "Ein Weltherrscher als vanitas-Exempel in imperial-ideologisch orientierter Zeit? Fragen und Beobachtungen zum *Strassburger Alexander*," in *Stauferzeit: Geschichte, Literatur, Kunst,* edited by Rüdiger Krohn and others (Stuttgart: Klett, 1978), pp. 144–180;

Ferdinand Urbanek, "Umfang und Intention von Lamprechts Alexanderlied," *Zeitschrift für deutsches Altertum und deutsche Literatur,* 99 (May 1970): 96–120.

# Thegan and the Astronomer

## (flourished circa 850)

Brian Murdoch
*University of Stirling*

MAJOR WORKS: *Vita Hludowici Imperatoris* (circa 837–838) and *Vita Hludowici Imperatoris* (circa 840)

**Manuscripts:** Manuscripts of Thegan's work include Vienna, Österreichische National-bibliothek, Cod. Vindob. 408; Trier, Stadtbi-bliothek, MS 1286, 43; those of the Astronomer's include Vienna, Cod. Vindob. 529; Vatican, Bibliotheca Vaticana, Cod. Reg. Christ. 637 and 692; London, British Library, BL Add. 21 109.

**Standard edition and first publication:** In *Monumenta Germaniae Historica/Scriptores II,* edited by Georg Heinrich Pertz (Hannover: Monumenta Germaniae Historica, 1829), pp. 585–648.

**Standard edition:** In *Quellen zur karolingischen Reichsgeschichte,* volume 1, edited by Reinhold Rau (Darmstadt: Wissenschaftliche Buchgesellschaft, 1966), pp. 213–281.

**Editions in English:** Thegan's life of Louis the Pious translated by J. R. Ginsburg and D. L. Boutelle, in Paul Edward Dutton, *Carolingian Civilisation* (Peterborough, Ont.: Broadview Press, 1993), pp. 141–155; the Astronomer's life translated by Allen Cabaniss as *Son of Charlemagne: A Contemporary Life of Louis the Pious* (Syracuse, N.Y.: Syracuse University Press, 1961).

The celebrated life of Charlemagne (*Vita Karoli Magni Imperatoris,* circa 830) by Einhard was matched not long afterward by two Latin prose lives of his son and successor, Louis the Pious; one was written by Thegan, a cleric who was probably from Trier, and the other by an anonymous writer known from one passage in the work as the Astronomer. As historical records of the age, these works go together with a lengthy historical poem by Ermoldus Nigellus, *De rebus gestis Ludovici Pii* (On the Deeds of Louis the Pious, circa 827), and the first part of Nithart's *Liber Historiarum* (843).

Thegan (also known as Theganbert and Degen) seems to have been a suffragan of noble birth in the diocese of Trier. He was celebrated in verse as a man of great knowledge by Walahfrid Strabo, who edited his work and corrected the Latin, which was grammatically questionable in places; it is, at all events, hardly up to the classical historiographic standard of Einhard, although Thegan knew the life of Charlemagne and cites it, as well as passages from Virgil. Walahfrid was also unhappy about Thegan's attitude toward the preferment within the ecclesiastical hierarchy of those not nobly born. In section 20 Thegan exhibits an old-fashioned snobbery about the dangers of elevating the lowborn to positions of authority, an attitude that echoes classical writing (in a secular context, a similar standpoint is found in Suetonius's comments on Claudius and Nero and in the *Augustan History* on Elagabalus). Thegan belabors the point with an amount of detail that is not found in some of the historical reporting in his work, and it is not a view of which Walahfrid – whose own origins were not high – could readily approve.

The *Vita Hludowici Imperatoris* was written around 837–838 – in Louis's lifetime – and it is, therefore, necessarily different from the work of Einhard, who wrote after his subject's death. Walahfrid noted that Thegan does not offer a rounded life in the manner of the earlier historian (who was influenced by the model of the classical biographer Suetonius) but a chronicle of deeds. The *Vita Hludowici Imperatoris* – which takes up fifty-eight paragraphs, most of them fairly brief – presents many incidents in a manner that corresponds largely to the year-by-year monastic annals of events. Section 26, for the year 820, for example, says little more than that Louis went to fight a Slav leader, defeated him, and came home again. Occasionally Thegan does expatiate, although his longer passages are not always to the point (as with his diatribe against the lowborn, for example). He nevertheless offers a general presentation of the appearance and character of Louis that is like (and contains material from) Einhard's life of Charlemagne. Thegan is intensely partisan; one of his almost adulatory descriptions – which is, moreover, of special relevance to German literature – is in section 19, which imitates Einhard's description of Charlemagne: Einhard says that Charlemagne "Graecam vero melius intellegere quam pronuntiare poterat" (could understand Greek better than he could speak it), and the phrase is used in almost identical form by Thegan of Louis. There is, however, one marked difference between the two emperors: Einhard says that Charlemagne ordered the old Germanic warrior tales to be collected and that he was interested in the Frankish language (that is, the German vernacular, as opposed to Latin), while Thegan says that Louis was actively opposed to such interests. "Poetica carmina gentilia quae in iuventute didicerat, respuit, nec legere, nec audire, nec docere voluit" (he despised the vernacular songs, which he had heard in his youth, and would neither read, hear, nor teach them), says Thegan. The passage in which this remark comes is, admittedly, designed to show Louis's learning and piety, and there may also be an echo here of Alcuin's question: "What has Ingeld to do with Christ?" If the passage reflects reality, it may account for the relative paucity (even by Old High German standards) of German writing from Louis's reign, and perhaps even for the loss of any of the *carmina gentilia* except for the lucky and still largely inexplicable preservation of the *Hildebrandslied* (Lay of Hildebrand, circa 825). How accurate the picture is, and how much of it reflects Thegan's views of what a prince ought to be, remains a matter of debate. Louis is shown as one who stands out above his subjects, a man invariably pious and grave – even when others laugh, he never does so. His close relationship with the papacy, too, is underscored. Thegan is equally clear-cut in his vilification of Louis's enemies: Ebo, Archbishop of Rheims, is a "turpissimus rusticus" (most vile peasant), "impudicus et crudelissimus" (impudent and extremely cruel), and, worst of all in Thegan's eyes, "ex originalium servorum stirpe" (of slave stock). In his desire to idealize his subject Thegan is also restrained on the conflict between Louis and his son, Lothar.

Max Manitius summarizes Thegan's *Vita Hludowici Imperatoris* as no more than "eine Parteischrift . . . nur mit Vorsicht zu gebrauchen" (a partisan document . . . to be used only with care).

The anonymous life of Louis by the so-called Astronomer is considerably longer than Thegan's, with sixty-four chapters; and it was written after the death of Louis (probably soon after), since it covers his entire life. The writer says in his prologue that he gained much of his information from a monk named Adhemar, who had been educated alongside Louis; whether the information came orally or from a lost work is unclear. The biographer also says that he had been at court himself. As a historian, thus, he cites his sources, and they are reputable. He stresses in the prologue the value of reading about the past deeds of princes for usefulness and for edification, but also as a warning. The work is, then, historiographical rather than propagandistic like the writing of Thegan. Little else is known about the anonymous biographer other than that he discussed astronomy with Louis in regard to the appearance of a comet and that he, like Thegan, knew Einhard's work on Charlemagne, which he, too, echoes from time to time. He refers to Charlemagne's campaign in Spain and alludes to the battle of Roncesvalles, commenting that it is not necessary to mention any names (such as that, presumably, of Roland) "quia vulgata sunt" (because everyone knows them) – an indication, perhaps, of the existence of songs of Roncesvalles at that date. It has been suggested that the Astronomer was a native of Aquitaine and that he came to court with Louis; the work is extremely detailed on Louis's early life. The chronology, however, is not always precise, and the work is less like a set of annals than was Thegan's. The Astronomer almost invariably provides more detail on historical events than does Thegan: the Slav campaign which the earlier biographer refers to briefly, for example, is treated far more fully (in section 33) by the Astronomer, who is also more specific on the various divisions between Louis and his sons. The emperor's piety is again stressed, though Thegan's intense adulation for Louis and complementary exaggerated vehemence toward the latter's enemies are absent from this far more sober history. There are no further details of Louis's attitudes toward German literature, however, and only at his death – which is described in some detail – does a word of the emperor's own language appear: in his last moments Louis turned his eyes to something and cried out, "hutz! hutz! quod significat foras" (*hutz! hutz!* which means out). The historian concludes that the pious emperor was seeing an evil spirit that he refused to tolerate. Louis then raised his eyes to heaven and smiled before he died.

**References:**

Wolfgang Haubrichs, *Die Anfänge,* volume 1/1 of *Geschichte der deutschen Literatur,* edited by Joachim Heinzle (Frankfurt am Main: Athenäum, 1988), pp. 143–144;

M. L. W. Laistner, *Thought and Letters in Western Europe AD 500–900* (London: Methuen, 1957), pp. 275–276;

Max Manitius, *Geschichte der lateinischen Literatur des Mittelalters,* volume 1 (Munich: Beck, 1911; reprinted, 1964), pp. 653–657;

Rosamond McKitterick, *The Frankish Kingdoms under the Carolingians, 751–987* (London: Longman, 1983), pp. 106–107;

Timothy Reuter, *Germany in the Early Middle Ages* (London: Longman, 1991);

Ernst Tremp, "Thegan und Astronomus," in *Charlemagne's Heir,* edited by Peter Godman and Roger Collins (Oxford & New York: Clarendon Press, 1990), pp. 691–700;

Tremp, *Die Überlieferung der Vita Hludowici Imperatoris des Astronomus* (Hannover: Monumenta Germaniae Historica, 1991).

# Theodulf
## *(circa 760 – circa 821)*

Linda Archibald
*Liverpool John Moores University*

MAJOR WORKS: *Libri Carolini* (after 790)

**Manuscripts:** The original working copy of the *Libri Carolini* is the Vatican copy, Vat. lat. 7207, but parts of it are missing, including the preface and book 4. Comments in the margins have been attributed to Charlemagne. The only surviving complete manuscript is Paris, Arsenal 663, a copy of Vat. lat. 7207. This copy was made for Hincmar at Reims in the 860s. A one-page fragment also exists: Paris, Bibliothèque Nationale, B.N. lat. 12125, folio 157.

**Standard edition:** In *Patrologia Latina,* 221 volumes, edited by Jacques-Paul Migne (Paris: Migne 1841–1879) CV.

*Ad iudices, Capitularies, Epistolae* (after 798)

**Standard edition:** In *Patrologia Latina,* 221 volumes, edited by Jacques Paul Migne (Paris: Migne, 1841–1879), CV: 187–380.

*Carmina* (circa 817)

**Standard edition:** "Carmina," edited by Ernst Dümmler, in *Monumenta Germaniae Historica Poetae,* volume 1 (Berlin: Weidmann, 1880), pp. 437–581;

**Edition in English:** Excerpts translated by Peter Godman, in his *Poetry of the Carolingian Renaissance* (Norman: University of Oklahoma Press, 1985; London: Duckworth, 1985), pp. 150–174.

Theodulf was a Visigoth, probably born in northern Spain around 760, who became a significant figure in the court of Charlemagne. Although he was not from Germany, or even from Frankish territory, his contribution to the intellectual output of the Carolingian court was profound. His surviving works are in Latin, and his skill in this language marks him as one of the leading figures of his time.

Not much is known about Theodulf's early life. It is clear from his later activities, however, that he was well educated in the classical tradition and had a preference for authors from Spain, such as

Isidore and Prudentius. He spent much of his adult life furthering the judicial, educational, and literary ideals of the Carolingian court society. It is likely that he was attracted by the stability and opportunity for learning at Charlemagne's court and wished to leave behind the troubled political situation in Spain. This distant part of Charlemagne's realm was still troubled by frequent attacks from Moorish armies.

Theodulf and Alcuin of York, both non-Franks, were opinion makers and spokesmen for Charlemagne and his court. In the last years of the eighth century these two scholars vied for the king's favor, taking part in the friendly rivalry of the poets' circle that Charlemagne encouraged by way of entertainment. Alcuin was Charlemagne's adviser on theological and educational matters, Theodulf on the law and on relations with Rome. Theodulf was steeped in pre-Christian traditions, and his eclectic approach, along with the contributions of the Italian and British factions at the court, meant that Charlemagne was provided with a spectrum of opinion and an assembly of some of the best minds available. Much of the early work of Alcuin and Theodulf is of a collaborative nature, and identification of their individual contributions is difficult. Theodulf devoted much time to the production of copies of the Bible, and his learning ensured that the copying was carried out accurately. The version of the Vulgate that he helped to prepare included variant readings, a radical scholarly approach in a time not noted for its originality.

Theodulf was concerned about doctrinal content, but he also valued the physical appearance of the copyists' work and paid particular attention to illustration and binding. He was noted for his knowledge of the principles of art and design, and frequent references in his works to pottery, mosaics, architecture, and manuscript illumination testify to his taste in such matters. Theodulf, unlike many of his more ascetically minded monastic contemporaries, celebrated the liberal arts and saw little conflict between study of these subjects and study of the Scriptures. In a poem dealing with his favorite authors, Theodulf cites the usual Christian canon: Gregory the Great, Augustine, Jerome, Ambrose, Cyprian, and Isidore for their prose works and Sedulius, Paulinus, Arator, Avitus, and Juvencus for their verse on biblical themes. He is more adventurous than most of his contemporaries, however, in going on to praise his countryman Prudentius, the grammarians Pompeius and Donatus, and the classical masters Virgil and Ovid. He lauds Prudentius's skill in composing in various meters, reveal-

ing an appreciation of literary techniques that reflects his classical education. He tries to maintain a bridge between the classical and Christian traditions of literary production, preferring to merge the two rather than make a choice, in Augustinian fashion, between eloquence and doctrine. But Theodulf was too much of a politician to ignore the potentially anti-Christian influence that the classical writers could provide. Alcuin was vehement in his condemnation of the old pagan writers, and this view was to gain in popularity when the Carolingian empire began to break up after 817. Theodulf acknowledges the trend but defends the value of the classical tradition:

> Et modo Pompeium, modo te, Donate, legebam,
> Et modo Virgilium, te modo, Naso loquax.
> In quorum dictis quamquam sint frivola multa,
> Plurima sub falso tegmine vera latent.
> Falsa poetarum stilus affert, vera sophorum,
> Falsa horum in verum vertere saepe solent. (lines 16–
> 21)

(And then sometimes I would read Pompeius and Donatus,
while at others I would study Virgil and wordy
Ovid.
Although there are many frivolities in their words,
much truth lies hidden under a deceptive surface.
Poets' writing is a vehicle for falsehood, philosophers'
brings truth;
they transform the lies of poets into veracity)

– translated by Peter Godman

In the pseudoclassical conceit of the court Theodulf was given the nickname "Pindar" in recognition of his learned and polished poetic style. By modern standards, Theodulf's poetry is probably the most accomplished of the Carolingian era.

The lifestyle of Charlemagne and his court was a nomadic one: as king and, after 801, as emperor he embarked on long summer campaigns to suppress rebellions and spent the winter in Aachen or some temporary residence. He also sent emissaries to all parts of the kingdom and, later, of the empire to carry out his chosen policies. His scholars were, consequently, on the move and had to communicate with each other and with the court in letters. Much of the literary (as opposed to educational and religious) material that has survived appears to have been designed to be passed from person to person for private delectation and also to be suitable for declamation before an assembly. Nicknames, private jokes, and references to the foibles of key figures in the retinue are signs of a well-developed literary club. Some of Theodulf's poems serve the same function as present-day cartoons, making serious points through comic and sometimes malicious remarks. Theodulf wittily depicts the short stature of one colleague, the rustic manner of another, and the fondness of some for food and drink, all in the context of praise for the emperor and the court. He appears particularly to enjoy satirizing the behavior of his English and Irish colleagues, whose enjoyment of alcohol often resulted in long evenings of storytelling and ribald jokes. One also reads of his impatience with poorly educated fighting men and the internal politics of the court. In one poem Theodulf reveals his views on two of the nationalities represented at court:

Ante canis lepores alet aut lupus improbus agnos,
    Aut timido muri musio terga dabit,
Quam Geta cum Scotto pia pacis foedera iungat. (lines 163–166)

(Sooner will the dog feed the hare or the cruel wolf feed
    the lambs,
or the cat turn and flee from the timid mouse,
than a Goth will join with an Irishman in a friendly
    treaty of peace).
                    – translated by Godman

Theodulf, the Goth whose name contains a reference to the wolf, displays a rather fierce disdain for a nation culturally distant from his own. It is one of the features of the Carolingian phenomenon that such a broad spectrum of attitudes could coexist and cross-fertilize, but Theodulf and Alcuin show that the interaction was not always cordial. The two competed to be chosen as Charlemagne's spokesman on the death of Pope Adrian I in 795: both poets wrote epitaphs, and Charlemagne chose Alcuin's version, though many scholars consider Theodulf's the better piece.

Theodulf was a master of poetic form, and he used and adapted classical and Christian models to great effect. His poems of praise of Charlemagne are models of technical correctness. There is always an undertone of Christian morality that balances the external radiance of the emperor – his physical stature, wealth, and power – with the inner qualities of wisdom and judgment he needs to maintain the stability of his realm. There is no mistaking his writings for the old pagan praise-poem genre.

In 790 Theodulf began his most significant work, the *Libri Carolini*. In 787 the Second Council of Nicaea had debated the issue of the worship of images, a doctrinal point that threatened to split the Eastern and Western branches of Christendom. Charlemagne saw himself as defender of the faith in the West, whose responsibility it was to counteract what he perceived as a pernicious tendency in the East to worship images. It was decided that a document would be composed arguing Charlemagne's position.

The resulting treatise is a compilation of the ideas of several people, but Ann Freeman has shown that Theodulf was the main author; the earlier view that Alcuin or some unnamed Gothic scholar was responsible is now discredited, and Theodulf is generally given credit for this work. References throughout the text to West Gothic liturgical sources rather than to Frankish or British ones point clearly to Theodulf, as do other West Gothic manuscript features. The arguments in the text display a deep understanding of the complex religious and political issues. A fine line had to be drawn between the assertion of Charlemagne's authority and the need to maintain good relations with the pope. The work is hampered somewhat by misunderstandings that appear to have crept in as a result of poor translations from Greek into Latin. This defect points to one major weakness in Carolingian religious scholarship: lack of effective command of the other two major biblical languages, Greek and Hebrew.

By 798 Theodulf had become increasingly useful as an emissary, traveling around the realm carrying out various tasks on behalf of Charlemagne. His literary and analytical talents were put to good use when he conducted a survey of judicial practices in the western areas of the kingdom that were causing unrest. He included many experiences from this journey in his satirical verse work *ad iudices* (To the Judges), sometimes also called *contra iudices* (Against the Judges), which gives an eloquent account of his task and includes some entertaining descriptions of the vices he encountered. The purpose of the work is, however, a serious one. The wit of the court poet is molded into a general exhortation regarding appropriate behavior for judges and officials who are responsible for ensuring that citizens are treated in accordance with Christian doctrine and natural justice. Biblical references are used to depict good and bad examples of judicial processes and to point out the gruesome punishments that corrupt judges once suffered and, by implication, now deserve. There are also many classical references, including some from Virgil and Ovid, that reflect Theodulf's breadth of learning and his willingness to look at pagan authors along with the usual Christian sources. There were conflicts between the pagan legal systems and traditions still in use in parts of Charlemagne's realm, on the one hand, and Christian law, on the other. Theodulf refuses to be drawn into these matters but concentrates on the more immediate problem of bad judges. He condemns judges who listen to their wives and servants, who have been bribed to pervert the course of justice, who turn up for work suffering the aftereffects of overindulgence.

One of only two non-Franks to be granted a bishopric by Charlemagne (Paulinus of Aquileia was the other), Theodulf was appointed to the See of Orleans. He undertook his duties with enthusiasm and was much loved by the people of his diocese. Two surviving elaborate ceremonial Bibles commissioned by Theodulf at Orleans reflect his appreciation of beautiful objects. Wall paintings, mosaics, and other artifacts, many of them based on classical themes, reveal his patronage of artists and craftsmen. His *Capitularies* (after 798) is a set of clear instructions to the clergymen under his jurisdiction on how to arrange the schoolroom and curriculum in such a way as to continue the progress achieved by Charlemagne and his circle at Aachen; he knew that he would often be absent on affairs of state, and the work was intended to advise his staff in their daily work. Here the concerns of the teacher are clear, along with a clear commitment to Christian values. Theodulf also wrote some theological works, notably on baptism and the Holy Spirit, but much of his time was taken up with his duties as bishop and as emissary for the emperor.

When Charlemagne died in 814, Theodulf at first enjoyed the favor of his son and successor, Louis the Pious. Theodulf, however, like many of those who enjoyed the "Renaissance" atmosphere around the court of Charlemagne, adapted badly to the monastic reforms and political paranoia of the new regime. Power struggles developed, and the differences that Charlemagne had united in a common purpose began to reemerge. Theodulf lost his bishopric in 814 and was charged with supporting enemies of the state. Regarded as a political enemy and a threat to Louis the Pious's religious and educational reforms, he was exiled to the monastery of Saint Aubin at Angers.

In his later years Theodulf wrote several pieces that reveal an increasing disappointment with life, especially despair at the political infighting. In one poem, using classical imagery, he writes of an imaginary battle between flocks of birds. The work is an allegory for the bitter struggles for control of the parts of the empire ruled by the various descendants of Charlemagne. The birds flutter to and fro, pleading for terms and conditions that will guarantee peace; the allusion to the role of emissary that he knew so well is clear. But the time for diplomacy has ended, and a bloody and senseless slaughter ensues. Theodulf laments the deaths of so many birds. The date of this poem, around 817, suggests that it may have been written as a defense of his own position and an attempt to show his loyalty to Louis the Pious and his hatred of war. It predicted the futile outcomes for the Carolingian dynasty of the power struggle and contains none of the fun of his earlier poems. Theodulf was released from Saint Aubin in 821 and died soon afterward.

Theodulf's contribution to the literature of the Carolingian period is incalculable. Much of his work has either not survived or is buried in the mass of official documentation produced by Charlemagne's advisers. Attempts to analyze documents that are joint efforts leave one unsure as to his true positions on various topics. It is clear, however, that he was a poet of exceptional talent, a theologian with a refreshingly liberal outlook on literary traditions, and a competent administrator and emissary. His determination as a teacher to defend the classical poets against dogmatic reform got him into trouble, but it benefited younger scholars.

**References:**

S. T. Collins, "Sur quelques vers de Théodulfe," *Revue Bénédictine,* 60 (1950): 214–218;

Ann Freeman, "Carolingian Orthodoxy and the Fate of the *Libri Carolini,*" *Viator,* 16 (1985): 65–108;

Freeman, "Further Studies in the *Libri Carolini,*" *Speculum,* 40 (April 1965): 203–293;

Freeman, "Theodulf of Orleans and the *Libri Carolini,*" *Speculum,* 32 (1957): 663–705;

Freeman, "Theodulf of Orleans and the Psalm Citations of the *Libri Carolini,*" *Revue Bénédictine,* 97, no. 3–4 (1987): 195–224;

Peter Godman, *Poetry of the Carolingian Renaissance* (London: Duckworth, 1985);

Hans Liebeschütz, "Theodulf of Orleans and the Problem of the Carolingian Renaissance," in *Fritz Saxl, 1890–1948: A Volume of Memorial Essays,* edited by Donald James Govdon (London: Nelson 1957), pp. 77–92;

P. Meyvaert, "The Authorship of the *Libri Carolini,*" *Revue Bénédictine,* 89 (1979): 29–57;

Thomas F. Noble, "Some Observations on the Deposition of Archbishop Theodulf of Orleans in 817," *Journal of the Rocky Mountain Medieval and Renaissance Association,* 2 (January 1981): 29–40;

Dieter Schaller, "Philologische Untersuchungen zu den Gedichten Theodulfs von Orléans," *Deutsches Archiv für Erforschung des Mittelalters,* 18 (1962): 13–91;

Schaller, "Vortrags- und Zirkulardichtung am Hof Karls des Grossen," *Mittellateinisches Jahrbuch,* 6 (1970): 14–36;

May Vieillard-Troiekouroff, "Germigny-des-Prés, l'oratoire privé de l'abbé Théodulphe," *Dossiers Archéologiques,* 30 (1978): 40–49;

Jan M. Ziolowski, "Poultry and Predators in Two Poems from the Reign of Charlemagne," *Denver Quarterly,* 24 (Winter 1990): 24–32.

# Walahfrid Strabo
## *(circa 808 – 18 August 849)*

Brian Murdoch
*University of Stirling*

MAJOR WORKS: Theological and liturgical texts; saints' lives in verse and prose; introductions to historical works by Einhard and Thegan; occasional, panegyric, and religious verse, including the *Visio Wettini* (829), *De imagine Tetrici* (829), and the *Hortulus.*

**Manuscripts:** Most of the works are represented in a variety of manuscripts; of particular importance are Saint Gall, Stadtbibliothek, Cod. Sangall. 869, with various works; Vatican, Biblioteca Vaticana, Cod. Reg. 469, with poems and the *Hortulus;* Saint Gall, Cod. Sangall. 446; Vatican, Cod. Pal. 1519; Oxford, Bodleian Library Laud misc. 410. The poem *De imagine Tetrici* is preserved only in Saint Gall, Stadtbibliothek Cod. Sangall. 869. Another Saint Gall manuscript, Cod. Sangall. 878, is a compilation by Walahfrid of the works of other authors.

**First publication and standard edition:** In *Patrologia Latina,* 221 volumes, edited by Jacques-Paul Migne, volumes 113 and 114 (Paris: Migne, 1852).

**Standard editions:** In *Monumenta Germaniae Historica/Poetae Latini Medii Aevi/Poetae Latini Aevi Carolini,* volume 2, edited by Ernst Dümmler (Berlin: MGH, 1884), pp. 259–473; *Monumenta Germaniae Historica/Epistolae,* volume 5, edited by Dümmler (Berlin: MGH, 1898).

**Edition in modern German:** *Der Hortulus des Walahfrid Strabo: Aus dem Kräutergarten des Klosters Reichenau,* translated by Hans-Dieter Stoffler (Sigmaringen: Thorbecke, 1978).

**Editions in English:** Selected poems translated by Helen Waddell, in her *Medieval Latin Lyrics* (Harmondsworth, U.K.: Penguin, 1952), pp. 122–129; in Peter Godman, *Poetry of the Carolingian Renaissance* (Norman: University of Oklahoma Press, 1985; London: Duckworth, 1985), pp. 214–216; *Walahfrid Strabo's Visio Wettini,* edited and translated by David A. Traill (Bern: H. Lang / Frankfurt am Main: P. Lang, 1974); in *Carolingian Civilization: A Reader,* edited by Paul Edward Dutton (Peterborough, Ont.: Broadview, 1993), pp. 375–387; in *Two Lives of Charlemagne,* translated by Lewis Thorpe (Harmondsworth, U.K.: Penguin, 1969), pp. 49–50.

Walahfrid Strabo – the second part of his name means "the squinter" – was born in Swabia in poor circumstances and educated at the monastery of the Reichenau on Lake Constance, which he remembered fondly in verses in the sapphic meter that have the repeated refrain "insula felix" (blessed island). He studied under Hrabanus Maurus in Fulda, where he complained of feeling cold and homesick. His fellow students at the famous school included Otfried von Weißenburg; Lupus of Ferrières, who shared his interests in classical writing; and Gottschalk of Orbais, who would become involved in a bitter theological controversy with Hrabanus. In 829 Walahfrid went to the Carolingian court to serve as tutor to the future King Charles the Bald, son of the emperor Louis the Pious and his wife, Judith (to whom Walahfrid dedicated some verses). In 838 he returned to the Reichenau as abbot. On the death of Louis in 840 he supported the eldest son, Lothar, for the succession; after the defeat of Lothar by his brothers, Charles the Bald and Louis the German, at Fontenoy in 841 he endured a period of exile in Speier, from which he wrote a poem to Lothar expressing his hopes in him. He was restored to his abbacy not by Lothar, however, but by Louis the German in 842. He died in France on a visit to his former pupil, Charles, on 18 August 849. His old teacher, Hrabanus, wrote his epitaph, praising his skill as a poet.

Walahfrid's literary and editorial output in his short life was extensive. The work that occupies most of the two volumes of his works in the *Patrologia Latina,* however – the *Glossa Ordinaria,* a commentary on the Bible compiled from the writings of earlier theologians – is actually much later. Walahfrid did, however, excerpt from the commentaries of earlier exegetes, including his teacher, Hrabanus.

"German literature" in the ninth century is a difficult concept; only in the most rigid of definitions can it be restricted to literary writings in the vernacular – of which there were few, in any case. Walahfrid does not seem to have composed in German but in the universally acceptable vehicle of Latin. His Latin style is polished; his varied verse forms are, for the most part, classical, and they echo writers such as Virgil. He also undertook editorial tasks, revising, introducing, and polishing texts and putting in headings and divisions.

Walahfrid's earliest work is an apocalyptic vision of Paradise and Purgatory experienced by one of his teachers at the Reichenau, Wetti, just before his death in 824. Wetti's vision was written down in prose, and the eighteen-year-old Walahfrid was encouraged to write a poetic version. He dedicated his *Visio Wettini* (Vision of Wetti, 829) to another teacher, his lifelong friend and patron, Grimald, an aristocrat and politician who would later become abbot of Saint Gall. This work is of some importance as the first vision-poem and has been referred to as a forerunner of Dante's *Divine Comedy* (1321). Wetti's vision includes Charlemagne in hell, having his genitals devoured by beasts as a punishment for lust. Walahfrid's implicit disapproval of Charle-

magne in this poem would turn later, in his prologue to Einhard's *Vita Karoli Magni Imperatoris* (Life of Charlemagne, 830), into references to him as "excellentissimus . . . rex" (a most glorious . . . emperor); Peter Godman says that this "volte-face" is "no less remarkable for the brazenness with which it was accomplished."

Not long after composing the vision-poem Walahfrid wrote a metrical life of the obscure fourth-century patron saint of Langres, Mammas (the spelling of his name varies) of Cappadocia, and another hagiographic poem on a contemporary figure, the Irishman Saint Blaithmac, who was killed in a Viking raid on Iona in Scotland around 825. Later in life Walahfrid was requested to revise or provide new versions of two further saints' lives in prose: that of Saint Othmar, written originally by Gozbert of Saint Gall (only Walahfrid's version is extant); and that of Saint Gall himself. Two versions of the life of Saint Gall had been written previously; one was anonymous, the other by Wetti. Walahfrid provided a radical revision, with occasional political comments added, in which the saint's miracles underscore the independence of the monastery of Saint Gall from the See of Constance. An anonymous metrical version of the life of Saint Gall closely based on Walahfrid's was written in 850, the year after he died; and Ratpert's German *Lobgesang auf den Heiligen Gallus* (Panegyric to Saint Gall), which is known only in a Latin translation by Ekkehard IV, was influenced by Wetti's version and possibly by Walahfrid's.

Walahfrid's editorial skill is represented by his introductions to two major biographies of Carolingian emperors: Einhard's life of Charlemagne and Thegan's of Louis the Pious (circa 837–838). While still a young man Walahfrid had written poems to Thegan, an aristocratic churchman who was probably from Trier; and he praises Thegan in the prologue, though he is unhappy about Thegan's criticism of nonaristocratic churchmen such as Walahfrid himself.

Walahfrid's theological works include *Libellus de exordiis et incrementis quarundam in rebus ecclesiasticis rerum* (A Little Book on the Beginnings and Developments of Some Church Practices, 841). A significant feature of this brief text is the philological interest it shows in borrowings among Greek, Latin, and German in ecclesiastical terminology.

At the beginning of the seventeenth century a set of Old High German glosses was published with the description "Hrabani Mauri, abbatus Fuldensis, glossae latino-barbaricae de partibus humani corporis . . . Walafridus Strabus . . . discipulus"

(Hrabanus Maurus, Abbot of Fulda, Latin-German glosses on parts of the body ... Walahfrid Strabo ... his pupil). Since the text glossed is one of the parts of Isidore of Seville's encyclopedia, the *Etymologies,* which Hrabanus took over into his *De naturis rerum* (On the Nature of Things), it is possible that these glosses consist of notes made by Walahfrid during his time at Fulda. Hrabanus's lectures at Fulda, "ego ... Strabus ... trevitate re penitus nemonia laberetur notavi" (which I ... Strabo ... have noted down from memory), also lie behind some Old Testament exegesis with glosses in Codex Sangall. 283. But the speculation that scribe *gamma* of the Old High German *Tatian* (circa 830) was Walahfrid – a judgment made on grounds of dialect – is unproven.

In 801 Charlemagne had brought to Aachen a bronze statue of the Gothic king Theoderic, who appears in German literature as Dietrich. The Goths were Arians, adhering to the belief that the Son of God was not eternal by nature, in contradistinction to the Catholic Franks. Moreover, Theoderic had persecuted and killed the philosopher Boethius. In Walahfrid's poem *De imagine Tetrici* (On the Image of Dietrich, circa 829) the poet and his muse Scintilla criticize Theoderic, contrasting him to Louis the Pious, who is compared to Moses. Walahfrid praises Judith, Louis's children, and other members of the court. The poem is, indeed, courtly poetry, not unlike that written a generation earlier at Charlemagne's court, where biblical and classical comparisons were also made.

Far longer is the poem known later by the title *Hortulus* (Little Garden) but actually called *Liber de cultura hortorum* (Book on Gardening). The work, probably a fairly early one, is dedicated to Grimald; the idea for it may have come from *De re rustica* (Country Matters), a treatise on agriculture by the first-century writer Lucius Junius Columella, the tenth book of which is a poem about gardening. There were copies of the work in Fulda and in the Reichenau. Twenty-three sections examine various plants with reference to their mythological, medicinal, and, sometimes, Christian implications. The dedicatory poem to Grimald is striking, picturing him in his small garden, shaded by apple trees, while the "ludentes pueri" (happy lads) of Grimald's school pick peaches and apples for him. Walahfrid asks Grimald that he might, while reading, "vitiosa seces, deposco, placentia firmes" (prune errors out, I pray; set firm the parts that please).

Walahfrid was a man of wide learning who corresponded with most of the leading intellectuals of his age. He was also ambitious and moved in the highest circles, most notably at the court of Louis the Pious while tutoring the future King Charles the Bald of the West Franks; his poetry reflects Frankish political events and issues. Forced to retire from his abbacy of the Reichenau because of his support for Lothar, he was able with the help of his old friend Grimald, by then chaplain to Louis the German, to make a successful comeback. In the prologue he supplied to the life of Charlemagne, Walahfrid says that Einhard "mira quadam et divinitus provisa libratione se ipsum Deo protegente custodierit" (had a marvelous knack – almost providential, and with God looking after him – of keeping his balance). The description might apply as well to Walahfrid.

**References:**

Erich Auerbach, *Literary Language and Its Public in Late Antiquity and the Early Middle Ages,* translated by Ralph Manheim (Princeton: Princeton University Press, 1963);

Georg Baesecke, "Hrabans Isidorglossierung, Walahfrid Strabus und das ahd. Schrifttum," in his *Kleinere Schriften zur althochdeutschen Sprache und Literatur,* edited by Werner Schröder (Bern & Munich: Francke, 1966), pp. 7–37;

Konrad Beyerle, ed., *Die Kulter der Abtei Reichenau,* 2 volumes (Munich: Münchener Drucke, 1924, 1925);

Bernhard Bischoff, "Eine Sammelhandschrift Walahfrid Strabos (Codex Sangall. 878)," in his *Mittelalterliche Studien,* volume 2 (Stuttgart: Hiersemann, 1967), pp. 34–51;

Arno Borst, *Mönche am Bodensee 610–1525* (Sigmaringen: Thorbecke, 1978);

Martin Brooke, "The Prose and Verse Hagiography of Walahfrid Strabo," in *Charlemagne's Heir,* edited by Peter Godman and Roger Collin (New York & Oxford: Clarendon Press, 1990), pp. 551–564;

Leopold Eigl, *Walahfrid Strabo* (Vienna: Mayer, 1908);

Godman, "Louis 'the Pious' and his Poets," *Frühmittelalterliche Studien,* 19 (1985): 239–289;

Godman, *Poets and Emperors: Frankish Politics and Carolingian Poetry* (Oxford: Clarendon Press, 1987);

Wolfgang Haubrichs, *Die Anfänge,* volume 1/1 of *Geschichte der deutschen Literatur von den Anfängen bis zum Beginn der Neuzeit,* edited by Joachim Heinzle (Frankfurt am Main: Athenaeum, 1988);

Otto Herding, "Zum Problem des karolingischen 'Humanismus' mit besonderer Rücksicht auf

Walafrid Strabo," *Studium Generale,* 1 (December 1948): 389–397;

M. L. W. Laistner, *Thought and Letters in Western Europe AD 500–900* (London: Methuen, 1957);

Max Manitius, *Geschichte der lateinischen Literatur des Mittelalters,* volume 1: *Von Justinian bis zur Mitte des zehnten Jahrhunderts* (Munich: Beck, 1911; reprinted, 1964), pp. 302–314;

Helmut Maurer, ed., *Die Abtei Reichenau* (Sigmaringen: Thorbecke, 1974);

Robert E. McNally, *The Bible in the Early Middle Ages* (Westminster, Md.: Newman, 1959);

F. J. E. Raby, *A History of Christian-Latin Poetry,* second edition (Oxford: Clarendon Press, 1953), pp. 183–189;

Raby, *A History of Secular Latin Poetry in the Middle Ages,* volume 1, second edition (Oxford: Clarendon Press, 1957), pp. 229–234;

Ernst Schröter, *Walahfrids deutsche Glossierung zu den biblischen Büchern Genesis bis Regum II und der althochdeutsche Tatian* (Halle: Niemeyer, 1926);

Peter K. Stein, "Poesie antique et poesie neoantique sous les regnes de Charlemagne, Louis le Pieux et Louis le Germanique: l'exemple de Walahfrid Strabo," in *La Représentation de l'antiquité au moyen âge,* edited by Danielle Buschinger and André Crepin (Vienna: Halosar, 1982), pp. 7–27;

Paul von Winterfeld, "Die Dichterschule St. Gallens und der Reichenau unter den Karolingern und Ottonen," in *Mittellateinische Dichtung,* edited by Karl Langosch (Darmstadt: Wissenschaftliche Buchgesellschaft, 1969), pp. 131–154.

# Williram of Ebersberg

*(circa 1020 – 1085)*

Brian Murdoch
*University of Stirling*

MAJOR WORKS: *Poems, Vita S. Aurelii*

**Standard editions:** Marie-Luise Dittrich, "Sechzehn lateinische Gedichte Willirams von Ebersberg," *Zeitschrift für deutsches Altertum,* 76 (1939): 45–63; "Vita S. Aurelii," in *Acta Sanctorum,* November, volume 4 (Brussels: Bollandists, 1925), pp. 137–141.

*Expositio in Cantica Canticorum* (circa 1060)

**Manuscripts:** There are more than twenty manuscripts of this work, dating from the eleventh to the sixteenth centuries, plus fragments. The most important of the early manuscripts include Wroclaw, Stadtbibliothek, Ms. 347, from the eleventh century; Munich, Bayerische Staatsbibliothek, Cgm. 10, from the eleventh century; Leiden, University Library, Ms. B. P. L. 130, from the eleventh century; Vatican, Bibl. Vaticana Pal. Lat. 73, from the eleventh and twelfth centuries; London, British Library, Har-

ley 3014, from the twelfth century; Dresden, Sächsische Landesbibliothek, A 167a, from the late twelfth century, contains only Latin.

**First publications:** Translated into Latin by Menrad Molther as *VVilrammi abbatis olim eberespergensis in Cantica Solomonis mystica explanatio* (Hagenau Seltz, 1528); *Willerami abbatis in Canticvm canticorvm paraphrasis germina,* edited by Paulus Merula (Leiden: Raphelengium, 1598).

**Standard editions:** *Willirams deutsche Paraphrase des Hohen Liedes,* edited by Joseph Seemüller (Strasbourg: Trübner, 1878); *The "Expositio in Cantica Canticorum" of Williram, Abbot of Ebersberg 1048–1083,* edited by Erminnie Hollis Bartelmez (Philadelphia: American Philosophical Society, 1967).

Williram was a Frank from a well-off and well-connected family. Born circa 1020, he was educated

*Page from one of the early manuscripts for Williram's commentary on the Song of Songs. The text of the Vulgate version is in the middle column; the left column is a Latin verse commentary on the passage; the right column is a German prose translation of the passage with a mixed German and Latin prose commentary (Munich, Bayerische Staatsbibliothek, Cgm. 10, fol. 64r).*

first in Bamberg (it is not clear where else) and became a monk in Fulda, a monastery linked with the imperial house and a major intellectual center. In 1040 he became head of the school in Bamberg and seems to have counted on the patronage of Emperor Heinrich III, who gave him the abbacy of the small monastery of Ebersberg in Bavaria in 1048. It was there that Williram composed his major work, the *Expositio in Cantica Canticorum* (Commentary on the Song of Songs), around 1060. Heinrich III had died in 1056, and although Williram sent a copy with a dedicatory Latin poem to his successor, Heinrich IV, probably in 1069, the latter appears not to have been sympathetic to Williram's pleas to let him return to Fulda. Williram's comments on Ebersberg are far from positive, but he remained there, an efficient and conscientious abbot, until his death in 1085. He wrote his own epitaph, in which he said, "correxi libros, neglexi moribus illos" (I corrected books, but neglected the moral lessons in them); it is included with the commentary on the Song of Songs in a manuscript from Ebersberg that is now in Munich. One of the works he "corrected" was a life of Aurelius, patron saint of the reforming monastery of Hirsau, which he revised at the request of the abbot, William. Apart from some Latin poems, however – including an epitaph for his relative, Heribert, bishop of Eichstätt – his major work remains the mixed Latin-German text of his commentary on the Song of Songs.

The *Expositio in Cantica Canticorum* belongs to the Latin genus of *opus geminatum* (double work), which, in the context of Carolingian and later Latin writings, means a juxtaposition of prose and verse. A well-known earlier example is Sedulius's fifth-century *Carmen Paschale,* a gospel poem with an accompanying prose version, the *Paschale opus.* Bede produced two versions of his life of Saint Cuthbert, and in the Carolingian period writers such as Alcuin and Hrabanus Maurus wrote in the genre. Williram's work, however, is not only in prose and verse but also in Latin and German. In the finely decorated eleventh-century palatine manuscript, after a Latin prologue, the manuscript page is divided into three by architectural columns with elaborated arches. In the center space is the Vulgate Latin text of the Song of Songs in large lettering. The left-hand space contains a Latin verse commentary, and on the right is a German prose text consisting of a rendering of the Vulgate verse into German, followed by a prose commentary in a mixture of German and Latin. Thus, for example, the Vulgate verse Song of Songs 4:11 declares that the lips of the beloved distill honey and that honey and

milk are under the tongue of the beloved; the fourteen lines of Latin poetry develop this idea, and the German prose then makes clear how the passage refers allegorically to the manner in which the doctors of the church explain the sweet teaching of the Bible in all its senses, the spiritual sense hidden under the merely literal: " 'Hónig unte míloh. ist únter dîner zúngon. . . .' Únter déro sélbon *doctorum* zungon. ist hónig únte míloh; uuante sîe dîe *perfectos instruunt* mít *spiritalis sensus dulcedine"* ("Honey and milk are under thy tongue. . . ." Under the tongues of those very teachers is honey and milk, for they instruct the initiated with the sweetness of the spiritual sense).

The columnar division is especially clear in the palatine manuscript because of the decoration, but other early manuscripts show the threefold layout equally well. Williram makes it plain in his preface, too, what he is doing. He says that he has decided to make the Song of Songs clearer with verses and with a German explanation, putting the corpus in the center and surrounding it with the others for ease of study, so that text and interpretation can be seen together. The Vulgate text is the main thing; the Latin verse offers an artistic but more difficult explanation; the German offers first a translation that is absolutely clear and then an exegesis in which the technical theological terminology is left in Latin. There are, thus, two kinds of Latin: Vulgate prose and verse; and two kinds of German: a translation and then a *Mischprosa* (mixed prose) of German and Latin that had already been used by Notker Labeo of Saint Gall and is also present in the brief eleventh-century work *Himmel und Hölle* (Heaven and Hell).

The work is preserved in many manuscripts – a striking number for an early text – and at least fourteen are complete versions. The work was copied down to the sixteenth century, but some of the later manuscripts have only the Vulgate and the Latin verse; in one case a partial Latin translation of the German prose is added; another has only the German (this version, clearly designed for those who knew no Latin, was perhaps intended for the use of nuns). The *Sankt Trudperter Hohes Lied* (Saint Trudpert Song of Songs), written about a century after Williram, is based on his work, although with the addition of mystical-speculative elements, and is part of a tradition of Latin-German versions of the Song of Songs.

The Song of Songs is a difficult Old Testament text for Christian interpretation, since it is a profoundly sexual love poem. Williram's approach is entirely traditional: he treats it as a dialogue between Christ and the Church as the bride of Christ. He took this interpretation from Latin commentaries, most notably that by Haimo of Auxerre, but used other works as well. He comments that he has added nothing of his own but has used various expositions by the fathers. His approach is conservative in a thoroughgoing sense; in the opening words of his prologue he deplores the modern decline in studies of the Bible, which he sees as disappearing under a flood of contentious overinterpretation. In this context he praises Lanfranc "in francia" (in France) for maintaining standards of straightforward interpretation; this comment allows Williram's time of writing to be dated to around 1060, since Lanfranc ran the important monastery school at Bec from 1059 to 1063, when he stopped teaching to become abbot of Caen (later he became archbishop of Canterbury under William the Conqueror).

Some of the manuscripts have headings that indicate who is speaking at any given point – primarily Christ and Ecclesia, but occasionally Synagoga and others. Sometimes, too, an indication is given of who is being addressed. In some of the manuscripts divisions are made other than the simple division of the biblical book into 149 verses used by Williram.

Williram's achievement is difficult for the modern reader to assess, seeming both unoriginal in content and too elaborate in form, especially as that form is rarely clear in printed versions. But Williram's work reminds the reader that biblical poetry is not independent of the biblical source, and that commentary is separate from and subordinate to both. In his time, and for centuries afterward, Williram's work was extremely well known as an exposition of the Vulgate text, and it was copied, adapted, and read in many contexts. In 1528, only a few years after it was last copied, it was edited and translated into Latin by Menrad Molther, and in 1598 it was edited by Paulus Merula.

## Biography:
Wilhelm Scherer, "Leben Willirams, Abtes von Ebersberg in Baiern," *Sitzungsberichte der Wiener Akademie der Wissenschaften, phil.-hist. Kl.,* 53 (1866): 197–303.

## References:
Erminnie Hollis Bartelmez, "Williram's Text of the Song of Solomon and Its Distribution," *Manuscripta,* 16 (1972): 165–168;

Marie-Luise Dittrich, "Die literarische Form von Willirams *Expositio in Cantica Canticorum*," *Zeitschrift für deutsches Altertum,* 84 (1952–1953): 179–197;

Dittrich, "Willirams von Ebersberg Bearbeitung der *Cantica Canticorum*," *Zeitschrift für deutsches Altertum,* 82 (December 1948): 47–64;

Gustav Ehrismann, *Geschichte der deutschen Literatur bis zum Ausgang des Mittelalters,* volume 2/1 (Munich: Beck, 1922), pp. 18–29;

Kurt Gärtner, "Zu den Handschriften mit dem deutschen Kommentarteil des Hoheliedkommentars Willirams von Ebersberg," in *Deutsche Handschriften 1100–1400,* edited by Volker Honemann and Nigel Palmer (Tübingen: Niemeyer, 1988), pp. 1–34;

Wolfgang Haubrichs, *Die Anfänge,* volume 1 of *Geschichte der deutschen Literatur,* edited by Joachim Heinzle (Frankfurt am Main: Atheneum, 1988), pp. 226–228, 276–279;

Nikolaus Henkel and Nigel Palmer, *Latein und Volkssprache im deutschen Mittelalter* (Tübingen: Niemeyer, 1992), pp. 199–222;

Max Manitius, *Geschichte der lateinischen Literatur des Mittelalters,* volume 2 (Munich: Beck, 1923; reprinted, 1965), pp. 592–599;

Brian O. Murdoch, *Old High German Literature* (Boston: Twayne, 1983), pp. 117–120;

Hans-Ulrich Schmid, "Nachträge zur Überlieferung von Willirams Paraphrase des Hohen Liedes," *Zeitschrift für deutsches Altertum,* 113, no. 4 (1984): 229–234;

Volker Schupp, *Studien zu Williram von Ebersberg* (Bern & Munich: Francke, 1978);

Joseph Seemüller, *Die Handschriften und Quellen von Willirams deutscher Paraphrase des Hohen Liedes* (Strasbourg: Trübner, 1877);

Lothar Voetz, *Eine bisher unbekannte Williram-Handschrift aus dem 15. Jahrhundert* (Göttingen: Akademie der Wissenschaften, 1990).

# Abrogans

## (circa 790 – 800)

### Albrecht Classen
*University of Arizona*

**Manuscripts:** The *Abrogans* is extant in three manuscripts: Saint Gall, Stiftsbibliothek, Codex Sangallensis 911, late eighth century (K); Paris, Bibliothèque Nationale, Codex latinus 7640, early ninth century (Pa); Karlsruhe, Landesbibliothek, Codex Augiensis XXI, early ninth century (Ra).

**First publication:** In *Diutiska: Denkmäler deutscher Sprache und Literatur, aus alten Handschriften,* volume 1, edited by Eberhard Gottlieb Graff (Stuttgart, 1826), pp. 128–279.

**Standard edition:** *Das älteste deutsche Buch: Die "Abrogans"-Handschrift der Stiftsbibliothek St. Gallen. Im Facsimile herausgegeben und beschrieben,* edited by Bernhard Bischoff, Johannes Duft, and Stefan Sonderegger (Saint Gall: Zollikofer Fachverlag, 1977).

In the early Middle Ages most theological texts were composed in Latin. The most important text was the Bible – the Vulgate – but students had to undergo a rigorous education program before they were allowed to approach this holy work. This program included the study of selected materials and their translations. During the Carolingian age an extensive education system was established throughout the Frankish empire that resulted in prolific book production. Teachers such as Saint Boniface at Fulda and Mainz, Hrabanus Maurus at Fulda, and Otfried von Weißenburg were aware of the difficulties their students faced in reading Latin texts, and they often offered help in the form of interlinear and marginal glosses in Old High German. For modern scholars these glosses provide information about the etymology, grammar, and vocabulary of Old High German and about early medieval culture in general.

In the second half of the eighth century the number of glosses increased, along with the growing number of manuscripts used in schools, and soon the glosses developed into separate lexicological works in the vein of the dictionaries that had been in use since the second century. Later centuries brought similar dictionaries, particularly in northern Italy, which were often geared toward rhetoricians and offered mainly synonyms. They were titled according to the first word listed, such as *Abba, Abavus,* or *Affatim.*

The Old High German *Abrogans* (circa 790–800) is a representative of this genre and is considered the first text written in German. It is a translation of an alphabetically arranged Latin dictionary of synonyms; the latter work, which today is at the Landesbibliothek Karlsruhe, was presumably composed around the middle of the seventh century in northern Italy by a Langobardic scribe and exported to the Bavarian language area in southern Germany soon afterward. Linguistic evidence indicates that the *Abrogans* was composed in southwestern Germany at the end of the eighth century, but where it was written is unknown. The most complete version is in the monastic library of Saint Gall. It is not known who inspired the creation of the bilingual dictionary; it could have been Bishop Arbeo of Freising, Bishop Virgil of Salzburg, or some Anglo-Saxon missionary. Langobardic influence is not excluded, since the Langobardic-Bavarian cultural center at the royal court in Pavia exerted a considerable influence far into Upper Austria and Bavaria. Before the end of the eighth century the *Abrogans* was imitated by some monks in Regensburg to form the *Samanunga uuorto fona deru niuuiun anti dera altun eu* (Collection of Words from the New and the Old Testaments).

The original text of the *Abrogans* is lost. All three extant versions are copies from a later period and were written in the Alemannic monasteries of Reichenau and Murbach. The Paris manuscript (designated Pa), which appears to be closest to the archetype and which combines the *Abrogans* with a purely Latin dictionary of synonyms titled *Abavus maior,* breaks off with the letter *i* (the fragmentation probably occurred in the seventeenth century). The Saint Gall manuscript, the most complete of the three, was given the designation K because of the now-rejected assumption that a monk named Kero wrote this Latin and Old High German glossary. Georg Baesecke coined the modern title for the book in 1930 according to the first word in Latin, *Abrogans*, thereby discarding the older title, *Keronisches Wörterbuch* (Kero Dictionary).

The *Abrogans* offers one of the largest and oldest linguistic databases for Old High German – 3,693 vernacular terms can be found in the three manuscripts combined – and is the oldest German glossary using the alphabet. Moreover, the *Abrogans* documents the coming of the Carolingian Renaissance, during which energetic efforts were made to revive the study of classical authors. This intellectual movement was based in the Benedictine monasteries in the Frankish empire and received strong support through the Anglo-Saxon missionaries, among whom the leading figure was Alcuin, Charlemagne's chief adviser and founder of the royal academy at the palace in Aachen.

The *Abrogans* consists of two parts. The older, designated Ka, is written in the archaic form of Old High German; the later part, Kb, shows influences from the Frankish-language area. *Abrogans* is a word of late antique Latin and means "to ask for forgiveness." The Old High German equivalent is given in the Saint Gall manuscript as *dheomodi* (repentant) and in the Paris manuscript as *aotmot* (humble). The second word, *humilis* (humble), is rendered into *samft moati* (gentle). The translator obviously had difficulty finding the most adequate Old High German terms to match the Latin words. The problem was not with an inexperienced or incompetent translator but with Old High German itself, a language that lacked the full development of Latin – particularly in abstract terms and in words for concepts, such as humility, that were foreign to the Germanic value system. In addition, dialect variations continued to dominate and hampered the emergence of a uniform language spoken over all Germanic areas. The Saint Gall manuscript, in which conservative and progressive linguistic elements are mixed, especially indicates the unstable condition of Old High German in the late eighth century. In some cases, however, the translator deliberately changed the content of the Latin phrase to adjust it to his Christian worldview. For instance, *clandestinum* (secret) is rendered into *uuitharzoami,* meaning inappropriate or immoral, because *secrecy* implied a break with the monastic rules and, thus, was condemnable. The translation of *occultum* (dark) not as the adjective *tunkal* but as the noun *tuncli* is another example of a deliberate change. The translator operated with a word-for-word strategy and did not consider the context except when serious problems arose. In many cases lack of an equivalent German term leads to Latin terms being rendered into Old High

German by way of explications, generalizations, or interpretations.

The anonymous author's interest was in providing translations for important Latin terms found both in religious texts and in secular ones such as the seventh-century grammar books by Virgilius Maro of Toulouse. The *Abrogans* constitutes a sort of encyclopedia of the culture of its time. Nevertheless, the overall religious framework must not be ignored: at the end of each series of words beginning with the same letter are explanations of biblical names. The *Abrogans* was quickly imitated and became the model for many other Old High German glossaries.

**References:**

Georg Baesecke, *Der deutsche Abrogans und die Herkunft des deutschen Schrifttums* (Halle: Niemeyer, 1930);

Baesecke, "Die Sprache des deutschen Abrogans," in his *Kleinere Schriften zur althochdeutschen Sprache und Literatur,* edited by Werner Schröder (Bern & Munich: Francke, 1966), pp. 181–220;

Rolf Bergmann, *Verzeichnis der althochdeutschen und altsächsischen Glossenhandschriften: Mit Bibliographie der Glosseneditionen, der Handschriftenbeschreibungen und der Dialektbestimmungen* (Berlin & New York: De Gruyter, 1973);

Werner Betz, *Der Einfluß des Lateinischen auf den althochdeutschen Sprachschatz. 1: Der Abrogans* (Heidelberg: Winter, 1936);

Bernhard Bischoff, "Paläographische Fragen deutscher Denkmäler der Karolingerzeit," *Frühmittelalterliche Studien,* 5 (1971): 101–134;

John Knight Bostock, *A Handbook on Old High German Literature,* revised by K. C. King and D. R. McLintock (Oxford: Clarendon Press, 1976);

Ursula Daab, "Die Affatimglossen des Glossars Jc und der deutsche *Abrogans,*" *Beiträge zur Geschichte der deutschen Sprache und Literatur* (Tübingen), 82, no. 2/3 (1961): 275–317;

Daab, "Zur althochdeutschen Glossierung des Abrogans (ab1)," *Beiträge zur Geschichte der deutschen Sprache und Literatur* (Tübingen), 88 (1967): 1–27;

Elisabeth Karg-Gasterstädt, "Zum Wortschatz des Abrogans," in *Altdeutsches Wort und Wortkunstwerk: Georg Baesecke zum 65. Geburtstag* (Halle: Niemeyer, 1941), pp. 124–137;

Gerhard Köbler, *Verzeichnis der Übersetzungsgleichungen von Abrogans und Samanunga* (Göttingen: Musterschmidt, 1972);

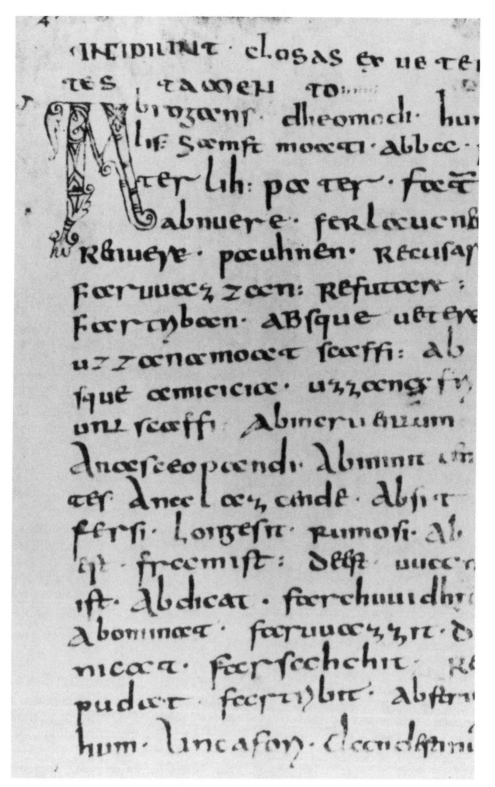

*Two versions of the opening of the Abrogans. Left: page from manuscript K (Saint Gall, Stiftsbibliothek, Codex Sangallensis 911), from the late eighth century; right: manuscript Pa (Paris, Bibliothèque Nationale, Codex latinus 7640), from the early ninth century. Although later, manuscript Pa is thought to be closer to the original, which has been lost.*

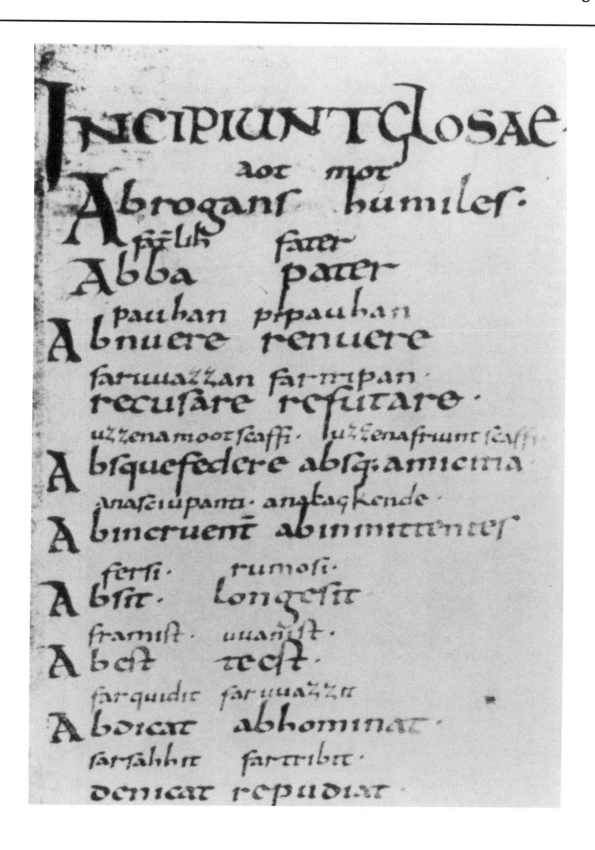

Elda Morlicchio, "L'*Abrogans:* analisi contrastiva lessicale latino-antico alto tedesco," *Studi Germanici,* 19-20 (1981-1982): 5-27;

Brian Murdoch, *Old High German Literature* (Boston: Twayne, 1983);

Heinz Rupp, "Forschung zur althochdeutschen Literatur 1945-1962," *Deutsche Vierteljahresschrift für Literaturwissenschaft und Geistesgeschichte,* 38 (1964): 1-67;

Hans Schwarz, *Präfixbildungen im deutschen Abrogans: Analyse und Systematik* (Göppingen: Kümmerle, 1986);

Stefan Sonderegger, *Althochdeutsche Sprache und Literatur: Eine Einführung in das älteste Deutsch, Darstellung und Grammatik* (Berlin & New York: De Gruyter, 1974);

Jochen Splett, "Abrogans deutsch," in *Die deutsche Literatur des Mittelalters: Verfasserlexikon,* second edition, volume 1, edited by Kurt Ruh and others (Berlin & New York: De Gruyter, 1978), cols. 12-15;

Splett, *Abrogans-Studien: Kommentar zum ältesten deutschen Wörterbuch* (Wiesbaden: Steiner, 1976);

Splett, "Der Abrogans und das Einsetzen althochdeutscher Schriftlichkeit im 8. Jahrhundert," in *Typen der Ethnogenese unter besonderer Berücksichtigung der Bayern,* volume 1, edited by Herwig Wolfram and Walter Pohl (Vienna: Verlag der Österreichischen Akademie der Wissenschaften, 1990), pp. 235-241;

Splett, "Zur Frage der Zweckbestimmung des Abrogans," in *Collectanea philologica: Festschrift für Helmut Gipper zum 65. Geburtstag,* volume 2, edited by Günter Heintz and Peter Schmitter (Baden-Baden: Koerner, 1985), pp. 725-735;

Josef Stalzer, "Zu den hrabanisch-keronischen Glossen," in Στρωματεις: *Grazer Festgabe zur 50. Versammlung deutscher Philologen und Schulmänner* (Graz: Selbstverlag des Festausschusses, 1909), pp. 80-90;

Wilhelm Wissmann, "Zum Abrogans," in *Fragen und Forschungen im Bereich und Umkreis der germanischen Philologie: Festgabe für Theodor Frings zum 70. Geburtstag,* edited by Elisabeth Karg-Gasterstädt (Berlin: Akademie Verlag, 1956), pp. 80-113.

# Annolied

## (between 1077 and 1081)

### Francis G. Gentry
*Pennsylvania State University*

**Manuscript:** No manuscripts of the *Annolied* survive. The 1597 and 1639 editions appear to be based on different manuscripts but not on different versions of the work.

**First publications:** Verses 19 to 78, in *De literis et lingua Getarum sive Gothorum*, edited by Bonaventura Vulcanius (Leiden: Ex Officina Plantiniana, apud Franciscum Raphelengium, 1597), pp. 61–64; complete poem in *Incerti poetae teutonici: Rhythmus de Sancto Annone colon. archiepiscopo*, edited by Martin Opitz (Danzig: Ex Officina Andr. Rünefeldii, 1639).

**Standard editions:** *Das Annolied: Hrsg. von Martin Opitz 1639. Diplomatischer Abdruck*, edited by Walther Bulst (Heidelberg: Winter, 1946); in *Die religiösen Dichtungen des 11. und 12. Jahrhunderts: Nach ihren Formen besprochen*, edited by Friedrich Maurer, volume 2 (Tübingen: Niemeyer, 1965), pp. 3–45; in *Deutsche Dichtung des Mittelalters*, volume 1:*Von den Anfängen bis zum hohen Mittelalter*, edited by Michael Curschmann and Ingeborg Glier (Frankfurt am Main: Fischer, 1987), pp. 92–147.

**Edition in modern German:** *Das Annolied: Mittelhochdeutsch und Neuhochdeutsch*, edited by Eberhard Nellmann (Stuttgart: Reclam, 1975).

Preserved only through most fortunate chance, the *Annolied* (Song of Anno, between 1077 and 1081) is one of the most fascinating works of the early Middle High German period and second only to the *Kaiserchronik* (Chronicle of the Emperors, circa 1147) for insights into important aspects of the medieval worldview, especially the concept of historical progression and its allegorical interpretation. The most pressing reason for the composition of the *Annolied*, however, was the glorification of Anno — the prince, the bishop, and the "good shepherd" of his Cologne flock. Anno is clearly being proposed as a candidate for sainthood, and his canonization did take place in 1183. The skillfulness of the poet in weaving the events of the bishop's life into the broad tapestry of the history of salvation and of the world is unique in early Middle High German poetry. It is conjectured that the immediate source for the "Anno" portion of the *Annolied* (strophes 34–48) was the now-lost *Vita Annonis* by Reginhard, the abbot of Siegburg (1076–1105). A most important source for the *Vita Annonis* are the *Annals* (circa 1078) of Lampert, a monk of Hersfeld. The poet makes a strong case for Anno's canonization and presents him as an ideal ruler who combined the best qualities of a religious and secular prince.

The identity of the *Annolied* poet is not known, nor can the place and time of composition be determined with certainty. Since Anno died in December 1075 and the text reports his death, there is, at least, a terminus a quo. Although scholarly opinion is divided, a consensus is forming that the work was composed sometime between March 1077 and December 1081 by a monk of the reform monastery of Siegburg. Support for this hypothesis is found in the text.

The date of composition is indicated in strophe 30, where, in the context of a description of various German cities, the poet writes:

Meginza was dû ein kastel,
iz gemêrte manig helit snel;
dâ ist nû dere kuninge wîchtûm,
dis pâbis senitstûl. (strophe 30, lines 11–14)

( In those days Mainz was a fortress,
[and] many a brave hero enlarged it.
Now it is the [ place of ] consecration of the kings,
[and] the location of papal synods.)

Aachen was the usual site of royal coronations. But during the early years of the Investiture Contest, when Emperor Heinrich IV was engaged in a long and bloody struggle with the German nobility, the antiking Rudolf von Rheinfelden was crowned in Mainz in March 1077, and in December 1081 the antiking Hermann von Salm was crowned in Goslar. Since the poet expressly says "Now it is the [place of] consecration of the kings," it is reason-

*Miniature of Archbishop Anno of Cologne (Darmstadt, Hessische Landes-
und Hochschulbibliothek, Ms. 945, fol. 4, circa 1180)*

able to postulate that the date of composition is to be found during Rudolf's brief period as the king chosen by the rebellious German nobility. It is theoretically possible that the time after the Mainz coronation of Heinrich V in 1106 is meant; but this conjecture has received little support following the seminal 1968 essay by Heinz Thomas, who demonstrates that the *Annolied* was the source of the description encountered in the *Gesta Treverorum* (1101) of the underground aqueduct that transported wine from Trier to Cologne. Therefore, it must have been written before 1101.

With regard to the place of composition: during his tenure as archbishop of Cologne from 1056 to 1075, Anno founded several monasteries, among them Siegburg in 1064. It was in Siegburg, on a hill southeast of Cologne, that Anno chose to spend the last years of his life, and he is buried there. The affection that Anno felt for the monastery and its brothers is expressed in strophe 37:

ci demi tiurin gotis lobe stiftir
selbo vier munister;
diz vunfti ist sigeberg, sîn vili liebi stat,
dar ûffe steit nû sîn graf. (strophe 37, lines 13–16)

(For the glory of [our] dear God,
he, himself, founded four monasteries.
The [a?] fifth is Siegburg, his favorite place.
His grave is located up there.)

The singling out of Siegburg and the emphasis placed on that monastery as Anno's "favorite place," even in death, buttress the hypothesis that a monk of Siegburg was the author of the *Annolied*.

It is, perhaps, fitting that the origins of the *Annolied* are enshrouded in uncertainty and mystery: the subject of the work was no stranger to controversy during his lifetime, and even now his character is the topic of lively debate among historians. Two incidents stand out in a life filled with momentous events: the abduction of the young king

Heinrich IV and the brutal quashing of the uprising of the citizens of Cologne. Anno's role in both episodes struck his contemporaries – and strikes modern historians – as morally ambiguous. The *Annolied*, on the other hand, presents these occurrences in a positive light.

Emperor Heinrich III died in 1056, leaving behind a not-quite-six-year-old son, Heinrich IV. The empress Agnes was the regent for her son, but she was not a skilled ruler and was deceived and manipulated by unscrupulous members of the nobility who were anxious to shore up their own power and authority at the expense of the monarchy. In 1062, in consort with other high nobles of the realm, Anno kidnapped the young king at Kaiserswerth and assumed the role of regent. For all practical purposes, Anno ruled the empire until Heinrich attained his majority in 1065. Whether the archbishop was prompted to participate in this coup by ambition and greed or whether he was concerned about the disarray in the government under Agnes and wished to provide a proper education for the young king cannot be determined, and it was a puzzle even to Anno's near contemporaries. In the Latin chronicle of Frutolf von Michelsberg, for example, which was written around the end of the eleventh century and the beginning of the twelfth (Frutolf, a monk of Michelsberg, died on 17 January 1103), it is said that the empress Agnes ruled wisely and well until several nobles, seduced by envy, took the boy from his mother and robbed her of authority over the empire. Archbishop Anno of Cologne joined the nobles and, in the vicinity of Kaiserswerth, brought the boy on board a ship and, thus, kidnapped him. Why he did so or whether God countenanced this action cannot be determined. But one thing is sure: since then much unrest has arisen and has increased in the empire as well as in the church. We witness, Frutolf says, the deterioration of monasteries, abuse of the clergy, and the collapse of justice and piety, and these conditions continue in the present. It is apparent that Frutolf believes that the action against the young Heinrich IV was unjust. This tampering with the correct order of things has led to chaos and strife in the empire and church and evidences no sign of abating. The conflict between papacy and empire and between Heinrich IV and his rebellious German nobles had been in progress for almost twenty-five years when Frutolf was writing his chronicle, and Frutolf indicts Anno's actions as the root cause of the discord prevalent in his own day.

In the *Annolied,* however, this episode assumes different contours. No mention is made of the abduction of the young king. Instead, attention is focused on Anno's role as regent and the reason for his acting in this role:

> Vili sêliclîche diz rîche alliz stûnt,
> duo des girihtis plag der heirre guot,
> duo her zô ci demi rîchi
> den iungen Heinrîche.
> wilich rihtêre her wêre. . . . (strophe 37, lines 1–5)

> (The whole empire was very fortunate
> when the gracious lord [Anno] attended to its administration,
> [and] when he was preparing
> young Heinrich for rule.
> What a regent he was. . . . )

Here there is no mention of the violence done to the young king, and the cause of the subsequent strife in the empire does not lie with Anno or his role as regent but with the king himself.

While Frutolf refrains from directly blaming Anno for the later tumult in the empire but does make rather obvious insinuations in this regard, the poet of the *Annolied* is quite clear as to who should bear the onus for the state of affairs in the realm:

> Dar nâch vîng sich ane der ubile strît,
> den manig man virlôs den lîph,
> duo demi vierden Heinrîche
> virworrin wart diz rîche.
> mort, roub unti brant
> civûrtin kirichin unti lant
> von Tenemarc unz in Apuliam,
> van Kerlingin unz an Ungerin.
> den nîman nimohte widir stên,
> obi si woltin mit trûwin unsamit gên.
> die stiftin heriverte grôze
> wider nevin unti hûsgenôze.
> diz rîche alliz bikêrte sîn gewêfine
> in sîn eigin inâdere.
> mit siginuftlîcher ceswe
> ubirwant iz sich selbe,
> daz dî gedouftin lîchamin
> umbigravin ciworfin lâgin
> ci âse den bellindin,
> den grâwin walthundin. (strophe 40, lines 1–20)

> (Then began the evil conflict
> in which many a man lost his life.
> At the time of Heinrich IV
> the empire was brought into total disarray.
> Murder, robbery, and arson
> devastated churches and lands
> from Denmark to Apulia,
> from France to Hungary.
> No one was able to withstand them,
> even if they wished to keep faith with each other.
> They organized great military campaigns

against relatives and countrymen.
The whole empire plunged its weapons
into its own innards.
With a victorious hand it [the empire]
overcame itself
so that the cadavers of the baptized
lay scattered and unburied
as carrion for the baying
gray wolves.)

These lines could refer to the disruptions in society brought about by the fierce and savage war against the Saxons, or they might be a hyperbolic reaction to the beginning of the Investiture Contest. Whatever the catalyst for their composition may have been, it is clear that the sympathies of the poet do not lie with Heinrich IV, for he is accounted the wellspring of calamity from which all the turmoil besetting the empire flows.

Dissatisfaction with the rather firm rule of the archbishop resulted in the uprising of the Cologne bourgeoisie in 1074. This rebellion was ruthlessly — and, apparently, brutally — quelled by Anno. In the eloquent and influential obituary of Anno in his *Annals,* Lampert of Hersfeld alludes to the uprising as one of the many trials that Anno had to face toward the end of his life. Lampert also personalizes the uprising by describing the events as physical attacks on the person of Anno or his confidants, many of whom were — according to Lampert — murdered. Only later, after reporting on a vision that Anno had (one that is recapitulated in the *Annolied*), does Lampert indicate that the archbishop was driven from Cologne by its citizens. Half a year before he died Anno had a dream in which he entered a beautiful house where several tribunes were set up as if at a solemn council of the church. There he saw many famous deceased bishops dressed in resplendent white episcopal garments. He, too, was dressed all in white, but on his breast there was a blemish that overshadowed the luster of the rest of his garments. Anno held a hand in front of this blot and went to the one unoccupied tribune in the room. He was stopped by a bishop who explained that the tribune was, indeed, reserved for him but that he could not occupy it until he had removed the stain on his garment. Anno was then dismissed from the room. The next morning an intelligent servant interpreted the vision for Anno: the stain reflected Anno's bitter thoughts about the citizens of Cologne who had ousted him from the city in the previous year; he should have forgiven them for their injustice. Anno thereupon had all those whom he had exiled summoned back to the city, where he restored them to the community of the church and returned

all confiscated goods. Thus were the bishop and his flock reconciled, and, it is to be assumed, the blemish was removed from his garments.

It is clear that Lampert is criticizing Anno only slightly and only because he neglected the principle of Christian forgiveness, not because he resorted to brutal actions. The *Annolied* reports on this situation in a similar vein. The poet laments Anno's faithless treatment by the Cologne bourgeoisie:

Dikki un anevuhtin dî lantheirrin,
ei iungis brâ iz got al ci sînin êrin.
vili dikki un anerietin,
dî une soltin bihuotin.
wî dikki une dî virmanitin,
dî her ci heirrin brâht havite!
ci iungis niwart daz niht virmidin,
her niwurde mit gewêfinin ûze dir burg virtribin,
als Absalon wîlin
virtreib vater sînin,
den vili guotin David.
disi zuei dinc, harti si wârin gelîch.
leidis unte arbeite genug
genîte sich der heirro guot,
al nah dis heiligin Cristis bilide. (strophe 39, lines 1–15)

(The lords of the land often attacked him.
At the end, [however], God turned everything to his honor.
Very often, those who were to protect him [Anno] planned attacks against him.
How often those whom he had exalted scorned him! Finally it came to the point that he was driven from the city with weapons, just as Absalom in former days had driven off his father, the good [King] David.
These two things [events] were very similar.
The good prince [Anno] had to bear much suffering and travail just like our Lord Christ.)

By portraying Anno as an *imitatio Christi,* and by employing the conventional image of Absalom and David — the ungrateful son and the loving father — the *Annolied* leaves no doubt about the perfidy of the inhabitants of Cologne. But here, too, in spite of the unjust actions taken against Anno, his garments are soiled. And, as in Lampert's *Annals,* Anno must become reconciled with the citizens of Cologne. The poet remarks tersely:

Kolnêrin virgab her sîni hulte.
daz her si hazzite, wî grôz daz wârin ere sculte! (strophe 43, lines 23–24)

(He dispensed his forgiveness to the people of Cologne.

That he had loathed them — how much that had been their fault!)

A good man and a pious churchman Anno built several churches and monasteries, was generous to widows and orphans, and cared for the ecclesiastical institutions in Cologne during his lifetime and made provision for them after his death. These aspects of Anno's character are also highlighted in the work.

The ostensible purpose of the *Annolied* is to present the case for canonization of Anno, and the work accomplishes this goal in a quite traditional manner by emphasizing Anno's life of sanctity and trial (*imitatio Christi*) and presenting the requisite miracle brought about by the good offices of the saint after his death. The miracle was the restoration of sight to Volprecht, the servant of a knight named Arnold. Because of an unspecified transgression, Volprecht lost the favor of his lord, and he began to doubt the goodness of God. He made a pact with the devil, who appeared to him and promised him aid in his difficulties with his master. All Volprecht had to do was to deny God and his good works. Also, he could not tell anyone that he was in league with the devil; should he do so, he would be torn to bits. On the following day Volprecht was with Arnold and began to carry out the devil's command by denying God and by being contemptuous of the saints. When, however, he began to revile Anno, a terrible retribution was visited upon him: his left eye melted in the socket. When still he did not repent, he was struck as if by a bolt of lightning, and his right eye burst forth from its socket. In great pain and consternation Volprecht professed his sins and prayed for Anno's intervention. His eyes miraculously regenerated in their sockets, bearing eloquent witness to the power of God and the efficacy of Anno. The miracle is all the more impressive since punishment was not inflicted on Volprecht until after he had mocked Anno, highlighting the closeness of the relationship between God and Anno.

The work is more than a hymn of praise to the Cologne prelate; of the forty-nine strophes, only the last sixteen deal exclusively with Anno's life and death and the miracle associated with him. The first thirty-three are concerned with history, both secular and redemptive. The overview of history culminates in strophe 33, where Anno is presented as the thirty-third bishop of Cologne — an assertion that is historically inaccurate but one that serves to link Anno in the medieval mind with Christ, who was thirty-three years old at the time of the Crucifixion. The *Annolied* begins:

Wir hôrten ie dikke singen
von alten dingen:
wî snelle helide vuhten,
wî si veste burge brêchen,
wî sich liebin vuiniscefte schieden,
wî rîche kunige al zergiengen,
nû ist  cît, daz wir dencken,
wî wir selve sulin enden.
Crist, der unser hero guot,
wî manige ceichen her uns vure duot,
alser ûffin Siegberg havit gedân
durch den diurlîchen man,
den heiligen bischof Annen,
durch den sînin willen.
dabî wir uns sulin bewarin,
wante wir noch sulin varin
von disime ellindin lîbe hin cin êwin,
dâ wir imer sulin sîn. (strophe 1, lines 1–18)

(We have often heard sing
of deeds of old:
how brave heroes fought,
how they destroyed mighty cities,
how cherished friendships came to an end,
[and] how powerful kings were laid low.
Now it is time that we should ponder
how we, ourselves, are to end.
Christ, our precious Lord: how many signs did he work before our eyes
as he did on the Siegburg
for the sake of [and] through [the instrument of ] that
    worthy man,
the blessed Bishop Anno.
That is a sign
that we must be on our guard,
for we must yet journey
from this troublesome life to eternity,
where we are to be forever.)

This strophe indicates that secular heroic poetry was enjoying continued popularity. The text provides the earliest and best evidence in the vernacular of the continuing, and doubtless oral ("we have often heard sing of deeds of old"), literary existence of profane themes, probably those centering about Dietrich von Bern (Theodoric) as well as other themes and figures of the Nibelung epic. Apart from Alcuin's caustic remark in the eighth century to the monks of Lindisfarne, "Quid Hinieldus cum Christo?" (What does Ingeld [a Heathobardic king mentioned in *Beowulf* ] have to do with Christ?), a more contemporary attestation to what certain churchmen considered the unseemly appreciation of heroic narratives can be found in the chiding of Bishop Gunther of Bamberg by Meinhard, the head of the cathedral school in Bamberg. Meinhard writes of the literary tastes of his bishop most disapprovingly: "semper ille Attilam, semper Amalungum et cetera id genus portare retractat" (He is always concerning himself with Attila, Amelung [Dietrich von Bern], and others of that sort). It is unclear from the context in the *Annolied,* however, if the poet is criticizing this type of literary pursuit or merely wishes to say that it is time for his listeners to think about their ultimate destiny.

Anno receives, as would be expected in the introductory strophe, prominent mention, and the special relationship between Christ and Anno is emphasized – Christ works miracles for Anno's sake. And the poet makes the rather unmistakable hint that one should take Anno as a model and prepare for life after death. The themes of moving beyond the concerns of the world and preparing for death are stock motifs of the memento mori genre (examples are the works of Notker von Zwiefalten and Heinrich von Melk), but in the second strophe the poet abandons this topic and embarks on an ambitious narration of the history of the world into which the city of Cologne and the figure of Anno will be convincingly integrated.

Strophes 2 and 3 recount the creation of the physical and spiritual worlds; the human being, composed of matter and spirit, forms a "third world":

duo deilti got sîni werch al in zuei:
disi werlt ist daz eine deil,
daz ander ist geistîn.
. . . . . . . . . . . . . . . .
duo gemengite dei wîse godis list
von den zuein ein werch, daz der mennisch ist,
der beide ist, corpus unte geist;
. . . . . . . . . . . . . . . . . . . . . . .
alle gescaft ist an dem mennischen,
sôiz sagit daz evangelium.
wir sulin un cir dritte werilde celin,
sô wir daz die Crîchen hôrin redin. (strophe 2, lines 5–10, 12–15)

(Then God divided his work in two.
This world is one part;
the other [part] is spiritual.
. . . . . . . . . . . . . . . . . . . . . .
Then the discerning power of God blended
from the two one work, the human being,
who is both body and spirit.
. . . . . . . . . . . . . . . . . . . . . .
All creation is in the human being,
as the Gospel says.
We should view him as a third world,
as we hear the Greeks say.)

Here the *Annolied* poet deviates from the Augustinian two-world theory and embraces the concept, espoused by the ninth-century philosopher John Scotus Eriugena, of the human being as a "tertius mundus" (third world). This theory owes much to

the Greek microcosm concept, as expounded by Aristotle, Plato, and the Neoplatonists, and is found in Eriugena's magisterial work *Periphyseon* (About Nature, circa 864–866). It is also encountered in his sermon on the prologue of the Gospel of Saint John (circa 875–877), which is doubtless the immediate source for the *Annolied* poet and explains the somewhat cryptic comment, "all creation is in the human being, as the Gospel says." In strophe 3 the poet disposes of the Fall of Humanity with the brief remark that Adam disobeyed God's command. God is described as being all the more incensed at this transgression since he sees that every other work of Creation is adhering to the commands that he set down for it. With the terse comment "dannen hûben sich diu leit" (from that time suffering took its origin), the poet moves in strophe 4 to the coming of Christ and his redemptive act:

Cunt ist wî der vîent virspûn den man,
zi scalke wolter un havin.
sô vuorter cir hellin
die vunf werlt alle,
unze got gesante sînin sun,
der irlôste uns von den sunden. (strophe 4, lines 1–6)

(It is well known how the Enemy [Satan] tempted the man.
He wanted to have him as a servant.
Thus he led to hell
all the five ages of the world,
until God sent his son
who freed us from our sins.)

The *Annolied* poet does not deem it necessary to deal extensively with Old Testament events and personages. Important for him is to present the two major episodes in the history of Salvation – Creation and Redemption – as well as the resultant spread of Christianity. Thus the poet is able to move quickly on to the redemptive act of Christ with merely a fleeting reference to the intervening time as the "five ages of the world," which, according to Saint Augustine, are: from Adam to Noah; from Noah to Abraham; from Abraham to David; from David to the Captivity in Babylon; and from the Captivity to John the Baptist and the birth of Christ. The sixth age is the present and extends from the birth of Christ to the hidden end of time. In strophe 4 the victory of Christ over Satan is depicted, and in strophe 5 the triumph of the Christian religion through the efforts of the Apostles is celebrated. In strophe 6 the poet shifts his gaze from the greater world to Cologne and rejoices in the Christianization of the city and in the presence of so many virtuous individuals throughout its history, such as the eleven thousand virgins and many saintly bishops – including Anno. Strophe 7 continues with a praise of Cologne as the "scônîstir burge / die in diutischemi lande ie wurde" (most beautiful city / that ever arose in German lands) and of Anno as "der vrumigste man" (the best man) who ever ruled there. In spite of the parochial tone of these two strophes, they serve to integrate Cologne into the beginnings of Christianity and to bring the name of Anno into contact with those of holy individuals, such as the virgins of Cologne and the Apostles, who were mentioned in strophe 5. But now that the connection has been made, and Anno and Cologne are firmly situated within the tide of redemptive history, the poet can move on to other aspects of history.

The aspect of history taken up next follows logically on the poet's musings about Cologne: the origin of the city. Reaching into the realm of the legendary, the poet describes the introduction of war by Ninus in strophe 8 and the conquest of all Asia and the founding of the city of Nineveh in strophe 9. Strophe 10 relates the building of Babylon by the wife of Ninus, Semiramis. Babylon was, the poet says, famed as the residence of many famous kings:

> in der burch sint wârin
> diu kunige vili mere.
> dâ havitin ir gesez inne
> Chaldêi die grimmin;
> die heritin afder lanten,
> unzi si Hierusalem virbranten. (strophe 10, lines 21–26)

(Since that time there were in the city
very famous kings.
There [too] resided the dreadful Chaldeans.
They laid waste the lands
until they burned Jerusalem.)

The latter reference is to the capture of Jerusalem by Nebuchadrezzar on 16 March 597 B.C. From this association it is only a short step to an account of the dreams of Daniel (Dan. 7–8) during the reign of Belshazzar, possibly a grandson of Nebuchadrezzar.

Daniel had two dreams in which beasts were the focus. The first was about a lion (interpreted as representing the Babylonian kingdom), a bear (representing the kingdom of the Medes), a leopard (the kingdom of the Persians), and a terrifying beast with iron teeth and ten horns (the empire of Alexander). On the fourth beast an eleventh horn developed, with eyes and a mouth that spoke against God. Daniel's second dream was about a ram with two horns (interpreted as representing the kingdoms of the Medes and Persians) that was conquered by a he-goat with one horn (representing Alexander the Great). The great horn of the he-goat breaks, and four smaller horns develop (interpreted as the division of Alexander's empire after his death). One horn grows to great size, reaches to Heaven, disrupts the Perpetual Sacrifice, and casts truth upon the ground. The struggle will last for years until the evil is conquered. Elements of both dreams are merged into one account in strophes 11 to 17 of the *Annolied*. Relying heavily on Jerome's commentary on the Book of Daniel, the poet identifies the lion as representing the Babylonians, the bear as representing the Medes and Persians, and the leopard as representing Alexander the Great. Daniel's mysterious fourth beast is identified as a boar and as representing the Romans. The boar's ten horns symbolize ten kings allied with the Romans, and the eleventh horn that reaches into Heaven and wages war against God is interpreted as the Antichrist. This theme of the four great empires, one succeeding the other, would later be expanded into the theory of the *translatio imperii,* the progression of empire from East to West. According to this theory, power progressed inexorably from its beginning in the East with the Babylonians to its ultimate decline in the West with the Romans, much as the sun progresses from east (morning) to west (evening). The *Annolied* provides the first confrontation in the vernacular with even a rudimentary form of the *translatio imperili* theory; it would be encountered again in the twelfth-century *Kaiserchronik.*

Strophes 14 and 15 afford the opportunity for yet another first encounter in the vernacular, an episode about the legendary feats of Alexander the Great. Its presence in the midst of a work constructed on completely different theoretical premises attests to the great popularity of and interest in the exploits of Alexander. It also suggests that the audience of the *Annolied* would be sufficiently versed in the story of Alexander to find enjoyment in this scene and would not find the account out of place in the work. The anecdote involves the familiar narrative of Alexander exploring the depths of the sea in a sort of ancient bathysphere. But in the *Annolied* something new is added: Alexander is betrayed by his faithless men and abandoned to die on the ocean floor. (Although occurring in later versions of the Alexander story, the motif of the faithless men is not attested in any sources up to the time of the composition of the *Annolied*.) After seeing fear-inspiring mermen and other marvels of the deep, Alexander devises a plan for his rescue: he causes some of his blood to spill into the water, and it irritates the ocean to the extent that it spits Alexander out on dry land.

Following the exploits of Alexander are several strophes dealing with the last empire, the Roman. Strophes 16 and 17 discuss Rome in terms of the last animal of Daniel's dream, the boar. In strophe 18 Caesar is sent off to wage war against the tribes of Germany. Strophes 19 to 23 describe Caesar's struggles against the Swabians, the Bavarians, the Saxons, and the Franks. The Saxons are castigated for their untrustworthiness, possibly an echo from the struggles of Charlemagne against the Saxons or the more contemporary wars of Heinrich IV against his Eastern neighbors. The Bavarians are depicted as brave and worthy opponents of Caesar. They also have a weapon, the *Noricus ensis,* which is described "in heidneschin buochen" (in heathen books), including Horace's *Odes,* Pliny's *Natural History,* and Petronius's *Satyricon. Noricus ensis* means "sword from Noricum," a region south of the Danube but in the Middle Ages considered synonymous with Germany. The Bavarians, according to the poet, originally came from Armenia, where Noah's Ark, which can still be seen, came to land; there are reports that people in this area still speak German. The Franks have an equally impressive ancestry:

> Cêsar bigonde nâhin
> zû den sînin altin mâgin,
> cen Franken din edilin;
> iri beidere vorderin
> quâmin von Troie der altin,
> duo die Criechin diu burch civaltin. . . . (strophe 22,
> lines 1–6)

> (Then Caesar came
> to his relatives of old,
> the noble Franks.
> The ancestors of them both
> came from Troy, the venerable,
> when the Greeks destroyed the city. . . .)

Aeneas escaped the destruction of Troy and, after many adventures and a long dalliance with Dido in Carthage, founded Lavinium; his son, Ascanius, founded Alba Longa, traditionally claimed as the city that later established Rome. The *Annolied* compresses the tale somewhat by having Aeneas build Alba Longa (strophe 23, lines 14–16). In addition, the poem provides further information about the fate of others of the exiled Trojans. Franko, the apparent progenitor of the Germanic tribe of the Franks and, in all likelihood, a relative of Aeneas, establishes a city:

> Franko gesaz mit den sîni
> vili verre nidir bî Rîni.
> dâ worhtin si duo mit vrowedin
> eini luzzele Troie.
> den bach hîzin si Sante
> nâ demi wazzere in iri lante;
> den Rîn havitin si vure diz meri.
> dannin wûhsin sint vreinkischi heri. (strophe 23, lines 17–24)

> (Franko settled with his people
> far away on the Rhine.
> There they built
> a little Troy.
> They called the stream Xanten
> in remembrance of the river in their homeland.
> They accepted the Rhine in place of the sea.
> Later the Frankish people originated from that place.)

Although conjectures about the Trojan origin of the Franks can be found in manuscripts since the seventh century, the details of the relationship appear here in the vernacular for the first time. These few lines in the *Annolied* serve the purpose of demonstrating the ties of blood between the Romans and the Franks, hinted at in the first lines of strophe 22, where Caesar was described as approaching "his relatives of old."

The close nature of the ties between the Franks and Caesar – that is, the Romans – is illustrated further through the aid that the Germanic tribes render Caesar in his struggles against Rome and in his decisive battle with Pompey in strophe 27. In strophe 28 the past presents yet another connection between the Germans ("diutischi liuti") and the Romans (here "Germans" should be understood as synonymous with "Franks"). To honor Caesar's primacy over Rome after his defeat of Pompey, the Romans greeted Caesar with a new form of address:

> Rômêre, dû sin infiengen,
> einen nûwin sidde aneviengin:
> si begondin igizin den heirrin.
> daz vundin simi cêrin,
> wanter eini duo habite allin gewalt,
> der ê gideilit was in manigvalt.
> den sidde hîz er duo cêrin
> diutischi liuti lêrin. (strophe 28, lines 5–12)

> (The Romans who greeted him
> came up with a new practice when they greeted him.
> They began to say "Ihr" [you – the familiar second
>     person plural] to the lord.
> They devised that to honor him
> since he now alone had all the power
> that previously was divided among many.

Then he had this practice taught to the
Germans as a sign of [his] esteem [for them].)

Thus, the Romans and the Franks are bound by ties of consanguinity, loyal service, and common linguistic custom. Not only do these bonds impute a special relationship between the Romans and Franks but, more important, they also attribute a political legitimacy to the Frankish empire that will be amplified and embellished in the *Kaiserchronik* as well as in the *Chronica* (circa 1147) of Otto von Freising.

With strophe 28 Caesar departs the scene to make way for Augustus, who is significant for two reasons. In the first place, Cologne was founded during his reign by a Prince Agrippa (Marcus Vipsanius Agrippa), after whom the city was also called "Agrippina" – or so the poet maintains in strophe 29. (It was actually named for Agrippina the Younger, wife of the Emperor Claudius, sister of Caligula, and mother of Nero.) Strophe 30 continues with extravagant praise of Cologne and its importance, mentioning the aqueduct that carried wine from Trier to Cologne as a gift for the powerful lords who resided there:

Triere was ein burg alt –
si cierti Rômêre gewalt –
dannin man unter dir erdin
den wîn santi verri
mit steinîn rinnin
den hêrrin al ci minnin,
die ci Kolne wârin sedilhaft:
vili michil was diu iri craft. (strophe 30, lines 18–25)

(Trier was an old city –
Roman might adorned it.
From there, under the earth
wine was sent
in stone conduits
as a gift of friendship to the lords who lived in
Cologne.
Great was their power.)

Once again, the poet is weaving the history of Cologne into secular history and stressing the overriding importance of the city and the prestige of those who ruled it. Having established this "fact," the poet moves on in strophe 31 to the second important event to have occurred during Augustus's reign: the birth of Christ, which had first been mentioned in strophe 4 in the midst of the narrative on redemptive history. And, as in strophe 5, so also in strophe 32 the tale is of the spiritual conquest of Rome by Saint Peter and the sending out of emissaries to preach: in the earlier strophe Christ sends out

his apostles to convert the Middle East, Africa, and India; in the later one Peter sends three missionaries to the Franks. On the way one of the missionaries, Maternus, is killed, but he is raised from the dead by the power of Saint Peter's staff. After preaching in Trier the three missionaries go to Cologne, where Maternus, who lived for forty years after his miraculous resurrection, becomes bishop. Strophe 33 concludes the historical part of the *Annolied,* and, as in strophes 6 and 7, the poet once again integrates Cologne into the broad framework of redemptive history, culminating in rather extravagant praise of Anno as the thirty-third bishop of Cologne.

The *Annolied* can justly be labeled a phenomenon of eleventh-century vernacular literature. It includes the first mention in the vernacular of a hitherto unknown aspect of the Alexander legend, as well as a fleshed-out account of the *translatio imperii,* a concept that would enjoy great popularity in later centuries but was by no means a pressing concern in the eleventh century. It is also an extraordinary work of art whose complexity and spirit of dedication inspire admiration and respect for the unknown monk-poet and his labor of love, as well as thanks to Martin Opitz for having rescued the tale.

**Bibliography:**

Francis G. Gentry, *Bibliographie zur frühmittelhochdeutschen geistlichen Dichtung* (Berlin: Schmidt, 1992), pp. 34–53.

**References:**

Gabriel Busch O.S.B., *Sankt Anno und seine viel liebe statt: Beiträge zum 900jährigen Jubiläum* (Siegburg: Reckinger, 1975);

Ernst Hellgardt, "Die Rezeption des Annoliedes bei Martin Opitz," in *Mittelalter-Rezeption: Ein Symposion* (Stuttgart: Metzler, 1986), pp. 60–79;

Doris Knab, *Das Annolied: Probleme seiner literarischen Einordnung* (Tübingen: Niemeyer, 1962);

Peter Knoch, "Untersuchungen zum Ideengehalt und zur Datierung des Annoliedes," *Zeitschrift für deutsche Philologie,* 83, no. 3 (1964): 275–301;

Ursula Liebertz-Grün, "Zum Annolied: Atypische Struktur und singuläre politische Konzeption," *Euphorion,* 74, no. 3 (1980): 223–256;

Eberhard Nellmann, *Die Reichsidee in der deutschen Dichtung der Salier- und frühen Stauferzeit: Annolied, Kaiserchronik, Rolandslied, Eraclius* (Berlin: Schmidt, 1963), pp. 35–81;

Heinz Thomas, "Bemerkungen zu Datierung, Gestalt und Gehalt des Annoliedes," *Zeitschrift für deutsche Philologie,* 96 (1977): 24–61;

Thomas, *Studien zur Trierer Geschichtsschreibung des 11. Jahrhunderts, insbesondere zu den Gesta Trevorum* (Bonn: Röhrscheid, 1968), pp. 119–134;

Gisela Vollmann-Profe, *Geschichte der deutschen Literatur von den Anfängen bis zum Beginn der Neuzeit,* volume 1/2: *Von den Anfängen zum Hohen Mittelalter* (Königstein: Athenäum, 1986);

Max Wehrli, *Geschichte der deutschen Literatur vom frühen Mittelalter bis zum Ende des 16. Jahrhunderts* (Stuttgart: Reclam, 1980).

# Cambridge Songs (Carmina Cantabrigensia)
## (circa 1050)

Brian Murdoch
*University of Stirling*

**Manuscripts:** Cambridge, University Library, MS Gg. V. 35, fols. 432r–441v (C). Some of the songs are in other manuscripts, notably Wolfenbüttel, Herzog-Ernst-Bibliothek, 3610 August. 56.16 (W); Paris, Bibliothèque Nationale, Lat. 111B; Vienna, Österreichische Nationalbibliothek, Cod. Vindob. 116; Verona, Biblioteca Capitolina, 88; Rome, Palatine Library, Vatican Lat. 3227.

**First publication:** In *The Cambridge Songs,* edited by Karl Breul (Cambridge: University Press, 1915).

**Standard edition:** *Die Cambridger Lieder,* edited by Karl Strecker, Monumenta Germaniae Historica / Scriptores rerum Germanicarum in usum scholarum (Berlin: Weidmann, 1926).

**Editions in English:** Poems XXIV, XXVII, and XL translated by Helen Waddell, in *Medieval Latin Lyrics* (New York: Holt, 1942; Harmondsworth, U.K.: Penguin, 1952); Poems XXIV, XXVII, and XL translated by Frederick Brittain, in *The Penguin Book of Latin Verse* (Harmondsworth, U.K.: Penguin, 1962); *The Cambridge Songs,* edited and translated by Jan M. Ziolkowski (New York: Garland, 1992).

The eleventh-century manuscript collection of around fifty poems or songs – some are provided with musical notation (neumes) and most seem to be meant for singing – in Latin, with two macaronic Latin-German pieces, known from its current location as the *Cambridge Songs* (*Carmina Cantabrigensia*), was probably copied at Saint Augustine's Monastery in Canterbury from a German original from the Rhineland. The original was perhaps compiled in the ambit of the Salian emperor Heinrich III, who reigned from 1039 to 1056. The collection includes a handful of classical extracts, but the later songs range largely from the mid tenth to the mid eleventh centuries (a few may be earlier); and although some of the songs are probably of Romance provenance, many are closely connected with German history, are set in Germany, or are partly composed in German. The *Cambridge Songs* have, therefore, long been of special interest to German studies. The collection's designation as a "goliard's songbook" – a collection of songs associated with the *vagantes* (wandering poets) – is, in view of the nature of the songs, no longer accepted. Within it there seems to be evidence of other earlier compilations and groupings that this compiler has taken over; several of the songs are found in other manuscripts, either in groups or singly, and some are alluded to elsewhere in medieval Latin writing in Germany – as in the *Sermones* of Sextus Amarcius, where a traveling singer performs the tale of the crafty Swabian and his wife.

It is not easy to determine precisely how many songs were originally included in the collection. One page has been removed from the manuscript, and some of the poems have been damaged to the point of irrecoverability. The collection includes religious poems; occasional or historical pieces, including the macaronic *De Heinrico* (Of Heinrich, circa 980?), a selection of comic tales in verse; love poems; an intriguing strophe added by mistake into one of the narrative poems; and several poems or extracts from the classical writers Horace, Virgil, and Statius and the sixth-century poet Venantius Fortunatus. Poems XXVIII and XXXIX were almost completely obliterated by medieval censors and are not preserved elsewhere; XXVIII is another macaronic poem mixing German and Latin, *Suavissima nunna* (Sweetest Nun), for which reconstructions have been attempted; attempts to restore the text with chemicals have caused further damage. Most of the medieval poems are anonymous.

The first piece in the collection is a single strophe of what is actually a longer poem that is also preserved in other manuscripts and sometimes falsely ascribed to Hrabanus Maurus. The strophe stresses how Christ took on flesh to eradicate the guilt of Adam and Eve – a brief expression of the whole cycle of Fall and Redemption and an appropriate opening for the collection:

Gratuletur omnis caro     Christo nato domino
qui pro culpa protoplasti     carnem nostra induit
ut saluaret quod plasmauit     dei sapientia

(Let mankind, made of flesh, give thanks, for Christ is
    born today,
who clothed Himself with human flesh for Eve's and
    Adam's sin,
so that the wisdom of the Lord might save what He had
    made.)

There follows a group of fourteen pieces, all but one of which are in the form of the sequence – a rhythmic song with a structure based on parallel, identical metrical units. The one poem not in this form, *Philomela* (X), is a nightingale poem with a single rhyme throughout; it is found elsewhere with musical notation and is sometimes ascribed to Fulbert of Chartes, an Italian who died in 1028. Four of the sequence poems appear together in the Wolfenbüttel manuscript, which has been taken as an indication that there was a formally based collection that both the Wolfenbüttel compiler and the original compiler used. The content of these sequence poems varies from religious to secular-historical to profane themes. There are classical and early medieval poems: three extracts from Statius's *Thebaid* (XXIX, XXXI, and XXXII), one from the *Aeneid*

(XXXIV), and songs by Horace (XLVI) and by Venantius Fortunatus (XXII); other historical poems that come later in the collection are clearly related to Germany. It has been suspected that another group of songs is French in origin, and the last fully readable poem, *O admirabile Veneris idolum* (O Wonderful Image of Love, XLVIII), an amorous song addressed to a *puerulus* (young boy), seems to be Italian. It is provided with neumes in the Cambridge manuscript, and with other notation in the Vatican manuscript, so that its main melody has been reconstructed.

Six poems apart from *De Heinrico* praise German kings and emperors; two of these commemorate coronations and three record deaths, while the remaining piece is in praise of a whole dynasty of emperors. Three of these panegyrics are in the sequence section at the start of the manuscript, but the thematic links do not coincide with the formal ones. Thus one of the sequence poems (III) was composed on the occasion of the imperial coronation of Konrad II on 26 March 1027, but that on the crowning of Henry III as German king on 14 April of the following year (XVI) is outside that subcollection. Both stress the role of God in the choice and anointing of the ruler. Two poems (IX and XVII) are concerned with the death of Heinrich II, known as "der Heilige" (the Saint), in 1024 and a third (XXXIII) with that of his successor, Konrad II, in 1039. The poem on the death of Konrad is by Wipo, the eleventh-century historian and court chaplain to Konrad, who wrote a biography of the emperor (*Gesta Chuonradi*) to which the poem is also appended. The *Modus Ottinc* (Tune on the Ottos, XI) celebrates the entire dynasty of Ottonian emperors (in the Wolfenbüttel manuscript, where this piece is also found, musical notation is provided) but concentrates on the last of the three Saxon emperors of that name, Otto III, in whose honor the song was presumably sung around 990 – certainly before he was crowned emperor in 996, or this event would doubtless have been mentioned. Six double strophes of ten lines and a coda praise the deeds of Otto the Great, especially his victory over the Magyars at the Lech in 955. Otto II gets only half a strophe; his treatment is a bit deprecatory, especially considering that it follows the valiant deeds of Otto I that were accomplished "parva manu" (with a few men only):

Adolescens
post hunc Otto
imperavit

multis annis
cesar iustus
clemens, fortis,
unum modo defuit:
nam inclitis
raro preliis
triumphabat.

(After this the
younger Otto
ruled the empire
for a long time
ruling justly,
fairly, firmly,
but he wanted for one thing:
very rarely
could he claim great
victories.)

His son, Otto III, is praised far more fulsomely in terms of the traditional virtues of a ruler "Bello fortis / pace potens" (strong in war and powerful in peace).

The poem on the Ottos is one of those in sequence form. Of the others in that mode, several are religious. The title of one of these in the Wolfenbüttel manuscript, *Modus qui et Carelmanninc* (Tune Which Is Also That for Carloman, V), presumably refers to a poem on Carloman, the name of various later Carolingian kings. The text of the poem in the Cambridge codex is, however, a compact survey of the Gospel narrative, and others of the sequence group are hymns – VII is from Cologne, VIII is from Xanten. Also in that group is a philosophical poem on Pythagoras (XII), giving a brief account of some of his ideas. There is another brief philosophical piece later in the codex, but it is only the first part of a much longer (twenty-five-strophe) poem (XXXVII).

Much attention has been paid to the story poems in the collection: the *Modus Liebinc* (Tune of the Snow Baby, XIV) and the *Modus Florum* (Tune of the Lie, XV), the sequence poem of Lantfrid and Cobbo (VI), and the stories of Alfrad and her donkey (XX), of Heriger of Mainz and the trickster (XXIV), of Proterius and his daughter (XXX), of the priest and the wolf (XXXV), and of Little John the hermit (XLII). The first is clearly a well-known folktale, set here in the town of Constance. A merchant described as a "Suevulus" (little Swabian), who has a lively wife, travels a great deal and leaves her alone. When he is away on a journey she becomes pregnant, after which she "filium / iniustum fudit / iusto die" (bore an illegitimate child in the legitimate time). When the merchant returns, the wife claims that she became pregnant by eating snow to keep from dying of thirst in the Alps. After some years the merchant goes on

another trip and takes the boy with him. He sells him to an Arab, and on his return he tells his wife that he was shipwrecked on a hot shore, and "niuis natus / liquescebat" (the snow-baby / melted). The story is told with economy, humor, and balance, ending with the cynical summation: "sic fraus fraudem uicerat" (thus fraud beat fraud).

The *Modus Florum* is described as a "cantilena mendosa" (lying story) designed for "pueruli" (schoolboys), and it, too, involves a Swabian. A king will marry his daughter to the man who can tell such fantastic lies that even he, the king, will call the man a liar. A Swabian tells how he hunted a hare and killed it, and when he cut off its head, pounds of honey and of peas fell from its ears; more to the point, says the Swabian to the king, under its tail was a document that stated that the king was the Swabian's slave. At this the king shouts "Mentitur . . . karta et tu!" (You're lying . . . you and your document!). The Swabian has, of course, won the contest. The tale is presented with narrative economy, in fewer than forty lines.

The story of Cobbo and Lantfrid tells how the two friends share everything. Cobbo asks for Lantfrid's wife and is given her. Lantfrid sings a song urging Cobbo not to shame his brother and then smashes his harp, at which Cobbo returns his wife. The poem is found in more than one other manuscript, and another poem is known about the two. The story of the nun Alfrad is a somewhat slighter tale in Adonic-rhymed lines in which a nun's donkey is devoured by a wolf; she and her sisters bewail the loss until she is told that "dominus aliam / dabit tibi asinam" (God / will provide another donkey). In the often-translated tale of Heriger, archbishop of Mainz from 913 to 927, a boaster reports to the prelate that he has visited hell and heaven; he says that John the Baptist acted as wine steward and Saint Peter as cook and that he stole some offal from the latter to eat. Heriger has him beaten for theft. The presence of a historical personage in a folk tale is an unusual feature.

In the story of Proterius a rich man from Caesarea has a daughter who is promised to a nunnery. A *seruulus* (insignificant wretch) falls in love with her and, by relinquishing his Christianity, conjures a devil to cause her to love him. Eventually the father agrees to the match, but after the marriage the young man confesses and is redeemed, the moral being that no sin is irredeemable. (In the Cambridge codex this poem is preceded by a brief piece that does not seem to be attached to it, in which all the words begin with *c;* an isolated line that seems to belong to this alliterative poem appears near the beginning of the collection.)

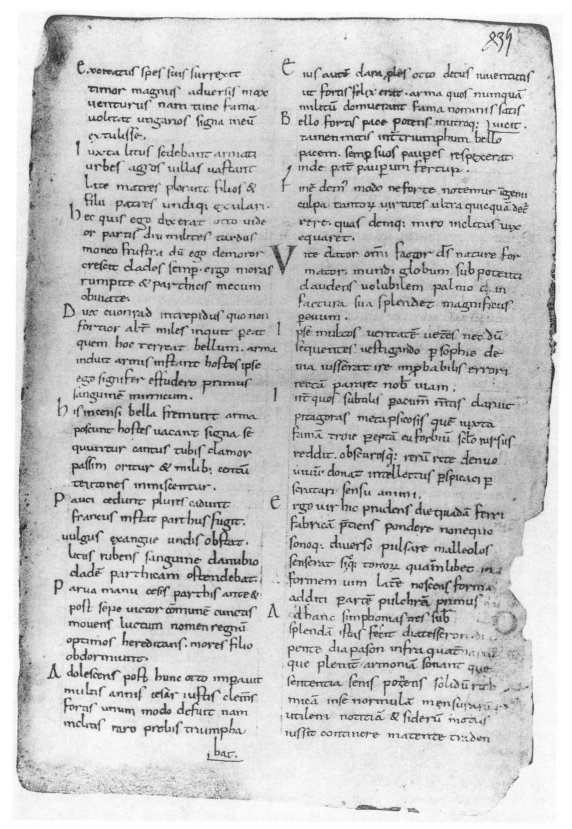

*Page from the manuscript for the* Cambridge Songs. *Strophes 2 through 6 of the* Modus Ottine *appear in the left column and in the top of the right column down to the large* V *(University Library, Cambridge, MS Gg. V. 35, folio 435r).*

The final two stories are in rhymed couplets and are humorous. The story of the priest's encounter with a wolf and his escape is one of many wolf or fox stories of the Middle Ages. The story of Little John concerns an eremitic monk who wants to be a saint and live without food or clothing. In spite of advice from an older anchorite he tries to do so, but after a while he realizes that it is impossible. Returning to the hut of the other hermit, he is made to wait outside in the cold until he learns his lesson: that he cannot be an angel, and so he must decide to be a good man. This story has been ascribed to Fulbert of Chartres. Different stories about Little John appear in other manuscripts.

Song XXV is a spiritual declaration in the form of a poetic letter, associated with Trier and directed at Archbishop Poppo of Trier on his return from Palestine in 1030. Song XXI is a brief statement about musical forms, and XVIII is a religious abecedarian poem that is also found in other manuscripts. The love poetry in the collection, though limited, has attracted considerable attention. Interpolated into the story of the snow-baby, and in the same rhythm, is a single strophe that expresses simply and vividly the longing of a woman for her departed lover. Peter Dronke suggests that it was written in the margin of the snow-baby story in the original manuscript because it would have been sung to the same tune; the Canterbury copyist included it in the text of the longer poem, partly because it refers to snow. A woman, "languens / amore tuo" (pining / for your love), arises at dawn and goes out barefoot into the snow, scanning the sea for the sight of a sail.

Particularly well known are two other love songs in the collection. *Iam dulcis amica, venito* (Come, My Beloved, XXVII), which is found with neumes in two other manuscripts, is an invitation in a complex rhythmical form to the beloved to "intra in cubiculum meum" (Come into my room), where everything is prepared for love. It has been referred to as combining Ovid with the Song of Songs; there are echoes of both, and perhaps some faint hints of Catullus. The manuscript is damaged in the later strophes, but the complete text appears elsewhere. *Levis exsurgit zephirus* (The West Wind Blows Softly, XL) foreshadows the work of poets such as Walther von der Vogelweide as the first-person speaker — sometimes categorized as a nun, though quite unnecessarily — contrasts the joys of spring with the absence of joys for the lovelorn. It has been suggested — and denied — that the poet was a woman.

A nun is present in the most intriguing piece of the codex, the heavily damaged macaronic poem XXVIII (with half lines first in Latin and then in German), sometimes referred to as "Cleric and Nun." That the woman is a nun can be made out from the surviving text, but her interlocutor in this love dialogue may or may not be a cleric. The man woos the lady, who resists him. In one of the few relatively legible passages the lady seems to declare that earthly delights will disappear like clouds, but Christ's kingdom will remain. In spite of convincing restoration attempts such as that by Dronke, the poem remains enigmatic, just as it remains puzzling why it was mutilated. Other pieces in the collection seem as likely as candidates for censorship as this one.

Not all the poems in the collection known as the *Cambridge Songs* are German, but several religious, secular, and narrative pieces clearly are. The collection shows what a song collection of the mid eleventh century could look like; and although it raises many problems, this Latin collection is of some importance in the consideration of a range of vernacular poetry from the earlier German historical poem *Ludwigslied* (Song of Louis, 881 or 882) to later developments in the hymn, the *Schwank* (humorous narrative), the religious *bispel* (moral example), and the *Minnesang*.

## References:

Peter Dronke, *Medieval Latin and the Rise of the European Love-Lyric,* 2 volumes, second edition (Oxford: Clarendon Press, 1968), I: 271–281, II: 353–356;

Dronke, *The Medieval Lyric* (London: Hutchinson, 1968);

Gustav Ehrismann, *Geschichte der deutschen Literatur bis zum Ausgang des Mittelalters,* volume 1 (Munich: Beck, 1922), pp. 364–374;

Annette Georgi, *Das lateinische und deutsche Preisgedicht des Mittelalters* (Berlin: Schmidt, 1969), pp. 62–72;

Anselm Hughes, *Early Medieval Music* (London: Oxford University Press, 1954), pp. 220–221;

Max Manitius, *Geschichte der lateinischen Literatur des Mittelalters,* 3 volumes (Munich: Beck, 1911–1931), III: 970–972;

Hans Naumann, "Der *Modus Ottinc* im Kreis seiner Verwandten," *Deutsche Vierteljahrsschrift,* 24 (1950): 470–482;

F. J. E. Raby, *A History of Secular Latin Poetry in the Middle Ages,* volume 1, second edition (Oxford: Clarendon Press, 1957), pp. 291–306;

Helen Waddell, *The Wandering Scholars,* sixth edition (Harmondsworth, U.K.: Penguin, 1952);

F. A. Wright and T. A. Sinclair, *A History of Later Latin Literature* (London: Routledge, 1931), pp. 281–286.

# Christus und die Samariterin

## (circa 950)

### Cyril W. Edwards
#### Goldsmiths' College, University of London

**Manuscript:** This anonymous fragment is preserved only in Vienna, Österreichische Nationalbibliothek, cod. 515, fols. 4v–5r. This small manuscript of eight leaves, which includes the "Lorsch Annals" of 794 to 803, originated in southwestern Germany, possibly at the monastery of Reichenau, where a copy of it was made in the early ninth century. The manuscript for *Christus und die Samariterin* dates from the middle of the tenth century; it immediately follows the Lorsch Annals, on fol. 5r, taking up the remaining – originally empty – part of the page. The text is written continuously in Carolingian minuscule, with occasional rhyme points. An additional single line, which the scribe accidentally omitted, is written on fol. 4$^v$; its correct place in the poem is indicated by a sign. The text is followed by three Latin responsories (fol. 5v) and a model sermon in Latin (fols. 6–8).

The text has been copied in incompetent fashion with many errors, erasures, corrections, and insertions. It has been argued, on the basis of variations in the size and formation of individual letters, that more than one scribe was involved in writing down the thirty-one lines, but this contention seems inherently unlikely. More probably the same unpracticed hand was responsible for the whole text, perhaps breaking off at intervals and then resuming its task. That this procedure reflects a process of poetic composition is highly unlikely, given the initial omission of the fifth line.

**First publication:** Edited by Peter Lembeck, in *Commentarii de Bibliotheca caesarea Vindobonensi,* volume 2 (Vienna: Typis M. Cosmerovij 1669), pp. 383–384.

**Standard editions:** As no. X in *Denkmäler deutscher Poesie und Prose aus dem VIII.–XII. Jahrhundert,* edited by Karl Müllenhoff and Wilhelm Scherer third edition, edited by Elias von Steinmeyer (Berlin: Weidmann, 1892; reprinted, Berlin & Zurich: Weidmann, 1964); as

no. XVII in *Die kleineren althochdeutschen Sprachdenkmäler,* edited by Steinmeyer (Berlin: Weidmann, 1916; reprinted, Berlin & Zurich: Weidmann, 1963); as no. XXIV in *Althochdeutsches Lesebuch,* edited by Wilhelm Braune, sixteenth edition, revised by Ernst A. Ebbinghaus (Tübingen: Niemeyer, 1978).

The thirty-one lines of verse of *Christus und die Samariterin* (Christ and the Woman of Samaria, circa 950) are based on John 4:4–20, the encounter between Christ and the Samaritan woman at the well. Christ has the woman draw water for him, although there is not normally any contact between the Jews and the Samaritans; in return, he tells her of the water of eternal life. The poem follows the Gospel passage – which formed the reading for the Friday after the third Sunday of Lent – closely, but not slavishly. After six opening lines of narrative, it takes the form of a lively interchange of dialogue. It omits, with one exception (line 24), the *verba dicendi* (formulas) that introduce the speeches of Christ and the woman in the gospel and in the more literal early-ninth-century *Tatian* prose translation. The alternating speeches are symmetrically structured in lines 6 to 23, though the symmetry seems to break down just before the end of the fragment. The poem is more compressed and moves at a faster pace than the biblical narrative. The emphasis on the distinction between Jews and Samaritans (John 4:9) is limited to one line, remarkable for the colloquial anachronism compelled by the rhyme:

iã ne niezant, uuizze Christ,      thie Iudon unsera uuist.

(The Jews, Christ knows, do not share our food.)

The sequence of ideas in the dialogue adheres to that of the Gospel, contrasting with the freer poetic rendering of the same passage in Otfried von Weißenburg's *Liber Evangeliorum* or *Evangelienbuch* (Gospel Book, between 863 and 871; II, 14).

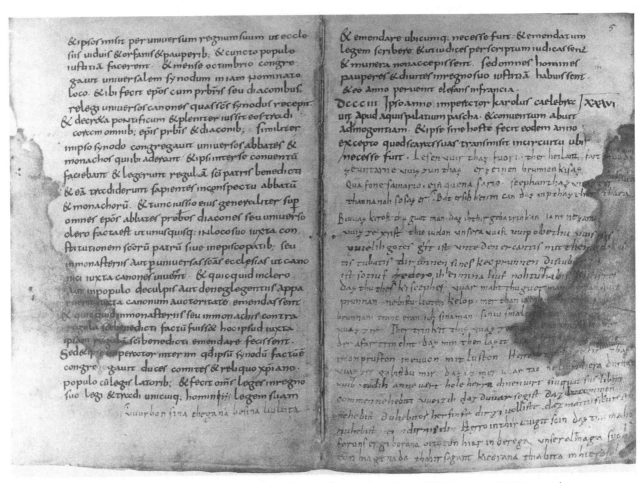

Manuscript for Christus und die Samariterin *(Vienna, Österreichische Nationalbibliothek, cod. 515, fols. 4v–5r)*

Otfried's more verbose treatment of the passage takes some sixty lines to reach the point at which *Christus und die Samariterin* breaks off.

The way in which the text has survived means that the possibility cannot be excluded that *Christus und die Samariterin* was originally part of a poetic enterprise on a larger scale, like the two ninth-century Gospel harmonies, Otfried's *Evangelienbuch* and the Old Saxon *Heliand* (circa 850). On the other hand, *Christus und die Samariterin* may be an isolated exercise in biblical poetry, like the tenth-century Bavarian paraphrase of Psalm 138. This possibility raises the question of why this passage should have been chosen for poetic rendition. Neither the *Christus* poet nor Otfried makes an attempt at an exegetical exposition of the passage, although in the case of *Christus und die Samariterin* an exposition might, of course, have followed after the end of the fragment. It may have been the doctrinal significance of the passage that inspired the poem's composition. It was a popular subject for patristic exegesis, above all because

of the emphasis implicit in the text on the universal mission of Christ. If this idea inspired the poem, however, the underplaying of the racial difference between Christ and the woman seems incongruous. Gustav Ehrismann suggests a link with the model sermon that follows in the manuscript, on the grounds that there is a reference in the third part of the sermon to the many miracles through which Christ revealed himself as the Son of God. Such a link appears somewhat tenuous. A clue to the poet's motive may be afforded by the introductory words, "Lesen wir" (We read), and by "uuizzun thaz" (let us know) in the following line. These phrases – didactic, perhaps homiletic in style – depend on a knowledge of the subject matter in written form that is common to both poet and audience. They contrast sharply with the formulas with which the older, alliterative poems the *Hildebrandslied* (Song of Hildebrand, circa 825) and the *Wessobrunn Prayer* (circa 775–825) begin, formulas that emphasize an oral tradition. The poem must have been inspired by study of the passage in the monastic schoolroom, and perhaps it needed no other inspiration.

The suffering humanity of Christ, stressed in the patristic exegetical treatment of the passage, is emphasized in the poem by the evocative compound *fartmuodi* (wearied by his journey) in the first line, and by the fact that Christ remains seated when the woman arrives: "thanna noh sō saz er" (he sat there still). The Samaritan woman initially addresses Christ as "guot man" (good man); this expression gives way to "herro" (Lord) as her respect for him increases. Several phrases in the poem, minor departures from the Gospel text, have what appears to be an idiomatic, colloquial ring: "ubar tac" (day after day); "tu dich anneuuert" (get thee hence).

The poet's masterly handling of dialogue has been compared with that in the *Hildebrandslied,* where there is a similar symmetrical grouping of speeches and the speakers also echo each other's words. It has been argued that this "balladesque" style is characteristic of Germanic epic style, but Latin rhythmic poetry is another possible source of influence. The paucity of poetic survivals from the Old High German period makes it difficult to assign such stylistic features to a single tradition.

The language of the text confirms the impression created by the hand in which it is written: that it is a copy of an older composition and is at least one and probably two removes from the original. Alemannic features combine in a seemingly arbitrary way with features pointing further north, to a Franconian dialect. The consensus is that an Alemannic scribe copied from a Franconian original, but it may well be that the dialect mix was present in the exemplar that confronted the most recent scribe. It has also been argued that the mixture of Alemannic and Franconian elements points to a border area or to a dialect in a state of flux. The nature of the discrepancies makes this notion unlikely; they include incompatible forms of the same pronoun in initial position in successive sentences, such as *ther* and *der* (lines 18–19). It is difficult to differentiate between what may be orthographic aberrations and what may constitute evidence for the original dialect of the poet.

The form of *Christus und die Samariterin* is the long line of Otfriedian verse, made up of two rhyming short lines, with four main stresses. The long lines, in turn, form units of varying length, sometimes termed strophes. The poem is characterized by a great deal of alliteration, which is regarded as being of an accidental, ornamental nature, as it does not fall into the patterns expected of Old High German alliterative verse, nor is it sustained from line to line. There would seem, however, to be at least an awareness of an older tradition of versification in this use of alliteration. The prevalence of impure rhyme and both vocalic and consonantal assonance reveals a more primitive technique than that of Otfried, and it has been argued that the poem's original may predate the *Evangelienbuch,* constituting evidence of a pre-Otfriedian tradition of rhyming verse. Comparisons between the vocabulary of the poem and that employed by Otfried reveal few common points. The basis for a relative chronology is slender, however, given current ignorance of the anonymous poem's exemplar. The neumes in the Heidelberg manuscript of the *Evangelienbuch* indicate that Otfriedian verse could be sung, and this possibility, despite the metrically irregular treatment of unstressed syllables, has also been argued with regard to *Christus und die Samariterin.*

**Bibliographies:**

Dieter Kartschoke, *Altdeutsche Bibeldichtung* (Stuttgart: Metzler, 1975);

Sydney Groseclose and Brian O. Murdoch, *Die althochdeutschen poetischen Denkmäler* (Stuttgart: Metzler, 1976);

David R. McLintock, "Christus und die Samariterin," in *Die deutsche Literatur des Mittelalters: Verfasserlexikon,* volume 1, edited by Kurt Ruh, second edition (Berlin: De Gruyter, 1978), cols. 1238–1241.

**References:**

Bernhard Bischoff, "Paläographische Fragen deutscher Denkmäler der Karolingerzeit," *Frühmittelalterliche Studien,* 5 (1971): 101–134;

Bischoff, *Die südostdeutschen Schreibschulen und Bibliotheken in der Karolingerzeit,* volume 1: *Die bayrischen Diözesen,* third edition (Wiesbaden, 1974);

J. Knight Bostock, *A Handbook on Old High German Literature,* second edition, revised by K. C. King and D. R. McLintock (Oxford: Clarendon Press, 1976);

Gustav Ehrismann, *Geschichte der deutschen Literatur bis zum Ausgang des Mittelalters,* part 1: *Die althochdeutsche Literatur,* second edition, reprinted (Munich: Beck, 1959);

Johannes Erben, "Textspezifische Gelegenheitsbildungen des Kompositionstyps Adjektiv + Substantiv in althochdeutschen Texten: Zu den Wertungen in Christus und die Samariterin sowie in Otfrids Evangelienbuch," in *Althochdeutsch: Festschrift für R. Schützeichel,* 2 volumes, edited by Rolf Bergmann (Heidelberg:

Carl Winter Universitätsverlag, 1987), I: 366–370;

Hanns Fischer, *Schrifttafeln zum althochdeutschen Lesebuch* (Tübingen: Niemeyer, 1966);

Wolfgang Haubrichs, *Geschichte der deutschen Literatur von den Anfängen bis zum Beginn der Neuzeit,* volume 1: *Von den Anfängen zum hohen Mittelal-* *ter. Teil 1: Die Anfänge: Versuche volkssprachiger Schriftlichkeit im frühen Mittelalter (ca. 700–1050/60),* edited by Joachim Heinzle (Frankfurt am Main: Athenäum, 1988);

Brian O. Murdoch, *Old High German Literature* (Boston: Twayne, 1983).

# De Heinrico
## *(circa 980?)*

### Brian Murdoch
#### *University of Stirling*

**Manuscript:** Cambridge University Library, MS. Gg. V.35, fol. 437r–v. Facsimile in Hanns Fischer, *Schrifttafeln zum althochdeutschen Lesebuch* (Tübingen: Niemeyer, 1966), p. 24.

**First publication:** Edited by Johann Georg von Eckhart, in *Veterum monumentorum quaternio* (Leipzig: Forester, 1720).

**Standard editions:** In *Denkmäler deutscher Poesie und Prosa aus dem VIII–XII Jahrhundert,* edited by Karl Müllenhoff and Wilhelm Scherer, third edition, edited by Elias von Steinmeyer (Berlin: Weidmann, 1892; reprinted, Berlin & Zurich, 1964); in *The Cambridge Songs: A Goliard's Song Book of the XIth Century,* edited by Karl Breul (Cambridge: Cambridge University Press, 1915), pp. 12–14; in *Die kleineren althochdeutschen Sprachdenkmäler,* edited by Steinmeyer (Berlin: Weidmann, 1916; reprinted, Berlin & Zurich: Weidmann, 1963); in *Die Cambridger Lieder,* edited by Karl Strecker (Berlin: Weidmann, 1926), pp. 57–60; in *Altdeutsche Texte,* edited by Heinz Mettke (Leipzig: Bibliographisches Institut, 1970), pp. 54–55; in *Althochdeutsches Lesebuch,* edited by Wilhelm Braune, sixteenth edition, edited by Ernst A. Ebbinghaus (Tübingen: Niemeyer, 1979).

**Editions in modern German:** In *Althochdeutsche Literatur,* edited by Horst Dieter Schlosser (Frankfurt am Main & Hamburg: Fischer, 1970), pp. 278–279; in *Älteste deutsche Dichtung und Prosa,* edited by Heinz Mettke (Leipzig: Reclam, 1976), pp. 252–255; in *Althochdeutsche Literatur,* edited by Hans Joachim Gernentz (Berlin: Union, 1979), pp. 202–203.

**Edition in English:** In J. Knight Bostock, *A Handbook on Old German Literature,* edited by K. C. King and D. R. McLintock (Oxford: Clarendon Press, 1976), p. 253.

The eleventh-century manuscript containing the brief poem *De Heinrico* (Of Heinrich, circa 980?) was probably copied in Canterbury from a German original from the Rhineland; it is now in Cambridge. The work is one of around fifty pieces, mostly in Latin, known as the *Cambridge Songs.* The poem is macaronic: most of its twenty-seven lines have the first part in Latin and the second in Old High German; in one or two lines the division is not as clear-cut, and there is some overlapping, notably in the opening line. Initial capital letters divide the poem into eight strophes, the first two and the sixth with four long lines, the rest with three. The halves of the long lines are linked by rhyme or assonance:

| | |
|---|---|
| *tunc surrexit Otdo* | ther unsar keisar guodo |
| *perrexit illi obuiam* | inde uilo manig man |
| *et excepit illum* | mid mihilon eron. (strophe 3) |

*(Then Otto arose, our good emperor.
He went to meet him with a large number of men
and received him with great honors.)*

The poem begins by invoking the Virgin Mary for help in telling the story of a duke named Heinrich who once ruled Bavaria. It then describes how a messenger came to Otto, announcing the arrival of Heinrich and instructing Otto to receive him. Otto does so, welcoming "ambos vos aequivoci" (you two of the same name, strophe 4, line 2) and taking Heinrich into the church to pray for grace. Otto then welcomes Heinrich again and confers great honors on him, "*preter quod regale* thes thir Heinrih nigerade" (*except the royal power* which Heinrich did not desire, strophe 6, line 4). Heinrich's advice is of the greatest importance, and he counsels Otto in everything; his judgments of everyone are appropriate.

Since the surviving manuscript is a copy of a collection, the date of composition of this particular poem is hard to determine. The anonymous poet was presumably a cleric, given the opening invocation and the form of the work. The eulogy of Heinrich, Duke of Bavaria, is neatly constructed, with a balanced distribution of ideas in the Latin and the German, as in strophe 7, lines 1–2:

| | |
|---|---|
| *quicquid Otdo fecit,* | al geried iz Heinrih |
| *quicquid ac omisit,* | ouch geried iz Heinrihc |

*(Whatever Otto did* was counseled by Heinrich, *and whatever he left undone* was counseled by Heinrich, too.)

Several of the German half lines are repetitive formulaic phrases that add little to the narrative — for example, "ther unsar keisar guodo" (our good emperor); "mid mihilon eron" (with much honor) — while some of the Latin parts read like formal phrases from chronicles. There are a few points where emendation is required: for example, in strophe 7, line 2, *omisit* (left undone) has been substituted for the manuscript's *amisit* (bestowed) (there is not complete agreement among the standard editions on these emendations). The dialect in the German parts seems to be Middle Franconian, and there are indications that the original was in Rhenish Franconian. There are a few Low German elements in the poem, some of them in passages where the emperor Otto is speaking; this feature has led to the suggestion that, since the only emperors to whom the poem could refer were Saxon, the speech is being depicted realistically.

The historical situation presented in the poem is clearly in the past, although how distant a past cannot be judged. The problem with the work — as virtually every recent critic has had to admit — is that the characters involved, and hence the events, are hard to identify, and clues in the work itself are limited. Since the early part of the tenth century nearly all the dukes of Bavaria had been named Heinrich, and three Ottos occupied the imperial throne during the century. There were also several conflicts and reconciliations between various emperors and dukes that might be reflected in the work.

Although the first editor considered the poem to be about the late-twelfth-century emperor Otto IV, this view was soon replaced by one that linked the work with Otto I, born in 912, king of the Germans from 936 and emperor after 962. His brother, Heinrich, rebelled and was even involved in a murder plot against him but was pardoned in 941 and created Duke Heinrich I of Bavaria. Weight was given to this identification of the situation in the poem by a misreading of the word *bringit* (he brings) in strophe 2, line 3, as *bruother* (brother). Once the misreading was clarified, however, the problems with this identification became clear: by the time Otto I became emperor, his brother was dead. This difficulty might be explained away as poetic license, but the reference to "two of the same name" is a problem, as is the fact that the Heinrich of the poem arrives in splendor, not as an unaccompanied penitent. The dominant role of Heinrich thereafter also does not fit the situation of Otto I and his brother. (The relationship between the brothers seems to have influenced other medieval German works, including *Herzog Ernst* [ Duke Ernst, circa 1190] and Konrad von Würzburg's *Heinrich von Kempten* [between 1261 and 1277].)

It is more likely that the poem refers to Duke Heinrich II of Bavaria, known as "der Zänker" (the Quarrelsome). During the short reign of his cousin, Emperor Otto II, from 973 to 983, Heinrich II rebelled, and he was deposed in 976. He was replaced as duke by another and unrelated Heinrich, usually designated Heinrich III — causing confusion with the son of Heinrich II, who became Duke Heinrich IV of Bavaria on his father's death in 995. There was no reconciliation of Heinrich II or Heinrich IV with Otto II, so he is unlikely to be the emperor in question. In 983 his three-year-old son Otto became German king, and he would be crowned emperor in 996. Heinrich der Zänker attempted to seize power during the king's infancy but failed to do so, and Otto's mother, Theophano, ruled as regent until her death in 991. Heinrich II was restored to the Duchy of Bavaria in 985, and this event has been suggested as the occasion referred to in the work.

*Manuscript for De Heinrico (University Library, Cambridge, Ms. Gg. V. 35, fols. 437r–v)*

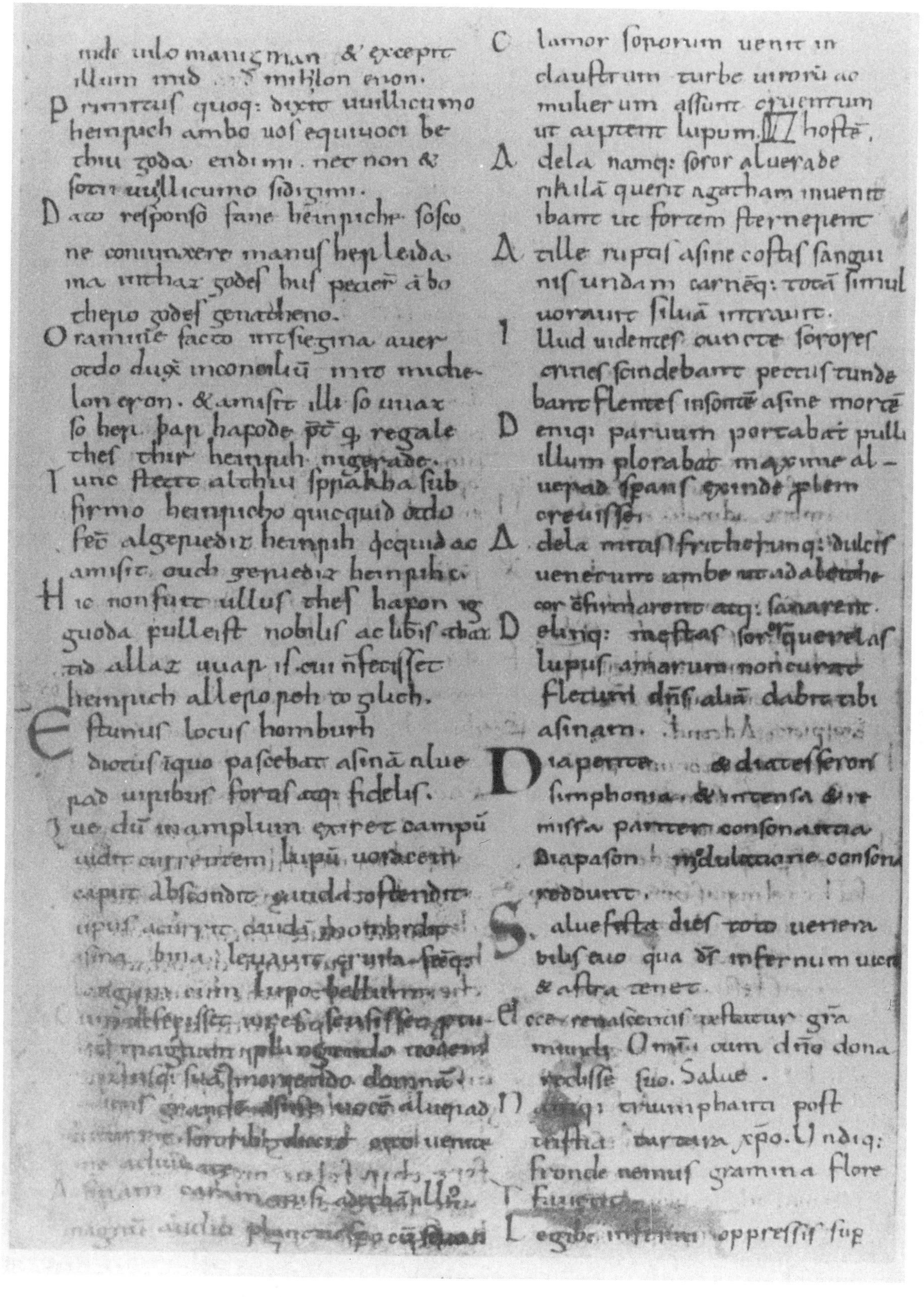

Associating the poem with the events of 985 requires an interpretation of the bestowal of honors on Heinrich and also demands that the line about his "not desiring" the regal honor be read as a piece of special pleading, since shortly beforehand he had given every sign of wanting precisely that. The poem would then be a political whitewashing of Heinrich der Zänker, and the "two of the same name" would refer to Heinrich II and his son, who was twelve years old in 985. The somewhat peremptory tone of the messenger to the emperor – although he did not yet have that rank – becomes acceptable when it is recalled that Otto III was only five years old in 985. The poem does not, however, refer specifically to the restoration of the dukedom, and Heinrich der Zänker's role in the business of government immediately after 985 was not as great as is implied here.

An alternative is to relate the poem to a later period: when the dowager empress Theophano died in 991 Otto III had not reached his majority, and a council of regents was set up; one of the regents was Heinrich der Zänker's son, the future Duke Heinrich IV of Bavaria. The poem might deal with this connection, then, between the emperor and Duke Heinrich IV. The poem says that Heinrich did not desire the royal power, and, indeed, Duke Heinrich IV did not seek the throne, although he was to become German king on the death of Otto III in 1002 and emperor, as Heinrich II (known as "der Heilige" [the Saint]), in 1014 (he would be crowned king by Archbishop Willigis of Mainz, who had played a major part in the regency council). If *De Heinrico* does relate to Heinrich IV, it was probably composed before his elevation to the German throne – that is, between 991 and 1002. The "two of the same name" would still refer to father and son, although the emphasis would be on the son. The occasion described, then, would be prior to 995, when Heinrich der Zänker died. Also, Otto acquired the title of emperor in 996, and the commanding tone of the messenger remains plausible as long as Otto was underage.

At all events the poem makes sense if it concerns Otto III before he attained his majority in 996. The likelihood is that it was written in the time of Duke Heinrich IV of Bavaria, probably before he became emperor; and its purpose is either to praise the duke himself or to place the reputation of his father, Heinrich der Zänker, on a better footing than it deserved.

The poem is not a panegyric in the formal sense and, given the macaronic form, might be no more than an academic exercise. It might, however, be a propaganda piece intended to emphasize the role and importance of the Bavarian dukes in the running of the empire. The precise occasion for which it was composed, which seems to have been one of some formality, is unlikely ever to be determined. Even though the *Ludwigslied* (Song of Ludwig, 881 or 882) mentions no dates or places, it can be placed in its historical context. The same is by no means true of *De Heinrico*.

**References:**

J. Knight Bostock, *A Handbook on Old High German Literature,* edited by K. C. King and D. R. McLintock (Oxford: Clarendon Press, 1976), pp. 252–256;

Helgard Christensen, "Das ahd. Gedicht De Henrico [*sic*]," *Kopenhagener Beiträge zur germanistichen Linguistik,* 10 (1978): 18–32;

Markus Diebold, *Das Sagelied* (Bern & Frankfurt am Main: Lang, 1974), pp. 16–18;

Marie-Luise Dittrich, "De Heinrico," *Zeitschrift für deutsches Altertum,* 84 (1952–1953): 274–308;

Gustav Ehrismann, "Zur althochdeutschen Literatur 2: *De Heinrico,*" *Beiträge,* 29 (1904): 118–126;

T. Grienberger, "Althochdeutsche Texterklärungen I, 4: *De Heinrico,*" *Beiträge,* 45 (1921): 226–230;

J. Sidney Groseclose and Brian O. Murdoch, *Die althochdeutschen poetischen Denkmäler* (Stuttgart: Metzler, 1976), pp. 90–94;

Wolfgang Haubrichs, *Die Anfänge,* volume 1/1 of *Geschichte der deutschen Literatur,* edited by Joachim Heinzle (Frankfurt am Main: Athenaeum, 1988), pp. 184–189;

Wolfgang Jugandreas, "De Heinrico," *Leuvense Bijdragen,* 57 (1968): 75–91;

Brian O. Murdoch, *Old High German Literature* (Boston: Twayne, 1983), pp. 100–102;

Ernst Ochs, "Ambo vos aequivoci: Zur Abfassungszeit des ahd.-lat. *Heinrichslieds,*" *Zeitschrift für deutsche Philologie,* 66 (1941): 10–12;

W. Sanders, "Imperator ore incundo saxonizans," *Zeitschrift für deutsches Altertum,* 98 (April 1969): 13–28;

Mathilde Uhlirz, "Der Modus de Heinrico und sein geschichtlicher Inhalt," *Deutsche Vierteljahrsschrift,* 26 (1952): 153–161;

Wolf von Unwerth, "Der Dialekt des Liedes *De Heinrico,*" *Beiträge,* 41 (1916): 312–331.

# Ecbasis Captivi
## (circa 1045)

Dennis M. Kratz
*University of Texas at Dallas*

**Manuscripts:** The poem survives in two manuscripts. The older – Brussels, Bibliothèque Royale MS 10615–10729 – was written circa 1250, probably in the monastery of Saint Eucharius-Matthias in Trier. The second manuscript – Brussels, Bibliothèque Royale MS 9799–9809 – was copied from the first circa 1275.

**First publication:** In *Lateinische Gedichte des X. und XI. Jahrhunderts,* edited by Jacob Grimm and Andreas Schmeller (Göttingen: Dieterich, 1838; reprinted, Amsterdam: Rodopi, 1967), pp. 243–285.

**Standard edition:** *Ecbasis cuiusdam Captivi per tropologiam,* Scriptores rerum germanicarum in usum scholarum ex Monumentis Germaniae Historicis separatim editi, edited by Karl Strecker (Hannover: Hahn, 1935).

**Edition in English:** Translated in prose by Edwin H. Zeydel as *Ecbasis cuiusdam captivi per tropologiam: Escape of a Certain Captive Told in a Figurative Manner* (Chapel Hill: University of North Carolina Press, 1964).

As the earliest surviving example of an attempt to transform the beast fable into a more ambitious literary form, the allegorical Latin narrative known as the *Ecbasis Captivi* (Escape of a Captive, circa 1045) occupies an important place in the history of medieval literature. By departing from the tradition of the brief animal fable, the anonymous monk who composed the poem in the mid eleventh century took a step toward the creation of a new literary genre: the beast epic. In the next century that genre would produce three major works: the French *Roman de Renart* (circa 1175); the Latin *Ysengrimus* (circa 1180); and the German *Reinhart Fuchs* (Reynard the Fox, circa 1180), by Heinrich der Glîchezaere.

The medieval European literary tradition of the animal fable is based ultimately on the short stories written in Greek that are attributed to Aesop. Although the Middle Ages did not know Aesop's fables in Greek, Latin collections of fables derived from them were extremely popular. Christian writers found them particularly useful as exempla to illustrate points of Christian doctrine and morality. Two influential collections were those of Phaedrus, written in verse in the first century, and of Avianus, written in prose around 400. Such collections were in all likelihood used as school texts, and many of the fables became well known.

The *Ecbasis Captivi,* unlike these collections of brief tales, tells one continuous and coherent story. The poem is composed in Latin leonine hexameters, that is, hexameters in which an internal rhyme occurs between the last syllable of the line and the last syllable of a word near the middle of the line. The author fashioned his elaborate narrative of 1,229 lines by blending two tales: the first recounts the capture of a calf by a wolf and the calf's rescue; the second is a fable, told by the wolf, explaining how he and the fox became bitter enemies. This antagonism between the fox and the wolf would play a central role in the cycle of narratives based on the adventures of Reynard the fox.

In the frame tale, or "outer fable," a calf left alone without his mother escapes from his stall and plays in the meadow until evening falls. He is captured by a wolf and taken to the wolf's cave – or castle, as it is later described – for slaughter. The wolf is joined by a hedgehog and an otter, and the latter is assigned to guard the captive. Even though he has been warned in a dream not to hurt the calf, the wolf persists in his plan to eat him. The wolf learns that the herd, having discovered the calf's disappearance, is coming with other animals to rescue him. The wolf says that of all the animals who are approaching he most fears his old enemy the fox, who is also his uncle. Asked to explain how he and the fox became such bitter enemies, the wolf tells the story that provides the "inner fable" of the *Ecbasis Captivi.*

The wolf says that at Easter time long ago the lion, king of the beasts, became ill. When every animal except the fox came to court and suggested a cure, the lion ordered the fox found and executed, and the wolf – the father of the wolf telling the story – prepared a gallows for the fox. Warned by his ally, the panther, the fox suddenly arrived at court with the excuse that he had been on a pilgrimage to the Holy Land seeking a cure for the ailing monarch. At the lion's insistence he revealed the cure: flay the wolf, apply salves to the lion, and use the wolf's pelt as a blanket. When the treatment proved successful, the lion raised the fox to a position of honor. Since the wolf had been killed to provide his pelt, the fox received his castle as a fief. In the intervening years, however, the wolf's son wrested the castle from the fox. It is to that castle that the wolf has brought his prey.

The rescuers, led by the fox and the bull, arrive. The wolf's cowardly accomplices desert him: the otter dives into the river; the hedgehog hides. The wolf also hides but is tricked by the fox into revealing himself to the rescuers and is killed by the bull. The fox regains his castle. The calf returns to his mother.

The date of the composition of the *Ecbasis Captivi* remains a matter of dispute. Werner Ross has argued that it was composed in the first half of the tenth century, but so early a date presents difficulties; Edwin H. Zeydel provides stronger arguments for a mid-eleventh-century date. The debate hinges on the identification of two rulers, Konrad and Henry, mentioned by the poet. Those rulers are most likely the German emperor Konrad II, who ruled from 1024 to 1039, and the French king Henry I, who ruled from 1031 to 1039. Zeydel points out also that hereditary enfeoffment, as exemplified in the reward of the fox for curing the lion in the inner fable, was not customary in Germany before the eleventh century.

Nothing is known of the author, although in the prologue he offers a few facts about himself: for example, that he is fond of daydreaming and that he is prone to criticizing others while overlooking his own faults. For the most part, however, these declarations appear to be topoi rather than candid information. One such topos in the prologue is the poet's assertion that he writes poetry to combat a tendency toward sloth. The poet employs another topos at the end of the work when he declares that he is ending the poem because he is tired. The narrative seems to reflect his familiarity with southern Germany, for it mentions Trier, the Moselle and Meuse rivers, and the Black Forest. Such comments suggest that the author was a Cistercian monk who spent at least part of his life near Toul, probably in the monastery at Saint Evre, where he taught in the monastic school, and that he was of Germanic stock, perhaps from the Black Forest region.

The "tale of the sick lion" that is the subject of the inner fable has a long history, tracing back to Aesop. The first medieval literary treatment of the tale is a Latin poem composed in the late eighth century by Paulus Diaconus (Paul the Deacon), a member of Charlemagne's court. Paul's version, however, differs in significant respects from that of the *Ecbasis Captivi*, the most important difference being that it is the bear and not the wolf who is outwitted by the fox. A tenth-century poem by Leo of Vercelli, of which only a few fragments survive, makes reference to the antagonism of the wolf and the fox. It is impossible to say whether the author of the *Ecbasis Captivi* knew of either work.

No literary source has been found for the story of the calf who is captured by a wolf. Although the Bible has references to a wolf in sheep's clothing (Matt. 7:15) and to lost sheep (Matt. 18:12, Luke 15:4), the Scriptures do not include any tale or parable of a calf rescued from a wolf. Zeydel has proposed that the author may have been inspired to invent the tale by a Latin hexameter known to have been used as a penmanship exercise as early as the tenth century: *infelix vitulus sudibus quam sepe ligatus* (the unfortunate calf tied up with ropes in its stall). Variations on this hexameter occur twice in the *Ecbasis Captivi*.

In the prologue the poet compares himself to the fettered calf of the narrative. This analogy has led a few scholars to conclude that the poem is autobiographical – that the poet had himself escaped from and been returned to the monastery. Zeydel points out, however, that "recaptured fugitives from monasteries were not as a rule employed as teachers and were hardly entrusted with anything as precious as parchment or other writing materials." Hans Robert Jauss makes the more plausible suggestion that the remark reflects the poet's sly humor: he is a captive of the demands of Latin verse when he would prefer to be romping freely in the meadows like the Muses. If so, the complaint is surely ironic, for the author displays both erudition and an uncommon mastery of Latin verse. He is extraordinarily adept at fashioning rhymed leonine hexameters by stitching together halves of unrhymed classical hexameters. Moreover, the poet is aware of his skill: at the conclusion of the prologue he declares that he will tell his story "non simplo stamine" (not with a simple thread, line 68). This metaphor, which compares the coming story to a woven fabric, invites at least four plausible interpretations: the poet will weave the outer and inner fables into a coherent story; he will weave fiction and autobiography; he will combine an amusing story about animals with a deeper allegorical lesson; or he will compose his Latin from lines and verses taken from other poets.

One of the most compelling features of the *Ecbasis Captivi* is the author's learned use of quotations from an impressive range of classical and patristic literature. He makes particular use of Horace — more than 250 lines, almost all from the *Satires* and *Epistles* — but there are also approximately 100 lines from Virgil as well as more than twenty lines apiece from the Christian Latin poetry of Prudentius, Juvencus, and Sedulius. Allusions to many other texts appear, among them the Bible and the Rule of Saint Benedict.

The combination of moral instruction and learned allusion that characterizes the *Ecbasis Captivi* led Zeydel to the conclusion that it was intended as a school exercise for the author's pupils. Jauss has offered another conjecture, that the *Ecbasis Captivi* arose as an Easter entertainment — a play or perhaps a school declamation. Ludwig Gompf has offered strong arguments that the *Ecbasis Captivi* was meant to be recited aloud by a small group of readers who were probably accompanied by a mime: he points to the frequent dialogues between characters and extended speeches by individual animals and to the prologue, where the poet promises a reward for the recitation — not the reading — of the entire work.

The full title, *Ecbasis cuiusdam Captivi per tropologiam* (The Escape of a Certain Captive Told Figuratively), found in the earlier of the two surviving manuscripts, may provide a clue to the poet's intent, although there is no evidence that he himself gave this title to the work. Actually, the manuscript reads "per topologiam"; this spelling, meaning "through the quotation of topoi," may be correct. All modern editors, however, accept Karl Strecker's emendation "per tropologiam." This phrase, whether written by the author or added by a later scribe, alerts the reader to the use of allegorical or metaphorical speech; commonly used in exegesis, it implies the need to search for a deeper spiritual meaning beneath the surface. Here the phrase, as Elisabeth Gulich has shown, clearly indicates that the reader should seek such a deeper level of meaning in the text, should regard the characters and their actions as *figurae* (signs) pointing to a moral lesson.

In the prologue the poet makes statements that seem to reinforce the implications of the title. Although he confesses that he is offering a "mendosam profero cartam," (fictional tale, line 40), he qualifies this declaration by advising the reader that the fiction contains much that is "utilia" (useful). *Utilia* in this context means "offering useful moral instruction" and is probably derived from Horace.

The word *ecbasis* has two possible meanings. The more general one is "escape" or "departure," and in other texts it is often equated with the more common Latin word *exitus;* but it also has a technical meaning in rhetoric as "a digression." *Ecbasis captivi,* therefore, can mean either "the escape of a captive," in which case it refers to the story, or "the digression of a captive," in which case it refers to the author.

The allegorical possibilities of the calf's adventures are readily apparent. On one level, the calf is a brother chafing under monastic discipline: he flees his monastery and is caught by the Devil (the wolf), only to be rescued by his abbot (the bull) and fellow monks (the herd). A more general reading *per tropologiam* would see the calf as humanity, lured from the protection of the church into the temptations of the world, again to be saved only by clerical intervention.

The *tropologia,* or allegory, of the inner fable is less obvious. Hartmut Hoffmann suggests that the poet was not only offering a general moral sermon but also satirizing specific individuals and political events of his day. If so, commentators have been unable to identify these targets. Whether or not the poet was satirizing particular individuals, the characters of the inner fable unquestionably serve as general *figurae*. The fox, for example, is the shrewd but unprincipled and self-serving adviser, while the lion represents the gullible ruler. The hedgehog and the otter may have been intended as caricatures of contemporary nobles, but they are also *figurae* of faithless allies.

In an attempt to provide an interpretation that reconciles the inner and outer fables, Jan M. Ziolkowski emphasizes the prominent role of Easter throughout the *Ecbasis Captivi*. The outer fable takes place during the Easter Eve Vigil and on Easter. As the narrative begins, the calf is unhappy both because he is fettered and because he longs to taste milk from his mother's udder; perhaps the latter desire refers to his impatience with observing his Lenten fast. Moreover, when the wolf captures the calf, he first declares that the calf deserves to be killed as a punishment for his sin (presumably, the sin was his flight from his pen – that is, from his monastic discipline). Later the wolf describes the unfortunate calf as his paschal meal. The wolf's hunger stems in part from his having abstained from eating meat for the past two months (the duration of the wolf's abstention from meat would be equal to the length of time most monks fasted during Lent). The outer fable, in this interpretation, tells the story of humankind under the Old Law, that is, before Easter. The wolf, as the Devil or, perhaps, the Old Law itself, believes that the calf's sin is irrevocable and unforgivable.

The inner fable, Ziolkowski suggests, is introduced by the poet to prove that the New Law takes precedence over the old. The wolf begins his explanation of his feud with the fox with a striking allusion to the New Testament. "Exiit edictum" (A decree went out, line 396), he says, that the beasts of the forest should come to the aid of the sick lion-king. The phrase *exiit edictum* brings to mind the beginning of the story of the birth of Christ (Luke 2:1): "And it came to pass that in those days a decree went out [edictum exiit] from Caesar Augustus."

References to Easter abound in this section of the *Ecbasis Captivi*. Christ's Resurrection is mentioned twice (lines 935 and 973); the nightingale reads a homily on the Passion (lines 859 to 905); and the birds sing paschal praises (line 946). Finally, before setting out to rescue the calf the animals chant "Salve festa dies" (Hail festive day, line 977), a line from a well-known Easter hymn by Venantius Fortunatus.

The fox both cures the lion and teaches him a new model for ruling. Specifically, he condemns the view that one act of transgression should doom the perpetrator. He proposes a new system that allows an individual three chances for redemption (the same number of opportunities to embrace salvation that Christ gave to Peter).

After curing the lion the fox says to him, "hora est surgendi; tua sunt quasi regia Croesi" (it is the hour of rising; your kingdom is like that of Croesus, line 729). This line provides an example of the poet's skillful interweaving of quotations to create a rhyming (*surgendi . . . Croesi*) hexameter line. The first half-line contains an allusion to Paul's admonition to the Romans to "rise from sleep, for now our salvation is nearer than we believed" (Rom. 13:11). The second half-line is taken from Horace (*Epistolarum* 1.II.2) and seems to be a reminder about the dangers of becoming absorbed in the riches of the mundane world.

As the day on which the New Law supplanted the Old Law, argues Ziolkowski, Easter provides the conceptual link between the outer and inner fables. The design of the story reflects the passage from the era before the Crucifixion to the era afterward, that is, the critical change in the world that Easter celebrates. The outer story presents the tale of the calf – representing *per tropologiam* a monk in particular and, on another level, humankind in general – who sins by straying from the safety of his stall to play in the meadow, that is, becomes enmeshed in the pleasures of the world. The wolf, perhaps meant to be read metaphorically as the Devil, follows the rules of the Old Law by demanding that the calf be punished for his transgression. Now the poet interrupts the story with the inner fable, which illustrates the teaching that sinners should have the chance to repent and reform. The setting free of the calf is connected, through the inner fable, with the idea that the wolf's law, the law before the Resurrection, is no longer valid. Now the outer story resumes, and the repentant calf is rescued.

This interpretation seems to complement the conjecture of Jauss and Gompf that the *Ecbasis Captivi* was created as an Easter entertainment to illustrate the coming of the New Law with the Resurrection of Christ. As such, it can be seen as the forerunner not only of the beast epic but also of the Easter plays that became so popular in medieval Europe.

The *Ecbasis Captivi* is a transitional work rather than a fully developed epic: it has been suggested that the medieval beast epic came into being when the animals received names, but the characters in the *Ecbasis Captivi* are allegorical figures lacking proper names or personalities. The narrative marks, however, a turning point in the history of the beast narrative in Western literature. Although it is impossible to trace any direct influence of the *Ecbasis Captivi* on later literature, several elements that it introduces play central roles in subsequent works: the antagonism of the fox and the wolf, the notion that the fox is the wolf's nephew, the role of the panther in warning his friend of the lion's edict, and the wolf's erection of a gallows for the execution of that edict. Finally, it is in the *Ecbasis Captivi* that an animal world is first described as a feudal society, where, for example, a king grants a castle as a fief to reward a particularly great service. More than in its anticipation of specific elements, however, the importance of the *Ecbasis Captivi* lies in its representing the first surviving step toward the creation of a new literary genre.

References:

Norman F. Blake, *The History of Reynard the Fox* (Oxford: Oxford University Press, 1970), pp. xi–xxi;

Ludwig Gompf, "Die *Ecbasis cuiusdam captivi* und ihr Publikum," *Mittellateinisches Jahrbuch,* 8 (1973): 30–42;

Elisabeth Gulich, "Die Bedeutung der Tropologia in der *Ecbasis Captivi,*" *Mittellateinisches Jahrbuch,* 4 (1967): 72–90;

Hartmut Hoffmann, "Poppo von Trier in der *Ecbasis cuiusdam Captivi?,*" *Archiv für Kulturgeschichte,* 40 (1958): 289–314;

Hans Robert Jauss, *Untersuchungen zur mittelalterlichen Tierdichtung* (Tübingen: Niemeyer, 1959);

Werner Ross, "Die *Ecbasis Captivi* und die Anfänge der mittelalterlichen Tierdichtung," *Germanisch-Romanische Monatschrift,* 35 (1954): 266–282;

Donald B. Sands, "The Flemish Reynard: Epic and Non-Epic Affiliations," in *The Epic in Medieval Society,* edited by Harald Scholler (Tübingen: Niemeyer, 1977), pp. 307–325;

Jan M. Ziolkowski, *Talking Animals: Medieval Latin Beast Poetry, 750–1150* (Philadelphia: University of Pennsylvania Press, 1993), pp. 153–197.

# *Georgslied*

## *(896?)*

Anatoly Liberman
*University of Minnesota*

**Manuscript:** The work is preserved on leaves 200v–201v of the Palatine manuscript of Otfried von Weißenburg's *Evangelienbuch,* Heidelberg, Universitätsbibliothek, Cod. pal. lat. 52. A facsimile of the first sixteen lines can be found in *Die ältesten deutschen Sprach-Denkmäler in Lichtdrucken,* edited by Magda Enneccerus (Frankfurt am Main: F. Enneccerus, 1897), p. 37.

**First publication:** In *Lectionum theotiscarum specimen,* edited by Bertel Christian Sandvig (Copenhagen: Horrebowii, 1783).

**Standard editions:** Edited by Friedrich K. T. Zarncke, in *Berichte über die Verhandlungen der Königlich Sächsischen Gesellschaft der Wissenschaften zu Leipzig: Philologisch-Historische Klasse,* 26 (1874): 1–40; edited by Rudolf Kögel, in his *Geschichte der deutschen Literatur bis zum Ausgange des Mittelalters,* volume 1, part 2 (Strasbourg: Trübner, 1897), pp. 100–102.

**Edition in English:** Translated by J. Knight Bostock, in his *A Handbook on Old High German Literature,* second edition, edited by K. C. King and D. R. McLintock (Oxford: Clarendon Press, 1976), pp. 223–224.

The Old High German *Georgslied* (Song in Honor of [Saint] George, 896?) is noted more for its deficiencies than for its merits. The scribe adopted an erratic system of spelling, and scholars have attempted to decipher the text. In modern editions the *Georgslied* is fifty-nine lines long, but the text appears as prose, without musical notation, on the last two leaves of the Heidelberg manuscript (Codex Palatinus) of Otfried von Weißenburg's *Evangelienbuch* (Gospel Book, between 863 and 871). Older Germanic poetry was often written continuously to save space. It is usually not difficult to divide such works into lines, for the reader is guided by either alliteration (as in *Beowulf*) or end rhyme (as in the present case).

Despite the confusing orthography and several cruxes, the content of the song is fairly clear. The narrative begins in medias res. George (variously spelled *Georio, Gorio,* and *Goriio*) went to a legal assembly, that is, to the royal court, with a great army. Many kings tried to persuade him to relapse into heathendom, but he would not listen to them. So he was thrown into prison. There he fed two women, saving their lives. He restored a blind man's eyesight, a lame man's ability to walk, a mute man's power of speech, and a deaf man's hearing. A pillar that had stood in the dungeon for years suddenly burst into flower. Enraged, the powerful Tacianus accused George of sorcery and had him stripped naked and struck with a sword that was "uunteruuasso" (wondrous sharp), but George raised himself up and preached. Again the mighty Tacianus flew into a rage. He had George bound and tortured on a wheel. Tacianus's men broke him in ten pieces, but he raised himself once more. Then Tacianus had George flayed and burned. His men threw the ashes into a well and put a heap of stones over it. They walked around his burial place and challenged him to rise, and he did. He also ordered another man to rise from the dead. Then he went to the palace and preached to the queen. Queen Elossandria was virtuous, bent her ear to George's sermon, and gave away her wealth. George put up his hand, and Abollinus (about whom nothing has been said up to this point) trembled. George commanded the hound of hell, and the hound went into the pit. Him. . . .

After *him* (*ihn*) the song breaks off; there follows a confession in Latin, "nequeo Vuisolf" (Wisolf is unable). This statement has given the unfortunate Wisolf great notoriety among students of German literature. Wisolf, it was held, either devised the incomprehensible orthography of the song but was overwhelmed by its complexity and stopped in the middle of a sentence, or he was a foreigner who bungled his work. The main features of the text are the chaotic use of capital letters – for example, *seGita* (said), *beGonta* (began) – and the transposition of the letter *h,* which, instead of preceding vowels, more often follows them: for example, *ihmil* for *himil* (heaven), *ehrte* for *herte* (steadfast), *ihez* for *heiz* (ordered), *orhter* for *hort'er* (he heard). *H* is frequently used when its presence is not called for, as in *fholko* for *folko* (people [instrumental case]), *ehngila* for *engila* (angels), and *tohuben* for *touben* (deaf [accusative case]). Less striking but also puzzling is the use of *c* for *z* and *h* for *k*. Not only letters but also lines sometimes seem to occupy wrong places in the text.

The hypotheses put forward in connection with the *Georgslied* are of two types. According to one school of thinking, the text was copied by a man called Wisolf, who, despite his (quite unusual) German name, was a speaker of some Romance dialect; or, if he was a German speaker, then he was hopelessly unqualified for his job. According to the other school, Wisolf knew well what he was doing and used a bizarre spelling system or even a cipher.

Opinions also differ as to the circumstances under which the text arose: it could have been dictated to an inexperienced scribe by a monk with a speech defect, recorded from memory, copied from an illegible manuscript, or rearranged by Wisolf. The authors of the most authoritative manuals of early German literature, including Rudolf Kögel and Gustav Ehrismann, vied with one another in heaping scorn on Wisolf, but J. Knight Bostock in 1936 and Fritz Tschirch in 1951 showed that the orthographic aberrations in the *Georgslied* form some sort of system. Not everything has been explained, but the idea of an ignorant or even crazy man producing chaos on paper has lost some of its appeal.

Wisolf's handwriting is that of a professional scribe (a point first made by K. Siemers), which means that he was aware of and responsible for the quality of his product. Francis A. Wood cited spellings of a student of his, who was talented but made mistakes resembling Wisolf's; today this student's writing habits would be diagnosed as a mild form of dyslexia. But as a dyslexic, Wisolf would hardly have stayed in his job or been entrusted with filling the leaves in a precious manuscript. It is more probable that he was qualified to copy a text of extraordinary difficulty. The spelling pattern to which he adheres does not betray a foreigner; nor are foreigners unable to copy a text they do not understand (the best-known late example is provided by the 1787 Thorkelin transcripts of *Beowulf*).

Separate elements of this spelling pattern occur in many other Old High German texts. Although modern Germans have less trouble with initial *h*'s than speakers of English dialects, *h*'s have been dropped with considerable regularity throughout the history of German, and it is not uncommon to see transposed and "spurious" *h*'s in Old High German and Middle High German manuscripts. The salient feature of the *Georgslied* is the abundance of such abnormalities. Even against the background of gratuitous variation typical of medieval texts, this poem is an exception. Someone seems to have followed a set of rules and used them – despite the extravagance of the result – with moderation, for proper names are not distorted.

Tschirch pointed out that in transposing *h*'s and in the use of capitals the scribe would carry out his method with great consistency for a while and then forget about it and write like everyone else. This observation makes the workings of the scribe's mind even harder to grasp. It appears as though he knew the traditional spelling and intentionally deviated from it, but all scholars who have discussed the *Georgslied* agree that, whether the scribe was Ger-

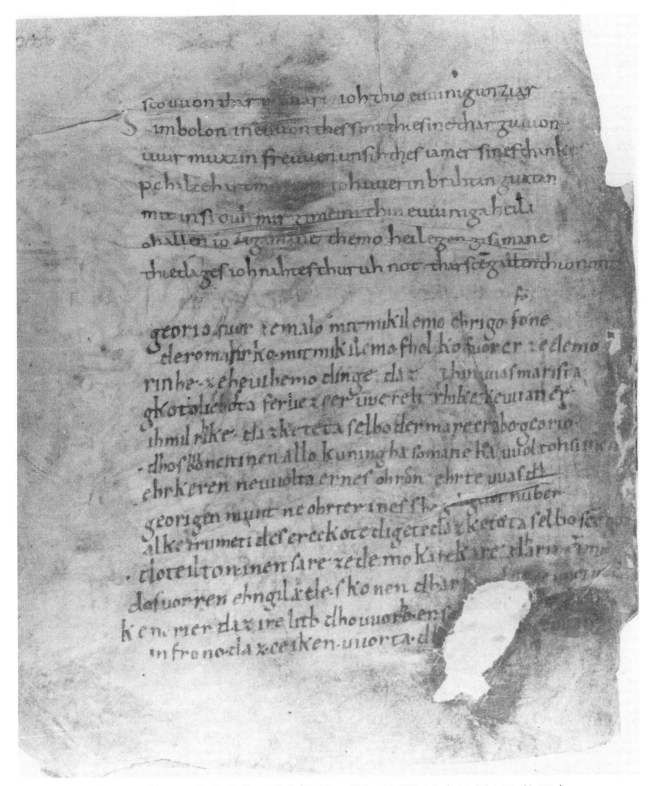

*First page of the manuscript for the* Georgslied *(Heidelberg, Universitätsbibliothek, Cod. pal. lat. 52, fol. 200v)*

man or French, he did not pronounce initial *h*'s and treated the letter *h* as a graphic embellishment, so he could hardly have put *h* in the same wrong place almost every time. It would also be more natural to suppose that a scribe who had the spirit of a reformer, like the thirteenth-century English monk Orm, would have been more in control of his spelling than Wisolf was; and the last leaves of Otfried's *Evangelienbuch* appear a singularly inappropriate place for a first experiment. Finally, some forms do make one think of a cipher or dyslexia, notably *psanr,* which occurs twice and has been decoded as *spran(g).*

"Nequeo Vuisolf " has been taken as Wisolf's confession of ignorance. If the *ihn* preceding these words is a German word, which seems likely, Wisolf must have given up copying in despair at this point: even he, the best scribe around, could not cope with such a task. His text is probably an accurate transcript of an impossible original; Douglas J. Guillam thinks that Wisolf was copying from a hardly legible manuscript whose dialect he did not know. Under such circumstances it is idle to speculate who composed the song, why it has such a strange appearance, and how many times it was copied before Wisolf.

The dialect of the *Georgslied* is Alemannic as it was spoken around the end of the eleventh century, and, in all likelihood, the song was composed either in the monastery of Saint Gall or in the abbey of the Reichenau. According to Bostock, "In 888 Abbot Hatto III of the Reichenau built a church at Oberzell on the Reichenau, dedicated to St. George. The supposed relics of the saint were given to Hatto by Pope Formosus when, as archbishop of Mainz, he accompanied [King] Arnulf to Italy. . . . The relics were translated to the Reichenau in 896 and are still preserved there. It is widely held that their translation was the occasion for the composition (or the present redaction) of the German poem." H. Brauer, who believed Wisolf to be a foreigner, found it almost sacrilegious that such a manuscript could have been produced at Saint Gall in the days of Notker III and connected it instead with the chancery of Queen Gisela, Konrad II's wife. Other scholars, such as Eduard Schröder, believe that since the text was entered in the Codex Palatinus, it was copied in Heidelberg.

Despite the use of rhyming couplets in the *Georgslied* and its association with the Codex Palatinus, nothing testifies to Otfried's direct influence on the poet, whose immediate source was a Latin passion of Saint George. Friedrich K. T. Zarncke's edition of the song (1874) precedes an edition of the

passion by Wilhelm Arndt in the same journal, so the texts can easily be compared. Several passages in the *Georgslied* make sense only if one knows the passion. This is especially true of lines 14–15, about the two starving women Saint George met in prison, and lines 42–47, about the resurrection of the dead man. It appears that the dead man's name was Jovis or Jovius and that on coming to life he declared the tyrant and his retainers to be deceived by the Devil. Abollinus, who appears suddenly in the *Georgslied,* is mentioned as one of the idols many times in the passion, where he is called Apollonus.

It is not improbable that the *Georgslied* poet knew other songs or homilies about the saint, for he slightly rearranges the events told in the passion. The author's independence of the alliterative style of Germanic epic poetry does not mean that he lacked popular roots: the song reinforces the fairytale character of the passion with the three executions, each more terrible than the preceding one. And the tyrannical king has a gentle, virtuous wife – another situation common in folklore.

The style of the song is akin to that of a ballad. The narrative begins in medias res, only the finale of the protagonist's career is described (in the tenth century Saint George was not yet venerated as a dragon slayer), and only the most dramatic moments – chiefly miracles – are recounted. The heroic songs of the thirteenth-century Old Icelandic *Elder Edda* also move in leaps from one narrative pinnacle to another, and some of those songs are direct precursors of Scandinavian ballads. Like the singers of the Eddic songs, the *Georgslied* poet addressed an audience (probably a lay one) familiar with the plot. The *Georgslied* appeals to the listeners' emotions and uses a form not alien to common people; but it stresses the hero's relations with God rather than with his fellowmen, and this feature distinguishes it from old songs. Saint George appears before the judges and is accompanied by many supporters, as defendants in those days always did; yet they are never mentioned as trying to help, let alone as dying with, their lord. They serve as part of an introductory epic formula and play no other role in the song. Strangely enough, the assembly at which George is tried is called most dear to God; this statement may be another empty formula, but perhaps the trial was pleasing in the eyes of God because in the end it redounded to the glory of Saint George. The hero performed everything for which he prayed, and the Lord granted him everything. If Wisolf had not despaired of his task, more would undoubtedly have been heard about heaven and hell.

The text of the *Georgslied* falls into several segments, for every episode is followed by concluding statements such as "daz ketæta selbo *hero* sancte Gorio" (This George did himself), "daz cunt uns selbo *hero* sancte Gorio" (This Saint George made known to us himself), and "dhie heidenen man kescante Gorio dhrate fram" (George put the heathens greatly to shame [the italicized words have been added by editors of the work]). These statements resemble refrains but appear at irregular intervals. None of the attempts to group the lines of the song into strophes has been fully convincing. Eduard Sievers regarded the *Georgslied* as an example of antiphone singing, with two choirs alternating as in a psalm; he designated one of them bass, the other tenor, but this reconstruction is mere intelligent guessing.

## References:

Wilhelm Arndt, "Passio Sancti Georgii," *Berichte über die Verhandlungen der Königlich Sächsischen Gesellschaft der Wissenschaften zu Leipzig: Philologisch-Historische Klasse,* 26 (1874): 43-70;

J. Knight Bostock, *A Handbook on Old High German Literature,* second edition, edited by K. C. King and D. R. McLintock (Oxford: Clarendon Press, 1976);

Bostock, "The Orthography of the Old High German *Georgslied,*" *Medium Ævum,* 5 (October 1936): 189-198;

H. Brauer, "Die Heidelberger Handschrift von Otfrids Evangelienbuch und das althochdeutsche Georgslied," *Zeitschrift für deutsche Philologie,* 55 (1930): 261-268;

Wilhelm Braune, *Althochdeutsches Lesebuch,* fifteenth edition, edited by Ernst A. Ebbinghaus (Tübingen: Niemeyer, 1969);

Gustav Ehrismann, *Geschichte der deutschen Literatur bis zum Ausgang des Mittelalters,* volume 1: *Die althochdeutsche Literatur* (Munich: Beck, 1918);

Douglas J. Guillam, "A Note on the Old High German *Georgslied,*" *Medium Ævum,* 7 (February 1938): 76-78;

Eduard Schröder, "Eine Nachspur von Otfrids Reimpraxis?," *Zeitschrift für deutsches Altertum und deutsche Literatur,* 71 (1934): 166-167, 265;

J. Seemüller, "Studie zu den Ursprüngen der altdeutschen Historiographie," in *Abhandlungen zur germanischen Philologie: Festgabe für Richard Heinzel* (Halle: Niemeyer, 1896), pp. 278-352;

K. Siemers, "Zum ahd. Georgslied," *Beiträge zur Geschichte der deutschen Sprache und Literatur,* 39 (1913-1914): 98-115;

Eduard Sievers, "Althochdeutsche Responsorientexte," *Beiträge zur Geschichte der deutschen Sprache und Literatur,* 52 (1928): 208-216;

Fritz Tschirch, "Wisolf – eine mittelalterliche Schreiberpersönlichkeit," *Beiträge zur Geschichte der deutschen Sprache und Literatur,* 73 (1951): 387-422;

Francis A. Wood, "Notes on Old High German Texts," *Modern Philology,* 12 (February 1915): 495-502;

Friedrich K. T. Zarncke, "Über den althochdeutschen Gesang vom heiligen Georg," *Berichte über die Verhandlungen der Königlich Sächsischen Gesellschaft der Wissenschaften zu Leipzig: Philologisch-Historische Klasse,* 26 (1874): 1-42.

# Graf Rudolf
*(between circa 1170 and circa 1185)*

Will Hasty
*University of Florida*

**Manuscripts:** Fourteen fragments of a single manuscript survive, composed by two scribes at the end of the twelfth century: α to δ are in Brunswick, Stadtbibliothek (Ms. 5), A to K are in Göttingen, Niedersächische Staats- und Universitätsbibliothek (Cod. Ms. philol. 184,7).

**First publication:** *Grave Ruodolf,* edited by Wilhelm Grimm (Göttingen: Dieterich, 1928 [Göttingen fragments]); revised as *Graf Rudolf* (Göttingen: Dieterich, 1844 [Göttingen and Brunswick fragments]).

**Standard editions:** In *Mittelhochdeutsches Übungsbuch,* edited by Carl von Kraus (Heidelberg: Winter, 1912); *Graf Rudolf,* edited by Peter F. Ganz (Berlin: Schmidt, 1964).

*Graf Rudolf* (Count Rudolph, circa 1170 or circa 1185), a poem dealing with the adventures of a young count in Europe and the Holy Land against the historical backdrop of the Crusades, is unique in the early history of court literature. Although sharing certain elements – such as the bridal-quest motif and oriental geography – with contemporary works such as *König Rother* (King Rother, circa 1150), *Graf Rudolf* is singular in its realistic portrayal of events. The anonymous author excluded the fantastic elements to be found in the so-called minstrel epics and also in the Arthurian works that would soon be the rage in court literature; and he composed his tale in an attractively simple and straightforward style. Although it deals with the Crusades, the work makes no attempt to impart a religious message. It is worldly through and through, and the Crusades serve more as a stage for the actions of the hero than as an event whose ethos requires moralizing or reflecting about the state of one's soul. Finally, *Graf Rudolf* is entirely different from another well-known work about the Crusades that was written at about the same time, the *Rolandslied* (Song of Roland, circa 1172) of Pfaffe Konrad, in its positive representation of Muslims, who are not the insidious, godless infidels of the chanson-de-geste tradition but chivalrous and courtly – in some instances more so than their Christian counterparts. Thus, the work seems to anticipate the idea of a universal knighthood and courtliness beyond confessional strife that achieves its most eloquent expression in Wolfram von Eschenbach's *Willehalm* (circa 1210–1220).

About fourteen hundred lines of *Graf Rudolf* survive in fourteen fragments. The beginning and end of the poem, which may have contained information about the poet, his literary source or sources, and his patron, are among the missing sections. The fragments are parts of a single copy of the work produced in the latter part of the twelfth century by two scribes, one writing the fragments designated α to δ and A to F, the other G to K. Despite their chronological proximity to the original and the care with which they were produced (they do not appear to contain any major errors), the fragments reveal little about the composition of the work, and what they do reveal is highly debatable. The dialect seems to belong to central Germany, although it is unclear whether the linguistic features (such as *n*-less infinitives) are those of Hessen or Thuringia. Even this thesis has not gone unquestioned: Willy Sanders – linking the name Irmengart, which the Muslim princess and lover of Rudolf assumes upon her baptism, to a saint of the same name who enjoyed a regional popularity along the lower Rhine – has posited that the work originated in the Cologne area. The names of many of the protagonists – such as Gilot, Beatrise, Bonthard, and Bonifait – and a passage that speaks of a "walschen mile" (French mile) make it clear that the poem was based on a French source; but although some other works, such as the Anglo-Norman *Boeve de Haumtone* (circa 1200), share some names and motifs with *Graf Rudolf,* the exact source remains unclear. Attempts have been made to identify historical events and figures on which the poem may have been based. The battles around Askalon between 1131 and 1143 may have provided the foundation for corresponding portrayals in the poem, while the traitor Hugo von Puiset, who fled to Askalon, has been posited as the model for Rudolf.

Perhaps the greatest amount of scholarly debate has involved the dating of the poem. The work's first editor, Wilhelm Grimm, placed it between 1148, the year of the first Christian siege of Askalon – an event that is mentioned in the work – and 1187, when Jerusalem was conquered by Saladin, since some mention of this momentous conquest would have been made if the work had been written after that year. A more specific dating of the poem to around 1170 to 1173 has been made on the basis of another passage (Db 36), which says of the emperor:

man saget ioch svene in durste
so schenke ime ein riche kunic
der is kreftic unde vrumec,
der trage von ime die crone.

(One says that when he is thirsty,
he is poured wine by a rich king,
who is powerful and able,
and who has received from him his crown.)

If this mention of a king who serves as a cupbearer is a reference to contemporary history, then perhaps this passage is based on the Bohemian *Reichsschenken* (imperial cupbearers), a ceremonial office held by the rulers of Bohemia since 1127. A period before 1173 suggests itself as a date for the poem, since from 1173 to 1198 there was a prince of Bohemia but no king. It is possible that the rich king was Wladislaw II, who ruled from 1158 to 1173. Peter Ganz has drawn attention to weaknesses in this dating of the work, noting that the portrayal of kings as servants of emperors is frequently employed to symbolize the great power and prestige of the latter; it is, then, likely that the German poet simply took this element from the French original without intending any specific reference to the king of Bohemia. Even if a reference to this king was intended, Ganz observes, the poet might still speak of kings as pourers of wine after 1173 because of the prestige such a description confers upon the emperor, which was perhaps more important to the poet than historical accuracy.

A later date for the poem, after 1199, has been suggested by Friedrich Wentzlaff-Eggebert, who believes that the words of the pope at the beginning of the poem refer to the fall of Jerusalem in 1187, and

that the pope's call to all people, "arme unde riche" (rich and poor), corresponds to the Crusade initiated by Innocent II. On the basis of a passage portraying a magnificent imperial festival, Volker Schupp has posited that the poem must have been written after the festival of 1184 in Mainz. An earlier dating is suggested by the use of archaic words such as *degen* and *recke* (both terms mean "warrior"), which appear side by side with more modern and trendy words borrowed from the French, such as *hövescheit* (courtliness) and *mâze* (measure). This mixture of archaic and modern terminology seems to indicate an early transitional phase rather than a later attempt to make the work seem folksy. Although the date of composition of the poem is important for appraisal of it – is it far ahead of its time or a later and much less original work? – a consensus on this point will be difficult to achieve.

The plot of the story is difficult to piece together. The fragments are in poor condition; many words and lines are unreadable and in need of editorial conjecture. As preserved in the fragments the work begins in Rome with the pope receiving a message, presumably bearing bad news about the state of affairs in the Holy Land. The pope begins the Crusade by calling together rich and poor from far and wide and asking them to liberate the Holy Sepulcher:

her sprach "*mine* vil li*e*ben,
ich biete uch ander *sunnen*
durch die *heiligen himel w*nne
daz ir wollet ledigen daz *grab*
da got sel*be inne lach*."

(he spoke: "My dear sons,
I ask you
for the sake of heavenly joy
to liberate the grave
in which God Himself lay.")

This passage is exemplary of some of the difficulties posed by the work. The lines are difficult to read in their entirety, and their completion is based on conjecture (the restored illegible sections are in italics). As they stand, the lines clearly portray the Holy Sepulcher as being in the hands of the infidel. It is, therefore, surprising that the Christians encounter no resistance when they enter the Holy City, which seems to be firmly in the control of the Christian king of Jerusalem.

Subsequent fragments deal with the announcement of the Crusade at Rudolf's court, preparation by the women of the court for the young count's departure, and the arrival of the Christian army before the gates of Jerusalem, where they encounter not the resistance of a determined heathen enemy but a jubilant reception. Count Rudolf, although the youngest of the Christian nobles, volunteers to lead an expedition against the city of Askalon, which has been occupied by the infidels. A war of six months ensues, in which there are notable demonstrations of valor and many casualties on both sides. There is also ignoble behavior – particularly on the part of the Christian king, who scorches the land, killing women and children like cattle. In his description of these hostilities the poet is interested not in the state of mind of the hero, as will be the case in later court literature, but in such strategic and political machinations as one notable tactic employed by the Muslims: when their reserves are depleted, they deceive the Christians by placing women with shorn hair on the walls. After Rudolf arranges a truce, a festival is held in Jerusalem. In the course of his description of this festival the poet reveals that Rudolf's homeland is Flanders.

In the next fragment Rudolf is conversing with, and then in the arms of, an unidentified woman, who is probably the daughter of the sultan Halap. It would seem that Rudolf, for unknown reasons, has turned his back on the Christian king, has granted his services to the Muslims, and has fallen in love with the daughter of his new lord. The sultan refuses the Christian king's request to have Rudolf delivered to him with his hands bound. Battles between the Muslims and Christians result from this refusal; Rudolf now fights among the ranks of the former, although it is noted that he does not fight with the edge of his sword: "mit vlacheme sverte / sluch er uf die cristenheit" (with the broad side of his sword / he attacked the Christians). The last fragments depict the baptism of the princess, the escape of the wounded Rudolf – described in agonizingly minute detail – from some unspecified form of captivity, and the heroic death of a young man named Bonifait, who had been entrusted to the count's supervision. The end of the work might

have portrayed the return of Rudolf and his converted wife to Flanders and their happy life there.

The work is free of the ideological fanaticism frequently associated with the Crusades. The poet is not troubled by the spiritual implications of a Christian count fighting in the army of a heathen against a Christian king. The oft-noted realism may be a by-product of this independence from concerns of a religious kind, as Wolfgang Mohr's appraisal of the poet suggests: "sein Blick ist erstaunlich wenig durch Heilswahrheiten beschränkt, und er kann die Dinge sehen, wie sie sind" (his view is astonishingly free of concern about the truths of salvation, and he can see things as they are). Whatever the circumstances that led to its production, *Graf Rudolf* is a work that was ahead of its time.

## References:

Johann Bethmann, *Untersuchungen über die mittelhochdeutsche Dichtung vom Grafen Rudolf* (Berlin: Palaestra, 1904);

Peter Ganz, "Graf Rudolf," in *Die deutsche Literatur des Mittelalters: Verfasserlexikon,* edited by Kurt Ruh, volume 3, no. 1 (Berlin: De Gruyter, 1987), cols. 212–216;

Stephen J. Kaplowitt, "The Non-literary Sources of *Graf Rudolf:* A Re-evaluation," *Studies in Philology,* 66 (July 1969): 584–608;

Wolfgang Mohr, "Zum frühhöfischen Menschenbild in *Graf Rudolf*," *Zeitschrift für deutsches Altertum,* 96, no. 2 (1967): 97–109;

Kurt Ruh, *Höfische Epik des deutschen Mittelalters,* volume 1 (Berlin: Schmidt, 1967), pp. 64–69;

Willy Sanders, "Zur Heimatsbestimmung des *Graf Rudolf, Zeitschrift für deutsches Altertum,* 95 (February 1966): 122–149;

Volker Schupp, "Zur Datierung des *Graf Rudolf*," *Zeitschrift für deutsches Altertum,* 97 (March 1968): 37–56;

Friedrich Wentzlaff-Eggebert, *Kreuzzugsdichtung des Mittelalters* (Berlin: De Gruyter, 1960), pp. 123–128.

# Heliand

(circa 850)

Anatoly Liberman
*University of Minnesota*

**Manuscripts:** C, Codex Cottonianus, British Museum, Cotton Caligula A. VII, probably from the tenth century, 5,968 lines divided into numbered chapters, or so-called fitts. M, Codex Monacensis, Munich, Bayrische Staatsbibliothek, Cgm 25, probably of the ninth century; it is incomplete. There are also two fragments that are independent of C and M and of each other: P, the Prague fragment, now in Berlin, Museum für Deutsche Geschichte, D 56/446, lines 958b – 1006a; V, Codex Vaticanus, Pal. lat. 1447, lines 1279–1358, as well as part of the Old Saxon *Genesis.* Both fragments are approximately contemporaneous with M.

**First publication:** *Heliand oder Die altsächsische Evangelien-Harmonie. Erste Lieferung: Text,* edited by J. Andreas Schmeller (Munich, Stuttgart & Tübingen: Cotta, 1830).

**Standard editions:** *Heliand,* edited by Eduard Sievers (Halle: Waisenhaus, 1878); *Heliand,* edited by Otto Behaghel, Altdeutsche Bibliothek, no. 4 (Halle: Niemeyer, 1882; reprinted, edited by Burkhard Taeger, Halle: Niemeyer, 1984).

**Editions in English:** Translated by Mariana Scott as *The Heliand: Translated from the Old Saxon* (Chapel Hill: University of North Carolina Press, 1966); translated by G. Ronald Murphy as *The Heliand: The Saxon Gospel* (New York & Oxford: Oxford University Press, 1992).

The longest extant (almost complete) text of the *Heliand* (circa 850), manuscript C, comprises about 6,000 lines; for comparison, the Old English *Beowulf* has 3,182 lines, the Middle High German *Nibelungenlied* (Song of the Nibelungs, circa 1220) more than 9,000. The *Heliand* (the title is Old Saxon for "Savior") recounts the life of Jesus. Most people who read this epic in the original react instinctively to the poet's ability to create mood, conjure up vivid scenes, and produce memorable descriptions. No amount of philological admiration can make up for the inherent boredom of Otfried von Weißenburg's *Evangelienbuch* (Gospel Book, between 863 and 871) or the Middle English *Ormulum,* but the *Heliand* belongs with *Beowulf,* the *Nibelungenlied,* and the Middle English *Sir Gawain and the Green Knight* (circa 1370): it is not a mere versified text to be explored and used for the compilation of grammars and compendia but a piece of literature, even though scholars, preoccupied with other problems, have seldom studied it as a work of art.

One such problem is the origin of the *Heliand.* The only possible reference to the work in older literature occurs in two Latin prefaces: *Praefatio in librum antiquum Saxonica lingua conscriptum* (Preface to a Compilation of Books in the Ancient Saxon Language) in prose; and *Versus de poeta et interprete huius codicis* (A Poem on the Poet and the Interpreter of This Work), in verse. According to the prose preface "Ludouuicus pijssimus Augustus," intent on promoting true religion and healthy minds among his subjects, commissioned a man of Saxon extraction known among his countrymen as a singer or poet "non ignobilis Vates" (of no mean repute *or* of noble origin) to narrate the Old and New Testaments in poetic form "in germanicam linguam" (in a Germanic language) so that not only the literate but also the uneducated would have exposure to the Scripture. The man obeyed willingly, for he had been advised by Heaven to do so. He began with the Creation, selected the most important facts, and added exegesis; the task was fulfilled in a truly masterful way. He divided his work into "vitteas" (fitts), that is, sections, corresponding to *lectiones* or *sententias.* The verse preface tells the story of the poet. He was a herdsman; in a dream a voice instructed him to narrate the sacral history and the dogmata in a language that would do justice to the

*Page from manuscript P for the* Heliand *(Berlin, Museum für Deutsche Geschichte, D 56/466)*

occasion. And he told the story of the Five Ages and the Advent of Christ, who rescued the world from hell by his blood.

The prefaces were published in 1562 by Matthias Flaccius Illyricus in the second edition of his *Catalogus testium veritatis* (Catalogue of the Testimonies of Truth). Flaccius Illyricus did not specify where he had found the texts. The origin of the prefaces, as well as their relation to each other and to the *Heliand* and the Old Saxon *Genesis,* is unknown. A detailed report by Paul Metzenthin (1922) denied the relevance of the prefaces to the *Heliand.* Willy Krogmann's more detailed survey (1948) had the opposite goal: Krogmann had no doubt that the work described in the prefaces was the *Heliand,* and he also attempted to reconstruct their history.

Only one point is incontestable: the prefaces are genuine documents of the Carolingian epoch, not a sixteenth-century fraud. They can, however, refer to an Old Saxon Bible harmony only if their author had before him the *Genesis* and the *Heliand,* for the *Heliand* is not the history of the world from its creation to its rescue from hell but deals only with the life of Jesus. Nor does it have much to offer in the way of dogma and exegesis. The Latin of the prose preface is awkward in some places while the surrounding sentences are irreproachable, and interpolations were suspected from the first. The verse preface's story of a divinely inspired herdsman who became a poet is reminiscent of the legend of Caedmon, an Old English poet whose hymn glorifying the Creator is extant, but it contradicts the tale of "a singer of no mean repute" or "of noble origin." Also, Old Saxon poetry does not seem to reflect any medieval Low German idiom, yet the goal of the harmony was supposed to be to familiarize the uneducated with the Holy Writ. There are several other questions and incongruities, such as: what is the *lingua germanica* chosen as the *Saxon* poet's language?

It appears that the author of the prefaces had access to an Old Saxon manuscript that is now lost. Flaccius Illyricus cannot have seen this manuscript; if he had, he would have given a description of it. For the prefaces to furnish a clue to the *Heliand,* their inconsistencies and stylistic infelicities must be edited away (both Krogmann and Eduard Sievers give their versions of the prose preface as it allegedly looked before the interpolator tampered with it). According to prevailing opinion, Ludouuicus pijssimus Augustus is Louis the Pious, who died in 840. But Richard Drögereit pointed out that Ludwig the German (843–876), an East Frankish king, could have been meant; this theory changes the ter-

minus a quo and the terminus ad quem of the poem, though both remain in the ninth century. If the prefaces are not related to the *Heliand,* the dating of the poem must be based only on internal evidence.

A modern investigator is unable to determine the native dialect of the *Heliand* poet, to locate the monastery at which the poem was written, or to define its audience in linguistic terms. The *Heliand* uses vowels and grammatical forms that belong to Saxon, Frisian, Franconian, and High German. Two types of hypotheses have been offered to account for the mixed language in the *Heliand:* first, that there must have been a place in which such a strange language was spoken; second, that the *Heliand* uses an artificial language created for the purposes of poetry.

The best-known proponent of the first approach was Ferdinand Wrede, who, by using the principles of linguistic geography, placed the *Heliand* in northern Thuringia, in the vicinity of Merseburg. Gertrud Geffcken, Wrede's early follower, discovered no words in the poem that would tie it unambiguously to one locality, though nothing in her findings contradicts Wrede's reconstruction. Anneliese Bretschneider passionately defended Wrede's general idea, but she paid special attention to the Franconian features in the *Heliand* and assigned the poem to Magdeburg. In her words, almost every modern Germanic scholar "hat es im Gefühl" (has the gut feeling) that the *Heliand* belongs to southern Ostphalia; this assertion is a strong overstatement.

According to the second approach, which has a long prehistory in Homeric and Germanic studies, the *Heliand* was produced at the height of a long tradition; it is so elaborate that even a thousand years later one discerns in its form, as in the form of *Beowulf,* traces of decadence (often referred to as "mannerisms"). The poet must have had countless predecessors, "singers of tales," who had extolled the virtues and heroic feats of Germanic chieftains and their retainers. A poetic tradition of such excellence sometimes presupposes a so-called koine, that is, a more-or-less artificial language combining various dialects and avoiding the peculiarities that are not understood outside of small areas. Such was, presumably, the Greek of the *Iliad.* The language of the great Middle High German poets has also been characterized as a koine, but Old High German poetry poses insuperable difficulties because some works from that period were recorded in "mixed dialects." According to Hermann Collitz, the language of the *Heliand* is "a mere literary and artificial mixture of dialects, similar to the combination of Low

Franconian with Middle High German in [Heinrich von] Veldeke's poetry, or to that of Aeolic with Ionic and other Greek dialects in the Homeric poems." Erik Rooth believed that, whatever the *Heliand* poet's native dialect might have been, he created with the help of Franconian orthography a new written language for the Saxons. (A parallel would be Norwegian spelled according to the rules of Danish orthography.) According to Walther Mitzka, the *Heliand* is a relic of an elevated language used all over the Germanic-speaking world at court, in religious services, and on other ceremonial occasions. Wrede's term *Biblical Saxon* might suggest that, regardless of his attempts to locate the place of composition of *Heliand,* he considered the possibility of approaching Old Saxon poetry from a similar angle; but to him the concept of Biblical Saxon was akin to that of Biblical Greek or Biblical Gothic: it did not presuppose a koine or language different in principle from that of a certain geographical area.

The monasteries that have most often been named in connection with the *Heliand* are Werden, on the Ruhr in southwestern Westphalia, and Fulda. In Rooth's opinion, the *Heliand* poet worked at Fulda; many others have held similar views, though there is a difference between recognizing the influence of Fulda on the poet and seeing him compose his work there. As J. Knight Bostock put it, "if two languages as different as those of the *Tatian* [circa 830] and the *Heliand* were being written at the same monastery at approximately the same time, it is difficult to see what standards can be established at all." The first to suggest Werden as the home of the *Heliand* was its first editor, Andreas Schmeller, and Krogmann and Drögereit have adduced weighty arguments in support of Schmeller's conjecture. In 1937 Krogmann brought out a book, half of which is devoted to the words *(h)leia* (rock, stone) and *pascha* (Easter). *Lei,* the modern reflex of *leia,* is still remembered because of such names as *von der Leyen* and *Lorelei* (literally, "roaring rock"). In present-day German *lei* is not used north of the Rhenish Slate Mountains (*Schiefergebirge*), and *pascha* (in contradistinction to *ostara*) was mainly current in the archdiocese of Cologne. Krogmann concluded that the *Heliand* must have been composed by someone who lived in the angle formed by the Rhine and Ruhr rivers. Paleographic evidence also points in the direction of Werden.

Some of the arguments traditionally used to determine the provenance of the *Heliand* deal with the vocabulary of the poem, others with its phonetic aspects (especially *g* versus *j* and *k,* and diphthongs versus monophthongs). Scholars have tried to find

an area where the language of the *Heliand* could have sounded natural (this is how Merseburg and Magdeburg happened to be likely sites for the composition of the *Heliand*) or a monastery at which the poet could have had access to all his putative sources. Those interested in cultural connections between the Old Saxons and medieval Europe tend to choose Fulda as an ideal environment for the *Heliand,* but Drögereit showed that the considerations brought forward in favor of the Fulda theory are shaky or too general to carry conviction. Much attention has been spent on the poet's treatment of the biblical landscape, social institutions (such as paying tribute), material culture, and industry (such as obtaining salt by evaporation of seawater). For example, he is fond of sea scenes: whenever an opportunity offers to describe fishermen, sand on the shore, a storm, and the like, he uses it to the full, which suggests that the poem was meant for seafaring people. The poet's "liberties" are also telling: thus, when the Gospels mention wheat, he substitutes rye.

Unfortunately, these findings often contradict one another. One looks for a speaker of Old Saxon who had a full command of the dialect of the Slate Mountains; was influenced by the usage of the archdiocese of Cologne; wrote in a mixture of Old Saxon, Old Frisian, Old Franconian, and Old High German; grew up on the shore or was at least taken for a native on the coast populated by the Saxons (though most inhabitants of coastal areas were Frisians); followed the paleography of the Werden scriptorium; and reflected the attitudes of great Fulda teachers. These are only a few of the requirements the *Heliand* poet must meet to satisfy modern scholars. Predictably, the home of the *Heliand* has never been found; in addition to Werden, Fulda, Merseburg, and Magdeburg, such locations as Münster, Paderborn, Corvey, Utrecht, Hamburg, Halberstadt, Bremen, and the mouth of the Loire have been suggested, and there have been attempts to combine elements of different theories: for example, that the poem was written in Franconian and translated into Old Saxon, or was started at one monastery and finished at another. It is true that only copies of the *Heliand* by unknown scribes, not the poet's copy, are extant, but comparison of manuscripts M, C, and the fragments proves that mixed forms were present in the original text.

In regard to the poet's sources, since the appearance of books by Ernst Windisch (1868) and C. W. M. Grein (1869) it has been recognized that the *Heliand* is in the main based on the *Tatian.* It appears that the *Heliand* is independent of the

Latin version of this gospel harmony produced at Fulda, which accords well with the fact that even the German translation of the *Tatian* corresponds to neither the accompanying Latin nor the Fulda Latin text. For the appreciation of the *Heliand,* however, it is less important to discover the text that supplied the poet with his material than to understand his background.

It is commonly believed that the *Heliand* poet read a good deal of exegetic literature and knew some apocryphal legends, but there is a marked discrepancy between the poet's supposed use of sophisticated writings and the many blunders he makes in referring to both Testaments. Several scholars (notably Franz Jostes and Wilhelm Bruckner) believed that such blunders betray a layman, but it is hard to imagine a lay author of the *Heliand* and even harder to believe that the work was a collaboration between the poet and a "professional" adviser. On the other hand, it is indeed puzzling how someone allegedly steeped in Hrabanus Maurus's commentary on Matthew and in the writings of Bede and Alcuin – that is, a seasoned theologian with a taste for subtleties of interpretation – failed to learn rather elementary facts from the Bible. The *Heliand* was, therefore, probably composed by a cleric but hardly by a scholar.

For years the one unassailable truth about the *Heliand* was its dependence on Old English poetry. Since the *Heliand* poet was believed to have made use of Hrabanus's commentary and to have worked at Fulda, the English hypothesis gained credibility, for Hrabanus was a pupil of the Englishman Alcuin. This "truth" was called into question in 1958 by Dietrich Hofmann, who pointed out that the *Heliand* presupposes a developed tradition of Old Saxon lay poetry and that impulses often went from, rather than to, the Continent. Little has been done to substantiate the second part of Hofmann's idea, but the traditional notion can no longer be taken for granted.

Even if the Latin preface published by Flaccius Illyricus refers to the *Heliand,* it is not known whether the poem was meant for a predominantly Christian audience or for prospective converts. To a modern reader versed in old literature, the *Heliand* contains many echoes of Germanic heroic poetry, and this effect must have been much stronger in the ninth century. The first investigators of the *Heliand* treated it as a Christian version of older Germanic poetry. The tone was set by A. F. C. Vilmar in 1845; the questions he raised remain at the center of *Heliand* scholarship, though the attitude toward medieval Germanic poetry has changed radically since 1845. At present the Christian element in the *Heliand* is viewed as its inalienable core.

With regard to the relations between the *Heliand* and older poetry, scholars have discussed two subjects in especially great detail: Christ as a pseudo-Germanic chieftain surrounded by loyal retainers, and fate – *metod* or *wurd* – as an active force in the lives of human beings. The Christian Germanic poets filled traditional words and formulas with new meanings, however, and scholars are often misled by associations stemming from etymology and are prone to Germanize medieval texts more than their authors did.

The very term *Germanization* is unfortunate. The *Heliand* poet does not try to falsify the spirit of the Gospels; he only stresses similarities between the mores as they appear in the Bible and those known to him and avoids scenes that could have ruined his mission. He describes the birth of John the Baptist and recounts (with many embellishments) the discussion of the name giving, but he does not mention the circumcision. Likewise, he does not say that Jesus entered Jerusalem on an ass, for he wants the story to arouse reverence, not obscene laughter or puzzlement. But he follows the interpretation of the New Testament – be it the role of Peter or predestination – as he learned it from his ninth-century teachers, whoever they may have been. He was not a singer of Eddic tales on biblical themes. G. Ronald Murphy's attempt to discover in the *Heliand* subtle allusions to the plight of the vanquished Saxons and Germanic myths is not convincing enough to change the prevalent opinion.

The centuries that have passed since the creation of the *Heliand* make it difficult to approach the poem as a work of art. A few dissertations and articles (of which only Andreas Heusler's 1920 work is still widely read) that analyze parallelisms, meter, and alliteration and scattered remarks in articles and monographs devoted to other subjects are all that *Heliand* scholarship has to offer students of the style of the poem. Contemporary narratology tends to search for the inner coherence of poems, romances, and sagas – whence the attention lavished on digressions in *Beowulf* – but the simple narrative line of the *Heliand* would hardly be the source of great discoveries; only the prominent place occupied by the Sermon on the Mount is immediately noticeable.

The most ambitious attempt to disclose a unifying principle of composition in the *Heliand* is Johannes Rathofer's endeavor to prove that a rigid numerical principle underlies the poem's structure. His hypothesis met with well-argued opposition from Krogmann and Burkhard Taeger. But even if Rathofer's case were stronger, his conclusions would not explain the appeal of the *Heliand* (to the extent that such things can be "explained"): the poem is too long to be read straight through from beginning to end, so its attractiveness must have been based on something other than number symbolism and the like. The artistry of the *Heliand* is, instead, to be sought in its language, rhythm, choice of details, calculated contrasts, and the structure of separate episodes, however imposing the architectonic of the entire edifice may be.

## Bibliography:

Johanna Belkin and Jürgen Meier, *Bibliographie zu Otfrid von Weißenburg und zur altsächsischen Bibeldichtung (Heliand und Genesis)*, Bibliographien zur deutschen Literatur des Mittelalters, no. 7 (Berlin: Schmidt, 1975).

## References:

J. Knight Bostock, *A Handbook on Old High German Literature*, second edition, edited by K. C. King and D. R. McLintock (Oxford: Clarendon Press, 1976);

Anneliese Bretschneider, *Die Heliandheimat und ihre sprachgeschichtliche Entwicklung*, Deutsche Dialektgeographie, no. 30 (Marburg: Elwert, 1934);

Wilhelm Bruckner, *Der Helianddichter ein Laie* (Basel: Reinhardt, Universitäts-Buchdruckerei, 1904);

Hermann Collitz, "The Home of the *Heliand*," *PMLA*, 16, no. 1 (1901): 123–140;

Richard Drögereit, *Werden und der Heliand: Studien zur Kulturgeschichte der Abtei Werden* (Essen: Fredebeul & Koenen, 1951);

Jürgen Eichhoff and Irmengard Rauch, eds., *Der Heliand*, Wege der Forschung, no. 321 (Darmstadt: Wissenschaftliche Buchgesellschaft, 1973);

William Foerste, "Otfrids literarisches Verhältnis zum Heliand," *Niederdeutsches Jahrbuch*, 71–73 (1950): 40–67;

Gertrud Geffcken, *Der Wortschatz des Heliand und seine Bedeutung für die Heimatfrage* (Marburg: Friedrich, 1912);

Hulda Göhler, "Das Christusbild in Otfrids Evangelienbuch und im Heliand," *Zeitschrift für deutsche Philologie*, 59 (1935): 1–52;

C. W. M. Grein, *Heliandstudien I: Die Quellen des Heliand. Nebst einem Anhang: Tatians Evangelienharmonie herausgegeben nach dem Codex Casselanus* (Cassel: Kay, 1869);

Albrecht Hagenlocher, *Schicksal im Heliand: Verwendung und Bedeutung der nominalen Bezeichnungen*, Niederdeutsche Studien, no. 21 (Cologne & Vienna: Böhlau, 1975);

Kurt Hannemann, "Die Lösung des Rätsels der Herkunft der Heliandpraefatio," *Forschungen und Fortschritte*, 15 (1939): 327–329;

Wolfgang Haubrichs, "Die Praefatio des Heliand: Ein Zeugnis der Religions- und Bildungspolitik Ludwigs des Deutschen," *Niederdeutsches Jahrbuch*, 89 (1966): 7–32;

Andreas Heusler, "Heliand, Liedstil und Epenstil," *Zeitschrift für deutsches Altertum und deutsche Literatur*, 57 (1920): 1–48; reprinted in his *Kleine Schriften*, volume 2, edited by Stefan Sonderegger (Berlin: De Gruyter, 1969), pp. 517–565;

Dietrich Hofmann, "Die altsächsische Bibelepik ein Ableger der angelsächsischen geistlichen Epik?," *Zeitschrift für deutsches Altertum und deutsche Literatur*, 89 (1959): 173–190;

Franz Jostes, "Der Dichter des Heliand," *Zeitschrift für deutsches Altertum und deutsche Literatur*, 40 (1896): 341–368;

Jostes, *Die Heimat des Heliand*, Forschungen und Funde, nos. 3 and 4 (Münster: Aschendorf, 1912);

Willy Krogmann, *Absicht oder Willkür im Aufbau des Heliand* (Hamburg: Wittig, 1964);

Krogmann, *Die Heimatfrage des Heliand im Lichte des Wortschatzes* (Wismar: Hinstorff, 1937);

Krogmann, "Die Praefatio in Librum Antiquum Lingua Saxonica Conscriptum," *Niederdeutsches Jahrbuch*, 69–70 (1948): 141–163;

Paul Metzenthin, "Die Heimat der Adressaten des Heliand," *Journal of English and Germanic Philology*, 21, no. 2 (1922): 191–228; no. 3 (1922): 457–506;

Walther Mitzka, "Die Sprache des Heliand und die altsächsische Stammesverfassung," *Niederdeutsches Jahrbuch*, 71–72 (1950): 31–39;

G. Ronald Murphy, *The Saxon Savior: The Germanic Transformation of the Gospel in the Ninth-Century Heliand* (New York & Oxford: Oxford University Press, 1989);

Johannes Rathofer, *Der Heliand: Theologischer Sinn als tektonische Form. Vorbereitung und Grundlegung der Interpretation* (Cologne & Graz: Böhlau, 1962);

Rathofer, "Zum Aufbau des Heliand," *Zeitschrift für deutsches Altertum und deutsche Literatur*, 93 (1964): 239–272;

Erik Rooth, "Zum Heliandproblem," in *Studia Germanica: Festschrift E. A. Kock* (Lund, Sweden: Blom, 1934), pp. 289–304;

Heinz Rupp, "Der Heliand: Hauptanliegen seines Dichters," *Der Deutschunterricht,* 8 (1956): 28–45;

Burkhard Taeger, *Zahlensymbolik bei Hraban, bei Hincmar und im Heliand?: Studien zur Zahlensymbolik im Frühmittelalter,* Münchener Texte und Untersuchungen zur deutschen Literatur des Mittelalters, no. 30 (Munich: Beck, 1970);

A. F. C. Vilmar, *Deutsche Altertümer im Hêliand als einkleidung der evangelischen geschichte: Beiträge zur erklärung des altsächsichen Hêliand und zur innern geschichte der einführung des christentums in Deutschland* (Marburg: Elwert, 1845);

Carl A. Weber, "Der Dichter des Heliand im Verhältnis zu seinen Quellen," *Zeitschrift für deutsches Altertum und deutsche Literatur,* 64 (1927): 1–76;

Juw von Weringha, *Heliand und Diatessaron,* Studia Germanica, no. 5 (Assen: Van Gorcum, 1965);

Ernst Windisch, *Der Heliand und seine Quellen* (Leipzig: Vogel, 1868);

Ferdinand Wrede, "Die Heimat der altsächsischen Bibeldichtung," *Zeitschrift für deutsches Altertum und deutsche Literatur,* 43 (1899): 333–360; reprinted in his *Kleine Schriften,* Deutsche Dialektgeographie, no. 60 (Marburg: Elwert, 1899).

# Das Hildebrandslied

## (circa 820)

### Brian Murdoch
*University of Stirling*

**Manuscript:** The work is preserved (incomplete) on the front and back pages (1r and 76v) of a collection of ecclesiastical writings in Kassel, Landesbibliothek, Cod. theol. fol. 54. Facsimile: In Hanns Fischer, *Schrifttafeln zum althochdeutschen Lesebuch* (Tübingen: Niemeyer, 1966), pp. 12–13.

**First publication:** J. G. Eckhart, *Commentarii de rebus Franciæ* (Würzburg: Magenav, 1729).

**Standard editions:** In *Denkmäler deutscher Poesie und Prosa aus dem VIII.–XII. Jahrhundert,* edited by K. Müllenhoff and W. Scherer, third edition, edited by Elias von Steinmeyer (Berlin: Weidmann, 1892); in *Die kleineren althochdeutschen Sprachdenkmäler,* edited by Steinmeyer (Berlin: Weidmann, 1916); in Georg Baesecke, *Das Hildebrandslied: Eine geschichtliche Einleitung für Laien, mit Lichtbildern der Hs., alt- und neuhochdeutschen Texten* (Halle: Niemeyer, 1945); in Siegfried Gutenbrunner, *Von Hildebrand und Hadubrand* (Heidelberg: Winter, 1976), pp. 11–33; in *Althochdeutsches Lesebuch,* edited by Wilhelm Braune, sixteenth edition, edited by Ernst Ebbinghaus (Tübingen: Niemeyer, 1979).

**Editions in modern German:** in *Älteste deutsche Dichtungen,* edited by Karl Wolfskehl and Friedrich von der Leyen (Frankfurt am Main: Insel, 1964), pp. 6–9; in *Deutsche Balladen,* edited by Konrad Nussbacher (Stuttgart: Reclam, 1967), pp. 3–8; in *Althochdeutsche Literatur,* edited by Horst Dieter Schlosser (Frankfurt am Main: Fischer, 1970), pp. 264–267; in *Älteste deutsche Dichtung und Prosa,* edited by Heinz Mettke (Leipzig: Reclam, 1976), pp. 78–83.

**Editions in English:** Translated by Bruce Dickins, in *Runic and Heroic Poems of the Old Teutonic Peoples* (Cambridge: Cambridge University Press, 1915), pp. 78–85; translated by Brian Murdoch as "From the Old High German: *Hildebrand,*" *Lines Review* (Edinburgh), 109 (June 1989): 20–22.

The author of *Das Hildebrandslied* (The Lay of Hildebrand, circa 820) is not known, nor is it known why it was written down on the blank front and back pages of a Latin manuscript from the monastery of Fulda in northern Germany in the early ninth century. Its immediate origin is also unknown, although the extant version clearly stands at the end of a long and complex process of transmission. It is incomplete; the story lacks the last few lines, although it is not difficult to reconstruct what is missing. It is written in an impossible mixture of High and Low German because someone has tried, but failed, to translate a High German original into Low German. This feature presents less of a problem for understanding the work than does its incompleteness and the misplacement of some lines toward the end. The poem, thus, requires a certain amount of editorial work before it is readable, but it then emerges not only as the sole surviving example in Old High German of a heroic warrior poem in alliterative verse – a genre that survives far more fully in Anglo-Saxon and Old Norse – but also as an extremely well-presented and tightly told narrative that deals with universal problems.

The story is simple and is told mostly in dialogue between the two protagonists. Two groups of warriors face each other, and from each a champion comes forward to fight in single combat. The winner will be entitled to the armor and battle gear of the other. Although the two armies do not play an active role in the narrative, they are always present and should never be forgotten: they are the social background that forces each man to fight, whether he wants to or not. Finally, the two champions are father and son; the audience of the poem knows the situation, but neither the champions nor their armies are aware of it at the beginning. The two champions parley before the combat, and Hildebrand realizes that Hadubrand is his son when Hadubrand tells him that his father was called Hildebrand, that he was a great warrior, and that he had fled with Dietrich (Theoderic) from the wrath of Odoacer, leaving a bride and a baby. This information has come to him from people who are now dead, and passing sailors have told him that Hildebrand died in battle.

Hildebrand tells his son who he is and offers him a token of friendship:

want her do ar arme   wuntana bauga,
cheisuringu gitan,   so imo se der chuning gap,
Huneo truhtin. . . . (lines 33–35)

(He took from his arm   a torque of twisted gold,
of imperial gold   given him by the king,
lord of the Huns. . . .)

It is significant that the narrator speaks these lines, since the protagonists are usually left to speak for themselves; only the scene setting at the start and the battle at the end are fully in the hands of an objective narrator. After telling the audience in line 4 that the pair are father and son (using the single Old High German word *sunufaturungo*) the poem launches almost at once into dialogue. Thus the description of the arm ring is shown to be crucial in the work. Apparently Hildebrand has fought, under Theoderic's command, for the Huns and has been rewarded for his bravery. But Hadubrand assumes that the older man is trying to throw him off his guard and that, since he is wearing Hunnish gold, he *is* a Hun who has survived so long only because he cheats in this way. Hadubrand's response is a sharp one:

mit geru scal man   geba infahan,
ort widar orte. ( lines 37–38)

(you should take such gifts   with a spear
point against point.)

He accuses Hildebrand of trying to trick him and (if a textual emendation is correct) goes on to say that Hildebrand can never have been the exile he claims to be. Hildebrand realizes that his situation and the presence of the silent watchers and listeners give him no choice; he will have to fight, either killing his son or being killed by him. Almost with a shrug, he bows to the inevitable:

welaga nu, waltant got . . . wewurt skihit ( line 49)

(alas, God above . . . cruel fate will take its course)[.]

The son reinforces his rejection of the trickery of this supposed Hun by restating, rather than surmising, that his father is dead, killed in battle, since the sailors had told him so. Once the older man realizes the impossibility of identifying himself to his son, he comments that only the most cowardly of the Eastern people — a reference to the Huns, perhaps — would refuse to fight, and the battle has to begin. Once again, as so often before, the only way Hildebrand can prove who he is — Hildebrand, the most famous warrior — is by fighting, and this time he has to do so by killing his only son. He can prove his identity only by destroying his family line. The winner in such a contest would have the right to take the armor from his dead adversary, and there is a massive irony in the father's final words: that the son can take his armor if he has any right to it, for the son has a legal right to the old man's belongings once Hildebrand is dead, but he now stands to obtain this inheritance by unknowingly killing his father. He speculates that this feat should be easy for the son, since he — Hildebrand — is so old. These words are the most poignant of the whole work, in which there are several expressions of the role of tragic necessity.

The poem breaks off in the midst of a brief (since the various stages are covered quickly) and somewhat stylized battle description. Some critics have taken the piece to be self-contained and not a fragment at all; at all events, it is not primarily a battle poem. Although theoretically various conclusions are possible — death of the son, death of the father, death of both men, or some kind of mediation that stops the fight — only the first fits into the context of the work. The story of the father/son conflict is an archetype in world literature — the best-known examples are the death of Sohrab in battle with Rustum in the Persian epic, known in English through Matthew Arnold's 1853 poem, and the killing of his son by Cuchullain in the Old Irish tale — and almost invariably ends this way, even though a thirteenth-century German version, the so-called *Jüngeres Hildebrandslied* (Later Lay of Hildebrand), has a reconciliation brought about by the mother. For the son to kill the father would be tragic, but not a tragedy, because the son has no reason to believe that this man is his father and is convinced that he has a Hun as an opponent. The pair could kill each other, but for the poem to end with a double death would be horror, not tragedy. Hildebrand clearly kills his son, his actual posterity, so that his reputation can live on. A series of strophes attached to a manuscript of the Old Norse *Saga of Asmund* and known in German as "Hildebrand's Sterbelied" (Death Song of Hildebrand) refers to the speaker's having killed his son, his own heir, against his will. That he is the greatest of warriors has at the last told against him; the gifts of the gods are always two-edged. The only thing that mitigates the tragedy is the one thing that — according to another Old

First page of the manuscript for the Hildebrandslied *(Kassel, Landesbibliothek, Cod. theol. fol. 54)*

Norse poem, the *Havamal* (Words of the High One) — does not die: the reputation of the warrior. The real inheritance left by Hildebrand is the *Hildebrandslied* itself, the song composed after the battle.

The monastery had Anglo-Saxon connections, which perhaps accounts for the use of Anglo-Saxon characters in the text (most notably the runic sign for *w*). The *Hildebrandslied* was probably written down in the third or fourth decade of the ninth century, seemingly by two different scribes, at Fulda. That the language was originally Old High German and that the attempt was made to adapt it into Low German (and not vice versa) was established only after years of scholarly debate when it was noted that one part alliterates only in Old High German. Furthermore, the extant text is clearly a copy of a written work, not a transcription of an oral one: when the scribe wrote the name Deotrihhe (Theoderic) in line 26 his eye obviously went back to the last occurrence of the name, in line 23, and he repeated a few words from that line.

The basic verse form is the heroic alliterative long line, found in Old Norse and Anglo-Saxon on a far greater scale than in Old High German, where there are only a few examples and where the form soon gave way to the Latin-influenced end-rhyming verse demonstrated so fully in Otfried von Weißenburg's *Evangelienbuch* (Gospel Book, between 863 and 871). The Germanic alliterative long line falls into two parts, with a strong caesura, and each half line typically contains two strong beats. The first beat of the second half line is the most important, and it carries the alliteration; that is, at least one and sometimes both of the strong beats in the first half line will begin with the same sound (an identical consonant or group of consonants, or any vowel alliterating with others). The final strong beat of the whole line rarely alliterates. The form is a regular and forceful one, and the weight of sense placed on the first strong beat of the second half is considerable:

mit *gé*ru scál man *gé*ba infáhan

(literally: with a spear should one gifts accept)[.]

The poem also uses formulas — set phrases that fit the meter and are convenient to use when no major point is being made. Some of the description of the arming of the two men and of the battle is told in lines that can be matched in Anglo-Saxon or Old Norse, and Hildebrand's asking the younger man about his father contains phrases used by Otfried

for the Devil's attempt to find out who Christ is. Some lines are repeated within the work itself.

In the version that has survived many lines are corrupt, parts seem to be missing or have been changed, and additions have been made. Just when these modifications were made is not known, nor is it known precisely when the translation into Low German was attempted. Any assertions about the earlier stages of the poem have to be speculative, since this is the only version in existence. Although some critics have insisted on keeping the text exactly as it stands, one particular editorial problem needs noting. Most of the poem is in dialogue, the speeches of the father alternating with those of the son. At one point, however, this alternation seems confused. Hadubrant says that his father is definitely dead (line 43):

tot ist Hiltibrant,   Heribrantes suno

(dead is Hildebrand,   Heribrand's son)[.]

The next line is a repeated formula that underscores, with the alliteration and the similar names (Heribrant, Hiltibrant, Hadubrant), the family relationship that is the point of the piece:

Hiltibrant gimahalta   Heribrantes suno

(Hildebrand spoke,   Heribrand's son)[.]

The placing is effective, but Hildebrand now apparently says that he can see from his adversary's armor that he has never been an exile. If this is really Hildebrand speaking, it is rather self-pitying; the argument has been made that these words really belong to Hadubrand and are part of his expression of disbelief that the man he sees before him can be his exiled father. Indeed, the line that follows this brief speech inserts, in addition to the somewhat anomalous reference to God, a metrically impossible indication of the fact that this is still Hildebrand speaking, as if the scribe or his predecessor realized at this point that things were confused. Just how the lines should be rearranged has never been established, but the comments on exile do look as if they should be spoken by the son and not the father.

The poem clearly has a long ancestry. The names Theoderic (Dietrich) and Odoacer (Ottokar) and the reference to the king of the Huns (Attila) place the story into the context of the Goths in the fifth century. The Goths, a Germanic tribe in southeastern Europe, were divided into two groups. The Visigoths (West Goths) moved westward and eventually took Rome. By the end of the fifth century

Rome was under the rule of Odoacer. He was killed in 493 at Ravenna by the Ostrogoths (East Goths) under Theoderic; a generation earlier the Ostrogoths had been allied with the Huns under Attila. Theoderic ruled the western part of the old Roman Empire until 526. His success led to a revision of the actual events that appears regularly in Germanic heroic stories for many centuries. In the literary tradition Theoderic had a right to rule in Rome but was wrongfully supplanted by Odoacer and went into exile with a few men (including Hildebrand) at the court of Attila. This distorted and anachronistic version is the background of the *Hildebrandslied*. A Gothic original has been presumed, and it is thought that the poem moved to Italy, where it was taken up by the Germanic successors of the Goths, the Lombards; the names of the central characters are Lombardic (Hildebrand's name, for instance, is spelled at least once as Hiltibraht). From northern Italy the poem might well have passed to Bavaria, and thence to Fulda in its final and least successful linguistic leap, to the would-be Low German form in which it now exists.

The poem is, in essence, fatalistic and pre-Christian; the few references to God are exclamatory and usually fail to fit the meter, and there is no afterlife in the poem except that of fame and reputation. Hildebrand does not even live on in his son. The work bears a straightforward interpretation as a tragedy, and within the context of father/son conflicts it is striking in the tightness of the noose drawn by fate around Hildebrand. Other interpretations of the work have been offered, however, which are linked with the attempt to explain why it was written down in Fulda in the first decades of the ninth century at a time when its style and content were clearly antiquated.

The work has been seen as the expression of a legal conflict (emphasizing the word *dinc* in line 32 as an equivalent to the Latin *causa* [case, legal dispute]). The proffered gift has been considered an attempt on Hildebrand's part to rejoin his clan. From another point of view the theme is Hadubrand's revenge for his father's abandonment of him and his mother. According to another related interpretation, the song may have been written down as a document to be used in the settlement of family feuds, indicating the possible consequences of neglecting one's familial responsibilities.

While Hildebrand's acceptance that he must kill his own son in the service of his overlord, Theoderic, has sometimes been viewed as the ultimate expression of the warrior virtue of loyalty, it has also been taken as a warning *against* the heroic ideal,

which can lead to tragedies of this nature. Further, Hadubrand's obdurate refusal to accept this man as his father has been taken as a condemnation of the Germanic warrior ethos, with Hildebrand's conciliatory attempt a rejection of those values and an embodiment of the Christian virtues of *sapientia et fortitudo* (wisdom and fortitude). This interpretation, however, overlooks the fact that Haduband has no reason to believe Hildebrand and every reason – probability, hearsay evidence, and the offer of an armband that associates his opponent with the Huns – not to do so. Also, the Lay of Hildebrand confirms, simply by existing, the reputation of the heroic warrior. In an Old Norse poem a character who knows that his life will be a tragic one seeks reassurance that the right songs will be sung about him after his death; he is comforted when he is told that this will be the case.

The style and content of the *Hildebrandslied* clearly look back to a time far earlier than the ninth century, possibly bespeaking an antiquarian interest on the part of the monks who wrote the work down, but the heroic ideal and the style of the poem were not quite as antiquated in the Saxon north as in the south. At all events the tragic necessity, the problem of identity, and the irony of fame are universals that have allowed the work to hold its literary value, even if the reasons for its appearance in Fulda remain obscure.

**Bibliographies:**

H. van der Kolk, *Das Hildebrandslied: Eine forschungsgeschichtliche Darstellung* (Amsterdam: Scheltema & Holkema, 1967);

J. Sidney Groseclose and Brian O. Murdoch, *Die althochdeutschen poetischen Denkmäler* (Stuttgart: Metzler, 1976), pp. 31–41.

**References:**

J. Knight Bostock, *A Handbook on Old High German Literature,* second edition, revised by K. C. King and D. R. McLintock (Oxford: Clarendon Press, 1976), pp. 43–82;

Ernst Ebbinghaus, "The End of the Lay of Hiltibrant and Hadubrant," in *Althochdeutsch,* volume 2, edited by Rolf Bergmann, Heinrich Tiefenbach, and Lothar Voetz (Heidelberg: Winter, 1987), pp. 670–676;

Ebbinghaus, "Some Heretical Remarks on the Lay of Hiltibrant," in *Festschrift Taylor Starck* (The Hague: Mouton, 1964), pp. 140–147;

A. T. Hatto, "On the Excellence of the *Hildebrandslied:* A Comparative Study in Dynamics," *Modern Language Review,* 68 (1973): 820–838;

Wolfgang Haubrichs, *Die Anfänge*, volume 1/i of *Geschichte der deutschen Literatur*, edited by Joachim Heinzle (Frankfurt am Main: Athenaeum, 1988), pp. 147–159;

Joachim Heinzle, "Rabenschlacht und Burgundenuntergang im *Hildebrandslied?*," in *Althochdeutsch*, volume 2, pp. 667–684;

Werner Hoffmann, "Das *Hildebrandslied* und die indo-germanische Vater-Sohn-Kampf-Dichtung," *Beiträge* (Tübingen), 92 (1970): 26–42;

Hoffmann, "Zur geschichtlichen Stellung des *Hildebrandsliedes*," in *Festschrift M.-L. Dittrich* (Göppingen: Kümmerle, 1976), pp. 1–17;

Herbert Kolb, "Hildebrands Sohn," in *Studien zur deutschen Literatur des Mittelalters*, edited by Rudolf Schützeichel and Ulrich Fellmann (Bonn: Bouvier, 1979), pp. 51–75;

Willy Krogmann, *Das Hildebrandslied in der langobardischen Urfassung hergestellt* (Berlin: Schmidt, 1959);

Hugo Kuhn, "Stoffgeschichte, Tragik und formaler Aufbau im *Hildebrandslied*" and "Hildebrand, Dietrich von Bern und die Nibelungen," in his *Text und Theorie* (Stuttgart: Metzler, 1969), pp. 113–140;

Richard H. Lawson, "The *Hildebrandslied*: Originally Gothic?," *Neuphilologische Mitteilungen*, 74 (1973): 333–339;

W. P. Lehmann, "Das *Hildebrandslied*, ein Spätzeitwerk," *Zeitschrift für deutsche Philologie*, 81 (1962): 24–29;

Rosemarie Lühr, *Studien zur Sprache des Hildebrandsliedes* (Frankfurt am Main & Bern: Lang, 1982);

Friedrich Maurer, "*Hildebrandslied* und *Ludwigslied*," *Der Deutschunterricht*, 9, no. 2 (1957): 5–15;

William C. McDonald, "Too Softly a Gift of Treasure: A Re-reading of the Old High German *Hildebrandslied*," *Euphorion*, 78 (1984): 1–16;

D. R. McLintock, "The Language of the *Hildebrandslied*," *Oxford German Studies*, 1 (1966): 1–9;

McLintock, "Metre and Rhythm in the *Hildebrandslied*," *Modern Language Review*, 71 (1976): 565–576;

McLintock, "The Politics of the *Hildebrandslied*," *New German Studies*, 2 (1974): 61–81;

H. H. Meier, "Die Schlacht im *Hildebrandslied*," *Zeitschrift für deutsches Altertum*, 119 (1990): 127–138;

Birgit Meineke, *Chind und Barn im Hildebrandslied vor dem Hintergrund ihrer althochdeutschen Überlieferung* (Göttingen: Vandenhoek & Ruprecht, 1987);

Brian Murdoch, *Old High German Literature* (Boston: Twayne, 1983), pp. 55–64;

Frederick Norman, *Three Essays on the Hildebrandslied* (London: Institute of Germanic Studies, 1973);

K. Northcott, "*Das Hildebrandslied*: A Legal Process?," *Modern Language Review*, 56 (1961): 342–348;

W. Perrett, "On the *Hildebrandslied*," *Modern Language Review*, 31 (1936): 532–538;

Alain Renoir, "The Armor of the Hildebrandslied," *Neuphilologische Mitteilungen*, 78 (1977): 389–395;

Renoir, "The Kassel Manuscript and the Conclusion of the *Hildebrandslied*," *Manuscripta*, 23 (1979): 104–108;

Renoir, *A Key to Old Poems: The Oral-Formulaic Approach to the Interpretation of West Germanic Verse* (University Park & London: Pennsylvania State University Press, 1988), pp. 133–156;

Werner Schröder, "Hildebrands tragische Blindheit und der Schluß des *Hildebrandsliedes*," *Deutsche Vierteljahresschrift*, 37 (1963): 481–497;

Schröder, "Ist das germanische Heldenlied ein Phantom?," *Zeitschrift für deutsches Altertum*, 120 (1991): 249–256;

Rudolf Schützeichel, "Zum *Hildebrandslied*," in *Festschrift Max Wehrli* (Zurich & Freiburg: Atlantis, 1969), pp. 83–94;

Ute Schwab, *Arbeo laosa: philologische Studien zum Hildebrandslied* (Bern: Francke, 1972);

Heather Stuart, "The *Hildebrandslied*: An Anti-heroic Interpretation," *German Life and Letters*, 32 (1978–1979): 1–9;

W. F. Twaddell, "The *Hildebrandslied* Manuscript in the USA," *Journal of English and Germanic Philology*, 73 (1974): 157–168;

Jan de Vries, "Das Motiv des Vater-Sohn-Kampfes im *Hildebrandslied*," *Germanisch-romanische Monatsschrift*, 34 (1953): 257–274;

N. Wagner, "*Cheisuringu gitan*," *Zeitschrift für deutsches Altertum*, 104 (1975): 179–188;

Roswith Wisniewski, "Hadubrands Rache: Eine Interpretation des *Hildebrandsliedes*," *Amsterdamer Beiträge zur älteren Gemanistik*, 9 (1975): 1–12.

# Kaiserchronik
## (circa 1147)

### Francis G. Gentry
*Pennsylvania State University*

**Manuscripts:** The manuscript tradition of the *Kaiserchronik* is impressive; no other twelfth-century German work was as successful. There are three main redactions: A, B, and C; B and C are revisions of A. A reflects the "old text" that breaks off with line 17283. There are three manuscripts and twelve fragments representing this redaction, ranging from the latter half of the twelfth century to the end of the fourteenth. The three main A-redaction manuscripts are: Vorau, Chorherrenstifts Vorau in Steiermark, Hs.276/1, parchment, folio, second half of the twelfth century (V); Munich, Bayerische Staatsbibliothek, cgm 37, parchment, quarto, fourteenth century (M); Heidelberg, Universitätsbibliothek, cpg 361, parchment, folio, thirteenth century (H).

**First publications:** *Der keiser und der kunige buoch oder die sogenannte Kaiserchronik,* edited by Hans Ferdinand Massmann (Quedlinburg & Leipzig: Basse, 1848/1849 [H]); *Die Kaiserchronik nach der ältesten Handschrift des Stiftes Vorau,* edited by Josef Diemer (Vienna, 1849 [V]).

**Standard edition:** *Die Kaiserchronik eines Regensburger Geistlichen,* edited by Edward Schröder (Hannover: Weidmann, 1892; third edition, Dublin & Zurich: Weidmann, 1969 [V]).

The *Kaiserchronik* is one of the most impressive literary achievements of the German Middle Ages. Most scholars agree that it was completed by a Regensburg cleric around 1147, in that it ends with Konrad III making preparations to lead the Second Crusade along with Louis VII of France. Since the work appears to end in midsentence — "der chunich niht langer netwelte" (the king did not tarry any longer) — it is unclear whether the poet intended to carry on with his writing at some later time or whether he merely brought his work to a rather

abrupt ending. Nonetheless, if the terminus ad quem can be conjectured with reasonable certainty, the terminus a quo cannot. Suggestions range from 1126, with the consecration of Kuno I as bishop of Regensburg, to a few years before the work's completion. Kuno was a former abbot of Siegburg, and it is conjectured that he had a copy of *Das Annolied* (Song of Anno, between 1077 and 1081) brought to Regensburg. Thus it would be reasonable to look to Kuno as a patron, since it is certain that the section dealing with Daniel's dream in the *Annolied* was used by the *Kaiserchronik* poet (lines 526–590 in the *Kaiserchronik* correspond to lines 175–260 of the *Annolied*). In addition, large sections of the Julius Caesar section of the *Annolied* were reproduced almost verbatim in the corresponding segment of the *Kaiserchronik* (lines 247–602). But Kuno died in 1132, and suitable patrons after him are not readily identifiable. Further, it is not difficult to imagine that the Regensburg poet found access to the *Annolied* through some other means. There is also uncertainty about the number of poets who might have been involved in the project, or whether the *Kaiserchronik* might have been given in dictation over the course of a few years. In making the latter proposal, Eberhard Nellmann points out that Otto von Freising dictated his *Cronica* (Chronicle, 1143–1146), which is more demanding and more massive, within the span of four years. These uncertainties, however, in no way affect the tremendous impact of the work, which is the first such chronicle in the vernacular and in verse. It provided the model for all the vernacular chronicles that followed.

Right from the start the poet leaves no doubt as to the intention of his work:

In des almähtigen gotes minnen
sô wil ich des liedes beginnen.
daz scult ir gezogenlîche vernemen;
jâ mac iuh vil wole gezemen

202

ze horen älliu frumichait.
die tumben dunchet iz arebait,
sculn si iemer iht gelernen
od ir wistuom gemêren.
die sint unnuzze
unt phlegent niht guoter wizze,
daz si ungerne hôrent sagen
dannen si mahten haben
wîstuom unt êre;
unt waere iedoch frum der sêle. (lines 1–14)

(For the love of Almighty God,
I now intend to begin a "rhymed work."
You should listen to it in a seemly manner.
Indeed it can only be good for you
to hear about all kinds of good works and behavior.
It always strikes the ignorant as tedious
whenever they should learn something
or increase their knowledge.
They are useless [to society]
and are not showing good sense
by not wanting to hear [about those things]
from which they could have
wisdom and honor,
and yet retain a God-fearing soul.)

These beginning lines of the prologue, which goes on to line 42, postulate the ideal audience for the work. (Given the use of the vernacular, it is likely that the target group was composed of members of the feudal nobility and ministerials, and possibly members of a cloister who were not versed in Latin.) They are the ones who wish to learn and profit from the good examples of others; as such, they are "useful" to the greater society – as opposed to the ignorant, who wish to learn nothing and are, consequently, "useless." This concept of usefulness is an expansion of the doctrine of the Christian society formulated in the late eleventh century by Pope Gregory VII – who, to be sure, was concentrating on the duties of kings. Gregory said that usefulness to the entire Christian society is the only criterion by which an individual – in this case, the king – can be judged. In the thirteenth and fourteenth centuries this concept would be taken up again and again by preachers such as Berthold von Regensburg and didactic poets such as Hugo von Trimberg and extended to all "orders" of society: those who do their duty are useful to society, whether they are kings or shoemakers. The poet is manipulating his audience by providing them with only one unattractive alternative to learning from his work: being classified among the useless members of society. The situation is not unlike that in the prologue to *Tristan und Isolde* (circa 1210), in which Gottfried von Straßburg addresses the "edele herzen" (noble hearts). Indeed, most "courtly" works are predicated on the usefulness of the knight to courtly society as a whole.

This notion is especially evident in the Arthurian works of Hartmann von Aue, as when he has Erec say to Mabonagrin: "bî den liuten ist so guot" (it is good to be among the people).

The *Kaiserchronik* poet goes on to explain his work as constituting a chronicle of the Roman Empire from the beginning to the present day. He will not be talking merely about the emperors but will also profile the popes, who played a role in the empire. Further, he will present both good and bad emperors and popes. Thus for the *Kaiserchronik* poet the Roman Empire must be viewed as the cooperative venture of Church and world, of pope and emperor.

Nowhere is this symbiosis made clearer than in the episode of Constantine and Sylvester. Constantine was stricken with leprosy, which could only be healed by the blood of innocent children. But because Constantine had such a noble nature, he dispensed with this grisly cure. Pope Sylvester baptized him, whereupon the emperor was restored to full health. Together he and Sylvester introduced Christianity and established it firmly in the Roman Empire. It was also Sylvester who blessed the imperial regalia and set the crown of empire on Constantine's head (lines 8116–8122), thereby reinforcing the thesis propounded by many popes, but most decisively by Gregory VII in his *Dictatus papae,* that only the pope may crown the emperor and that without this act the individual is not the emperor. Further, while Constantine was busy building Constantinople, Sylvester remained in Rome as quasi-administrator (in lines 10410–10411 Constantine says to the pope: "ich bevilhe dir mîn rîche, unz ich wider zuo dir chom" [I entrust my empire to you until I shall return to you]) and resolutely defended and established the Christian faith.

The story of Charlemagne has many similarities with that of Constantine. Pope Leo was Charlemagne's brother. (This is the first suggestion in German literature that Charlemagne and Leo were related.) When Leo was mistreated by the Roman mob, Charlemagne was admonished by a voice in his dreams to go to Rome, rescue Leo, and secure him on Saint Peter's throne. After the troubles in Rome had been put down, Charlemagne was anointed emperor by Leo.

In the prologue the poet castigates the singers of "lugene" (lies), that is, secular tales (lines 27–42). Those miscreants will surely end up in the fires of hell, especially since they will teach their tales to the next generation, who will then hold lies for truth:

lugene unde ubermuot
ist niemen guot.

rinmarc wil wille si in des ware.
Also der edel Hespanian. di bure
ze hierin gewvan. di iude.n er uir
kaufen hiel. unde nihr da des uerliel.
des der nutze. oder frum was. daz liet
saget uor war daz. vil schiere er
sih beratte. daz her hiel er latten.
engengen babylonie: hedem aller
wurften kunic. der in dirre werlte:
under disen himele iender lebete.
Der kunic Milian. hieh sin her inge-
gen in uz uarn. er uor in ingegene.
mit michelr menige. er hete mani
gen helt kunen. manigen uanen
grünen. manigen wïh unde rot. si
komen ingrole not. da mahte man
sehen gulilen manige halfperge wi-
te. manigen guldinen schilltes rant. da was in
manich ————— hett wol gar. Gutus J gant
nam romate uan. vil schiere rant
er den an. der den uanen da uorlu
te. den brahter legrolen arbatten.
daz sper er durch in stach. daz wart
er uermellenlichen sprah. ledic sint
dinu lehen. du nemaht dinem her
ren. niemer nehain mere der uon
gesagen. ih ist mit dir unfanft er
haben. den schilt er uf ruhte. den ua

die wîsen hôrent ungerne der von sagen.
nû grîfe wir das guote liet an. ( lines 39–42)


( Lies and arrogance
bring no one any good.
Wise people [never] listened to such things willingly.
Now we will take up this efficacious tale.)

The poet addresses a similar topic much later in his discussion of the emperor Zeno and his dealings with Dietrich von Bern ( Theodoric). Dietrich is presented here in a much harsher light than in other works of literature, probably reflecting the conflict between the Arian Ostrogoths and the Catholic Romans in general more than the inherent wickedness of Dietrich. According to the poet, demons took Dietrich's body and threw it into a volcano, where it will burn until the Last Judgment. After disposing of Dietrich in this rather spectacular way, the poet takes one more poke at the Dietrich legend. Those who claim that Dietrich and Etzel (Attila) were contemporaries are sadly mistaken; Etzel was dead forty-three years before Dietrich was born:

do der chunic Ezzel ze Ovene wart begraben,
dar nâch stuont iz vur wâr
driu unde fierzech jâr,
daz Dietrîch wart geborn.
ze Chriechen wart er rezogen,
dâ er daz swert umbe bant,
ze Rôme wart er gesant,
ze Vulkân wart er begraben.
hie meget ir der luge wol ain ende haben.
(lines 14179–14187)


(After King Etzel was buried at Oven,
forty-three years elapsed
[before] Dietrich was born.
He was raised in Greece,
[and] when he put on the sword,
he was sent to Rome.
He was buried at Vulkan.
With this [explanation of the facts] you can put an end to this lie.)

These lines further support the opinion that the secular tales mentioned by other religious writers of the early Middle High German period revolved around the exploits of Dietrich and parts (at least) of the tale of the Nibelungen.

While the poet is extremely exact with regard to chronology in his attempt to demonstrate the "lies" of secular literature, he is less so when he wished to support his own view of the Roman Empire. The poet was determined to dismiss the legitimacy of Greek rule after Zeno's death in 491. Yet Justinian, for example, is an East Roman emperor

of whom the poet approves because of his willingness to heed the good advice of his wife, Tharsilla, and honor his nobles. Justinian, however, was emperor *after* Zeno. Therefore, the poet alters chronology and places Justinian as emperor before Theodosius (379–395).

The *Kaiserchronik* is replete with such fanciful tales and distortions of history. In addition to spurious emperors such as Faustinianus or nonexistent relationships such as Charlemagne and Leo as brothers, the work brims with fascinating real or imagined episodes from the lives of real or imagined Roman emperors. (The German emperors were apparently less interesting to the poet; after spending 14,240 lines on the Romans, he allots 3,001 lines to the Germans, of which Charlemagne receives 809 lines while the remaining 2,192 lines are meted out among the remaining eighteen emperors.) After Zeno's death the Greek emperors are not viewed as legitimate rulers of Rome, and the imperial crown remained "ûf sante Pêters altâre" (on Saint Peter's altar, line 14283) until the coming of Charlemagne. With the advent of Charlemagne and his acceptance of the crown from his brother, Pope Leo, the *translatio imperii* (transfer of power) is complete. For because of their "proven" kinship with the first Roman emperor, Julius Caesar, the Germanic Franks have the right to assume the imperial crown and rule the Romans as part of their own far-flung empire.

Perhaps it would be more accurate to say that the empire has been "restored," since Charlemagne is regarded as the heir of Constantine and Sylvester. One of Charlemagne's first acts as emperor is to reinstitute the laws of Constantine: "jâ was vergezzen harte/der pfahte Constantînî" (indeed, the imperial laws of Constantine had been sorely neglected, lines 14782–14783). Not only, then, did Charlemagne receive Constantine's crown but he also set about to reintroduce and revitalize Constantine's laws, thereby reinforcing the Latin Christian essence of the Roman Empire.

Two fascinating episodes deal with the victimization of a woman by her brother-in-law: the tale of the fictitious emperor Faustinianus and his wife Mechthild, and the tale of Crescentia. Faustinianus and Mechthild have two sons, Faustinus and Faustus. Claudius, the emperor's brother, desires Mechthild. She retains her virtue, but, fearing for her sons' safety, she persuades Faustinianus to send the children away to study. They are shipwrecked, rescued by a fisherman, and sold into slavery. They are bought by a childless noblewoman who adopts them as her own sons. Meanwhile, Mechthild has given birth to a third son, Clemens, the future pope and martyr. Disturbed that she has not heard from her two sons, she sets out in search of them. She, too, is shipwrecked and saved. She goes to work for an ill noblewoman, whom she serves well. Faustinianus, wondering where his family has disappeared to, goes out looking for them and is shipwrecked. He is found, naked, by a merchant, who feeds and clothes him. Faustinianus accepts service in a noble's house and is well liked. Meanwhile, the unsavory Simon Magus has gained control over Faustinus and Faustus. Saint Peter frees them. Faustinianus and Mechthild, reduced to beggary, meet Clemens and Peter, and Peter reunites the family amid great joy. Faustinianus and Mechthild return to Rome, where Claudius is ruling. They give all their goods to Peter and enter a cloister.

Crescentia is loved by two brothers named Dietrich: one is handsome, the other is not. She marries the latter, who is the emperor. Once, when he is away, his brother makes advances to Crescentia. She rejects him and devises a stratagem that will provide her with respite from her brother-in-law. Under the pretext of wanting to sleep with him, she causes him to construct and provision a tower with a good lock. She tricks him and locks him up until her husband returns two years and two months later. Released from the tower, the brother-in-law accuses Crescentia of being unfaithful to her husband. The emperor orders her death, and his brother throws her off a bridge. She is rescued by a fisherman and brought to a duke's court. The duke's viceroy has lascivious designs on her, but she retains her virtue. The viceroy kills the duke's child but makes it look as if Crescentia has done it. She is thrown from the battlements but miraculously survives. All who have mistreated Crescentia are struck with leprosy, and she becomes a holy woman. She demands that all who have wronged her make a public confession; they do, and they are cured of their leprosy. The viceroy does not live to enjoy his restored health, however, because now it is his turn to be thrown from the battlements; he is then drawn and quartered. In due course she makes herself known to her husband but refuses all carnal contact. It is her will that they both enter a cloister and lead religious lives, and they do.

Aside from the intrinsic charm of the tales, there is an unmistakable message: a religious life is far superior to life in the world, even life as an emperor. Also, in both episodes women are victims of abuse, and only after enduring great privation and torment are Mechthild and Crescentia restored – but to a "higher" life. The *Kaiserchronik* poet may have

been disturbed by the sexual nature of women, which makes them a threat to men; thus, he ennobles Mechthild and Crescentia at the end by removing their sexuality from them.

Another reaction of the poet to what he perceived as distorted sexuality can be found in the section on Nero (lines 4083–4300). The section starts:

> das buoch kundet uns mêre:
> daz rîche besaz duo Nêre;
> der was der aller wirste man
> der von muoter in dise werlt ie bekom. (lines 4083–4086)

> (the book relates further that Nero led the empire at that time.
> He was the worst of all men
> who ever came into this world from a mother.)

It continues with the standard tales of Nero's cruelties, plus something new: Nero wanted to have a child. His doctors brewed him a potion, and he became pregnant: "in im wahsen began / wider der manne natûre / ein wurm ungehûre (lines 4140–4142) (there began to grow in him, / contrary to the nature of a man, / a monstrous worm). Gender roles were taken seriously in the Middle Ages by thinkers as disparate as Hildegard of Bingen and Alan of Lille; transgressions of the properly assigned roles were roundly condemned. Sodomy was condemned not solely as a sin but also because in the commission of the act one of the parties went against his or her nature and adopted the role of the opposite sex: a man effected the passive "female" role in a homosexual union, or a woman assumed the aggressive "male" role in a lesbian relationship – a grave offense against the divinely established order. By wanting to bear a child, Nero went against his masculine nature and, thus, compounded his sin. Possibly as repayment for his unnatural and dissolute life, Nero suffered greatly from a variety of illnesses before his death – gout, severe arthritis, and leprosy. Finally, his cadaver was dragged by the citizens of Rome to a ditch, where a legion of devils collected his soul and the wolves ate his flesh.

Nero's end is probably the most spectacular in the *Kaiserchronik,* and some, if not all, of the dreadful things said about him were no doubt known to the majority of the poet's audience. By this time Nero had become a "type" – much as the mention of Absalom would conjure up the image of the faithless child or the name Job would invoke the virtue of patience, reference to Nero would summon all sorts of negative associations in the minds of the listeners. It would be impossible to have a Nero episode without some of these excesses being luridly and lovingly recounted.

But the main purpose of the *Kaiserchronik* was to depict rulers, both pagan and Christian, who could be taken as worthy role models for the secular nobility at the poet's time. The emperor Trajan is an excellent example of such a role model. The picture of Trajan in the *Kaiserchronik* is consonant with the one developed by the historians of late antiquity. Trajan is the epitome of the just ruler, who respected his nobles (something of which the poet approves and something that the later Heinrich IV, of whom the poet does *not* approve, did not do) and ruled all levels of society justly and without bias: "er rihte vil rehte / dem hêrren unde dem cneht" (he judged justly / both lords and servants) (lines 5845–5846). In fact, Trajan was so just that when he died Pope Gregory interceded on behalf of his soul. As a result, even though he was a pagan, Trajan's soul was saved from hell and put into Saint Gregory's care until the Last Judgment. The poet then addresses his audience directly:

> Nû suln alle werltkunige
> dâ bî nemen pilede,
> wi der edel kaiser Trâjan
> dise genâde umbe got gewan,
> want er rehtes gerihtes phlegete
> di wîl er an dirre werlte lebete. (lines 6083–6088)

> (Now should all kings of the world
> take note
> how the noble emperor Trajan
> gained this grace from God.
> [He gained it]
> because he exercised just judgments,
> all the while he lived in this world.)

The story of Trajan exemplifies the main concerns of the poet: the ruler must respect his nobles and must be just in all his pronouncements; otherwise, he is an unjust ruler and "useless" to society – in the Gregorian sense – because he is not fulfilling his chief duty as sovereign.

Of course, those emperors, like Constantine and Charlemagne, who worked closely with their respective popes – who were, coincidentally, their brothers – are the individuals most worthy of emulation. But paramount in the poet's concept of sovereignty was the obligation of the ruler, whether pagan or Christian, to uphold the laws of the empire, ranging from the administration of the emperor's house to maintaining distinctions among the levels of society (for example, Charlemagne's sumptuary laws regarding peasants, lines 14791–14813). *Kaiserchronik* has no equal in the vernacular, and it is one more magnificent example of the concern of the medieval church for the establishment and preservation of a just society in which each, high or low, would receive his or her due.

**References:**

Gustav Ehrismann, *Geschichte der deutschen Literatur bis zum Ausgang des Mittelalters,* volume 2, part 1: *Frühmittelhochdeutsche Zeit* (reprint, Munich: Beck, 1966);

Eberhard Nellmann, "Kaiserchronik," in *Die deutsche Literatur des Mittelalters: Verfasserlexikon,* volume 4, edited by Kurt Ruh and others (Berlin & New York: De Gruyter, 1983), col. 949–964;

Nellmann, *Die Reichsidee in der deutschen Dichtung der Salier- und frühen Stauferzeit: Annolied, Kaiserchronik, Rolandslied, Eraclius* (Berlin: Schmidt, 1963), pp. 82–163;

Ernst Friedrich Ohly, *Sage und Legende in der Kaiserchronik: Untersuchungen über Quellen und Aufbau der Dichtung* (reprint, Darmstadt: Wissenschaftliche Buchgesellschaft, 1968);

Gisele Vollmann-Profe, *Geschichte der deutschen Literatur von den Anfängen bis zum Beginn der Neuzeit,* volume 1, part 2: *Von den Anfängen zum Hohen Mittelalter* (Königstein: Athenäum, 1986);

Max Wehrli, *Geschichte der deutschen Literatur vom frühen Mittelalter bis zum Ende des 16. Jahrhunderts* (Stuttgart: Reclam, 1980).

# Ludus de Antichristo

### (circa 1160)

## Wolfgang Hempel
### University of Toronto

**Manuscript:** The *Ludus de Antichristo* is preserved in only one manuscript, a small (sixteen-by-twelve-centimeter) codex compiled between 1160 and 1186 in the monastery of Tegernsee in Bavaria and containing a variety of material probably used in the monastery's school. The codex, Clm 19411, is now in Munich, Bayerische Staatsbibliothek. In the manuscript the play is untitled. *Ludus de Antichristo* is the title most commonly used, but in older German literature the title *Tegernseer Antichristspiel* occurs frequently.

**First publication:** "Ludus Paschalis de adventu et interitu Antichristi in scena adhibitus saeculo XII," edited by Bernardus Pez, in *Thesaurus anecdotorum novissimus,* volume 2 (Augsburg: Veith, 1721) pp. 187–196.

**Standard edition:** *Ludus de Antichristo,* 2 volumes, edited by Gisela Vollmann-Profe, Litterae: Göppinger Beiträge zur Textgeschichte, no. 821 (Lauterberg: Kümmerle, 1981).

**Edition in English:** *The Play of Antichrist,* translated by John Wright (Toronto: Pontifical Institute of Medieval Studies, 1967).

The *Ludus de Antichristo* (Play of the Antichrist, circa 1160) stands outside the evolutionary paths of German and Latin literature, following no discernible models and having no apparent successors. But as a work of art it encapsulates the highest aesthetic and ideological values of the political-social elite during the efflorescence of medieval civilization under the Hohenstaufen dynasty from 1138 to 1254.

The *Ludus de Antichristo* is anonymous. Earlier attempts at identifying the author with one of the literary names of the time, such as the Archpoet, Wernher der Garrte, or Metellus of Tegernsee, have failed to gain common acceptance. In any case, they would not have yielded much biographical insight, since nothing is known about these authors. One can, however, reconstruct a personality from the text and its social-historical background. The author's close familiarity with feudal customs and ceremonies and with imperial politics, and his advocacy of the theocratic ideology of Friedrich Barbarossa suggest a person of chivalric background with close affinities to the imperial administration. His extensive knowledge of the Scriptures, of theological literature, and of liturgy show a man with a higher clerical education or even of high ecclesiastic position. These characteristics point to a type of person quite common among the elite of the time, a clergyman who held feudal or administrative offices. The author of the *Ludus de Antichristo* in all likelihood moved in the circles of the ecclesiastic princes (bishops and abbots with the status and power of imperial feudal lords) who were one of the main power bases of the Salian and Hohenstaufen emperors. As befits a member of this class, the author, besides having great literary talent and ability at disputation, had an independent and self-assured mind – characteristics revealed by the play's many dramatic and theatrical innovations, by its imaginative and unconventional use of verse, and above all by its masterful reshaping of the legendary material.

The dating of the *Ludus de Antichristo* is problematic, the only certainty being, for palaeographic reasons, a date before 1186. Most scholars have settled on about 1160, a time at which the political-historical situation was most similar to the one reflected in the play.

The *Ludus de Antichristo* presents the events immediately preceding the end of the world and the Last Judgment, dramatizing the reign of the Last Roman Emperor and the rule and fall of the Antichrist. The basic plot is simple: the Emperor restores the Roman Empire by bringing all Christian kings under his sovereignty and defeating the pagans; he then resigns his crown and his office to God. At that moment the Antichrist takes over the world, making all kings his lieges through force, bribes, or deception and martyring those who denounce him; but at the moment of his final triumph he is suddenly toppled by a crash of thunder from

208

above. This simple and clearly structured framework of two stories, that of the emperor and that of the Antichrist, is so richly endowed with characters and subplots, with ceremonial actions and chants, and with pantomime and music that the play becomes a microcosm of the medieval universe, complex and rich in detail yet strictly ordered and of stately majesty.

The stage is set to represent the whole medieval world: eight "seats" (platforms with thrones) are arranged in a circle. In the east stands the Temple of the Lord, with the seat of the King of Jerusalem to one side of it and the seat of the personification of the Jewish faith to the other. On the west side is the seat of the Roman Emperor, and around it those of the French King and the German King. At the south there is the seat of the King of Babylon and perhaps that of the King of the Greeks. (The manuscript is ambiguous about this last seat, which may be at the north or, leaving the north side as the place for the audience, at the east.)

The play begins with the processional entrance of the personae with their retinues. First come the personifications of the three faiths, each persona chanting her confession while ascending her throne: Gentilitas (Paganism) with the King of Babylon, Synagoga (Judaism) with the Jews, and Ecclesia (Christianity) with Misericordia (Compassion) on her right and Justitia (Justice) on her left, followed by the Apostolicus (Pope) on the right and the Imperator (Emperor) on the left with the militia behind them. Last to enter are the King of the Franks and the King of the Greeks with their armies. The Emperor sets out to reconstitute the power of the old Roman empire and sends envoys first to the King of the Franks, ordering him to pay homage, swear fealty, and do service as required of a feudal vassal. The King refuses but is defeated in a battle and led to the Emperor's throne, where he submits to the Emperor's seigniory and is invested in his kingdom. The King of the Greeks readily follows the command, pays homage to the Emperor, and is invested as a vassal. The same happens with the King of Jerusalem. A universal Christian empire having thus been established, the King of Babylon decides to destroy the competing faith and sets out to besiege Jerusalem. When the Emperor is called to help by the King of Jerusalem he gathers his army and marches against the invaders. In the ensuing battle the King of Babylon is defeated and flees, and the Emperor enters the temple. After worshiping he lays down his regalia on the altar, resigning his empire to God as his sovereign lord. He then returns to his throne as King of the Germans.

After this establishment of an ideal secular order, while Ecclesia, Gentilitas, and Synagoga repeat their introit chants, the Hypocritae (religious hypocrites) sneak in and gain the favor and trust of the King of Jerusalem and his court. At this point the Antichrist enters, accompanied by his helpers, Hypocrisis (Hypocrisy) and Haeresis (Heresy), and is welcomed by the Hypocritae. They urge him to assume power and enthrone him in Jerusalem, expelling the King of Jerusalem, who seeks refuge with the German King, and Ecclesia, who returns to the apostolic throne. Reversing the empire's expansion, the Antichrist now sends the Hypocritae as messengers to the kings, ordering them to worship him as the returned Christ. The Greek King, threatened with force, pays homage and is reinvested as the Antichrist's vassal. The Hypocritae use gifts to induce the French King to accept vassalage, but when they try this strategy with the German King they are rebuffed as frauds and liars. The Antichrist sends his vassal kings with their armies to attack the German King, but they are defeated. Finally, the Antichrist resorts to miracles: he heals a cripple and a leper and "revives" a man who pretends to have been killed in the battle. These feats convince the German King, and he, too, becomes the Antichrist's liege man. He even helps his lord in his world conquest by defeating the King of Babylon and forcing him and Gentilitas to submit to the Antichrist's lordship. When all kings have returned to their thrones, the Hypocritae are sent to win over the third faith, and Synagoga, convinced that the Antichrist is the Messiah, submits to him. Now God's messengers, the prophets Henoch (Enoch) and Elia (Elias), approach Synagoga, open her eyes, and reconvert her. They are all taken to the Antichrist's court, and, because they still denounce him, he has them killed. At the height of his world dominance, the Antichrist summons all his people to his court to worship him as God. But as soon as he proclaims the world's peace and security, a crash over his head topples him, and his helpers flee. All people now return to the faith and to Ecclesia, who leads them in a final Te Deum.

A modern reader will not be able to experience the impact that a play such as the *Ludus de Antichristo* had on its audiences. A medieval spectator's mind-set included several major conceptual predispositions on which the play worked. Above all, the play's subject matter possessed enormous import and topicality for its time. The main moving force of central European political history in the Middle Ages was the struggle for political dominance between the supreme secular and spiritual powers, the emperor and the pope. Since Charlemagne, the Frankish and, later, the German kings had regarded themselves as the heirs to the late Roman Empire and had begun, with increasing success since Otto I (who ruled from 936 to 973), to establish a theocracy like that of late Rome under Constantine the Great. Such a theocracy would see the emperor as the sole representative of the divine power and as the supreme authority in both the secular and the religious realms. The papacy resisted, claiming supremacy for the church, in whose service and defense the secular power was to act. In particular, the popes tried to break up the symbiosis of German secular and ecclesiastical powers that existed in the "Imperial Church," the bishops and abbots who were invested in their dominions by the German king and Roman emperor and formed their main power base. After the bitter Investiture struggle in the eleventh century, in which the papacy tried to gain the right of investiture of the prelates, a temporary truce and compromise had been reached. But the antagonism flared up again when Friedrich Barbarossa, after his coronation in 1152, began a new drive, led by his chancellor Rainald von Dassel, toward a theocratic *Sacrum Imperium Romanum* (Holy Roman Empire). The ensuing political and military struggle was to last until the end of the Hohenstaufen dynasty in 1254 and ended with the exhaustion and loss of political supremacy for both the empire and the papacy. In the theological-political discussion during this conflict each side accused the other of fighting God's order, thus of being an incarnation of the Devil and his principal sin of *superbia* (egocentrism and self-aggrandizement, causing separation from God). The main biblical and patristic support for these arguments was found in the motif of the Antichrist.

The myth of the Antichrist is based on several passages in the Bible, mainly on the dreams and visions of Daniel (chapters 2, 7, and 11), on Revelation (chapters 11 and 13), and on predictions of Christ (Matt. 24) and Saint Paul (2 Thess. 2). From these passages and from later prophecies (the "Sybilla Tiburtina" and the "Pseudo-Methodius," which expanded the motif of the Last Emperor), there developed over the centuries a rich and multifarious mythological complex around the central ideas that world history was divided into the ages of four successive empires, of which the Roman Empire was the last; that the rule of the Antichrist was to follow; and that on his destruction the world was to be brought to an end by God in the Last Judgment. Interest in this eschatology was greatly increased, of course, by the approach of the millen-

nium, and it lasted for a long time thereafter. From the tenth through the thirteenth centuries the concepts of the Last Emperor and the Antichrist were central to all political and historical discussion. The standard source for the entire legendary complex was the *Libellus de Antichristo,* a letter written in the latter part of the tenth century by Adso, abbot of Montier-en-Der, in reply to an obviously anxious request from Queen Gerberga of France. Adso's compilation, which is somewhat disorganized and rambling, includes all the motifs and concepts current in his time. One-third of his account dwells on the origin, upbringing, and nature of the Antichrist; most of the rest describes the Antichrist's three-and-a-half-year tyranny. Only a short passage (one-tenth of the whole) deals with the Roman Empire, saying that its remnants are still maintained by the French kings; that the last of them will lead the empire to its completion and, after a happy reign, will deposit his crown in the temple; and that all the kingdoms will then defect from the empire and the Antichrist will come.

The author of the *Ludus de Antichristo* has used these sources with great liberty. Indeed, he has written a virtually new story, leaving out much of the Antichrist material and expanding the Emperor's part so extensively that it dominates the play. This new story has a complex but clear and coherent organization. Its basic structure derives from an opposition of Emperor and Antichrist, characters whose actions are antithetical. The author has built up the first part of the play, for which the tradition gave him only the motifs of reconstitution of empire and resignation, to contrast with the Antichrist story, whose outline was fixed by the tradition. But since the Emperor part has chronological priority and prefigures the second part, the reader has the impression that the Antichrist is a parody or perversion of the Emperor. By thus making the Antichrist into an Antiemperor, the *Ludus de Antichristo* creates an ingenious syllogism in the spectator's mind: "If the Antichrist is the antithesis of Christ (as tradition has it), and the Emperor is the antithesis of the Antichrist (as the play shows), then the Emperor is an image of Christ."

The formal structure of the play is one of stately regularity and symmetry, like that of a Romanesque cathedral. The dramatic action consists of many small modules, that is, actions and movements between which the action seems to pause briefly in *tableaux vivants*. These actions are separated in the manuscript by the then-unusual marking device of a period followed by a capital letter, and they are mostly introduced by words such

*Illustrations from the manuscript for the* Ludus de Antichristo. *Top to bottom: the Antichrist beheads the prophets Henoch and Elia; he tempts kings, priests, and common people with sumptuous gifts; he performs false miracles, making leaves suddenly appear on a tree, fire rain down from the sky, and a storm agitate the sea (Munich, Bayerische Staatsbiblioteck, Clm 19411, fol. 241v).*

as *then* (tunc) or *and* (et). The rubric (stage direction) that describes the battle between the Emperor and the French King, for instance, reads: "Et statim ordinatis aciebus vadil ad expugnandum regem Francorum. Qui sibi occurens congreditur cum eo. Et superatus captivus reducitur ad sedem Imperatoris. Et sendente Imperatore stat coram eo cantans." (And immediately, after having organized his army, [the Emperor] goes to vanquish the French King. Who, rushing against him, clashes with him. And, after having been beaten, he is led back to the Emperor's throne. And while the Emperor is seated, he stands before him and sings, line 86a). Here a series of single actions, such as mobilizing, marching, and fighting, combine to form a larger event, a war. Such composite events, which consist of a fixed set of actions (sometimes interspersed with variants that give the plot a measure of unpredictability), are the building blocks of the play. The most frequent is the composite action "embassage," which always consists of these parts: lord instructs messengers; envoys travel; envoys present message; envoys return in the entourage of the recipient or, in case of a refusal, alone; and envoys present reply.

This sequence occurs eleven times and would have been a dominant visual component in any performance. Most embassages are, in turn, part of a larger fixed complex that one might call "vassalization." This subplot, which is repeated eight times in the play, consists of: the embassage; journey of vassal-to-be to the lord's seat; vassal's submission (with genuflection and formula); investiture; and vassal's return home. Two of the eight vassalization subplots contain a variation: refusal to pay homage followed by battle, defeat, and submission. The embassage and homages closely reflect real customs, procedures, and ceremonies, but here they are so standardized and repetitive that they are the main reason for the play's often-noted liturgical or ceremonial character.

The impression of a cathedralesque architecture also results from a combination of parallelism and opposition. The play has the basic structure most common in medieval literature (for example, in the Arthurian tale), that of two parallel segments — in this case, the Emperor story and the Antichrist story. Both begin with the same three confession hymns, show the creation of an empire and its defense against attackers (the King of Babylon and the prophets, respectively), and end with the completion of an empire. In essence, however, they are antithetical: the first ruler submits to God, the second considers himself God; the first accepts the limits of his mission (he leaves the pagans alone and does

not try to convert the other faiths), the second strives for absolute and universal power; the first is restrained and magnanimous toward the vanquished, the second is ruthless and murderous; the first empire exhibits great order, the second is less orderly and harmonious.

The interpretation of the *Ludus de Antichristo* has always been a matter of much controversy. Most of the critics have held a "symbolist" position, regarding the play as a parable expressing the imperial ideology of the Hohenstaufen circle. Others have seen it solely as a dramatization of eschatology. A few critics have suggested that the play is ambivalent, vacillating between being symbolic and historical. None of these views is quite satisfactory. The symbolist and eschatological views are too one-dimensional and reductionist to do justice to the many-faceted work, and the "indeterminist" view, while acknowledging two realms of meaning, implies, by using terms such as *vacillation* and *ambivalence,* that there is a fault or shortcoming in the play. Actually, the fault is in these interpretations, which are based on modern mental predispositions and disregard still another medieval mind-set from which the play must be viewed: the putative audience of the *Ludus de Antichristo* was well versed and practiced in the medieval hermeneutical method of "allegorism," a way to find God-given meaning behind the literal sense of the Scriptures.

This method was based on the Neoplatonic view of creation as a strictly ordered system that gradually materialized from the transcendent principles and ideas emanating from God. These principles or universals (*universalia*) exist in all elements of creation, whether things (from angels and humans to animals and inanimate objects) or events. And all things throughout space and time that have a universal in common are linked with one another. The purpose of the human mind is to strive toward God by searching for these universals. In the Scriptures God has given humanity a teaching book that shows how things and events point and refer to (*significare*) more-essential, universal facts. Scriptural texts, thus, have two levels of meaning: first, there is the literal sense (*sensus litteralis*), in which words have their direct and normal meaning — where, for instance, *saxum* means "stone"; then there is the spiritual sense (*sensus spiritualis*), in which these meanings, in turn, signify other meanings — where a stone may point to a tyrant, the universal inherent in both being "intransigence." On the spiritual level, medieval exegesis distinguished three areas: the allegorical sense (*sensus allegoricus* or *figuralis*), in which things signify elements of history; the moral sense (*sensus moralis*), in which they signify ethical precepts; and the anagogic sense (*sensus anagogicus*), in which they signify transcendental truths. The standard example was *Jerusalem*. In the literal sense this word signified the material, historical town in Palestine; in the allegorical sense the town, in turn, signified and referred to the Christian Church; in the moral sense it signified the devout Christian; and in the anagogic sense it signified the celestial city of God. The universal common to all four significations was "Christ's abode." An audience consisting of clergy and educated laity, accustomed to search for the spiritual sense in all Scripture and scholarly writing, cannot but have perceived the *Ludus de Antichristo* allegorically, since it was thought to be a presentation of scriptural lore. A medieval audience would, thus, have understood the play on several planes at the same time.

The *sensus litteralis* of the *Ludus de Antichristo* consists, of course, in the events presented in the play. The salient point here is that for a contemporary recipient, this plot was not a story but history. While a modern reader might see the *Ludus de Antichristo* as a cleverly constructed and creative piece of propaganda, the author probably shared the general notion of his time that a writer's duty was to present the factual truth about the world and that any invention was a cardinal sin. An author's mission was, to put it in modern terms, factual, expository writing, while fiction was taboo. For the author of the *Ludus de Antichristo* and his audience, therefore, the play was not a fictional dramatization of utopian ideas but a quasi-liturgical preenactment of future history as it had been told in the Scriptures. All that the author did was to concentrate on certain aspects of the sanctioned material; arrange it to reveal its hidden order; and interpolate details that logically seemed to belong in it or that were found elsewhere in the Scriptures, such as the many biblical and liturgical quotations with which the text is saturated. It is conceivable that the author was a sophisticated manipulator of his audience who did not think that he was writing history but was aware that he was creating a story for propaganda purposes. Even in that case, however, his audience must be assumed to have perceived the play with the normal medieval mind-set. The *Ludus de Antichristo,* therefore, should be read not as a parable or an allegory but as a factual "docudrama" – which, to be sure, was meant to be interpreted by the allegorical method.

The *sensus spiritualis* of the *Ludus de Antichristo* can easily be discerned in its three aspects. The *sensus moralis* could be found in the antithetical features of the Emperor and the Antichrist – the former's *humilitas* (humility) and the latter's *superbia,* the autarchic egocentricity that dooms the Antichrist, as Ecclesia declares after his fall: "Ecce homo qui non posuit deum adintorem suum!" (See here, a man who did not make God his helper!, line 415). The *sensus anagogicus* would have been discovered in the universals embodied in the characters and situations of the literal level. For example, the universal of the "Just King" (*rex iustus*), epitomized in God's lordly function, would be incorporated in the character and the acts of the Emperor; the Roman Empire would signify the Kingdom of God (*civitas Dei*). The Antichrist, on the other hand, was the typical embodiment (*typos*) of the Devil, and the Antichrist's dominion was the typification of the *civitas diaboli* (Kingdom of the Devil). The main political thrust of the play, however, seems to lie in the *sensus allegoricus,* because this level comprises the relationship between scriptural events (in this case, the story of the two empires) and events and figures of nonscriptural history (in this case, the contemporary political situation). For example, the two wars against the King of Babylon in the *Ludus de Antichristo* and the first two Crusades of the twelfth century are manifestations of the universal "Soldiery for God" (*militia Dei*), which was one of the strongest theological justifications for the chivalric mode of life. In this way, many elements in the play can be typologically related to contemporary issues. The figures of Hypocrisis and the Hypocritae, to take one particularly potent instance, carried an extensive and severe condemnation of the religious reform movement that was strongly opposed to the fusion of secular and ecclesiastical power in the Imperial Church. All in all, an allegorical exegesis of the *Ludus de Antichristo* would see the reign of the Last Emperor as a secular reflection of the transcendent *civitas Dei* and as a future but preordained example that the Hohenstaufen empire was duty-bound to emulate. A modern and a medieval understanding of the play are, thus, diametrically opposed: while for a modern critic the *Ludus de Antichristo* may be a dramatization of imperial ideology, for the medieval interpreter it was the opposite. The author, or at least the audience, would see the imperial ideology as a reflection of universals that were also visible in the episode of future history enacted in the play.

There is yet another respect in which the modern reader is at a disadvantage compared with a medieval spectator: the reader lacks the experience of a performance of the play. The modern reader's attention may be focused more on the impressive recited text with its sonorous rhythms than on the less conspicuous rubrics, especially since present editions number only the verse lines. For the medieval audience, however, accustomed to seeing a plethora of symbolic acts in daily life, the actions and ceremonies in the play probably had a stronger impact than the chanted declarations and pronouncements, since these ideas and tenets were standard fare. A modern reader should try, therefore, to imagine the play in performance. Opera may be the modern theatrical form that comes closest to the synthesis of arts displayed in a *Ludus de Antichristo* performance. The reader must imagine a pageantry that encompassed many art forms and must have been a sensually overwhelming spectacle and display of power and majesty. There was the background of Romanesque architecture, as the play was most likely staged inside a cathedral. There were splendid costumes (ceremonial vestments, armor, exotic dress) and imposing props (crowns and other regalia, ornate thrones, an idol, an altar). There was the choreography of the processions, marches, and battles, which were based on old popular traditions and had a balletic character. There was much pantomime, for instance in the false miracles, in the cajolery of the hypocrites, and whenever the text describes emotions such as anger, doubt, or triumph. And there was the music, ranging from chants (perhaps in the Gregorian tradition) to arias (for instance, surrealistically, an angel on high sings a biblical love song while the martyrs are being killed), from hymns and chorals to marching songs, all possibly accompanied by an organ, trumpets, and drums. Even the spoken passages contributed to the composition with their strong rhythms of rhymed couplets. Given the belief that all material and sensual things are only a reflection and a symbol of a superior world, the overall effect of this event must have been altogether spellbinding.

The *Ludus de Antichristo* has been staged in modern times, mainly in Germany during the 1920s and early 1930s. But these attempts have not left lasting impressions in the critical literature and probably were not adequate to the play. To bring the *Ludus de Antichristo* to theatrical life again would take a composer, a choreographer, and a director who were not only in sympathy with the author but also equally gifted.

**Bibliography:**

Carl J. Stratman, *Bibliography of Medieval Drama,* second edition (New York: Ungar, 1972).

**References:**

Klaus Aichele, *Das Antichristdrama des Mittelalters, der Reformation und der Gegenreformation* (The Hague: Nijhoff, 1974);

Aichele, "The Glorification of Antichrist in the Concluding Scenes of the Medieval *Ludus de Antichristo,*" *Modern Language Notes,* 91 (April 1976): 424–436;

Heinrich Appelt, *Die Kaiseridee Friedrich Barbarossas* (Vienna: Böhlau, 1967);

Richard Axton, *European Drama of the Middle Ages* (London: Hutchinson, 1974);

G. Barraclough, *The Medieval Empire: Idea and Reality* (London: Historical Association, 1950);

Amelia Jane Carr, "Visual and Symbolic Imagery in the 12th Century Tegernsee 'Ludus de Antichristo,' " Ph.D. dissertation, Northwestern University, 1984;

Edmund Kerchever Chambers, *The Medieval Stage* (Oxford: Oxford University Press, 1903);

W. Couch, "The Dramatic Structure of the *Ludus de Antichristo,*" *Revue de l'université d'Ottawa,* 42 (1972): 272–278;

Richard Kenneth Emmerson, *Antichrist in the Middle Ages: A Study of Medieval Apocalypticism, Art, and Literature* (Seattle: University of Washington Press, 1981);

Francois Louis Ganshoff, *Feudalism,* translated by Philip Grierson, third edition (New York: Harper, 1964);

Wolfgang Greisenegger, *Die Realität im religiösen Theater des Mittelalters,* Wiener Forschungen zur Theater- und Medienwissenschaft, no. 1 (Vienna: Braumüller, 1978);

Gerhard Günther, *Der Antichrist: Der staufische Ludus de Antichristo* (Hamburg: Wittig, 1970);

Karl Hauck, "Zur Genealogie und Gestalt des staufischen *Ludus de Antichristo,*" *Germanisch-Romanische Monatsschrift,* new series 2 (1951): 11–26;

Friedrich Heer, *The Holy Roman Empire,* translated by Janet Sondheimer (London: Weidenfeld, 1968);

Wolfgang Hempel, "Die allegoretische Struktur des *Ludus de Antichristo,*" in *Momentum dramaticum: Festschrift for Eckehard Catholy,* edited by Dietrick, Linda, and David G. John (Waterloo, Ont.: University of Waterloo Press, 1990), pp. 55–74;

W. T. H. Jackson, "Time and Space in the *Ludus de Antichristo,*" *Germanic Review,* 54 (Winter 1979): 1–8;

Wilhelm Kamlah, "*Der Ludus de Antichristo,*" *Historische Vierteljahrsschrift,* 28 (1934): 53–87;

Thomas Kirchner, *Raumerfahrung im geistlichen Spiel des Mittelalters* (Frankfurt am Main: Lang, 1985);

Markus Litz, *Theatrum sacrum und symbolische Weltsicht: Der staufische "ludus de antichristo"* (Frankfurt am Main: Lang, 1990);

Wilhelm Meyer, "*Der Ludus de Antichristo* und über die lateinischen Rythmen des 12. Jahrhunderts," in *Gesammelte Abhandlungen zur mittellateinischen Rythmik,* volume 1 (Berlin: Weidmann, 1905), pp. 136–170;

Peter Munz, *Frederick Barbarossa: A Study in Medieval Politics* (London: Eyre & Spotiswood, 1969);

Horst Dieter Rauh, *Das Bild des Antichrist im Mittelalter: Von Tyconius zum deutschen Symbolismus,* Beiträge zur Geschichte der Philosophie und Theologie des Mittelalters: Texte und Untersuchungen, new series (Münster: Aschendorf, 1973);

Josef Riedmann, "Ein neuaufgefundenes Bruchstück des 'Ludus de Antichristo,' " *Zeitschrift für bayrische Landesgeschichte,* 36 (1976): 16–38;

Helmut Rosenfeld, "Die Bühne des Tegernseer Antichristspieles als Orbis Terrarum," in *Literatur und Sprache im europäischen Mittelalter: Festschrift für Karl Langosch* (Darmstadt: Wissenschaftliche Buchgesellschaft, 1973), pp. 63–74;

Karl Schulze-Jahde, "Zur Literatur über das Tegernseer Antichristspiel," *Zeitschrift für deutsche Philologie,* 57 (1932): 180–183;

Bruno Stäblein, "Zur Musik des *Ludus de Antichristo,*" in *Zum 70. Geburtstag von Joseph Müller-Blattau,* edited by Christoph Mahling (Kassel: Bärenreiter, 1966), pp. 312–327;

Theo Stemmler, *Liturgische Feiern und geistliche Spiele: Studien zu Erscheinungsformen des Dramatischen im Mittelalter* (Tübingen: Niemeyer, 1970);

Helmut Weidhase, "Regie im *Ludus de Antichristo,*" in *Festschrift für Kurt Herbert Halbach,* edited by Rose Beate Schäfer-Maulbetsch and others, Göppinger Arbeiten zur Germanistik, no. 70 (Göppingen: Kümmerle, 1972), pp. 85–143;

John Wright, *The Play of Antichrist* (Toronto: Pontifical Institute of Medieval Studies, 1967);

Karl Young, *The Drama of the Medieval Church,* 2 volumes (Oxford: Clarendon Press, 1933).

# *Ludwigslied*
### *(881 or 882)*

Anatoly Liberman
*University of Minnesota*

**Manuscript:** Valenciennes, France, Bibliothèque de la Ville, MS 150, 141v–143r.

**First publications:** "Laudes Ludovici regis," edited by Karl Lachmann, in *Specimina linguae Francicae in usum auditorum* (Berlin: G. Reimeri, 1825), pp. 5–17. Facsimiles in *Die ältesten deutschen Sprach-Denkmäler in Lichtdrucken,* edited by Magda Enneccerus (Frankfurt am Main: F. Enneccerus, 1897), pp. 40–43; in *Schrifttafeln zum althochdeutschen Lesebuch,* edited by Hanns Fischer (Tübingen: Niemeyer, 1966), pp. 22–25.

**Edition in English:** Translated by J. Knight Bostock in his *A Handbook on Old English Literature,* revised by K. C. King and D. R. McLintock (Oxford: Clarendon Press, 1976), pp. 239–241.

The *Ludwigslied* (Song of Louis, 881 or 882) celebrates the victory of a king named Ludwig or Hluduig (Louis) over invading Northmen; the poet does not say where or when the battle took place. The king grew up without a father and ruled jointly with his brother Karlemann. He was away at the time of the invasion, returned home, and, at the head of the Frankish army, defeated the enemy. The names Ludwig (Louis) and Karlemann (Carloman) recur with such regularity in the Frankish royal family that as late as 1856, when Jacob Grimm's note on the *Ludwigslied* was published, some uncertainty remained as to which king and which battle inspired the song. The situation was clarified by Ernst Dümmler in 1865: Ludwig is Louis III of the West Franks, who routed the Danes at Saucourt-en-Vineu on 1 or 3 August 881.

Louis II (the Stammerer) died in 877, leaving three sons: Louis, the hero of the song, who was then seventeen years old; Carloman, who was a year younger; and Charles, who was born posthumously. Resistance on the part of some nobles did not prevent the two older brothers from being proclaimed kings: Louis took the northern part of France, and Carloman inherited Burgundy and Aquitaine. In 879 Louis and Carloman set off to the south to protect their territory from a usurper, Count Boso of Vienne. While Louis was thus engaged, the Danes ravaged France. Louis put the invaders to flight at Saucourt. Both Louis and Carloman died young: Louis on 5 August 882, Carloman in 884. The poem wishes the king a long life, so it must have been composed after the battle but before Louis's death, that is, between 1 or 3 August 881 and 5 August 882. The manuscript, however, is later, for it has a dedication to Louis's memory.

The song opens with an introduction and a retrospect. The Lord became the fatherless child's guardian and gave him a throne among the Franks. God wanted to test his servant, and so he let heathen men attack the Franks; this attack was also a punishment for the sins of the Christians. Many people perished; the sinners (thieves, robbers, liars, lechers) who survived repented. God commanded Louis to help his people, and Louis obeyed.

The introduction and retrospect take up twenty-six lines of the poem. The next twenty-eight lines are allotted to the preparation for the battle and the battle itself. At home the king is met with jubilation. He addresses his countrymen in a speech in which he recognizes God's authority over life and death and promises a reward to those who will follow him. He sings a holy song, and his warriors join in with kyrie eleison. The victory is won. The song ends with a praise of God and his saints.

The most surprising thing about the *Ludwigslied* is its provenance. Louis III was indeed a Frankish king, but he ruled over the *West* Franks, that is, over France. God gave him "stuol hier in Vrankon" (line 6), which means either "the throne here among the Franks" or, more likely, "the throne here in France." Although copied and preserved at Saint-Amand, a French monastery, the song glorifies the king of France in German; the dialect is Rhenish Franconian with an admixture of Low and Middle Franconian. The same scribe copied the ninth-cen-

*Page from the manuscript for the* Ludwigslied *(Valenciennes, France, Bibliothèque de la Ville, MS 150, fol. 142r)*

tury Old French *Sequence of Saint Eulalia.* At the end of the ninth century, Franconian was apparently still known in the western part of Charlemagne's former empire, at least at court. One must assume that the *Ludwigslied* was composed in France.

Grimm viewed the *Ludwigslied* as a modernized specimen of Germanic mythological and heroic poetry: it reminded him of the songs of the Old Icelandic *Elder Edda,* especially of the episodes in which the gods appear as the foster parents of human beings. In the *Ludwigslied* God and Ludwig converse freely: "Ludwig, my king, help my people! The Northmen have them hard pressed." "Lord, if death does not hinder me, I will do as Thou commandest" (lines 23 to 26a).

Nineteenth-century scholarship attempted to remove the Christian "overlay" from Germanic poetry and expose its pagan core. The main trend in later, especially post–World War II, studies has been to demonstrate that the Christian element in Germanic poetry is its essence. *Beowulf* (date debated), the *Heliand* (Savior, circa 850), and minor literary monuments such as the *Ludwigslied* have been reread against the background of contemporary religious treatises and declarations, and the authors of the long and short poems have emerged as shrewd theologians versed in patristic literature, always ready to drop topical hints disguised as harmless statements. The problem is that, however sophisticated the modern decoding of medieval Germanic poetry may be, in the end it comes to the predictable conclusion that Anglo-Saxon and German poets who lived between the eighth and eleventh centuries were educated Christians (usually clerics) familiar with traditional songs. This characterization is true of the *Ludwigslied* poet, who used the Otfriedian verse, that is, rhyming couplets. A meticulous investigation by Erika Urmoneit shows that, with the possible exception of the word *wunna* (enjoyment?, virtue?), his vocabulary and usage were the same as those in other works of that period. The attempt by Theophil Melicher to mine the *Ludwigslied* for old legal terms was less than completely successful because no mechanism prevents scholars from reading into neutral words the connotations they seek.

The danger of interpreting the same words as invested with a specifically Christian meaning and of hearing hidden theological overtones in them is equally great. W. Schwarz regarded the *Ludwigslied* as a political manifesto; he noted that the song was written at a time when the church was fighting for supremacy and would not allow a monarch to rule without its blessing but that there was a party that

looked on kingship as given only by God. In light of this controversy, the dialogue between God and Louis can be understood as supporting the position that Louis did not need the authority of the powerful Hincmar, archbishop of Rheims, to occupy the throne "in Vrankon": God's sanction was sufficient. Even if the poet went to the Old Testament rather than to popular songs for his inspiration and for models of God's direct commands, it does not follow that the *Ludwigslied* is a political document. Finally, it is hard, however, to believe that the dialogue between God and Louis is the song's main message.

In the *Ludwigslied* the king is represented as an *imitatio Christi:* God speaks to Louis as Louis later speaks to his warriors, though Louis's address is like many others in old songs in which the chieftain urges his retainers to be brave and promises to reward their loyalty. An encomium of a Christian monarch, the *Ludwigslied* is a blend of epic poetry and a sermon, as Gustav Ehrismann put it. Nothing testifies to the existence of ancient encomiums in German in the style of Icelandic *drápur* (long poems extolling kings); even if they existed at one time, by the ninth century they had gone out of fashion and had been supplanted by Latin hymns and songs of praise, from which the author of the *Ludwigslied* learned his art. Even skaldic encomiums could have been partly influenced by Latin hymns.

The poet's goal was not to record events but to glorify the faithful servant of God, King Louis, and he chose his effects accordingly. He mentions no names except Louis's and Carloman's. The engagement is described in the traditional language of heroic lays: "Blood suffused the fields [or cheeks?], the Franks fought; each distinguished himself, but none like Louis. Swift and brave: such was his nature. He pierced some and stabbed others" (lines 48b to 52). Although indifferent to details, the author of the *Ludwigslied* made every effort to bring out the meaning of the events described. The Northmen's attack is presented as a punishment for the Franks' sins, and Louis's victory is depicted as a reward for Louis from God.

In such songs realistic niceties interested neither the author nor his audience; but even if he had tried to give a trustworthy account of a battle, he would not have known how to do it. Heroic poetry could describe current events only by referring to a parallel from the past. For example, King Hrothgar's poet extols Beowulf's victory over Grendel by speaking of Sigemund (a positive example) and Heremod (a negative example). Beowulf himself is not even mentioned in the song. In familiar fashion, the Icelandic skald (poet) Egill glorified King Eiríkr without citing a single specific detail. Formulaic touches permeate most of the *Ludwigslied*. In addition to the battle scene, the king's speech that precedes it, and Louis's wish to ask his counselors' advice (though he had already had the "advice" of God himself and unhesitatingly followed it), all of which is formulaic, it is said that Louis "quickly poured out bitter drink to his enemies"; this phrase also occurs in *Beowulf, Andreas,* and the *Nibelungenlied* (Song of the Nibelungs, circa 1200).

Louis's biography is reminiscent of an epic hero's life or of that of a Christian saint; it develops in the poem according to the formulaic fairy-tale theme of "male Cinderella." It is true that Louis lost his father at a rather early age, but he did not, as the *Ludwigslied* claims, grow up an orphan. The author has nothing to say about the mutinous feudals, internecine strife, the horror of the Vikings' raids, or the dramatic course of the battle of Saucourt (the Franks were almost overpowered just when victory seemed within reach), but he mentions Carloman, who did not participate in the engagement. It apparently seemed important to him that Louis, like so many other characters in fairy tales, should have a younger brother. Misfortune happened at home when the "adult" was away – another feature of the fairy tale. The poet makes these clichés of oral tradition serve his aim: the destitute child was not left alone, for God became the boy's guardian and gave him valor, a splendid following, and a kingdom. It is in the poet's ability to combine elements of various traditions that signs of his mastery must be sought.

The technical perfections and imperfections of the *Ludwigslied* are hard for a modern reader to evaluate. The song must have been commissioned, which means that its author enjoyed the reputation of a professional poet. He has a good command of the Otfriedian verse, the main medium of German monks-turned-poets around the end of the first millennium, though his rhyming sometimes differs from Otfried's. He skillfully alternates parataxis in the descriptive episodes and hypotaxis in the king's speech and knows how to arrange his material. Hans Eggers has attempted to show that the first forty-seven verses obey the "law of the golden section" (18+11+18), but the *Ludwigslied* does not fall into obvious segments. J. Seemüller and Rudolf Kögel emphasize the ballad style of the poem, that is, its highlighting of the peaks at the expense of details.

The poet must have been close to Louis's court, though not necessarily a participant in the battle, for one need not witness an event to describe it in formulaic terms. Lines 13 to 19, about the repentance of thieves and other sinners, are usually interpreted as showing that the poet was a cleric. Scholars who insist on the political message of the *Ludwigslied* have suggested that the poet belonged to circles engaged in the drafting of the Capitularies of 862 and 889 and even that Gauzlin, Louis's chancellor, had commissioned the song. Hucbald (Hukbald, Hugbald) of Saint-Amand has often been named as the most probable author of the *Ludwigslied*, but no proof of his authorship has been found. In 1929 Eduard Sievers revived this hypothesis; he also ascribed the *Sequence of Saint Eulalia* to Hucbald. Sievers's reliance on his method of *Schallanalyse* (sound analysis) guaranteed his conjecture a short life, but the problems that puzzled him – who could have felt equally at ease copying Old French and Old High German texts, why this person spoke Rhenish Franconian at Saint-Amand, and what kind of dialect West Franconian was – are the most important ones in the linguistic study of the *Ludwigslied*.

**References:**

Heinrich Beck, "Zur literaturgeschichtlichen Stellung des althochdeutschen Ludwigsliedes und einiger verwandter Zeitgedichte," *Zeitschrift für deutsches Altertum und deutsche Literatur,* 103 (1974): 37–51;

Elisabeth Berg, "Das Ludwigslied und die Schlacht bei Saucourt," *Rheinische Vierteljahrsblätter,* 29 (1964): 175–199;

J. Knight Bostock, *A Handbook on Old High German Literature,* second edition, edited by K. C. King and D. R. McLintock (Oxford: Clarendon Press, 1976);

Wilhelm Braune, *Althochdeutsches Lesebuch,* edited by Ernst A. Ebbinghaus (Tübingen: Niemeyer, 1969);

Rosemary Combridge, "Zur Handschrift des Ludwigsliedes," *Zeitschrift für deutsches Altertum und deutsche Literatur,* 97 (1964): 33–37;

Ernst Dümmler, *Geschichte des Ostfränkischen Reichs,* volume 2 (Berlin: Duncker & Humblot, 1865);

Hans Eggers, "Der Goldene Schnitt im Aufbau alt- und mittelhochdeutscher Epen," *Wirkendes Wort,* 10 (1960): 193–203;

Trude Ehlert, "Literatur und Wirklichkeit – Exegese und Politik: Zur Deutung des Ludwigsliedes," *Saeculum,* 32 (1981): 31–42;

Gustav Ehrismann, *Geschichte der deutschen Literatur bis zum Ausgang des Mittelalters,* part 1, *Die althochdeutsche Literatur,* Handbuch des deutschen

Unterrichts an höheren Schulen, no. 6 (Munich: Beck, 1918);

Hanns Fischer, *Schrifttafeln zum althochdeutschen Lesebuch* (Tübingen: Niemeyer, 1966);

Wiebke Freytag, "Ludwigslied," in *Die Deutsche Literatur des Mittelalters: Verfasserlexikon,* second edition, volume 5, edited by Kurt Ruh and others (Berlin & New York: De Gruyter, 1905), cols. 1035–1039;

Jacob Grimm, "Über das Ludwigslied," *Germania,* 1 (1856): 233–235;

Ruth Harvey, "The Provenance of the Old High German Ludwigslied," *Medium Ævum,* 14 (1945): 1–20;

Holger Homann, "Das Ludwigslied – Dichtung im Dienste der Politik?," in *Traditions and Transitions, Studies in Honor of Harold Jantz,* edited by Lieselotte E. Kurth, William H. McClain, and Homann (Munich: Delp, 1972), pp. 17–28;

Johann Kelle, *Geschichte der Deutschen Litteratur von der ältesten Zeit bis zur Mitte des elften Jahrhunderts* (Berlin: Herz, 1892);

Raimund Kemper, "Das Ludwigslied im Kontext zeitgenössischer Rechtsvorgänge," *Deutsche Vierteljahrsschrift für Literaturwissenschaft und Geistesgeschichte,* 56 (1982): 161–173;

Rudolf Kögel, *Geschichte der deutschen Litteratur bis zum Ausgange des Mittelalters* (Strasbourg: Karl Trübner, 1897);

Paul Lafrancq, *"Rhythmus teutonicus" ou "Ludwigslied"?: De la decouverte de Mabillon (Saint-Amand, 1672). A celle d'Hoffmann von Fallersleben (Valenciennes, 1837)* (Paris: Droz, 1945);

Friedrich Maurer, "Hildebrandslied und Ludwigslied," in his *Dichtung und Sprache des Mittelalters: Gesammelte Aufsätze,* second edition (Bern & Munich: Francke, 1971), pp. 157–167;

Theophil Melicher, "Die Rechtsaltertümer im Ludwigslied," *Anzeiger der phil.-hist. Klasse der österreichischen Akademie der Wissenschaften,* 18 (1954): 254–275;

Brian O. Murdoch, "Saucourt and the *Ludwigslied:* Some Observations on Medieval Historical Poetry," *Revue belge de philologie et d'histoire,* 55, 3 (1977): 841–867;

Rudolf Schützeichel, "Ludwigslied; Das Heil des Königs," in his *Textgebundenheit: Kleinere Schriften zur mittelalterlichen deutschen Literatur* (Tübingen: Niemeyer, 1981), pp. 45–67;

Schützeichel, "Das Ludwigslied und die Erforschung des Westfränkischen," *Rheinische Vierteljahrsblätter,* 31 (1967): 290–306;

W. Schwarz, "The 'Ludwigslied,' a Ninth-Century Poem," *Modern Language Review,* 42 (October 1947): 467–473;

J. Seemüller, "Studie zu den Ursprüngen der altdeutschen Historiographie," in *Abhandlungen zur germanischen Philologie: Festgabe für Richard Heinzel* (Halle: Niemeyer, 1896), pp. 278–352;

Eduard Sievers, "Elnonensia," in *Philologisch-Philosophische Studien: Festschrift für Eduard Wechssler zum 19. Oktober 1929,* Berliner Beiträge zur Romanischen Philologie, no. 1 (Jena & Leipzig: Gronau, 1929), pp. 247–277;

Erika Urmoneit, *Der Wortschatz des Ludwigsliedes im Umkreis der althochdeutschen Literatur,* Münstersche Mittelalter-Schriften, no. 11 (Munich: Fink, 1973);

Max Wehrli, "Gattungsgeschichtliche Betrachtungen zum Ludwigslied," in *Philologia Deutsch: Festschrift zum 70. Geburtstag von Walter Henzen,* edited by Werner Kohlschmidt and Paul Zinsli (Bern: Francke, 1965), pp. 9–20;

Fritz Willems, "Der parataktische Satzstil im Ludwigslied," *Zeitschrift für deutsches Altertum und deutsche Literatur,* 85 (1954): 18–35.

# *Muspilli*
## (circa 790 – circa 850)

### Robert G. Sullivan
*University of Massachusetts at Amherst*

**Manuscript:** The fragmentary work is preserved only on the endleaves (61r, 120v, and 121rv) and two lower margins (119v and 120r) of a manuscript of the pseudo-Augustinian *Sermo de symbolo contra Iudaeos paganos et Arianos,* which is itself part of a larger codex, Munich, Staatsbibliothek, clm 14098. The *Sermo* was copied between 825 and 836, and the *Muspilli* was entered at a later date by a different hand. Its legibility has sharply decreased since its discovery by J. B. Docen in 1817.

**First publication:** *Muspilli: Bruchstück einer alliterierenden Dichtung vom Ende der Welt mit einem Faksimile des Originals,* edited by J. A. Schmeller, *Neue Beiträge zur vaterländischen Geschichte, Geographie und Statistik,* no. 1 (Munich: G. Jaquet, 1832), pp. 89–117.

**Standard edition:** In *Althochdeutsches Lesebuch,* edited by Wilhelm Braune, revised by Ernst A. Ebbinghaus, sixteenth edition (Tübingen: Niemeyer, 1979), pp. 86–89.

**Edition in English:** In A. Robert Bell, "*Muspilli:* Apocalypse as Political Threat," *Studies in the Literary Imagination* 8, no. 1 (1975): 102–104.

The *Muspilli* (circa 790–circa 850), a fragmentary and anonymous poem of only 103 lines, has fascinated and confounded students of medieval German literature since its rediscovery in the early nineteenth century. Even the meaning of the title of the poem, which its first editor, J. A. Schmeller, derived from a word in line 57 (*muspille*), has been a source of controversy. Scarcely more agreement has been reached on the interpretation of the poem itself, which depicts the end of the world and the Last Judgment. Indeed, the history of the scholarly investigation of the poem provides, in miniature, a sketch of the changing fashions and interests of the study of older German literature. As one of the few surviving Old High German alliterative poems and a work unique in the vernacular literature of its time, the *Muspilli* holds a central place in the study of early medieval literature and religious and social history.

The exact date of composition of the *Muspilli* cannot be determined; linguistic evidence in the poem provides only a vague dating of sometime in the ninth century, probably the first half and certainly after 790. The Latin theological tract in which the *Muspilli* is preserved, the pseudo-Augustinian *Sermo de symbolo contra Iudaeos paganos et Arianos* (A sermon on the creed against The Jews, Pagans, and Arians) yields somewhat more precise information about when the *Muspilli* was written down. The carefully written manuscript for the *Sermo* was the property of Louis the German, the ruler of the East Franconian kingdom, and was presented to him by Adalram, Bishop of Salzburg from 821 until 836. Louis probably received the manuscript sometime after his arrival in the east as duke of Bavaria in 825 and before Adalram's death in 836. A date closer to 825 is most likely since Adalram addresses Louis in some dedicatory verses as "summe puer" (most noble boy). A later date, and inspired perhaps by a connection he perceived between the poem and the treatment of eschatological themes in the *Sermo,* a different and far inferior scribe added the *Muspilli* on the blank pages and lower margins of the Latin work. The older hypothesis that Louis himself or his wife copied the *Muspilli* onto the pages of his splendid Latin manuscript is unsubstantiated. The most persuasive conclusion one may draw is that the poem was entered sometime in the quarter century after Louis's death in 876. The introduction and conclusion to the poem were likely to have been written on the front and back covers of the *Sermo,* and were probably lost when the Latin work was attached to a larger codex, which eventually became the possession of the monastery of Saint Emmeram in Regensburg.

The author of the *Muspilli* is unknown. Orthographic irregularities and mistakes in the text strongly imply that the scribe was copying from another written version and not, as has occasionally been supposed, from an oral version. Whether this earlier written version was in turn a compilation of two separate works, as some scholars claim, can only be answered by an interpretation of the thematic unity of the poem. The dialect of the poem is generally Bavarian; some puzzling exceptions include a few instances of the diphthong *ua,* characteristic of the Alemannic and South Rhenish Franconian dialects, instead of the Bavarian *uo,* and the occasional, seemingly arbitrary use of *h* before vowels. The text is also inconsistent in its rendering of geminated, or doubled, consonants, which were pronounced separately in Old High German. These peculiarities and inconsistencies are doubtless best attributed to the scribe.

The original author of the *Muspilli* had a clear interest in and access to somewhat obscure eschatological traditions; whether these traditions were Christian or pagan can only be decided by the interpretation of the poem and its sources. Most likely the poet had a monastic education. Frequent use of legal terminology in the poem reveals a writer well acquainted with contemporary judicial practices, and the poet's criticism of legal abuses implies an acquaintance with similar Carolingian strictures. The alliterative verse form of the *Muspilli,* however inadequate, shows that its author was familiar with native poetic forms, either from missionary interest or simply because these forms were generally popular. One may, thus, imagine the author of the *Muspilli* to have been a somewhat, or perhaps highly, learned Bavarian monk of independent mind who had contact with powerful members of lay society and who felt a deep need to preach on theological and legal and social problems.

The *Muspilli* is for the most part written in the accentual and alliterative verse (*Stabreim*) characteristic of Germanic poetry. Germanic alliteration is typically determined by the third stress of the long line, which contains a total of four stresses and is divided by a caesura into two half lines. The third stress alliterates with either or both of the first two stresses and, less frequently, the fourth stress. Line 14 of the *Muspilli,* in which only the first and third stresses alliterate, provides an ideal example: "dar ist líp ano tód, líoht ano fínstri" (There there is life without death, light without darkness). The *Muspilli* poet's use of alliteration, however, is neither consistent nor devoid of obvious flaws. He frequently transgresses the ideal form by misplacing

the alliterative stresses, as in line 15, in which the fourth stress, rather than the third, determines the alliteration. He writes what would seem excessively long lines (such as line 60, which contains seventeen syllables) and combines end rhyme with alliteration (for example, in lines 7 and 37). In line 61 he even substitutes end rhyme for alliteration: "diu marha ist farbrunnan, diu sela stet pidungan" (The land shall be burned; the soul shall stand in sorrow). Indeed, lines 61–62 are an instance of the non-Germanic, rhyming verse that Otfried von Weißenburg used. (Paradoxically, however, line 14 of the *Muspilli,* an example of traditional Germanic alliterative verse, also occurs in Otfried's *Evangelienbuch* [Gospel Book, between 863 and 871], I, 18, 9.) As a result of these irregularities, the alliterative verse of the *Muspilli* is typically described as transitional or, less favorably, as decadent.

The poem presents a fairly cohesive unity, even if the transitions between the parts are sometimes abrupt or seemingly illogical. It is unlikely, therefore, that the missing introduction and conclusion were of great length. The overall thematic structure is clear: lines 1 to 30 describe the fate of the individual soul at death; lines 31 to 36 depict the summons to the Last Judgment; lines 37 to 62 are an account of the battle between the Antichrist and Elijah and its consequences; lines 63 to 72 warn of judicial abuses; and lines 73 to 103 portray the Last Judgment. Georg Baesecke claimed on philological, metrical, and thematic grounds that lines 37 to 62 are interpolated from a second poem (the so-called *Muspilli II* hv), but the evidence for this thesis is inconsistent and ambiguous. Scholars today tend to place less confidence in such speculative editorial practices and argue instead for the necessity of treating the received text as a whole. It may be that the text of the *Muspilli* is corrupt or even a compilation, but a convincing and historical interpretation must be empirically based on the existing text and not on a postulated version that claims to present the original author's intention.

The ostensible theme of the *Muspilli,* the end of the world and the Last Judgment, is not unique. Fears and hopes for the imminent end of the world obsessed the early Christians, who were influenced in their eschatological speculations by passages in the Old Testament as well as by other Jewish and Christian apocalyptic writings, which, although frequently obscure, were highly imaginative in detail. The canonical Christian apocalyptic text is, of course, the New Testament Revelation of Saint John the Divine, also known as the Apocalypse. With the demise of pagan persecution and the grad-

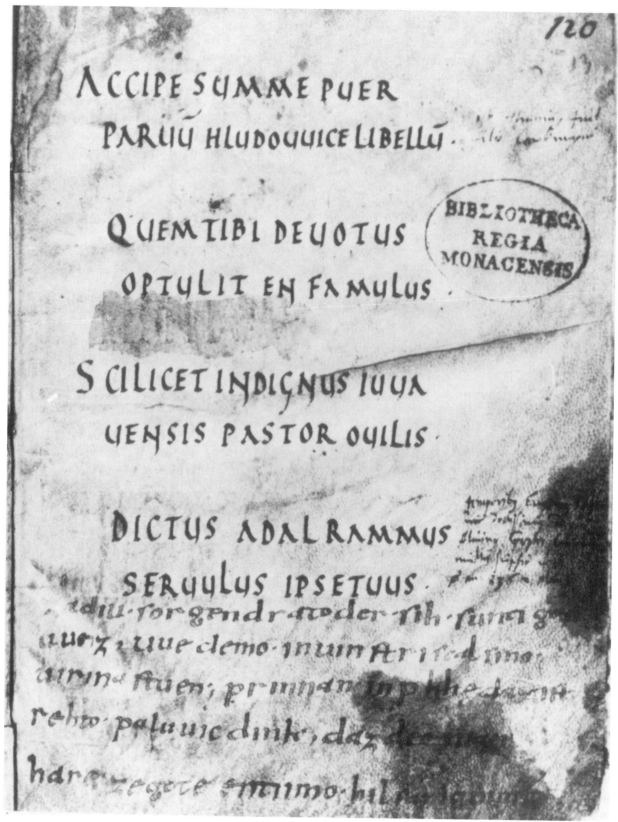

*Dedication by Bishop Adalram of Salzburg to King Louis the German, and lines 23–27 of the poem, from the manuscript for the* Muspilli
*(Munich, Bayerische Staatsbibliothek, clm 14098, fol. 120r)*

ual establishment of Christianity as the state religion in the fourth century, however, apocalyptic fervor was not only generally discouraged but often actively suppressed. The doctrine of "delayed eschatology" safely postponed the Second Coming to an unknown later time, and in the hands of many of the Latin church fathers popular speculations on the end of the world became sober and learned theological discussions. The topic nevertheless continued to fascinate scholars, preachers, and laypeople, and parallels have been drawn between the *Muspilli* and the Old English poem *Christ III* (ninth century). In the ninth century, aside from many treatments and theological discussions in Latin, both Otfried von Weißenburg and the anonymous author of the Old Saxon *Heliand* (Savior, circa 850) discussed the Second Coming of Christ in detail in their poetic versions of the Gospels. When German literature was revived in the late eleventh century, vernacular interest in universal and particular eschatology commenced anew, beginning with Jacob's prophecy to his sons in the *Vienna Genesis* (circa 1075), lines 5667 to 5745 and Notker von Zwiefalten's *Memento mori* (circa 1080). One would, however, be mistaken in associating any of these works with the popular, often revolutionary millenarian movements that arose in the late eleventh century. None of the poems betrays an eschatological urgency, nor can they be called revolutionary. Rather, these vernacular works discuss eschatological themes as part of church dogma or, more typically, in a homiletic fashion. Their purpose is less to announce the end of the world or the advent of the New Jerusalem than to instill righteous conduct in their readers and listeners by means of the frightful description of the consequences of evil and injustice. The *Muspilli* thus stands firmly in a long and established tradition.

What distinguishes the *Muspilli* from other eschatological works is its marked interest in and peculiar treatment of certain details of the vision of the end of the world. A deeper knowledge of Western apocalyptic tradition, however, has deflated many of the earlier claims about the absolute uniqueness of the poet's version of the Last Judgment. For example, the apparent contradiction between the vivid description of the war between the demonic and heavenly hosts for the individual soul after death (lines 1 to 30) and the universal judgment pronounced by Christ at the end of the world (lines 73 to 103) can be resolved theologically by the notion of purgatory. First codified in the twelfth century, the doctrine of purgatory was foreshadowed by Augustine and other patristic writers, especially Pope Gregory the Great. According to Greg-

ory, the soul is judged immediately after the death of the person and sent to heaven, hell, or a place in upper hell where it should strive to purge itself of its worldly sins until the Last Judgment, after which, if successful in its penitence, it will reside in heaven. The *Muspilli*, thus, portrays these two temporally distinct steps in the judgment of the individual soul. While the details of purgatory were often vague and differed from writer to writer, the concept was well known, as may be seen from Bede's *Historia Ecclesiastica Gentis Anglorum* (Ecclesiastical History of the English People, 731, V, 12), which relates the story of a man named Drycthelm who came back from the dead and gave a detailed report of what he had seen.

The most puzzling aspects of the eschatology of the *Muspilli* are in lines 37 to 62, on the fight between the Antichrist and Elijah and its consequences. Rev. 11:1–13, the ultimate source of the description, tells of "two witnesses" who will prophesy at the end of the world and then be slain by "the beast from the bottomless pit." After three and a half days, they will arise from the dead and ascend to heaven in a cloud. But the account in Revelation is far from clear. Early Christian tradition identified the nameless witnesses as Enoch and Elijah, who, according to the Old Testament, had never died but had been taken up by God to heaven (Gen. 5:24; 2 Kings 2:11–12); the beast was understood to be the Antichrist, who is later to be defeated by Christ (Rev. 17:11–14). The *Muspilli* poet gives two different accounts of the battle. According to the *weroltrehtwison* (those knowledgeable about earthly justice, line 37), he says, Elijah alone will defeat the Antichrist; the "gotman" (followers of God, line 48), however, say that Elijah will be wounded, perhaps fatally, in the battle. This second view, to which the poet adheres, is closest to the biblical account and to the main Western tradition. Elijah (usually together with Enoch) defeats the Antichrist, on the other hand, only in a handful of sources. The one most explicit and similar to the *Muspilli* is the Coptic translation of an originally Greek *Apocalypse of Elijah* from the late third century. Some isolated Western instances have also been discovered, most notably in Cassiodorus's commentary on the Psalms (*Expositio in Psalterium*, circa 540–548) where it is mentioned in an aside that the Antichrist is to be defeated by the "duo viri sanctissimi" (two most holy men), Enoch and Elijah. One plausible reading of the poem's two contrasting versions of the battle between Elijah and the Antichrist relates them to the poet's concern with justice and his criticism of contemporary legal practice. In this view the *weroltrehtwison* see the battle as a trial by combat or judicial ordeal, in which Elijah, as the representative of God, must prevail. The *gotman* reject this interpretation as contrary to the biblical account and because they know that God's perfect justice will be fully realized only at the Last Judgment itself.

No less unusual than the inclusion of the tradition of Elijah's victory over the Antichrist are lines 50–51 of the *Muspilli*. The manuscript is torn at this point, but according to the traditional emendations the lines read: "[so da]z Eliases pluot in erda kitriufit, / [so] inprinnant die perga, poum ni kistentit" ([When] Elijah's blood drips to the earth, / [then] the mountains will burn, not a tree shall stand). These emendations are convincing, yet they introduce a causal relation between Elijah's blood and the fiery destruction of the world that is unknown to most traditional accounts. The few exceptions include an eighth-century Spanish formulary, which says that the flames that will consume the world will arise from the blood of Enoch and Elijah. Similar legends persisted in medieval Russia and Siberia as late as the nineteenth century.

One solution to the difficulties presented by the *Muspilli* is the hypothesis that the poet's sources or inspiration were Germanic in origin. Parallels have been drawn, for example, between the poem and the Germanic vision of the end of the world in the Old Norse *Voluspá* (late tenth to early eleventh century) in the *Elder Edda* or with Snorri Sturluson's account of the battle between Thor and the world serpent in the *Prose Edda* (circa 1220–1230). Those who hold this view hoped to gain support for it by attempting to give a pagan interpretation to the word *muspille* in line 57: "dar ni mac denne mak andremo helfan vora demo muspille" (There no relative can help another in the face of the *muspilli*). No word in the poem has received more attention or been interpreted more diversely: the standard edition (1979) lists more than fifteen etymological conjectures and combinations. The word occurs nowhere else in Old High German, but there are two instances of it in the Old Saxon *Heliand,* where it means either "the end of the world" ("mûdspelli," line 2591) or perhaps "Christ at the Second Coming" ("mûtspelli," line 4358). In Old Norse, Muspell is the pagan name of either a giant or the realm of fire from which the "sons of Muspell" will ride out to battle against the gods at the end of the world. Based in part on these cognates and etymological reconstructions, *muspilli* is most frequently understood to mean "the fire at the end of the world." It is impossible to determine whether the word would have had pagan associations in ninth-century Bavaria, and in view of the parallels between the *Muspilli* poet's eschatology and certain, admittedly isolated, strands of Christian tradition, some scholars treat the Germanic interpretation of the poem with caution.

Despite its often obscure eschatological detail, the purpose of the *Muspilli* is strikingly clear and no less Christian than other early-medieval German vernacular works on the end of the world: to castigate sins and to admonish listeners to reform their lives and do penance. Even if these homiletic demands are corrupt additions to or distortions of the original poem, they now constitute the thematic core from which the interpretation of the poem must proceed. Judicial perversions are especially attacked in the poem – for example, in lines 66 to 68, where "denner mit den miaton marrit daz rehta" (he who impedes justice by proffering bribes, line 67) is warned of his fate at the Last Judgment. These lines also help to situate the poem in its historical context as well as in the history of German literature. Line 67 is nearly identical to injunctions in an early-ninth-century capitulary for Charlemagne's "missi dominici" (special envoys). Using a Latin form of the Old High German verb *marren* (to impede), the capitulary similarly prohibits the impeding of justice ("iustitiam marrire") by bribes. The word for judicial bribes in line 67, *miata,* moreover, is used by Otfried (V, 19, 57) in a nearly identical context and in the early Middle High German period became almost a technical term (*miete*) for this frequently criticized abuse. Such examples show that the *Muspilli* poet's vision of the end of the world serves as a warning and that his description of the Last Judgment provides the standard against which the sin of injustice in this world is measured and condemned.

## Bibliographies:

Gustav Ehrismann, *Geschichte der deutschen Literatur bis zum Ausgang des Mittelalters,* part 1: *Die althochdeutsche Literatur,* second edition (Munich: Beck, 1932), pp. 147–148;

Hans-Hugo Steinhoff, "Muspilli," in *Die deutsche Literatur des Mittelalters: Verfasserlexikon,* second edition, edited by Kurt Ruh, vol. 6 (Berlin: de Gruyter, 1987), cols. 821–828.

## References:

Georg Baesecke, "Muspilli II," *Zeitschrift für deutsches Altertum und deutsche Literatur,* 82 (1948–1950): 199–239;

Charles M. Barrack, "*Muspilli:* A Dilemma in Reconstructuring," *Folia Linguistica,* 8 (1975): 255–269;

A. Robert Bell, "*Muspilli:* Apocalypse as Political Threat," *Studies in the Literary Imagination,* 8, no. 1 (1975): 75–104;

J. Knight Bostock, *A Handbook on Old High German Literature,* second edition, revised by K. C. King and D. R. McLintock (Oxford: Clarendon Press, 1976), pp. 135–154;

Hilda R. E. Davidson, *Gods and Myths of Northern Europe* (Harmondsworth, U.K.: Penguin, 1964), pp. 202–210;

Rudolf van Delden, "Die sprachliche Gestalt des 'Muspilli' und ihre Vorgeschichte im Zusammenhang mit der Abschreiberfrage," *Paul/Braune Beiträge zur Geschichte der deutschen Sprache und Literatur,* 65 (1941): 303–329;

A. C. Dunstan, "*Muspilli* and the Apocryphal Gospels," *German Life and Letters,* 11 (1958): 270–275;

Heinz Finger, *Untersuchungen zum "Muspilli"* (Göppingen: Kümmerle, 1978);

A. Gross and Thomas D. Hill, "The Blood of Elias and the Fire of Doom: A New Analogue for Muspilli, vvs. 52 ff.," *Neuphilologische Mitteilungen,* 81 (1980): 439–442;

Dieter Kartschoke, *Geschichte der deutschen Literatur im frühen Mittelalter* (Munich: Deutscher Taschenbuch Verlag, 1990), pp. 134–138;

Herbert Kolb, "Himmlisches und irdisches Gericht in karolingischer Theologie und althochdeutscher Dichtung," *Frühmittelalterliche Studien,* 5 (1971): 284–303;

Kolb, "*Vor demo muspille:* Versuch einer Interpretation," *Zeitschrift für deutsche Philologie,* 83, no. 1 (1964): 2–33;

Kolb, "dia weroltrehtwîson," *Zeitschrift für deutsche Wortforschung,* 18 (1962): 88–95;

John G. Kunstmann, "Some Unprofessional Remarks on the Elijah-Episode of the Old High German *Muspilli,*" *Duquesne Studies: Annuale Mediaevale,* 1 (1960): 5–21;

Wolfgang Lauer, "*Muspilli,* ein Wort christlicher oder vorchristlicher germanischer Eschatologie," in *Althochdeutsch,* volume 2, edited by Rolf Bergmann (Heidelberg: Winter, 1987), pp. 1180–1194;

Cola Minis, *Handschrift, Form und Sprache des Muspilli* (Berlin: Schmidt, 1966);

Wolfgang Mohr and Walter Haug, *Zweimal "Muspilli"* (Tübingen: Niemeyer, 1977);

Rudolf Schützeichel, "Zum Muspilli," in *Festschrift für Ingo Reiffenstein zum 60. Geburtstag,* edited by Peter K. Stein and others (Göppingen: Kümmerle, 1986), pp. 15–29;

Klaus von See, *Germanische Verskunst* (Stuttgart: Metzler, 1967), pp. 72–74;

Herbert W. Sommer, "The *Muspilli*-Apocalypse," *Germanic Review,* 35 (1960): 157–163;

Sommer, "The Pseudepigraphic Sources of Muspilli II," *Monatshefte,* 55 (1963): 107–112;

Karl A. Wipf, ed. and trans., *Althochdeutsche poetische Texte* (Stuttgart: Reclam, 1992), pp. 344–351.

# Old German Genesis and Old German Exodus
## (circa 1050 – circa 1130)

Robert G. Sullivan
*University of Massachusetts at Amherst*

*Old German Genesis* (circa 1050–circa 1075)

**Manuscripts:** The complete *Old German Genesis* exists in two illustrated manuscript versions: the *Vienna Genesis,* Vienna, Nationalbibliothek, Codex 2721, folios 1r–129v; and the *Millstatt Genesis,* Klagenfurt, Austria, Kärntner Landesarchiv, Geschichtsverein für Kärnten, Handschrift 6/19, folios 1r–84v. A third manuscript, Styria, Austria, Chorherrenstift Vorau, Codex 276, folios 78rb–87vb, includes only the *Vorau Joesph* as part of the *Vorauer Bücher Mosis.* The three manuscripts, all from the twelfth century, are also major sources for most of the important Early Middle High German religious poems.

**First publication:** *Vienna Genesis,* edited by Eberhard Gottlieb Graff as "Metrische Bearbeitung eines Theils des ersten Buchs Moses," in *Diutiska: Denkmäler deutscher Sprache und Literatur,* volume 3 (Stuttgart & Tübingen: Cotta, 1829), pp. 40–112.

**First complete editions:** In *Deutsche Gedichte des 12. Jahrhunderts und der nächstverwandten Zeit, Bibliothek der gesamten deutschen National-Literatur von der ältesten bis auf die neueste Zeit,* volume 3, part 2, edited by Hans F. Massmann (Quedlinburg & Leipzig: Basse, 1837), pp. 235–310 (*Vienna Genesis*); in *Fundgruben für Geschichte deutscher Sprache und Literatur,* part 2, edited by Heinrich Hoffmann von Fallersleben (Breslau: Grass, Barth, Aderholz, 1837), pp. 9–84 (*Vienna Genesis*); in *Genesis und Exodus nach der Milstätter Handschrift,* 2 volumes, edited by Joesph Diemer (Vienna: Gerold, 1862), pp. 1–116(*Millstatt Genesis*); "Geschichte Joseph's in Aegypten nach der Vorauer Handschrift," edited by Diemer, *Sitzungsberichte der kaiserlichen Akademie der Wissenschaften: Philisophisch-Historische Klasse,* 47 (1864): 636–687 (*Vorau Joseph*).

**Standard editions:** *Die altdeutsche Genesis: Nach der Wiener Handschrift,* edited by Viktor Dollmayer (Halle: Niemeyer, 1932 [*Vienna Genesis*]); *Die frühmittelhochdeutsche Wiener Genesis,* edited by Kathryn Smits (Berlin: Schmidt, 1972 [*Vienna Genesis*]); in *Genesis und Exodus nach der Milstätter Handschrift,* 2 volumes, edited by Joesph Diemer (Vienna: 1862), pp. 1–116 (*Millstatt Genesis*); "Geschichte Joseph's in Aegypten nach der Vorauer Handschrift," edited by Diemer, *Sitzungsberichte der kaiserlichen Akademie der Wissenschaften: Philosophisch-Historische Klasse,* 47 (1864): 636–687 (*Vorau Joseph*); "Das Gedicht von Joseph nach der Wiener und der Vorauer Handschrift," edited by Paul Piper, *Zeitschrift für deutsche Philologie,* 20 (1888): 257–289, 430–474.

*Old German Exodus* (circa 1120–1130)

**Manuscripts:** The *Old German Exodus* is preserved in two manuscript versions: lines 1–1480, known as the *Vienna Exodus,* in Vienna, Nationalbibliothek, Codex 2721, folios 159r–183r; and the complete work, known as the *Millstatt Exodus,* in Klagenfurt, Austria, Kärntner Landesarchiv, Geschichtsverein für Kärnten, Codex 276, Handschrift 6/19, folios 102r–135r.

**First publications:** In *Deutsche Gedichte des 12. Jahrhunderts und der nächstverwandten Zeit, Bibliothek der gesamten deutschen National-Literatur von der ältesten bis auf die neueste Zeit,* volume 3, part 2, edited by Hans F. Massmann (Quedlinburg & Leipzig: 1837), pp. 326–342 (*Vienna Exodus*); in *Fundgruben für Geschichte deutscher Sprache und Literatur,* part 2, edited by Heinrich Hoffmann von Fallersleben (Breslau, 1837), pp. 85–101 (*Vienna Exodus*); in *Genesis und Exodus nach der Milstätter Handschrift,* 2 volumes, edited by Joseph Diemer (Vienna: 1862), pp. 117–164 (*Millstatt Exodus*).

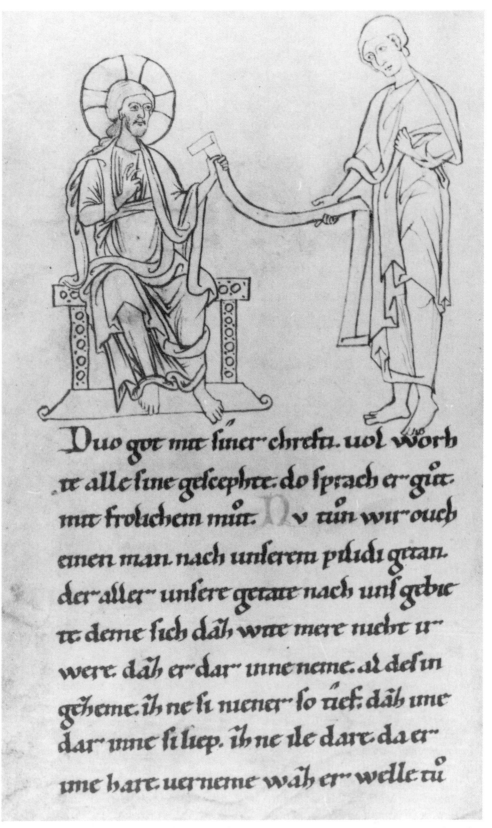

Duo got mit siner chrefti. uol worh
te alle sine gescephte. do sprach er gúte
mit frolichem mût. Nv tûn wir ouch
einen man nach unserem pilidi getan.
der aller unsere getate nach uns gebie
te deme sich dáh wie mere nieht ir
were. dáh er dar inne neme. al des in
geheime. ih ne si niener so tief. dáh ime
dar inne si liep. ih ne ile dare da er
ime hare uer neme. wáh er welle tû

*Page from the manuscript for the* Vienna Genesis *(Vienna, Nationalbibliothek, Codex Vindob. 2721, fol. 5v)*

**Standard edition:** *Die altdeutsche Exodus,* edited by Edgar Papp (Munich: Fink, 1968).

Often subsumed under the title of "the Old German biblical epics" to distinguish them from the *Old Saxon* and *Old English Genesis* poems, the early Middle High German verse narratives based on the Old Testament Books of Genesis and Exodus are among the most fascinating and important works of the precourtly period (circa 1050–circa 1170). As the longest eleventh-century German vernacular work, and one of the oldest, the *Vienna Genesis* version of the *Old German Genesis* (circa 1050–circa 1075) has naturally received the most attention; philologists and linguists, especially, have sought in this work answers to their questions about the evolution of the German language and its narrative and poetic forms. But the *Vienna Genesis* and the other versions of the Old German biblical epics have an appeal of their own. None of these poems is a mere translation of the Bible; rather, they are filled with allusions to or reflections of contemporary society, religiosity, and popular theology and are invaluable sources for historians. When one further considers the precariousness and difficulty with which vernacular literature became established in the medieval German-speaking lands after the fruitful but erratic Old High German period, one sees that the importance of the biblical epics cannot be overestimated. Indeed, if it is possible to speak of a continuity of German literature from the Middle Ages to the present, then its beginnings are to be discovered, in large part, in these poems.

Although usually and rightly considered together, the anonymous German biblical epics are two distinct works: the *Old German Genesis,* of which there are two complete versions, the *Vienna Genesis* and the *Millstatt Genesis,* and a partial version, the *Vorau Joseph;* and the *Old German Exodus* (circa 1120–1130), which exists in an incomplete version, the *Vienna Exodus,* and a complete one, the *Millstatt Exodus.* The various versions are named for the manuscripts in which they are preserved. The Vienna manuscript is the oldest, perhaps even earlier than 1150; the Millstatt manuscript, from the Millstatt Abbey and presently located in Klagenfurt, is from the last quarter of the twelfth century; and the Vorau manuscript is dated circa 1180 to 1200. There are seven uncolored drawings before and at the beginning of the *Vienna Genesis;* the eighty-seven drawings in the *Millstatt Genesis* and the thirty-two in the following poem, the *Physiologus,* make the Millstatt codex one of the first extensively illustrated German vernacular manuscripts. In the seventh Vienna drawing God is seated on a throne, handing a scrolllike band to a standing figure. Strikingly similar to this picture is the first Millstatt drawing, in which, however, the second figure has wings and a nimbus. From the resemblance between these drawings and the fact that the older Vienna manuscript contains empty spaces for further illustrations, mostly corresponding to the placing of the Millstatt drawings, Hella Voss concluded that the illustrators of the Millstatt manuscript were acquainted with the iconographic plan of the Vienna codex. Voss saw in the drawings the influence of the Salzburg school of painters and placed their origin in the late twelfth century in Austria, perhaps in the monastery of Millstatt. Hermann Menhardt, however, claimed that the style of the illustrations, the iconography of which he thought Byzantine in origin, is that of the Regensburg-Prüfeninger school in Bavaria. According to Menhardt's conjectures, Heinrich der Löwe (Henry the Lion), Duke of Saxony and Bavaria, had probably brought back an older illustrated Greek version of the octateuch (the first eight books of the Bible) from his 1172 visit to Constantinople. This copy would, then, have been used at Heinrich's court in Regensburg and have become the source for the Vienna and Millstatt illustrations, which Menhardt thought were completed in the late twelfth century. Literary scholars have generally withheld judgment on the contradictory evidence of the art historians, and in their efforts to place the biblical epics they have confined themselves to an investigation of the language of the manuscripts, which they conclude is the Bavarian-Austrian dialect of early Middle High German, a transitional form between Old High German and Middle High German. Hence, although some have argued for the presence of a more western substratum in the Millstatt poems, most contend that the texts of the manuscripts, if not the drawings, were completed in Austria – in Carinthia or, perhaps, in Styria.

Whoever the patrons or authors responsible for these manuscripts were, and whether they were religious or laypersons, the existence of the manuscripts reveals the continued importance and reception of the biblical epics in the latter half of the twelfth century and suggests that Austria had become a refuge for precourtly literature. Furthermore, it is clear from their present arrangement that the biblical epics were considered an integral part of a vernacular account of salvation history. Thus the Vienna manuscript begins with the *Old German Genesis,* followed by the *Physiologus,* a bestiary in prose that was seen as an amplification of the Genesis account of Creation, and concludes with the *Old Ger-*

*man Exodus.* The Millstatt codex is more ambitious: it initially maintains the same order as the Vienna manuscript, although its version of the *Physiologus* is rhymed, but it then continues with a rhymed sermon, "Vom Rechte" (On Justice); "Die Hochzeit" (The Wedding), an allegory of the marriage of the soul with Christ; "Die Millstätter Sündenklage" (The Millstatt Lamentation of Sins); "Die Auslegung des Vaterunsers" (The Exegesis of the Lord's Prayer); and the fragmentary poem "Die Beschreibung des himmlischen Jerusalem" (The Vision of the Heavenly Jerusalem).

The Old German biblical epics are representatives of a genre that arose in late antiquity and remained popular through the early nineteenth century, including such masterpieces as John Milton's *Paradise Lost* (1674) and Friedrich Klopstock's *Der Messias* (The Messiah, 1773). Throughout the long history of the biblical epic, the basic form remained constant: a verse narrative in the vernacular based on the Bible, usually on one or all of the first five books of the Old Testament or on the Gospel accounts of the life of Jesus. The oldest known biblical epic, primarily inspired by the Gospel of Matthew, was written in Latin hexameters at the beginning of the fourth century by the Spanish priest Juvencus, who took as his poetic model Virgil's *Aeneid.* Juvencus's purpose, which was both apologetic and pastoral, was to show that Christians could produce a work equal to the best in pagan literature and to offer a suitable and edifying alternative to that literature. In the early Middle Ages the authors of biblical epics shared a similar intent. Their principal rival was no longer classical Roman letters but a native non-Christian – and later, only superficially Christian – oral poetry, whose distracting and corrupting influence provided the Christian poets with a justification for creating a new literature based on the Bible and written not in the sacred language of Latin but in the vernacular. The new dawn of German literature in the second half of the eleventh century opens with the biblical epic.

For both of the Old German biblical epics the Latin Bible is the principal source, but it is a Bible seen through the eyes of the medieval exegetical tradition. The German poets did not use specific biblical commentaries; instead, their works seem to have been most influenced by exegetical commonplaces typically found in medieval sermons. The German poets differed in their emphases, but like the authors of the Latin Old Testament biblical epics of late antiquity they tended to concentrate on the historical narrative. Nonetheless, the author of the *Old German Genesis,* in particular, was familiar with the patristic interpretive division of the Bible into four levels or senses: the historical or literal sense, the tropological or moral sense, the allegorical sense, and the anagogic or mystical-eschatological sense.

The knowledge of the Bible and its interpretation revealed in the biblical epics indicates that their anonymous authors were monks or clerics and that their audiences were probably monastic, but the possibility that their listeners included or consisted of laypersons, either the lay brethren of the reformed monasteries or noblemen and noblewomen outside the monasteries, is not to be rejected, and in the case of the *Old German Exodus* it is quite likely. It has been frequently claimed that the biblical epics were probably composed for liturgical readings – the *Genesis* for the pre- and early Lenten period, the *Exodus* for Easter – but this thesis remains speculative.

The Vienna and Millstatt versions of the *Old German Genesis,* the first Old Testament biblical epic in German, are mostly identical in extent and purpose, differing in subtle yet important ways. The Vienna version is certainly the older, for its language and form are far more archaic. The writer of the Millstatt version has modernized the language and rhyme of his source, and either he or his illustrators have added 131 chapter headings of two to ten short lines that are usually keyed to the illustrations. Each version includes sections or phrases that are missing from the other. The first half of the story of Joseph in the Vorau manuscript has essentially the same form as in the *Vienna Genesis,* but in its latter half it has much in common with the Millstatt version. In their attempts to trace the transmission of the *Old German Genesis,* therefore, scholars usually postulate an archetype called *WM (for *Wien* [ Vienna] and *Millstatt*) as the source of the Vienna and Millstatt redactions and an older version, *WMV, as the ultimate source of all three poems.

It is generally supposed that the original *Genesis* must have been composed before 1122, the date of the Concordat of Worms, because it contains a passing reference to the custom of the king investing bishops with ring and staff (lines 144–145), which the Concordat prohibited. The poem's uncontroversial mention of this central symbol of the Investiture Controversy has been used to argue that the poem must be even older, from before 1075 – the year the controversy began with Pope Gregory VII's order forbidding investiture by laymen. But this historical argument is questionable: there are instances of bishops being invested with ring and staff by the king even after 1122. Nonetheless, linguistic evidence, while not beyond reproach, makes the pre-1075 dating highly probable.

The verse and form of the *Old German Genesis* were the subjects of acrimonious debates between Friedrich Maurer and Werner Schröder and their students, with Schröder arguing that the verse consists of rhyming short lines similar to, but more primitive than, those used in the high courtly epics. Maurer maintained that the verse should be read as syntactically complete, internally rhyming long lines and, further, that the colored initials of the Vienna and Millstatt versions prove that the poem is arranged in strophes, not merely paragraphlike sections, of varying length. Behind this quarrel lies the question of the continuity and authorship of early-medieval German literature. Maurer saw an immediate connection between the verse form of the oldest early Middle High German works and the Old High German rhyming long-line works, especially Otfried von Weißenburg's *Evangelienbuch* (Gospel Book, between 863 and 871), while Schröder maintained that the evidence is too ambiguous and sporadic to postulate such a continuity. Maurer's thesis has some probability for the *Old German Genesis,* but the occurrence in the poem of enjambment, syntactical units that overstep the postulated long lines, presents difficulties.

The *Old German Genesis* is generally divided into six sections, which were once seen as having been written by six different authors: the Creation and the Fall (lines 1–526), Cain and Abel (lines 527–685), Noah and the Flood (lines 686–787), Abraham and his sons (lines 788–1056), Isaac and his sons (lines 1057–1710), and Joseph (lines 1711–3037). The anonymous and — as all agree today — sole author of the work has made a judicious selection from the Book of Genesis, usually concentrating on the narratively interesting and coherent strands, notably the story of Joseph, which claims almost half the poem. The biblical genealogical reports, in particular, are excluded — for example Gen. 36, about which the poet says in lines 1711–1712:

> Daz an dem buoche stât gescriben  des muozzen wir sumelichez uberheven.
> chunde wirj ouch wol scopphen  sô scolte wir doch ettewaz uberhupphen.

> (We must leave out some of what is written in the Book.
> Even if we could set it into verse, we should still jump over some parts.)

The poet also either excises material that is especially pertinent to Judaic theology or else reinter-

prets it as a prefiguration of Christianity. For example, Gen. 17, in which God renews his covenant with Abraham and establishes the rite of circumcision, is quickly glossed over by the poet, who concludes his discussion in lines 869–870 with the remark: "der site ist hiute under judiskem liute, / unde ist ire geloube iz sî in bezzere denne diu touffe" (This is now the custom among Jewish people / who believe that is better for them than baptism); and Abraham's washing the feet of his angelic guests is related to Christ's action at the Last Supper and the establishment of the "mandatum novum" (new commandment) of love in John 13:34: "die vuozze er in dwuog. / bedaz er getete die mandâte" (He washed their feet; / with this he upheld the commandment, lines 878–879).

The author of the *Old German Genesis* adds many amplifications of his biblical source, especially in his account of the Creation, including fantastic etiological accounts of the origin of black people and of such fabulous creatures as the one-footed sciopedes; in both cases their present appearance is said to have been caused by their ancestors' having eaten forbidden herbs (lines 646–660). The poet also explains that "scalche" (slaves) first arose from Noah's curse of his son Ham (lines 752–768) and that "chaltsmide" (Gypsy[?] merchants), who are harshly condemned for their greed, descend from Ishmael, the son of Abraham and his maid Hagar (lines 856–864 and 916–921). The customs of paying the tithe and of ecclesiastical immunity, which stem from Joseph's enslavement of the Egyptians during the seven years of famine and his exemption of the priests, provoke the poet's ironic remark: "sô stuont iz bî den heidinen, ich neweiz ub iz die christâne sô meinen" (So it was among the pagans; I do not know if Christians feel the same about it, line 2637). It appears that the author of the Millstatt version was sufficiently perturbed by Joseph's actions to alter the biblical account and have Joseph refuse to enslave any of the Egyptians.

Sources for some of the *Old German Genesis* poet's amplifications can be found in the Latin biblical epic *De spiritalis historiae gestis* (The Deeds of Spiritual History), by Alcimus Ecdicius Avitus, who died in 518, although scholars no longer consider this work to have been his primary inspiration or model. Parallels have also been drawn to passages in patristic writings, biblical commentaries, and such encyclopedic works as the *Etymologiae* of Isidore of Seville, though these sources were probably known to the poet only at second hand or even third hand. Thus even those additions that appear popular or unlearned should be viewed in the light of learned Christian tradition – for example, lines 146–148, which explain the purpose of the little finger, which Isidore calls the "auricularis" (ear finger):

> Der minneste finger  der nahât ambeht ander
> newane sôs wirt nôt  daz er in daz ôre grubilet,
> daz iz ferneme gereche  swaz ieman spreche.

> (The smallest finger has no other purpose
> but to dig in the ear when necessary
> so that one can properly hear what others are saying.)

In many instances the German poet transposes his own feudal society and its customs and concepts into the ancient world of the biblical patriarchs. God's angels are described as his "holden" (vassals, line 28), with whom, like a feudal lord, he meets for "rât" (counsel, line 40). Laban gives a "grôzze wirtscaft" (great courtly feast, line 1295) for his kinsman Jacob, who has fallen in "minne" (love) with Laban's daughter, and the poet comments: "ich weiz er si vil minnechlîche chuste" (I know that he kissed very lovingly, line 1275). Joseph is called "der helt balt" (the bold hero) in line 1738, and the biblical title for his position with Potiphar, "praepositus" (overseer), becomes "dienestman" (ministerial, line 18420). In lines 1939–1940 Joseph himself addresses two "hêrren" (high servants) of "der chunich" (king) – that is, Pharaoh – with the usual precourtly term for knight:

> Jâ jâ, ir guoten chnehte,  iz nevert umb iuch nieht rehte.
> ir gehabet iuch hiute ubile,  iz nezâme nieht adale.

> (Well, you knights, this isn't right.
> Your behavior is wrong today and doesn't befit your nobil
> ity.)

The *Vienna Genesis* is, furthermore, the first literary text in German to use the courtly word for knight, *rîter*. It, too, occurs in connection with Joseph, who is described in line 2533 as riding out to meet his father Jacob "mit ... manich rîter gemeit" (with ... many a fair knight). (The later *Millstatt Genesis* even substitutes *rîter* [line 77, 7] where the *Vienna Genesis* describes Potiphar as a "hêrr" [line 1840].) The poet's topical references are by no means confined to the socially powerful, however, and he knowingly describes the plight of impoverished land workers in his portrait of Adam and Eve after the Fall (lines 593–598).

Although the Book of Genesis is his main source, the poet has enclosed the biblical narrative within the framework of Salvation history from the Creation to the Last Judgment. After a short prayer (lines 1–4), the poem opens with God's creation of the choirs of angels and the fall of Lucifer; the creation of humankind is explained as a substitute for the fallen tenth choir, an interpretation that was a commonplace of early Middle High German religious literature and was later mentioned by Hartmann von Aue in one of his Crusade songs (circa 1189–1197, strophe 211, lines 3–7). The poem concludes with Jacob's blessing of his twelve sons (lines 2698–2970), in which the often-obscure biblical text becomes the occasion for an extended allegorical meditation. In lines 2771–2773 the poet comments on Jacob's blessing of Judah:

> Diz ist ein tiefiu rede,  ich wâne si iemen irrechin mege.
> chund ich daz firnemen  daz ich dar ubere hân gilesin,
> gerne ich denne sagiti,  welihi bizeichinunge si habiti.

> (This is a profound saying. I imagine that no one can
>    fully explain it.
> If I might understand what I have read about it,
> then I should gladly say what it symbolizes.)

In the following line he gives the meaning of the blessing: "Judas ... bizeichinit dich, Christ unser hêrre" (Judah ... prefigures you, Christ our Lord). After explaining the mission of Jesus, the poet incorporates into Jacob's blessing of Dan a sketch of the coming of the Antichrist and the end of the world.

Typical of the exegesis of Jacob's blessings, and of the *Old German Genesis* as a whole, is the poet's emphasis on the moral or tropological interpretation of the biblical story. The lengthiest and most frequent digressions draw the moral lesson of the stories of Genesis and are used to admonish the listeners of the need for contrition and penance and to console them with the promise of God's grace and mercy. For example, God's establishment of the rainbow as a sign to Noah that he will never again destroy the world with a flood is first interpreted as an allegory of the wine and water of Communion (lines 728–733), which in turn represent the water of baptism. The poet then warns that we too often lose the grace of baptism by sinning and that we can only regain it and quench the fires of damnation by our cleansing tears of repentance (lines 734–737). Far from providing merely an entertaining and instructive summary of the Bible, therefore, the poet has transformed his material into a homiletic explanation of the meaning and obligations of the human condition.

The *Old German Exodus* is usually held to have been written around 1120 to 1130. The *Vienna Exodus* is the older of two versions but contains a gap of some fifty lines and breaks off at line 1480, leaving the reverse side of page 183 of the manuscript blank. Unlike the *Millstatt Genesis* the Millstatt redaction of the *Old German Exodus* closely parallels the Vienna version, only sparingly modernizing its language, rhymes, and meter. The *Millstatt Exodus,* however, obviously could not have been copied from the fragmentary Vienna version; rather, both versions of the *Exodus* are probably derived from a lost poem that was transmitted together with the original *Old German Genesis* and the *Physiologus.*

The *Old German Exodus* differs substantially from the *Genesis* in its treatment of the biblical source. Whereas the *Genesis* poet used the entire Book of Genesis but freely excised or amplified his material to develop his moral theme more clearly, the *Exodus* poet adapted only the first fifteen chapters of the Book of Exodus, the story of Moses and the deliverance of the Israelites from Egyptian bondage. Aside from some misunderstandings, he generally reproduces those chapters faithfully, but he centers the action on the conflict between Moses and Pharaoh. The most noticeable alteration, the fusion of the third and the fourth plagues of Egypt into a plague of "hundesfliegen" (dog flies), is trivial, and its purpose is to propel the narrative. Unlike the *Genesis* poet, furthermore, the *Exodus* poet makes little immediately visible effort to Christianize his source: his heroes are "diu isrâheliske diet" (the Israelites) or simply "die iuden" (the Jews). Only twice in the narrative part of the poem does the author explicitly reveal his Christian perspective: in the first instance God calls Passover "die ôsteren" (Easter, line 2826), while the second instance is anachronistically ascribed to Pharaoh, who complains of the Israelites in lines 84–86:

> ir chint si besnîdent
> an dem ahttoden tage;
> ze touffe wellent si daz haben.

> ( They circumcise their children
> on the eighth day
> and would have it considered as baptism.)

Possible Christian additions or reinterpretations occur in lines 2947–2956, in which Joseph's bones are described in terms reminiscent of relics — "daz was heilich unde reine" (they were holy and pure) — and in lines 2569–2572, where God's commandment to Moses to observe the Passover "in eternity" (Exod. 12:24) is shortened to "ze manigen hundert iâren" (for many hundred years) — that is, presumably, until the coming of Christ; but later (line 2599) the expression is changed to "ze uil manigen êwen" (for eternity).

The most striking additions to the biblical source are connected to the feudal and martial vocabulary with which the *Old German Exodus* poet embellishes his material. For example, Pharaoh says of the Israelites in lines 95–96: "si sint guote chnehte, / geturren wole uehten" (They are good warriors [or knights] / and know how to fight well), and Moses' killing of an Egyptian is described in lines 286–290 in terms of the blood feud. In lines 1482–1484 the dog flies are described as "gotes rîtere" (the knights of God), and in lines 2175–2177 the locusts of the eighth plague are called "uil guote wîgande, / uil snelle helede" (great warriors / and intrepid heroes). The longest metaphoric addition, including the first occurrence in German of the courtly word for knighthood, is reserved for the frogs of the second plague, which are a "her uile chlein" (very little army), but with neither

> . . . scilt noch daz swert,
> noch die hutten noch gezelt,
> helm noch die brunne,
> neheiner rîterscephte wunne. . . . ( lines 1343–1346)

> ( . . . shield nor sword,
> neither huts nor tents,
> nor helmet, nor hauberk
> nor any delight of knighthood. . . .)

But these latter additions are probably merely ironic, unlike the culminating description of the flight of the Israelites and their pursuit by Pharaoh and his followers, which bristles with military terms, perhaps under the influence of the fifth book of Avitus's Latin biblical epic. In lines 2871–2938 and 3039–3074 both the Israelites, who are "âne allerslahte ubermuot" (without any kind of pride, line 2928), and the "vermezzen" (presumptuous, line 3075) Egyptians, among whom are "herzogen unde grâuen" (dukes and counts), are accoutred with every kind of medieval armor and weapon, to which the poet twice calls the attention of his audience — for example, in lines 2907–2908: "Nû uernemet, mîne hêrren, / ich wil iw sagen mêre" (Now listen, my lords; / I want to tell you more) — a likely indication that his listeners included laymen.

Aside from the lengthy study by Dennis Howard Green (1967), interpretation of the *Old German Exodus* has been neglected. Green argues that the poem is a pre-Crusading epic, justifying this interpretation in part by reference to the poet's bellicose additions. Pharaoh is indeed called a "heiden" (heathen) throughout the poem, and his army contains "die alswarze môre" (the completely black Moors, line 3043). Green's thesis has been questioned, although the claim that the *Exodus* might at least breathe of the Crusading spirit cannot be dismissed. One should, nonetheless, take the poet at his word: he explains his purpose at the end of the poem (lines 3297–3301) when he says of Moses' song of thanksgiving:

> mit ime sô tuo wir same,
> daz ouch wir muozzen uarn
> uon diseme ellende
> heim ze deme lande,
> zuo der himelisken Jerusalem.

> (Let us do the same with him
> so that we should also journey
> from this exile
> home to the land,
> to the heavenly Jerusalem.)

It is tempting to regard this passage as an assertion that the poem is an extended allegory, but this is no doubt too strong a word to describe the author's intention and method. Some isolated comments in the poem (lines 602, 1140, 2490, and 2801) have been used to argue that the poet was acquainted with allegorical interpretation. But in all of these examples (the third of which is simply a paraphrase of Exod. 12:13) the author merely says that a name or an act has, as he puts it in line 602, "einen tiefen sin" (a deep meaning). Only once in the poem is there a glimmer of allegorical thinking: in lines 2509–2514 God tersely commands that the Israelites should gird their loins "mit guotem gedanche" (with good thoughts). This absence of explicit allegory is all the more surprising in that much of the Book of Exodus had received standard allegorical interpretations in the Middle Ages (many of which were derived from such New Testament passages as 1 Cor. 10:1–11).

Following Max Wehrli, one should, perhaps, see the *Exodus* poem as a narrative embodiment of the typological and analogical understanding of history, for it is this understanding that finally justifies and explains the anachronistic additions and alterations in both the *Old German Genesis* and the *Old German Exodus*. The story of the latter, thus, presents an epic prefiguration and not an elaborate and concealed allegory. The poet's plan may best be seen in his transformation of the biblical leitmotiv of God's hardening of Pharaoh's heart against the Israelites. In all but two instances the *Exodus* poet substitutes for the biblical explanation of Pharaoh's behavior direct speeches by Pharaoh in which the biblical word *servi* (servants) is given various carefully differentiated translations. Thus, Pharaoh calls the Israelites his "eigenlîche" (bondsmen), "choufscalche" or "scalche" (slaves) who must serve him without recompense ("dienôn âne allerslahte lôn," lines 2253–2254), but for his own servants he reserves the more positive word *chnehte* (for example, in line 1912). Yet Pharaoh's terms are a distortion of the true status of the Israelites, whom God in his power has preserved for "urîtuom" (freedom, line 1219) and who are described by the poet in lines 127–130 as "hêrlîche chnehte" (lordly warriors) and "von adele" (of nobility). They are "gotes scalche" (slaves [only] to God, line 1753) and, hence, "gotliebe hêrren" (God's beloved lords, line 3021). Moses, their liberator, is the type or prefiguration of Christ, who will free us from our earthly servitude. The theme of the *Old German Exodus* poet may be summed up by the Pauline assertion in lines 227–228 of "Die Auslegung des Vaterunsers": "verschelchet hat uns der alte man, / gevrien muoz uns der niwe man" (The old man [Adam] enslaved us, / the new man [Christ] will free us). The epic concentration and style of the *Exodus* poet, including, of course, his martial interests, would provide a model to later, more mundane German poets, but his own purpose was, above all, spiritual.

**Bibliography:**

Francis G. Gentry, *Bibliographie zur frühmittelhochdeutschen geistlichen Dichtung* (Berlin: Schmidt, 1992), pp. 112–126.

**References:**

Siegfried Beischlag, *Die Wiener Genesis: Idee, Stoff und Form,* Sitzungsberichte der Akademie der Wissenschaften in Wien, Philosophisch-historische Klasse, no. 220 (Vienna: Holer-Pichler-Tempsky, 1942);

Helmut de Boor, *Die deutsche Literatur von Karl dem Großen bis zum Beginn der höfischen Dichtung. 770–1170,* volume 1 of *Geschichte der deutschen Literatur,* by de Boor and Richard Newald (Munich: Beck, 1964), pp. 133–158;

Eugene Egert, "The Curse of the Serpent in the Middle High German 'Genesis' Poems," *Amsterdamer Beiträge zur älterern Germanistik,* 24 (1986): 29–37;

Gustav Ehrismann, *Geschichte der deutschen Literatur bis zum Ausgang des Mittelalters,* part 2, section 1: *Die mittelhochdeutsche Literatur: Frühmittelhochdeutsche Zeit* (Munich: Beck, 1922), pp. 78–91;

Josef Essler, *Die Schöpfungsgeschichte in der "Altdeutschen Genesis" (Wiener Genesis V. 1–231):*

*Kommentar und Interpretation* (Göppingen: Kümmerle, 1987);

Dennis Howard Green, "Epic Expansion and the Problem of Rhyme in the *Millstätter Exodus*," *Medium Aevum,* 43, no. 3 (1974): 234–251;

Green, *The Millstätter Exodus: A Crusading Epic* (London: Cambridge University Press, 1967);

Green, "The *Millstätter Exodus* and its Biblical Source," *Medium Aevum,* 38, no. 3 (1969): 227–238;

John S. Groseclose, "Passion Prefigurations: Typological Style and the Problems of Genre in German Romanesque Poetry," *Monatshefte,* 67 (Spring 1975): 5–15;

Peter W. Hurst, "The Evocation of Paradise in the 'Wiener Genesis' and in the 'Tristan' of Gottfried von Strassburg," in *Studien zur frühmittelhochdeutschen Literatur. Cambridger Colloquium 1971,* edited by L. P. Johnson and others (Berlin: Schmidt, 1974), pp. 215–234;

Evelyn Margaret Jacobson, " 'Triuwe' and 'Minne' in the Millstätter Genesis," *Germanic Notes,* 12, no. 4 (1981): 51–54;

Hugo Kuhn, "Gestalten und Lebenskräfte der frühmittelhochdeutschen Dichtung," in his *Dichtung und Welt im Mittelalter* (Stuttgart: Metzler, 1969), pp. 112–132;

Friedrich Maurer, "Die Formen der religiösen Dichtungen des 11. und 12. Jahrhunderts," in *Die religiösen Dichtungen des 11. und 12. Jahrhunderts,* volume 1, edited by Maurer (Tübingen: Niemeyer, 1964), pp. 1–60;

Hermann Menhardt, "Die Bilder der Millstätter Genesis und ihre Verwandten," in *Beiträge zur*

*älteren europäischen Kulturgeschichte: Festschrift für Rudolf Egger* (Klagenfurt: Verlag des Geschichtsvereines für Kärnten, 1954), pp. 248–371;

Brian Murdoch, *The Fall of Man in the Early Middle High German Biblical Epic: The "Wiener Genesis," the "Vorau Genesis" and the "Anegenge"* (Göppingen: Kümmerle, 1972);

Kenneth J. Northcott, " 'Tougen minne' in the *Genesis,*" *Modern Language Notes,* 74 (1959): 151–153;

Werner Schröder, "The 'Altdeutsche Exodus': A Crusading Epic?," *Modern Language Review,* 64 (April 1969): 334–339;

Schröder, "Zu alten und neuen Theorien einer altdeutschen 'binnengereimten Langzeile,' " *Beiträge zur Geschichte der deutschen Sprache und Literatur,* 87 (1965): 150–165;

Gisela Vollmann-Profe, *Wiederbeginn volkssprachlicher Schriftlichkeit im hohen Mittelalter (1050/60–1160/70),* volume 1, part 2, of *Geschichte der deutschen Literatur von den Anfängen bis zum Beginn der Neuzeit,* edited by Joachim Heinzle (Königstein: Athenäum, 1986), pp. 86–93;

Hella Voss, *Studien zur illustrierten Millstätter Genesis* (Munich: Beck, 1962);

Max Wehrli, *Geschichte der deutschen Literatur vom frühen Mittelalter bis zum Ende des 16. Jahrhunderts,* second edition (Stuttgart: Reclam, 1984);

Alfred Weller, *Die frühmittelhochdeutsche Wiener Genesis nach Quellen, Übersetzungsart, Stil und Syntax* (Berlin: Mayer & Müller, 1914).

# Old High German Charms and Blessings

Brian Murdoch
*University of Stirling*

**Manuscripts:** The *Merseburger Zaubersprüche* are preserved in Merseburg, Domstift, Codex 136, fol. 85r. The *Contra vermes* is in Munich Bayerische Staatsbibliothek, Clm 18, 524, fol. 203v. The epilepsy charm is in Munich, Bayerische Staatsbibliothek, clm 14, 763, fol. 88v. Those for a sore throat and for sore eyes are in Munich, Bayerische Staatsbibliothek, clm 23,390, fol. 59v. The Zurich blood charm is in Zurich, Kantonalbibliothek, ms. 51, fol. 23v. Horse charms are in Vienna, Österreichische Nationalbibliothek, cod. 751, fol. 188v; Trier, Stadtbibliothek, Hs. 40, vol. 36v; and Vatican, Palatine Library, Cod. Pal. 1158, fol. 68. The *Lorscher Bienensegen* is in the Vatican, Palatine Library, Cod. 220, fol. 58r. The *Wiener Hundsegen* is in Vienna, Österreichische Nationalbibliothek, cod. 552, fol. 107r. The *Innsbruck Pharmacopoeia* is in Innsbruck, Universitätsbibliothek, ms. 652. The *Zurich Pharmacopoeia* is in Zurich, Stadtbibliothek, Hs. C 58/275. The *Cambridge Eye-Charm* is in Cambridge, Peterhouse College, Cambridge University, ms. 130, fol. 219v. The *Graz Hail-Blessing* is in Graz, Universitätsbibliothek, ms. 41/12, fol. ult. The *Zurich House-Blessing* is in Zurich, Kantonalbibliothek, ms. C 176, fol. 154r. Various charms and blessings are in Paris, Bibliothèque Nationale nouv. acq. lat. 229. The *Bamberger Blutsegen* is in Bamberg, Dombibliothek, Cod. med. 6, fol. 139. The *Weingartner Reisesegen* is in Stuttgart, Landesbibliothek, Bibl. 25.

**Standard editions:** In *Denkmäler deutscher Poesie und Prosa aus dem VIII.-XII. Jahrhundert,* edited by Karl Müllenhoff and Wilhelm Scherer, third edition, edited by Elias von Steinmeyer (Berlin: Weidmann, 1892; reprinted, Berlin & Zurich: Weidmann, 1964); *Die kleineren althochdeutschen Sprachdenkmäler,* edited by Steinmeyer (Berlin: Weidmann, 1916); in *Denkmäler deutscher Prosa des 11. und 12. Jahrhunderts,* edited by Friedrich Wilhelm

(Munich: Callwey, 1916); in *Frühmittelalterliches Deutsch,* edited by Fritz Tschirch (Halle: Niemeyer, 1955), pp. 35–38; in Carol Ann Miller, "The Old High German and Old Saxon Charms and Blessings," Ph.D. dissertation, Washington University, 1963; in *Altdeutsche Texte,* edited by Heinz Mettke (Leipzig: Bibliographisches Institut, 1970), pp. 45–50, 97; in *Althochdeutsches Lesebuch,* edited by Wilhelm Braune, sixteenth edition, edited by Ernst Ebbinghaus (Tübingen: Niemeyer, 1979); in *Sammlung kleinerer althochdeutscher Sprachdenkmäler,* edited by Gerhard Köbler (Gießen: Arbeiten zur Rechtsund Sprachwissenschaft, 1986), pp. 116–117, 262–263, 508–510, 528–529, 544–545, 570–575, 592–593.

**Editions in modern German:** In *Älteste deutsche Dichtungen,* edited by Karl Wolfskehl and Friedrich von der Leyen (Frankfurt am Main: Insel, 1964), pp. 30–41; in *Althochdeutsche Literatur,* edited by Horst Dieter Schlosser (Frankfurt am Main & Hamburg: Fischer, 1970), pp. 251–261; in *Älteste deutsche Dichtung und Prosa,* edited by Heinz Mettke (Leipzig: Reclam, 1976), pp. 84–101; in *Althochdeutsche Literatur,* edited by Hans Joachim Gernentz (Berlin: Union, 1979), pp. 84–89.

The Old High German charms and blessings, the best known of which are preserved in a manuscript of the tenth century now in the library of the Bishopric of Merseburg, are short pieces of prose or poetry designed either to ameliorate a situation that already exists – for example, curing an ailment – or to prevent something unpleasant from happening. About thirty such texts are extant. Those designed to cure are usually referred to as *Zaubersprüche* (magic charms), those whose intent is prevention as *Segen* (blessings) – a genre virtually impossible to distinguish from the *Gebet* (prayer). Indeed, the overlap between all three terms in the Old High German period is considerable, and the terminology applied to

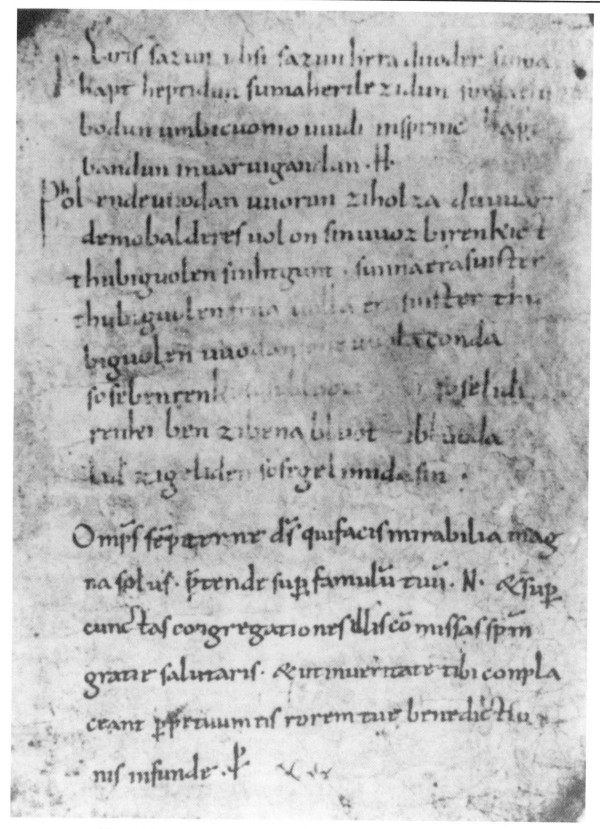

*Manuscript for the* Merseburger Zaubersprüche *(Merseburg, Domstift, Codex 136, fol. 85r)*

these pieces is confused and often artificial. All the works are designed, however, to have an effect through the power of the word. They may be contrasted with recipes or prescriptions, with which they are often found side by side in the manuscripts and which are also designed to ameliorate; the difference is that recipes require the use of ingredients and do not work by the power of the word alone. Nor is it always helpful to insist on the distinction between healing and prophylaxis, which is sometimes used to separate charms from blessings or prayers: insofar as they are written down, the Old High German charms, even when ostensibly concerned with a situation that already obtains, are obviously for use at a future time when such a situation will arise again.

All the surviving Old High German charms and blessings are Christian; a few of the earliest contain references to Germanic gods; but even those pieces are found in monastic manuscripts, and their context is invariably Christian. The manuscripts in which the charms are recorded are rarely earlier than the tenth century; most are later and are, therefore, from a Christian culture that had been established for many centuries.

Although anthologies, especially those that offer modern German translations, invariably highlight the Old High German parts of any given charm, the Old High German charms all contain integral Latin elements that must not be ignored. The two *Merseburger Zaubersprüche* (Merseburg Charms), for example, are accompanied by a Latin prayer that is rarely printed. An early charm that exists in High German and in Low German has the Latin title *Contra vermes* or *Pro nessia,* both of which literally mean "against worms" but actually mean "against disease." The precise meaning of the German portion is not quite clear, since the last word may refer to a horse's hoof or to an arrow that was, perhaps, to be fired away, taking the disease with it:

> Ganz uz, Nesso,  mit niun nessichilinon,
> uz fonna marge in deo adra, vonna den adrun in daz
>     fleisk,
> fonna demu fleiske in daz fel,  fonna demo velle in diz
>     tulli.
>
> (Go out, worm, with your nine little ones
> out from the marrow into the vein, from the vein into
>     the flesh,
> from the flesh into the skin, from the skin into this hoof [or
>     arrow]).

(There are parallels to this section of the charm in an ancient Indian work, the *Atharva-veda.*) But the charm is not just these three lines of German: not only is the Latin title part of the work, but at the end are the words *Ter Pat n̄r,* which mean that the Paternoster, the Latin version of the Lord's Prayer, has to be repeated three times as part of the charm. These words have sometimes been minimized as the "sole Christian element" in the text, but three full repetitions of the Lord's Prayer would far outweigh the three lines of German. Although the German seems to prescribe an action and include a command for the disease to leave by magic, the Latin Lord's Prayer is the dominant element; and that prayer does not contain a command but, rather, the request "fiat voluntas tua" (Thy will be done). The Old High German charm preserves what is probably older pagan material, but as it exists it is entirely Christian. The Low German form of the charm ends with the words "Drohtin, werthe so" (Let it be, O Lord), which is equivalent to the liturgical *amen,* which means "so be it."

The church was not against magic of this kind. There are frequent condemnations in religious literature of black magic, storm raising, cursing, and so on, but there is nothing of this kind in Old High German; the charms and blessings are invariably for positive purposes. The role of the church is important in determining the possible use of the Old High German charms. There are, for example, similarities between the charms and the collects – prayers used in the liturgy to make special requests, such as for the healing of sickness or the prevention of misfortune. These prayers were read, sometimes in groups of three or seven, before the lesson at certain masses. The pattern of the collects corresponds well to that of many of the Old High German charms. Critics examining only the German portions of the charms have stressed the supposedly magical command, by which the healing was supposed to be effected. In the surviving pieces, that command is modified by an invocatory request that God should permit the healing.

The pre-Christian Germanic elements preserved in some of the charms were presumably for oral use, and since the charms usually contain a liturgical prayer they, too, were probably intended to be spoken – perhaps by a priest – like the collects. That some of the charms for curing horses call for the user to whisper the charm in the horse's ear does not mean, as some scholars have surmised, that all the charms were whispered; there seems to be a difference in this regard between veterinary and human charms. A charm against epilepsy prescribes certain actions in addition to the speaking of the words; these actions have a distinctly ritual character.

*Manuscript for the* Bamberger Blutsegen *(Bamberg, Dombibliothek, Cod. med. 6, fol. 139)*

It is possible that some of the charms were used as amulets. In Latin many charms exist in which nonsense or abracadabra words were written down to be carried as talismanic protection. In Christian societies names (for example, the traditional names of the Three Wise Men) and prayers were written down for this purpose; and to an illiterate person, of course, all written words would be nonsense words. There are some Old High German charms containing nonsense words; but there is no clear evidence of a periaptic (talismanic) intent, and the Old High German charms and blessings depend on speech. These pieces of practical literature are the first stage of a continuum in German; precisely similar charms to those found in Old High German are found also, and in larger numbers, in Middle High German and, indeed, in modern German.

The two Merseburg Charms are a tenth-century addition to a ninth-century manuscript (now in the Cathedral Chapter in Merseburg) that includes liturgical material, including a Franconian baptismal oath. The German portions of the two charms contain references to pagan deities, but the Christian context is clear. Critics have for many years confidently described the first of the two as a charm to conjure magically the release of prisoners and the second as designed to cure a horse's sprained foot; both views are questionable. Neither piece is given a title. The Old High German material is followed by a lengthy Latin prayer (in a neater version of what is probably the same scribal hand) asking God to help a person whose name can be inserted at specific points and to guard the congregations of the faithful. This prayer presumably makes respectable the references in the Old High German part to the pagan gods.

The first charm describes how *idisi,* women roughly equivalent to the Norse Valkyries, took prisoners, harrowed an army, and picked at fetters. This triadic description, which is not very clear, is followed by a command: "insprinc haptbandun / inuar uigandun" (burst asunder fetters, / escape the foe). Taken at face value, this phrase seems to be associated with an escaping prisoner, and there are references in Old Norse literature to prisoners escaping by magic; but such references are, precisely, in *literature.* Later in the Middle Ages amulets were carried into battle by soldiers to protect them from death or capture, but prisoners did not escape in that way. It is far more plausible to see the fetters and captivity as metaphors for disease. There is at the end of this part of the text what might be the letter *N* for *nomen* (name), indicating that the sick person is to be named here.

The German portion of the second Merseburg Charm is also built on a triadic pattern. In alliterative verse, like the first charm, it describes Phol and Wodan riding in the woods. The first name is obscure; it might be Apollo or Paul, although in neither case would the alliteration of the line work. (In fact, the scribe who wrote the charm down was unsure himself, since the *h* has been added later.) In the next line Balder's horse goes lame, leading one to assume that Phol and Balder, a known Germanic god, are one and the same. There follows a three-line section in which goddesses try to conjure a cure by incantation, and then Wodan does so. Five names are mentioned, not all of them recognizable from other sources. The first two pairs of names may be appositional: for example, "Friia Uolla ira suester" may mean "Freya, who is Folla's sister" rather than "Freya and Folla, her sister"; thus three rather than five goddesses may be involved. The third section makes a general statement about the healing of any kind of disorder, whether of humans or of horses:

> sose benrenki,  sose bluotrenki,
>     sose lidirenki:
> ben zi bena,  bluot zi bluoda,
> lid zi geliden, sose gelimida sin!
>
> (be it bone-wrench, be it blood-wrench
>     be it limb-wrench
> bone to bone, blood to blood
> limb to limb, let them be locked!)

Versions of the same charm may be found all over Europe, though the male participants in the narrative vary; often they are Saint Peter and Christ, with Christ effecting the cure, and these versions complete the Christianization process begun, perhaps, in the Merseburg manuscript. The triadic "bone to bone, blood to blood, limb to limb" formula appears in many other languages and is clearly of some antiquity. Not all of the similar charms refer to the cure of horses, and there is no need to link the Merseburg Charm with horses only. A parallel Old High German example from Trier is directed against an equine ailment called *spurihalz,* presumably some kind of lameness; here Christ cures Saint Stephen's horse, but the "bone-to-bone" passage is not present. The Trier charm, like that from Merseburg, adds two Christian prayers, the standard Latin Paternoster and a German prayer asking Christ to cure the present horse as he did Saint Stephen's. The second Merseburg Charm has been interpreted in many ways, even as the reflection of a horse sacrifice. It is not known whether the Merseburg scribe understood the real sense of the Germanic parts or whether he just felt them to be of impressive antiquity and acceptable in a Christian society as long as a Christian element was attached.

It is worth asking at this point whether the charms worked. In general terms the Old High German charms (and a good many in other languages, such as Anglo-Saxon) are preserved together with medical recipes, and this supports the idea that they were felt to be efficacious. Most of the Old High German pieces are to do with bleeding (which does stop), sprains (which again improve with rest), epileptic attacks (which, though frightening, are temporary and can actually be helped by soothing the patient, with familiar prayers, for example), or perhaps for general sickness. More specifically prophylactic pieces and prayers – those designed to prevent misfortunes that have not yet happened – will, of course, always be felt to be useful if the misfortune does not happen or does not last.

Only one other charm seems to preserve some elements of pre-Christian thought: the charm against epilepsy, which has the Latin title *Contra caducum morbum* (Against the Falling Sickness) in one of its two surviving versions. Both versions are in relatively late manuscripts, one currently in Paris, the other in Munich. In the Paris manuscript the charm is attached to a medical tract; the Munich manuscript is a miscellany in which the charm, together with some Latin charms against bleeding and against fevers, follows a grammatical treatise. The content of the German portion of the charm, which is in prose, seems to indicate that neither scribe was entirely sure what he was writing. In the Paris version Latin instructions follow the title, telling the practitioner to stand over the patient and to say the charm three times. The charm itself opens with what may be the name of the Germanic god Donar but might have become an abracadabra word by the time the charm was written down. The rest seems to be Christian, although the sense is unclear: the Devil's son came to Adam's bridge, but Adam's son defeated him; Peter sent Paul, his brother, to heal the sick (Peter and Paul appear as brothers in some apocryphal writings and are often in conflict with the pagan archmagician, Simon Magus); a garbled Latin phrase, *pontum patum,* might refer to a bridge or to Pontius Pilate; the help of Christ is asked for the patient; there are instructions to touch the sides of the patient, who is to be commanded in God's name to stand up ("got der gebot dir ez" [God bids you do so]). The charm is completed by the Our Father, with its request that God's will be done. By the

time this charm had been completed the patient would probably have recovered from the seizure on his or her own, and the charm would have received the credit.

References are found to genuine biblical incidents, such as the piercing of Christ's side, but much use is made of nonbiblical stories: legends of the infancy of Christ, the tale of how the Jordan ceased to flow at Jesus' baptism, additional miracles such as the restoring to life of a fish. Besides Peter and Paul, other saints play a role in charms, just as they do in liturgical prayers, specific saints being invoked for particular illnesses. The *Münchener Halsentzündungssegen* (Munich Charm for the Healing of a Sore Throat) invokes Saint Blaise, who saved the life of a child who was choking. On the other hand, a hemostatic charm from a now-lost Strasbourg manuscript, the *Straßburger Blutsegen* (Strasbourg Blood Charm) invokes "ter heilego Tumbo" (Saint Dumb), whose name plays on the Latin *stupidus,* which in turn plays on *stupere* (to step). The Strasbourg manuscript contained another charm that presumably refers in garbled form to an incident from Christ's youth.

Many extant charms are designed to stop bleeding, and quite often nosebleeds are specified. A medical recipe from the eleventh century, the end of the Old High German period, in an Innsbruck medical manuscript calls for ground eggshell to be inhaled through a hollow reed; it is followed by a charm, and the juxtaposition of these texts indicates their intended similarity of function. (The recipe would probably work.) The charms against bleeding in Old High German are of three main types, although they are by no means always clearly distinguished. One group refers to an incident in the youth of Jesus, in which Jesus and someone else – often Judas – are playing with spears; they cut themselves, and Jesus heals his own wound. The second group, the Longinus charms, refers to the soldier who pierced Christ's side in John 19:34 and was, according to legend, himself healed of blindness. Third are the Jordan charms, alluding to the apocryphal story that the river stopped flowing when Jesus was baptized in it. All are common in Latin and in other languages, and all are contained in the *Bamberger Blutsegen* (Bamberg Blood Blessing), a composite or extended charm in another medical manuscript in which the charms are headed "pro pauperes" (for the poor). The Old High German text first gives the Judas and Jesus story (which is probably that which is found in garbled form in the Strasbourg text), then refers to the river Jordan. There follows a verse about the healing of Christ,

aliquantos autem· annos pax ecclesiae est reddita

quae statim ut ecclesia gloriam pacis accepit·:

Domum suam ecclesiam fecit· Cui omnes opes suas

ad xpianorum requiem derelinquens fecit ipsam

ecclesiam heredem xpo· Qui cum do patre & spu sco

aequalis uiuit & regnat in unitate uirtutis·

in scta sctorum·        E X P L I C I T

Christ uuart gaboren· er² uuolf ode deiob· douuas sce maria

christas hirtider heiligo christ unta sce marti dergauuerdo

uualten hinta dero huuro dero Zohono· bazin enuolf noh

uulpa zascedin uert lanne me gi se uuara se ze louf an uualdes

ocle uueges· ocle heido der heiligo christ unta sce marti defru

mamirsa hinto allaheraheim gasunta·

Contra serpente inxpi nomine qu intra desia maria

naria Ziso dno Ziso pcante naria nartancilla sup

fargartha uidens si esse ___ nomine; Dextera dni;

Sup aspide et basiliscu·:·

*Manuscript for the* Wiener Hundsegen *(Vienna, Österreichische Nationalbibliothek, Cod. 552, fol. 107r)*

and then a conjuration of the blood to stop flowing in the name of the five wounds of Christ.

A succinct version of the wounding and healing of Christ appears in a Low German blood charm in the same Trier manuscript as the Christ and Saint Stephen piece against *spurihalz*:

> Ad catarrum dic:
> Christ uuarth giuund  to uuarth he hel gi ok gesund
> that bluod forstuond  so duo thu bluod
>      amen Ter Pater noster Ter

> (For nosebleeds, say:
> Christ was wounded, he became whole and
>   healthy again
> that blood stopped, do you likewise, o blood.
>      three amens, three Our Fathers)

There is an Old High German version of the Jordan charm in the same Paris manuscript that contains the epilepsy charm; the Latin heading specifies that the charm is for a nosebleed. Christ commands the Jordan to stop flowing until he and Saint John have crossed it, a story reminiscent of the parting of the Red Sea by Moses. The Longinus story is found in several charms, including the eleventh-century *Innsbruck pharmacopoeia* and as part of the *Münchener Wundsegen* (Munich Wound Charm), written in the latter part of the twelfth century, where it is combined with a soteriological nonbiblical narrative much used in blood charms, the story of the "three good brothers" who meet Christ, the healer, when they are out looking for herbs. Sometimes the various stories merge, and the mixture of Latin and German in the charms is well illustrated by what Elias von Steinmeyer calls "ein ziemlich unverständlicher Blutsegen" (a pretty well incomprehensible blood charm) in a tenth-century manuscript in Zurich that also contains Latin sermons. Between two Latin fever charms and the story of the woman with an issue of blood in Matt. 9:20–22 is a composite charm that includes German words (the Latin abbreviations are resolved as far as possible, sometimes by guesswork, and in the translation the Latin is in italics):

> Longinus miles. lango zile. cristes thegan ast astes. Adiuro sanguis per patrem et filium. et spiritum sanctum vt ne fluas. plus quam iordanis aha . . . quando Christus. In ea baptizatus est et a . . . a [alleluia?]. III uicibus Pater noster cum gloria.

> (*Longinus the soldier*. long [?]. Christ's warrior . . . grace [?] *I abjure you, blood, in the name of the father and the Son and the Holy Spirit to stop flowing like Jordan river . . . when Christ*

*was baptized and . . . [?]. Three times Our Father with the Gloria.*)

The language and the content seem equally confused, but this state of affairs is not unusual with the charms.

Other Old High German charms are concerned with various, not always identifiable, misfortunes. *Contra malum malannum* (Against a Tumor[?]) invokes the Father and the Son; the precise nature of the disease is unclear. One against *uberbein* (bone spur), which Steinmeyer groups with some recipes against gout, invokes the Holy Cross. An early piece preserved in Munich and a twelfth-century charm in Cambridge deal with sore eyes. The first adds an *amen* to the injunction to bathe the eyes in running water; the second offers a litany — no action is prescribed, but the *amen* is again present. The even later *Gothaer Fiebersegen* (Gotha Fever Charm) invokes all the saints and concludes with a selection of triple prayers. Charms against diseases in general, thought to be caused by worms, are sometimes accompanied by specific instructions in Latin on their use. Their closeness to recipes is apparent.

Some charms clearly refer to animal diseases, frequently of horses; here, too, the use of the Our Father and the *amen* are normal. The German text is sometimes incomprehensible, being reduced to a series of magic words. Such is the case in the confused *Contra rehin*, directed presumably against a kind of lameness, in a group of animal charms added to the twelfth-century *Zurich Pharmacopeia;* three Our Fathers are clearly called for, however. Identifying the horse diseases is not always easy, but many seem concerned with lameness or stiffness. One notable example, found in the same Paris manuscript as the epilepsy charm, has the title *Ad equum errehet* (For a Lame Horse). Three rhymed German quatrains describe a man with a lame horse who encounters Christ; the latter instructs the man to perform various actions, including whispering in the horse's ear and stepping on its hoof. Instructions in Latin call for the same actions; the words to be spoken to the horse are in German but are preceded by a Paternoster. Another series of charms in a medical manuscript, also in Paris, contains little German; these charms specify various actions, as well as the repetition of the Paternoster ten times. There are warnings against the use of the charm (or *Medicina,* the medicine, as it is called in the text) on other animals. Other charms are concerned with the banishing of worms — that is, disease — from horses and from animals in general, and some are supposed to

*Manuscript page including the* Lorscher Bienensegen, *written upside down at the bottom (Vatican, Palatine Library, Cod. Pal. 220, fol. 58r)*

banish worms from human beings; there are Latin and German examples of the last type, usually with the repeated Paternoster. One of these charms in the Paris group invokes Saint Germain, asking that the sun should not shine until the worms leave the animal.

*Spurihalz* is the subject of a horse charm in a ninth-century manuscript in Vienna that calls for a preliminary Paternoster (or perhaps three of them) and a concluding *amen*. The text refers to Christ's healing of a fish, perhaps alluding to one of the apocryphal stories in which a dried fish is brought back to life. Two horse charms written in the twelfth century in a manuscript that is now in the Vatican ask for the cure of an unknown equine disease, *morth;* the first gives a rudimentary narrative of a previous healing, the second invokes Christ, and both demand a threefold Paternoster.

The distinction between charms and blessings is, at best, one of intent: the former are aimed at situations that have already come into being, the latter at preventing situations from arising. It is not possible to distinguish between blessings and prayers; the collects, for example, are prayers that can request both healing and prevention. There are Old High German blessings that exhibit the same mixture of Latin and German, and add the same official prayers or liturgical utterances as the charms. Possibly the earliest general request for a blessing is the runic inscription on the Osthofen fibula, which may ask God for protection against the Devil. Mixed in with a series of Latin charms of a particularly liturgical nature in a tenth-century manuscript now in Zurich is the enigmatic *Hausbesegnung* (House Blessing) – a Latin title indicates that the piece protects the home against demons. Two alliterative long lines in German exorcise the demon by making use of its inability to say the word *chnospinci;* what the word means has been long and inconclusively debated. Two blessings have to do with animals: the *Wiener Hundesegen* (Viennese Dog Blessing) invokes Christ and Saint Martin to protect dogs, and the *Lorscher Bienensegen* (Lorsch Bee Blessing) asks bees, in the name of the Virgin, not to swarm. Bee charms are found in various early cultures – not surprisingly, given the enormous importance of honey in those cultures.

One group of pieces comes close to liturgical prayers. Old and early Middle High German has preserved several *Reisesegen* (travel blessings), the best known being one from Weingarten, in a twelfth-century prayer book that also includes litanies. The *Weingartner Reisesegen* is quite impressive in literary terms. It opens with a formal Latin blessing

(and instructions to make the sign of the cross) and asks for the safety of the traveler in the name of Christ, the Virgin, and Saint Ulrich. Later in the Middle Ages come the longer *Tobiassegen* (Tobias Blessings), which read like litanies of protection, and the similar double Munich *Ausfahrtssegen* (Departure Blessing). Blessings and whole masses for those undertaking a journey are common in missals and sacramentaries in the Old High German period (the fragmentary Saint Gall sacramentary is one example), as are invocations regarding the weather. In addition to Latin collects on the latter theme there is a brief and sometimes incomprehensible piece in German against hailstorms in a manuscript in Graz dating from the twelfth century: the *Grazer Hagelsegen* (Graz Hail Blessing) contains the usual demands for Paternosters.

Distinctions among charms, blessings, and prayers are hard to make; it is easier to distinguish between charms, blessings, and prayers, on the one hand, and recipes, on the other, although all are closely related, in aim at least, and it must be recalled that charms and blessings often survive in medical manuscripts. Judgments of what the form and function of charms might have been in pre-Christian Germanic society have to be speculative, because no pre-Christian charms survive as such. Virtually all the surviving Old High German charms have been Christianized.

**References:**

Jean Paul Allard and Jean Haudry, "Du second charme de Mersebourg au Viatique de Weingarten," *Études Indoeuropéenes,* 14 (September 1985): 33–59;

Peter Assion, *Altdeutsche Fachliteratur* (Berlin: Schmidt, 1973), pp. 133–151;

Isaac Bacon, "Versuch einer Klassifizierung altdeutscher Zaubersprüche und Segen," *Modern Language Notes,* 67 (April 1952): 224–232;

Georg Baesecke, "*Contra caducum morbum,*" *Beiträge,* 62 (1938): 456–460;

J. Knight Bostock, *A Handbook on Old High German Literature,* second edition, edited by K. C. King and D. R. McLintock (Oxford: Clarendon Press, 1976), pp. 26–42;

Wilhelm Boudriot, *Die altgermanische Religion in der christlichen kirchlichen Literatur* (Bonn: Rohrscheid, 1928);

Gerhard Eis, *Altdeutsche Zaubersprüche* (Berlin: De Gruyter, 1964);

Eis, "Der Millstätter Blutsegen in einer Memminger Handschrift," *Studia Neophilologica,* 36 (1964): 207–210;

Marianne Elsakkers, "*Contra caducum morbum:* 2 maal vallen en opstaan," *Amsterdamer Beiträge zur älteren Germanistik,* 29 (1989): 49–60;

Oskar Erdmann, *Blut- und Wundsegen in ihrer Entwicklung dargestellt* (Berlin: Mayer & Müller, 1903);

Adolph Franz, *Die kirchlichen Benediktionen im Mittelalter* (Freiburg: Herder, 1909);

Susan D. Fuller, "Pagan Charms in Tenth-Century Saxony?: The Function of the Merseburg Charms," *Monatshefte,* 72 (Summer 1980): 162–170;

Manfred Geier, "Die magische Kraft der Poesie: Zur Geschichte, Struktur und Funktion des Zauberspruchs," *Deutsche Vierteljahresschrift,* 56 (1982): 359–385;

Felix Genzmer, "Germanische Zaubersprüche," *Germanisch-Romanische Monatshefte,* 1 (October 1950): 21–35;

Genzmer, "Die Götter des zweiten Merseburger Zauberspruchs," *Arkiv for Nordisk Fililogi,* 63 (1948): 55–72;

T. Grienberger, "Althochdeutsche Texterklärungen," *Beiträge,* 45 (1921): 212–238;

J. Sidney Groseclose and Brian O. Murdoch, *Die althochdeutschen poetischen Denkmäler* (Stuttgart: Metzler, 1976), pp. 48–58;

Barbara Kerewsky Halpern and John Miles Foley, "The Power of the Word: Healing Charms as an Oral Genre," *Journal of American Folklore,* 91 (October–December 1978): 903–924;

Irmgard Hampp, "Vom Wesen des Zaubers im Zauberspruch," *Der Deutschunterricht,* 13, no. 1 (1961): 58–76;

Wolfgang Haubrichs, *Die Anfänge,* volume 1, part 1 of *Geschichte der deutschen Literatur,* edited by Joachim Heinzle (Frankfurt am Main: Athenaeum, 1988), pp. 412–436;

R-M. S. Heffner, "The Third Basel Recipe (BaIII)," *Journal of English and Germanic Philology,* 46 (1947): 248–253;

Karl Helm, "Zur althochdeutschen 'Hausbesegnung,' " *Beiträge* (Halle), 69 (1947): 358–360;

J. A. Huisman, "*Contra caducum morbum:* Zum althochdeutschen Spruch gegen Fallsucht," *Amsterdamer Beiträge zur älteren Germanistik,* 17 (1982): 39–50;

Adolf Jacoby, "Der Bamberger Blutsegen," *Zeitschrift für deutsches Altertum,* 54 (1913): 200–209;

Wolfgang Jungandreas, "*God fura dih, deofile,*" *Zeitschrift für deutsches Altertum,* 101, no. 1 (1972): 84–85;

Rolf Ködderitzsch, "Der Zweite Merseburger Zauberspruch und seine Parallelen," *Zeitschrift für celtische Philologie,* 33 (1974): 45–57;

H. W. J. Kroes, "Zum Lorscher Bienensegen," *Germanisch-Romanische Monatsschrift,* new series, 10 (1960): 86–87;

Willy Krogmann, "*Pro cadente morbo,*" *Archiv,* 173 (1938): 1–11;

Georg Manz, *Ein St Galler Sakramentar-Fragment (Cod. Sangall. No. 350)* (Münster: Aschendorff, 1939);

Achim Masser, "Zum Zweiten Merseburger Zauberspruch," *Beiträge* (Tübingen), 94 (1972): 20–25;

Hermann Menhardt, "Der sogenannte Millstätter Blutsegen aus St. Blasien," *Zeitschrift für deutsches Altertum,* 85 (1954–1955): 197–202;

Hugo Moser, "Vom Weingartner Reisesegen zu Walthers Ausfahrtsegen," *Beiträge* (Halle), 82 (1961): 69–89;

Murdoch, "But Did They Work?: Interpreting the Old High German *Merseburg Charms* in Their Medieval Context," *Neuphilologische Mitteilungen,* 89, no. 3 (1988): 358–369;

Murdoch, "Drohtin, uuerthe so!: Funktionsweisen der altdeutschen Zauberspüche," *Literaturwissenschaftliches Jahrbuch der Görres-Gesellschaft,* 32 (1991): 11–37;

Murdoch, *Old High German Literature* (Boston: Twayne, 1983), pp. 45–54;

Murdoch, "*Peri hieres nousou:* Approaches to the Old High German Medical Charms," in *"Mit regulu bithuungan": Neue Arbeiten zur althochdeutschen Poesie und Sprache,* edited by John L. Flood and David N. Yeandle (Göppingen: Kümmerle, 1989), pp. 142–160;

Kenneth Northcott, "An Interpretation of the Second Merseburg Charm," *Modern Language Review,* 54 (January 1959): 45–50;

F. Ohrt, *Die ältesten Segen über Christi Taufe und Christi Tod in religionsgeschichtlichem Lichte* (Copenhagen: Levin & Munksgaard, 1938);

Robert Priebsch, "A Rhymed Charm against 'Mort' in Horses," *Modern Language Review,* 17 (October 1922): 415–417;

Rainer Reiche, *Ein rheinisches Schulbuch aus dem 11. Jahrhundert* (Munich: Arbeo-Gesellschaft, 1976);

Lynn L. Remly, "Murder at a Gallop: The Second Merseburg Charm," *Midwestern Journal of Language and Folklore,* 2 (Spring 1976): 31–39;

Hellmut Rosenfeld, "*Phol ende Wuodan Vuorun zi holza:* Baldermythe oder Fohlenzauber?," *Beiträge* (Tübingen), 95 (1973): 1–12;

Hubert Schiel, "Trierer Segensformeln und Zaubersprüche," *Trierisches Jahrbuch* (1953): 23–36;

Arno Schirokauer, "Der Eingang des Lorscher Bienensegens," *Modern Language Notes,* 57 (January 1942): 62–64;

Schirokauer, "Form und Formel einiger altdeutscher Zaubersprüche," *Zeitschrift für deutsche Philologie,* 73, no. 3 (1954): 353–364;

Bernhard Schnell, "Das 'Prüler Kräuterbuch': Zum ersten Herbar in deutscher Sprache," *Zeitschrift für deutsches Altertum,* 120, no. 2 (1991): 184–202;

Anton Schönbach, "Segen," *Zeitschrift für deutsches Altertum,* 24 (1880): 65–84;

Carl Selmer, "An Unpublished Old German Blood Charm," *Journal of English and Germanic Philology,* 51 (1952): 345–354;

Gerd Sieg, "Zu den Merseburger Zaubersprüchen," *Beiträge* (Halle), 82 (1960): 364–370;

Stefan Sonderegger, *Althochdeutsch in St Gallen* (Saint Gall, 1970), pp. 75–77;

Heather Stuart and F. Walla, "*Eoris sazun idisi* – or did they?," *Germanic Notes,* 14, no. 3 (1983): 35–37;

Stuart and Walla, "Die Überlieferung der mittelalterlichen Segen," *Zeitschrift für deutsches Altertum,* 116, no. 1 (1987): 53–79;

Wolf von Unwerth, "Der Zweite Trierer Zauberspruch," *Zeitschrift für deutsches Altertum,* 54 (1913): 195–199;

Heinrich Wesche, *Der althochdeutsche Wortschatz im Gebiete des Zaubers und der Weissagung* (Halle: Niemeyer, 1940);

K. A. Wipf, "Die Zaubersprüche im Althochdeutschen," *Numen,* 22 (1975): 42–69.

# The *Old High German Isidor*
## (*circa 790 – 800*)

Alfred R. Wedel
*University of Delaware*

**Manuscripts:** The Old High German translation of Isidore of Seville's *De fide Catholica ex vetero et novo testamento contra Judaeos* has been preserved in two medieval manuscripts: Paris, Bibliothèque Nationale, Ms. lat. 2326 (eighth and ninth centuries) and Vienna, Österreichische Nationalbibliothek, Codex 3093 (ninth century), also known as the *Monsee-Vienna Fragments.* The first of these manuscripts contains most of the translation. A vertical line divides each of the first thirty-three pages; on the left side of the page the Latin text appears, on the right side the German translation. The German text is discontinued after page 22, which corresponds to chapter 9 of the first book in Isidore's text. The second manuscript consists of only five pages.

**First publications:** "Althochdeutsche, im cod. Paris. 2326 enthaltene, Ubersetzung eines Theils des isidorischen Traktats *de nativitate domini,*" edited by Eberhard Gottlieb Graff, *Germania,* 1 (1836): 57–89; *Die altdeutschen Bruchstücke des Tractats des Bischofs Isidorus von Sevilla, De fide catholica contra Judaeos, Nach der Pariser und Wiener Handschrift,* edited by Karl Weinhold (Paderborn: Schöningh, 1874).

**Standard editions:** "Der althochdeutsche Isidor, Facsimile-Ausgabe des Pariser Codex nebst critischem Texte der Pariser und Monseer Bruchstücke, mit Einleitung, grammatischer Darstellung und Glossar," edited by George A. Hench, *Quellen und Forschungen,* 72 (1893): i–xix, 1–194; *Der althochdeutsche Isidor, nach der Pariser Handschrift und den Monseer Fragmenten,* edited by Hans Eggers (Tübingen: Niemeyer, 1964).

Isidore of Seville was born circa 560, succeeded his brother Leander to the bishop's seat of Seville around 600, died on 4 April 636, and was canonized in 1598. Called "the Last of the Church Fathers of the West" and the *Doctor Hispaniae* (Teacher from Spain), during the Middle Ages he was celebrated as the most learned man of Europe and today is best known to the scholarly world as the author of the *Etymologies,* a medieval-style encyclopedia that he completed in 636. Isidore's works became known throughout Europe even before the Muslim invasion of Spain in 711 forced many Spanish scholars to seek refuge in England and France. He collected the knowledge of the classical authors in his works and transmitted this knowledge to those parts of Europe where it had been lost in the tumultuous migrations of peoples during the fifth century. Thus, it was Isidore who made the study of the liberal arts in the medieval schools possible.

Among his many writings, only one was translated into German less than two centuries after his death in 636: the treatise *De fide Catholica ex vetero et novo testamento contra judaeos* (On the Catholic Faith, Based on the Old and New Testament, against the Jews, 615), a work that had been composed to defend the Christian dogmas against the objections raised by the Jews during the Visigothic domination of Spain. The German translation, made between about 790 and 800, was used to attack the arguments raised by the adherents of Adoptionism, a heresy that was gaining followers throughout Europe during the early years of Charlemagne's reign. In both cases a central issue was the doctrine of the Holy Trinity.

The Visigoths — that is, the Goths of the west — were already Christians when they entered the Spanish province of Tarraconensis as allies of Rome a few years before the collapse of the West Roman Empire in 476. These Romanized barbarians were followers of the heresy of Arianism. The Arians denied the Trinity and regarded Christ as subordinate to God. The Hispano-Roman population of the Iberian Peninsula living under Visigothic rule was Catholic, adhering to the articles of faith proclaimed by the Council of Nicea in 325 and the Council of Constantinople in 381. Those articles condemned Arianism and proclaimed that the Father, the Son, and

*Page from the Paris manuscript for the* Old High German Isidor. *The Latin text of Isidore of Seville's* De fide Catholica ex vetero et novo testamento contra Judaeos *appears in the left-hand column, the German translation on the right (Paris, Bibliothèque Nationale, Ms. lat. 2326, fol. 2v).*

the Holy Ghost were three persons but only one substance. The Visigothic king Leovigild tried, without success, to achieve the spiritual unity of Spain by imposing Arianism on all of his subjects; his son Reccared did the exact opposite, converting to Catholicism at the Third Council of Toledo in 589. During the council, at which Isidore was present, the monarch instructed his bishops to convert the Jews of the realm. Anti-Jewish legislation was formulated but not put into effect until Sisebut ascended the throne in 612. In his *Historia Gothorum* (History of the Goths, 619) Isidore expresses a deep regret at the king's decision to use force instead of persuasion and at the false conversions that resulted.

Isidore dedicated *De fide Catholica* to his sister Florentine, a nun. It was an apologetic work written to convert the Jews. The treatise is divided into two books. The first four chapters deal with the Holy Trinity; the second part of the first book describes the birth of Christ, his life, and his work of Redemption. In chapter 62, the epilogue to the first book, Isidore points out the blindness of the Jews in refusing to recognize that the coming of Christ fulfilled messianic prophecies of the Old Testament. The first eighteen chapters of the second book are an invitation to Jews and gentiles to accept the Catholic faith. The second part of the second book interprets the Old Testament from a mystical point of view. The treatise ends with an epilogue in which Isidore laments the precarious situation of the Jewish people because of their unbelief.

The Old High German translation of Isidore's treatise was undertaken at the instigation of Charlemagne to combat the Adoptionist heresy propagated by the Spaniards Elipando, archbishop of Toledo, and Félix, bishop of Urgel. The Adoptionists believed that Christ was an extraordinary human being who had been elevated to the Godhead by the grace of God: the son of Mary was, therefore, the Son of God not by nature but by adoption. Charlemagne's zeal to put an end to this heresy was due to the fact that he had taken upon himself the mission of re-creating the territorial and spiritual unity that existed during the latter part of the West Roman Empire.

It has been asserted that the *Old High German Isidor* was produced for the purpose of using the biblical prophesies quoted by Isidore against the arguments of the Adoptionists at the councils of Regensburg in 792 and Frankfurt in 794. But these councils were held in Latin; a translation would seem superfluous, unless the Latin text, which appears alongside the German, was read aloud to a mixed audience of clerics and laypersons, as George Nordmeyer has proposed. Herta Kowalski-Fahrun, however, is of the opinion that the *Old High German Isidor* was undertaken not for an apologetic or dogmatic but for a practical purpose: the treatise explains concisely the basic Christian beliefs in both Latin and the vernacular and makes the connection between the Old and the New Testament understandable; it could, therefore, have served as instructional material for young clerics and as sermons for the lay population. It is significant that the word *Judaei* (Jews) of the original text is left out and the word *unchilaubendun* (unbelievers) is added in two passages; this change shifts the focus from the conversion of Jews to the conversion of unbelievers in general. These unbelievers included all Jews, heretics, and pagans in Charlemagne's realm.

The two extant incomplete Old High German manuscripts are copies of an original translation that no longer exists and that may have carried the translation of Isidore's treatise beyond the ninth chapter of the first book, where the longer manuscript ends. The name of the translator and the place where the translation took place remain unknown. The regularity of the orthography and the choice of terms to express theological concepts reveal an expert hand. The translation is not a slavish rendering of the original text, as are so many other translations of the period. On the contrary, there are frequent deviations from the Latin text that show a desire on the part of the translator to make certain passages more understandable. Richard Kienast believes that the translator had the Old Germanic alliterative poetry in mind when he rendered the Latin text into a rhythmic and dynamic Old High German prose. Since the *Old High German Isidor* shows traces of the Alemannic dialect, Gustav Nutzhorn suggests that the work was composed in Murbach in Alsace; but the Lorraine area would also qualify as the birthplace of the translation since, as Rudolf Kögel points out, a school existed in Metz under the supervision of Archbishop Angilram, the court chaplain of Charlemagne. Finally, Wilhelm Bruckner suggests that the *Old High German Isidor* could have been produced in Alcuin's academy at Tours, in the Loire region, where a French-German bilingual population existed that had been educated in the Latin tradition.

The *Old High German Isidor* stands out as a masterpiece of German prose during a time in which the writing centers of the Carolingian period were making their first attempts to create a written vehicle for the German language. It is, however, by no means clear to what degree the *Old High German*

*Isidor* contributed to the development of German literature. One could argue that the German version of Isidore's treatise was too utilitarian to inspire the development of a literature of entertainment; it cannot be denied, however, that the *Old High German Isidor* proved that German was, after all, not such a barbaric language.

**References:**

Restituta Ansprenger, "Untersuchung zum adoptianischen Streit im 8. Jahrhundert," Ph.D. dissertation, Freie Universität, Berlin, 1953;

Georg Baesecke, "Unerledigte Vorfragen der ahd. Textkritik und Literaturgeschichte, III," *Beiträge,* 69 (1947): 367–409;

Ernest Brehaut, *An Encyclopedist of the Dark Ages: Isidore of Seville* (New York: Columbia University Press, 1912);

Wilhelm Bruckner, "Zur Orthographie der althochdeutschen Isidorübersetzung und zur Frage nach der Heimat des Denkmals," in *Festschrift Gustav Binz* (Basel: Schwabe, 1935), pp. 69–83;

Manuel C. Diaz y Diaz, ed., *Isidoriana* (Leon: Centro de estudios San Isidoro, 1961);

Hans-Joachim Diesner, *Isidor von Sevilla und das westgotische Spanien* (Berlin: Akademie, 1977);

Gustav Ehrismann, *Geschichte der deutschen Literatur bis zum Ausgang des Mittelalters,* volume 1 (Munich: Beck, 1932), pp. 273–286;

Jacques Fontaine, *Isidore de Séville et la culture classique dans L'Espagne wisigothique,* 2 volumes (Paris: Etudes Augustiniennes, 1959);

Fontaine, *Tradition et actualité chez Isidore de Séville* (London: Variorum Reprints, 1988);

Richard Kienast, "Zur frühesten deutschen Kunstprosa: Der Prosarhythmus der althochdeutschen Isidor-Übersetzung," in *Festschrift für Wolfgang Stammler* (Berlin: Schmidt, 1953), pp. 11–24;

Rudolf Kögel, *Geschichte der deutschen Litteratur bis zum Ausgange des Mittelalters,* volume 1 (Strasbourg: Trübner, 1897), pp. 478–479;

Herta Kowalski-Fahrun, "Alkuin und der ahd. Isidor," *Beiträge,* 47 (1923): 312–324;

George Nordmeyer, "On the OHG *Isidor* and Its Significance for Early German Prose Writings," *PMLA,* 73 (March 1958): 23–35;

Nordmeyer, "Syntax Analysis of the Old High German *Isidor,*" in *Festschrift Hermann J. Weigand* (New Haven: Department of Germanic Languages, Yale University, 1957);

Gustav Nutzhorn, "Murbach als Heimat der ahd. Isidorübersetzung und der verwandten Stücke," *Zeitschrift für deutsche Philologie,* 44 (1912): 265–320, 430–476;

Max Rannow, *Der Satzbau des althochdeutschen Isidor im Verhältniss zur lateinischen Vorlage* (Berlin: Weidmann, 1888);

E. A. Thompson, *The Goths in Spain* (Oxford: Clarendon Press, 1969);

Alfred R. Wedel, "Subjective and Objective Aspect: The Preterit in the *Old High German Isidore,*" *Linguistics,* 123 (1 March 1974): 45–58;

Wedel, "Syntagmatische und paradigmatische Mittel zur Angabe des lateinischen Perfekts im althochdeutschen *Isidor* und *Tatian,*" *Neuphilologische Mitteilungen,* 88, no. 1 (1987): 80–89.

# Petruslied
## (circa 854?)

Anatoly Liberman
*University of Minnesota*

**Manuscript:** The *Petruslied* is preserved in Munich, Bayrische Staatsbibliothek, Clm 6260: leaf 158v, copied around 900.

**First edition:** In *Miscellaneen zur Geschichte der teutschen Literatur,* volume 1, edited by Bernard Joseph Docen (Münich: Schererche Kunst- und Buchhandlung, 1807), pp. 3–4. Facsimiles in *Die ältesten deutschen Sprach-Denkmäler*, edited by Magda Enneccerus (Frankfurt am Main: F. Enneccerus, 1897), plate 39; in *Schrifttafeln zum althochdeutschen Lesebuch*, edited by Hanns Fischer (Tübingen: Niemeyer, 1966), pp. 20, 22*–23*.

The *Petruslied* (Song of [Saint] Peter, circa 854?) was copied at Freising, on the verso of the last leaf of a manuscript of Hrabanus Maurus's commentary on Genesis, by a different scribe. The song consists of three strophes, each followed by the refrain "Kyrie eleyson, Christe eleyson" (Lord have mercy on us, Christ have mercy on us):

Unsar trohtin hat farsalt  sancte Petre giuualt,
daz er mac ginerian  ze imo dingenten man.
 Kyrie eleyson,  Christe eleyson.
Er hapet ouh mit uuortun  himilriches portun
dar in mach er skerian  den er uuili nerian.
 Kirie eleison  Criste *eleyson.*
Pittemes den gotes trut  alla samant uparlut,
daz er uns firtanen  giuuerdo ginaden.
 Kirie eleyson,  Criste eleison.

Our Lord gave Saint Peter the power
To save those who believe in him,
Kyrie Eleyson, Christe eleyson.
He controls with his words [*or* He controls especially *or* expressly] the gates of Heaven.
He will admit those whom he wants to save.
Kyrie eleyson, Christe eleyson.
Let us all together pray to God's friend [Saint Peter] very loudly,
That he in his mercy pardon us sinners.
Kyrie eleyson, Christe eleyson.

Since the song was written down in Freising, it is natural that its dialect is Bavarian, but in the last line of the exhortation (line 8) two words have Franconian prefixes, and, instead of *taz, daz* occurs. Also, the text does not display the paleographical features one would expect from a scribe of the Freising school. On the evidence of the language, the Freising copy has been dated to approximately the year 900; it is less clear when the original was composed. The use of end rhyme ties the song to the Otfriedian tradition, and Otfried von Weißenburg completed his *Evangelienbuch* (Gospel Book) not later than 871. In the song, the line with Franconian prefixes and unshifted *d* coincides with *Evangelienbuch* I. 7, 28, and the contexts are almost the same. The Annunciation scene in *Evangelienbuch* I. 7, 25–28 ends: "Let us pray to the Virgin, to Saint Mary, that she intercede for us with her son in all eternity. John, God's friend, will also deign to be merciful to us, sinners."

Earlier scholarship, until the time of Georg Baesecke, tended to hold that the exhortation in the *Petruslied* was derived from Otfried, but this view has almost been abandoned. The rhyme in the *Petruslied* (*firtanen/ginaden*) is better than in the *Evangelienbuch* (*firdanen/ginadon*). It is hard to imagine that the *Petruslied* poet quoted a chance line from the *Evangelienbuch* for the finale of his song; both authors may have drawn on a common stock of formulas. Owing to its vagueness, the phrase *gotes* [or *druhtines*] *trut* (God's [or the Lord's] friend) could be applied widely; Otfried uses it about Abraham, Moses, and Christ, in addition to Saint Peter. If the *Petruslied* is older than the *Evangelienbuch,* the hypothesis that Otfried was the creator of end rhyme in German falls. The question, however, remains unresolved. Identical arguments are used to prove opposite views. Ulrich Pretzel believed that since the rhyme is so polished, the song must be later than the *Evangelienbuch,* but it is equally possible that a popular text was corrupted through multiple copying and inept imitation. The reasoning of those who defend the song's antiquity carries more conviction. Of special importance are Hermann Fränkel's state-

*The manuscript for the* Petruslied *(Munich, Bayerische Staatsbibliothek, Clm 6260, fol. 158v)*

ment of the case and Lee Stavenhagen's detailed analysis. Both argue for the song's relatively old age, and the same view is presented in the widely read histories of German literature by Helmut de Boor and the encyclopedia of the German literature of the Middle Ages, *verfasserlexicon*.

The *Petruslied* must have been composed by a Frankish poet and only copied at Freising; otherwise it is hard to account for the Franconian features. Inasmuch as in the ninth century the only language of worship was Latin, the *Petruslied* is a litany of Saint Peter rather than part of the liturgy. The lines were probably sung by a priest and the refrain by the lay public. The idea that the *Petruslied* served as a pilgrim's song has no foundation in fact. The refrain kyrie eleison was very popular in the Middle Ages and was not exclusively connected with pilgrims' processions.

The *Petruslied* could have been composed on the occasion of consecration of a church bearing Peter's name. Under Bishop Erchambert such a church was erected in Freising around 850, but the extant copy is half a century later. German songs of this type usually had Latin sources, and W. Mettin pointed to an Ambrosian hymn, *Aurea luce et decore roseo,* that he considered to be a source of the *Petruslied.* His theory became a commonplace, but despite the agreement in the wording the hymn has no end rhyme, and Stavenhagen has thrown doubt on Mettin's theory. The origin of the *Petruslied* is probably impossible to discover, since the popular tradition of early rhyming poetry in German is lost.

In the manuscript the *Petruslied* is provided with neumes, which means that the melody remains a matter of reconstruction. Three such reconstructions exist: by Joseph Müller-Blattau, 1935; Otto Ursprung, 1952; and Ewald Jammers, 1957. Jammers points out that, contrary to the usual practice, the neumes of the *Petruslied* are not determined by the rhythm, so the scribe may have been ignorant of singing technique and put them in mechanically. Jammers suggests that the neumes were originally meant for a Latin song and transferred to the German text later. In any case, according to Jammers, the neumatic notation of the *Petruslied* exhibits no dependence on Otfried's recitative. Curiously, the refrain, which must have been sung by the uneducated people, has a neume, called a *quilisma*, designating a rather complicated portamento. Although the text has both words and notes, musicologists are unable to clarify the problems that puzzle literary scholars.

Over the text of the *Petruslied,* one can discern the name Suonhart. Nothing is known about the man who bore this name or of his relation to the manuscript.

## References:

Georg Baesecke, "St. Emmeramer Studien," *Beiträge zur Geschichte der deutschen Sprache und Literatur,* 46 (1922): 431–494;

Helmut de Boor, *Die deutsche Literatur von Karl dem Grossen bis zum Beginn der höfischen Dichtung* (Munich: Beck, 1949);

Hermann Fränkel, "Aus der Frühgeschichte des deutschen Endreims," *Zeitschrift für deutsches Altertum und deutsche Literatur,* 58 (1921): 41–64;

Ewald Jammers, "Das mittelalterliche deutsche Epos und die Musik," *Heidelberger Jahrbücher,* 1 (1957): 31–91;

E. Karg-Gasterstädt, "Petruslied," in *Die deutsche Literatur des Mittelalters: Verfasserlexikon,* volume 5, edited by Karl Langosch (Berlin: De Gruyter, 1955), cols. 885–887;

Helmut Lomnitzer, "Petruslied," in *Die deutsche Literatur des Mittelalters: Verfasserlexikon,* second edition, volume 7, edited by Kurt Ruh and others (Berlin & New York: De Gruyter, 1987), cols. 521–525;

W. Mettin, "Die ältesten deutschen Pilgerlieder," in *Philologische Studien: Festgabe für Eduard Sievers zum 1. Oktober 1896* (Halle: Niemeyer, 1896), pp. 277–286;

Joseph Müller-Blattau, "Zu Form und Überlieferung der ältesten deutschen geistlichen Lieder," *Zeitschrift für Musikwissenschaft,* 17 (1935): 129–146;

Ulrich Pretzel, *Frühgeschichte des deutschen Reims,* volume 1: *Allgemeiner Teil, Besonderer Teil 1: Die Entwicklung bis zur Volltonigkeit des Reims,* Palaestra, no. 220 (Leipzig: Becker & Eler, 1941);

Rudolf Schützeichel, "Petruslied: Die Macht der Heiligen," in his *Textgebundenheit: Kleinere Schriften zur mittelalterlichen deutschen Literatur* (Tübingen: Niemeyer, 1981), pp. 29–44;

Lee Stavenhagen, "Das Petruslied: Sein Alter und seine Herkunft," *Wirkendes Wort,* 17 (1967): 12–28;

Otto Ursprung, "Das Freisinger Petrus-Lied," *Die Musikforschung,* 5 (1952): 17–21.

# Physiologus
## (circa 1070 – circa 1150)

Alfred R. Wedel
*University of Delaware*

**Manuscripts:** The two longer German prose translations of the Latin version of the *Physiologus* known as the *Dicta Chrysostomi de naturis bestiarum* are included in two manuscripts, both in Vienna, Österreichische Nationalbibliothek: Codex Vindobonensis 223 (eleventh century) and Codex Vindobonensis 2721 (twelfth century). The first of these translations, *Der ältere Physiologus,* is a fragment, covering only twelve of the twenty-seven chapters of the *Dicta Chrysostomi de naturis bestiarum.* The second, *Der jüngere Physiologus,* renders into German all twenty-seven chapters of the Latin version. Another manuscript, *Die Millstätter Reimfassung,* Klagenfurt, Austria, Geschichtsverein für Kärnten im Kärntner Landesarchiv, document 6/19, dating from the twelfth century and written in verse, also contains all the chapters found in the Latin version. Finally, there is a short manuscript fragment, Schäftlarn, Bavaria, Benedictine monastery, Document Clm 17195, known as the *Schäftlarner Fragment,* from the twelfth century, which mentions just two of the animals found in chapters 3 and 5 of the Latin version. Facsimiles can be found in *Codex Vindobonensis 2721,* edited by Edgar Papp (Essingen-Lauterburg: Kümmerle, 1980) and *Millstätter Genesis und Physiologus Handschrift,* volume 2, edited by Alfred Kracher (Graz: Akademischer Druck- und Verlagsanstalt, 1967).

**First publications:** *Der ältere Physiologus,* edited by Eberhard Gottlieb Graff, in his *Diutiska,* volume 3 (Stuttgart, 1829), pp. 22–39; *Der jüngere Physiologus,* edited by Hans Ferdinand Massmann, in his *Deutsche Gedichte des zwoelften Jahrhunderts* (Quedlinburg & Leipzig: Basse, 1837), pp. 311–325; *Die Millstätter Reimfassung,* edited by Theodor Georg von Karajan, in his *Deutsche Sprach-Denkmale des zwölften Jahrhunderts* (Vienna: Braumüller & Seidel, 1846), pp. 72–106.

**Standard editions:** *Der ältere Physiologus,* edited by Elias von Steinmeyer, in his *Die kleineren althochdeutschen Sprachdenkmäler* (Berlin: Weidmann, 1916), pp. 124–134; *Der ältere Physiologus, Der jüngere Physiologus,* and the "Schaftlärner Fragment," edited by Friedrich Wilhelm, in his *Denkmäler deutscher Prosa des 11. und 12. Jahrhunderts* (Munich: Hueber, 1960), pp. 4–28, 46–47; *Der altdeutsche Physiologus: Die Millstätter Reimfassung und die Wiener Prosa, nebst dem lateinischen Text und dem althochdeutschen Physiologus,* edited by Friedrich Maurer (Tübingen: Niemeyer, 1967).

**Edition in English:** Translated by Michael J. Curley as *Physiologus* (Austin: University of Texas Press, 1979).

The *Physiologus* (circa 1070–circa 1150) is a Christian adaptation of ancient stories of diverse origins that deal with stones, plants, and the properties of real and mythical animals. The Latin title is a translation of the Greek *Physiologos,* which refers to a person engaged in the study of nature – that is, a scientist. In the Christian context the title suggests, however, someone who is more than just an authority in the natural sciences; it refers to one who is an interpreter of the transcendent significance of things found in nature. Most chapters of the book begin with a biblical reference containing the name of a given mineral, plant, or animal. Consequently, the *Physiologus* can be understood as a theological treatise for the instruction of the lay population that uses allegories dealing with plants, animals, and stones.

Judging from the four hundred or so extant medieval manuscripts of this work in diverse languages of Europe, Africa, and Asia, the *Physiologus* was the most widely read Christian work until the appearance of Isidore of Seville's *Etymologies* in the seventh century. Although some of the manuscripts mention an author – among them the Greek philosopher Aristotle; the church fathers Epiphanius,

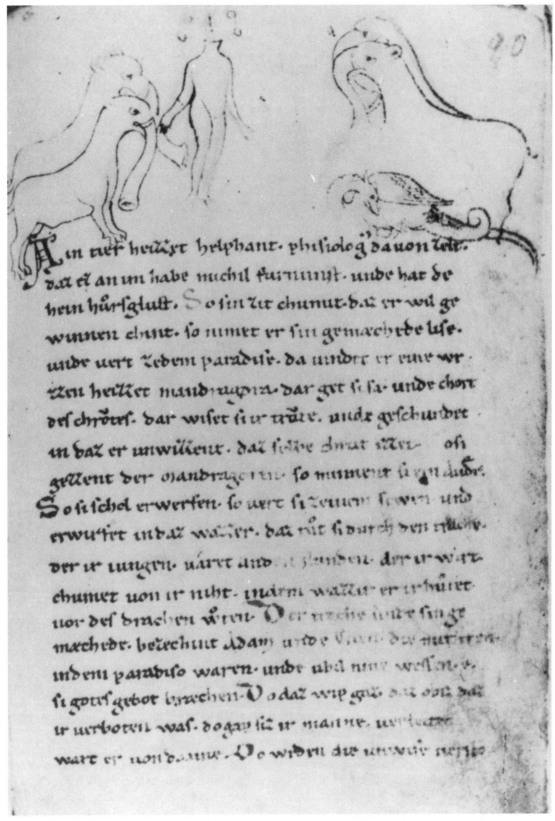

Pages from the manuscript for the Millstätter Reimfassung of the Physiologus *(Klagenfurt, Austria, Geschichtsverein für Kärnten im Kärntner Landesarchiv, document 6/19, fols. 90r, 96v)*

Man sol miden die lere. die gelart haben diese er
rare. Arrins. Sabillins. Maredoni. Manchi.
Homeians. Montanus. Valentin. Basiles. Maer
donins. Fortanus. Unde ander irrare. wande un
reht was ir lere. ir lere die was lugelich. unde
ist widerwartien richur warheite. ich meine die
war ein gotheite.

Phisiolog seit von dem
Igele er spricht dorne
habet er arme. variu ubil
grean kumt der gut under
wingarten e der trager st
... her ... til der bere. herabe er die ber
schuret. se war er vur der ber überwalget. die
agen suet er tehunde unde trert si seurn iun
grun Der igel beleichet den ... bart. der
... sinen wingarten. das gutslichv weder
... schiren. daz in werlelich achut ihe ...
... der dorniger ruste ihr ursluche. sinv gutlich
weder noch sinen wingarten urt unde. tel uon
...

John Chrysostom, Ambrose, and Jerome; King Solomon; and even a nonexistent Saint Physiologus – nothing is known about the author of the original *Physiologus*. It is generally accepted that the work was composed in Greek in the Hellenistic city of Alexandria, Egypt, in the last quarter of the second century. Some of the stories in the book came from ancient India and some from the remote Egyptian past.

The version of the *Physiologus* that served as the text for the four medieval German translations names John Chrysostom as its author. This version, as its title, *Dicta Chrysostomi de naturis bestiarum* (Sayings of Chrysostom on the Nature of Animals), indicates, deals exclusively with animals; consequently, the German versions make no mention of plants or stones. Twenty-nine animals, real and imaginary, are described in twenty-seven chapters: lion, panther, unicorn, niluus, siren and ass-centaur, hyena, wild ass and monkey, elephant, antelope, swordfish, viper, lizard, stag, goat, fox, beaver, ant, hedgehog, eagle, pelican, owl, heron, partridge, ostrich, hoopoe, chalandrius, and phoenix. (The standard Greek version of the *Physiologus* has forty-nine chapters, each dealing with a separate animal, mineral, or plant.)

Hermann Menhardt is of the opinion that the Codex Vindobonensis 223, the manuscript of *Der ältere Physiologus* (The Older *Physiologus*), was taken from the Benedictine monastery of Hirsau in the Black Forest to the newly founded daughter institution of Saint Paul in Kärnten. He also believes that the entire manuscript was written by the same hand. He explains the fact that chapters 1 through 8 reveal linguistic characteristics of Alemannic, whereas chapters 9 through 12 show traces of Rhenish-Franconian, by claiming that Hirsau was near the linguistic border that separated these two Old High German dialects. Nikolaus Henkel, however, insists that the presence of two dialects does not prove that Hirsau was the place of origin of the manuscript; he theorizes that the manuscript, which dates from the end of the eleventh century, was a copy of an older original and was produced by two scribes and that the dialectal differences are due to the native dialects of the scribes.

*Der ältere Physiologus* is a free translation of the *Dicta Chrysostomi de naturis bestiarum;* it represents, especially in the first eight chapters, an abbreviated version of the Latin original. The Old High German text concludes toward the middle of chapter 12, on the lizard, and does not have the section on the monkey that constitutes the second part of chapter 7 in the *Dicta Chrysostomi de naturis bestiarum*. An-

other version, *Der jüngere Physiologus* (The Younger *Physiologus*), appears in the Codex Vindobonensis 2721 between Old High German translations of Genesis and Exodus. *Der jüngere Physiologus* is a complete translation of the *Dicta Chrysostomi de naturis bestiarum*. It does not render the Latin syntax slavishly into German but uses simple German sentences that convey the meaning of the original. The place of origin of *Der jüngere Physiologus* remains unknown. The document was written by a single hand, and the dialect is basically Bavarian with some traces of Swabian. The composition date has been fixed as around 1130 to 1150.

*Der jüngere Physiologus* served as a model for *Die Millstätter Reimfassung* (The Millstatt Rhymed *Physiologus*). This early Middle High German version is an attempt to render *Der jüngere Physiologus* into verse. The scholar Ulrich Pretzel deplores the poor technique of the versification and considers the work one of the most unpolished in German literature. This manuscript, which is richly decorated with pen drawings and is known as document 6/19 of the Kärnten National Archives, does not follow the usual arrangement in which each verse is placed below the preceding one to form rhymed couplets; instead, each verse follows the previous one horizontally, as in prose. Most of the rhymes are assonance rather than pure rhyme: the vowel of the last syllable of the first half line is identical with the vowel of the last syllable of the second half line, while the final consonants are not identical. For example, in the first long line of chapter 1 *Jacob* rhymes with *gesegenot*. The place of origin of the document, which is in the Bavarian-Austrian dialect, is unknown. A comparative study of the drawings in this manuscript with those in other manuscripts led Hella Voss to conclude that the document must have been composed either in Kärnten or in Styria around 1180 to 1200.

The document Clm 17195 in the library of the Benedictine monastery of Schäftlarn dates from the twelfth century and includes a fragment in verse of another German *Physiologus* version. It, too, uses assonance rather than pure rhyme, but it was composed independently of *Die Millstätter Reimfassung*. The purpose of inserting this fragment into the text of an unrelated theological treatise is unknown. The *Physiologus* text was added – by a different hand – to a blank space in chapter 33. This fragment deals briefly with the ass-centaur and the unicorn, which in the *Dicta Chrysostomi de naturis bestiarum* are treated in chapters 3 and 5, respectively.

Judging from the *Physiologus* translations undertaken not only in Germany but also in other parts of Europe – including England, Iceland, France, and Spain – there is no doubt about the popularity of the work; but it leaves one with the question of whether the medievals literally believed these fantastic tales regarding the properties of animals. Henkel does not think so; he quotes Isidore of Seville, who says in his *Etymologies* (XII, 3, 3), "Falso autem opinantur qui dicunt mustelam ore concipere, aure effundere partum" (Those people are wrong who believe that the weasel conceives through its mouth and gives birth to its young through one ear). The purpose of the treatise was to teach not zoology, but theology. The story of the weasel, for instance, which was a widely known fable in the ancient world, was told to explain Ps. 58: 4–5: "They are like the deaf asp which stops its ears, and will not listen to the sound of the charmer." After hearing about the properties of this animal, the reader is told "Some believers are like the weasel, after receiving the holy communion through their mouth, they will cast the Word of God out of their hearing."

In the three lengthier German versions of the *Physiologus,* chapter 11 deals with the viper. The chapter begins with the passage in Matt. 3:7 where the Pharisees are said to be a "viper's brood," followed by the animal story: the male viper introduces its head into the mouth of the female viper to copulate, after which the female bites off the head of her mate; the young will eventually eat their way out through their mother's belly, causing her death. The text of *Der Jüngere Physiologus* explains that the Pharisees are like these vipers: "si irsluogen ir uater den heiligen christ. unt âhten ir muoter der heiligen christenheit" (they killed their father, the holy Christ, and scorn their mother, the church). This type of allegorical exegesis was undoubtedly a useful means of instructing the lay population in the Christian faith and explains the enormous popularity of the *Physiologus* during the Middle Ages.

**References:**

Emma Brunner-Traut, "Altägyptische Mythen im Physiologus," *Antaios,* 10, no. 2 (1968): 184–198;

Robert James Glendinning, "A Critical Study of the Old High German Physiologus and Its Influence," Ph.D dissertation, University of Manitoba, 1959;

Max Goldstaub, "Der Physiologus und seine Weiterbildung, besonders in der lateinischen und byzantinischen Litteratur," *Philologus,* supplementary volume 8 (1899–1901): 339–404;

Nikolaus Henkel, *Studien zum Physiologus im Mittelalter* (Tübingen: Niemeyer, 1976);

Heinz Jantsch, *Studien zum Symbolischen in frühmittelhochdeutscher Literatur* (Tübingen: Niemeyer, 1959), pp. 108–179;

Friedrich Lauchert, *Geschichte des Physiologus* (Geneva: Slatkine Reprints, 1974);

Florence McCulloch, *Medieval Latin and French Bestiaries* (Chapel Hill: University of North Carolina Press, 1962);

Hermann Menhardt, *Der Millstätter Physiologus und seine Verwandten* (Klagenfurt: Verlag des Landesmuseums für Kärnten, 1956);

Menhardt, "Wanderungen des ältesten deutschen Physiologus," *Zeitschrift für deutsches Altertum und deutsche Literatur,* 84, no.1–2 (1937): 37–38;

Ulrich Pretzel, *Frühgeschichte des deutschen Reims* (Leipzig: Becker & Erler, 1941), pp. 244–256;

Hella Voss, *Studien zur illustrierten Millstätter Genesis* (Munich: Beck, 1957);

Alfred R. Wedel, "The Complexive Aspect of Present Reports in the Old High German *Physiologus*," *Journal of English and Germanic Philology,* 82 (October 1983): 488–499;

Max Wellmann, "Der Physiologus: Eine religionsgeschichtlich-naturwissenschaftliche Untersuchung," *Philologus,* supplementary volume 22 (1931): 1–116.

# Ruodlieb
## (circa 1050 – 1075)

Dennis M. Kratz
*University of Texas at Dallas*

**Manuscripts:** Two manuscripts exist, both fragmentary. The more important, known as the "Munich" manuscript, Bayerische Staatsbibliothek, Clm 19486, was written by the author of the poem. Fragments of a manuscript evidently copied from the original are in the Saint Florian (Austria) Chorherrenstift.
**First publication:** In *Lateinische Gedichte des X. und XI. Jahrhunderts,* edited by Jacob Grimm and Andreas Schmeller (Göttingen: Dieterich, 1838; reprinted, Amsterdam: Rodopi, 1967), pp. 129–198.
**Standard edition:** *The Ruodlieb: Linguistic Introduction, Latin Text and Glossary,* edited by Gordon B. Ford, Jr. (Leiden: Brill, 1966).
**Editions in English:** Translated in prose by Edwin H. Zeydel as *Ruodlieb: The Earliest Courtly Novel, after 1050* (Chapel Hill: University of North Carolina Press, 1959); translated in prose by Gordon B. Ford, Jr., as *The Ruodlieb: The First Medieval Epic of Chivalry from Eleventh-Century Germany* (Leiden: Brill, 1965); translated in verse by Dennis M. Kratz, in his *Waltharius and Ruodlieb* (New York: Garland, 1984), pp. 73–199.

The *Ruodlieb,* a Latin narrative poem composed in southern Germany between around 1050 and 1075, is not only an innovative work of art that has resisted all efforts to categorize it but also a rich source of information about life in the eleventh century. It contains, for example, detailed and apparently realistic depictions of a judicial proceeding, a marriage ceremony, the proper treatment of guests, and even one of the earliest descriptions of chess to be found in Western literature. The importance of the *Ruodlieb* rests equally on its anticipation of several elements of plot and theme that would become essential to the twelfth-century vernacular romance:

the adventures of a wandering knight, an emphasis on the ennobling power of mutual love, and the depiction of a new kind of heroism based on Christian values and courtly behavior.

The text was discovered in 1803 by B. J. Docen of the Royal Bavarian Library in Munich on irregularly cut parchment strips in the bindings of manuscripts from the monastery of Tegernsee; his successor as librarian, Andreas Schmeller, found additional fragments. The eighteen fragments that the two men collected now constitute the major manuscript of the *Ruodlieb.* They range from a few lines on fragment 10 to more than six hundred on fragment 5. The evidence suggests that the author himself wrote this manuscript, making corrections in and glosses on the text. Approximately twenty-three hundred verses of the *Ruodlieb* survive; many are incomplete, and a major issue in editing the *Ruodlieb* involves the necessity of completing these mutilated lines. A second issue concerns the proper ordering of the fragments to form the most coherent narrative, perhaps the narrative originally designed by the poet.

The identity of the author remains a mystery; a few conjectures about him can be made based on evidence in the poem. German was the poet's native language: a few German words occur in the text, and in four instances the poet gives German glosses to explain unusual Latin words. In all likelihood he composed the *Ruodlieb* at Tegernsee. He may have been educated there, for the education offered at Tegernsee included the study of classical literature, including topoi drawn from classical and patristic authors. Although the extent of the author's knowledge of classical literature is uncertain, he had obviously read the *Aeneid.* The efforts of modern scholarship have found no direct citation of a classical author other than Pliny, whom the poet claims as the source of his information about the miraculous

260

herb *buglossa;* but no mention of *buglossa* appears in the extant works of Pliny (or anyone else). Certain poetic themes, such as the extended complaint concerning the horrors of old age in fragment 15 and the formulaic *tot/quot* (as many/so many) declarations about love and the denial of love in fragment 17 have a long history in Latin literature. His acquaintance with such topoi implies that the poet had at least read excerpts from the works of several classical authors.

The *Ruodlieb* also contains an impressive range of material drawn from legend and folklore. The encounter of a warrior or king with a dwarf who knows the whereabouts of a treasure is a relatively common theme in Germanic heroic legends: one version of the *Eckenlied* (Song of Ecke, circa 1250), for example, mentions a king named Ruotliep who is given a sword stolen from three dwarfs, and the Norwegian *Thidreksaga* (Saga of Theodoric, circa 1250) includes a tale about a dwarf and a king named Rozeleif. Perhaps one of these stories provided the *Ruodlieb* poet with the name of his hero and the inspiration for the events in its last surviving fragment. Other folkloric elements, such as the properties of *buglossa* and the procedures for transforming the urine of a lynx into sparkling jewels (fragment 5, lines 99–129), have no identifiable source.

Among the episodes that seem to reflect the poet's adaptation of oral traditions, the dream of Ruodlieb's mother (fragment 17, lines 89–101), in which she sees Ruodlieb threatened by wild boars and then crowned by a dove who flies to him as he sits in a linden tree, has much in common with prophetic dreams recounted in other works, including the *Nibelungenlied* (Song of the Nibelungs, circa 1200) and the Norse *Heimskringla* (Ring of the World, circa 1230).

Opinion is divided as to whether the author was a cleric or a layman. Werner Braun has argued, on the basis of the favorable treatment of monks in the narrative, that he was a monk. Braun sees the ethos of the poem as an expression of the ideals of Cluniac monasticism applied to the secular world. On the other hand, since the *Ruodlieb* contains many descriptions of life at court, Karl Hauck suggests that the poet was a nobleman who had spent time at an imperial court. Perhaps it was at court that he gained his knowledge of the extraordinary range of folklore that graces the *Ruodlieb.* The most likely court is that of Heinrich III, who ruled as emperor from 1039 to 1056, approximately the time during which many scholars agree that the *Ruodlieb* was composed. Indeed, Hauck proposes that Heinrich

III provided the model of the noble king who welcomes Ruodlieb to his court circle.

The *Ruodlieb* has received many, often contradictory, interpretations. The question of its genre has attracted a profusion of answers, most stressing the originality of the narrative. Helena M. Gamer, for example, sees it as the first realistic novel, while for Edwin H. Zeydel it is the first courtly novel. Most modern readers, however, have regarded it either as a transformation of the epic or as a forerunner of the romance. Franz Brunhölzl takes the position that the *Ruodlieb* is a failed attempt to write a Virgilian epic, its departures from the *Aeneid* a reflection of incompetence rather than ambition. Dennis M. Kratz, on the other hand, suggests that the departures reflect the poet's conscious attempt to reshape the epic tradition to express new heroic values. Peter Dronke, who praises the poet as an innovator of the highest order, suggests that the *Ruodlieb* is best understood as a "poetic experiment" in which elements of realism and fantasy are woven into an utterly new literary form.

The *Ruodlieb* is composed in Latin leonine hexameters, that is, hexameters in which an internal rhyme occurs between the last syllable of the line and the last syllable of a word near the middle of the line, usually the third foot. The Latin is difficult to understand and occasionally (by classical standards, at least) ungrammatical, but it possesses an unusual vitality. Brunhölzl dismisses the poet's idiosyncratic Latin as proof of his inability to write in a Virgilian style, but Dronke and others have taken the more sympathetic view that the poet was attempting to create a new Latin suitable to the unique nature of his subject matter and the new genre of literature that he may have been trying to invent.

The poet's Latin is now recognized as one of the most alluring facets of the *Ruodlieb.* The author is particularly adept at characterization through dialogue. Some of the dialogues in the *Ruodlieb* are delicate and courtly, such as the tactful interrogation of Ruodlieb by a retainer of the Greater King (fragment 1, lines 73–117) and the Greater King's interview with Ruodlieb concerning his conduct of peace negotiations with the ruler of a defeated people (fragment 4, lines 80–230). Others rival the vivacity and coarse humor of the best vernacular fabliaux. For example, one character, the redheaded man, seduces the wife of his host by claiming that he has been sent by a wealthy young nobleman to rescue her from her elderly husband; as payment for his deed he demands that she have sexual intercourse with him three times. " 'Si decies possis, fac,' " ("Do it ten times, if you can"), the willing woman replies, " 'vel quotiens vis' " ("or else as often as you like," fragment 7, line 86).

The choice of Latin hexameter suggests that the poet intended at least at the beginning of his poem to be regarded as part of the classical epic tradition. The opening scene contains the most concentrated clustering not only of recognizably epic themes but also of Virgilian echoes. The first strokes of the poet's portrait of Ruodlieb recall the *Aeneid* and its hero, Aeneas; the first line of the *Ruodlieb,* like that of the *Aeneid,* identifies its hero simply as "vir" (a man). His values as the narrative begins are those associated with the heroic tradition. He has served his various lords well in whatever tasks they have assigned him, "aut ulciscendum causaeque suae peragendum" (whether seeking vengeance or transacting business, fragment 1, line 7). Unfortunately, not only has his service to his lords failed to win Ruodlieb adequate payment, but it has also embroiled him in feuds that now threaten his safety; and so,

> Nusquam secure se sperans vivere posse,
> rebus dispositis cunctis matrique subactis,
> tandem de patria pergens petit extera regna.
>     (fragment 1, lines 15–17)

> (Thinking that he could live nowhere safely,
> after putting his affairs in order and placing them in
>     his mother's care,
> he left his homeland and set out for foreign lands.)

The phrase *petit extera regna* alludes to Virgil's description of Aeneas as forced "extera quaerere regna" (to seek foreign lands, *Aeneid* 4.350). While Aeneas's journey is caused by the enmity of Juno, Ruodlieb must leave because he has incurred enmities through serving faithless lords who broke their promises to reward him.

Once he leaves home, the hero seems to move from the world of epic into the world of romance, and his travels can be understood as occurring simultaneously on the physical and the spiritual planes. The king whose realm he enters is identified only as the Greater King (Rex Maior). Geographically, this principality would seem to be situated in southern Italy; the poet describes it as "apud Africanos" (among the Africans), but since Ruodlieb reaches the kingdom traveling by land, the phrase is probably meant to indicate a territory surrounded by Saracens of African origin. Symbolically, as John Hirsh was the first to point out, the realm of the Greater King reflects the values of God, the Greatest King. At this court Ruodlieb will see the proper relationship between a lord and his subjects; here he will begin his growth toward a new kind of heroism based upon Christian principles.

Evidence of the poet's interest in a new form of narrative suited to a new vision of heroism appears almost immediately. Ruodlieb quickly becomes a favorite of the Greater King by demonstrating his skill as a hunter and fisherman using the herb *buglossa.* An unprovoked attack on the Greater King's realm by the forces of a neighboring ruler, the Lesser King (Rex Minor), provides the poet with an opportunity to display the hero's prowess on the field of battle. The poet, however, gives no such description, even though Ruodlieb is the commander of the army that defeats the invaders. The reader only learns of the war's outcome through the brief report of a messenger.

The poet offers, instead, a detailed narration of the peace negotiations that follow the victory. In these negotiations Ruodlieb articulates the values that he has learned from his new lord. First, he strongly condemns the "stulta superbia" (foolish pride) and desire for self-glorification that, he says, motivated the leader of the defeated force. Ruodlieb declines, however, to inflict any punishment upon his foe:

> Princeps respondit: "rex noster non ita iussit,
> aut se dedentem vel captum perdere quemquam,
> sed, si possumus, captivis erueremus
> cum praeda pariter, quae fecimus ambo decenter.
> Vincere victorem, maiorem vult quis honorem?
> Sis leo pugnando par ulciscendo sed agno!
> Non honor est nobis, ulcisci damna doloris.
> Magnum vindictae genus est, si parcitis irae."
>     (fragment 3, lines 7–14)

> (The commander answered: "Our king did not order
>     us
> to kill anyone who either surrendered or was captured,
> but, if we could, to rescue prisoners
> and booty alike.
> Who wishes greater honor than to vanquish a victor?
> Be a lion in battle but like a lamb in avenging!
> We get no honor from avenging grievous losses.
> The best kind of vengeance is to spare your anger.")

Ruodlieb, who previously had been willing to seek vengeance on behalf of his lords, now eschews vengeance. His reference to the lamb underscores the Christian basis of the story. Moreover, this man, who at the beginning of the narrative was disappointed at the failure of his old lords to give him honors, now describes a higher form of honor, and he attributes his new values to the teaching of his new lord.

The *clementia* (forgiveness) that Ruodlieb learns from the Greater King is but one of three

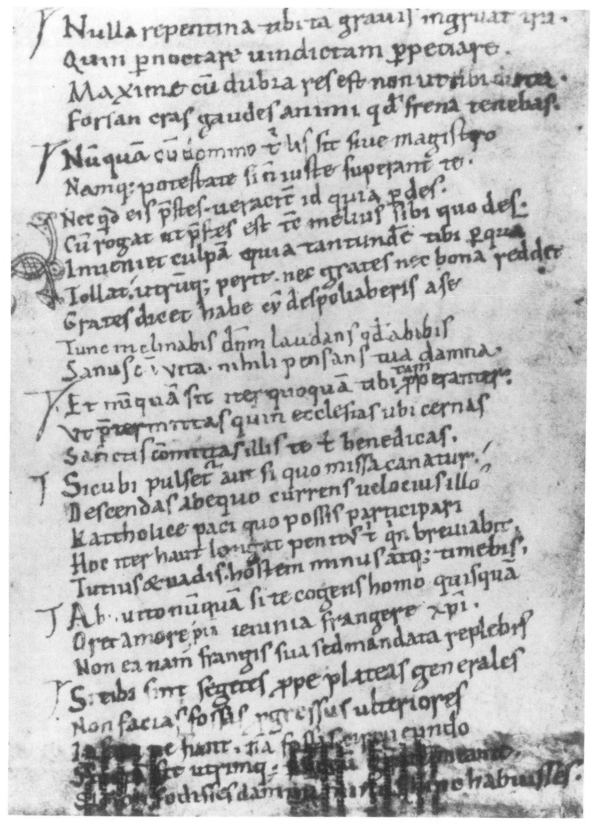

*Page from the "Munich" manuscript for the* Ruodlieb, *in the hand of the author of the poem (Munich, Bayerische Staatsbibliothek, Clm 19486)*

manifestations of *virtus* (virtue) that his new lord exhibits. At the end of the negotiations the Lesser King thanks the Greater King for his gracious treatment. The Lesser King praises the Greater King for displaying three forms of virtue: *pietas* (piety), *sophia* (wisdom), and *clementia;* through his demonstration of these qualities the Greater King serves as the earthly representative of Christ.

During and after the negotiations with the defeated king, the Greater King not only displays *virtus* in his own behavior but also criticizes Ruodlieb when the latter's actions fall short of this ideal. He chides the knight for gaining wealth by defeating the Lesser King and his nobles at chess while serving as the Greater King's envoy. On the other hand, when the Lesser King offers a sumptuous array of presents to his conqueror, the Greater King refuses all except a pair of dancing bears that seem to signify harmony and the need to control the baser desires. Later Ruodlieb reinforces the implied role of the Greater King as the figure of Christ when he tells his lord, " 'Pascha fuit tecum mihi semper cottiduanum' " ("Every day with you has always been Easter for me," fragment 5, line 305).

A letter from Ruodlieb's mother brings the news that all his enemies have died or been branded criminals, and the lords of his native land wish him to return. Giving Ruodlieb permission to leave, the Greater King offers him a choice between two forms of reward for his service: wealth or wisdom. Ruodlieb replies, " 'non volo peccuniam, sitio gustare sophiam' " ("I have no wish for money, but I thirst for wisdom," fragment 5, line 445). This choice leads to Ruodlieb's receiving both wisdom and wealth: the king hides a generous supply of gold and jewels in two loaves of bread that he instructs his departing servant not to open until he reaches home; the wisdom takes the form of twelve maxims to guide Ruodlieb's future behavior. These pieces of advice range from the philosophical to the mundanely practical, from an admonition always to attend mass while traveling to a warning against digging ditches in fields next to public roads. The poet may have intended the maxims to provide the frame for the rest of the narrative, and the fragments that follow do illustrate the correctness of the first three maxims. The rest of the narrative, however, involves only a few of the other maxims. The poet may have changed his mind or been unable to complete his design.

The first maxim warned the knight against associating with redheaded men; nevertheless, soon after leaving the court Ruodlieb allows himself to be accompanied by a redheaded man whose rash actions have disastrous consequences. As the Greater King serves as a positive model of knightly action, the redheaded man, described as "vanus nimiusque superbus" (vain and very arrogant), serves as a negative model. When the two travelers arrive at a village, the redheaded man seeks lodging at the home of an old man and his young wife, a situation against which the second of the Greater King's maxims had warned Ruodlieb. He seduces the woman by telling her that he will take her to a rich young lover if she has sex with him. So bold is his pursuit that he even caresses her breasts and legs as her husband looks on, though later he will falsely claim that she seduced him. The affair leads to the murder of the old man. Although the portion of the story that deals with the redheaded man's punishment is missing, it would seem that he is sentenced to death for the crime. The redheaded man's sexual liaison with the young wife of his host presumably illustrates the folly of failing to control one's baser carnal instincts and one's pride.

In contrast to the redheaded man, Ruodlieb, following another of the Greater King's maxims, finds lodging with a married couple who provide a model of harmony and mutual respect. The same ideals of generosity and festivity that prevailed at the court of the Greater King also exist at the house of the young husband and old wife who offer hospitality to Ruodlieb. The two sojourns are linked: Ruodlieb had called his time with the Greater King a continuous Easter; the young man tells Ruodlieb that he celebrates any day that God sends him a guest as Easter.

In the final portion of his journey home Ruodlieb meets and befriends a young man who turns out to be his nephew. He persuades the young man to join him. Ruodlieb and his nephew stop at the castle of a wealthy widow, who turns out to be the godchild of Ruodlieb's mother. At the castle Ruodlieb demonstrates his skill with *buglossa* and his virtuosity as a harpist. When the nephew falls in love with the daughter of their hostess, Ruodlieb supervises their courtship with the same tact that he displayed in negotiating peace between the two kings. The pair discover their affection for each other while dancing; as they dance, the poet compares them to a falcon and a swallow. The image not only calls attention to his strength and her graceful beauty but also foreshadows his attempts to snare her in marriage. The relationship of the young couple provides another example of the theme of harmony based on mutual respect that pervades the narrative. The young woman, far from being submissive, affirms her role as equal partner. When the lovers play dice, she wins the first game; after losing the second, she takes a ring from her finger and tosses it to her lover. The ring does not fit him, but he can wear it, she tells him, if he is willing to adjust it. This scene, especially its emphasis on the absence of any submissiveness on the part of the young woman, prefigures the wedding of the two later in the narrative.

Hirsh has suggested that the *Ruodlieb* has a three-part design: the knight's journey to and exploits at the court of the Greater King, his adventures on his return home, and events after he reaches home. The final section continues the poet's exploration of the themes of heroism and harmony. After arriving home Ruodlieb discovers the treasure hidden in the two loaves of bread. The young knight who left home because he had received too few rewards now realizes that God has "locupletare vel honoribus amplificare" (enriched and magnified him with honors, fragment 13, line 69).

The beginning of the poem focused on the grief of Ruodlieb's mother as her son left home; now her grief is turned to joy. His noble treatment of his mother brings God's favor on Ruodlieb, a favor soon to be translated into further honors; and Ruodlieb's mother plays a central role in his gaining them. She tries to convince her son to find a wife; as part of her argument she describes the horrors of growing old alone, and Ruodlieb agrees to seek a suitable wife. One of his men declares that he knows of such a woman. Ruodlieb agrees to court the woman, but he discovers that she is having an illicit affair and breaks off the courtship. Meanwhile, God reveals to Ruodlieb's mother in a dream her son's impending success. She correctly interprets the dream, saying, "nunc scio maiores nacturus eris quod honores" ("now I know that you will attain greater honors," fragment 17, line 123). Thus, the poet returns to the theme of honors with which he began the epic, suggesting that Ruodlieb's lessons from the Greater King have led to these greater rewards.

The *Ruodlieb* ends abruptly, as a dwarf, whom the knight has apparently just captured, is about to tell him the location of a magnificent treasure. The poet's failure to complete the poem has evoked a wide range of conjectures, ranging from the assumption that he lacked the narrative skill to complete the work to the more complimentary and attractive suggestion of Gordon B. Ford, Jr., that he ended abruptly on purpose, leaving the implied triumphant conclusion to the reader's imagination.

The poet's departures from his apparent classical model, the *Aeneid,* provide the starting point for most modern interpretations of the *Ruodlieb.* Dronke's suggestion that the *Ruodlieb* is an experiment helps give the modern reader a sense of the

poet's striking, if isolated, accomplishment. The opening scenes lead the reader to expect an epic adventure; instead, the poet fashions a narrative structure more familiar to readers of the later romances of authors such as Chrétien de Troyes and Hartmann von Aue. In the romance the hero typically departs from court, overcomes a series of challenges, and returns to court. Ruodlieb departs from home and goes to court; he then departs from court, overcomes a series of challenges, and returns home. As the narrative ends he has departed from home again and is confronting a new challenge.

As part of this new narrative design, the poet eschews the expected "epic" descriptions of battle, replacing such scenes, on the one hand, with a detailed depiction of peace negotiations and, on the other hand, with the metaphoric battlefield of a chessboard. He describes in detail, moreover, Ruodlieb's skill as a hunter and fisherman, but in these scenes the hero uses the herb *buglossa* rather than force to capture his prey.

The poet has also given women an unusually prominent role in the narrative. The list of memorable women in the *Ruodlieb* is long. Some – the hero's mother; the rich old widow who marries the poor young man; the chatelaine; her daughter, who marries Ruodlieb's nephew – are of noble character. Others – the young woman who has a sexual liaison with the redheaded man and the woman who is the object of Ruodlieb's ill-fated marriage proposal – are alluring but dangerous.

The king's advice, especially when it concerns women, is far from perfect. His precepts about marriage, in particular, are inconsistent with other remarks made by or attributed to him, and his advice is clearly undercut by the experience of the married couples whom Ruodlieb encounters after leaving the court. The Greater King says, in essence, that the secret of a happy marriage lies in the husband's maintaining control over his wife:

> ". . . illi tamen esto magister,
> litigium cum te ne quod praesumat habere;
> nam vitium nullum maius valet esse virorum,
> quam si subiecti sint, quis debent dominari."
>   (fragment 5, lines 490–493)

(". . . be her [your wife's] master,
so that she will not dare to have an argument with you;
Because there can be no worse disgrace for men,
than to be controlled by those whom they should rule.")

Moreover, the king continues, even if the two of you are living in perfect harmony, " 'numquam . . . sibi pandere totum' " ("do not . . . tell her everything," fragment 5, line 495). If you are ever angry with her, he concludes, keep your temper and " 'pernoctare vindictam perpetiare' " ("delay your vengeance overnight," fragment 5, line 499). This advice is inconsistent with the Greater King's earlier teaching that vengeance is to be eschewed, not just put off overnight; and keeping things hidden from one's wife is a form of *fraus* (deception), which is condemned elsewhere in the narrative. The validity of the king's advice about marriage is apparently subverted by the poet's description of the two happy marriages that Ruodlieb encounters as he travels back home. The relationship of the widow and her young husband is based on mutual respect, not the domination of one by the other; they rule each other: the husband "nunc dominatur ei, servivit cui vice servi" (now rules over her whom he once served, fragment 6, line 26), but at the same time, "matrem iam dominam vocat" (he calls his mother [that is, his wife] lord, fragment 6, line 108). And the wedding ceremony of Ruodlieb's nephew and his bride includes a remarkable scene in which the bride demands that their marriage be based on mutual trust and not on her subjugation to him. The groom begins by swearing his fidelity and seeking not only the same oath from her but also the right to cut off her head should she ever be unfaithful. She refuses to swear this oath until she has extracted the same oath from him. As part of her argument she uses a scriptural reference:

> Quae satis astute iuveni respondit et apte
> "Iudicium parile decet ut patiatur uterque.
> Cur servare fidem tibi debeo, dic, meliorem,
> quam mihi tu debes? Dic, si defendere possis,
> si licuisset Adae, maecham superaddat ut Evae,
> unam cum costam faceret Deus in mulierem."
>    (fragment 14, lines 70–75)

> (Both quite cleverly and fittingly she answered her
>    young man:
> "It is right that each of us obey an equal rule of law.
> Why should I, tell me, be more faithful
> to you than you to me? Speak, if you can maintain
> that Adam was allowed to have a mistress in addition
>    to Eve,
> when God formed his rib into just one woman.")

(The reference to Eve recalls the unhappy marriage of the young wife who has sexual intercourse with the redheaded man: when she later repents, she declares that the redheaded man tricked her and now seeks to "exemplaris Adam, qui culpam vertit in Evam" ["follow the example of Adam, who cast the blame on Eve," fragment 8, line 37] by claiming that she seduced him.) Having won the debate, the bride extracts from the groom his pledge that she has the right to cut off his head should he ever be unfaithful to her. Only then does she agree to be united with him in a union "sine fraude" ("without deceit," fragment 14, line 86). The poet concludes this episode by asking: "Qualiter inter se concordent, quid mihi curae? (What worry could I have how they will harmonize? fragment 14, line 99). Lack of deceit, in a marriage as in politics, produces harmony.

Marriage and honesty form the main themes of the final fragment of the *Ruodlieb*. The last lines of the narrative are a plea from the wife of a dwarf Ruodlieb has captured. The dwarf has sworn to tell Ruodlieb the location of a treasure and a bride that are destined to be his. The dwarf emphasizes the absence of deceit among dwarfs ("absit ut inter umquam nos regnaverit haec fraus," fragment 18, line 18) and urges the hero to trust him, and his wife offers to be Ruodlieb's hostage as proof of her husband's trustworthiness.

At the conceptual center of the *Ruodlieb,* then, are the intertwined concepts of heroism and harmony. The loss of harmony, caused in part by his adherence to a heroic ethos, forces Ruodlieb away from home. At the court of the Greater King he learns a new form of heroism based on forgiveness, wisdom, and piety. His application of these values in the peace negotiations following the brief war restores the lost harmony between neighboring countries. On his journey home Ruodlieb discovers the joys of one harmonious marriage and helps bring about another marriage, founded on mutual respect, in which the partners will live in harmony. The poet thus shows harmony at both the greater and the lesser levels of society.

If the author was a member of the lay nobility, perhaps he intended the *Ruodlieb* as a didactic "mirror for rulers," a guide to a more harmonious earthly kingdom. The poem does not, after all, condemn the older heroic values as much as it urges their infusion with higher, Christian standards of behavior. If the author was a monk, perhaps the harmony of this world was meant to be understood as a reflection of the harmony of heaven. In any case, although the poet's creation had no discernible influence on later medieval literature, in retrospect it can be called the first medieval romance.

It cannot be said that the experiment is without flaws — for example, the poet's apparent abandonment of his design in which the maxims of the Greater King were to provide a frame for the later adventures of Ruodlieb. The flaws appear related to the boldness of the poet's ambition, the profusion of material that he attempted to weld into a coherent whole. The ingredients of the narrative include a didactic vision of knighthood, a picaresque adventure, a folktale exemplifying proverbial maxims, a fabliau involving adultery and its dubious rewards, a love story that ends happily in marriage, and, in Dronke's words, "at the last a fairy-tale of dreams and dwarfs and treasure hoards." A bold failure deserves more admiration than a timid success. The *Ruodlieb,* ahead of its time, is a powerful and admirable artistic achievement.

## References:

Werner Braun, *Studien zum Ruodlieb* (Berlin: De Gruyter, 1962);

Franz Brunhölzl, "Zum *Ruodlieb, Deutsche Vierteljahrschrift für Literaturwissenschaft und Geistesgeschichte,*" 39 (1965): 506–552;

Peter Dronke, *Poetic Individuality in the Middle Ages* (Oxford: Clarendon Press, 1970), pp. 33–65;

Helena M. Gamer, "The Earliest Evidence of Chess in Western Literature: The Einsiedeln Verses," *Speculum,* 29 (1954): 734–750;

Gamer, "The *Ruodlieb* and Tradition," *ARV: Journal of Scandinavian Folklore,* 11 (1955): 65–103;

Christian Gellinek, "Marriage by Consent in Literary Sources of Medieval Germany," *Studia Gratiana,* 12 (1967): 554–579;

Karl Hauck, "Heinrich III. und der *Ruodlieb,*" *Beiträge zur Geschichte der deutschen Sprache und Literatur,* 70 (1948): 372–419;

John Hirsh, "The Argument of *Ruodlieb,*" *Classical Folia,* 27 (1973): 74–83;

Dennis M. Kratz, "Ruodlieb: Christian Epic Hero," *Classical Folia,* 27 (1973): 252–266;

Paul Schach, "Some Parallels to the Tree-Dream in *Ruodlieb,*" *Monatshefte für deutschen Unterricht,* 46 (December 1954): 353–364;

Benedikt K. Vollmann, "*Ruodlieb* Fragment XII," in *Lateinische Dichtungen des X. und XI. Jahrhunderts,* edited by Walter Berschin and Reinhard Düchting (Heidelberg: Lambert Schneider, 1981), pp. 227–248;

Hans Walther, "Quot-tot: Mittelalterliche Liebesgrüsse und Verwandtes," *Zeitschrift für deutsches Altertum,* 65 (December 1928): 257–289.

# "Spielmannsepen"

## (circa 1152 – circa 1500)

### Maria Dobozy
#### University of Utah

*König Rother* (circa 1152–1180)

**Manuscripts:** Two manuscripts of this verse narrative are preserved from the twelfth century: Heidelberg, Universitätsbibliothek, cpg 390, comprising 5,181 lines written in Middle German with Bavarian elements, is almost complete; Munich, Bayerische Staatsbibliothek, cgm 5249, Nr. 1, is fragmentary. The Nuremberg Fragment, Nuremberg, Germanisches Nationalmuseum, Hs 27744, survives from the thirteenth century. Another manuscript, which provides the final lines (5134–5197), is Berlin, Staatsbibliothek der Stiftung Preußischer Kulturbesitz, mgf 923, Nr. 20, from the fourteenth century.

**First publication:** *König Rother,* edited by Heinrich Ruckert (Leipzig: Brockhaus, 1872).

**Standard editions:** *König Rother,* edited by Theodor Frings and Joachim Kuhnt, Rheinische Beiträge und Hülfsbücher zur germanischen Philologie und Volkskunde, vol. 3 (Bonn & Leipzig: Schroeder, 1922); *Rother,* edited by Jan de Vries (Heidelberg: Winter, 1922).

**Edition in English:** Translated by Robert Lichtenstein as *King Rother* (Chapel Hill: University of North Carolina Press, 1962).

*Herzog Ernst* (circa 1190)

**Manuscripts:** There are three medieval traditions of the story in German: A, B, and D (tradition C is a parallel Latin translation, represented in both prose and hexameters and extant from the thirteenth century). A is the earliest version, originating in the first half of the twelfth century and represented in four manuscript fragments in rhymed couplets. Two of these fragments, called the Prag frag. I–V, written in Middle Franconian, were originally part of a single manuscript dating from the beginning of the thirteenth century. That manuscript was cut up, and the fragments are now located in different libraries: Berlin, Staatsbibliothek der Stiftung Preußischer Kulturbesitz, mgo 225 (Prag I–II, 127 verses), and Prague, National Library, MS XXIV C2 (Prag III–V, 194 verses). There are also Krakow, Biblioteka Jagielloriska, mgq 1303,5, formerly in Berlin, which contains sixty-eight verses, from the end of the twelfth century; and Wroclaw, University Library, cod. IV oct. 11$^d$, from the last quarter of the thirteenth century. B, the best-known version, dates from 1198 to 1208. It is composed in Middle High German rhymed couplets and exists in three manuscripts: Nuremberg, Germanisches Nationalmuseum, N, Hs. 998, formerly Hs. 2285, dated 1441, written in Middle Franconian, is bound together with illuminated texts of Konrad von Würzburg's *Trojanerkrieg* and Rudolf von Ems's *Willehalm von Orlens;* the text of *Herzog Ernst* is not illustrated. The Wels fragment, Wels, Stadtarchiv, Schl. Nr. 1227, dates from the mid fourteenth century. D probably originated in the second half of the thirteenth century. A single manuscript from the beginning of the fifteenth century survives in Gotha, Historisches Staatsarchiv, Schloß Friedenstein, cod. Chart. B 48, but contains a few small gaps. The rhymes indicate Middle German provenance with coloring from several dialects.

**First publication:** *Herzog Ernst,* edited by Karl Bartsch (Vienna: Braumüller, 1869 [A and B]).

**Standard editions:** *Herzog Ernst,* edited by Karl Bartsch (Vienna: Braumüller, 1869; reprinted, Hildesheim: Olms, 1969 [B]); *Herzog Ernst: Ein mittelalterliches Abenteuerbuch,* edited by B. Sowinski (Stuttgart, 1979 [A]); *Herzog Ernst D (wahrscheinlich von Ulrich von Etzenbach),* edited by Hans-Friedrich Rosenfeld (Tübingen: Niemeyer, 1991 [D]).

**Edition in English:** Translated by J. Wesley Thomas and Carolyn Dussère as *The Legend of Duke Ernst* (Lincoln: University of Nebraska Press, 1979 [B]).

*Münchener Oswald* (circa 1430)

**Manuscripts:** The most important manuscripts representing the verse epic tradition are Innsbruck, Ferdinandeumsbibliothek, Ms. 1114, circa 1435; Munich, Bayerische Staatsbibliothek, cgm 719, circa 1444, written in Bavarian; a fragment, Munich, Bayerische Staatsbibliothek, cgm 5377, circa 1477; and Vienna, Österreichische Nationalbibliothek, cod. 12540, from the first half of the fifteenth century.

**First publication:** *Der Münchener Oswald: Text und Abhandlung,* edited by Georg Baesecke, Germanistische Abhandlungen, vol. 28 (Breslau: Marcus, 1907).

**Standard editions:** *Der Wiener Oswald,* edited by Georg Baesecke (Heidelberg: Winter, 1912); *Der Münchener Oswald. Mit einem Anhang: Die ostschwäbische Prosabearbeitung des 15. Jahrhunderts,* edited by Michael Curschmann (Tübingen: Niemeyer, 1974).

**Edition in English:** Translated by J. Wesley Thomas as "The Munich Oswald," in *The Strassburg Alexander and the Munich Oswald: Precourtly Adventure of the German Middle Ages* (Columbia, S.C.: Camden House, 1989), pp. 83–118.

*Salman und Morolf* (circa 1475)

**Manuscripts:** A Dresden manuscript, LB, Mscr. R, 52$^u$m, 4, possibly illustrated, from the mid fifteenth century, was lost during World War II. Still preserved are the Eschenburg illuminated manuscript produced in 1479 by the Frankfurt patrician and goldsmith Hans Dirmstein, Frankfurt am Main, Staatsbücherei und Universitätsbibliothek, Ms. germ. qu. 13; the Marburg Fragment, Marburg, Hessisches Staatsarchiv, 147 Hr.8, from the second half of the fifteenth century; a manuscript originating in Strasbourg, Paris, Bibliothèque de l'Arsenal, Ms. 8021, dated from the end of the fifteenth century; and two more from the sixteenth century.

**First publication:** *Von kunig salomon vnd siner huß frouwen Salome* (Strasbourg: Mathis Hupfuff, 1499).

**Standard edition:** *Salman und Morolf,* edited by Alfred Karnein (Tübingen: Niemeyer, 1979).

*Orendel* (circa 1477)

**Manuscript:** The work survived in Strasbourg in a single Alsatian manuscript, dated 1477, that was destroyed in a fire in 1871. A manuscript copy by C. M. Engelhardt is in Berlin, Stiftsbibliothek der Stiftung Preußischer Kulturbesitz, mgq 817a.

**First publication:** *Ein hubsche Historie zu lesen von vnsers herre rock: wie der wunderbarlich einem konig (Orendel genant) worden ist* (Augsburg: Hans Froschauer, 1507).

**Standard editions:** *Orendel,* edited by Hans Steinger (Halle: Niemeyer, 1935); Orendel: *Ein deutsches Spielmannsgedicht mit Einleitung und Anmerkungen,* edited by Arnold E. Berger (Bonn: Weber, 1888).

Five poems erroneously grouped together early in the nineteenth century as the *Spielmannsepen* (minstrel epics) have been known by this designation ever since. They comprise *König Rother* (King Rother, circa 1152–1180), *Herzog Ernst* (Duke Ernst, circa 1190), the *Münchener Oswald* (Munich Oswald, circa 1430), *Salman und Morolf* (circa 1475), and *Orendel* (circa 1477). In the nineteenth century *Ortnit* (circa 1225–1250) and others were also included. Originally the designation *Spielmannsepos* was used to refer to works thought to be situated between the heroic poetry of the early medieval period and the thematically and structurally harmonious courtly romances of the High Middle Ages. Scholars judged the poems stylistically inept and repetitive and condemned the language as coarse, the scenes as burlesque, the narrative as inconsistent, and the treatment of themes as superficial. The *Spielmänner* (minstrels) were held responsible for the poor quality of the poems since they were thought of as itinerant, poorly educated performers for hire who, in striving to astonish and please audiences, would adapt stories and embellish them with unexpected turns of plot and fantastic exploits and characters. At first the minstrels were considered mere transmitters, incapable of composing the works; but eventually it was admitted that they could have composed them. Once that admission occurred, the minstrels came to be criticized as the creators of the poems. Soon thereafter, the term *Spielmannsepos* became a widely accepted genre designation. Defining a literary genre according to a particular class and type of author is not terribly unusual, for information about the author's life has frequently been used to interpret and evaluate texts, to assess their innovations relative to their chronology, and to locate texts politically. But because those poems existed in oral form for centuries before they were written down, it is impossible to make any conjectures about the authors. Consequently, these premises have been rethought since the end of the nineteenth century.

The first major objection to the minstrel thesis is that minstrel activity does not characterize these poems exclusively, for most medieval literature was performed. The converse is also true: transmission of these texts did not depend solely on minstrels, even though their reception was shaped strongly by the minstrels' performances. Second, the term *Spielmann* has, until recently, been a broad concept implying a homogeneous group; consequently, positing a minstrel as author provides no insight into the texts whatsoever. It is now known that the group referred to as minstrels was anything but homogeneous; all evidence demonstrates that the term subsumes a wide range of status, class, ability, activity, and modes of existence. Minstrels do not fit neatly into categories because entertainment or minstrelsy was not a profession but a service role. Once a text was written down, anyone could perform it without license from any institution or profession, unlike the regulations controlling the work of lawyers, doctors, theologians, and other members of established medieval professions.

Because literature was primarily experienced by audiences through performance, the impact of such performances should not be underestimated. A convincing rendition can round out a personality or steer audience sympathy from one character to another with little change in the text. Phrases written into a manuscript to replicate for the reader the performer's typical interjections indicate a desire to have the reader play the role of performer and to re-create a professional performance. Therefore, minstrels' performances – and, consequently, their interpretations – had a formative influence on literature.

Even though the theory of the minstrel as artless transmitter has been abandoned, the texts are still kept together under the label *Spielmannsepen.* The reason is not simply that the term is now entrenched; more significantly, it is because the poems do not share enough essential characteristics with other narratives of the twelfth and thirteenth centuries to allow them to be accommodated satisfactorily in other categories, such as heroic epic, romance, or hagiography, but exhibit some similarities with all three genres. The grouping is not totally misleading, however, for the poems do have some characteristics in common: they all contain the bridal-theft or courtship plot; and from Germanic tradition they inherited character names such as Orendel, Asprian, Witold, and Dietrich and figures such as giants, mermaids, and dwarfs, and from classical myth the cyclops and pygmies. Magic occurs frequently. Furthermore, in contrast to earlier vernacular poetry, they all convey a keen acceptance of the temporal world and the ambition to

control it. Even Orendel's and Oswald's march to sainthood is characterized by active service to God rather than by the contemplative life. The contemporary themes they address include political and religious aspects of the Crusade mission and perspectives on a changing kingship. Finally, each poem has a historical event or person at the center, just as do Pfaffe Konrad's *Rolandslied* (Song of Roland, circa 1172) and Pfaffe Lamprecht's *Alexander* (circa 1150).

*Historical legend* might be a useful designation for these works: each has a historical kernel or starting point and attachment to a specific location and, therefore, some claim to historical accuracy. *Orendel* is connected with Trier, the *Münchener Oswald* with Regensburg, *König Rother* with Bari, *Herzog Ernst* with Bavaria, and *Salman und Morolf* with Jerusalem. As in a legend, there are few moments of reflection, no agonizing regrets, and no rationalizing of events or actions. The narratives also have occasional supernatural aspects. The stories tell of faraway places, satisfying people's curiosity about foreign lands; but basically these poems use the foreign and the exotic as a negative contrast by which to define the borders of the familiar.

The poems also have a strong political foundation and could well be called state epics. Like the *Alexander* and the *Rolandslied,* they explore the role of kingship and record its progressive institutionalization by experimenting with the best means of incorporating the new kingship model into the inherited literary forms of the epic and the saint's life. In addition, they describe events in which entire societies can take part. The wars described are not only attempts to convert nonbelievers but also to extend and consolidate the Christian empire and to safeguard its population. Thus, the poems convey a sense of public service. It is significant that in most of these works (*Orendel,* the *Münchener Oswald, Herzog Ernst,* and *König Rother*) the leader (a king or exiled warrior) loses his entourage and must assemble a new one. To succeed this time he must draw on a much broader base of supporters; consequently, his performance is evaluated in terms of his ability to sustain cooperation within the body politic. The implication is that if the realm is to achieve stability, a carefully structured social organization is required. For example, Ernst's revolt casts a pall over the empire because the emperor has allowed distrust to arise between the central authority and the barons.

All five so-called minstrel epics are likely to have originated in the twelfth century, although manuscripts of that period exist only for *Herzog Ernst* and *König Rother*. Hence, their earliest but undocumented versions are contemporary with many heroic epics but earlier than the courtly romances. They represent a large portion of the first wave of secular vernacular poetry written in Germany. The spotty textual transmission of several epics and the plethora of versions of *Herzog Ernst* make it difficult to assign to these poems a precise date and literary-historical position.

The second half of the twelfth century was a period of rapid economic growth and rapid development in the arts. The proliferation of texts and genres during this period attests to an explosion in literary activity. The minstrel epics reflect the literary experimentation of the time. Lacking the concepts of *minne* (courtly love) and *aventiure* (knight-errantry), the minstrel epics are not yet infused with a codified set of courtly ideals of conduct and love typical of the romance genre. The heroes take part in genuinely deadly battles, not knightly jousts; the theft of the bride is an act of force to which she is completely vulnerable.

One factor that influenced the creation of these works was the increasing piety of the laity in the twelfth century. Local miracle stories enjoyed ever-greater popularity as opposed to those relating miracles in faraway places. In Germany the number of pilgrims increased, pilgrimage churches multiplied, and the number of relics brought back by the crusaders grew. All of this activity stimulated the production of local saints' legends as well as the proliferation of stories recounting the discovery of relics.

The bridal-quest narrative found in the minstrel epics and other vernacular texts exhibits a basic pattern: the royal councillors advise the king to marry for the purpose of providing a successor. Only one princess, who is usually a pagan, has the qualifications of rank, wealth, beauty, and virtue; but her father refuses to let his daughter marry and imprisons or executes all suitors and envoys. This situation poses a challenge for the protagonist, and in each poem he plans and accomplishes the courtship and abduction of the princess in a different way. The suitor usually arrives incognito to woo the princess. He usually tries to win her approval, but ultimately it is the threat of force that compels her to consent. The abduction requires a battle, often an invasion of the pagan territory, but in the end the suitor carries the bride home.

In the minstrel epics this plot is normally doubled. On the couple's return home the husband loses his new wife. In *König Rother* her father has her abducted, and Rother must return, at great risk, to retrieve her. In *Orendel* the heathens imprison

Queen Bride during the Crusade. In the *Münchener Oswald* the abduction in part 2 is transformed into a miracle story – Christ arrives at the wedding feast and asks Oswald for his possessions, including his new wife. Composed against the background of the Crusade ideology, which promoted the Christian mission to convert Muslims, the poems show that to save the young woman from paganism it is justifiable to wrench her from the protection of her kin. For doing so, the "suitor" achieves purification and, almost always, salvation. The hero's attainment of salvation brings these narratives into proximity to the saint's legend. The battles against the infidels are depicted explicitly as Crusades. Rother fights the Saracens and, toward the end of his life, retires to a monastery. Ernst returns from a Crusade having achieved atonement and is then reconciled with his emperor. Oswald and Orendel become saints by the end of their stories for their active role in the Crusades. Salman, too, must fight pagan kings, but *Salman und Morolf* inverts the plot: here the heathen king besieges a Jerusalem ruled by the Christian king Salman to abduct his enchantingly beautiful wife, Salme. She is eventually recovered by the wily tricks of Morolf, Salman's brother and adviser.

The name of the hero of *König Rother* reaches far back into Germanic history, deriving from those of the Langobard kings Authari of the sixth century and Rothari of the seventh century; the latter fought wars against the emperor of Constantinople. A possible contributor to the character of Rother was the early-twelfth-century Norman ruler Roger II, who was unsuccessful in establishing a marriage between his son and a Byzantine princess. The flattering portrayal of Rother as a just king supported, intentionally or unintentionally, the imperial ideology of Friedrich Barbarossa by making Rother the progenitor of Charlemagne.

The manuscript tradition connects *König Rother* with Bavaria, based on family and territorial names mentioned, but the dialect mixtures in the manuscripts indicate a link with the lower Rhine. The text in the form in which it is known today originated probably between 1152 to 1180; its continuing popularity is attested by manuscripts that span three centuries.

The story follows the bridal-quest plot closely. King Rother's councillors advise him to marry to ensure an heir to the throne of Bari. One of the nobles suggests the daughter of the Byzantine emperor Konstantin and offers to lead a group of emissaries to ask for her hand on Rother's behalf. When they state their mission to Konstantin, he has them imprisoned. Rother goes looking for them disguised as

Ich sage der wunders craft · Hi zo constanti
nopole · Der vil mern burge · Was ein recker
herre · vnde plach grozer ern · Daz schinit
mir immir an · Her hat mer michil guot ge
tan · Ime waren die uorsten alle holt · Her
gaf in daz erotage golt · Daz re sichein man
zo dere werlde gewan · Sin hof stunt offin
wromeliche · Den armin vnde den richen
Die uvndin an deme gotin · Uatir vnde
motir · Sin wille was zo gebine · Her ne
rochte nicht zolebine · Diz sicheinis scazzis
vberhite · Dar hetter urloge mite · Her sante
in nacht vnde tac · Sver indusint phunde
bat · Her gab sie ime also ruuge · Also zwene
penninge · Beide herre ich wil dir sagin ·
war umbe ich die rede han u'hauen ·

other der gerne vunam · Waz her selbe
hette getan · Do sprach der riche mere · Ich

*Page from the Heidelberg manuscript for König Rother (Heidelberg, Universitätsbibliothek, cpg 390, fol. 53v)*

the warrior Dietrich, who has been banished from Rother's court. In Constantinople, as he displays his fighting prowess and gives freely of his wealth, he rapidly makes himself popular with all but the emperor. Hearing his praises, the princess sends for him and divulges her desire to marry Rother. Rother divulges his identity to her. Soon thereafter the Babylonian army attacks Konstantin, and Rother takes responsibility for defending the city. Victorious over the invaders, Rother leaves the taking of prisoners to Konstantin and sails home to Bari with the princess.

The second cycle begins when Konstantin sends a minstrel to lure his daughter onto a ship and bring her back to Constantinople. Rother must return immediately to claim her because she is to be married to the son of the Babylonian king. While reconnoitering at Konstantin's court Rother is quickly discovered. The emperor has him taken out to be hanged, but Rother's men, hidden a short distance up the coast, come to his aid and defeat the emperor's army. The Eastern Empire and Western Empire make peace, and the young couple produce an heir to the throne. In their later years Rother and his queen withdraw to the monastic life.

*König Rother* has repeatedly been judged one of the most successful poems of the "minstrel" canon. Its relatively consistent narrative leads directly from the goal stated at the outset to its culmination in the establishment of a direct line of succession to Charlemagne. The lines of thematic development break down, however, when it becomes evident that the means employed are not appropriate to the goals. Even though Rother and the princess have agreed to her abduction, Rother's dealings with Konstantin lead repeatedly to acts of force. From the beginning the use of force lies at the heart of his thinking, imbued as it is with the warrior ethic. He sets off for Byzantium disguised as Dietrich, the heroic warrior who lives for combat. The volatile giants who accompany him flaunt their weapons and strength, making Konstantin shrink back in fear and frustration. Force is used for the purpose of gaining possession of the princess, who is reduced to a piece of valuable property: Rother steals her, Konstantin's men abduct her, Konstantin attempts to marry her off against her will, and, finally, Rother's army attacks to secure Rother's proprietorship over her.

The political considerations of succession motivate the action, but the warrior ethos, the traditional heroic use of force, becomes the means by which the aims are pursued. The giants, the symbol of violent strength, act in accordance with the ethos

of retribution, which justifies force. After defeating Konstantin's army they want to slay the emperor, and Konstantin fully expects to be dealt a mortal blow. But the victorious Rother reverses his tactic: he shows restraint and treats Konstantin with all due decorum, leaving his giants in frustrated rage.

The rejection of force is also shown in the courtly pageantry of the procession of elegantly dressed ladies at the conclusion of the battle in which the young wife is ceremoniously presented to Rother. This scene completely undercuts the force that had been exercised up to this point to attain the bride and anticipates the courtly romances. Kingship is shown to have advanced beyond the hero-king stage; the hero's personal strength and the use of force are no longer adequate for governing an empire and establishing political relationships. Rother and his men initiate the reversal of the old ethos, underscoring the intellectual and moral superiority of the Western over the Eastern Empire.

The *Münchener Oswald* is based on Oswald, king of Northumbria, who was baptized on Iona in the Hebrides, returned to England, conquered Cadwalla, began to Christianize the country, and fell in battle in 642 against the pagan king Penda of Mercia. Soon after his martyrdom, miracles at his grave were reported, and he was venerated as a saint from that time on. His cult spread to Germany as early as the seventh century and came to be centered among the nobility of Regensburg. At the beginning of the fourteenth century his cult experienced renewed popularity in Regensburg among a broader audience when he was given a place among the fourteen saints known as "aids in need." As a result, the most popular version of the story is Bavarian. The year 1300 is the earliest date for the archetype of the extant manuscripts.

The story is similar to *König Rother:* King Oswald is advised to marry to produce an heir to the throne. An ancient pilgrim knows of the ideal woman – a pagan princess, Paug, who is secretly a believer in Christ. But her father, Aron, puts all suitors to death, and Oswald cannot find a messenger who would dare carry his suit for him. The pilgrim tells Oswald that a talking raven has been sent by God to help with the courtship. The raven agrees to fly to the lady with the letter asking for her hand. In the letter Oswald also asks for advice on how best to steal her away. She replies, via the raven, that he should bring an army, a stag with golden antlers, the raven, and goldsmiths.

When Oswald arrives he releases the gilded stag; while the entire pagan court rides off in pursuit of the animal, the princess slips out of the gate, which is opened by divine hands, and joins Oswald at his ships. They sail off but are soon overtaken by her father. A battle ensues in which all of Aron's men are killed. To convert Aron, Oswald asks God to resurrect the warriors; they tell Aron what pain they suffered during their short sojourn in hell and request to be baptized immediately. Aron has no recourse but to join them. Thus, the courtship becomes a mission of conversion.

Arriving home with his bride, Oswald gives a great wedding feast at which, as was customary, he feeds the poor. At the feast Christ, in the guise of a beggar, asks for all of Oswald's possessions – even his new wife – in the name of Christ. Oswald gives them unhesitatingly. Christ reveals himself, returns what he was given, adjures the couple to remain celibate, and assures them of salvation.

In this text, too, the political considerations of securing a queen for the realm and an heir for the throne prompt the wooing expedition. But from the outset the overarching value of service to God governs the action. Oswald's exceptionally close alliance with God is established at the beginning. Orphaned at a young age, Oswald, like Ludwig in the *Ludwigslied* (Song of Louis, 881 or 882) is taken on as God's ward. Thenceforth, Oswald, like Ludwig, does not plan his own course of action; he needs merely to discern and carry out God's will. Divine guidance and aid are available at every turn and overcome every obstacle. The aid arrives unsolicited, first with the ancient pilgrim who tells Oswald whom to court and then in the form of the talking raven. The final sign of divine intervention is the testing of Oswald by Christ. Once Oswald has shown himself willing to part with his wife, it is clear that God's will takes priority and justifies Oswald's actions. But the political needs of the realm appear to be incompatible with God's will: the celibacy of the young couple will make the production of an heir to the throne, and hence an orderly succession, impossible.

Princess Paug has been given more freedom to act and make decisions than most other women in these epics. She embraces Christianity freely and is willing to act on her faith. Although Oswald initiates the process, she arranges for her abduction by devising a plan and instructing Oswald in it. When they are escaping the city, she prays, and the gate is opened by God. Once on board Oswald's ship, however, she loses her independence and becomes a dutiful, pious, submissive wife who acquiesces to all of Oswald's wishes.

On 1 May 1196 what was purported to be the seamless cloak of Christ was deposited in the main altar of the Trier cathedral. *Orendel* tells the tale of the loss of the robe, its discovery by Orendel, and its deposition in Trier; it thus documents the authenticity of the relic. The legend of Orendel is, however, older than the deposition of the relic and appears to have originated with Archbishop Bruno in 1124; an even older heroic song may have formed the base on which Bruno forged the legend. Segments of the plot derive from the late Roman story of Apollonius's shipwreck and bondage to a fisherman. The discovery of the seamless robe comes from a story in which Saint Helena finds the true cross of Christ and from a second story in which she fashions the robe. The first written version is thought, because of its rhymes and style, to have originated in the second half of the twelfth century. On the other hand, the slightly more modern vocabulary points to the thirteenth century. After a time the relic was forgotten; but interest revived when the cloak was rediscovered in 1512, the year in which two printed editions of the poem appeared. It is this version that is known today.

The work reflects the two primary narrative directions: the Germanic heroic and the hagiographic. The Strasbourg *Heldenbuch* (Book of Heroes) mentions Orendel in the company of Alexander the Great, Siegfried, and Dietrich, indicating that the text was considered properly placed among heroic epics. And yet, the poem also has the tone of a saint's life. A now-lost manuscript from Heidelberg, dated 1447, contained Ulrich Boner's *Edelstein* (1350), an explicitly edifying text; *Dietrichs Flucht* (Dietrich's Escape, circa 1290) and *Die Rabenschlacht* (The Battle of Ravenna, circa 1290), two traditional heroic epics; and *Orendel,* under the title *ein hübsch buoch genant der graw rock* (A Proper [or Courtly] Book Called The Gray Robe). The title directs the reader's attention to the robe as the focus of the poem. One may infer that *Orendel* is included because it was deemed a transition piece between epic-heroic texts and morally uplifting ones.

The unifying symbol in the narrative is the seamless robe of Christ. After a short recapitulation of the vicissitudes of the robe, the story concentrates on Orendel's bridal quest and his continuous battles against the infidel. Prince Orendel of Trier decides to wed Bride, Queen of Jerusalem, and prepares a Crusade to the Holy Land. He is shipwrecked and loses his ships, army, gold, and even his clothing. A fisherman takes him in. While fishing, Orendel finds the robe in the belly of a fish; he grasps immediately that it is meant for him. Arriving in Jerusalem, he proceeds to the Holy Sepulcher and pledges his service. He then borrows a horse and weapons from a chess player and frees Jerusalem from a heathen siege. Bride gratefully offers to marry her rescuer.

Bride is a female warrior who becomes his partner in battle as well as in their chaste bed, and the remainder of the story is a series of confrontations between heathen and Christian. In one episode Orendel rescues Bride when she is captured and abused by the infidel. When Jerusalem is freed a second time, the couple are told by an angel to remain chaste until they are conducted to heaven in six months.

When Bride offers Orendel marriage and sovereignty over Jerusalem, the political requirement of the monarchy to provide for succession, normally met by the bride theft, is supplanted by a mission to incorporate all of heathendom into a Christian realm. The serious threat of pagan encroachment is demonstrated when Orendel and Bride are called to defend Westphalia, which is situated in the center of the Holy Roman Empire. Clothed in the robe, Orendel accepts divine protection and a new identity: he comes to be known as the Grey Robe. This union of man and relic symbolizes his transformation into a viceroy of God. The robe constantly reminds the audience of God's involvement in human affairs. From this point on, Orendel embodies theocratic kingship.

This theme is left undeveloped as battle follows battle. No single act of Orendel's is stressed; there is no decisive victory, no climax to the story, and no stability established in the kingdom. Once the military enterprise is allied with service to God, the combination gains the focus of attention and supplants the goal of marriage. It may be that the breakdown of epic form functions as a commentary on the customary unfolding of the courtship, in which the powerful male ruler chooses his bride, uses force to overpower any resistance, and appropriates her person and lands. Here that use of force is broken: Bride offers her hand and realm, they void the marriage by remaining celibate, and they become equal partners in the military struggle to expand Christendom.

The hagiographic thread becomes explicit when Orendel dedicates himself to Christ. His pious service to the Holy Grave dictates his martial activities and allows for chaste equality between him and Bride. At the same time, it undercuts the courtship and marriage as well as the imperial project, for in the end both rulers are transported to heaven, and their subjects are left to fend for themselves.

The elements that give the work its hagiographic coloring also undermine the concept of heroic kingship. The constant divine intervention that pulls Orendel out of serious danger eliminates the need for heroism on his part. Thus, the ideal is not heroism but ascetic piety.

The historical kernel of *Salman und Morolf* is the Christian Kingdom of Jerusalem, which existed from 1100 to 1187. The work is, however, a mixture of the Talmudic tradition of Solomon battling demons, the theme of the sage enthralled by the beauty of a woman, and Slavic, German, and Ibero-Arab ingredients. French romances and other German epics share with *Salman und Morolf* specific motifs such as the chess game in *Huon de Bordeaux,* the ploy of suspended animation or *Scheintod* (apparent death) as a means of abduction in Chrétien de Troyes's *Cliges,* the attempted hanging and rescue of Rother in *König Rother,* and the throwing of the husband's body into the wife's lap in chapter 38 of the Norwegian *Thidreksaga* (Saga of Dietrich of Bern, circa 1250).

The strophic form of *Salman und Morolf* reveals its origins in oral traditional poetry, even though the extant texts are late medieval. It is the only one of the minstrel epics consistently transmitted in this form. It is also unique in that the illustrations were apparently always part of its manuscript transmission.

The story inverts the typical plot: Salman (Solomon), Christian king of Jerusalem, has abducted, baptized, and married the captivating Salme (Salome). But the heathen king Fore (Pharaoh), enthralled by her beauty, plans to abduct her. His assault on Jerusalem is repulsed, he is taken prisoner, and Salme is assigned to guard him. He wins her love with magic, and she enables him to escape so that he can arrange for her abduction. The abduction is accomplished by a magic root that causes Salme to fall into a deathlike state; her "dead" body is then spirited away. Because Salman is inconsolable, his brother, the magician Morolf, sets off to find the abducted wife and bring her back. Disguised as a pilgrim, he plays a game of chess with Salme; he is recognized and imprisoned but escapes by drugging his captors. He returns to Salman, who leads an army to Fore's realm. Salman enters the enemy court alone, disguised as a pilgrim, and is immediately identified and imprisoned. He is guarded by Fore's sister, Affer, until he is taken to be hanged the next morning. As they reach the gallows his men appear on the horizon and rescue him. Salme and Affer are brought to Jerusalem, where Affer is baptized.

Seven years later essentially the same events recur: Salme is abducted by the heathen king Princian; Morolf finds her and forcibly returns her to

Salman. This time the action relies more heavily on magic. Morolf agrees to bring Salme back on the condition that he be allowed to punish her with death. He defeats the heathen king, decapitates him, and throws the head scornfully into Salme's lap. Back in Jerusalem he opens her veins while she bathes; he then arranges for Salman to marry Affer.

The story, as most interpreters view it, revolves around the enslaving power of feminine beauty. In its most destructive form such beauty debilitates masculine strength and royal power, and for this reason Salme must die. Because of beauty's affinity with magic, Morolf is the only person able to withstand her attraction since he, too, has knowledge of magic. The theme of Christian Crusade against pagan encroachment on Jerusalem is overshadowed by Salman's concern for recovering his wife, but it does determine the ethical assessment of the characters. The work raises questions about the efficacy of baptism and the missionary program: is Salme's swift reversal to paganism a result of magic, or of a lack of genuine conversion (which, in any case, would have made her immune to magic)? Is she a metaphor for the inadequacy of the missionary program or for the political and military reversals occurring in the Christian territories of the Middle East in the late twelfth century?

One might say that the problem lies with the ruler who decides to marry a woman who must be forcibly seized: Salman has stolen Salme from her father, Fore steals her from her husband, and Princian does likewise. Each time Morolf fetches her, she appears not to want to return to Jerusalem. One may interpret *Salman und Morolf* as a cautionary tale warning against taking a wife by force and against forcing conversion to Christianity. (Forcing people to convert on pain of death was a practice revived by each new group of Crusaders on arriving in the Holy Land.) Salme's willingness to escape from Jerusalem may well stem from her unwillingness to convert to Christianity. Affer, in contrast, symbolizes the results of a different approach to courtship – one exemplified by Rother and Oswald – where the woman is given a choice. Kind and completely submissive, Affer is the preferable partner for Salman. Like Paug, she is the paragon heathen woman in Crusade narratives who exhibits compassion and harbors Christianity in her heart even before she is baptized.

The charm of the Salman story lies in its comic aspect – in Salman's helplessness and in the pranks of Morolf, a trickster hero of the Nordic Loki type who has an evil and dangerous side. His pranks and disguises do not always lead directly to his goal; they can be vicious or funny, and many are gratuitous as far as the plot is concerned. He simply enjoys getting the better of others: for example, after drugging the entire heathen court he tonsures the knights, dumps the sleeping king on the floor of the bedroom, and puts a priest into bed with Salme.

Magic is prominent in the narrative and cannot be ignored in interpreting it. It represents superior knowledge that is dangerous and is, therefore, an ambiguous force at best. Both the heathen kings and Christian characters such as Morolf are capable of strong magic; for this reason magic cannot by itself be the cause of Salme's infidelity and relapse into paganism. Morolf's frequent use of magic and Salme's attempts to protect herself from it form the overarching dramatic tension of the poem. As he comes closer to his goal of executing her he becomes more aggressive and demonic, and she becomes increasingly passive, like a sacrificial animal unable to defend itself. Magic is central to the work, yet its use is so ambivalent that no particular character can be condemned for using it.

Several conflicts are recorded from the tenth, eleventh, and twelfth centuries that could have inspired *Herzog Ernst,* the story of a revolt by a duke against the Holy Roman emperor. The revolt of Liudolf, Duke of Swabia, against Otto I occurred in 953; and the revolt of Ernst II, Duke of Swabia, against his stepfather Konrad II occurred in 1026. The Hohenstaufen duke Friedrich II revolted against Lothar III, and the two were reconciled in 1135. Strife between Friedrich Barbarossa and Heinrich der Löwe (Henry the Lion) fits the pattern as well but may have occurred too late to be a stimulus.

The story of Ernst's revolt and travels survives in the largest number of reworkings of any material in German except, perhaps, the story of Faust. Versions spanning three centuries differ greatly. The so-called A version is shorter than the later ones but contains the oriental journey with its many elements taken from the antique tradition of Homer, Pliny, Isidor, and the Latin romance of Alexander: Magnet Mountain, ruse to escape from griffins, cyclops, pygmies, giants. Both versions A and B include the Crusade, with the typical stops made along the way: Byzantium, Babylon (Cairo), Alexandria, and Jerusalem. Only version B combines the theme of revolt and conflict between ducal power and central authority with the oriental odyssey.

Version B comprises a frame story, which takes place within the empire, and the central narrative relating Duke Ernst's journey. Ernst enjoys a good education and matures into a worthy nobleman. Emperor Otto weds Ernst's mother and favors him at court, but Ernst suddenly becomes the object of Otto's wrath when he is maligned by the Count Palatine. After killing the count, Ernst suffers the full power of the emperor's army. He defends his lands heroically against the emperor but eventually recognizes that defeat is inevitable and prepares to leave the realm. Together with his trusted retainers he embarks on a Crusade, but the sea voyage becomes a lengthy odyssey. He is shipwrecked, loses most of his men to griffins, and meets cyclopses, flathooves, crane people, longears, pygmies, and giants. After fighting bravely for a deserving ruler and earning a dukedom, he finally reaches the Holy Land to fight against the infidel. When Ernst returns home, the emperor, moved by his barons to clemency, receives him back into the court and reinstates him in his former rank and lands.

The interpretation of *Herzog Ernst* depends on how one perceives the connection between the historically based frame story and the fantastic oriental voyage. At first they appear to be only loosely connected: the frame focuses on the political conflict between Ernst and the emperor, and the central story relates the fantastic exploits of Ernst the hero. The odyssey can be understood as a series of exploits that constantly force comparison between the Holy Roman Empire and the lands outside it. For example, the story examines courtship: even though *Herzog Ernst* is not based on the courtship pattern, in the frame story Emperor Otto carries out a straightforward courtship and offer of marriage in a civilized manner so that the chosen lady has an opportunity to accept or reject the offer. In contrast, the crane people in Grippia exhibit civilized behavior and follow formal protocol and decorum but are insensitive to the pain of others: their brutal bride theft causes the death of the bride's father and ends with their stabbing the sobbing maiden to death with their bills. Such scenes make manifest the function of the oriental travels: the voyage charts the "civilized world" outside the empire; some peoples are uncivilized and others civilized, but most reveal shortcomings so that the empire compares favorably with them.

Above all, however, Ernst's voyage is a religious pilgrimage. When he recognizes that no one can prevail against the emperor, he opts to retreat with honor by going on a Crusade; his other reason for making this choice is that by revolting against the emperor he has opposed God's will.

His return with his trophies is the evidence of successful completion of his mission. The purpose of the journey, as of all Crusades, is the Christianization of nonbelievers; but in this case it is also the civilizing of the Oriental peoples so that they and their lands may become incorporated into the world order of the empire.

Although the poem clearly favors imperial authority, it shows the effects of the ruler's susceptibility to jealous calumny and court intrigue. It would appear then, that the successful ruler must, above all, attain the ability to judge character and to select reliable and capable supporters to help him consolidate and expand his realm. Failure to do so causes strife and war, at great cost to the empire.

Even if he were not to be pardoned, Ernst must return; his return demonstrates the universality of the empire in that he cannot exist outside it. From the Orient he brings specimens of the marvelous inhabitants of the exotic places he has visited as well as a precious gem, the *Waise*. The *Waise* is set into the imperial crown, and the wondrous creatures become symbols of the expanse of the empire. By giving a place to these trophies, the empire redefines itself through its new boundaries. The text of the story of Ernst's journey is commissioned by Otto at the end; it is a cultural artifact that becomes the final definition of the realm. The poem, then, recreates in words what Ernst established through his deeds. Thus, the concern of the text lies not in transmitting information about foreign realms and peoples; rather, the exotica of the odyssey define the familiar.

**References:**

Rolf Bräuer, *Literatursoziologie und epische Struktur der deutschen "Spielmanns-" und Heldendichtung: Zur Frage der Verfasser, des Publikums und der typologischen Struktur des "Nibelungenliedes," der "Kudrun," des "Ortnit-Wolfdietrich," des "Buches von Bern," des "Herzog Ernst," des "König Rother," des "Orendel," des "Salman und Morolf," des "St.-Oswald-Epos," und der "Tristan-Dichtungen"* (Berlin: Akademie, 1970);

Michael Curschmann, *"Spielmannsepik": Wege und Ergebnisse der Forschung von 1907–1965. Mit Ergänzungen und Nachträgen bis 1967* (Stuttgart: Metzler, 1968);

Maria Dobozy, "Das Bild der Heidin in der deutschen Kreuzzugsdichtung," in *La Croisade: Réalités et Fictions. Actes du Colloque d'Amiens, 1987,* edited by Danielle Buschinger (Göppingen: Kümmerle, 1989), pp. 111–118;

Dobozy, *Full Circle: Kingship in the German Epic. "Alexanderlied, Rolandslied, 'Spielmannsepen'"* (Göppingen: Kümmerle, 1985);

Dobozy, "The Theme of the Holy War in German Literature, 1152–1190: Symptom of the Controversy between Empire and Papacy?," *Euphorion,* 80, no. 4 (1986): 341–362;

Christian Gellinek, *"König Rother": Studie zur literarischen Deutung* (Munich: Francke, 1968);

Walter Haug, "Struktur, Gewalt und Begierde: Zum Verhältnis von Erzählmuster und Sinnkonstitution in mündlicher und schriftlicher Überlieferung," in *Idee; Gestalt; Geschichte: Festschrift Klaus von See. Studien zur europäischen Kulturtradition,* edited by Gerd Wolfgang Weber (Odense, Denmark: Odense University Press, 1988), pp. 143–157;

Karl-Bernhard Knappe, *Repräsentation und Herrschaftszeichen: Zur Herrscherdarstellung in der vorhöfischen Epik* (Munich: Arbeo-Gesellschaft, 1974);

Ingeborg Köppe-Benath, "Christliches in den Spielmannsepen König Rother, Orendel, Salman und Morolf," *Beiträge zur Geschichte der deutschen Sprache und Literatur,* 89 (1967): 200–254;

Jürgen Kühnel, "Zur Struktur des Herzog Ernst," *Euphorion,* 73, no. 3 (1979): 248–271;

Karl Helmut Kuhnert, *Die Geschichte von dem Rock Christi: Die symbolische Bedeutung des mittelhochdeutschen Epos vom König Orendel (in Trier)* (Frankfurt am Main: Fischer, 1979);

Claude Lecouteux, "Kleine Beiträge zum Herzog Ernst," *Zeitschrift für deutsches Altertum,* 110, no. 3 (1981): 210–221;

Uwe Meves, *Studien zu König Rother, Herzog Ernst und Grauer Rock (Orendel)* (Frankfurt am Main: Lang, 1976);

Otto Neudeck, "Ehre und Demut: Konkurrierende Verhaltenskonzepte im 'Herzog Ernst B,'" *Zeitschrift für deutsches Altertum,* 121, no. 2 (1992): 177–208;

Walter Johannes Schroeder, *Spielmannsepik* (Stuttgart: Metzler, 1962);

Hans Simon-Pelanda, *Schein, Realität und Utopie: Untersuchungen zur Einheit eines Staatsromans (HE B)* (Frankfurt am Main & New York: Lang, 1984);

Wilhelm Störmer, "'Spielmannsdichtung' und Geschichte: Die Beispiele Herzog Ernst und König Rother," *Zeitschrift für bayerische Landesgeschichte,* 43 (1980): 551–574;

Ferdinand Urbanek, *Kaiser, Grafen und Mäzene im König Rother* (Berlin: Schmidt, 1976);

Armin Wishard, *Oral Formulaic Composition in the Spielmannsepik: An Analysis of "Salman und Morolf"* (Göppingen: Kümmerle, 1984).

# The Strasbourg Oaths
### (14 February 842)

Brian Murdoch
*University of Stirling*

*The Strasbourg Oaths (Die Straßburger Eide,* 14 February 842)

**Manuscript:** The oaths are included in book 3, chapter 5 of the *Historiarum libri quatuor* by Nithard, which survives in a single manuscript, Paris, Bibliothèque Nationale, Lat. 9768, fols. 13a–13b, from the late tenth century. The manuscript is not the original, and the scribe did not know German, so that the German text of the oaths is somewhat confused regarding word division.

**First publication:** In *Denkmäler deutscher Poesie und Prosa aus dem VIII–XII Jahrhundert,* edited by Karl Müllenhoff and Wilhelm Scherer, third edition, edited by Elias von Steinmeyer (Berlin: Weidmann, 1892; reprinted, Berlin & Zurich: Weidmann, 1964).

**Standard editions:** In *Althochdeutsches Lesebuch,* edited by Wilhelm Braune, sixteenth edition, edited by Ernst Ebbinghaus (Tübingen: Niemeyer, 1979); in *Die kleineren althochdeutschen Sprachdenkmäler,* edited by Elias von Steinmeyer (Berlin: Weidmann, 1916); in *Altdeutsche Texte,* edited by Heinz Mettke (Leipzig: Bibliographisches Institut, 1970), pp. 20–21; in *Sammlung kleinerer althochdeutschen Sprachdenkmäler,* edited by Gerhard Köbler (Gießen: Arbeiten zur Rechts- und Sprachwissenschaft, 1986), pp. 581–583.

**Editions in modern German:** In *Älteste deutsche Dichtung und Prosa,* edited by Heinz Mettke (Leipzig: Reclam, 1976), pp. 118–123; in *Althochdeutsche Literatur,* edited by Horst Dieter Schlosser (Frankfurt am Main: Fischer, 1989), pp. 290–293.

Nithard, *Historiarum libri quatuor* (843)

**Manuscript:** Paris, Bibliothèque Nationale, Lat. 9768.

**First publication:** In *Patrologia Latina,* volume 116, edited by Jacques-Paul Migne (Paris: Migne, 1864).

**Standard edition:** In *Monumenta Germaniae Historica, Scriptores rerum Germanicarum in usum scholarum,* edited by Ernst Müller (Berlin: MGH, 1907).

**Edition in English:** Translated by Bernard Walter Scholz and Barbara Rogers as "Nithard's Histories," in *Carolingian Chronicles* (Ann Arbor: University of Michigan Press, 1970), pp. 129–174.

Angilbert, *Versus de bella quae fuit acta Fontaneto* (date unknown)

**Manuscript:** Paris, Bibliothèque Nationale, Lat. 1154.

**First publication:** In *Monumenta Germaniae Historica/Poetae Latini Medii Aevi/Aevi Carolini,* volume 2, edited by Ernst Dümmler (Berlin: MGH, 1884), pp. 136–139.

**Standard edition:** In *Monumenta Germaniae Historica, Scriptores rerum Germanicarum in usum scholarum,* edited by Ernst Müller (Berlin: MGH, 1907).

**Editions in English:** Translated by Helen Waddell as "Poem of Fontenoy," in her *Medieval Latin Lyrics* (Harmondsworth, U.K.: Penguin, 1952); translated by Peter Godman as "Poem of Fontenoy," in his *Poetry of the Carolingian Renaissance* (Norman: University of Oklahoma Press, 1985; London: Duckworth, 1985); translated by Brian Murdoch as "Poem of Fontenoy," in his *Walthari: A Verse Translation of the Medieval Latin Waltharius* (Glasgow: Scottish Papers in Germanic Studies, 1989), pp. 113–114; translated by Paul Edward Dutton as "Poem of Fontenoy," in his *Carolingian Civilization* (Peterborough, Ontario: Broadview, 1993), pp. 363–365.

The oaths of mutual nonaggression sworn by two of the sons of Louis the Pious and their respective followers at Strasbourg on 14 February 842 belong to the period of the breakup of the empire of Charlemagne and the birth of modern Western Europe. They are of philological interest as a monument in Old High German, more so as they are accompanied by equivalent oaths in Old French and occur in a contemporary record, Nithard's *Historiarum libri quatuor* (Four Books of Histories, 843), written in Latin by an eyewitness. Finally, the events leading up to the swearing of the oaths – in particular the hugely important battle of Fontenoy – are the subject of one of the most memorable and poignant Latin historical poems of the period, *Versus de bella quae fuit acta Fontaneto* (Verses on the Battle of Fontenoy, date unknown), also by an eyewitness, about whom all that is known is his name, Angilbert.

The last years of the reign of Louis the Pious, who succeeded Charlemagne as emperor in 814, were troubled by the beginnings of internecine strife that pitted the emperor, his named imperial heir, Lothar, and his youngest son, Charles, King of Neustria (later Charles the Bald, King of France), against Louis's second son, Louis, King of Bavaria (later Louis the German, King of Germany), and Pépen II, King of Aquitaine, the son of Louis the Pious's third son, Pépen I, who had died in 838. When Louis the Pious died in 840 the alliances shifted, and a civil war – which led to the dissolution of the empire – broke out at a time when the Vikings were attacking the territories of the Franks. Lothar, allied by this time with Pépen II, demanded the right to rule the empire. On 25 June 841 Lothar's army, supported by Pépen II, met the joint forces of Charles and Louis the German at Fontenoy, near Puisaye. Although the battle was not decisive Lothar retreated, and the following February, Charles and Louis met at Strasbourg to swear an oath of mutual nonaggression and mutual support against Lothar. This alliance would enable them to keep the territories they held, which roughly corresponded to modern France and Germany, respectively. The oath of support was sworn by the brothers, and an affirmation was then sworn by their followers. This ceremony necessitated the use of two vernaculars: *lingua teudisca,* the Rhenish Franconian dialect of Old High German; and *lingua romana,* Old French, spoken in Charles's territories. Louis, as the older of the brothers, swore the oath first, speaking in French so that his brother's followers would understand what he was saying; then Charles did the same in German. A form of the oath was then sworn, in their own languages, by the followers of the two kings. The oath sworn by the brothers is formal, invoking God and the Christian people and vowing to give aid to the other brother and not to make common cause with Lothar. The oath sworn by the followers is briefer, depends on the leaders' keeping their pledges to each other, and

releases the men from their own feudal vows should their leader break his oath. The two brothers were stronger than Lothar, and in 843 the Treaty of Verdun established France and Germany and gave Lothar the central portion that still bears his name: *Lothari regnum* (Lorraine).

The oaths sworn on 14 February at Strasbourg are the only ones for which a vernacular text exists, and the document in which they appear is important in its own right. Nithard was close to the events he describes, and he may, indeed, have had a hand in drafting the oaths. His father, Angilbert – not to be confused with the author of the *Versus de bella quae fuit acta Fontaneto* – was a prominent scholar at the court of Charlemagne and later the lay abbot of Saint Riquier; Nithard was one of two illegitimate sons of Angilbert by Bertha, the daughter of Charlemagne and, therefore, a grandson of the emperor. Nithard was well educated and enjoyed a prominent position at court as a politician, an ambassador, a mediator between the warring brothers, and a warrior. At Fontenoy he fought for Charles the Bald under the command of Adalhard. Charles had given him the task of writing a history of the times; Nithard did so intermittently, taking his *Historiarum libri quatuor* as far as 843. His account of the battle and of the events leading up to it gain in vividness by his description of his own roles as envoy and fighter.

Nithard's work begins with the death of Charlemagne and gives an account of the divisions of territory proposed by Louis the Pious after the birth of Charles. The first book ends with Louis's death. The second book considers the struggle between the brothers and concludes with the battle in 841, emphasizing the effective role of Adalhard, "quibus haŭd modicum supplementum Domino auxiliante Prebui" (to whom I was able with God's help to give not a small amount of assistance.) The third book opens with a confession of shame at having to record details of a conflict within his own family and moves on to the close relationship between Charles and Louis the German and then to the Strasbourg Oaths. The fourth book opens with Nithard expressing his desire to conclude his work as a chronicler and to retire "ab universa re publica" (from public life); after presenting further developments on the political stage he reports how an earthquake opened the tomb of Angilbert, whose body proved to be uncorrupted after twenty-nine years (an indication of sainthood), and mentions how Angilbert had fathered him and his brother Hartnid by Bertha. After recording the marriage of Charles in 843 he launches into a bitter reflection on the times, contrasting the good days under Charlemagne,

*Page from the manuscript for the* Strasbourg Oaths, *included in Nithard's* Historiarum libri quatuor *(Paris, Bibliothèque Nationale, Lat. 9768)*

when the people walked in the way of God and "pax illis atque concordia ubique erat" (there was peace and concord everywhere then). Now, however, "ubique dissensiones et rixae sunt manifestae" (dissent and strife are everywhere); abundance and joy have been replaced by penury and sadness. The work ends with an eclipse of the moon and does not mention the Treaty of Verdun. The work is clearly partisan – Nithard was an acknowledged follower of Charles – and M. L. W. Laistner has suggested that so much space is given to the recording of the Strasbourg Oaths because of the need felt by Nithard to emphasize the alliance between the brothers against Lothar, "the villain of the piece." Nithard appears to have died in the battle of Angoumois between Charles and his nephew Pépen II on 15 June 844.

The battle of Fontenoy is presented as God's judgment on Lothar in *Versus de bella quae fuit acta Fontaneto,* a Latin *planctus* (lament in fifteen three-line strophes, each beginning with the next letter of the alphabet) by another, and otherwise unknown, Angilbert. This man fought on Lothar's side in the battle, which is depicted as a victory for Lothar that could not be sustained because he was let down by others. The poem is enormously impressive. Pagan and Christian elements are contrasted: the battle is on a Saturday, the day of the pagan god Saturn, not on the Christian Sabbath, and the laws of Christ are broken on the field of Mars. What comes out especially in the poem is the internecine nature of the battle, with brother killing brother in defiance of natural love. The abecedarian strophes present a series of abrupt images, and one group culminates in the wish that the day on which the battle was fought be cursed and that no sun shine on it; the night, too, is one of sorrow, and then on the next day the corpses of the valiant dead can be seen. The ending is equally abrupt:

> Ploratumque et ululatum nec describo amplius
> unusquisque quantum potest restringatque lacrimae
> pro illorum animabus deprecemus dominum.

> (Past all lamenting, I can write no more.
> Let men cope as they can with their own tears
> and let us all pray to God for the souls of the fallen.)

Angilbert's poem is a fitting response to what would not be the last battle fought between brothers in

that part of the world. The Strasbourg Oaths, which followed the battle, hardly solved the problem.

## References:

J. Knight Bostock, *A Handbook on Old High German Literature,* second edition, edited by K. C. King and D. R. McLintock (Oxford: Clarendon Press, 1976), pp. 187–188;

Peter Classen, "Die Verträge von Verdun und Coulaines, 843 als politische Grundlagen des westfränkischen Reiches," *Historische Zeitschrift,* 196 (1963): 1–35;

Gustav Ehrismann, *Geschichte der deutschen Literatur bis zum Ausgang des Mittelalters,* volume 1 (Munich: Beck, 1922), pp. 354–355;

Peter Godman, *Poets and Emperors: Frankish Politics and Carolingian Poetry* (Oxford: Clarendon Press, 1987), pp. 151–153;

Wolfgang Haubrichs, *Die Anfänge,* volume 1/1 of *Geschichte der deutschen Literatur,* edited by Joachim Heinzle (Frankfurt am Main: Athenaeum, 1988), pp. 194–195;

M. L. W. Laistner, *Thought and Letters in Western Europe AD 500–900* (London: Methuen, 1957);

Max Manitius, *Geschichte der lateinischen Literatur des Mittelalters,* volume 1 (Munich: Beck, 1911), pp. 657–660;

Brian O. Murdoch, *Old High German Literature* (Boston: Twayne, 1983), pp. 18–19;

Janet L. Nelson, "Public *Histories* and Private History in the Work of Nithart," *Speculum,* 60 (April 1985): 251–293;

Timothy Reuter, *Germany in the Early Middle Ages* (London: Longman, 1991);

Florus van der Rhee, "Die Straßburger Eide, altfranzösich und althochdeutsch," *Amsterdamer Beiträge zur älteren Germanistik,* 20 (1983): 7–25;

Ruth Schmidt-Wiegand, "Eid und Gelöbnis im mittelalterlichen Recht," in *Recht und Schrift im Mittelalter,* edited by Peter Classen (Sigmaringen: Thorbecke, 1977), pp. 55–90;

Wolfgang Wehlen, *Geschichtsschreibung und Staatsauffassung im Zeitalter Ludwigs des Frommen* (Lübeck & Hamburg: Matthiesen, 1970).

# Tatian
## (circa 830)

Karen Konyk Purdy
*University of Pennsylvania*

**Manuscripts:** The work is preserved in three manuscripts: Manuscript G, Saint Gall, Stiftsbibliothek, Nr. 56, 171 leaves, written in the second half of the ninth century at Fulda; Manuscript B, Oxford, Bodleian Library, Ms. Junius 13, a copy of a manuscript that was owned in 1597 by the Dutch scholar Bonaventura Vulcanius but is now lost; and Manuscript P, Paris, Bibliothèque Nationale, Ms. lat. 7641, leaves 4b–16a, from the tenth century, probably written in northern France. Two other manuscripts are now lost: Cod. Pal. 55, listed in the catalogue of the Bibliotheca Palatina in Heidelberg, was sent from there to the Vatican Library in 1623 but was lost after 1798; a manuscript owned by the Cathedral of Langres has been lost since 1689. Another lost manuscript, *Evangelio theudisco,* from the ninth century in France, listed in the *Liturgica historica* (1918) by Edward Bishop, is probably the same one that was once at Langres.

**First publications:** In *Originum Francicarum Libri VI (in quibus praetor),* edited by Johann Isaac Pontanus (Amsterdam: Hardervici, ex officina T. Henrici, impensis H. Lavrentii, 1616), pp. 588–598 (based on Manuscript B); *Ammonii Alexandrini quae et Tatiani dicitur Harmonia evangeliorum,* edited by Johann Andreas Schmeller (Vienna: Beck, 1841 [based on Manuscript G]).

**Standard edition:** *Tatian, lateinisch und altdeutsch mit ausführlichen Glossar,* edited by Eduard Sievers (Paderborn: Schöningh, 1872).

The Old High German *Tatian* (circa 830) is the most important prose translation of the post-Carolingian period. Written in the early ninth century at the centrally located Fulda monastery, it is a vital tool for the study of early Old High German phonology and grammar. Like the *Old High German Isidor* (790–800), it reflects the intellectual and religious interest of its time and provides some of the best examples of early Old High German vocabulary in these spheres. Furthermore, it shares subject matter and probable sources with the great poetic works *Heliand* (Savior, circa 850) and Otfried von Weißenburg's *Evangelienbuch* (Gospel Book, between 863 and 871).

The original was written by a second-century Syrian Christian, Tatian, who, after spending some time in Rome with Saint Justin Martyr and then associating with the heretical Encratites, returned home. There he wrote his *Diatessaron* (Gospel Harmony) by carefully combining the four Gospels — and, according to some, including Georg Baesecke, a fifth Hebrew gospel — to present the story of Jesus to the common people of his own church. His Gospel harmony was often copied and was translated into many Eastern as well as Western languages; it was never condoned by the church hierarchy for official use but was instead banned in favor of the canonized Gospels. In the sixth century Victor of Capua happened upon an untitled Latin Gospel harmony; he had a revised copy made, bringing the language into conformity with that of the Vulgate, and wrote a preface in which he cautiously named Tatian as the probable author, summarized the early Christian's life, justified the use of the text despite Tatian's connection with heretical beliefs, and explained the changes he had made. A sixth-century manuscript of Victor's text was brought to Fulda, supposedly by Saint Boniface; it is known as the *Codex Fuldensis.* In the second half of the ninth century a manuscript was produced at Fulda that contains an Old High German translation of the *Tatian* in parallel columns with the Latin version. This manuscript, which includes Victor of Capua's preface, is known as Manuscript G.

Eduard Sievers's edition of Manuscript G appeared in 1872. His claim that the *Codex Fuldensis* was the original Latin text of the *Tatian* was generally accepted until a series of studies and textual comparisons by both biblical and literary scholars,

Quoniam quidem multi
conati sunt ordinare
narrationem quae in nobis
complexae sunt rerum
sicut tradiderunt nobis
qui abintio
ipsi uiderunt & ministri
fuerunt sermonis,
uisum est & mihi assecuto
a principio omnibus diligenter
& ordine tibi scribere
optime theophile
ut cognoscas eorum
uerborum dequibus
erudiris et ueritatem,

In principio erat uerbum
& uerbum erat apud dm
& ds erat uerbum,
hoc erat In principio
apud dm. Omnia per ipsum
facta sunt & sine ipso
factum est nihil;
quod factum est
In ipso uita erat;
& uita erat lux hominum.
& lux In tenebris
lucet & tenebrae
eam non comprehenderunt.

Fuit In diebus herodis regis
Iudeae quidam sacerdos
nomine zacharias
deuice Abia

bi thiu uuanta manage
zilotun ordinon
saga thio In uns
gifulta sint rahhono
so uns sictan
thie thar fon anaginne
selbon gisahun Inti ambahta
uuarun uuortes.
uuas mir gisehan gifolgentemo
fon anaginne allem gern lihho
after antrertu thir scriben
thu bezzisto theophile
thaz thu fora stantes thero
uuorto fon them
thu gilerit bist uuar.
In anaginne uuas uuort
Inti thaz uuort uuas mit gote
Inti got selbo uuas thaz uuort.
thaz uuas In anaginne
mit gote. Alliu thuruh thaz
uuirdun gitan. Inti uzzan sin
ni uuas uuiht gitaner,
thaz thar gitan uuas
thaz uuas In imo lib;
Inti thaz lib uuas lioht manno.
Inti thaz lioht In finstarnessin
liuhta. Inti finstarnessi
thaz nibi griffun.
uuas In tagun heroder ther cuninges
Iudeno sumer biscof
namen zacharias
fon themo uuehsle abiane

*Page from manuscript G of the* Tatian *(Saint Gall, Stiftsbibliothek, Nr. 56, p. 25)*

beginning in 1894, proved that it was simply the oldest existing Latin manuscript. Many attempts have been made to reconstruct the original Latin and Syriac versions. The Latin of Manuscript G varies significantly from the *Codex Fuldensis,* and the Old High German translation varies just as markedly from the Latin next to it. Many conjectures have been made regarding the relationship of the Old High German to the two Latin versions; Baesecke, Wilhelm Wissmann, and Anton Baumstark suggest that the source of the Old High German *Tatian* is neither the *Codex Fuldensis* nor the Latin of Manuscript G but a source common to both. More recently, Gilles Quispel has concluded that despite the discrepancies, the *Codex Fuldensis* is the most likely main source of the Latin of Manuscript G and that the latter, in turn, is the main source of the Old High German *Tatian.* A possible explanation for the differences between the Latin and the translation may be the use of other Gospel harmonies to fill in lines or verses that were missing in the main source.

Studies of the development of the East Franconian dialect indicate that the Old High German *Tatian* was written at Fulda around 830, while Hrabanus Maurus was abbot. The number of people who worked on the translation is greatly disputed. The text shows variations in Old High German vocabulary and in the method of translation, but little phonological variation; some sections are close to an interlinear style, while others show a much freer style and a real feel for the German language. Handwriting variations show that Manuscript G was produced by seven scribes, six of whom worked simultaneously on separate sections; the sixth scribe also made corrections throughout the text, while the seventh concentrated on the punctuation. The seventh scribe is thought to have been Hrabanus Maurus himself.

The Old High German *Tatian* provides vital data in the early Germanic and Christian vocabulary. Erich Gutmacher's study of the 2,030 words that appear in the text reveals compelling similarities among the *Tatian,* the *Abrogans* (circa 790–800) in the south, and Anglo-Saxon documents to the north. Some 280 words in the *Tatian* are missing in other High German texts, while 40 words common to other High German texts do not appear in the *Tatian,* and 120 words are common only to the *Tatian* and Old English, Old Saxon, and Old Low Franconian. Some scholars have suggested that the Anglo-Saxon vocabulary was borrowed, but Gutmacher and Wilhelm Braune have proved that the *Tatian* contains many common West Germanic words

that had died out earlier in most High German dialects while remaining in use in the Anglo-Saxon and North Germanic areas.

The *Tatian* influenced the literature that followed. Its subject matter was the basis for the straightforward poetry of the *Heliand.* It is also likely that Otfried, a student of Hrabanus Maurus at Fulda, was familiar with it.

**References:**
Georg Baesecke, *Die Überlieferung des althochdeutschen Tatian* (Halle: Niemeyer, 1948);

Anton Baumstark, *Die Vorlage des althochdeutschen Tatian,* edited by Johannes Rathofer, Niederdeutsche Studien no. 12 (Cologne: Böhlau, 1964);

Bernhard Bischoff, "Eine Sammelhandschrift Walafrid Strabos (Cod. Sangall. 878)," in *Aus der Welt des Buches: Festgabe zum 70. Geburtstag von G. Leyh* (Leipzig: Harrassowitz, 1950), pp. 30–48;

Helmut de Boor and Richard Newald, *Geschichte der deutschen Literatur,* volume 1: *Die deutsche Literatur von Karl dem Grossen bis zum Beginn der höfischen Dichtung,* ninth edition (Munich: Beck, 1979);

J. Knight Bostock, *A Handbook on Old High German Literature* (Oxford: Clarendon Press, 1955);

Wilhelm Braune, "Althochdeutsch und Angelsächsisch," *Beiträge zur Geschichte der deutschen Sprache und Literatur,* 43 (1918): 361–445;

Gustav Ehrisman, *Geschichte der deutschen Literatur bis zum Ausgang des Mittelalters,* volume 1 (Munich: Beck, 1954);

Peter Ganz, "Ms. Junius 13 und die althochdeutsche Tatianübersetzung," *Beiträge zur Geschichte der deutschen Sprache und Literatur* (Tübingen), 91 (1969): 28–76;

Erich Gutmacher, "Der Wortschatz des althochdeutschen Tatians in seinem Verhältnis zum Angelsächsischen, Altsächsischen, und Altfriesischen," *Beiträge zur Geschichte der deutschen Sprache und Literatur,* 39 (1914): 1–83, 229–289, 571–577;

Diether Haacke, "Evangelienharmonie," in *Reallexikon de deutschen Literaturgeschichte,* second edition, volume 1, edited by Werner Kohlschmidt and Wolfgang Mohr (Berlin: De Gruyter, 1958), pp. 410–413;

Elisabeth Karg-Gasterstädt, "Tatian," in *Die deutsche Literatur des Mittelalters: Verfasserlexikon,* second edition, volume 4, edited by Kurt Ruh and others (Berlin: De Gruyter, 1953), pp. 370–373;

Friedrich Köhler, *Lateinisch-althochdeutsches Glossar zur Tatianübersetzung* (Paderborn: Schöningh, 1914);

Richard H. Lawson, "Paratactic *thô* in Old High German *Tatian*," *Neuphilologische Mitteilungen,* 81 (1980): 99–104;

Lawson, "The Prefix *Gi-* as a Perfectivizing Future Significant in OHG Tatian," *Journal of English and Germanic Philology,* 64 (1965): 90–97;

Lawson, "A Reappraisal of the Function of the Prefix *Gi-* in Old High German *Tatian*," *Neuphilologische Mitteilungen,* 69 (1968): 272–280;

Lawson, "Weak-Verb Categories and the Translator Problem in Old High German *Tatian*," *Amsterdamer Beiträge zur älteren Germanistik,* 14 (1979): 33–41;

Heinz Mettke, "Zum Wortschatz von Tatian-δ," *Jahrbuch des Vereins für Niederdeutsche Sprachforschung,* 84 (1961): 35–42;

William Moulton, "Scribe δ of the Old High German *Tatian* Translation," *PMLA,* 59 (June 1944): 307–334;

Curt Peters, *Das Diatessaron Tatians, seine Überlieferung und sein Nachwirken im Morgen- und Abendland, sowie der heutige Zustand seiner Erforschung* (Rome: Pont. institutum orientalium studiorum, 1939);

Daniel Plooij, *A Primitive Text of the Diatessaron: The Liege Manuscript of a Mediaeval Dutch Translation* (Leyden: A.W. Sijthoff, 1923);

Gilles Quispel, *Tatian and the Gospel of Thomas: Studies in the History of the Western Diatessaron* (Leiden: Brill, 1975);

Rathofer, "Die Einwirkung des fuldischen Evangelientextes auf den althochdeutschen 'Tatian,' " in *Literatur und Sprache im europäischen Mittelalter: Festschrift für Karl Langosch zum 70. Geburtstag,* edited by Rathofer, Alf Önnerfors, and Fritz Wagner (Darmstadt: Wissenschaftliche Buchgesellschaft, 1973), pp. 256–308;

Rathofer, "Ms. Junius 13 und die verschollene Tatian-Hs. B," *Beiträge zur Geschichte der deutschen Sprache und Literatur* (Tübingen), 95 (1973): 13–125;

Rathofer, "Zum althochdeutschen Tatian," *Colloquia Germanica* (1973): 55–57;

Margot Schmidt, "Zum althochdeutschen Tatian: Forschungslage," *Colloquia Germanica* (1972): 1–16;

Ernst Schröter, *Walahfrids deutsche Glossierung zu den biblischen Büchern Genesis bis Regum II und der althochdeutsche Tatian* (Halle: Niemeyer, 1926);

Karl Stackman, "Die Göttinger Abschriften des St. Gallen 'Tatian': Über die Mühsal althochdeutscher Studien in papoleonischer Zeit," in *Althochdeutsch,* edited by Rolf Bergmann and others, volume 2 (Heidelberg: Winter, 1987), pp. 1504–1520;

Heinrich Joseph Vogels, *Beiträge zur Geschichte der Diaterssaron im Abendland* (Münster: Aschendorff, 1919);

Wilhelm Wissmann, "Zum althochdeutschen Tatian," in *Indogermanica: Festschrift für Wolfgang Krause zum 65. Geburtstag* (Heidelberg: Winter, 1960), pp. 249–267;

Theodor Zahn, "Zur Geschichte von Tatian's *Diatessaron* im Abendland," *Neue kirchliche Zeitschrift,* 5 (1894): 85–120.

# Waltharius
## (circa 825)

### Dennis M. Kratz
*University of Texas at Dallas*

**Manuscripts:** The *Waltharius* is preserved in complete form in four manuscripts, of which three are descended from a common archetype. These three are Brussels, Bibliothèque Royale, 5380–5384, from the late eleventh or early twelfth century; Paris, Bibliothèque Nationale, Latin 8488A, from the late eleventh century; and T – Trier, Stadtsbibliothek 2002, from the fifteenth century. The fourth manuscript, Karlsruhe, Landesbibliothek Rastatt 24, from the twelfth century, which was destroyed by fire in 1945, was from a less reliable tradition. **First publication:** In *Lateinische Gedichte des X. und XI. Jahrhunderts,* edited by Jacob Grimm and Andreas Schmeller (Göttingen: Dieterich, 1838; reprinted, Amsterdam: Rodopi, 1967). **Standard edition:** Edited by Karl Strecker, in *Monumenta Germaniae Historica, Poetae Latini Aevi Carolini,* volume 6, part 1 (Weimar: Bohlau, 1951), pp. 36–85. **Editions in English:** Excerpts translated in verse by Charles W. Jones, in *Medieval Literature in Translation* (New York: McKay, 1950), pp. 193–208; translated in prose by H. M. Smyser and Francis P. Magoun, Jr., as "The Poem of Walter," in *Walter of Aquitaine: Materials for the Study of His Legend,* Connecticut College Monographs, no. 4 (New London: Connecticut College, 1950), pp. 4–37; translated in verse by Dennis M. Kratz, in *Waltharius and Ruodlieb* (New York: Garland, 1984), pp. 3–71.

A fine literary achievement in its own right, the Latin epic poem *Waltharius* (circa 825) also occupies an important place in medieval literary history as an early example of the Christian response to the allure of the Germanic and classical heroic traditions. The poet, whose identity remains a matter of intense scholarly debate, weaves classical, Germanic, and Christian threads to form an extraordinary artistic fabric.

The 1,456-line narrative falls naturally into three parts, approximately equal in length. In the first section (lines 1 to 418) the army of Attila the Hun is sweeping through western Europe. Three kings agree to ransom their kingdoms with tribute and hostages. The hostages are Walther of Aquitaine; his betrothed, Hiltgunt of Burgundy; and the Frankish warrior Hagen, who is sent in place of the infant prince Gunther. In time the hostages rise to positions of prominence in the Hun court; Walther, the greatest of Attila's warriors, commands his army. When Hagen learns that Gunther has not only become king of the Franks but has also rescinded the treaty with Attila, he escapes and returns to his lord. Soon thereafter Walther sponsors a lavish banquet at which the Huns drink themselves into a stupor. While they sleep Walther and Hiltgunt escape with two coffers crammed with Hun treasure.

In the second section (lines 419 to 1061) the flight of Walther and Hiltgunt takes them through the land of the Franks. Hagen is pleased to discover that his friend has escaped, but the greedy Gunther thinks only of the treasure that they are transporting through his territory. Despite Hagen's objections and his warnings about Walther's prowess, Gunther gathers eleven men and sets out to rob Walther. Hagen is one of the eleven, but he declares that he will not participate in any attack. Meanwhile, Walther and Hiltgunt have sought refuge in a mountain pass. After vainly demanding that Walther hand over the treasure, Gunther orders his men to attack, but the pass is so narrow that only one warrior can approach Walther at a time. In a series of individual combats Walther kills each of the men, one of whom is Hagen's nephew. Now only Gunther and Hagen are left to continue the fight.

In the third section (lines 1062 to 1456) Hagen agrees to attack Walther to avenge the death of his nephew. He and Gunther lure Walther onto open ground by pretending to leave. In the ensuing fight Walther hacks off Gunther's right leg, but Hagen intercepts the next blow with his helmet, causing Walther's sword to shatter. When the frustrated Walther throws the useless hilt away, Hagen cuts off his right hand. Undaunted, Walther draws a dagger with his left hand and gouges out Hagen's right eye and six of his teeth. The men abruptly lay down their weapons, drink wine served by Hiltgunt, tell jokes about one another's injuries, and depart. The poet says that Walther will reach home, marry Hiltgunt, and rule happily in Aquitaine for thirty years.

The author of the *Waltharius* drew the main elements of the story from the same body of legends that a later poet would use to compose the *Nibelungenlied* (Song of the Nibelungs, circa 1200). The latter contains three apparent references, if not to the *Waltharius* itself, at least to the tale that it recounts. In the first passage Etzel (Attila) recalls the time when Walther, Hagen, and Hiltgunt were his hostages (line 1756, canto 28). Although Hagen escapes in the *Waltharius,* in the *Nibelungenlied* Etzel says that he sent Hagen home. Later a warrior remembers the glory won by Hagen and Walther while they were members of Etzel's court (line 1798, canto 29). Finally, another warrior criticizes Hagen for that time in the past when Hagen sat on his shield while Walther was killing so many of Hagen's friends (line 2344, canto 39). Also the surviving fragments of the Old English epic *Waldere,* which was probably composed in the eighth century, seem to describe the moments immediately preceding the attacks on Walther by Gunther's retainers.

It is extremely unlikely that the author of the *Nibelungenlied* knew the Latin *Waltharius* or that the *Waltharius* poet knew the *Waldere.* The evidence suggests that each poet was drawing on the same widely known body of legendary tales. No other work of medieval literature mentions the disfigurement of the three men that plays so prominent a role in the *Waltharius;* the most reasonable assumption would seem to be that the *Waltharius* poet invented this element of his story.

Scholarly disagreement swirls about almost every aspect of the *Waltharius,* but the circumstances of its composition have drawn particular attention. Jacob Grimm, the first editor of the *Waltharius,* placed it in the tenth century and identified the author as Ekkehard I of Saint Gall. He based this identification on a statement by Ekkehard IV in the eleventh-century chronicle *Casus S. Galli* that, while a schoolboy, the earlier Ekkehard had composed an

exercise titled *vitam Waltharii manu fortis* (The Life of Walther of the Strong Hand) and had subsequently revised and polished it. Grimm believed that the *Waltharius* was that revised work. Recent criticism, however, has challenged this identification on two grounds. First, the mature artistry of the poem and the breadth of its author's knowledge not only of patristic but also of classical literature indicate that the work could hardly have been a young student's school assignment. Second, the idea, first proposed by Karl Strecker, that the *Waltharius* is a product of the ninth-century Carolingian Renaissance rather than of the tenth century has gained wide acceptance. For example, Otto Schumann has pointed out that none of the many classical and Christian works the poet cites was written later than 900. The composition of the poem has been dated between 835 and 860 by Wolfram von den Steinen on the basis of historical references in the narrative; also, the poet's mastery of classical Latin and his imitation of classical forms reflect the literary values of the ninth rather than the tenth century. Dieter Schaller and Alf Önnerfors, although differing on the identity of the author, agree that the quality of the Latin and the style of the poem reflect Carolingian rather than tenth-century culture. Önnerfors, moreover, points out that between 785 and 810 the Huns were a subject of considerable interest at the court of Charlemagne.

If not Ekkehard I, then who is the author of the *Waltharius?* The three most reliable manuscripts contain a twenty-two-line preface by a monk who gives his name as Geraldus, dedicating the *Waltharius* to a prelate named Erkambald; it seems reasonable to assume that Geraldus composed the *Waltharius* as well. The assumption that the epic was composed by a monk for other monks is buttressed by the fact that the poet, in the first line, addresses his intended audience as "fratres" (brothers). Scholars have, however, been unable to find a plausible candidate for the Erkambald whom Geraldus addresses. Furthermore, almost every scholar agrees that the dedication is rather badly written; in Peter Dronke's words, a "Geraldus who is expert at epic verse but deadly at dedications is hard to imagine." Schaller suggests that Geraldus's poem was meant to accompany, and praise, the work of another poet that he was sending to Erkambald.

Following Dronke, Schaller argues that the poet need not have been a monk, and he interprets the word *fratres* as having the broader sense of "fellow Christians"; he believes that the poet is the same member of Charlemagne's court at Aachen who composed the epic *Carolus Magnus et Leo Papa*

(Charlemagne and Pope Leo), which displays a similar mastery of Latin hexameters. In that case, however, how the manuscript tradition became so strongly associated with Saint Gall remains a mystery. Önnerfors has argued that the poem could have been composed by another member of the court: Grimald, the teacher of the Latin poet Walahfrid Strabo. Grimald became abbot of Saint Gall, and Ekkehard I's decision to write about Walther could have been influenced by the existence there of a Carolingian *Waltharius* composed by Grimald. The conjectures of both Schaller and Önnerfors are plausible, if unprovable.

The *Waltharius* was, then, probably composed in the first half of the ninth century. If the author was a monk, the manuscript tradition suggests that he composed the poem in southern Germany, either in the cloister of Reichenau or in that of Saint Gall. Whoever composed the *Waltharius* was an unusually well-read and gifted poet. Hennig Brinkmann initiated modern literary study of the poem in a seminal 1928 essay arguing that the *Waltharius,* up to then regarded as a school exercise of mainly historical interest, is, in fact, a carefully designed work in which the poet calls attention to his artistic control. The design of the *Waltharius* is based on two intertwined principles: the recurring use of the number three and a successive narrowing of the focus of the narrative. The first of the three sections begins with the Huns sweeping across Europe, which the poet calls "tertia pars orbis" (one third of the world, line 1), then turns to the three kings who send three hostages to Attila. The second section provides a detailed account of Walther's battle against Gunther's men. The third section deals with the fight of the final three warriors – Walther, Hagen, and Gunther – among themselves. The poet interrupts the narrative on several occasions to remind the reader of his artistic control. He adds to his initial mention of Gunther a declaration that "quam postea narro" (I will tell more later, line 15). When Walther uses a double-bladed ax against one of Gunther's warriors, the poet assures his audience that "istius ergo modi Francis tum arma fuere" (the Franks in those days had this kind of weapon, line 919). In his description of Walther's weaponry as he flees the court of Attila, the poet notes that Walther had a two-edged sword on his left thigh and on his right thigh a sword with one cutting edge (lines 336–338); in the climactic battle Walther grabs this one-edged sword, and the poet takes this opportunity to remind the reader that "qua dextrum cinxisse latus

memoravimus illum" (we mentioned that he had strapped this to his right side, line 1391). Karl Stackmann, the other pioneer of *Waltharius* criticism, argued that the key to the reader's understanding the poem is his recognition that the poet was both imitating and transforming his classical models. Modern critics have built on the insights provided by Brinkmann and Stackmann, developing the picture of a poet who was consciously creating a multilayered work of art for a sophisticated reader who would appreciate his use of a wide range of sources.

There is no question that the poet wished the *Waltharius* to be regarded as an epic poem. He follows the language, form, and content of the classical epic genre and bases the design of his work on three earlier epics: Virgil's *Aeneid* (19 B.C.), Statius's *Thebais* (circa 91), and the *Psychomachia* (circa 392) of the Christian poet Prudentius. Writing in Latin dactylic hexameter, the *Waltharius* poet imitates both general epic conventions and specific scenes from the earlier works. Theodore Andersson has examined the poet's use of his two classical models in his descriptions of warfare. In the battle scenes, as in the epic as a whole, the poet steadily narrows the focus of the narrative. The *Waltharius* contains two extended descriptions of fighting between armies. Each begins with a panoramic view of the battlefield, then describes the two armies as they approach one another, then offers descriptions of close combat between various sets of fighters, and concludes with the exploits of a single warrior.

The imitation of classical sources extends to other stylistic elements as well. The *Waltharius* poet demonstrates his mastery of the simile, an obligatory feature of the Latin epic style. In the longest of the eight similes in the *Waltharius* Walther, under savage attack by Hagen and Gunther, is compared to a bear surrounded by dogs:

Haud aliter Numidus quam venabitur ursus
et canibus circumdatus astat et artubus horret
et caput occultans submurmurat ac propiantes
amplexans Umbros miserum mutire coartat,
tum rabidi circumlatrant hinc inde Molossi
comminus ac dirae metuunt accedere belvae,
taliter in nonam conflictus fluxerat horam. (lines 1337–1343)

(Not otherwise when a Numidian bear is hunted,
it stands surrounded by dogs and bares its claws
and growls, lowering its head, and grabs the dogs
that come too close and makes them yelp in pain.
Here, there, on every side the raging hounds are barking,

but they are afraid to move in close and attack the
    awful beast:
just so the battle wavered into the ninth hour.)

The classical source for this simile is Virgil's comparison in *Aeneid* 10.707-715 of the Italian warrior Mezentius to a wild boar harassed by hunting dogs afraid to venture too near the enraged beast. Earlier Hagen has had a dream in which, after a protracted battle, a bear bites off Gunther's leg and rips out one of Hagen's eyes (lines 617-627). This dream foretells the conclusion of the *Waltharius,* and the image of the bear in the simile clearly invites the reader to recall Hagen's vision.

The poet's sense of humor has also drawn much attention. Gareth Morgan has explored the poet's predilection for puns, especially ones that require a knowledge of both German and Latin: since *Hagedorn* is the German word for "hawthorn," he refers to Hagen as "spinosus" (thorny, line 1421); in the heat of combat Walther calls Hagen, who is pressing the attack with his sword, as " 'o paliure, vires foliis, ut pungere possis' " ("a hawthorn with stabbing leaves," line 1351). The epic concludes on a comic note with the three warriors joking about the wounds they have received. When they depart for their respective homes, the poet writes "sic redierunt disiecti" (line 1445), a double entendre that can be translated as "they went their separate ways" and as "they left mutilated."

Dronke and Dennis M. Kratz have demonstrated the convergence of the poet's sense of humor and his imitative skills in the scene depicting Attila's discovery that Walther and Hiltgunt have fled. The banquet at which Walther induces such inebriation among the Huns that they sleep through his escape is based on the banquet given by Dido in honor of Aeneas (*Aeneid* 1.637-756). Attila's complaint, when he awakens to both a hangover and news of Walther's departure, gains a new level of comic meaning for the reader who recognizes the poet's use of literary allusions. In his despair, Attila "ex humeris trabeam discindit ad infima totam" (rips his entire robe from the shoulders to the hem, line 382). The language recalls Virgil's description of an act of grief by Aeneas: "tum pius Aeneas humeris abscindere vestem" (*Aeneid* 5.685). The next line strengthens the association between Attila and Aeneas: Attila "et nunc huc animum tristem, nunc dividit illuc" (directs his saddened mind now here, now there, line 383). The language is borrowed almost verbatim from Virgil's description of Aeneas's response to the directive to leave Carthage for Italy: "atque animum nunc huc celerem nunc dividit illuc" (*Aeneid* 4.285). The two images share the image of tearing; in the first Attila physically tears his robe; in the second he is metaphorically torn between possible courses of action.

The next image, which compares Attila's internal distress to a raging storm – "ac velut Aeolicis turbatur arena procellis" (just as the sand is stirred up by Aeolian storms, line 384) – also seems Virgilian. But this line, as Dronke first noted, is not from the *Aeneid* but from a satiric poem by the Christian poet Venantius Fortunatus (circa 530-600), where it describes the gastric distress of a gluttonous abbot ("non sic Aeoliis turbatur harena procellis"). The association would have undercut Attila's heroic stature for any reader who understood the allusion. The image, with its implied mockery of Attila, begins a series of descriptive touches that seem serious but take on a comic undertone for the reader who recognizes the *Waltharius* poet's use of the *Aeneid*. Attila is fiercely angry, unable to eat or drink (a reinforcement, perhaps, of the previous allusion to the abbot with an upset stomach). The phrase describing his inability to sleep – "nec placidam membris potuit dare cura quietem" (and anxiety stripped soothing quiet from his limbs, line 390) – repeats verbatim Virgil's description of the lovesick Dido (*Aeneid* 4.5). The rest of the passage reinforces the association between Attila and Dido by describing Attila's restless wanderings through the city in language that also recalls Dido: the enraged king and fearsome warrior has been reduced to a woman suffering the pangs of passion.

The treatment of Attila in this scene provides a preview of the depiction of the poem's main male characters: Gunther, Hagen, and Walther. The poet uses references to other works of Latin literature to cast an ironic, critical light on the apparently heroic actions of the three. This ironic stance provides the solution to an issue that has evoked particularly intense discussion: the poet's ability to weave the various threads of his epic into a Christian fabric. The view that the Christian elements are incidental to a poem that displays an essentially pagan ethos, represented by George F. Jones, has found little support; most modern readers have agreed that the poet was attempting to use the Latin epic as a medium for the expression of Christian values, though they have differed on his approach. One school of thought holds that the poet attempts to portray Walther as a positive exemplar of Christian heroism, the other that he takes a critical stance toward Walther and the values associated with the heroic code.

Rosemary Katscher sees the Christian theme of the epic in a new kind of heroism that Walther exemplifies. She points to his relationship with Hiltgunt and to his treatment of his vanquished enemies: during the many days and nights of their flight from Attila's court Walther refrains from sexual contact with his betrothed, earning the poet's praise for his self-control (lines 426-427); in one episode Walther utters a statement of contrition after he has killed eleven of Gunther's men, and in another, during a brief respite from the onslaught against him, he fits the heads of several decapitated warriors to their appropriate trunks and prays for his victims.

This reading of the *Waltharius,* however, encounters several difficulties. If Walther is intended as a Christian hero, it is difficult to explain his more frequent examples of decidedly unchristian behavior and his continuing adherence to heroic values: he steals two boxes of treasure from Attila and vows to fight to the death rather than give them up; he makes several strong and clear statements that the twin motivators of his behavior are glory and wealth; finally, as Max Wehrli first pointed out, the poet attacks avarice as a sin throughout the epic but also makes it clear that avarice provides the primary motivation for all the heroic characters, including Walther.

A third interpretation takes a middle ground, agreeing both with those who say that Walther is not a Christian hero and with those who find the poem Christian in spirit: Kratz has shown that the *Waltharius* is an ironic work that seeks to display the inadequacy rather than the glory of the heroic ethos; the poet uses citations from the *Aeneid,* the *Psychomachia,* and the Bible to criticize the outmoded values associated with both Germanic and classical epic. As in his treatment of Attila, the poet undercuts the apparent nobility of the epic's three main characters: Gunther, Hagen, and – especially – Walther. The poet offers a relentlessly negative picture of Gunther, labeling him "stupidus" (stupid), "avarus" (greedy), and "superbus" (arrogant). He becomes Pride personified as he hastens toward Walther and his treasure. When Gunther "cornipedem rapidum saevis calcaribus urget" (goads his swift-footed charger on his savage spurs, line 515), the poet is making an unmistakable reference to Prudentius's description of Superbia (Pride) on her own charger "rapidum calcaribus urget, / cornipedem" (*Psychomachia,* lines 253-254).

Gunther matches his arrogance with his avarice. When he learns that Walther is traveling through his domain, Gunther thinks only of the treasure that is being transported across his realm.

When Walther offers a portion of the treasure for his safe passage, Gunther says that he will be satisfied with nothing less than all of it. After the loss of all his retainers except Hagen, Gunther finally enters the battle. His performance in the final battle, however, is described by Walther as " 'tepide atque enerviter' " (tepid and nerveless, line 1415).

Hagen and Walther receive more balanced portraits. Both are guided in their actions by the heroic ethos, which is described in essentially the same terms in both classical Latin and medieval German literature. The twin motivators of this ethos are glory and wealth. The goal of the heroic individual is to gain glory – that is, a reputation for excellence – through the performance of bold deeds. Part of that reputation rests on the necessity to avenge injury to oneself or to one's lord. Material wealth is sought not for its own sake but as a symbol of the esteem the hero has earned. The importance that the *Waltharius* poet attached to these two motivators can be discerned in his comment that not one of Attila's warriors dared to pursue the fleeing Walther however much each wished "laudem captare perennem" (to capture everlasting fame, line 411) and "gazam infarcire cruminis" (to stuff moneybags with treasure, line 412).

Revenge and a concern for reputation, recurring themes throughout the *Waltharius,* can be seen especially in the sequence of attacks against Walther by Gunther's warriors. After Walther kills the first warrior, the second fights to avenge the death of the first. One of Gunther's men cuts off a lock of Walther's hair; Walther decapitates his foe, even as the wounded man begs for mercy, to prevent him from boasting that he gave Walther a bald spot (lines 979-981).

Hagen, too, acts in accordance with the heroic ethos. At first he refuses to join in the attack on his friend because he believes that Gunther is acting wrongly. Eventually he is drawn into the battle against Walther, but only to avenge the death of his nephew. The poet's introduction and criticism of Hagen's decision exemplifies his narrative technique: Hagen attempts to dissuade his nephew from attacking Walther, but "laudem captare cupiscens" (a desire to win glory, line 855) lures the young man forward. As he watches his nephew advance toward his inevitable death, Hagen delivers an impassioned criticism of avarice as the root of all evil:

"O vortex mundi, fames insatiatus habendi,
gurges avaritiae, cunctorum fibra malorum!" (lines
867-868)

*First page of the Karlsruhe manuscript for the* Waltharius, *which was burned in 1945 (from Gero von Wilpert,* Deutsche Literatur in Bildern, *1957)*

("O whirlpool of the world, voracious lust of having,
Abyss of avarice, the root of every evil!")

The first line of this speech contains a direct allusion to Prudentius's description of greed in the *Psychomachia* as "amor insatiatus habendi" (the voracious love of having, line 478). Hagen goes on to decry his nephew's " 'vili pro laude' " (desire for cheap praise, line 871) as a form of greed: " 'Instimulatus enim de te est, o saeva cupido' " (For he is prodded on by you, o savage greed, line 870). By characterizing the desire for glory as a form of greed, the poet implies that the heroic code itself is founded on avarice. Moreover, this equation of glory with greed provides the basis for the poet's condemnation of Hagen's behavior. Although Hagen expresses his lack of interest in Walther's treasure, he later gives two reasons for entering the battle against Walther: to avenge his nephew and to do " 'aliquid memorabile' " (something noteworthy, line 1279). Hagen is, thus, guilty of the same avarice of which he accuses others, although the flaw lies less with him than with the greed-based code that guides his actions. He receives an ironically appropriate punishment for his behavior: he loses an eye and six teeth. Few readers (especially the audience of monks for whom many scholars think the *Waltharius* was written) would have missed the appropriateness of these wounds or the poet's allusion to the biblical injunction of "an eye for an eye, a tooth for a tooth" (Exod. 21:22–25).

Like Hagen, Walther is presented as following the dictates of the heroic value system. Within the limits of those values he is, in many respects, presented admirably. He exhibits *fortitudo* (boldness) in battle and *sapientia* (intelligence) in his strategic decisions. All his actions are consistent with the ethos of heroism. He takes treasure from Attila as his due and later vows to fight to the death to avoid both poverty and the dishonor of having the treasure wrested from him:

"Incassum multos mea dextera fuderat hostes,
si modo supremis laus desit, dedecus assit.
Est satius pulchram per vulnera quaerere mortem
quam solum amissis palando evadere rebus." (lines
    1215–1218)

("In vain my right hand would have slain many foes,
if in the end dishonor is present and praise absent.
It is better to seek a noble death by wounds
than to escape, my wealth lost, and wander all alone.")

Walther makes clear his adherence to heroic values. To escape without his possessions or glory is un-

thinkable. He places his hope for success not in God but in his own right hand. Once he has taken the treasure from Attila, he is preoccupied with keeping it and avoiding the shame of losing it. From the Christian perspective of the poet, such concern for wealth and reputation is a form of greed.

The final episode of the *Waltharius* serves both as the key to the design of the entire poem and as a particularly vivid demonstration of the poet's two most praised poetic skills: his use of literary allusion and his sense of humor. The three warriors have been battling ferociously for the treasure; grievously wounded, they suddenly call off the fight. The two main elements of this episode are the wounds suffered by the three men and the sudden cessation of hostilities. The wounds are humorously symbolic: Hagen, fighting for vengeance, loses an eye and teeth; Gunther, who rushed after Walther's treasure, loses a leg; Walther, who vowed that his right hand would protect the treasure, loses that hand.

The poet then guides the reader to another layer of meaning by offering a catalogue of the wounds:

Postquam finis adest, insignia quemque notabant:
illic Guntharii regis pes, palma iacebat
Waltharii nec non tremulus Haganonis ocellus.
sic sic armillas partiti Avarenses! (lines 1401–1404)

(After the fighting ceased, marks branded each.
There lay Gunther's foot, the hand
of Walther and Hagen's still twitching eye.
Thus thus they shared the Avars' treasures!)

The poet's moral exclamation (including the implied pun linking Avars with avarice [Latin *avaritia*]), combined with the detail of the list, underscores the importance of the passage. The list, however, seems inaccurate, or at least incomplete, a troubling lapse by a poet who has several times interrupted the narrative to point out his accuracy and control. Hagan lost teeth as well as an eye, and Walther hacked off Gunther's entire leg, not just his foot. The changes are not, in fact, an error. They are intended to remind the reader of Mark 9:42–48: "And if your hand causes you to sin, cut it off; it is better for you to enter life maimed than with two hands to go to hell, to the unquenchable fire. And if your foot causes you to sin, cut it off; it is better for you to enter life lame than with two feet to be thrown into hell. And if your eye causes you to sin, pluck it out; it is better for you to enter the kingdom of God with one eye than with two eyes to be thrown into hell, where the worm does not die, and the fire is not quenched." The biblical allusion indicates that the wounds suffered by the warriors should be regarded as symbolic punishments for valuing worldly goods, such as treasure and fame, over spiritual goods.

The sudden cessation of the fighting and the warriors' bantering humor refer the reader to Prudentius's allegorical epic, in which the Virtues rest after defeating the Vices in a series of individual combats. The Virtue Operatio (Good Works) explains that rest is now possible because they have defeated Avarice. In her praise of moderation she advises her colleagues not even to carry a wallet when they set out on a journey but to trust in God to supply their needs. The medieval audience would perceive in the reference an implied criticism of Walther's insistence on taking two treasure boxes when he set out from Attila's court. The combined allusions to Mark and to the *Psychomachia* suggest that the wounds suffered by the warriors can be understood as punishments for their avarice.

That the warriors desist from battle so quickly, making no further mention of the treasure for which they were fighting, has puzzled many readers. The ending has been explained by saying that the poet was dealing with traditional material that he could not alter even though it made little sense. The conclusion does make sense, however, in the context of the condemnation of the outmoded heroic values associated with epic poetry as manifestations of the sin of avarice.

If the poet was a monk writing for monks, then his denunciation of worldly values is not difficult to understand, nor does it seem unlikely that his audience would have understood the implications of his allusions to Christian sources. The interest in German heroic literature not only among members of Charlemagne's court but also among the clergy of the period is well known: Alcuin exclaims, in a letter to the bishop of Lindisfarne criticizing his monks for their love of Germanic heroic tales, "quid Hinieldus cum Christo?" (What does Ingeld [a Heathobardic ruler who appears in *Beowulf*] have to do with Christ?). One can imagine the *Waltharius* as one monk's artful reply to the question. His challenge was to transform the Latin epic into a vehicle for the expression of Christian values; his solution was to fashion a narrative that, like the *Psychomachia*, offers adventure on the surface and also, for the reader who recognized the implications of the allusions embedded throughout the text, a morally satisfying condemnation of classical and Germanic standards of heroic behavior. The result was a poem of extraordinary importance for modern readers interested in the artistic resolution of the problem of adapting classical and Germanic traditions to Christian purposes.

**References:**

Theodore Andersson, *Early Epic Scenery* (Ithaca, N.Y.: Cornell University Press, 1976);

Hennig Brinkmann, "Ekkehards Waltharius als Kunstwerk," *Zeitschrift für deutsche Bildung*, 43 (1928): 625–636;

Peter Dronke, "Functions of Classical Borrowing in Medieval Latin," in *Classical Influences in European Culture: A.D. 500–1500*, edited by R. R. Bolgar (Cambridge: Cambridge University Press, 1971), pp. 159–164;

Dronke, "Waltharius – Gaiferos," in *Barbara et Antiquissima Carmina*, edited by Dronke and Ursula Dronke (Barcelona: Universidad Autonoma de Barcelona, 1977), pp. 29–79;

George F. Jones, "The Ethos of the *Waltharius*," in *Middle Ages – Reformation, Volkskunde: Festschrift for John G. Kunstmann* (Chapel Hill: University of North Carolina Press, 1959), pp. 1–20;

Rosemary Katscher, "Waltharius – Dichtung und Dichter," *Mittellateinisches Jahrbuch*, 9 (1976): 48–120;

Dennis M. Kratz, *Mocking Epic: Waltharius, Alexandreis and the Problem of Christian Heroism* (Madrid: Porrua, 1980);

Gareth Morgan, "Walther the Wood-sprite," *Medium Aevum*, 41 (1972): 16–19;

Alf Önnerfors, "Das Waltharius Epos: Probleme und Hypothesen," in *Scripta Minora 1987–88: 1* (Lund: Publikationen der Königlichen Gesellschaft der Geisteswissenschaften, 1989);

Dieter Schaller, "Geraldus und St. Gallen: Zum Widmungsgedicht des Waltharius," *Mittellateinisches Jahrbuch*, 2 (1965): 74–84;

Schaller, "Von St. Gallen nach Mainz?: Zum Verfasserproblem des Waltharius," *Mittellateinisches Jahrbuch*, 24/25 (1989/1990): 423–438;

Bernd Scherello, "Die Darstellung Gunthers im Waltharius," *Mittellateinisches Jahrbuch*, 21 (1986): 88–90;

Otto Schumann, "Zum *Waltharius*," *Zeitschrift für deutsches Altertum*, 83 (1951): 12–40;

Karl Stackmann, "Antike Elemente im *Waltharius*," *Euphorian*, 45 (1950): 231–248;

Wolfram von den Steinen, "Der *Waltharius* und sein Dichter," *Zeitschrift für deutsches Altertum*, 84 (1952): 1–47;

Max Wehrli, "Waltharius: Gattungsgeschichtliche Betrachtungen," *Mittellateinisches Jahrbuch*, 2 (1965): 63–73;

Gero von Wilpert, *Deutsche Literatur in Bildern* (Stuttgart: Kröner, 1957).

# Wessobrunner Gebet
## (circa 787 – 815)

Cyril W. Edwards
*Goldsmiths' College, University of London*

**Manuscript:** The Wessobrunn Prayer survives in a single manuscript, Munich, Bayerische Staatsbibliothek, clm. 22053, fols. 65v–66r.

**First publication:** In Bernhard Pez, *Thesaurus anecdotorum novissimus,* volume 1 (1721), pp. 417–418.

**Standard editions:** As no. 1 in *Denkmäler deutscher Poesie und Prosa aus dem VIII–XII Jahrhundert,* third edition, edited by Elias von Steinmeyer (Berlin: Weidmann, 1892; reprinted, Berlin & Zurich: Weidmann, 1964); as no. 2 in *Die kleineren althochdeutschen Sprachdenkmäler,* edited by Steinmeyer (Berlin: Weidmann, 1916; reprinted, Berlin & Zurich: Weidmann, 1963); as no. xxix in *Althochdeutsches Lesebuch,* edited by Wilhelm Braune, sixteenth edition, revised by Ernst A. Ebbinghaus (Tübingen: Niemeyer, 1978).

**Editions in English:** Translated by K. C. King in J. Knight Bostock, in *A Handbook on Old High German Literature,* second edition, revised by King and D. R. McLintock (Oxford: Clarendon Press, 1976), pp. 129–130; edited and translated by Brian O. Murdoch, in his *Old High German Literature* (Boston: Twayne, 1983), p. 66.

The anonymous *Wessobrunner Gebet* (Wessobrunn Prayer, circa 787–815), also known as the *Wessobrunner Schöpfungsgdicht* (Wessobrunn Creation Poem), exists in a manuscript of ninety-nine leaves that came to Munich from the monastery of Wessobrunn, southwest of Munich, after its dissolution in 1803. The ultimate provenance of the manuscript is uncertain; the destruction of Wessobrunn in the tenth century suggests that it is unlikely to have originated there. Linguistic evidence and the interest in Bavaria shown throughout the manuscript point to a Bavarian scriptorium. Attempts to link it on paleographic grounds with manuscripts of

established provenance have proved unsuccessful. It may be a by-product of an important Bavarian center such as Regensburg, or it may emanate from a minor schoolroom such as Neuburg – a diocese mentioned in the manuscript but of uncertain location.

The prayer reads, in its entirety:

De Poeta
Dat *ga*fregin ih mit firahim firi uuizzo meista.

Dat ero ni uuas noh ufhimil.
noh paum noh pereg niuuas.
ninohheinig noh sunna nistein.
noh mano niliuhta. noh der março seo.
Do dar niuuiht niuuas enteo ni uuenteo.
*enti* do uuas der eino almahtico cot.
manno miltisto. *enti* dar uuarun auh manake mit inan

cootlihhe geista. *enti* cot heilac.
Cot almahtico du himil *enti* erda *ga* uuorahtos.
*enti* du mannun so manac coot for*ga*pi.
for gipmir indino ganada rehta galaupa.
*enti* cotan uuilleon. uuistóm *enti* spahida.
*enti* craft. tiuflun za uuidar stantanne.
*enti* arc zapi uuisanne. *enti* dinan uuilleon za
*ga*uurchanne.

(Of the Creator
This my questioning among men determined, greatest
   of wonders.
That there was neither earth nor heaven,
Nor tree, nor mountain was there,
Nor anything, nor did the sun shine,
Nor the moon beam, nor the glorious sea,
When there was nothing of ends nor turnings.
And then there was the one Almighty God,
Kindest of men. And there were also many with him,

Divine spirits. And God Holy.
God Almighty, you who created heaven and earth,
And you who bestowed so many good things upon
   men,
Bestow upon me in your grace true belief,

And good will, wisdom and intelligence,
And power to withstand devils,
And to shun evil, and to work your will.)

The prayer opens with a formula suggesting that an oral tradition lies behind it; such formulas also introduce sections of two other Old High German alliterative poems, the *Hildebrandslied* (Lay of Hildebrand, circa 825) and the *Muspilli* (circa 790–circa 850). It proceeds to describe the void that preceded the Creation. The powerful simplicity of this sequence of negatives has led scholars to search for analogues as far afield as the Old Icelandic *Voluspá* and the Sanskrit *Rig-Veda*. The natural phenomena whose presence is negated are, for the most part, found in the first chapter of Genesis; other biblical descriptions of the beginning and of the end of the world (Jer. 4:23–26; Psalm 104; Job 26) might also have inspired the poet. The depiction of the void is summed up in the fifth line; the rhyme pair *enteo ni uuenteo* may derive from Gen. 1:2, "formless and void," where both the Greek and the Hebrew versions have a rhyme pair (*aoratos kai akataskeuastos* and *tôhuwābōhû,* respectively). The presence of the Creator and the angels is then revealed. The final six lines ask God, by virtue of the power shown in the Creation, to show forgiveness and guidance to the supplicant – a request similar to those found in the Old High German charms. The wording is reminiscent of that of the *Fränkisches Gebet* (Frankish Prayer), written down in 821 at the behest of Baturich, bishop of Regensburg. This similarity suggests that the poem possessed a liturgical function, although the possibility that it was conceived as a private prayer, an act of personal devotion, cannot be excluded, given the singular pronoun *mir* in line 12.

The *Wessobrunner Gebet* and the *Hildebrandslied* are the two oldest German poems. The prayer forms part of a small surviving corpus of Old High German alliterative poetry. *Stabreim,* the alliterative long-line verse form that was also cultivated in Anglo-Saxon, Old Norse, and Old Saxon, was virtually extinct in Germany by the end of the ninth century. The *Wessobrunner Gebet* and the *Muspilli* employ this form to treat two key Christian concepts, the Creation and the Apocalypse, respectively. Both themes are also found in Anglo-Saxon alliterative poetry, and it seems probable that the impulse behind the *Wessobrunner Gebet* derives from Anglo-Saxon England, whose missionaries played a central role in the Christanization of Germany in the eighth century. An Anglo-Saxon tradition of alliterative lays concerning the Creation is attested by the seventh-century *Cædmon's Hymn,* nine lines in praise of the Creator; by the reference in *Beowulf* (circa 700) to a minstrel who sang of the Creation; and by the alliterative poem *The Wonders of Creation* in the Exeter Book of the early eleventh century. Resemblances in vocabulary and formulaic diction, such as the echo of *Beowulf* in *manno miltisto* (in Old English, *manna mil ost*) and the stress placed on asking questions as the basis of wisdom in *The Wonders of Creation,* point to a link between the *Wessobrunner Gebet* and this Christian Anglo-Saxon tradition.

Against this hypothesis, a "Germanicizing" school of thought, inspired initially by nationalist feeling in the nineteenth century, has argued that the depiction of the void in the opening lines of the prayer belongs to a pagan, pre-Christian tradition, and the description of the beginning of the ages in the *Voluspá* has been adduced as supportive evidence. The late transmission of the *Voluspá* and the probability that the depiction of the beginning of the world in the first chapter of Genesis was known to both authors undermine the "pagan" argument. It has, however, been revived by Carola L. Gottzmann, who relates the natural phenomena negated in the prayer to Germanic cult beliefs and thus seeks to reestablish the poem as a subtle piece of missionary propaganda denying the presence of these objects of pagan worship at the beginning of the world. The poem could not have had such a conversion function in late-eighth- or early-ninth-century Bavaria, but if it is a copy of, or in part derived from, an earlier text, then such a line of argument is sustainable.

The consensus is that the prayer is a copy of an earlier exemplar. This position is confirmed by the scribal emendation of *perec* to *pereg* (line 3); by the ẹ in *marẹo,* which belongs more properly in the following word, *seo* (line 5); and by a downward stroke from the *o* of *ero* in line 2, which suggests the scribe's consciousness of an error (one would expect *erda,* as in line 9). The assumption of discrepancies between the exemplar and the prayer as it has been transmitted has led to divergent arguments relating to the content, meter, and language of the original prayer. The Germanicizing argument would claim that the opening lines are a relic of a pagan alliterative poem. The alliterative meter is defective when compared to the conventions observed by longer alliterative poems; it has even been argued that the last six lines of the text are prose, although they clearly contain elements of alliteration and end rhyme. But metrical deficiencies also affect the first part of the poem. Eric G. Stanley argues that shorter works such as prayers and charms were

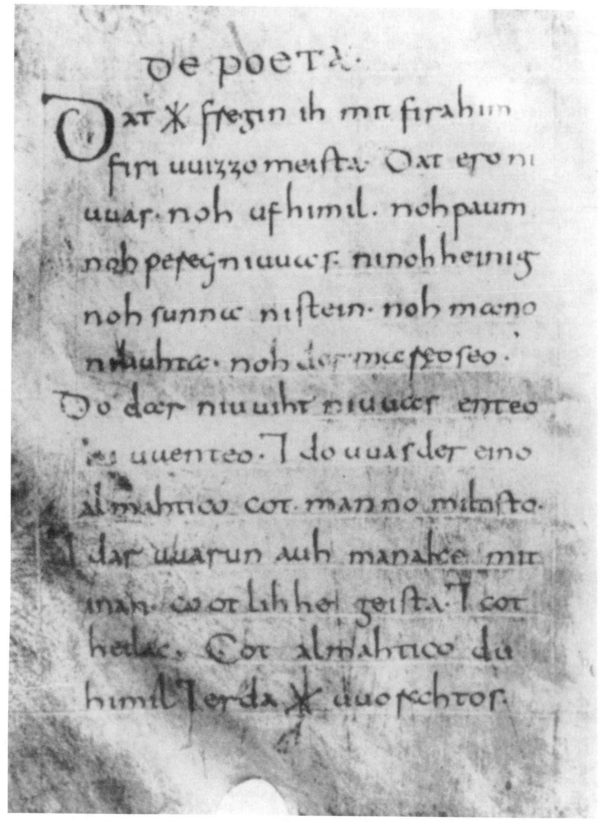

*First page of the manuscript for the* Wessobrunner Gebet *(Munich, Bayerische Staatsbibliothek, dm. 22053, fol. 65v)*

not subject to the same metrical constraints as works on a larger scale. Nevertheless, lacunae are posited in the standard editions in lines 3, 4, and 9, and there have been many conjectural attempts to restore the poem's supposed original alliterative perfection.

The twenty-one lines in the manuscript have been subjected to various attempts at subdivision, particularly by those who claim that the early lines are pagan in origin. Formal, stylistic, and linguistic arguments have been adduced in favor of such subdivision, the most popular being that a later prose Christian prayer has been added to a fragment of an earlier alliterative pagan lay. Perhaps the strongest evidence against the unity of the poem as it is preserved is the apparent syntactic break between the end of the ninth line, "enti cot heilac," and the following line, with which the prayer proper begins: "Cot almahtico, du himil enti erda gauuorahtos."

The shift in subject matter from the stark negation of the created phenomena to the assertion of the presence of God and the angels, and the appeal to God's power and grace with which the prayer ends, may be considered sufficient justification for the stylistic and syntactic variations that have been observed. The text, as preserved, presents a convincing sequence of thought, but whether this sequence was integral to the poem's original composition remains open to argument.

The language of the prayer is primarily Bavarian, but some features – such as the first word (*Dat*) and the scribal emendation of *perec* to *pereg* – point to an origin elsewhere; whether these features indicate that the original of the prayer was composed in a German dialect from further north, in Anglo-Saxon, or in an earlier form of Bavarian, has been the subject of much debate. The lack of comparable linguistic evidence from eighth-century Bavaria makes resolution of the issue highly difficult. Willy Krogmann argues that the prayer is in a uniform Bavarian dialect of the seventh century the linguistic form of which predates all other survivals from the area.

The vocabulary of the prayer includes a few words and phrases that are unique or rare in Old High German literature but have parallels in Anglo-Saxon and Old Norse alliterative poetry, such as *uʃhimil* (Old Norse *upphiminn*) and *cootlihhe geista* (Anglo-Saxon *halige gastas*). This evidence is too slight for one to be certain whether the poet is drawing on a common stock of Germanic poetic vocabulary – the *Rhapsodensprache* (rhapsodist language) of the *scop* (court minstrel) – or whether these words derive from a foreign model. Krogmann maintains

that they are part of the Old Bavarian vocabulary that is now otherwise lost; it seems more probable that they reflect an Anglo-Saxon poetic tradition.

The *Wessobrunner Gebet* is the only continuous text in the manuscript written entirely in German, though there are several Bavarian glosses and proper names in other texts. The Latin rubric *De Poeta,* written in uncial letters above the prayer, resembles, in format, titles assigned to other items in the manuscript. Its meaning, however, is open to debate and raises the question of the role of the prayer in the manuscript. The manuscript contains a miscellany of material with which its compiler – one hand is dominant throughout – must have become acquainted in the monastic schoolroom. The contents, most of which derive from patristic sources, include a version of the "Discovery of the Holy Cross," with crude illustrations; encyclopedic material, generally in the form of excerpts, derived from Bede, Isidore, and other church fathers; geographical glosses derived from Saint Jerome; and parts of sermons of Saint Augustine. On folio 63r there is a list of the seven liberal arts with definitions. The second art, *redthorica,* is glossed: "id est poetica. *Kazungali." Kazungali,* an abstract noun derived from *zunga* (tongue), has a parallel, *gizungilo,* in Otfried von Weißenburg's *Evangelienbuch* (Gospel Book, between 863 and 871 [I, 2, 33]), where it means "eloquence." The word is preceded by two botched attempts at the star rune, the first erased, the second with a horizontal rather than the correct vertical stroke through it. The star rune, apparently thought by the scribe to correspond to the sound *ka,* occurs only here and in the *Wessobrunner Gebet,* where it corresponds to *ga.* It may derive from Anglo-Saxon scribal practice, like the Tironian *et* abbreviation for the Bavarian *enti* – though Irish scribal influence may lie behind both these features, which do not occur in other Old High German texts. In other respects the hand is a characteristic example of early Carolingian minuscule.

The star rune and the conjunction with *poetica* have led to the interpretation of *De Poeta* as "by the poet," and of the prayer as an example of poetry to illustrate the definition of that art. This interpretation seems unlikely in view of the sections *De Mensuris* and *De Chronica,* which intervene between the list of the arts and the prayer (folios 65v–66r). It seems more likely that *De Poeta* means "concerning the Creator," showing the influence of Greek; the compiler displays knowledge of Greek elsewhere in the manuscript.

Immediately following the prayer in the manuscript, on folio 66v, is a charter in which one Jacob frees his slave Herimot, with the permission of "riholfo magistro" and of Charlemagne, in a place called Hesilinloh. The hand of the charter is similar to, if not identical with, that of the prayer, and it provides the best guide for dating and locating the scribe, if not the poet. The charter (or its exemplar) was written before the death of Charlemagne in 814 – possibly before his coronation as emperor in 800, as he is referred to as *rex* rather than as *imperator.* "Riholf" has been identified as Rihulf, archbishop of Mainz from 787 to 813 and so overlord of the diocese of Augsburg, in which it has been possible to identify two places named Hesselohe. The notes on the final leaf of the manuscript (99v) refer to the years 814 and 815. The manuscript is likely to have been compiled over a period of years, perhaps even in different monasteries, but the prayer was probably copied into it in a Bavarian monastery between 787 and 815. The gap between scribe and poet, as with most of the short Old High German texts, places the identity of the author beyond the reach of scholarship.

**Bibliography:**

Sydney Groseclose and Brian O. Murdoch, *Die althochdeutschen poetischen Denkmäler* (Stuttgart: Metzler, 1976), pp. 45–68.

**References:**

Georg Baesecke, "St. Emmeramer Studien," *Beiträge zur Geschichte der deutschen Sprache und Literatur,* 46 (1922): 430–494;

Bernhard Bischoff, *Die südostdeutschen Schreibschulen und Bibliotheken in der Karolingerzeit,* volume 1: *Die bayrischen Diözesen,* third edition (Wiesbaden: Harrasowitz, 1974);

Cyril Edwards, "*Tôhuwabohû:* The *Wessobrunner Gebet* and its analogues," *Medium Aevum,* 53 (1984): 263–281;

Edwards and Jennie Kiff-Hooper, "*Ego bonefacius scripsi:* More Oblique Approaches to the *Wessobrunn Prayer,*" in "*mit regulu bithuungan*": *Neue Arbeiten zur althochdeutschen Poesie und Sprache,* edited by John L. Flood and David N. Yeandle, Göppinger Arbeiten zur Germanistik no. 500 (Göppingen: Kümmerle, 1989), pp. 94–132;

Gustav Ehrismann, *Geschichte der deutschen Literatur bis zum Ausgang des Mittelalters. Erster Teil: Die althochdeutsche Literatur,* second edition (Munich: Beck, 1959);

Hanns Fischer, *Schrifttafeln zum althochdeutschen Lesebuch* (Tübingen: Niemeyer, 1966);

R. A. Fowkes, "Eastern Echoes in the *Wessobrunner Gebet,*" *Germanic Review,* 37 (January 1962): 83–90;

P. F. Ganz, "Die Zeilenaufteilung im *Wessobrunner Gebet,*" *Beiträge zur Geschichte der deutschen Sprache und Literatur* (Tübingen), special issue (1973): 39–51;

Carola L. Gottzmann, "Das *Wessobrunner Gebet:* Ein Zeugnis des Kulturumbruchs vom heidnischen Germanentum zum Christentum," in *Althochdeutsch: Festschrift für R. Schützeichel,* edited by Rolf Bergmann, 2 volumes (Heidelberg: Winter, 1987), I: 637–654;

F. D. Gräter, "Das älteste teutsche Gedicht," *Bragur,* 5, no. 1 (1796): 118–155;

Jacob and Wilhelm Grimm, eds., *Die beiden ältesten Gedichte aus dem achten Jahrhundert: Das Lied von Hildebrand und Hadubrand und das Wessobrunner Gebet* (Cassel: Thurneissen, 1812);

Johannes A. Huismann, "Das Wessobrunner Gebet in seinem handschriftlichen Kontext," in *Althochdeutsch: Festschrift für R. Schützeichel,* 2 volumes (Heidelberg: Winter, 1987), I: 625–636;

Willy Krogmann, "Die Mundart des Wessobrunner Gebets," *Zeitschrift für deutsche Mundartforschung,* 13 (1937): 129–149;

D. R. McLintock, "The Negatives of the 'Wessobrunn Prayer,'" *Modern Language Review,* 52 (July 1957): 397–398;

W. Perrett, "On the *Wessobrunner Gebet* – I and II," *London Medieval Studies,* 1 (1937–1938): 134–138; 2 (1939): 139–149;

Ute Schwab, *Die Sternrune im Wessobrunner Gebet: Beobachtungen zur Lokalisierung des clm 22053, zur Hs. BM Arundel 393 und zu Rune Poem V.86–89,* Amsterdamer Publikationen zur Sprache und Literatur no. 1 (Amsterdam: Rodopi, 1973);

Leslie Seiffert, "The Metrical Form and Composition of the *Wessobrunner Gebet,*" *Medium Aevum,* 31 (1962): 1–13;

Eric G. Stanley, "Alliterative Ornament and Alliterative Rhythmical Discourse in Old High German and Old Frisian Compared with Similar Manifestations in Old English," *Beiträge zur Geschichte der deutschen Sprache und Literatur,* 106 (1984): 184–217;

Glenys A. Waldman, "The Wessobrunn Prayer Manuscript clm 22053: A Transliteration, Transcription and Study of Parallels," Ph.D. dissertation, University of Pennsylvania, 1975.

# The Legends of the Saints and a Medieval Christian Worldview

*An Overview of Old and Middle High German Hagiographic Literature from Its Beginning until the Onset of the High Courtly Period (850–1190)*

James K. Walter
*Ohio Northern University*

Wir hôrten ie dikke singen
von alten dingen:
wî snelle helide vuhten,
wî si veste burge brêchen,
wî sich liebin vuiniscefte schieden,
wî rîche kunige al zegiengen.
nû ist cît, daz wir dencken,
wî wir selve sulin enden. (*Annolied,* lines 1–8)

( We've often heard songs
about ancient things:
how brave heroes fought,
how they laid waste to fortified cities,
how close friendships came to an end,
how powerful kings all declined.
Now it is time that we think
how we ourselves will meet our end.)

Reminding his audience of the songs about the great figures of antiquity and their end, the composer of the *Annolied* (Song of Anno, between 1080 and 1081) urges his listeners to consider their own eternal destiny; his work continues with a summary of the development of God's revelation in religion and in political structures, culminating in the life and work of the eleventh-century bishop of Cologne, Anno. Anno provides the writer with an example of a life and of deeds equal in value to those of centuries past. Approximately a century later the writer of the *Oberdeutsche Servatiuslegende* (Upper German Life of Saint Servatius, circa 1185) strikes a similar note: he briefly describes the deeds of the heroes of pre-Christian times – warfare, the building of cities, composing of verse – then explains:

ûf dehein diu zuoversiht
diu den ewigen lîp bræhte
wan daz man ir gedæhte
mit dem zergänchlichen lobe.
von diu unbilde niemen obe
wir von den gereden chunden
die die werlt habent überwunden

unt mit got êwichlîch sint,
als Servâtius sîn erweltez chint. . . . (lines 30–38)

( With none of them rests the hope
which brings eternal life,
only that they be remembered
with transitory praise.
Therefore let no one take offense
if we can speak of those
who have overcome the world
and are eternally with God,
such as Servatius, his chosen son. . . . )

Noteworthy is the repeated argument for the production of works about holy men and women. Such works, the legends of the medieval period, are defined by Hellmut Rosenfeld as "die dichterische Widergabe des irdischen Lebens heiliger Personen" (the poetic rendering of the earthly life of holy persons). Rolf Schulmeister argues that all religious literature of the medieval period has at its base the concepts of *ædificatio* (explication of spiritual truths and instruction through them) and *imitatio;* in the legend, however, this conceptual framework is tied to the central figure of the saint, by which the audience is instructed and moved to imitation. Siegfried Ringler emphasizes that this single figure serves, through his or her holiness and activity, to demonstrate God's working in the world. Thus it is not surprising that the writer of the *Annolied* and the writer of the *Oberdeutsche Servatiuslegende* insist on the value of their work by comparing it favorably to that of the ancient world. Rosenfeld points out that the legend can be understood as a religious parallel to the secular heroic sagas: God's "heroes" replace the heroes of antiquity. The central figures of the legends include the heroes of the Old Testament, Jesus, the Virgin Mary, the Apostles, and religious men and women from the apostolic era to the Middle Ages. This article will focus on vernacular works dealing with

300

the latter group of saints and, besides providing an overview of several of these legends from the beginnings of German literature until the onset of the period of courtly literature around 1190, will demonstrate how the saint functions within the framework of salvation history. These holy men and women can be understood as heroes or champions in a spiritual struggle.

The earliest German works that resemble the legend in content are the *Petruslied* (Song of [Saint] Peter, circa 850) and the *Georgslied* (Song [in Honor of Saint] George, 896?). The *Petruslied*, in three short strophes, glorifies Peter as gatekeeper of Heaven and for his ability to save those who call on him. Since each of the two-long-line stanzas ends with a Kyrie Eleison as a refrain, the song may have functioned as a processional. The saint's ability to act from Heaven for the benefit of Christians is a frequent theme of fuller saints' lives and an important element in the propagation of the cult of the saint. In its ten extant strophes the *Georgslied* tells of the martyrdom of Saint George, historically a fourth-century bishop of Cappadocia (in the *Georgslied* he is a count). George, famous in the later Middle Ages for his slaying of the dragon (of which there is no mention here), is a type of saint known for his inability to be killed, regardless of torture or means of execution. The Old High German work tells of George's attempt to convert to Christianity the ruler Dacian and of Dacian's subsequent fury and determination to put George to death. The "mare crabo Georio" (famous count George) travels to a meeting of the powerful of the land, where he is tempted to abandon the Christian faith. Thrown in prison, he performs a series of miracles. Dacian has him cut to pieces, but George rises from the dead and continues to preach. Breaking George's body on the wheel produces the same result. Dacian has the saint ground into powder and burned and the ashes tossed into a well, atop which large stones are piled. Water gushes from the well, and with it George, who preaches on. He convinces Dacian's wife to undertake acts of charity and causes hell itself to quake. The Old High German poem ends here. As in the *Petruslied*, there are refrainlike verses that are not part of the narrative (their form varies, but all begin with the word *Daz* [That]). The poem may, therefore, have had a liturgical function. The saint is portrayed as a religious hero who supernaturally resists the power of a worldly ruler. George accepts suffering, turns it into active intervention, and thus serves as a conduit for God's power into the world.

The author of the *Annolied*, working in the Cluniac monastery at Siegburg near the end of the eleventh century, strives to win his audience over to a Christian view of world history and to turn its attention from the songs of the classical world to one about a holy man of God. The *Annolied* marks the real beginning of German literature about saints. Bishop Anno of Cologne is worthy of consideration by Christians because he, by his example and the power he wields on earth and from Heaven, can be of help in the all-important question of one's eternal destiny. The *Annolied*, however, does not begin with Anno and his deeds but with a history of revelation from the Creation and of political development from the founding of the first city to Anno's rule in Cologne. At line 577 the "Anno Legend" proper begins, telling of the bishop's exemplary reign. The third part of the poem, starting at line 789, tells of the miracles connected with Anno after his death. The second part features the element of the saint's life that is prevalent in the *Georgslied*: the saint as a religious champion who has influence with the world's rulers; the third section has the same emphasis as the *Petruslied*: the ability of the now-departed saint to act from Heaven. The *Annolied* is the first example of hagiographic writing in German in which the many aspects of a saint's life found in later such writings are combined, and it may have been a model for much of that later work. Anno, by God's grace, achieves a powerful position in the world, reaching the status of the kings and warriors of classical lore:

> alsi diu sunni dut in den liufte,
> diu inzuschin erden unti himili geit,
> beidin halbin schînit,
> alsô gieng der bischof Anno
> vure gode unti vure mannen.
> in der phelinzin sîn tugint sulich was,
> daz im daz rîch al untersaz,
> ci godis diensti in den geberin,
> samir ein engel wêri.
> sîn êre gehîltir wole beidinthalb.
> dannen ward her ci rehtimi hêrtûmi gezalt. (lines 586–596)

> (As the sun, which goes in the sky
> between earth and heaven,
> illuminates both halves,
> so did Bishop Anno
> go before God and mankind.
> In the palaces his virtue was such
> that all the realm was inferior to him;
> at God's service his behavior
> was as though he were an angel.
> His honor he maintained on both sides,
> whence he was counted among true rulers.)

Kings from distant lands send Anno gifts, and his fame spreads without causing his soul any harm. The *Annolied* presents the example of a holy man whose exploits are equal or superior to those of

*Saint Sylvester (Pope Sylvester I) as depicted in a detail from a mid-thirteenth-century fresco at the Chiesa di SS. Quatro Coronati in Rome*

any legendary hero, accompanied by an assurance that Anno can still act from Heaven. By placing this image of an active saintly hero in the context of God's providential ordering of history, the author impresses his audience with a world in which God's holy men and women are the true heroes worthy of attention, emulation, and reverence.

In the century following the *Annolied* several legends dealing with saints were written in Middle High German. While not all of them present the broad context of salvation history found in the *Annolied,* these works share with it the glorification of a holy man or woman who acts on behalf of God in the world. Judging from those works, among the most popular figures were Saints Aegidius, Alban, Alexius, Crescentia, Juliana, Veronica, Sylvester, Vitus, Andrew, Ulrich, Servatius, Patrick, and the emperor Charlemagne. Some of these works exist only in fragmentary form from the twelfth century and in complete form only from a later period. The fragments of *Andreas* (circa 1175), the legend of Saint Andrew, describe the apostle's martyrdom on a cross. The fragments of *Patricius* (circa 1160), part of a work about the fifth-century Irish saint Patrick, depict several miracles, including the return to life of a dead man. This man's retelling of his experiences beyond the grave reveals the development of the doctrine of purgatory in the eleventh and twelfth centuries. The fragmentary *Veit* (circa 1170), a life of Saint Vitus, is long enough only to describe Veit's infancy and baptism. Like all saints (except those who must repent of sinful beginnings), he is dedicated to God from infancy and chooses to be baptized even though his parents are not Christians. In his prologue, a prayer, the author says that he will tell

> fon einem heiligem man,
> fon dem guoten sancte Vite.
> er dienet dir alle zite
> in siner chintheite
> er was ie gereite
> ze dinem dieneste. (lines 214–217)

> (of a holy man,
> of the good Saint Vitus.
> He served you all the time.
> In his childhood
> he was ever ready for your service.)

Vitus is encountered in later versions which describe his exemplary life and final martyrdom under the emperor Diocletian.

The *Alexius* fragments (late 1100s) point to interest in the legends about this saint in the twelfth century; it is a complete, rather well-composed legend that was written around 1300, possibly by a woman. *Alexius* is the story of a rich young man, the son of a king, who gives up his wealth and privilege, as well as his young bride (leaving her on their wedding night), to live as a holy beggar. He returns to the house of his parents and lives there incognito until his death. His bride dies some years later and is buried next to Alexius's remains, which shine brilliantly when exhumed – a proof of holiness. (In later versions his long-dead arms embrace her corpse as they are united in the grave.) *Alexius* emphasizes the rejection of worldly status:

irdischiu dinge dûhten uns ein mist:
gein diu, diu ze himel sint,
disiu hie sint gar ein wint. (lines 248–250)


(Earthly things seem like manure to us;
compared to those which are in heaven,
these here are no more than wind.)

Alexius's rejection of his family's high position shows that obedience to God's calling and ideals makes any exploits of worldly heroes, and any status those heroes might achieve, meaningless.

Expositions of this rejection of the world in order to overcome it exist in more-fully preserved twelfth-century legends of saints. *Aegidius* (1150) is a legend of a "reluctant saint" who seeks to remain a recluse, working miracles and involving himself with other people only under duress. He is motivated by a desire to avoid the praise and recognition of the world, for Aegidius believes that it is impossible to receive such recognition and retain God's favor:

daz ouch nechein man
die zwei lon nemac han
daz in die werlt lobe
uñ her doch gotis hulde behabet. (lines 159–162)


(also that no man
may have the two rewards –
that the world praise him
and he still retain God's favor.)

The author of the *Aegidius* must justify why the saint finally agrees, no matter how reluctantly, to take on the cares of others in the world, even becoming an abbot and a priest. Thus, he presents the opposing view:

iz geschichit dicke beide,
daz man den gotis schalc lobit
vñ her doch gotis hulde behabet. (lines 164–166)


(Both things frequently happen,
that a servant of God is praised
and he still retains God's favor.)

Here the author indicates the fundamental motivation behind the writing of hagiographic literature: to praise holy men and women by drawing a clear contrast between their lives and those of others.

*Albanus,* the Middle High German legend of Saint Alban, survives in two fragments totaling 119 lines and was probably written about 1180. The full Latin version of the legend reveals that Alban is the result of the incestuous union of an emperor and his daughter. Alban is abandoned after birth and found by the king of Hungary. He is raised as heir to the

throne of that country and subsequently married to the emperor's daughter – his own mother. When the second incest is discovered, Alban kills his father and mother, does penance for all the sin in his life, and withdraws into seclusion. He is murdered, and after his death his corpse shows all the customary proofs of holiness. Alban is a "holy sinner," a type much better known from Hartmann von Aue's *Gregorius* (circa 1187). The first fragment of the Middle High German work tells of the discovery of the infant Alban in Hungary, his rise to prominence, and his marriage to his mother. As a young man Alban already reflects the praiseworthy attributes of a hero, religious or not:

inde als er sine kintliche dage hatte uvergangen,
du begunder harde mannen,
du begunde man in van dugenden inde van eren
  uver al dad riche mæren
so dad in minneden grozliche
alle die waren inme riche. (lines 43–48)


(and as he outgrew his childhood days
he then truly grew to be a man;
then they began to make known concerning
  him his virtues and honors
throughout the whole realm,
so that he was greatly loved
by everyone in the kingdom.)

The second fragment begins with a meeting of the emperor, his daughter, and Alban after they have discovered the second incest. The young man, altogether praiseworthy in the world's eyes, must bear the consequences of the sins of others and of his own sin. He becomes a saint of God by overcoming adversity and ill fortune and, turning his back on the life of the world, achieves a state of holiness through penance. The greatest worldly honors are made meaningless by spiritual concerns.

A priest named Arnolt composed his *Juliana* around 1150. Like Saint George, Juliana is a saint who withstands torture. The daughter of a non-Christian king, Juliana is pressed into marriage to another non-Christian ruler, Count Aulesius. Juliana refuses to marry Aulesius unless he sincerely converts to the Christian faith. Her father, furious, has her whipped and sent to Aulesius's court. There, refusing to change her stance, she is beaten with rods, hung by her hair, and bound so that blood spurts from her fingertips. Pitch is poured on her, but an angel protects her from burning. She is thrown into prison, where the Devil awaits her. Stronger than the power of hell, she withstands the

Devil's challenges not only verbally but also physically:

> si wart so chuone,
> vieng in pi den lochen,
> si pegunde in vast druchen,
> si warf in uf die erde,
> . . . . . . . . . . . . . . . .
> si chniete im uf die pruste,
> si pant in vil faste. (lines 23, 4–7; 24, 1–2)

> (She grew so bold
> she caught him by his locks,
> she began to oppress him grievously,
> she threw him to the ground
> . . . . . . . . . . . . . . . . . . . . . .
> she knelt on his chest,
> she tied him up quite securely.)

The relative weakness of the Devil and of the pagan gods of Juliana's father and fiancé as compared to God is a recurring theme in *Juliana;* when the saint is first threatened, she denounces her father's god and declares her love for God alone:

> den ich zu lieb wil haben,
> daz ist der lebendige got,
> der din ist pos und ein getroch.
> der got Appollo
> der lit in der helle
> und mag niemen scade gesin,
> sin verhenge den der min. (lines 6, 12–18)

> (He whom I wish to have as a lover
> is the living God,
> yours is wicked and a deception.
> The god Apollo
> lies in hell
> and can be of harm to no one,
> unless mine permits him to be.)

Juliana is brought from prison and broken on the wheel, but an angel mends her bones. She is then plunged into molten lead, which feels like cool dew to her. In a rage Aulesius finally has Juliana beheaded, ending her travails. As just retribution, Aulesius is later drowned at sea; his body is cast up on shore and eaten by animals. Juliana is a saint who, empowered by God, is mightier than any torment found in the world. Once again, the power of the saint to be a true and fearless hero for God is at the center of the story. In her struggle with the Devil, Juliana is described as *chuone* (bold), a word frequently encountered in Middle High German literature in descriptions of male warriors.

Another holy woman who gains salvation for herself and others by her long suffering is Crescentia.

The story is best preserved in the *Kaiserchronik* (Emperor Chronicle, circa 1147; lines 11352–12812); but it also existed independently, as evidenced by three manuscripts. Crescentia, the daughter of an African king, is sought after as a wife by two princes of Rome, twin brothers who are both named Dietrich but nicknamed "sconer (Handsome) Dietrich" and "ungetaner (Ugly) Dietrich." Crescentia chooses the latter; by a previous agreement, this choice makes him the sole king of the land. Ugly Dietrich goes on a journey, leaving Crescentia in the care of his brother, who promptly attempts to seduce her. The clever Crescentia convinces him that he should build a tower where they can carry out their tryst; then she tricks him inside and locks him in. When her husband returns, his brother, with the support of false witnesses, accuses her of unfaithfulness. Ugly Dietrich condemns her and has her thrown into the Tiber. Crescentia does not drown but is rescued by a fisherman. In time she comes to the attention of the local duke, and her innate goodness and superiority cause her to rise to prominence at his court. A wicked knight seeks her attentions, is rejected, and plans her undoing. At night he cuts off the head of the duke's infant son and places it in the lap of the sleeping Crescentia. In the morning she is condemned for the murder, and the duke throws her into the sea; he and the wicked knight are thereupon stricken with leprosy. Up to this point Crescentia's story has appeared not to fit a hagiographic mold, lacking any mention of God's working or of Crescentia's piety. But now Crescentia identifies herself as a "wretched woman" who suffers unjustly and who trusts in Christ's grace and power:

> nû bin ich ain ellendez wîp,
> verworht hân ich den mînen lip.
> ich hân daz wol besuochet,
> daz mîn got niene ruochet
> von diu nevurhte ich den tôt,
> want ich âne sculde in dize nôt
> chomen bin in allen gâhen.
> welt ir mich haizen hâhen,
> in daz wazzer werfen,
>
> des nemach mir niemen gehelfen,
> iz enwelle bedenchen der hailige Crist,
> der aller witwen vogit ist. (lines 12289–12300)

> (Now I am a wretched woman,
> I have cursed myself.
> I have well deserved it,
> that God in no way helps me.
> Therefore I do not fear death,
> for I have come in all speed

into this difficulty without guilt.
If you wish to have me hanged,
or thrown into the water,

no one can help me there,
unless holy Christ
would consider it.)

She is saved once more from drowning by a fisherman: Saint Peter, who grants her the power to heal those who confess their sins – particularly, it seems, their sins against her. She returns to the duke's castle, hears his confession, and heals him; she also heals the wicked knight, humbly acknowledging the source of her ability:

ich pin ze ainer suntærîn gezalt,
doch hân ich von mînem trehtîn den
    gewalt. . . . (lines 12587–12588)

( I am counted as a sinful woman,
yet from my Lord I have this power . . . .)

The duke takes Crescentia back to Rome, where both Dietrichs have been stricken with leprosy. The brothers confess their sins and are healed. Crescentia convinces the king to give up his kingdom and retire to the monastic life, then does so herself. At death she achieves the status of sainthood, praying:

nû heven wir ûf die hende
unt piten si, daz si unser niht vergezzen,
wande si daz himelrîche hânt besezzen. (lines 12806–
    12808)

(Let us raise up our hands
and pray them that they not forget us,
for they have possessed the kingdom of Heaven.)

Crescentia is called away from a secular life, because of undeserved punishment, to the justice of God; the audience is invited to consider where true justice lies.

In the legend of Anno one's eternal fate is shown to be more important than the heroic glory that was central in the tales of the ancients. Anno is a holy man who influences the affairs of the world without being corrupted by this activity and, thus, acts as a servant of God in the salvation of humanity; in the legends that come after the *Annolied* the conflict between holy living and worldly life is sharper. Alexius, Alban, and Crescentia are exceptional young people who are fully capable of gaining high status in the world but who, by choice or misfortune, are led to a Godly existence. By her ability to accept physical pain, Juliana shows the superiority of the Christian faith over the cults of the gods of antiquity. Though Aegidius prefers isolation from the world, he is forced by the demands of those in need to take a more-active role, and the author argues that such involvement is possible without loss of divine favor. All of these saints' legends praise the rejection of secular norms and look to their replacement by a more systematic Christian worldview, with heroes to match the new outlook.

Several legends of the twelfth century demonstrate the triumph of Christianity over Roman paganism or Judaism by intellectual rather than miraculous means. God's working in history through the intellectual superiority of one of his saints is the central focus of the *Trierer Silvester* (after 1150). This legend exists in fragmentary form as an independent work but has as its source lines 7806 through 10,400 of the *Kaiserchronik*. In the *Kaiserchronik* Sylvester, pope under Emperor Constantine, plays a pivotal role – the episode is in the middle of the chronicle – because it is the pope's steadfast defense of the Christian faith that leads Constantine, and with him the Roman Empire, to adopt the new religion. The Trier version begins, after a prologue, with Constantine ill in Rome. A Jewish doctor advises him to have all children two years old and under killed and to bathe in their blood. Constantine begins the preparations for this monstrous act but then selflessly rejects the plan and is rewarded by God:

"bezzer ist, daz ich eine irsterbe,
dan durch mich uirwerde
alsus manic kindelin. . . ."
. . . . . . . . . . . . . . . . . . . .
des uroweten sich werliche
die engele in hiemilriche,
daz der heidene man
so guten willen ie gewan.
iz ne wart geuristet nicht langir;
sine gnade ime got sante. (lines 98–100, 120–125)

("It's better that I, one man, die,
than that for my sake
so many little children perish. . . .")
. . . . . . . . . . . . . . . . . . . . . . . .
Truly did rejoice
the angels in heaven
that the unbelieving man
ever gained such good will.
It was not delayed any longer;
God sent him his grace.)

In a dream Saints Peter and Paul tell Constantine to find Pope Sylvester and be healed. Constantine relates the dream to Sylvester, who explains the Christian faith to the emperor. Constantine believes, is baptized, and is healed. Thus converted, the emperor has the statues of the Roman gods removed. An argument is made for the primacy of Rome among Christian churches, and a Christian conception of knighthood is advanced. In this episode the basic institutions of the Christian Middle Ages – a Christian Roman Empire, a Roman papacy, and the ideal of the Christian warrior – are given "historical" grounding and justification. The *Trierer Silvester* is an apologetic work; its saint-hero does not work miracles but converts unbelievers by his words; the miraculous healing of the emperor follows, rather than precedes, Sylvester's instruction. The *Trierer Silvester* shares with *Juliana* an utter scorn for the useless and demonic gods of pagan Rome:

> e bette wir al gemeine
> an holz vnde an steine:
> daz was des tuuiles getroc. (lines 417–419)

(Previously we prayed all in common
to wood and stone;
that was the Devil's deception.)

The *Trierer Silvester* breaks off in the middle of the saint's defense of Christianity against both pagan Roman religion and Judaism. The *Kaiserchronik* goes on to describe how the non-Christian learned men are confounded and how Constantine's mother, Helena, is converted. Sylvester fights God's battles in the intellectual arena, armed with the truth. The prologue to the *Trierer Silvester* makes clear that teaching the truth is a central purpose of the work:

> gnvge ir denkint in lvgene
> vnde uugent die ze samene
> mit schoflichen worten.
> ich uorchte uil harte,
> daz die sele drumme muze brinnen.
> iz ist al wider gotis minne.
> vnde lerit man die lugene die kint
> die nach in kunftic sint,
> die wollent sie also behaben
> vnde wollint sie uur war sagen. (lines 19–28)

(Plenty of them believe
in lies and combine them
with pretty words.
I fear very much
that souls will burn over this.
It is all against the love of God.
And should they teach the lies to their children
who come after them,
these will possess them

*Saint Veronica and her cloth as depicted in a panel from the fifteenth-century triptych* The Adoration of the Magi, *by Hans Memlinc (Hôpital Saint Jean, Bruges)*

and will pass them on as true.)

A similar purpose – to discredit the religions that preceded Christianity – pervades two legends written around 1180 by the so-called Wilder Mann (Wild Man): *Veronica* and *Vespasian*. *Veronica* is actually a life of Christ, of which the Veronica episode makes up a small part (sections 5 through 9). Veronica asks Saint Luke to draw her a picture of

Jesus on a cloth that she has. His attempts fail utterly, but Jesus, knowing of Veronica's goodness, visits her and wipes his face on the cloth, leaving a permanent image. In *Vespasian,* the old Roman emperor of that name is stricken ill. A Jewish man tells him of Jesus' healing of the sick. Vespasian sends his son, Titus, to Palestine to bring Jesus to Rome, but Jesus has been crucified by the time Titus arrives. Titus finds Veronica and her cloth and brings them to Rome, where application of the cloth heals Vespasian. The story then takes an anti-Jewish turn as Vespasian and Titus go to Palestine with a large army and conquer and raze Jerusalem as revenge for Christ's death. To praise this brutal triumph of Christianity over Judaism appears to be the Wilder Mann's purpose in writing *Vespasian:*

> "alse der kunic von der megede wirt geborn,
> so ist alli judisc riche virlorn"
> des vunden si urkunde gnuch,
> bisehin si di aldin buch,
> so solden si si wol birihten
> dat ich di warheit dihten. (lines 10, 1–6)

("When the king is born of the virgin,
then will all the Jewish kingdom be lost."
They would find enough documentation of that,
if they examine the old books.
Thus they would easily report
that I compose the truth.)

In *Vespasian* and *Veronica* the central figures are not saints; God's power is exercised by the miraculous cloth and by Roman legions, and Vespasian does not convert to Christianity. The Christian faith's superiority over the pre-Christian Roman religion and over Judaism informs all of the medieval German hagiographic writings, but in the *Trierer Silvester* and in the works of the Wilder Mann it is of greater importance than the figure of any particular holy man or woman.

The *Rolandslied* (Song of Roland) of Pfaffe Konrad, probably composed around 1172, can also be classed as a saint's life, because Charlemagne and Roland assume in it roles customarily found in writings about the saints in this period. An angel informs Charlemagne that he was chosen while in the womb to be God's servant. Charlemagne was officially declared a saint in 1165 by the Cologne archbishop Rainald of Dassel, and in the prologue Konrad celebrates him as such because of his military victories over non-Christians. The poem, Konrad says, is

> uon eineme turlichem man,
> wie er daz gotes riche gewan:

> daz ist Karl der cheiser.
> vor gote ist er,
> want er mit gote uber want
> uil manige heideniske lant. . . . (lines 9–14)

(about a splendid man,
how he gained the kingdom of God:
that is, the emperor Charles.
He is in God's presence
because, with God, he overcame
a great many heathen lands. . . .)

For Konrad, Charlemagne's battles in Spain against the Muslim Moors are not merely political; they are a war between God's forces and the forces of the Devil. Charlemagne has God's approval for his campaign in Spain, for an angel tells him:

> Karl, gotes dinist man,
> ile in Yspaniam!
> got hat dich irhoret,
> daz lút wirdit bekeret;
> di dír abir widir sint.
> die heizent des tuvelis kint
> unt sint allesamt uirlorin:
> die slehet der gotes zorn
> an libe unt an sele. (lines 55–63)

(Charles, God's vassal,
hurry to Spain!
God has heard you,
the people will be converted.
Those who oppose you, however,
they are called children of the Devil
and are altogether lost:
God's wrath will strike them down,
body and soul.)

In this spiritual warfare against the Devil's children, there is a martyr: Charlemagne's beloved nephew Roland. This loss is as grievous to Charlemagne as the loss of his own life would be. Konrad depicts Roland's death in language usually associated with a martyred saint; after Roland has prayed for Charlemagne and his people,

> dem alwaltigen herren
> dem beualch er sine sele. . . .
> . . . . . . . . . . . . . . . . . . . . . . .
> Do Rolant uon der werlt verschît;
> uon himil wart ain michel liecht.
> sa nach der wile
> chom ain michel ertpibe,
> doner unt himilzaichen. (lines 6918–6919; 6924–6928)

(To the Almighty Lord
he commended his soul. . . .
. . . . . . . . . . . . . . . . . . . . . . .
Then Roland departed the world;

there was a great light from heaven.
Right after that
there was a great earthquake,
thunder and signs in the sky.)

Charlemagne and Roland are secular military heroes; they do not reject earthly life but employ their prowess for the cause of the Christian religion. Thus Konrad's heroes closely resemble, in many respects, the saints of other twelfth-century legends, and the *Rolandslied* has not only thematic but also ideological similarity to such works.

Toward the end of the twelfth century several legends of considerably greater length appeared: *Ulrich*, by Albert of Augsburg (1,605 lines); *Sente Servas*, by Heinrich von Veldeke (6,206 lines); and another treatment of that saint by an anonymous writer, the incomplete *Oberdeutsche Servatiuslegende* (3,548 lines). Unlike the earlier legends, which deal only with selected episodes in the saints' lives, these works purport to cover the saint's entire career, from birth to death and beyond. The representation of saints in the late twelfth century parallels developments in the genre of the romance: artistry and a fuller treatment of the character of the saint replace simple propaganda for the saint's cult. Of the three longer saint's lives, *Ulrich* remains the furthest from the romance; Veldeke's *Sente Servas* legend approaches that form more closely, the *Oberdeutsche Servatiuslegende* even more so.

Though the purity of its rhyme shows a proximity to courtly literature, Albert of Augsburg's *Ulrich* does not compare favorably to the Servatius legends in narrative technique. It is a straightforward reworking of a Latin life of Saint Ulrich of Augsburg, who in 993 became the first officially canonized saint of the Roman church. Ulrich, typically, is set apart for God's service from childhood:

in den kintlichen tagen
vil mêzlichen begonder sich betragen.
Gotes uorhte liebeter sere,
den vriunden irbot er ere.
getelosicheit er virmeit;
als vil er mohte uor siner kintheit
vzen zeiget er an den geberden wol
wes sin herze was innen vol (lines 145–152)

(In his childhood days,
he started the habit of eating very moderately.
He very much loved the fear of God,
he paid honor to his relatives.
He avoided lack of restraint.

As much as possible, being a child,
he clearly showed on the outside by his actions
what his heart was full of on the inside.)

After instruction at Saint Gall, Ulrich becomes bishop of Augsburg. Much of the narrative concerns the proper behavior of bishops, priests, and Christians in general as preached and exhibited by Ulrich, and most of the miracles in the legend are visions of deceased holy men and women. A high point of Ulrich's career as bishop is reached when Augsburg is besieged by the Huns; after Ulrich leads a procession inside the city walls, Augsburg is miraculously rescued by the emperor Otto the Great. Ulrich's procession is compared to that of Joshua, the Israelite general:

Iosue hiez die ewarten
an deme tragenne harten
die arcken mit busunen schellen
daz lut mit schrienne hellen. . . .
. . . . . . . . . . . . . . . . . . . . . . . . . . . .
Als truc sente Vlrich gotes arck
in deme herzen reine. (lines 947–950; 952–953)

(Joshua ordered the priests
to do the hard work
of bearing the Ark while accompanying it with trumpet
    blasts;
the people [he ordered] to yell loudly. . . .
. . . . . . . . . . . . . . . . . . . . . . . . . . . . . . . . .
Thus did Saint Ulrich bear God's ark
in his pure heart.)

Ulrich's heart is full of an inward holiness that corresponds to the Ark of the Covenant, an outward sign of God's holy presence. Later, when Ulrich walks across a body of water without getting wet, his actions are again placed in an Old Testament military context: that of God leading the Hebrew people through the Red Sea. After his death Ulrich metes out punishments from Heaven on those who fail to observe his feast day and performs acts of mercy and healing. Unlike earlier saints' lives, *Ulrich* does not attempt to show the superiority of its saint over the heroes of classical legend; rather, Ulrich is compared to Old Testament events. In this way Ulrich's active role as a servant of God is emphasized.

*Sente Servas* and the *Oberdeutsche Servatiuslegende* tell the story of the fourth-century bishop Servatius. Born in Asia Minor, Servatius manifests holiness as a youth and is called to be bishop of the city of Tongeren in Belgian Limburg. He rules there laudably, but the citizens expel him. He is later received at Maastricht, where, after a long career and a journey to Rome to intercede for his people, he dies and is buried. Following his death Servatius miraculously answers many prayers.

Both Servatius legends are translated from Latin sources: Veldeke's is a fairly faithful rendering of the *Vita Sancti Servatii* (Life of Saint Servatius), and the *Oberdeutsche Servatiuslegende* is a close translation of the *Gesta S. Servatii* (Deeds of Saint Servatius). The two versions differ not only because of their different sources but also because the authors allow their own interests to influence their writing. Veldeke's keenness for the propagation of the Servatius cult is not shared by his Upper German counterpart, who downplays some of the legend's stronger claims for the saint. Veldeke feels a personal attachment to Servatius, and he makes the clearest statement yet seen of an author's participation in the cult of a saint:

in dutschen dichte di Henric
de van Veldeken was geboren:
he hadde sente Servase erkoren
te patrone ende te heren.
des makede'r heme dit te eren. (lines 6172–6176)

(This was composed in German by Heinrich,
who was born van Veldeke;
he had chosen Saint Servas
for his patron and his lord.
Therefore, he did this to honor him.)

The Upper German writer, who claims no connection to the Servatius cult, adorns his translation with descriptive passages and expressive language. When Servatius is consecrated bishop in Tongeren he wears a marvelous breastplate. The *Gesta* remarks only that the breastplate resembles one worn by Aaron, brother of Moses and high priest of Israel, as told in the book of Exodus. In the *Oberdeutsche Servatiuslegende* the biblical text is the point of departure for an extravagant and lengthy description (lines 521–579) of the beauty of the breastplate's gems; no allegorizing or moralizing tendencies are present. The Upper German author exhibits this same tendency when writing military scenes. After Servatius's death Tongeren is besieged and destroyed by the Huns as divine punishment for having expelled the bishop. Veldeke, much more interested in the religious significance of his work, does not describe the siege in detail but tells of the Huns' swath of destruction in general terms. The Upper German poet, however, focuses on the siege at some length (lines 1756–1808), painting a vivid picture of the Huns' war machines, of their ferocity,

of the final fall of the city, and of the plight of its citizens, particularly the women:

Dehein aht was der flüste
die die burgære hêten tägljîch:
der frowen leben was chläglîch
die die tiefen wunden
ir lieben vriunden bunden,
unt si mit dem tôde sâhen teun
unt unzällichen niderstreun,
ir chint unt ir mâgen. (lines 1776–1783)

(No consideration was given to the losses
which the citizens suffered daily:
the life of the women was lamentable,
who bound the deep wounds
of their dear loved ones,
and saw wrestling with death
and lying about in countless numbers
their children and their kinsmen.)

A few episodes later Charlemagne makes one of his frequent appearances in Middle High German literature, battling an army of Saracens who have invaded his empire. The emperor is victorious after commending himself and his cause to God and to Servatius. Charlemagne later visits the Servatius Church in Maastricht, where he witnesses a miracle and becomes even more convinced of Servatius's efficacy as an intercessor in Heaven. The scenes of the battle against the Saracens have no direct source in the *Gesta;* once again, the Upper German poet's predilection for descriptive narration has come to the fore. The scene reminds some scholars of the depiction of warfare in the *Rolandslied*, others of that in the *Alexander* (circa 1150) of Pfaffe Lamprecht. In any case, the author is under the influence of literary works other than the typical legend:

wie die helm lûhten,
die berge rôt dûhten
von den goltvarwen schilten.
Diu zeichen ob in spilten,
diu in dem lufte fluzzen:
diu herhorn duzzen,
dâ die schar zesamne runnen. (lines 2031–2037)

(how the helmets glistened,
the hills appeared red
because of the gold-colored shields.
Above them fluttered the insignia,
which flew in the air:
the battle-horns sounded,
as the hosts charged each other.)

These lines, which convey some sense of the excitement and anticipation at the start of a battle, display the Upper German author's skills.

Veldeke elaborates on his source by placing enormous stress on Servatius as an intercessor before the throne of God. Servatius's ability to release souls from the consequences of sin results from the saint's journey to Rome to pray at Saint Peter's for his people. The chief Apostle himself appears to Servatius in a vision and presents him with a wondrous key, which symbolizes the power the saint will have after his death to unlock the gates of Heaven for those who ask. That Veldeke lifts this ability from its immediate context (salvation for the doomed citizens of Tongeren) and gives it seemingly absolute application can be seen in Servatius's explanation of his gift:

> alle di selve gewalt
> di sente Peter hevet van gode,
> di gaf mich der godes bode,
> dat ich bunde ende entbunde
> bit suliken urkunde
> alse ich et wale tounen mach. (lines 2738–2743)

> (All the same power
> which Saint Peter has from God,
> that God's apostle gave to me,
> that I may bind and unbind
> with such a sign of proof,
> as I can very well demonstrate.)

Regardless of the freedoms they allow themselves, both authors of Servatius legends remain focused on production of hagiographic works that will assist the propagation of the saint's cult. Like the *Annolied,* their works begin with a history of God's work in the world (though theirs are more limited in scope), which is followed by the events of the saint's earthly existence, accompanied by many proofs of holiness. Servatius's career has many stages; he is not only an excellent bishop but also a holy hermit, a pious pilgrim, a learned teacher, and a devout intercessor. The works end with a description of miraculous interventions and prayers that have been answered by the saint after death. In *Servatius* and the *Oberdeutsche Servatiuslegende* this section is the most substantial, making up more than the half total work, and continuing to emphasize Servatius's activity in combination with a prayerful and contemplative existence. With both quiet holiness and mighty miracles Servatius is God's champion, a defender and example of the faith.

The writings about the saints, from the Old High German quasi-liturgical *Petruslied* and *Georgslied* to the longer Middle High German legend-novels of the end of the twelfth century, provide their audiences with examples of holy lives for imitation and with extensive indoctrination in the Christian life. Like the heroes of secular tales, Anno and later saints lead ex-emplary lives; but, unlike the ancients, they also punish or reward and, thus, instruct all members of Christian society. Figures worthy of imitation, from an emperor such as Charlemagne to a simple poor woman such as Veronica, are offered for all. In Charlemagne one has a depiction of the ideal emperor; in Anno, Ulrich, and Servatius the ideal priest and bishop; in Aegidius the ideal hermit; in Juliana and George the ideal martyr; in Sylvester the ideal apologist and teacher; in Alban the ideal penitent; in Roland the ideal warrior; in Alexius the ideal mendicant; and in Crescentia's suffering an ideal of patience. The legends of the holy men and women, heroes in the struggle for the Kingdom of God, infused medieval German audiences of every status with the idealism inherent in the medieval concept of Christian society.

**References:**
Karl Bartsch, "Der Trierer Aegidius," *Germania,* 26 (1881): 1–57;

Gerhard Eis, *Beiträge zur mittelhochdeutschen Legende und Mystik* (Berlin: Ebering, 1935), pp. 256–303;

Theodor Frings and Gabrielle Schieb, eds., *Die epischen Werke des Henric van Veldeken,* volume 1: *Sente Servas: Sanctus Servatius* (Halle: Niemeyer, 1956);

Karl-Ernst Grith, ed., *Albert von Augsburg: Das Leben des Heiligen Ulrich* (Berlin: De Gruyter, 1971);

Carl Kraus, ed., "Der Trierer Silvester," in *Deutsche Chroniken und andere Geschichtsbücher des Mittelalters,* volume 1/2 (Berlin: Weidmann, 1895);

Friedrich Maurer, *Die religiösen Dichtungen des 11. und 12. Jahrhunderts,* volume 3 (Tübingen: Niemeyer, 1970), pp. 10–51, 532–549, 606–613, 616–619;

Eberhard Nellmann, ed., *Das Annolied* (Stuttgart: Reclam, 1975);

Siegfried Ringler, "Zur Gattung Legende: Versuch einer Strukturbestimmung der christlichen Heiligenlegende des Mittelalters," *Würzburger Prosastudien,* 2 (1975): 255–270;

Hellmut Rosenfeld, *Legende* (Stuttgart: Metzlersche Verlagsbuchhandlung, 1982);

Edward Schröder, ed., "Die Kaiserchronik," in *Deutsche Chroniken und andere Geschichtsbücher des Mittelalters,* 1/1 (Berlin: Weidman, 1964);

Rolf Schulmeister, *Ædificatio und imitatio: Studien zur internationalen Poetik der Legende* (Hamburg: Ludke, 1971);

James K. Walter, "The Upper German 'Life of St. Servatius': Text, Notes and Commentary," Ph.D. dissertation, University of Wisconsin–Madison, 1989;

Carl Wesle, ed., *Das Rolandslied des Pfaffen Konrad* (Tübingen: Niemeyer, 1985).

# The Illustration of Early German Literary Manuscripts, circa 1150 – circa 1300

Julia Walworth
*University of London Library*

**Manuscripts discussed:** Vienna, Österreichische Nationalbibliothek, Cod. 2721. Comprises *Genesis, Prose Physiologus,* and *Exodus.* Consists of 183 folios (130 x 205 mm), text in one column. Seven colored pen drawings at the beginning of the *Genesis,* thereafter spaces for illustrations left blank in both the *Genesis* and *Physiologus.* Originated in southern Bavaria or Austria in the last quarter of twelfth century;

Klagenfurt, Kärntner Landesarchive, Geschichtsverein für Kärnten, Ms. 6/19, known as the *Millstätter Handschrift.* Includes *Genesis, Physiologus, Exodus, Vom Rechte,* and *Die Hochzeit.* Consists of 167 folios (122 x 199 mm), text in one column. One hundred nineteen colored pen drawings, preceded by rubrics, integrated into the text column, illustrating the *Genesis* and *Physiologus.* Originated in southern Bavaria or Austria (Kärnten?) circa 1200;

Heidelberg, Universitätsbibliothek, Cod. Pal. Germ. 112. Comprises Pfaffe Konrad's *Rolandslied.* Consists of 123 folios (207 x 147 mm), text in one column. Thirty-nine pen drawings inserted, without frames, in spaces left in the text area. Originated in Bavaria, circa 1170;

Berlin, Staatsbibliothek Preußischer Kulturbesitz, Ms. germ. fol. 282. Comprises Heinrich von Veldeke's *Eneidt.* Consists of seventy-four folios (250 x 175 mm), text in three columns. Thirty-five folios (all originally in bifolios) of illustrations, with an additional full-page introductory illustration on folio 1r. The illustration folios, mostly in two registers, alternate with text folios and depict 136 scenes. Three folios of illustration and seven folios of text, as well as the whole final gathering, are now lost. Originated in Bavaria, circa 1220–1230;

Munich, Bayerische Staatsbibliothek, Cgm 51. Comprises Gottfried von Straßburg's *Tristan und Isolde* and Ulrich von Türheim's continuation, both texts in an abridged redaction. Consists of 109 folios (205-238 x 145-165 mm), text in two columns. Fifteen separate leaves of full-page pen-and-wash illustrations, arranged in horizontal registers and depicting more than 117 scenes, are interspersed throughout the text. Large zoomorphic initial G at beginning of text, most other initials (in gold with pen flourishes) positioned to form geometric patterns across openings. Several folios of text (and almost certainly of illustrations) are missing. Originated in south Germany (text may have originated in the eastern Allemanic region), mid thirteenth century;

Munich, Bayerische Staatsbibliothek, Cgm 19. Comprises Wolfram von Eschenbach's *Parzival, Titurel* (fragments), and two *Tagelieder.* Consists of 75 folios, text in three columns. A bifolium (folios 49r - 50v) of full-page illuminations depicting fourteen scenes from the final events of *Parzival* arranged in three horizontal registers is all that remains of what was probably an extensive sequence of illustrations tipped into the text. Colored initials in text positioned to form geometric patterns. Originated in south Germany (text may have originated in the eastern Allemanic region), mid thirteenth century;

Heidelberg, Universitätsbibliothek, Cod. pal. germ. 389. Comprises Thomasîn von Zerclære's *Der welsche Gast.* Consists of 226 folios (175 x 115 mm), text in one column. One hundred eight miniatures in the margins, orientation and size varying depending on the composition and subject. Originated in Bavaria or Austria, circa 1250–1260;

Munich, Bayerische Staatsbibliothek, Cgm 63. Comprises Rudolf von Ems's *Willehalm von Orlens.* Consists of 111 folios (151 x 210 mm), text in two columns. Opening author portrait

*Page from the Millstatt Genesis manuscript, with illustrations depicting the animals leaving the ark (top) and Noah offering a sacrifice to God (Klagenfurt, Kärntner Landesarchiv, Geschichtsverein für Kärnten, Ms. 6/19, fol. 22r)*

and twenty-seven full-page illuminations in two registers, depicting fifty-four scenes. Much of the paint has come away from the parchment, revealing underdrawings and, in some cases, written instructions to the artist. Gold initials mark the beginning of each book, with smaller initials at subdivisions. The last gathering and one internal folio (including, probably, an illumination) are missing. Originated in southwest Germany, late 1260s-1280?;

Munich, Bayerische Staatsbibliothek, Cgm 18. Comprises Wolfram von Eschenbach's *Parzival*. Consists of 107 folios, text in two columns. A single miniature, depicting two scenes, at the foot of folio 1v. Spaces left in the top and bottom margins of other folios indicate that perhaps 100 more miniatures were planned. Originated in Bavaria(?), 1270s;

Munich, Bayerische Staatsbibliothek, Cgm 8345. Comprises Rudolf von Ems's *Weltchronik*. Consists of 268 folios (225 x 155 mm), text in two columns. Single leaf illuminated on both sides added at the beginning of the manuscript. Folio 1r: full-page author portrait in opaque colors on gold ground; folio 1v: Genesis scenes in three registers, in opaque paint on colored grounds. Throughout the text, until folio 193r, sixty-five unframed pen-and-wash drawings in the lower and side margins. Originated in southwest Germany or the Upper Rhine, circa 1270-1280, folio 1 circa 1280-1290?;

Munich, Bayerische Staatsbibliothek, Cgm 6406. Comprises Rudolf von Ems's *Weltchronik*. Consists of 240 folios (320 x 200 mm), text in two columns. One hundred fifty-eight miniatures on gold ground, in space provided in the upper or lower half of the page. The format of the miniatures varies, from single scenes that extend the full width of the page, to 2/3 of the page, to smaller juxtaposed scenes, and occasional full-page illuminations. Originated in southern Bavaria or Austria (Vienna?), circa 1300;

Saint Gall, Stadtbibliothek und Bibliotheca Vadiana, Ms. 302 Vad. Comprises Rudolf von Ems's *Weltchronik* and Der Stricker's *Karl der Große*. Consists of 291 folios (305 x 210 mm), text in two columns. Fifty-eight miniatures on gold ground, mostly in double registers, some almost full-page. Twelve large filigree initials at divisions in the text. Originated in Zurich(?), shortly after 1300;

Heidelberg, Universitätsbibliothek, Cod. Pal. Germ. 848, known as the Codex Manesse or Große Heidelberger Liederhandschrift. Comprises 140 groups of texts of lyric poetry, arranged by author. Consists of 426 folios (355 x 250 mm), text in two columns. One hundred thirty-seven full-page illuminations (author portraits), ground left blank. Originated in Zurich, first third of the fourteenth century;

Munich, Bayerische Staatsbibliothek, Cgm 193/III, and Nuremberg, Germanisches Nationalmuseum, Graphische Sammlung Hz 1104–1105 Kapsel 1607. Comprises fragments of Wolfram von Eschenbach's *Willehalm*. Eleven fragments from ten leaves of a lost manuscript, recovered from bindings. Original size: 295–303 x 210–225 mm. Text in one column (always on the inner side), illustrations in outer margin, usually three scenes per page. Originated in Thuringia or Saxony, circa 1270;

Budapest, Széchényi-National Library, Cod. Germ. 92. Comprises fragments of an unfinished illustrated manuscript of lyric verse (recovered from a binding). One bifolio and a single leaf (215 x 155, and 215 x 140 mm), text in one column. Three full-page preparatory pen drawings: author portraits. Originated in Bavaria or Austria, circa 1300;

Frankfurt am Main, Stadt- und Universitätsbibliothek, Ms. Germ. oct. 13. Comprises Rudolf von Ems's *Weltchronik*. Fragment of a bifolio recovered from a binding, trimmed (original size approximately 280 x 200 mm), text in two columns. On folio 1v an unfinished double-register miniature (Jacob traveling to Egypt and Jacob's reunion with Joseph), compositionally close to the corresponding miniature in Saint Gall cod. 302. Text by one of the scribes of Saint Gall cod. 302. Originated in Zurich, circa 1300;

Heidelberg, Universitätsbibliothek, Cod. Pal. Germ. 164. Comprises fragments of Eike von Repgau's *Sachsenspiegel*. Consists of thirty folios (single leaves, 300 x 235 mm), text in one column. Colored pen drawings in the outer and bottom margin, usually four or five scenes per page. Originated in Upper Saxony(?), first quarter of the fourteenth century;

Berlin, Staatsbibliothek Preußischer Kulturbesitz, Ms. germ. fol. 623. Comprises fragments of Rudolf von Ems's *Weltchronik* and Der Stricker's *Karl der Große*. Consists of twenty-

*One of the Budapest Fragments (Budapest, Széchényi National Library, Cod. Germ. 92, fol. 3r)*

*Page from the Saint Gall manuscript for Der Stricker's Karl der Große. Roland is depicted receiving the crown and standard from Charlemagne and planting the standard in rock (Saint Gall, Stadtbibliothek und Bibliothek Vadiana, Cod. 302 Vad., fol. 26v).*

three-folios (single leaves, 270 x 185 mm), text in two columns. Twenty-three full-page miniatures on gold ground, some in double registers. Originated in Swabia(?), beginning of the fourteenth century;

Private collection: Wolfram von Eschenbach's *Willehalm*. Single leaf recovered from a binding (miniature measures 191 x 142 mm), text in two columns. Full-page miniature in two registers (extremely worn), probably depicting Rennewart carrying the tub of water and killing the mocking page. Originated in west central Germany, second half of the thirteenth century. (Sotheby's sale, London, 20 June 1989, lot 25);

Private collection: Rudolf von Ems's *Weltchronik*. Two single leaves, both trimmed (155 x 132 mm; 210 x 161 mm), with two double-register miniatures (Doeg before Saul, the killing of the priest; Joab and Abner meet, Joab stabs Abner). The miniatures are stylistically close to some of the miniatures in Saint Gall Vad. cod. 302 and are presumably from a closely related manuscript. Originated in Zurich, circa 1300. Fragments published by Dr. Jörn Günther in his *Mittelalterliche Handschriften und Miniaturen: Katalog und Retrospektive* (Hamburg: 1993).

The study of illustrated German literary manuscripts is an expanding field, since evidence of previously unknown illuminated works continues to come to light; nevertheless, the number of illustrated literary manuscripts remains small relative to the number of unillustrated ones from the same period. The illustrated works, however, display a variety of styles and approaches, are far from insignificant, and deserve close critical attention. They offer insights into the reception of well-known literary works as well as into the visual imagination and ideals of the aristocracy for which they were produced.

The earliest surviving German literary manuscript with illustrations – Vienna, Nationalbibliothek, cod. 2721, from the second half of the twelfth century – was left unfinished. There are seven pen drawings, five of which are full page, at the beginning of the *Genesis*, but spaces left by the scribe indicate that 115 additional illustrations were planned for the *Genesis* and the *Physiologus*. Some idea of what may have been intended can be gathered from the related Millstatt *Genesis* and *Physiologus*, in which 119 colored pen drawings are integrated into the text column. The pictures, depicting the succession of

biblical events described in the *Genesis* and the animals discussed in the *Physiologus*, respectively, are accompanied by descriptive rubrics and placed in close proximity to the appropriate text. A similar arrangement of text and image, though without rubrics, is found in the earliest surviving illustrated manuscript of the *Rolandslied* (Song of Roland, composed circa 1172) of Pfaffe Konrad. Evidence for the existence of additional illustrated manuscripts of this text (drawings of an illustrated *Rolandslied* that was destroyed in Strasbourg in 1870 and a lost fragment in which spaces were left for illustrations) suggest that the artist was working from an existing model.

The first illustrations of epic romances occur in manuscripts from the thirteenth century. Most of the "classic" works are represented, though usually by a single manuscript: Heinrich von Veldeke's *Eneit* (composed circa 1185), Gottfried von Straßburg's *Tristan und Isolde* (composed circa 1210), Wolfram von Eschenbach's *Parzival* (composed circa 1200–1210) and *Willehalm* (composed circa 1210–1220), and Rudolf von Ems's *Willehalm von Orlens* (composed circa 1235–1243). In the cases of *Eneit*, *Tristan und Isolde*, and *Willehalm von Orlens* the earliest surviving nearly complete manuscripts are those with illustrations. Unlike the twelfth-century manuscripts, most of the illustrated romances include lengthy and highly original picture cycles, arranged in two or three registers filling the whole page. In the earlier of the thirteenth-century works, *Eneit* and the Munich *Tristan und Isolde* and *Parzival* (Cgm 19), the illustrations are on separate folios or bifolios that were added to the completed text and almost form an additional – pictorial – version of the story.

The thirteenth century also saw the development of several illustration cycles that would be adapted in manuscripts during the next century: Thomasîn von Zerclære's *Der welsche Gast* (The Italian Guest, composed 1215–1216) and, later, Eike von Repgau's *Sachsenspiegel* (Saxon Mirror, composed 1220–1235), in the former of which the illustrations were probably part of the author's original concept. Similarly, two of the best-known and artistically most spectacular groups of illuminated codices produced at the beginning of the fourteenth century had their roots in the thirteenth: the luxury manuscripts of Rudolf von Ems's *Weltchronik* (Chronicle of the World, composed circa 1235–circa 1243) and the compilations of lyric poetry that culminated in the Manesse Codex or Große Heidelberger Liederhandschrift. The Budapest fragments provide evidence of a collection of lyric verse

*Page from the earliest surviving manuscript for Pfaffe Konrad's* Rolandslied, *with illustration showing Roland striking a heathen soldier with his war horn (Heidelberg, Universitätsbibliothek, Cod. Pal. Germ. 112, fol. 93v)*

*Facing pages from the Heidelberg manuscript for Thomasin von Zerclære's* Der welsche Gast, *in which the illustrations of the falconer's loss of his bird and the husband's loss of his wife complement and reinforce each other (Heidelberg, Universitätsbibliothek, Cod. Pal. Germ. 389, fols. 62v–63r)*

accompanied by full-page "author portraits" (courtly scenes), the basic arrangement found in the later, more ambitious manuscripts. The earliest surviving *Weltchronik* manuscript, Munich Cgm 8345, with many line drawings in the margins, also documents an early phase of a series of illustrated manuscripts. With their large format and extensive use of gold and expensive colors, the *Weltchronik* manuscripts from the period around 1300 match the artistic quality of any of the contemporary liturgical manuscripts. The linking of salvation history and imperial history, together with the ethos of Christian knighthood contributed by Der Stricker's epic *Karl der Große* (Charlemagne, composed 1217–1225), which accompanies the *Weltchronik* in two instances, gave these manuscripts a special status. These texts were undoubtedly deemed worthy of the great sums expended on the manuscripts.

When, where, and for whom the illustrated German literary manuscripts of the twelfth and thirteenth centuries were made are questions that have vexed scholars for generations. While the names of patrons are occasionally mentioned by poets in their works, the manuscripts themselves provide no explicit information about their places of production or the identities of their original owners. The contexts in which these manuscripts may have been made and used is, therefore, a matter of conjecture, based on evidence provided by dialect, script, and the style of the illustrations and other decoration. Unlike the illuminated prose romances from France and Italy, which from the second half of the thirteenth century were produced in relatively large numbers and which are attributable to several identifiable centers of production, illustrated German manuscripts do not constitute a unified continuous tradition of secular illustration. Certainly there does not seem to have been any one major center producing luxury literary manuscripts. For the majority of these works, localization and dating continue to be the subject of study and debate.

Even when several manuscripts can be linked in one way or another, the relationship is usually not straightforward, nor is the problem of localization solved. The two earliest illustrated German manuscripts, the Vienna and Millstatt *Genesis,* for instance, contain related groups of texts, and the illustrations follow by and large the same plan. The spaces left for illustrations in the Vienna manuscript correspond with the placement of the illustrations in the Millstatt manuscript. Although the script and artistic style indicate that the Vienna manuscript is the earlier of the two, it cannot be localized, other than generally to southern Bavaria, while the Millstatt drawings exhibit certain similarities with work from Salzburg. It is possible that the Vienna manuscript was among several sources used by the creators of the Millstatt manuscript, but it is also possible that both manuscripts have a common source in an earlier model.

A similarly puzzling picture emerges even when the texts of the illuminated manuscripts concerned are closely related. The principal scribe of the Munich *Parzival* (Cgm 19) was also responsible for writing most of the text of the Munich *Tristan und Isolde* and has been identified as the scribe of a fragment of another *Parzival* manuscript (Munich, Cgm 194/III) and fragments of *Willehalm von Orlens* (Salzburg, Saint Peter, a VI 56). Paleographic and dialect evidence suggests that these manuscripts were written by members of a chancery or court scriptorium in the eastern Alemannic/Bavarian region, but, although the Munich *Tristan* and *Parzival* are similarly constructed of separate text and illustration folios, the illustrations are in quite different styles, for neither of which can close parallels in other secular or liturgical works be found. Thus, the artistic evidence does not as yet contribute to a more precise localization of the manuscripts, and the identification of the patron and origin of the illustrations remains a problem.

By the end of the thirteenth century the greater number of surviving manuscripts facilitates the interpretation of evidence for localization. The scriptorium that appears to have organized the production of at least three *Weltchronik* manuscripts (Saint Gall, Stiftsbibliothek und Bibliotheca Vadiana, Ms. 302 Vad. and the closely related fragments in Frankfurt and in the Sotheby's sale) can, through one of the scribes, be localized to Zurich.

The evidence currently available suggests that southern Germany – taken in the broadest sense to include present-day southwest Germany, Switzerland, Swabia, Bavaria, and Austria – was the region in which most of the surviving early illustrated literary manuscripts were made. (The predominance of pen drawings in the early illustration of literary manuscripts could be explained by their being a less expensive alternative to color illumination and, therefore, perhaps appropriate for vernacular and secular texts, but also by their production in southern Germany, where this technique flourished, particularly in the twelfth century and in the first half of the thirteenth century.) Patrons might, therefore, have been found in the imperial Hohenstaufen or Hapsburg households; in the ducal courts of the region; at the episcopal courts of Strasbourg, Basel, or Constance; or

*Page from the Berlin manuscript for Heinrich von Veldeke's* Eneit, *with illustration showing Lavinia pondering her unexpected feelings for Aeneas (Berlin, Staatsbibliothek Preußischer Kulturbesitz, Ms. Germ. fol. 282, fol. 66v)*

among the higher *Ministerialen,* some of whom are known to have had literary interests.

Generally speaking, the text of a given manuscript is best understood as only one among several "sources" used by the artist or whoever was responsible for planning the decoration. The cycle of illustrations in the Millstatt *Genesis,* for instance, is related to Genesis illustrations devised hundreds of years earlier. In creating illustrations for secular texts artists often adapted pictorial formulas familiar from religious and secular art, but they also invented entirely new compositions inspired by the narratives they were illustrating. Although examples of secular imagery are relatively scarce, it is clear from manuscripts such as the Munich *Tristan und Isolde* or *Willehalm von Orlens,* or the Heidelberg *Der welsche Gast,* that a vast repertory of secular formulas existed by the mid thirteenth century. The "language" in which the pictorial story is told is often highly conventional; traditional conventions and the development of new conventions or formulas play a large role in aiding the artist to illustrate new subject matter and in enabling the viewer to understand significant actions. The need to communicate new ideas often generates new conventions, for example, the iconography of knighting or of courtly love.

The selection of scenes for illustration and the way they are depicted may reflect a particular understanding of the text. The simple line drawings that highlight certain places in the text in the Heidelberg *Rolandslied,* for instance, contain little detail and are often so general that the identification of the scenes depends on the nearby text; but when the work is viewed as a whole, the choice of scenes illustrated emphasizes the fight of the Christian soldiers against the heathens and the role of Archbishop Turpin.

In other cases, the type of episode or scene may have helped determine what was selected for illustration and how it was treated. Those episodes, such as scenes of single combat, that occur in several versions of a narrative or in several narratives, or which were derived from biblical narratives in the case of *Weltchronik* manuscripts, may have had a visual tradition of their own. Similarly, some types of scenes, such as ceremonies and battles, were almost certainly familiar to the artists from other contexts and provided ready-made images that could be inserted as needed to fit the requirements of the plot. At a more sophisticated level, familiar types could also be used pointedly to augment, or change, the significance of a scene in a particular context. The availability and popularity of such pictorial formulas may have influenced the choice of scenes to be illustrated, as well as their visual presentation.

In some instances pictorial and literary topoi intersect, lending additional significance to the text for the practiced viewer. The illustrations in *Der welsche Gast,* for example, are intended to clarify, augment, or exemplify didactic points made in the text. Images taken from other contexts, whether using sophisticated classical iconography or the imagery of courtly love, would often be especially appropriate for Thomasîn's task. On the opening of folios 62v and 63r the two separate illustrations, each exemplifying the pain of loss, complement and reinforce each other visually, for the falconer's loss of his bird and the husband's loss of his wife to another man bring to mind the literary metaphor equating woman (in the role of lover) and falcon.

The appearance in the thirteenth century of illustrated manuscripts of texts, such as epic romances, associated with the lay aristocracy, raises questions about changes in patterns of book ownership and usage among this social group. Throughout the thirteenth century most people would have known these texts through oral recitation, though some could probably read, and some undoubtedly wanted to possess and look at copies of the books themselves, whether they could read or not. One of the immediately striking features of the early illustrated epic romances *Eneit, Tristan und Isolde, Parzival,* and *Willehalm von Orlens* is the number of pages devoted solely to illustrations. Each of these manuscripts employs a different means of integrating the picture pages with the text. In the Berlin *Eneit* illustration and text are carefully coordinated, so that at almost every opening (except in the center of each gathering) the viewer is confronted with a picture page on one side and the roughly corresponding text on the other. Text and image are linked in another way by the inclusion in the illustrations of often lengthy speech scrolls, without which some of the images would be incomprehensible. The speech scrolls allow the figures depicted to express thoughts as well as speech, as on folio 66v, where Lavinia ponders her unexpected feelings for Aeneas. Either the illustrations or the text could be enjoyed on their own, but the *Eneit* manuscript would be most fully experienced by those who could follow both text and pictures.

The experience of the Munich *Tristan und Isolde,* on the other hand, could not easily have involved such a coordinated joint use of text and images. Here, as in the Berlin *Eneit,* separate picture pages have been added to the text, but the pictorial narrative is more autonomous; it is physically inter-

*Page from the Munich manuscript for Gottfried von Straßburg's* Tristan and Isolde, *showing Tristan cutting out the dragon's tongue; the steward attacking the dead dragon; and the steward returning with the dragon's head, planning to take credit for the kill (Munich, Bayerische, Staatsbibliothek, Cgm 51 fol. 67 r )*

Page from a manuscript fragment for Wolfram von Eschenbach's Willehalm with illustration showing Willehalm receiving the imperial banner, Rennewart taking leave of the king, and Rennewart with the queen and Alice (Munich, Bayerische Staatsbibliothek, Cgm 193/III, fol. 3r)

spersed with the written narrative but progresses at its own pace. Unlike the *Eneit* manuscript, which presents and dramatizes without full continuity a lengthy series of selected scenes from the story, the *Tristan und Isolde* illustrations are noteworthy for their attempts to depict movement through time and space and to link events. For a viewer acquainted with the Tristan story, the illustrations in the Munich manuscript present few problems of interpretation as far as the basic story line is concerned. The reader of the *Tristan und Isolde* (whether reading aloud in a small group or privately) would arrive from time to time at picture pages that might recapitulate what had already occurred or summarize what was about to come; the flow of the written narrative is, thus, constantly interrupted by the flow of the pictorial narrative. In practice either the text or the images might have been the main method of communication of the story; and in contrast to many illustrated manuscripts the *Tristan und Isolde,* by the nature of its illustrations, accomodates the nonreader almost as well as the reader.

The surviving illuminated bifolium from the Munich *Parzival* (Cgm 19) does not reveal how the illustrated leaves would have been incorporated into the manuscript, assuming that a complete or even somewhat abridged pictorial cycle was originally planned. The use of a separate bifolium for the illustration, however, clearly links this manuscript in concept with the *Tristan und Isolde* and *Eneit* manuscripts. Although the Munich *Willehalm von Orlens* manuscript, in which the illuminated leaves are integral with the text gatherings, differs in many respects from the *Eneit, Tristan und Isolde,* and *Parzival* manuscripts, one of the deciding factors in the placement of the illuminations was, again, even distribution throughout the text: there are, with few exceptions, two illuminated pages per gathering.

A completely different manifestation of interest in the linking of text and illustration is found in the fragments of the manuscript of Wolfram's *Willehalm* made in Thuringia: here, illustrations of selected scenes are placed side by side with the text they accompany. A further link between text and image is made by placing, in close proximity to the illustration, an initial corresponding to the initial at the beginning of the relevant section of the text. This technique is also used in the illustrations of the well-known legal text, the *Sachsenspiegel* of Eike von Repgau. Although the earliest surviving manuscript of the *Sachsenspiegel* postdates the *Willehalm,* it seems possible that the layout and other features of the *Willehalm* were influenced by an earlier illustrated version of the *Sachsenspiegel* that is no longer extant.

If this unusual *Willehalm* manuscript were complete and were illustrated in the same density as the surviving fragments, it would contain some thirteen hundred individual scenes – certainly one of the most ambitious German manuscripts!

Whether a manuscript was planned on a huge scale with a large picture cycle, like the *Willehalm,* or whether it was a more modest undertaking, such as the Heidelberg *Rolandslied,* the presence of illustrations in literary manuscripts is in itself a consequence of a culture in change: people who had previously listened to readings from books had begun to want to own and look at them. Signs of heavy wear and tear indicate that these manuscripts were considered not just luxury objects for show but were handled and perused by their medieval owners. While these manuscripts were probably not solely used for what today would be thought of as private reading, they do present the possibility of privately experiencing what was previously, or usually, a group experience. Similarly, while most other works of art were, by their nature, experienced in public or in small groups, solitary enjoyment of manuscript illuminations was perfectly possible. The early illustrated literary manuscripts of the twelfth and thirteenth centuries represent aural, visual, and social experiences made not only tangible but also, potentially, private. Private use was not the only function of illuminated literary manuscripts, however, because by 1300, at least, it is clear that some vernacular codices were intended for presentation and ostentatious display.

**Facsimiles:**

Gottfried von Straßburg, *Tristan und Isolde: Faksimile Ausgabe des Cgm 51 der Bayerischen Staatsbibliothek München,* edited by Ulrich Montag and Paul Gichtel (Stuttgart: Müller & Schindler, 1979);

Heinrich von Veldeke, *Eneas-Roman: Vollfaksimile des Ms. germ. fol. 282 der Staatsbibliothek zu Berlin Preußischer Kulturbesitz,* edited by Andreas Fingernagel and Nikolaus Henkel (Wiesbaden: Reichert, 1993);

Pfaffe Konrad, *Das Rolandslied des Pfaffen Konrad: Faksimile des Codex Palatinus Germanicus 112 der Universitätsbibliothek Heidelberg,* edited by Wilfried Werner and Heinz Zirnbauer, Facsimilia Heidelbergensia, no. 1 (Wiesbaden: Reichert, 1970);

Walter Koschorreck and Wilfried Werner, eds., *Faksimile Ausgabe Heidelberg Universitätsbibliothek Cod. Pal. Germ. 848* (Kassel, 1981);

Alfred Kracher, ed., *Millstätter Genesis und Physiologus Handschrift: Vollständige Faksimileausgabe der Sammelhandschrift 6/19 des Geschichtsvereins für*

*Kärnten im Kärntner Landesarchiv, Klagenfurt,* Codices selecti, no. 10 (Graz: Akademische Druck- und Verlagsanstalt, 1967);

Rudolf von Ems, *Weltchronik: Der Stricker, Karl der Große. Faksimile-Ausgabe der Handschrift 302 der Vadiana,* edited by Ellen J. Beer and others (Lucerne: Faksimile Verlag, 1987);

Thomasîn von Zerclære, *Der welsche Gast: Codex Palatinus Germanicus 389 der Universitätsbibliothek Heidelberg,* edited by Friedrich Neumann and Ewald Vetter, Facsimilia Heidelbergensia, no. 4 (Wiesbaden: Reichert, 1974);

*Die Weingartener Liederhandschrift,* edited by Wolfgang Irtenkauf and others (Stuttgart: Müller & Schindler, 1969);

Wolfram von Eschenbach, *Parzival, Titurel, Tagelieder: Cgm 19 der Bayerischen Staatsbibliothek München,* edited by Gerhard Augst and others (Stuttgart: Müller & Schindler, 1970);

Wolfram von Eschenbach, *Willehalm: Die Bruchstücke der Großen Bilderhandschrift: Bayerische Staatsbibliothek München Cgm 193, III, Germanisches Nationalmuseum Nürnberg, Graphische Sammlung Hz 1104-1105 Kapsel 1607,* edited by Ulrich Montag (Stuttgart: Müller & Schindler, 1985).

**Studies:**

Joachim Bumke, *"Epenhandschriften: Vorüberlegungen und Informationen zur Überlieferungsgeschichte der höfischen Epik im 12. und 13. Jahrhundert,"* in *Philologie als Kulturwissenschaft: Festschrift für Karl Stackmann zum 65. Geburtstag,* edited by Ludger Grenzmann and others (Göttingen: Vandenhoeck & Ruprecht, 1987), pp. 45-59;

Bumke, *Mäzene im Mittelalter* (Munich: Beck, 1979);

Michael Curschmann, "Hören-Lesen-Sehen: Buch und Schriftlichkeit im Selbstverständnis der volksprachlichen literarischen Kultur Deutschlands um 1200," *Beiträge zur Geschichte der deutschen Sprache und Literatur,* 106, no. 2 (1984): 218–257;

Curschmann, *"Pictura laicorum litteratura?:* Überlegungen zum Verhältnis von Bild und volkssprachlicher Schriftlichkeit im Hoch- und Spätmittelalter bis zum Codex Manesse," in *Pragmatische Schriftlichkeit im Mittelalter,* edited by Hagen Keller, Klaus Grubmüller, and Nikolaus Staubach (Munich: Fink, 1992), pp. 211-229;

Dorothea and Peter Diemer, "Zu den Bildern der Berliner Veldeke-Handschrift," *Münchner Jahrbuch der bildenden Kunst,* third series 43 (1992): 19-38;

Bettina Falkenberg, *Die Bilder der Münchener Tristan Handschrift,* Europäische Hochschulschriften, Reihe 28, no. 67 (Frankfurt am Main: P. Lang, 1986);

Hella Frühmorgen-Voss, *Text und Illustration im Mittelalter,* edited by Norbert H. Ott, Münchner Texte und Untersuchungen zur Deutschen Literatur des Mittelalters, no. 50 (Munich: Beck, 1975);

Reiner Hausherr and Christian Väterlein, eds., *Die Zeit der Staufer: Geschichte, Kunst, Kultur,* 4 volumes (Stuttgart: Württembergisches Landesmuseum, 1977);

Thomas Klein, "Ermittlung, Darstellung und Deutung von Verbreitungstypen in der Handschriftenüberlieferung mittelhochdeutscher Epik," in *Deutsche Handschriften 1100-1400,* edited by Volker Honemann and Nigel F. Palmer, Oxforder Kolloquium 1985 (Tübingen: Niemeyer, 1988), pp. 110-167;

Klein, "Die Parzivalhandschrift Cgm 19 und ihr Umkreis," in *Wolfram Studien XII: Probleme der Parzival-Philologie, Marburger Kolloquium 1990,* edited by Joachim Heinzle and others (Berlin: Schmidt, 1992), pp. 32-66;

Monika Lengelsen, "Bild und Wort: Die Federzeichnungen und ihr Verhältnis zum Text in der Handschrift P des deutschen Rolandsliedes," Ph.D. dissertation, University of Freiburg im Breisgau, 1972;

Elmar Mittler and Wilfried Werner, eds., *Codex Manesse: Katalog zur Ausstellung, Universitätsbibliothek Heidelberg* (Heidelberg: Braus, 1988);

Florentine Mütherich and Karl Dachs, eds., *Regensburger Buchmalerei: Von frühkarolingischer Zeit bis zum Ausgang des Mittelalters. Ausstellung der Bayerischen Staatsbibliothek München und der Museen der Stadt Regensburg* (Munich: Prestel, 1987);

Norbert H. Ott, "Typen der Weltchronik-Ikonographie," *Jahrbuch der Oswald von Wolkenstein Gesellschaft,* 1 (1980/1981): 29-34;

Nigel F. Palmer, *German Literary Culture in the Twelfth and Thirteenth Centuries: An Inaugural Lecture Delivered before the University of Oxford on 4 March 1993* (Oxford: Clarendon Press, 1993);

Palmer, "Von der Paläographie zur Literaturwissenschaft," *Beiträge zur Geschichte der deutschen Sprache und Literatur,* 113, no. 2 (1991): 212–250;

Karin Schneider, *Gotische Schriften in deutscher Sprache* (Wiesbaden: Reichert, 1987);

Julia Walworth, "The Illustrations of the Munich *Tristan* and *Willehalm von Orlens:* Bayerische Staatsbibliothek Cgm 51 and Cgm 63," Ph.D. dissertation, Yale University, 1991.

# German Literature and Culture from Charlemagne to the Early Courtly Period

Francis G. Gentry
*Pennsylvania State University*

Translated by Wayne K. Wilson

*Translated and revised from* Deutsche Literatur: Eine Sozialgeschichte, *volume 1, edited by Horst Albert Glaser (Reinbek: Rowohlt, 1988).*

## The Disintegration of the Roman Empire in the West

The disintegration of the Western Roman Empire in 476 had a greater influence on modern Europe than on the populations in Italy and Gaul that were immediately affected. The fall of the empire may have been a shock for many contemporaries, but whether they perceived the event as the end of their civilization – perhaps of their culture – is questionable. The reason is that, with few exceptions, conditions in the western part of the empire had been chaotic for quite some time. In 476 the Roman army was already Germanic, as can be seen, for example, in the large number of mercenaries (*foederati*) who were paid to fight for Rome. The refusal of the fifth-century mercenary soldier Odoacer, who had been declared king, to accept the title of emperor and his return of the imperial regalia to Byzantium is evidence of the "usurpatory" Germanic tribes' sense of justice as well as of their realistic assessment of the condition of the Western Roman Empire. The eastern part had become economically and politically superior to the western part long before the definitive collapse. In 476 the Roman Empire still had an emperor in Byzantium, whose influence on the affairs of the western empire was gradually diminishing; that influence virtually vanished with the coronation of Charlemagne as emperor in 800. A few centuries had to pass, nonetheless, before the West felt strong enough to free itself symbolically and politically from the authority of the Eastern Roman emperor.

Although there was no longer an emperor in the West, one institution survived that maintained the continuity with the past: the Christian Church. Its importance for European history of the Middle Ages cannot be overestimated. Political continuity was reestablished only on the basis of the Romano-Christian past when Charlemagne was crowned emperor.

## Papal and Secular Theories of Government

Since the decrees of the emperors Theodosius I and Valentinian II in 390 proclaiming Christianity the state religion of the Roman Empire, the pope in Rome exercised governing functions, although the Roman church itself was neither officially established nor proclaimed authoritative; that is, the church in Rome could make no claim to a higher position among the other Christian churches. The special position of the Roman church and of the papacy developed slowly but also quite systematically. Not until the fifth century was the papal doctrine of the special rights of the Roman bishop within the church proclaimed: the Leonic thesis, named for Leo I (pope from 440 to 461), grew out of the assumption that since Peter had suffered martyrdom in Rome, at the beginning of the Christian church a special symbolic relationship between the first pope and Rome had been formed. The biblical confirmation of this special function of the church can be found in the well-known passage in Matthew 16:18–19, where Christ raised Peter to be the head of his church and gave him the right to bind and loose. According to the church, Christ founded thereby not only a distinct *societas* but also gave it an appropriate form of government – a unique event in the history of states and governments. Leo based his thesis of papal authority on a forged letter of Pope Clement I to Saint James, a Greek document from the second century that was translated into Latin in the fifth century. In this letter Clement reports that Peter, before his death and in the presence of the Christian community of Rome, passed on his right of binding and loosing to Clement. It seemed obvious, therefore, that Clement's successors had the right to exercise the power that Christ gave exclusively to Peter, because Peter had publicly given it to Clement. To counter the objection that Christ gave this power to Peter alone because Peter had been the first to recognize Christ as God at Caesarea Philippi, Leo devised a new formulation of the papal office: he admitted that no successor of Peter deserved to share the merit of having been the first to recognize Christ as God; this honor is reserved for Peter. In this sense, every successor is an *indignus haeres beati Petri* (an unworthy heir of Saint Peter). Every new pope is, therefore, a direct successor of *Peter*, not of the pope's immediate predecessor. The merit of Peter is reserved for Peter alone, but his power is constantly passed on anew, through him, to each succeeding Roman bishop. By this means the authority residing in the papal office was separated from the person holding that office. As an unworthy heir to the first pope each new pope receives his power and authority from God, as did Saint Peter himself – not from other humans. The Church, that is, the entire Christian *societas*, is like a minor child that the pope rules for God. The pope, therefore, acted on his own authority; he was not responsible to anyone but God. Thus, one finds, as early as the fifth century, the basis of the papal theory of empire. At this point, however, the pope was too weak to transform this thesis into reality and legitimize it. It was only in the eleventh century that the Roman bishop was able to make these imperial claims and, for a time, to realize them.

The basis of the secular theory of empire can be found in the concept of the monarchy held by the Byzantine emperors. The Eastern Roman emperor, too, considered himself the representative of Christ on earth, chosen by God to rule. Only he was entitled to uphold the sacred beliefs of Christianity. He was priest as well as emperor and participated in important liturgical ceremonies. Only he was entitled to convene church councils; only he was entitled to legislate; and

when he did, the laws were given the attribute "holy." Christ was the "pantocrat" (ruler of all); the emperor was the autocrat, the "cosmocrat" (ruler of the created world), chosen by God himself to rule God's people and realm. From the vantage point of the pope, the weakness of the secular theory of the rule was that it was based in secular history, while the papal thesis found its validation in "true" – that is, divine – history, which must take precedence.

It was to be expected that the papal claims would find little resonance at the imperial court in Constantinople (today Istanbul, Turkey), and as long as the Eastern Roman Empire remained relatively strong the popes were not able to realize them effectively. The great turning point in the politics of the Roman church and in the history of western Christianity came during the papacy of Gregory the Great from 590 to 604. Gregory, who before his selection as pope was an ambassador to the imperial court in Constantinople, recognized that at that time it was impossible to transform the imperial form of government into a papal one. Gregory was farsighted enough to know that if the claims of the papacy were to have a chance to be realized, the pope had to attempt to spread his theories and gain acceptance for them in regions that were not under the hegemony of the eastern emperor. Those regions were in the West. For this reason Gregory sent his monks to Gaul and to England with the mission of proclaiming the papal imperial theory along with the gospel of Christ. The monks succeeded in awakening sympathy for the claims of the papacy, and it is at that point that the actual history of the European Latin West begins. Since the monks brought the Latin Bible with them, Latin became the leading scholarly language of Europe. At the same time, the papal theory of empire was reinforced; after all, Latin was also the language of Rome. Barely one and a half centuries later the papacy harvested the first fruits of these monastic efforts in the Frankish empire.

### From Odoacer to Charlemagne

In 493 Odoacer was murdered near Ravenna, either by Theodoric the Great himself or at his behest. Theodoric then ruled Italy until his death in 526. Although the Goths were Christians, they followed the Arian heresy while those they ruled confessed to orthodox Christianity. For this reason an assimilation of the two ethnic populations never came about. The future belonged to another Germanic tribe, the Franks. On

Christmas 497 or 498 the Frankish tribal chief Clovis of the Merovingian dynasty (named for its founder, Merovech, who died in 458), submitted to baptism, along with his people, as orthodox – that is, Roman – Christians. His orthodoxy made it possible for Clovis to assimilate the Gallo-Romans into his newly conquered regions and to found a united state; such an accomplishment was not possible for his Ostrogoth neighbor Theodoric, and after Theodoric's death the Goths would disappear as a power in Italy.

In accordance with Frankish custom, after Clovis's death in 511 his empire was divided among his sons. In spite of various attempts to reunite the empire, the power and reputation of the Merovingian dynasty steadily declined; a corresponding decline occurred in religious, moral, and cultural life. Only with the rise of the Carolingian mayors of the palace – beginning with Pépin I around 635, and continuing from 714 with his grandson Charles Martel – did the period of great expansion and prestige of the Frankish kingdom begin, a period that reached its high point in the reign of Charlemagne. By the middle of the eighth century the Merovingian monarchy had become powerless, and the mayor of the palace had long wielded the power of government. Charles Martel's son, Pépin III, sent a message to the pope asking whether he had the right to become king. Pope Zacharias replied that whoever exercises the actual power of government should also be the king. This response was cause enough for Pépin III to send the last Merovingian king, Childeric III, to a monastery and have himself anointed king by the pope. That act was the decisive step on the part of the papacy to free itself of the claims of supreme authority of the eastern emperor and to realize the papal theory of empire: later it would be assumed that the king only became king by being anointed by the pope and that, therefore, the king actually received his power from the pope. Pépin was certainly not aware of the fateful nature of his action, and it did not take long before the great conflict between pope and king threatened to tear apart the empire. But in the meantime, to lend this interpretation the appearance of legitimacy the pope could cite the so-called Donation of Constantine, which – mirabile dictu – appeared in Rome at about this time.

According to this document – which was dated in the fourth century but actually composed in the middle of the eighth century – shortly before moving to Constantinople the emperor Con-

stantine delivered to Pope Sylvester I all the insignia of the empire because he recognized the pope as the true head of Romano-Christian society; Constantine even wanted to put the imperial crown on Sylvester's head, but the pope declined. The symbols of empire, through this purported action by Constantine, thus became the property of the pope. And, as Constantine wore a crown in Constantinople, one had to assume that the pope had lent him papal property – that is, the crown. The pope, therefore, was the actual head of the empire, and the emperor only received his office from the pope. As long as the emperor obeyed the Roman church and protected it, he could remain Roman emperor. If he did not, he was just a Greek king. The eastern emperor was unable to counter this interpretation effectively because western Europe had long been Latin and, therefore, looked to Rome and not to Constantinople. With this forgery began a new period in the Latin West.

## Cultural and Literary Life before Charlemagne

In the Frankish empire of the sixth century a cultural life like the one that was to flourish under the Carolingians hardly existed. There were, it is true, men and women who produced literature (in the broadest sense of the word), but their number was small. For that reason the voices of the women of late antiquity and the early Merovingian period stand out in particular. In recent years many studies have revealed that the later development of European Middle Ages is inconceivable without the active involvement of these important women of the fourth to the sixth centuries.

In spite of Saint Paul's strict admonitions (for example, in 1 Timothy 2:11–12), several women of late antiquity succeeded in raising their voices in the praise of God. Even Saint Jerome (circa 345–420) recognized that the education of women had to be counted among the duties of a true teacher. According to Jerome, women – meaning, of course, women of the upper classes – had to receive such instruction from wise men. They needed to learn Latin and Greek early, so that their speech would not be corrupted by the vernacular and so that they could understand the word of God and the Psalms. In addition, they should become literate so that they could understand Holy Scripture and the writings of the fathers of the church. It should not be surprising, then, that the writings of women of this period that have survived are of an exemplary and didactic character. The travel account of the Spanish nun Egeria, who lived around the end of the fourth century and the beginning of the fifth, can serve as an example. Egeria's *Itinerarium* is, at first glance, a report of her pilgrimage to the Holy Land directed to her "sisters" (perhaps nuns at home in Galicia). Aside from the stylistic characteristics of her description, which show similarities to the later chanson de geste, the *Itinerarium* is remarkable for the confident, almost joyfully naive attitude of the writer. Egeria's reports are full of admiration of the holy places she visited. Again and again she stresses that the reality actually does agree with the descriptions she had read in the Bible. Her report is animated by curiosity and by the happiness she feels when her observations confirm her faith. The reader learns few personal details about Egeria from her account, and she reports only the joys of the trip, not its difficulties: she was not writing for posterity but for a circle of people with whom she was well acquainted, so she did not have to give information about herself; and her "sisters" would have been aware of the hardships of a pilgrimage from Spain to the Holy Land in the late fourth and early fifth centuries. Egeria's objective was not to keep a travel journal in which all sorts of remarkable and extraordinary details were recorded but to assure her readers that the image of the biblical home that they had gained from the Bible and other religious writings was correct. It is, nonetheless, possible to form an image of this pious pilgrim. One can picture Egeria as a woman of education, enterprise, and courage, a convinced and confident Christian who is happy to find confirmation of everything that she has held as true. Egeria awakens in later readers sympathy and admiration that are not lessened by the great temporal distance that separates her from them.

More than a span of time separates Egeria from Radegunda, the Germanic queen and founder of many monasteries and abbeys. Radegunda, a Thuringian princess, was taken prisoner in 529 by the Frankish king Chlotar I after his victory over her uncle, King Herminafrid, and shortly thereafter she was forced to marry her captor. Although Radegunda resisted the marriage from the beginning – Chlotar often complained he had obviously married a nun instead of a queen – she remained with the king until he had her brother murdered. After that she retreated to Sainte Croix, the convent she had founded near Poitiers, where she lived until her death. In her time Sainte Croix became one of the few centers of intellectual life in the Merovingian Frankish empire: kings and bishops came to Radegunda for advice and support; some of the most productive years of the poet Venantius Fortunatus were spent in her presence there. Few men among the Franks were interested in monastic life or scholarly learning; it was, above all, the women who embraced monastic life, and they did so for a practical reason: to escape the bloody power struggles that were the order of the day. Of course, not every woman who took the veil was filled with the same religious fervor as Radegunda, who was later canonized. Rebellions of nuns, even at Sainte Croix after Radegunda's death, are no rarity in contemporary reports (for example, in Gregory of Tours's *Historiarum libri X*, book 10, chapters 15–16). Nonetheless, Sainte Croix was a genuine institution of learning. Radegunda introduced the rule, devised by Saint Caesarius of Arles (circa 470–542), according to which it was mandatory for girls entering the convent to have had some previous education: they were supposed to be further educated at the convent, not to start their education there. While the others worked, one of the sisters would read to the girls; when they were not being read to, the girls were to think about the Scriptures. In convents such as Sainte Croix the noble ladies of the Merovingians were able to enjoy a standard of living commensurate with their place in society while serving God and retreating from the troubles of their times.

The writings that have been preserved from this time are in Latin, although it can be assumed that there was also a wealth of popular secular songs and heroic epics that were part of an oral tradition and not written down. Among the writers of the period was Radegunda's friend Venantius Fortunatus. Coming from upper Italy, Fortunatus studied rhetoric and grammar in Ravenna. In 565 he hiked over the Alps to make a pilgrimage to the grave of Saint Martin in Tours, where he sought healing for his sight (accounts say that he was in fact healed). Thereafter he went from one Merovingian court to another, where he was always well received. To show his gratitude for the friendly treatment, he composed poems in honor of the various kings until he made the acquaintance of Radegunda. He remained in the service of the abbey for several years; from his time there come many occasional poems, poems written in the name of Radegunda, lives of saints, hymns, and satiric verse. Some of his works show great poetic gifts, among them his *Martinsvita* (Life of Saint Martin) and two hymns that quickly gained entrance into the liturgy, the passion hymn *Pange, lingua, gloriosi* and the processional hymn *Vexilla regis prodeunt*. After his being named bishop of Poitiers around 600 he apparently ceased writing. Nevertheless, his poetic fame lived on, first with the Anglo-Saxons, through whom it reached the Frankish empire of the Carolingians, where Fortunatus became the model for Carolingian authors.

The second great literary personality of the sixth century was Gregory, who came from a well-respected Gallo-Roman family, became bishop of Tours in 573, and remained at that post until his death in 594. In his ambitious work *Historiarum libri X* (History in Ten Books) he paints in rather glaring colors the raw and barbaric conditions that characterized the Merovingian empire; thanks to Gregory posterity possesses generally reliable information regarding the early days of the Merovingian dynasty. His history treats a succession of kings, queens, concubines, pious men and women, bishops, and abbesses, as well as lesser-known people, against the background of an age of change in which the basis of the later Germanic and Roman society of the Middle Ages was created. His history reads much like a modern novel; it is filled with intrigues, murders, bloody revenge, and such. Nonetheless, the reader cannot overlook the quiet humor, sincerity, and zeal of the author. Above all, Gregory wants to report the truth about his time. In his preface he gives his reason for undertaking this task: "As the cultivation of the arts is in a state of decline, possibly even of collapse, no grammarian experienced in the art of rhetoric can be found to portray in prose or in verse what has transpired among us, and yet much has in fact happened. . . . Some have complained and said: 'It is a pity that in our days the cultivation of learning has declined to such an extent, and there is no one of us to write down what has happened in these times.' When I considered that such things are often said, I could not help but try to bring to light both as a commemoration of the past and for the information of future generations even the struggles of the dastardly and the life of the righteous."

Gregory is exaggerating the extent of the decline of learning; in any case, he especially regrets the lack of educated grammarians who would be capable of writing correctly, that is, in the classical style and without errors. He also notes that his contemporaries are not capable of understanding philosophizing orators but only understand the speech of the simple man. Therefore, untalented though he is (he can only express himself, he says, in simple and unadorned speech), he must

write his history not only for contemporaries but, above all, for those who will come after. In the first two books he briefly presents the history of the world from the Creation to the death of Clovis. The nearer he comes to his own time in the last eight books, the more extensively he describes historical events and personalities as well as all sorts of miraculous occurrences. The history ends with the year 591. In the last paragraphs he names himself and his writings and implores his unknown successors not to destroy his work. They could perhaps rewrite it in verse form, he says, but otherwise the work should remain intact. Whether Gregory's report on his age is historically reliable or not, it presents a lively picture of his society and its customs without which an understanding and appreciation of the Carolingians would not be possible.

### The Anglo-Saxons

The cultural neglect about which Gregory complained was not to be found everywhere. In 597 Saint Augustine (not to be confused with the church father and bishop of Hippo, who died in 430) and some companions landed in England. After initial difficulties Augustine, who became the first archbishop of Canterbury in 601, and his successors spread the Christian religion among the population. The uninterrupted history of the English church up to the Reformation of the sixteenth century begins with the synod of Whitby in 663, where the primacy of the Roman over the Celtic church was established. The next centuries brought a flourishing of scholarly and literary activity the like of which one seeks in vain on the Continent. Above all, these centuries are noteworthy for the production of literature in the vernacular. In addition to the epic *Beowulf* (circa 700), the period brought forth countless primarily religious compositions: biblical epics, lives of saints, allegorical and didactic poetry, chronicles, and so forth. The unique development in England of the vernacular into a literary language can be attributed to the insight of leading scholars – above all, Bede – that it was not enough for only those fluent in Latin to be instructed in the Christian religion; there should also be priests and teachers who could impart the basic tenets of the Christian message to the people in their own language. How important this idea was to Bede is shown in his life of the natural talent Caedmon in book 4, chapter 24 of his *Historia ecclesiastica gentis Anglorum* (Ecclesias-

*Saint Radegunda entering the monastic life (top) and holding a book in her cell, an illustration from an eleventh-century manuscript (Poitiers, Bibliothèque Municipale, MS 250, fol. 31v)*

tical History of the English People, 731). Caedmon, who died around 680, was a simple shepherd; he was not known to be poetically gifted until the night he was divinely inspired to compose a hymn of praise to his Creator. He recited it the next day, to the astonishment of all present, and Hilda, the great abbess of Whitby, became his patroness and convinced him to enter the abbey. That God helped Caedmon to compose his hymn not in Latin but in the vernacular shows that the vernacular is a suitable vehicle for praising God. The full effect of Bede's efforts to promote the use of the vernacular is found with his pupils – above all, Bishop Egbert of York, who founded a school that soon became one of the most important educational centers in England. His greatest pupil was Alcuin, who became a scholar and adviser at the court of Charlemagne.

### The Educational Reform of Charlemagne

It was important to the Carolingian rulers – above all, to Charlemagne, who became king in 768 and emperor in 800 – to reform the Frankish church and its institutions and to establish a program of education to spread the word of God among the people. Charlemagne's promotion of these reforms was motivated not solely by religious zeal but also by the political idea of a Christian empire. The prerequisite for a unified empire was a unified religion, and this unity was to be strengthened through close cooperation between king or emperor and the Frankish church. On the basis of this alliance bloomed first the Frankish and later, with the appearance of the Saxon Ottonian dynasty, the German empire. The long period of stability and relative peace ended only when, as a result of the Investiture Struggle, the German church had to yield to the authority of the Roman church. The rule of Charlemagne formed the beginning of a period of cultural and theological renewal whose high point was reached under his successors, especially his grandson Charles the Bald.

Charlemagne gained the assistance of the best-known scholars from Italy, Gaul, England, and Ireland. Men such as the rhetorician Peter of Pisa, who instructed Charlemagne in grammar; Paul the Deacon, who wrote the history of the Langobards; Theodulf of Orléans; Paulinus of Aquileia; and Einhard, who composed the first biography of Charlemagne, the *Vita Karoli Magni Imperatoris* (830), spent time at the court of Charlemagne and taught at the so-called palace school in Aachen. But the most influential among the scholars at Charle-

magne's court and, next to Charlemagne, the driving force behind the educational and monastic reform in the Frankish empire was the Anglo-Saxon Alcuin of York, the student of Egbert who had, in turn, been Bede's student. Alcuin composed many Latin theological works, some lives of saints (for example, the *Vita Willibrordi* and *Vita Martini*), and important didactic works on the cultivation of language (for example, *Dialogus Saxonis et Franconis* and *De orthographia*), on rhetoric, and on the Christian virtues; he also wrote dialogues between himself and Charlemagne (*De rhetorica et virtutibus, De dialectica*) and between himself and Charlemagne's son Pépin (*Disputatio regalis et nobilissimi iuvenis Pépini cum Albino scholastico*). Like most other scholars at Charlemagne's court, he wrote many letters, and he composed several hundred poems.

Although an active cultural life flourished at the court, most of these famous teachers stayed at Charlemagne's court for only a few years. The greatest work was done by unknown scholars who led the schools that Charlemagne commanded to be founded; by anonymous scribes who copied the precious manuscripts in an artistic but quite legible script, the Carolingian minuscule; and by writers of sermons, saints' lives, and schoolbook collections. These obscure persons carried out the educational program of the ruler and his advisers, spread it, and continued it long after the death of Charlemagne.

But it was Charlemagne himself who set the educational project in motion. The two documents that contain an outline of his plans, the *Admonitio generalis* (789) and *De litteris colendis* (circa 780–800), show clearly that his efforts for the cultivation of (above all, Latin) language were aimed at church and monastic reform. Although Charlemagne hesitated to interfere with the sphere of action of his clergy, he considered himself a Christian king who was responsible for the church in his realm – indeed, who was called by God to do so, just as his biblical predecessor Josiah (whom he mentions in the preface to his *Admonitio generalis*), through the introduction of the Deuteronomic law, caused the Israelites to turn away from heathen gods and customs and return to the true faith. Charlemagne admonished bishops to send priests out into all regions of their dioceses to baptize and confirm believers and hear their confessions. Priests should not only forbid heathen practices but actively fight against them. They should teach the people the Lord's Prayer and the correct singing of the Psalms. Believers should be taught to show respect to God's house, to help the priest in cleaning and repairing it, to go to mass regularly, and to wait until the end of the sermon before leaving the church. Schools should be available so that children of every class could learn to read and, perhaps, to write. There were well-known schools before the Carolingian era, such as the *domus ecclesiae* of Caesarius of Arles, the *Vivarium* of Cassiodorus, and Bede's school at Wearmouth-Jarrow in the British Isles; the new development was that the schools in the Carolingian empire were under the supervision of the ruler. This engagement of the Carolingian rulers ensured the success of the reforms. Even if – or, rather, because the ninth century was peaceful neither within the empire nor outside it, the rulers kept a watchful eye on the welfare of the church and the other institutions of state where their subjects were taught how a Christian empire should function.

### Vernacular Literature

In his *Vita Karoli Magni Imperatoris* Einhard reports Charlemagne's order to collect the old "barbaric" songs in a so-called *Heldenliederbuch* (Book of Heroic Songs). According to tradition, the book was later destroyed by Charlemagne's son Louis the Pious. Whether such a book ever actually existed is disputed; it is possible that Einhard invented the incident. Whatever the truth of this matter may be, this passage in Einhard's work is proof of the existence of an oral tradition of worldly poetry in the vernacular, of which only a fragmentary example has survived: the *Hildebrandslied* (Lay of Hildebrand, circa 825).

The *Hildebrandslied* stands at the end of the development of the heroic song, a genre that had its origin with the Germanic peoples of the time of the "migration of the peoples" – that is, between the defeat of the Ostrogoths by the Huns in 375 and the sixth century. Aside from the Old High German *Hildebrandslied,* the only other works that permit insight into the original form of the heroic song are to be found in the old Icelandic collection, the *Edda Saemundar* (after 1220). The extant examples tell primarily about historic events of the heathen early period. Yet the poets did not just want to report facts but also to teach and entertain. The heroic songs are works of art, not examples of folk literature. The poets were warriors at the courts, and the songs were composed for the king and his entourage. Since they were transmitted orally rather than written down, it is difficult, if not impossible, to determine the original text of any heroic song. The song was altered each time it was sung, and sometimes significant changes were made in the text. Only with the written recording of the text does the

song become fixed in form and content. But the written mode of presentation did not dominate even then: the heroic song remained primarily an oral tradition until the late Middle Ages.

The heroic song portrays the exceptional warrior hero who, on behalf of his tribe or people, undertakes tasks or withstands hardships that far exceed the normal demands placed on individuals and that call forth admiration and terror in the hearer or reader. The form of the heroic poem, alliterative long-line verse, is well suited to oral transmission. This form was also used for the Old High German biblical epics, which had the same goal of instruction and entertainment and of which many more examples in the vernacular have survived.

The *Hildebrandslied* was written down at the end of the eighth or beginning of the ninth century by two monks at the monastery of Fulda, on the first and the last pages of a Latin theological codex. The monks only wrote down as much as would fit on the two pages, so that the end of the song is missing. In the song Dietrich of Bern (Theodoric the Great), the rightful king of Italy, is driven out of the land by the usurper Otacher (Odoacer). After thirty years in exile at the court of Etzel (Attila), Dietrich returns to Italy to fight Otacher and try to reconquer his realm. The two armies meet at Ravenna, where the leaders choose champions to represent them in single combat: Hildebrand is Dietrich's man, and Hadubrand is Otacher's. From their conversation – a standard element of the heroic encounter, which permits the opponents to learn each other's background, social class, and standing – Hildebrand discovers that he and Hadubrand are *Sunufaterungo* (son and father), respectively. Hildebrand attempts to convince his son Hadubrand of their relationship but is unsuccessful. Finally, Hadubrand reproaches Hildebrand by saying that the latter is not willing to fight because he is too old and too cowardly. This insult to his honor leaves Hildebrand no choice. He laments the hard fate that forces him to fight his own son: "welaga nu, waltant got, wewurt skihit!" (Oh ruling God, fate must run its course!). The song breaks off in the middle of the fight, but there can be no doubt about the outcome: in the old Icelandic *Hildebrands Sterbestrophe* (Hildebrand's Death Strophe, circa 1200) Hildebrand, on his deathbed, laments the fact that he had to kill his own son. According to the Germanic ethos Hildebrand has no choice but to fight his own son: if he does not fight, he proves Hadubrand's accusations correct; but if he does fight and is victorious, he not only takes on the great stigma of blood guilt, of murdering someone from his own family or tribe, but – since Hadubrand is his only child and has no offspring – he also destroys his own posterity. To show this dilemma was the task of the poet of the *Hildebrandslied.*

There still remains the question of why the historical facts were altered in the song. For an answer, one might look to the presumably Gothic origin of the work. The first singer probably wanted to show that Theodoric had a right to rule Italy; but Odoacer, who had been recognized as the king of Italy by the Eastern Roman emperor, was killed by the Ostrogoths during an armistice. The version of events in the *Hildebrandslied* is much more agreeable to the Germanic sense of justice and shows Theodoric as well as the Ostrogoths in a more favorable "ethical" light. That this consideration did not interest the Fulda monks can be seen by the fact that they left off the end of the poem. In all probability, the writing down of the *Hildebrandslied* was a penmanship exercise and not a conscious attempt to preserve a secular poem for posterity.

Secular vernacular literature was – as can be seen from Alcuin's admonition to the monks of Lindisfarne, "Quid Hinieldus cum Christo?" (What has Ingeld [a Heathobardic king and a character in *Beowulf*] to do with Christ?) – largely neglected and despised by the leading representatives of culture; the reading of it was considered useless as a guide to Christian conduct, if not positively sinful. This view continued to be dominant until the courtly period. It was quite different with the vernacular literature of a religious content. This tradition was brought to the Continent by the Anglo-Saxon monks and nuns, above all by Hrabanus Maurus, abbot of Fulda from 822 until 847 and bishop of Mainz from 847 until his death in 856.

With the exception of the *Hildebrandslied* and the *Merseburger Zaubersprüche* (Merseburg Charms, before 750), the Christian religion determined the content of Old High German literature. The purpose of the literature was initially to promote the process of conversion and later to strengthen believers in their faith. But if Old High German was to be used for missionary purposes, priests, monks, and preachers had to have a sufficient command of the language to recognize in translations of Latin writings possibilities of new word formations, of investing existing words with new connotations, and of the necessity, on occasion, of borrowing foreign words. Therefore, it should not be surprising that the first known German writing is a glossary: the *Abrogans* (circa 790–800) is a list of words that was found in a manuscript from the monastery of Saint Gall and is named after the first Latin key word,

which means "to ask for forgiveness." The *Vocabularius Sancti Galli,* constructed around 790 in Saint Gall, is a Latin-Greek word list that has been changed into a Latin–Old High German list. In the ninth century glossaries became somewhat more sophisticated, including complete interlinear texts. Among the best known are the *Murbacher Hymnen,* the Saint Gall *Benediktiner Regel* (Benedictine Rule), the *Kasseler Glossen,* and, in the tenth century, the *Pariser Glossen,* which was intended for travelers in the German linguistic area.

While the glossaries served to help the monks in the composition of vernacular texts, the texts themselves were intended for a wider audience. One of the oldest is the eighth-century *Weißenburger Katechismus,* which contains the Lord's Prayer, a confessional, and a creed, all of which the new Christian was expected to memorize. In view of the various theological controversies the creed was of special significance.

At the end of the eighth century, perhaps to fight against the Adoptionism heresy (which held that one had to make a distinction between the divine and the human nature of Christ), the so-called *Old High German Isidor* was written; the work is a translation, with the Latin and German in parallel columns, of the *De fide catholica contra Iudaeos* (On the Catholic Faith, against the Jews) of the bishop Isidore of Seville (circa 575–636). Old Testament references to the divinity of Christ form the center of this work. It cannot be determined with certainty whether the translation was made in one of the well-known monastic scriptoria or elsewhere; the effortless reproduction of the original in the vernacular and the consistent orthography create a great stylistic distance between the *Old High German Isidor* and other glossaries of its time. It is assumed that the *Old High German Isidor* originated in the inner circle of Charlemagne's court, where the doctrine of the Trinity was much discussed. Although the teachings of the *Isidor* were quite suitable for sermons to the congregation, its immediate audience was probably not the common people but the educated class of the empire. Remarkably, the *Isidor* had no immediate successors; only about two hundred years later, with Notker Labeo, is such a subtle and gifted translator found again on German soil.

The ambitious prose translation of the period is the Old High German *Tatian.* Tatian was a Syrian Christian of the second century, to whom is attributed a Gospel harmony that was translated several times over the centuries and found a wide reception. The German translation was completed between 825 and 830 in the Fulda monastery under the direction of its abbot, Hrabanus Maurus. Since its founding in 744 by Saint Boniface I, Fulda was an important educational center of the empire and was influential in the cultivation of the vernacular. This promotion of the vernacular was fostered by the first abbot, Sturmi, and by many Bavarian monks, as well as by Alcuin's student Hrabanus Maurus. Stylistically the *Tatian* is not on the same high level as the *Old High German Isidor,* but it is important for linguistic studies of Old High German because it attempts to define a form of Old High German that is not strongly influenced by dialect. Significant, too, is the enhancement of the language through its rich vocabulary.

While the vernacular efforts of the eighth century – other than the *Old High German Isidor* – are glossaries and interlinear works, the ninth century was a time of poetic creativity, especially in the area of the biblical epic. This genre goes back to Juvencus, who might be considered the founder of the Christian epic in general. Around 330 this Spanish priest wrote his *Evangelium Libri IV* (Gospel in Four Books) in Latin as a Christian answer to heathen literature. His example was followed in several vernacular languages; in Old High German the primary examples are Otfried von Weißenburg's *Evangelienbuch* (Gospel Book, between 863 and 871) and some important fragments of biblical epics. In the Old Saxon there exists, other than the mighty *Heliand* (Savior, circa 850), only a Genesis fragment. All biblical epics and fragments were either composed or written down in Fulda or inspired by the efforts of the Fulda monks on behalf of the vernacular. All, with the exception of Otfried's *Evangelienbuch,* are in long-line verse with alliteration.

The *Wessobrunner Gebet* (Wessobrunn Prayer, circa 775–825) is written in a Latin codex from the monastery of Wessobrunn in Bavaria. The title is misleading, because the first nine alliterating long lines are definitely the beginning of a biblical epic which has the Creation as its theme. After these nine lines the epic breaks off, and there follows a modest prose prayer that has nothing in common with the previous lines. There can be no doubt that the poem is based on an Anglo-Saxon model, which indicates Fulda as a possible place of composition. The epic part describes the universe before the Creation, portraying the chaos that existed when the natural order of the cosmos was lacking (italics indicate conjectures made where the manuscript is illegible):

Dat gafregin ih mit firahim firiuuizzo meista,
Dat ero ni uuas noh ufhimil,

noh paum, noh pereg ni uuas,
ni *sterro* nohheinig, noh sunna ni scein,
noh mano ni liuhta, noh der marȩo seo.
Do dar niuuiht ni uuas enteo ni uuenteo,
enti do uuas der eino almahtico cot,
manno miltisto, enti dar uuarun auh manake mit inan
cootlihhe geista, enti cot heilac.

(This I have found to be the greatest wonder,
that there was no earth, no sky,
no tree, no mountain,
not a single star shone, not even the sun,
neither the moon shone nor the sparkling sea,
when there was nothing that could be understood as the beginning or the end,
there had been the almighty God for a long time
who is rich in grace. There were many
magnificent spirits, but before them [was] the holy God.)

As a text for those to be converted, the *Wessobrunner Gebet* was well suited. The emphasis on the eternity of the Christian God had as its goal to demonstrate the Christian God's primacy over the Germanic gods. Borrowing a typical formula from the heroic epic, the prayer presents God as a ruler with his entourage (the angels) in an attempt to express this difficult concept in terms that would be understood by the listeners.

The *Muspilli,* on the other hand, has the end, rather than the beginning, of the world as its theme. Originating in the late ninth century, the *Muspilli* (the title may mean "world fire") is directed to a quite different audience than the *Wessobrunner Gebet.* If the *Wessobrunner Gebet* can be understood as an example of conversion literature, the *Muspilli* can be considered literature for the already converted. Its theme is just actions on earth; only through correct behavior can a person hope to attain the heavenly reward:

Pidiu ist de*mo* manne so guot, denner ze demo mahale quimit,
daz er rahono *uu*eliha re*h*to arteile.
Den*ne* ni dar*f*er sorgen, den*ne* er ze deru suonu qui*mit.*

(Therefore it is good for a person who goes before the Last Judgment
[himself previously] to have judged righteously in all things.
Then he need not worry when he stands before this court.)

The poet admonishes the judges, probably the secular nobility, to practice their office on earth justly, especially with regard to the needs of the poor and the socially weak, if their hope for paradise is to be fulfilled. This connecting of just actions on earth with the promised heavenly reward became a firm part of literature intended for the nobility. A sense of justice was counted among the most important attributes of the ruler, who was conventionally called *rex iustus et pacificus* (just and peaceful king), as of the nobility in general, and this theme increased in importance in later centuries. The appearance of this theme in the late ninth century was a sure sign that vernacular literature no longer stood just in the service of conversion efforts but rather served the deepening of belief. The *Muspilli* contrasts two groups who are contending in a theological controversy, the so-called Elias struggle: the "experts of secular law," presumably the laity, and the "servants of God," presumably the clergy. The experts of secular law say that the prophet Elias will win the fight with the Antichrist; they interpret the struggle as a divine judgment, while the servants of God believe that Elias will be injured in the fight: "*so daz Eliases pluot in erda kitriufit, so inprinnant die perga*" (when Elias's blood drops to the earth the mountains will begin to burn), and the world will go up in flames. That in the ninth century a circle of laymen could defend its position with as much energy as the clerics shows the increasing intellectual maturity in the land. In this respect the experts of secular law are worthy heirs of the Carolingian rulers, who, since the time of Charlemagne, intervened in such matters and thereby enriched the intellectual climate of the time.

### An Old Saxon Intermezzo

A fascinating chapter of German literary history was written not in Old High German but in Old Saxon. A massive biblical epic, the *Heliand* (Savior, circa 850) and a biblical epic fragment known as *Genesis A* (circa 850), are the only surviving records of an Old Saxon Christian literature. Of the two works, the *Heliand* is of greater interest. Although the conclusion and some other lines are missing, the *Heliand* still contains 5,983 lines in which the life of Christ is narrated in alliterative epic verse with many stylistic devices borrowed from the Germanic heroic epic. One is tempted to view the *Heliand* as the "Germanization" of the Christian message, revealing mainly a Germanic-heathen ethos and only subliminally a Christian one. But this view would completely misrepresent the purpose of the work. It is true that Christ is described in such Germanic feudal terms as *drothin* (lord), *uualdand* (ruler), *uualdandes barn* (child of the ruler), *thiodo drothin* (lord of the peoples), and *mildi mundboro* (generous protector) and that the Apostles – with the exception of Judas – are characterized as excellent noble atten-

dants; but one should interpret these designations as an attempt to reach a compromise with the expectations and literary tastes of the heathen Saxons who lived on the outer edges of the empire and who only yielded to conversion after a violent struggle with the Carolingian Franks. The work's Christian message of love for one's neighbor, justice, and peace remains unaltered by the Germanic-heathen form.

Virtually nothing is known about the poet or the place of composition of the *Heliand*. The latest scholarship points to the monastery Werden on the Ruhr, although one may assume that the *Heliand* was created under the influence of the literary and theological works from Fulda: one of the main sources for the poet is the commentary on the Gospel of Saint Matthew by Hrabanus Maurus, and Fulda was at this time the center of poetic efforts in the vernacular language.

Two Latin prefaces, one in prose and one in verse, may give clues as to the background of the author and his reason for writing the work. These prefaces became known only in 1562, when the humanist Matthias Flacius Illyricus printed them in the second edition of his *Catalogus testium veritatis*. The prose preface says that a poet, a man who was not unknown among the Saxons, in response to the decree of "Ludouuicus piissimus Augustus" (Louis the Pious?) had taken upon himself the task of translating the Old and New Testaments into German. In the verse preface this poet – in an apparent allusion to Bede's Caedmon story – is described as a simple shepherd who was instructed by God in a dream to write of holy things. It is uncertain whether this preface refers to the *Heliand* poet and possibly to the *Genesis* poet, but it can be stated with some certainty that the prefaces are not forgeries by Matthias Flacius: they are written in Carolingian Latin, not in the Latin of the humanists.

### *Otfried von Weißenburg and His Time*

During the time – about 863 until 871 – in which Otfried von Weißenburg was creatively active, political conditions were quite different from those that existed during the time of the author of the *Heliand*. The sons of Louis the Pious had divided the Frankish empire into an eastern empire, a middle empire, and a western empire. The *Strasbourg Oaths,* sworn on 14 February 842, cemented an alliance between Charles the Bald, ruler of the western empire, and Louis the German, of the eastern empire, against their brother Lothar, of the middle

*Charlemagne, statue by Agostino Cornacchini (Chiesa di San Pietro, Rome)*

empire. They also demonstrate that the empires were linguistically divided. Each recited the oath to his brother in the latter's language. First Louis the German spoke his oath in West Frankish (Old French): "Pro deo amur et pro christian poblo et nostro commun saluament, d'ist di in auant, in quant deu sauir et podir me dunat, si saluarai eo cist meon fradre Karlo et in aiuhda et in cadhuna cosa, so cum om per dreit son fradra saluat dist. . . ." Then Charles recited the same oath in East Frankish (Old High German): "In godes minna ind in thes christianes folches ind unser bedhero gehaltnissi, fon thesemo dage frammordes, so fram so mir got geuuizci indi maht furgibit, so haldih thesan minan bruodher, soso man mit rethu sinan

bruodher scal. . . ." Each ruler promised not to attack the other and to give the other support in the struggle against Lothar. Similar oaths were sworn by their respective armies in the language of their counterparts.

Hrabanus Maurus's student Otfried von Weißenburg was justifiably regarded as the most illustrious vernacular poet of this period. Influenced by Latin hymns, he was the first to use end rhyme rather than alliteration. In his 7,000-line Old High German *Evangelienbuch* he selects mainly episodes from the Gospel of Saint John and explains them allegorically, revealing the hidden sense that lies beneath the literal meaning of the text. Discussing the wedding in Cana, for example, he explains that the stone jugs represent the hearts of the disciples of God; they are hollow inside and filled with Holy Scripture so that they always offer something delectable to drink. The audience addressed by such an interpretation would have been a monastic one. As Max Wehrli says in his *Geschichte der deutschen Literatur vom frühen Mittelalter bis zum Ende des 16. Jahrhunderts* (History of German Literature from the Early Middle Ages until the End of the Sixteenth Century [Stuttgart: Reclam, 1980], p. 79): "Die Dichtung gründet auf der klösterlichen Praxis der Bibellektüre und Meditation, anhand der Lehren der Väter und vertieft durch das Gebet, in welchem sich erst der Kreis zwischen dem Sprechen des Menschen und dem Sprechen Gottes schließt. Letztes Ziel ist die Kontemplation, als Vorbereitung auf die ewige Seeligkeit" (Literature was based on the monastic practice of reading from the Bible and meditation, with the teachings of the church fathers and deepened by prayer, in which the circle between the speaking of the person and the speaking of God is only then completed. The final goal is contemplation as a preparation for eternal bliss).

The *Evangelienbuch* is, however, quite the opposite of a dry reading for a monastic circle. A humane, benevolent spirit accompanied by deep piety informs the work. Of great interest culturally are Otfried's prefaces to Louis the German, Archbishop Liutbert of Mainz, and Bishop Salomon of Constance, as well as his comments on why he wrote his Gospel book in the vernacular. In the dedication to Louis, whom he considers a model ruler, Otfrid enumerates the most important characteristics of a monarch: as a special favorite of God, who chose him to lead his people as he had once chosen David, he overcomes all difficulties with God's help; and like Job, the much-tested king bears his trials with patience and becomes a servant of God. The undivided empire of Charlemagne no longer exists, and his grandchildren are fighting one another; yet the picture of the ruler as the representative of God, as head of a Christian *societas*, remains unaltered.

In the Latin preface to Liutbert, Otfried mentions that his work was undertaken at the bidding of a certain "venerandae matronae" named Judith, who is not further identified, and several "probatissimorum virorum" to counter the pernicious influence of the secular vernacular songs. To accomplish this goal he had to write in the vernacular himself. His declaration at the beginning of the *Evangelienbuch* itself is even more significant: all culturally advanced peoples, such as the Greeks and the Romans, have, according to Otfrid, presented

and preserved their deeds in books. They have shown their grand abilities by mastering the rules of literature. Why should only the Franks refrain from singing God's praise in their own language? The Franks are not inferior to the Romans or the Greeks in courage, intelligence, or riches. No one dares to lead a war against the Franks, who belong to the lineage of Alexander the Great. It appears that Otfried is attempting to rekindle the glow of the great, powerful, and unified empire in the consciousness of his contemporaries.

A similar intent is to be found in the *Ludwigslied* (Song of Louis), which was composed around 881 or 882. The song in praise of the West Frankish king is written in the East Frankish dialect (Old High German) and is found in a West Frankish manuscript that also contains the Old French *Eulalia* sequence. Therefore, one may assume that the language of the eastern part of the empire was still alive in the western part at this time, at least in the noble circles.

The picture of Louis the German shows evidence of the Christian concept of the role of a ruler. The relationship between God and the ruler is immediate and direct; God does not just appear to the ruler, he speaks with him. The Franks are the new Israelites, the new chosen people, and Louis is the new Moses. Louis was orphaned as a child, and God became his *magenzogo*. This word, which is usually translated as "master," signifies much more; it implies someone from the same family or clan, a relative — perhaps an uncle — on the maternal side. Therefore, God and Louis are, metaphorically, related by blood. Louis is "rex dei gratia" (king by the grace of God) because the Lord called him and gave him industriousness, magnificent liege men, and the throne in Franconia. Because the Frankish people had sinned, God let them be sorely tested (that is, he let the Normans invade the empire), then had mercy on them and commanded Louis to save them: "'Hluduig, kuning min, Hilph minan liutin!'" ("Louis, my king, help my people!"). The Christian warriors do not go into battle like the old Germans, who, according to Tacitus, had the *barditus* on their lips; instead, they sing the *Kyrie Eleison*.

Among the many vernacular works of the Old High German period, such as prayers, baptismal vows, and confessional forms, the magic incantations stand out. Most of them show the fusing of the Christian religion with orally transmitted pre-Christian folk wisdom. That they were collected at a relatively late time — the ninth and tenth centuries — shows that they were able to adjust and maintain their popularity in a Christian but largely rural and conservative society. Instead of the Germanic gods, the powers appealed to are Christ, the Virgin Mary, or a saint. The magic is no longer contained in a formula (although these can still be found; for example, in the *Wurmsegen* [Worm Blessing]) but in a supplication to the divinity, perhaps to protect a shepherd's dog or to heal a lame horse. Only the *Merseburger Zaubersprüche,* in a tenth-century manuscript from the Merseburg cathedral, provide insight into the magical world of Germanic antiquity. For example, the second charm reads:

> P*h*ol ende Uuodan uuorun zi holza.
> du uuart demo Balderes uolon sin uuoz birenki*t*.
> thu biguol en Sin*th*gunt, Sunna era suister,
> thu biguol en Friia, Uolla era suister,
> thu biguol en Uuodan, so he uuola conda:
> sose benrenki, sose bluotrenki, sose lidirenki,
> ben zi bena, bluot zi bluoda,
> lid zi geliden, sose gelimida sin!

> (Phol and Wodan rode into the forest.
> Then Balder's foal sprained his leg.
> Then Singund spoke a magic verse to heal it [and]
>   Sunna, her sister,
> then Frija spoke a magic verse to heal it [and] Volla,
>   her sister,
> then Wodan spoke a magic verse to heal it, as well as
>   only he could:
> Just as the sprain of the leg so the irregularity of the
>   blood and that of the whole limb!
> Bone to bone, blood to blood, limb to limb,
> as if they had been melded together!)

The first section (lines 1–5), containing the anaphors, reports a situation in epic form. The second section (lines 6–8) contains the magic charm. The power of the charm depends on the magical power of the words, which are expressed as a command. It is through this command that such charms differ from Christian prayer and other sayings that were influenced by Christianity. With the *Merseburger Zaubersprüche* one is still in a Germanic-heathen landscape, and they permit a modest glance into the otherwise closed cult life of the pre-Christian era.

### Latin Literature of the Carolingian and Ottonian Empires

Though the emphasis here has been on the vernacular literature, one should not conclude that the vernacular was the typical language for literary production during the early Middle Ages. On the contrary, Latin was still the medium for cultivated international communication. While many important Old High German works have been handed down only in fragmentary form, rather insignificant Latin works exist in multiple, even hundreds of manuscripts. The monastic scriptoria produced a flood of manuscripts. Some contain original texts, such as Bible commentaries, theological tracts, sequences, and hymns, while others contain copies of the writings of the church fathers, of the Bible, or of other such documents. In many manuscripts works of Latin authors of antiquity are to be found. The Saint Gall monastic library contains, in addition to the oldest Alcuin Bible and the oldest copy of the pure text of the Benedictine Rule, an especially impressive collection of the great writers of antiquity: Terence, Lucretius, Sallust, Cicero, Caesar, Virgil, Horace, Ovid, Vitruvius, Persius, Lucan, Quintilian, Statius, and Juvenal. The exchange of manuscripts among scholars and monasteries for the purpose of copying was commonplace. It is, unfortunately, not possible to reconstruct the manuscript collections of all of the sixteen significant cathedrals and thirty most important monasteries in the greater Carolingian empire of the ninth century; manuscript catalogs from this time are available only for the Freising, Cologne, and Würzburg cathedrals and the Saint Gall, Reichenau, Murbach, Lorsch, Fulda, Saint-Riquier, and Saint Wandrille monasteries. Nevertheless, one may assume that the other institutions could also claim respectable collections.

That the Carolingian rulers and the women of the ruling houses, especially Empress Judith, the second wife of Louis the Pious, promoted literature through their patronage is attested by the many dedications of works to them. In addition, there were many nonliterary accomplishments during this epoch, such as the book illuminations and the extraordinary building activity: between 768 and 855 27 cathedrals, 417 monasteries, and 100 royal castles were constructed.

The rich Latin literature of the Carolingian age includes two outstanding works: Einhard's biography of Charlemagne, the *Vita Karoli Magni Imperatoris,* and Dhuoda's *Liber Manualis* (Handbook, 843). The son of a nobleman, Einhard was born around 770 in Maingar, educated at the monastery in Fulda, and then sent, around the end of the century, to the royal court in Aachen. There he studied with Alcuin, was soon elevated to the position of teacher in the court school, and became the emperor's adviser in literary and mathematical matters. He remained in favor with Charlemagne's son Louis the Pious, but when the relationship between Louis and his sons became increasingly strained and Einhard's attempts at reconciliation failed, he withdrew in 830 to Seligenstadt am Main. He died there on 14 March 840.

Written after 830, the *Vita Karoli Magni Imperatoris* is probably the most mature product, in the field of historiography, of the Carolingian cultural reform. Suetonius's biographies of the Roman emperors serve as Einhard's model as he depicts Charlemagne as an ideal ruler. To stress the uniqueness of his lord, Einhard implies that Charlemagne became emperor by God's grace, not as the result of anointing or coronation by the pope. He writes of the coronation of the emperor in 800 that Charlemagne came to Rome, and "quo tempore imperatoris et augusti nomen accepit" (at that time he received the appellations emperor and Augustus). This passage says that Charlemagne received the title, not the office, in Rome. And in another passage one finds the following words: "Post susceptum imperiale nomen . . ." (After accepting the title of emperor. . .)." For Einhard, Charlemagne was the highest lord of Roman Christianity; the title he received from the pope confirmed but did not confer that status. Einhard's descriptions of Charlemagne's efforts on behalf of the church and his charitable activities create the image of a Christian ruler who not only honors and protects the church but rules as a representative of God. This concept of the ruler was maintained and expanded by the Ottonian dynasty and the early Salian kings. In the Investiture Struggle it would be shaken and would undergo a fundamental change.

Dhuoda's *Liber Manualis* is a book of advice for her son. The manual reveals much about conditions in the Carolingian Empire and about the life of a woman in that time. She reports that she married Bernard of Septimania on 29 June 824. Shortly after her marriage she was taken to an estate of her husband in Uzès on the lower Rhône, where she lived in exile. On 29 November 826 her first son, William, was born; on 22 March 841 she bore a second son, Bernard. Her husband took the second child away from her even before the christening; it is not known why he treated her in this fashion. In the summer of 841 her husband sent William as a sort of hostage to the court of Charles the Bald, a custom of that time meant to ensure peace. She wrote the book for William between 30 November 841 and 2 February 843. It is not known when she died.

Although the manual represents an early form of a Prince's Mirror, it really is a work sui generis that gives the modern reader insight into the way of thinking of the Carolingian era. Aside from telling her son how to behave in society and how to serve his lord, Charles, she tries to explain the meaning of the Christian religion. She often discusses the hidden meaning behind numbers and names; for example, she interprets the name *Adam* by using Greek words for the letters: *A* stands for *anathole* (the east), *D* for *dysis* (the west), *A* for *arktos* (the north), and *M* for *mesembrios* (the south). If one adds up the numbers that are associated in Greek with these letters, the sum, forty-six, is exactly the number of years that were needed to rebuild the temple in Jerusalem. One recognizes that Dhuoda was an educated woman who was familiar not only with the Bible but also with the writings of scholars such as Alcuin and Isidore of Seville. She is an impressive product of the Carolingian educational reforms. William must also have been able to read, for she often admonishes him to read her little book, although he already owns many books and will own even more in the future. She also hopes that others after William may read her manual and profit from it.

The work ends with the final words of Christ on the cross, "consumatum est" (It is finished); and with the death of Louis the Child in 911 one can say the same of Frankish influence in the eastern part of the former greater empire of the Carolingians. With the selection of Heinrich I as king in 919, the hegemony in the future German empire went from the Franks to the Saxons. Although it can be assumed that vernacular literature continued in oral form, from 918 until about 1050 literature was mainly written in Latin. In this period the impetus for literary activity came from the monasteries, and women at the imperial court played a significant role as patronesses. From the convents came magnificent illuminated manuscripts, such as the *Hitda Codex* from Meschede, the *Evangeliar* of the abbess Svanhild of Essen, the *Quedlinburger Evangelienbuch,* and the precious processional crosses of the Ottonian abbesses Saint Matilda and Saint Theophano of Essen. These abbeys were led by women of the Saxon aristocracy; Matilde, the mother of the emperor Otto I, made the convent in Quedlinburg an important cultural center; Adelaid, the second wife of Otto I, was the patroness of Ekkehard II of Saint Gall; her daughter Mathilde was also abbess of the Quedlinburg convent; Gerberga, the niece of Otto I, was the abbess of Gandersheim at the time of Hrotsvit. The role of noblewoman in the religious and cultural life of the Saxon imperial period was, clearly, an important one.

With the reigns of Otto I, II, and III from 936 to 1002 came a renaissance in literature. Latin was still the language of literary communication, and secular themes came to be expressed in Latin. The *Carmina Cantabrigensa* (Cambridge Songs, circa

1050), so named from the location of the manuscript, comprises forty-seven songs, some of which are of German origin. Among them are secular *sequentiae* (sequences), such as the *Modus Ottinc,* which proclaims the deeds of the three Ottos, and the *Modus Liebinc* (The Snow-Baby), a farce about a clever Swabian. The poetic *sequentia* was developed by Notker Balbulus, a monk of Saint Gall, from a mnemonic device for monks who had to sing the long final *a* of the *Alleluia* after the gradual of the Mass; the melody of the *a* was complicated, and the sequence provided the monks a way to remember it. Such texts existed long before Notker, but he created a new poetic form with his texts. (From this form the Middle High German *Leich* [lay] developed.) An example of a religious sequence that is still known today is the *Dies Irae.*

Another Notker from Saint Gall was Notker III (circa 950–1022), also known as Notker Labeo (the Thick-lipped) or Notker Teutonicus (the German). He was the leader of the Saint Gall monastery school and a brilliant translator from Latin into German. He begins with a Latin sentence that he sometimes changes syntactically to make it easier to understand. He differentiates in the German between long and short vowels and adorns the stressed syllables with an acute accent. He tried to introduce a uniform orthography and invented the "Notker Anlautgesetz") (initial-sound law), which says that initial *b, d,* and *g* alternate with *p, t,* and *k,* respectively, according to whether the final sound of the previous word is voiced or unvoiced. He translated *The Consolation of Philosophy* of Boethius, the *Categories* and *Hermeneutics* of Aristotle, the first two books of the *Marriage of Mercury with Philology* of Martianus Capella, and the Psalms. In 1022 he died of the plague just after completing his translation of the commentary on Job that was probably written by Pope Gregory the Great; this work has been lost. Especially appealing in Notker's work are his clear and idiomatic translations and a syntax that is German, not Latin. Notker had no successors in his efforts on behalf of the German language, and it would be 150 years before the "barbarica lingua" achieved new expressive possibilities.

Two Latin epics, the *Waltharius* and *Ruodlieb* (circa 1075), frame the Ottonian epoch. Ekkehard IV (980–1060) reports in his chronicle of Saint Gall that a monk named Ekkehard I (circa 909–973) wrote in his youth a Latin Waltharius epic on this basis, the work has been dated about 930. But in three of the twelve manuscripts there is a prologue by one Geraldus, who says that he presented the epic to Bishop Erchambaldus. It is not clear whether

Geraldus meant that he composed the epic or that he merely gave it to the bishop; if the former is the case, there are several persons named Geraldus and Erchambaldus who could be the individuals involved, and the dating of the work would vary from around 850 to 918.

There is some controversy as to whether the *Waltharius* is a heroic poem that has been reworked in a Christian manner and, therefore, is an excellent example of the monastic reception of secular, probably originally vernacular, literature. There are allusions to classical mythology, as well as detailed reports of the bellicose exploits of the hero, Walther, that are related with obvious relish. The *Waltharius* theme of conflict between faithfulness to friend and loyalty of vassals has its origin in the Nibelung legends. As children, Walther, Hagen, and Hiltgunt are sent from their respective homelands – Aquitaine, Francia, and Burgundy – as hostages to the court of Attila the Hun for the purpose of achieving peace. There the three grow up together, and the two boys swear an oath of friendship to one another. The two achieve great fame as commanders of Attila's armies, while Hiltgunt watches over Attila's treasure. One night Hagen escapes to enter the service of the new Frankish king Gunther. Soon thereafter Walther and Hiltgunt also escape, taking the treasure of the Huns with them. To reach Spain they have to ride through Francia, where Gunther, over Hagen's objections, leads a band of warriors in an attempt to steal the treasure. After much hand-to-hand combat, Walther has killed all the Franks except Gunther and Hagen. The latter had not taken part in the battle because of the oath of friendship he and Walther had sworn. Only when the king begs for his help does he agree to fight, but he makes it clear to Gunther that he is prepared to break the oath of friendship only because of his vassal loyalty. On the other hand, he tells Walther that he is fighting only because the latter has slain his sister's son – in other words, out of loyalty to his kin. The inexorable tragedy of the typical heroic song is lacking at the end of the epic: instead, the three severely wounded men sit around the campfire, make grotesque jokes about their injuries, and make peace with one another – a Christian element that is quite foreign to the ethos of the heroic song.

*Ruodlieb* is the product of a different historical and literary epoch. It is no longer concerned with Germanic heroes but with German knighthood a century before the rise of French courtly culture; for this reason it has been called the first medieval novel. Incomplete at 2,300 lines, *Ruodlieb* provides many insights into medieval life. One learns detailed information about social classes, table manners, conditions of village streets, the importance of farming, marriage customs, diplomacy, the life of rich peasants, judicial procedures, forms of punishment (including death by fire, drowning, burial alive, and maiming), jewelry, games, and life at court.

The work portrays the ideal secular ruler through the example of the *rex maior* (Greater King). Ruodlieb enters the latter's service after being treated disloyally by his lords at home. In contrast to Ruodlieb's former lords, the *rex maior* is the embodiment of the *rex iustus et pacificus* who always returns good for evil. After winning a devastating war against the unjust *rex minor* (Lesser King), the *rex maior* offers the *rex minor* an honorable and generous peace; the *rex minor* humbly and gratefully accepts. His message to the *rex maior* is the best expression of the secular-ruler thesis that had gradually taken form in the West from Charlemagne through the Saxon emperors and reached its peak in the Salian dynasty on the eve of the Investiture Struggle: the *rex minor* proclaims through a messenger that in Christ's stead, the *rex maior* is the strong pillar of society (line 154). When the two kings meet at the former scene of battle to celebrate the peace, an altar stands ready for mass, adorned with the diadem and cross of the *rex maior*, symbolizing the close relationship of the king to God. When Ruodlieb finally wants to return to his former lords with an offer of reconciliation, the *rex maior* gives him two silver bowls. One of them is filled with gold coins on which is engraved Christ placing his hand in blessing on the symbol of imperial power. The secular concept of the ruler could not be stated more clearly.

## The Investiture Struggle

*Ruodlieb* shows the direction that literature probably would have taken around the middle of the eleventh century had it not been for the confrontation between the papacy and the emperor known as the Investiture Struggle. This struggle had deep and far-reaching effects on Germany that are today hardly imaginable; it was a blow from which the empire would suffer long after the "official" end of the struggle in the Concordat of Worms in 1122. The struggle cannot be understood in terms of a modern struggle between church and state, because at that time the institutions were not clearly distinguished. It was, rather, a contest between pope and emperor for primacy in the leadership of Christian society. Through the Investiture

Struggle the theocratic side of the German monarchy was put to an end once and for all. The result was a twofold emancipation – the church freed itself from secular domination, and the monarchy was released from archaic bonds – and the dawn of a new age.

From this long and bloody struggle, however, it was neither the monarchy nor the church but the German nobility that really profited: it gained about fifty years to free itself of the authority of the emperor. By 1100 Germany was the most feudal country in Europe, with a colorful multiplicity of territorial fiefdoms that were wholly independent of both the monarchy and the church. The strivings of the Saxon and Salian emperors for a centralized authority had been shattered; the real power in the land was with the princes.

## Early Middle High German Religious Literature

The designation *early Middle High German religious literature* is applied to about ninety works written from about 1060 – after nearly 150 years from which no written works in the vernacular, with the exception of Notker III's translations, have survived – to about 1180. Among them are biblical epics, commentaries on the Song of Songs, penitential sermons, laments for sin, moral-allegorical tracts, historical literature, zoological treatises, minstrel epics, litanies, and commentaries on the Mass.

The ascendancy of vernacular literature at this time is related to the changed role of the church after the Investiture Struggle. Instead of being concerned with the afterlife, as it had been previously, the church directed its attention to life in this world and claimed the right to lead secular society; therefore, it was forced to come to terms with questions about the duties of the various social classes, especially of the nobility, and these are the main themes of the literature of this period. To influence the laity, the church had to use the vernacular language. In addition, the circle of patrons of literature expanded: in the twelfth century the great princely houses began commissioning works; the Latin-speaking imperial court and great imperial monasteries were no longer the most important centers of literary production.

The first known German work of the period is the so-called *Ezzolied* (Song of Ezzo, circa 1060), written by a cleric named Ezzo at the behest of Bishop Gunther of Bamberg. The *Ezzolied* is preserved in two manuscripts: the earlier one, in Strasbourg, contains only the first seven stanzas; the later one, in Vorau, contains thirty-four stanzas. In the Strasbourg manuscript Ezzo directs his work to "iu herron" (my lords) – that is, to an aristocratic audience. He says that he wants to tell a true story, in contrast to the secular literature that is filled with lies. The song moves rapidly from the Creation and the Fall of Man to the birth, miracles, passion, death, and resurrection of Christ. The focus is on Christ's act of redemption, because through it the kingdom of Heaven is assured to all believers. Still, the mood is not one-sidedly otherworldly. The ultimate goal of life is to attain paradise, but the world is valued positively.

A completely different tone predominates in the short work (seventy-three long lines in nineteen stanzas), written around 1080 by an author named Noker, which bears the misleading title used by its discoverer: *Memento mori*. It was probably intended for a noble audience during a time of fasting. Noker begins with the admonition: "nu denchent, wib unde man, war ir sulint werdan" (Now think, woman and man, where you want to end up). The theme, however, is not redemption in the hereafter but the dangers one encounters on the journey through life. Noker complains that the poor do not get *reht* (that which they deserve). The rich and powerful, who fail to follow the command of God to love their neighbors, are to blame for this deplorable state of affairs. If they do not change their lives, they will be condemned forever. In spite of this threat (which is made only twice, in two contiguous stanzas), Noker observes a moderate tone throughout the work. The rich and powerful must fulfill the command to love one's neighbor by using their wealth to help the poor; only in this way can they lead a Christian life and attain Paradise.

These two works express the most important themes of the moral-didactic literature of this epoch: worldly affairs are not evil in themselves, but the purpose of earthly existence is more than just to live a pleasant and self-centered life; and the weaker members of society have certain rights that must be respected. The duty of the powerful is to help them secure their *reht* so that people will be able to live in harmony.

The anonymous author of the so-called *Summa theologiae* (circa 1100) incorporates the second theme into his portrayal of the story of Redemption. He uses, probably for the first time in German literature, the metaphor of the body to demonstrate the unity of humanity. God, he writes, has created our limbs to serve one another. The members that are apparently of the least worth, such as the feet, are needed the most, because the sublime members such as the eyes would be able to accomplish little without the mobility that is provided by the feet. The author concludes that there are gradations of rank in society and that the higher could exercise their functions in only a limited way without the lower ones.

The biblical epic enjoyed some popularity at this time. From the Old Testament come works based on Genesis and Exodus, as well as the *ältere* and *jüngere Judith* (The Older and Younger Judith) and the *Drei Jünglinge im Feuerofen* (Three Youths in the Oven). The earliest work based on Genesis is the *Wiener Genesis* (Vienna Genesis, 1060–1070); the latest is the *Millstätter Genesis* (Millstatt Genesis, presumably from the late twelfth century), and the middle position is occupied by the *Vorauer Bücher Mosis* (Vorau Books of Moses, circa 1120–1140). (*Vienna, Millstätt,* and *Vorau* refer to the locations of the manuscripts in which the works are written.) In the *Wiener Genesis,* which served as a model for the others, the author relates biblical events to the present and speaks to his listeners, who presumably came from noble circles, in images that were familiar to them from their own experiences. He describes the Garden of Eden, for example, as an ideal medieval tree and herb garden. As the chosen people of God, the Israelites prefigure the Germans. The Old Testament figures are portrayed as heroes and princes in a service-and-reward relationship to God, not as the simple peasants and shepherds that they actually were; the armies could just as well be knightly crusaders. The obvious joy in storytelling which already points to the precourtly epic writers is not to be mistaken and is a sure sign of the new age.

The history of salvation and the history of the world are interwoven in two works of this period, the *Annolied* (Song of Anno, between 1077 and 1081) and the *Kaiserchronik* (Chronicle of the Emperors, circa 1147). The *Annolied,* which has survived only in the printed version of Martin Opitz (1639), tells of the deeds of the eleventh-century bishop Anno of Cologne, who was one of the most powerful imperial princes and, as a result of the abduction of the minor Heinrich IV, ruled in the king's stead from 1062 to 1065. He was a controversial political personality, a sponsor of the monastic reform movement and an avid founder of churches and monasteries. The *Annolied,* which originated at the Siegburg monastery, can be considered as propaganda for Anno's beatification; the bishop is frequently referred to in the song as "sent Anno" (Saint Anno). As the canonization did not take place until 1183, this designation is rather premature.

According to the song, Anno was the thirty-third bishop of Cologne, and the actual story of Anno begins with the thirty-third stanza (thirty-three was the number of years of Christ's life). In the previous thirty-two stanzas the author describes the history of the world and the story of Redemption, which cannot be separated from one another: the Creation, the fall of Lucifer, original sin, and the birth of Christ. This history is complemented by secular events: founding of the city (Nineveh), construction of the Tower of Babel, episodes from the Alexander material, Daniel's dream of the four animals (in the interpretation of which the lion, bear, leopard, and boar signify the four realms of the world – the Babylonian, Persian, Macedonian-Greek, and Roman, respectively, of which each had historically succeeded the previous one), and the origin of the four significant German tribes in Franconia, Saxony, Bavaria, and Swabia (perhaps in an echo from the time of the great struggles between Charlemagne and the Saxons, the Saxons come off badly). Anno is portrayed as the ideal ruler because he combines the most important attributes of justice and love of one's neighbor. Like a lion, writes the poet, he had the first place among the princes, but like a lamb he goes among the poor. In this way he serves God and the world.

Wehrli describes the monumental (17,283 lines) *Kaiserchronik,* written in Regensburg, as the "großartige[n] Versuch, die Geschichte des Reichs von der Gründung Roms und speziell von Caesar an bis zur Gegenwart [1147] durch eine Sammlung der verschiedensten Überlieferungen darzustellen, als systematische Zusammenfassung des offiziellen abendländischen Erzählstoffs überhaupt" (grand attempt to present the history of the empire from the founding of Rome, and especially from Caesar, until the present [1147] through a collection of diverse records, as a systematic compilation of all the official western narrative material). The author introduces his audience to the idea of a Christian empire in which the imperial and papal powers are one. Attention is always focused on the moral dimension, especially on the virtue of justice. Even heathen emperors were capable of possessing the necessary virtues: Trajan was saved because he "rehtes gerihtes phlegete" (judged righteously), and all kings should take him as an example if they want to attain the heavenly kingdom. Salvation, thus, does not depend on outward membership in the Christian Church but on the inner moral substance of the individual. This emphasis on the individual is a sign of the new spirit of the twelfth century. The traditional wisdom of antiquity is admired in the work of Otto von Freising, the arme Hartmann's *Rede vom heiligen Glauben* (Tract Concerning [Our] Sacred Faith, between 1140 and 1160) and Priester Arnold's *Loblied auf den Heiligen Geist* (Song of Praise of the Holy Ghost, circa 1150); earthly wisdom, even if it is not sufficient to open the heavenly gates, is still important. This new attitude toward earthly and individual matters is far from the early Christian view that earthly knowledge is useless and vain, if not sinful. Worldly knowledge and the products of human effort are valued within the limits set by Christian belief.

This relaxed attitude with respect to worldly matters is also to be found in the works of the first woman poet in the German language who is known by name, Frau Ava. Ava probably came from a noble family and, as a widow, withdrew to a hermit's cell at the monastery in Melk; she died in 1127. Her oeuvre consists of four works, totaling 3,338 short lines, that form a whole: *Johannes, Leben Jesu* (The Life of Jesus), *Antichrist,* and *Das Jüngste Gericht* (The Last Judgment). Her work is a song of praise by a pious Christian of Christ's act of Redemption. She does not take the rhetorical approach of lamenting the modest poetic gifts she, as a woman, possesses; the humility formulas that one frequently encounters in the writings of other medieval poets are not found in Ava's writings. She considers her poetic activity a natural outcome of her beliefs, and this view was no doubt shared by the noble audience that she addresses as "lieben mine herren" (my dear lords).

The subjectivity found in Ava's writings pervades the great prose work of pious introspection of the twelfth century, the *Sankt Trudperter Hohelied* (Saint Trudpert Song of Solomon), which was presumably written in the upper German linguistic area around 1160. The manuscript was preserved in the Benedictine monastery of Saint Trudpert in the Black Forest. The anonymous poet interprets the seemingly erotic Song of Solomon by stressing the significance of the concept of the bride. First Christianity is the bride, then the Virgin Mary, and finally the soul of the believing individual. As a didactic exegesis for a Benedictine congregation of nuns, this interpretation fits in quite well. These women regarded themselves as brides of God who yearned for union with the Divine Bridegroom. The work is freed from the reserved erudition of earlier interpretations of the Song of Solomon; the erotic language and sensuous images of the biblical text now enter the vernacular. This work's equal in the portrayal of the inner person and of the soul that passionately loves God is not found in German until that of Mechthild von Magdeburg in the thirteenth century.

# Books for Further Reading

Bloch, Marc. *Feudal Society*. Translated by L. A. Manyon. New York: Routledge, 1989.

Bostock, J. Knight. *A Handbook on Old High German Literature,* second edition, revised by K. C. King and D. R. McLintock. Oxford: Clarendon Press, 1976.

Buntz, Herwig. *Die deutsche Alexanderdichtung des Mittelalters*. Stuttgart: Metzler, 1973.

Curtius, Ernst Robert. *European Literature and the Latin Middle Ages*. Translated by Willard R. Trask. Princeton: Princeton University Press, 1990.

De Boor, Helmut, and Richard Newald. *Die deutsche Literatur von Karl dem Großen bis zum Beginn der höfischen Dichtung,* volume 1 of *Geschichte der deutschen Literatur*. Edited by de Boor and Newald, fourth edition. Munich: Beck, 1969.

Dronke, Peter. *The Medieval Lyric*. London: Hutchinson, 1968.

Dronke. *Poetic Individuality in the Middle Ages: New Departures in Poetry, 1000–1150*. Oxford: Clarendon Press, 1970.

Dronke. *Women Writers of the Middle Ages: A Critical Study of Texts from Perpetua (d. 203) to Marguerite Porete (d. 1310)*. Cambridge: Cambridge University Press, 1984.

Eggers, Hans. *Das Althochdeutsche und das Mittelhochdeutsche,* volume 1 of his *Deutsche Sprachgeschichte*. Reinbek: Rowohlt, 1986.

Ehrismann, Gustav. *Geschichte der deutschen Literatur bis zum Ausgang des Mittelalters,* 2 volumes in 4. Munich: Beck, 1918–1935.

Fleckenstein, Josef. *Early Medieval Germany,* translated by Bernard S. Smith. Amsterdam: North Holland, 1978.

Gentry, Francis G. *Bibliographie zur frühmittelhochdeutschen geistlichen Dichtung*. Berlin: Schmidt, 1992.

Godman, Peter. *Poets and Emperors: Frankish Politics and Carolingian Poetry*. Oxford: Clarendon Press, 1986.

Groseclose, J. Sidney and Brian Murdoch. *Die althochdeutschen poetischen Denkmäler*. Stuttgart: Metzler, 1976.

Heusler, Andreas. *Die altgermanische Dichtung*. Berlin-Neubabelsberg: Akademische Verlagsgesellschaft Athenaion, 1924.

Laistner, M. L. W. *Thought and Letters in Western Europe AD 500–900*. London: Methuen, 1931.

Manitius, Max. *Geschichte der lateinischen Literatur des Mittelalters,* 3 volumes. Munich: Beck, 1911–1931; reprinted, 1964–1965.

McKitterick, Rosamond. *The Frankish Kingdoms under the Carolingians, 751–987*. New York & London: Longman, 1983.

Murdoch, Brian O. *Old High German Literature.* Boston: Twayne, 1983.

Raby, F. J. E. *A History of Secular Latin Poetry in the Middle Ages,* 2 volumes. Oxford: Clarendon Press, 1934.

Reuter, Timothy. *Germany in the Early Middle Ages.* London: Longman, 1991.

Ruh, Kurt, ed. *Die deutsche Literatur des Mittelalters,* second revised edition, 7 volumes to date. Berlin: De Gruyter, 1978– .

Waterman, John. *A History of the German Language: With Special Reference to the Cultural and Social Forces That Shaped the Standard Literary Language.* Seattle: University of Washington Press, 1976.

Wehrli, Max. *Geschichte der deutschen Literatur vom frühen Mittelalter bis zum Ende des 16. Jahrhunderts,* second edition. Stuttgart: Reclam, 1984.

Wipf, Karl A., ed. and trans. *Althochdeutsche poetische Texte.* Stuttgart: Reclam, 1992.

Ziolkowski, Jan M. *Talking Animals: Medieval Latin Beast Poetry, 750–1150.* Philadelphia: University of Pennsylvania Press, 1993.

# Contributors

Linda Archibald ................................................................*Liverpool John Moores University*
Jeffery Ashcroft...............................................................*University of Saint Andrews*
Whitney Bolton ...............................................................*Rutgers University*
Albrecht Classen...............................................................*University of Arizona*
Maria Dobozy .................................................................*University of Utah*
Cyril W. Edwards ...........................................*Goldsmiths' College, University of London*
Sabina Flanagan ..............................................................*University of Adelaide*
Jerold C. Frakes ..........................................*University of Southern California*
Francis G. Gentry............................................*Pennsylvania State University*
Will Hasty .....................................................................*University of Florida*
Wolfgang Hempel ...........................................................*University of Toronto*
Ernst Ralf Hintz...........................................*Pennsylvania State University*
Dennis M. Kratz ...........................................*University of Texas at Dallas*
Robert Levine ................................................................*Boston University*
Anatoly Liberman ...........................................................*University of Minnesota*
Albert L. Lloyd ...........................................*University of Pennsylvania*
William C. McDonald......................................*University of Virginia*
Brian Murdoch...............................................................*University of Stirling*
Karen Konyk Purdy.........................................*University of Pennsylvania*
Robert G. Sullivan .......................................*University of Massachusetts at Amherst*
J. Wesley Thomas .........................................*University of Kentucky*
James K. Walter...............................................*Ohio Northern University*
Julia Walworth.............................................*University of London Library*
Alfred R. Wedel ...........................................*University of Delaware*
Katharina Wilson ...........................................................*University of Georgia*

# Cumulative Index

*Dictionary of Literary Biography,* Volumes 1-148
*Dictionary of Literary Biography Yearbook,* 1980-1993
*Dictionary of Literary Biography Documentary Series,* Volumes 1-11

# Cumulative Index

**DLB** before number: *Dictionary of Literary Biography,* Volumes 1-148
**Y** before number: *Dictionary of Literary Biography Yearbook,* 1980-1993
**DS** before number: *Dictionary of Literary Biography Documentary Series,* Volumes 1-11

## A

Abbey Press .......................DLB-49

The Abbey Theatre and Irish Drama,
  1900-1945 ....................DLB-10

Abbot, Willis J. 1863-1934 ..........DLB-29

Abbott, Jacob 1803-1879 ............DLB-1

Abbott, Lee K. 1947- ...........DLB-130

Abbott, Lyman 1835-1922 .........DLB-79

Abbott, Robert S. 1868-1940 ....DLB-29, 91

Abelard, Peter circa 1079-1142 .....DLB-115

Abelard-Schuman .................DLB-46

Abell, Arunah S. 1806-1888 ........DLB-43

Abercrombie, Lascelles 1881-1938 ...DLB-19

Aberdeen University Press
  Limited .....................DLB-106

Abish, Walter 1931- ...........DLB-130

Abrahams, Peter 1919- .........DLB-117

Abrams, M. H. 1912- .............DLB-67

*Abrogans* circa 790-800 .............DLB-148

Abse, Dannie 1923- .............DLB-27

Academy Chicago Publishers .......DLB-46

Accrocca, Elio Filippo 1923- ......DLB-128

Ace Books .......................DLB-46

Achebe, Chinua 1930- ..........DLB-117

Achtenberg, Herbert 1938- .......DLB-124

Ackerman, Diane 1948- .........DLB-120

Acorn, Milton 1923-1986 ..........DLB-53

Acosta, Oscar Zeta 1935?- .......DLB-82

Actors Theatre of Louisville .........DLB-7

Adair, James 1709?-1783? ..........DLB-30

Adam, Graeme Mercer 1839-1912 ...DLB-99

Adame, Leonard 1947- ..........DLB-82

Adamic, Louis 1898-1951 ...........DLB-9

Adams, Alice 1926- ................Y-86

Adams, Brooks 1848-1927 .........DLB-47

Adams, Charles Francis, Jr.
  1835-1915 ................... DLB-47

Adams, Douglas 1952- .............Y-83

Adams, Franklin P. 1881-1960 ...... DLB-29

Adams, Henry 1838-1918 ....... DLB-12, 47

Adams, Herbert Baxter 1850-1901 ... DLB-47

Adams, J. S. and C.
  [publishing house] ............. DLB-49

Adams, James Truslow 1878-1949 ... DLB-17

Adams, John 1735-1826 ........... DLB-31

Adams, John Quincy 1767-1848 ..... DLB-37

Adams, Léonie 1899-1988 .......... DLB-48

Adams, Levi 1802-1832 ........... DLB-99

Adams, Samuel 1722-1803 ...... DLB-31, 43

Adams, William Taylor 1822-1897 .. DLB-42

Adamson, Sir John 1867-1950 ...... DLB-98

Adcock, Arthur St. John
  1864-1930 ................... DLB-135

Adcock, Betty 1938- ........... DLB-105

Adcock, Betty, Certain Gifts ....... DLB-105

Adcock, Fleur 1934- ........... DLB-40

Addison, Joseph 1672-1719 ........ DLB-101

Ade, George 1866-1944 ........ DLB-11, 25

Adeler, Max (see Clark, Charles Heber)

Adonias Filho 1915-1990 ......... DLB-145

Advance Publishing Company ...... DLB-49

AE 1867-1935 ................. DLB-19

Ælfric circa 955-circa 1010 ........ DLB-146

Aesthetic Poetry (1873), by
  Walter Pater .................. DLB-35

After Dinner Opera Company .........Y-92

Afro-American Literary Critics:
  An Introduction .............. DLB-33

Agassiz, Jean Louis Rodolphe
  1807-1873 .................... DLB-1

Agee, James 1909-1955 ......... DLB-2, 26

The Agee Legacy: A Conference at
  the University of Tennessee
  at Knoxville ....................Y-89

Aguilera Malta, Demetrio
  1909-1981 ...................DLB-145

Ai 1947- .....................DLB-120

Aichinger, Ilse 1921- ............DLB-85

Aidoo, Ama Ata 1942- .........DLB-117

Aiken, Conrad 1889-1973 ....DLB-9, 45, 102

Aikin, Lucy 1781-1864 ............DLB-144

Ainsworth, William Harrison
  1805-1882 ...................DLB-21

Aitken, Robert [publishing house] ...DLB-49

Akenside, Mark 1721-1770 ........DLB-109

Akins, Zoë 1886-1958 ..............DLB-26

Alabaster, William 1568-1640 ......DLB-132

Alain-Fournier 1886-1914 ..........DLB-65

Alarcón, Francisco X. 1954- ......DLB-122

Alba, Nanina 1915-1968 ...........DLB-41

Albee, Edward 1928- .............DLB-7

Albert the Great circa 1200-1280 ...DLB-115

Alberti, Rafael 1902- ...........DLB-108

Alcott, Amos Bronson 1799-1888 .....DLB-1

Alcott, Louisa May
  1832-1888 ...............DLB-1, 42, 79

Alcott, William Andrus 1798-1859 ....DLB-1

Alcuin circa 732-804 ..............DLB-148

Alden, Henry Mills 1836-1919 ......DLB-79

Alden, Isabella 1841-1930 .........DLB-42

Alden, John B. [publishing house] ....DLB-49

Alden, Beardsley and Company .....DLB-49

Aldington, Richard
  1892-1962 ........... DLB-20, 36, 100

Aldis, Dorothy 1896-1966 .........DLB-22

Aldiss, Brian W. 1925- ..........DLB-14

Aldrich, Thomas Bailey
  1836-1907 ......... DLB-42, 71, 74, 79

Alegría, Ciro 1909-1967 ..........DLB-113

Alegría, Claribel 1924- .........DLB-145

Aleixandre, Vicente 1898-1984 .....DLB-108

Aleramo, Sibilla 1876-1960 ........DLB-114

# B

## O

# Q

## S

# Y

# Z

ISBN 0-8103-5709-7

90000

## Documentary Series